WHICH

I felt nauseous	or	I felt nauseated
She is one of those girls who have never known	or	She is one of those girls who has never known
There is no more difficult a field	or	There is no more difficult field
Also he married, to everyone's surprise	or	And also he married, to everyone' surprise

When you are troubled by a construction, a word or a phrase that seems not quite right, MODERN AMERICAN USAGE is the reference book you need. In it, Wilson Follett has gathered hundreds of answers no dictionary gives to puzzling questions of English usage. He points out distinctions of word meaning, norms of grammar and syntax, and shows you how orderly thinking can help you identify errors when you meet them. With this expert guidance, your writing can become more precise, vivid and easy to understand.

WILSON FOLLETT
MODERN
AMERICAN
USAGE

Edited and Completed by
JACQUES BARZUN
In Collaboration With

CARLOS BAKER   **JAMES D. HART**
FREDERICK W. DUPEE   **PHYLLIS McGINLEY**
DUDLEY FITTS   **LIONEL TRILLING**

WARNER BOOKS

A Warner Communications Company

WARNER BOOKS EDITION

Copyright © 1966 by Hill and Wang, Inc.
All rights reserved

Library of Congress Catalog Card Number: 66-18993

ISBN 0-446-81529-2

This Warner Books Edition is published by
arrangement with Hill & Wang, Inc.

Cover design by The New Studio Inc.

Warner Books, Inc., 75 Rockefeller Plaza, New York, N.Y. 10019

 A Warner Communications Company

Printed in the United States of America

Not associated with Warner Press, Inc. of Anderson, Indiana

First Printing: April, 1974

Reissued: September, 1977

10 9 8 7 6 5 4 3 2

Contents

Publisher's Note

WILSON FOLLETT devoted his last years to composing a book on the subject he had studied all his life—American usage. When Wilson Follett died, he left more than two-thirds of the manuscript in first draft. To those who had read it, it was intolerable to think that his book would never be published. Jacques Barzun, among others of Wilson Follett's friends and correspondents, had followed the manuscript's progress from the beginning, and he accepted the task of revising and finishing the work on the understanding that he would be aided by a small group of writers and teachers of English— Carlos Baker, Frederick W. Dupee, Dudley Fitts, James D. Hart, Phyllis McGinley, and Lionel Trilling. Each of them gave *Modern American Usage* the benefit of his literary skill and educated judgment.

The talent and energy that Follett put into this work obviously implied an intense concern and a characteristic tone. Mr. Barzun and his collaborators shared this concern but none could—or would have tried to—imitate the tone. *Modern American Usage*, though lacking Wilson Follett's final hand, remains his in conception, his in much of its execution, and—the publisher hopes—his in spirit.

Editor's Note

WE WISH to thank the persons who have helped us in the task of making a book in which detail is paramount and in which the intentions of the absent author had to be preserved. This aid was given in many ways. Professor Theodore Caplow and Dr. Wendell H. Taylor read the proofs and made suggestions for improvement, not only in matters of grammar and usage but also of social and physical science. Mrs. Daniel Bell scrutinized both the typescript and the successive proofs with a trained eye for error and a fine ear for style. So did Mr. Arthur W. Wang, whose long friendship with Wilson Follett made him an invaluable helper. Finally, Miss Violet

Serwin bestowed her remarkable skill as decipherer and typist on several versions of the script, and later Mr. James Parsons proofread the galleys with expert attentiveness to form, spacing, and typography.

To the Reader

THE INTRODUCTORY CHAPTER attempts to give the reader some idea of the assumptions that underlie this book and to clear up certain current notions about usage and grammar, purism and pedantry. But though these matters enter into every judgment embodied in the book, a knowledge of them is not required for making a day-to-day use of the guide.

That use is simple. For any word or phrase about which you may feel uncertainty, turn to the Lexicon and look for what you seek in its alphabetical place. The entry may refer you to a more general article, in which several similar locutions are treated together. These longer articles are usually divided into numbered sections corresponding to the successive aspects of the topic.

For light on broad grammatical questions, such as *adverbs, antecedents, number, sequence of tenses, subjunctive,* look under those words in the Lexicon, where you will find a discussion of the principal difficulties attending those elements of syntax. Other syntactical points receive attention under the word they are connected with; for example, *as*; *that, which, relative*; *which* and *and which*.

For matters of style, consult the list of articles grouped under that heading in the Inventory below and find the title of the article or articles that seem pertinent; for example, *jargon, journalese, popularized technicalities.* At many points in the book an entry on a word will refer you to an article, and conversely an article will end with a reference to one or more word entries. This arrangement is designed to help readers who are interested in stylistic points to reach their goal whether they think first of a troublesome word or of a general difficulty. Note that in any article, words in SMALL CAPITALS (other than entire headlines quoted from news-

8

papers) show that there is an entry on the subject in its alphabetical place.

The Inventory will repay a little study by the reader who wishes to pursue a longer or shorter consecutive treatment of related points. Under the first subhead (*Diction*), only the chief words dealt with are listed. Most of the common particles (*a, an, as, but, like, the*, etc.) do not appear in that list but will be found in their alphabetical places in the Lexicon.

Because of its length, the discussion of the complex usage governing *shall* and *will*, *should* and *would* is printed as an appendix (pp. 455–479); and because of the advantage of treating the conventions of punctuation in one place rather than scattered alphabetically under the names of the marks, that subject is likewise given as an appendix (pp. 480–528).

Inventory of Main Entries in the Lexicon

I. DICTION

abbreviations
-able, -ible
accept
accolade
account for
accuse
acknowledge, admit
acquiesce
adequate
admission,
    admittance
advance, -d, -ment
affinity
allege
allergic
allude
alternate,
    alternative
ambiance
ambivalent
amplify
and/or
appreciate

approximate
assure, ensure,
    insure
-athon, -thon
avail
average
back formation
balance
barbarisms
belie
beneficient
bespeak
bourgeois
careen
case
catalog
character
check (verb)
chivalric
cohort
colleague
communicate
compare

compatible
compose, comprise
concept
conferee
connive
connotations
constant(ly)
contact (verb)
contemporary
context
continual
controversial
converse, obverse,
    reverse
convict (verb)
convince
council, counsel,
    consul
covering words
dangerous pairs
defensibles
definitely
delineate

demean, bemean
diction
dilemma
disinterested
doubt
drastic
dubious
echelon
-edly, adverbs in
education
-ee, -er
endings
expound
false singulars
felicitous
financial
fiscal
forbidden words
foreword
forgiveness
format
Frankenstein
French words and
    phrases
-ful
fund (-ing)
gambit
genteelism
helpmate
historic (al)
hopefully
human
humanism
icecap
identical
identify
if and when
if's and an's
illy
impinge
implement (verb)
implicit, explicit
imply, infer
include
inculcate

indicate
initial
insigne
in terms of
ironic
irregardless
-ism
-itis
judicial, judicious
key
Latin and Greek
    plurals
level
limited
locate
lost causes
major, minor
make sense
malaprops
masterful
meaningful
meld
minister (verb)
modern (istic)
momently, -arily
moonlighting
nature
needless words
nonleakable
nympho, psycho,
    etc.
oblivious
obviate
ology
only
overly
permafrost
personal
popular
popularized techni-
    calities
practical
pragmatic (al)
prestigious
prior to

proselyte
purge
qualification
quote, unquote
rack, wrack
range
rarebit
rationale
reaction
realistic
recap
recommend
redolent with
rehabilitate
repeat
reportedly
represent
resource person
respective (ly)
restive
roadability
same
sanction
sanguinary
scholar, -ship
self-addressed
    envelope
senior citizens
sex
shortenings
skill(s)
specific(s)
spelling
spirit of adventure,
    the
swimsuit
telescopings
tenderfoot
that, which, relative
that, who, relative
tick
togetherness
too
transpire
trigger (verb)

II. IDIOM

III. SYNTAX

IV. STYLE

ambiguity
argot
critics' words
educationese
emphasis
etymology
-ing
initialese
-ion, -ness, -ment
jargon

journalese
linking
logic
matching parts
metaphor
noun-plague
Operation X
oxymoron
pedantry
persons

popularized techni-
   calities
pronunciation
prose, the sound of
scientism
spelling
split infinitive
understatement
vogue words

Short Titles of Books Cited in the Text

FOWLER:
> *A Dictionary of Modern English Usage*, by H. W. Fowler. Oxford: The Clarendon Press, 1926.

THE FOWLERS:
> *The King's English*, by H. W. Fowler and F. G. Fowler. Oxford: The Clarendon Press, 1906.

SHORTER ENGLISH DICTIONARY:
> *The Shorter Oxford English Dictionary*, 3rd ed., 2 vols. Oxford: The Clarendon Press, 1947.

OXFORD ENGLISH DICTIONARY:
> *A New English Dictionary on Historical Principles*, 13 vols. Oxford: The Clarendon Press, 1933.

WEBSTER (or THE NEW INTERNATIONAL):
> *Webster's New International Dictionary of the English Language*, 2nd ed. Springfield: G. & C. Merriam Co., 1934.

WEBSTER'S THIRD EDITION:
> *Webster's Third New International Dictionary of the English Language*. Springfield: G. & C. Merriam Co., 1961.

WEBSTER'S COLLEGIATE:
> *Webster's New Collegiate Dictionary*, based on *Webster's New International Dictionary*, 2nd ed. Springfield: G. & C. Merriam Co., 1956.

NEW WORLD WEBSTER (or NEW WORLD DICTIONARY):
> *Webster's New World Dictionary of the English Language*. Cleveland and New York: World Publishing Co., 1951.

AMERICAN COLLEGE:
> *The American College Dictionary*. New York: Random House, 1947.

WILSON FOLLETT was born in North Attleborough, Massachusetts, on March 21, 1887. He was graduated *cum laude* in 1909 from Harvard University, where he had been a Jacob Wendell Scholar in 1906. He was married three times: to Grace Parker in 1909, to Helen Thomas in 1913, and to Margaret Whipple in 1931. After graduating from Harvard he taught English at Texas Agricultural and Mechanical (1909-1912), Dartmouth College (1912-1914), and Brown University (1914-1918).

In the 1920's he began a second career—that of editor. He worked for the Yale University Press and Alfred A. Knopf. At the end of the decade he left Knopf but returned during World War II for several years. His last publishing position was held at New York University Press, in the midfifties. Wilson Follett contributed to many magazines, among them the *Atlantic Monthly, Harper's, Saturday Review, Yale Review*, and the *Virginia Quarterly Review*. He edited several books: the one-volume Century Biographical Dictionary (not signed), *The Works of Stephen Crane* (12 vols., 1925-1926), Crane's *Collected Poems* (1930), and a collection of stories by Thomas Beer. He is the author of *Joseph Conrad: A Short Study, Some Modern Novelists* (with Helen Thomas Follett), *The Modern Novel, No More Sea*, and *Zona Gale: An Artist in Fiction*. He translated from the French *Molière: The Man Seen Through the Plays* by Ramon Fernandez.

He began writing *Modern American Usage* in the summer of 1958 and worked on it steadily until his death in January 1963.

I

INTRODUCTORY

1 / ON USAGE, PURISM, AND PEDANTRY

DESPITE THE MODERN DESIRE to be easy and casual, Americans from time to time give thought to the language they use —to grammar, vocabulary, and gobbledygook. And as on other issues they divide into two parties. The larger, which includes everybody from the proverbial plain man to the professional writer, takes it for granted that there is a right way to use words and construct sentences, and many wrong ways. The right way is believed to be clearer, simpler, more logical, and hence more likely to prevent error and confusion. Good writing is easier to read; it offers a pleasant combination of sound and sense.

Against this majority view is the doctrine of an embattled minority, who make up for their small number by their great learning and their place of authority in the school system and the world of scholarship. They are the professional linguists, who deny that there is such a thing as correctness. The language, they say, is what anybody and everybody speaks. Hence there must be no interference with what they regard as a product of nature; they denounce all attempts at guiding choice; their governing principle is epitomized in the title of a speech by a distinguished member of the profession: "Can Native Speakers of a Language Make Mistakes?" (A. W. Read, *Abstract for the Linguistic Society of America Meeting*, Dec. 28–29, 1964).

Within the profession of linguist there are of course warring factions, but on this conception of language as a natural growth with which it is criminal to tamper they are at one. In their arguments one finds appeals to democratic feelings of social equality (all words and forms are equally good) and individual freedom (a man may do what he likes with his own speech). These assumptions further suggest that the desire for correctness, the very idea of better or worse in speech, is a hangover from aristocratic and oppressive times.

17

To the linguists change is the only ruler to be obeyed. They equate it with life and accuse their critics of being clock-reversers, enemies of freedom, menaces to "life."

Somewhat inconsistently, the linguists produce dictionaries in which they tell us that a word or an expression is standard, substandard, colloquial, archaic, slang, or vulgar. How do they know? They know by listening to the words people use and by noticing—in conversations, newspapers, and books—how and by whom these words are used. Usage, then, is still real and various, even though the authorities refuse to point openly to a set of words and forms as being preferable to others. "Standard" gets around the difficulty of saying "best" or "correct."

It is nonetheless the best usage that decides the meaning of words. When the *New Yorker* reprints as an amusing tidbit *A symposium sponsored by the IEEE computer group will present a dearth of material on technologies, logic and memory implementations . . .* , it is because most of those who use *dearth* continue to believe that it means *scarcity* and not, as the writer thought, *abundance*. That writer was undoubtedly a native speaker, yet he seems to have made what used to be called a mistake. Very likely his mind was momentarily distracted from the word *wealth*, and he wrote *dearth*.

Such slips of the mind, tongue, or pen occur by the million every day without any effect but a smile or a slight embarrassment. The accepted meaning of the word that is misused remains untouched; and hence also the idea of *accepted:* it must signify what in freer days people dared to call *correct*.

But if usage rules in obvious cases of this sort, it is conceivable that a usage also exists about finer points—such matters as ingrained connotations, distinctions between close synonyms, suggestions of tone, applicability to concrete or figurative situations, indications of time or purpose or action; in short, the many hints and echoes that words carry within them and that a good speaker or writer brings out as if he were playing on a keyboard. Skill in expression consists in nothing else than steadily choosing the fittest among all possible words, idioms, and constructions. These differ in the qualities that usage has bestowed upon them; and the qualities, in turn, are known by the speaker or writer because he has attended to words and forms as they occur normally, in the company of other words spoken or written.

This choosing among words is made by every user of the language, and not exclusively by professional speakers and writers. A truck driver does not talk to a policeman as he does to his fiancée or to his pals, and we change our verbal as well as our facial expressions when we pass from a wedding to a funeral. In personal relations this adjustment is called tact. In the attempt to make the best use of words, the same mental work is performed. Yet it would be a mistake to suppose that a writer or speaker switches from one complete language or usage to another when he adapts his words to a situation or to the expectation of his audience. All the usages, standard and other, can be drawn on and mixed. It is this bewildering abundance, coupled with the insidious strength of bad examples, that makes most people speak and write carelessly and clumsily, even while they respect clarity and good usage.

Hence, in the task of "communicating," to which everybody these days is strenuously invited—the task of producing so-called effective English—we have to think not only of rules but also of the infinite requirements of tact. Readers even more than hearers respond to what is well put, whether or not they perceive what makes it so. Actually, language is made logical and clear by observing the norms of grammar and syntax; and it is made precise, vivid, and easy ("readable") by respecting the demands of idiom, connotation, tone, rhythm, and the other more fugitive virtues.

Accordingly, a book on usage such as this seeks to serve two related purposes. By analyzing structural errors and ambiguities it reminds writers and speakers of grammatical norms that are frequently flouted; and by discussing words and idioms it provides a list of distinctions and suggestions in the realm of tact. In neither department can it be complete; it does not pretend to be a grammar book, nor does it profess to discuss every failure of judgment or subtlety in the use of words. It concentrates on the prevailing faults of current speech and prose. And the most useful service it can render is to make its readers think for themselves on these matters. To become sensibly self-conscious about words is more important than to memorize and act on this or that suggestion without thought. For, once again, tact is the overriding concern, and a locution deserving of reproof at large may yield the needed effect when put in the right place, as Shaw demonstrated when he wittily used *contact* as a verb: *Etonian toffs and Polytechnic cads should contact each other only in street fights, the organization of which might be regarded as a legitimate part of their physical exercise.*

But, it will be asked, is tact not an individual gift, therefore highly variable in its choices? And if that is so, what guidance can a manual offer, other than that of its author's prejudices—mere impressionism? The more such a writer makes a point of his preferences the more he will be likely to produce a system of purism and pedantry. Would it not be better to ascertain statistically what the people of this generation actually say and write when they are being careful but not too careful? And since this is what certain dictionaries do, why not go straight to a good dictionary?

The first and obvious reply is that a dictionary does not give reasons even when it gives examples of varying usage in one or two brief quotations. Often, what makes a word preferable is its relation to others in a passage. The narrow context of a dictionary sentence gives too few clues to the force and versatility of a particular word. Definitions must be supplemented with discussion. This discussion draws its authority from the principle that good usage is what the people who think and care about words believe good usage to be. They have—and their critical reading and listening verifies—the impression that *dearth* means *scarcity*, that such a word as *escalation* is pedantic, that X. writes like a purist with a taste for the archaic, and that such and such expressions are slang or vulgarisms, or again that they may be allowable in loose colloquial speech but would jar or mislead on other occasions. The fact that those who attend to language disagree on many points does not alter the nature and force of good usage, any more than the diverse judgments of critics about fine art or of courts about the law alter the nature and force of art and of law.

The correctness of educated impressions was strikingly shown not long ago in the outcry against the statement made by the editors of Webster's New International Dictionary, Third Edition, that *ain't* is "used orally in most parts of the U.S. by many cultivated speakers, especially in the phrase *ain't I?*" The impression was general among such speakers that the statement was contrary to fact; and when the statistics on which the assertion rested were looked up by Professor Sheridan Baker of Michigan, everybody who read his article understood why the impression was more reliable than the statistics. ("The Art and Science of Letters," *Papers of the Michigan Academy of Science, Arts, and Letters*, vol. L, pp. 521 ff.)

The claim of scientific objectivity about usage begs the question. How can science know who the cultivated are and what number suffices to make them many? The "scientist" here goes by just the same impressions as his opponent. In opinions on usage, cogency and reasoning, not numbers, are what give weight to the decisions arrived at, just as in judicial opinions. And since in the realm of usage there is no police power to enforce the right, no one suffers, except perhaps in skill, by ignoring it.

Consider the bookdealer who in his catalogue of rare works describes one as adorned *with hitherto unpublished photographs of amorous Hindu sculpture.* The reader familiar with usage understands what is meant, but knows that *amorous* is the wrong word. The writer should have used *erotic; amorous* can only be used of persons and, by extension, of words or scenes in which actual persons are involved. Recourse to a dictionary will not help, for the definitions generally assemble rather than separate synonyms. Only the reading of literature—or of a guide that makes a point of it—will tell the uninformed what that distinction is.

Some may object that if the bookdealer's wording was readily understood, the distinction is silly and he who makes it is a prig. Why raise a fuss over *any* expression that is intelligible? The answer is that a language has chosen ways of putting things and rejects others equally clear. *We does* is intelligible but not English; and in the pair of epithets before us a second substitution clinches the point: if *amorous* is just as good as *erotic,* we should be able to say *loving* as readily as *amorous.* But what would the least sophisticated of readers think if he were told of a book *with photographs of loving Hindu sculpture?* He would suppose the writer to be foreign; and why? Because the phrase is not English. It is no more true English, though perhaps less visibly false, when *amorous* appears where *erotic* should be.

So much for the positive effect of usage and misusage. Negative discrimination is nowadays even more important for anyone who dislikes pedantry and who wants to avoid falling into it. The temptation to that fall is very great, for science and scholarship dominate the intellectual world and confer prestige on whoever imitates their literal mind and abstract tongue. The worst enemy of modern languages is the universal desire to show off in this pretentious way. Thus the telephone girl who speaks on tape for the Weather Bureau tells you about the day's *precipitation probability.* What she and her principals mean is *likelihood of rain.* She feels no discomfort in saying the pompous phrase, for her talk and her reading are peppered with pedantries. The ads tell her to buy a cosmetic that will give her face *subcutaneous stimulation,* and the news story says that a collision in mid-air was narrowly missed thanks to the pilot's *evasive action.*

It is a commonplace that the professions tend to develop jargons, but it is less often recognized that the modern professions make their jargons pedantic, as the older jargons of sailors, farmers, and thieves were not. Today, a person interested in the public schools is exposed to reading a report on the playing of background music in classrooms which says: *The hypothesis, therefore, is that music can reduce the intensity dimension of the student so that he remains in the range of effectiveness along the continuum.* And a person interested in the fine arts is invited to consider the merits of a painter who says: *I work to qualify a surface, to qualify a reality in terms of my human experience which is given form in abstract conception. . . . The determinant has changed to coordinate with the human condition. And that condition . . . has become increasingly synthetic and structural.*

In both extracts the pretentious words string together half-realized metaphors, a mode of thought that now characterizes educated and uneducated alike and shows them to be—at least in words—pedants who only half-think. The danger to the language, therefore, does not come from those unhappily sunk in ignorance and vulgarity; it comes from the entire range of the population, which is sunk in the swamp of jargon, and which complains of it without knowing how to extricate itself. This holds good for both sides of the Atlantic. While an American publisher invites an author to write for him by saying *The platform, booklength, can be about as flexible in size as you desire,* an English statesman exhorts the nation to *plus up its integrity image.* It would be far better for the common mother tongue if Webster's latest edition were right and educated speakers did go in for such simplifications as *ain't I,* instead of saying *the time factor is against me, the trouble between us is semantics, can you make yourself available?* and *in my frame of reference I can visualize no place for yours.*

Any revulsion from jargon should ideally take the speaker back to direct colloquial speech, but human recoil is extremist, and the effort to avoid error often lands the self-improver in what is known as purism. The difference between purity and purism is as hard to define as that between modesty and prudery, but in either domain the foolish excess is easily distinguished. Purism is another form of the pedantic. It singles out in the language of science and scholarship what is literal and minute, as pedantry does the abstract and long-winded. Purism haggles over trifles and refuses to know when errors and confusions no longer matter. We all understand what a *spiral staircase* is; the purist reminds us that a spiral lies flat in one plane, so that our staircase is properly a *helix.* But even if each of us has his one or two pet pedantries, collectively we shall not go down the helical staircase. We shall continue to *drink a cup of coffee* and assuredly not a *cupful;* we shall speak of *captions below the text,* though *caption* by a confused etymology suggests *head;* we shall refer to *the proverbial man of straw,* though he is not the subject of a proverb; we shall speak of being *buttonholed* by a bore and not *buttonheld,* from the supposedly correct *buttonhold;* we shall say *it is no use* when we speak, though we may want to write *it is of no use;* we shall certainly *cross the bridge* (but not till we come to it), instead of agonizing over the truth that it is the river that is crossed and not the bridge. And if the world, faced with a new and inspiriting phenomenon, wants to say *outer space,* we shall not affect to be puzzled on the plea that space cannot be inner or outer. If there is an *outer darkness* there can be an *outer space,* which we may even hope to visit.

In these and dozens of other instances (see FRANKENSTEIN; ONLY; SCOOP; and PEDANTRY), the reason for letting go the pure or pedantic truth of the matter is that it no longer serves (or never did serve) an expressive purpose. Conversely, the reason for urging the thoughtful to retain the strict sense of CONNIVE and DISINTERESTED is that the new, creeping abuse threatens to rob us of an expressive instrument. The confusion between two words or two senses may be an old one repeatedly cleared up, as in *perspicuous* and *perspicacious*—words that no one is obliged to use, but that everyone who does should keep straight, like *dearth* and *wealth;* or confusion may come from ignorant innovation, as when *viable* suddenly replaces *possible* at every turn. It is worth noting that when a distinction is commonplace, even though of trivial effect, the advocates of laxity do not overlook it. The young foreigner who apologizes for the fact that the chocolates he has brought as a gift are *molten* is told with a smile that that is not English: the right word is *melted.* Similarly, we are bound to say *awestruck* and *grief-stricken.* If we are to be bound when it makes as little difference as this, we should be able to comply with good grace when it makes much more.

For it often happens, as in *disinterested,* that the meaning now being threatened by confusion was arrived at by a distinction not originally felt. When it was at last made, it presumably answered a need, and in all probability that need still exists. Hence, for the orderly mind, the return to the earlier and blurred meaning is uneconomical and unwise; it robs us of something valuable. Almost always, the move toward a distinction, the positive work of mind on language, is a gain. The negative change, away from distinct ideas, is generally the result of heedlessness or ignorance, and hence a loss.

It follows that the appeal to the catch phrase "change means life" needs reconsideration. Change means death too, and in our own bodies we take steps to arrest or reverse certain changes by medicine, inoculation, surgery, and other strong measures. We choose what we want to preserve and what we want to slough off. In fact, analogies from life and evolution are poor ways of thinking about language. Change is inevitable in language as in other institutions—a truth known and accepted long before modern linguistics—but change is only a name for changes in the plural; that is, change affects the manifold elements of language unevenly and unpredictably. A language does not move as a solid mass like a glacier. In English, a very large number of forms and words have not changed for six hundred years—which is why with a little help an English speaker can read Chaucer at sight. And throughout much of this period the persistence of a standard has prevented some equally persistent deviations from becoming good usage: *scarcely . . . than* has been written for nearly two centuries without becoming acceptable; *hand me them pliers* has been said over and over again without breaking down the distinction between the adjective and the pronoun form.

There is, in short, more to the history of language than the restless agitation of molecules of speech, out of which the best of all possible worlds of language must emerge. Conscious purpose and reason have interfered with "nature," and the result has been embodied in the written tradition. Present-day linguistic theory writes off the written, saying it is not language at all; only speech is language. If this were so, the materials of linguistic science would go back only as far as the invention of the phonograph: everything before then would be irrelevant, and the boasted evolution itself would be irrecoverable for lack of records. Babel, moreover, would long ago have overtaken us, for the rate of change in spoken sounds is very rapid, and only the written language—indeed, only a fixed conventional spelling —now enables us to understand Shakespeare and to share (as we say) the English language with him.

It is useless to speculate about the motives of students whose zeal for enshrining the slip of the tongue makes them despise the richest source of fact about their subject. But it is important in the middle of the twentieth century to reassert the worth of the alphabet. The spoken language is not independent of the written. One need only listen to colloquial talk to discover how much the mother tongue owes to the conscious work that writers have always felt entitled to perform upon it. No scientific pretensions can remove that right. It would be a curious state of affairs if only those who seldom think about the words they use, who read little, and who "cannot be bothered" with distinctions should be the only ones with full powers over vocabulary and syntax.

Even on grounds of free democratic choice the hands-off attitude about language receives no support. If the citizen as taxpayer, parent, teacher, motorist, litigant, reader of poetry, or user of gadgets were delighted with the millions of words he endures annually, there might be some reason for letting everything alone and scrapping freshman English together with manuals of usage. But on the contrary the articulate public continually complains. The children, we hear, are badly taught and cannot read, spell, or write; employers despair of finding literate clerks and typists; the professions deplore the thickening of jargon which darkens counsel and impedes action; scientists cry out in their journals that their colleagues cannot report their facts intelligibly; and businessmen declare many bright people unemployable for lack of the ability to say what they mean in any medium. This is enough warrant for dozens of remedial measures; many are suggested and followed; but most of them are of the mechanical-miraculous kind which in the end prove futile.

Resisting the tide, then, is not antidemocratic but simple self-preservation against the decay of mind itself. Some wonder what is the good? On this point individual temperament decides. Brave writers resist chiefly by example and sometimes by precept: Rex Stout has one of his characters say *"Contact" is not a verb under this roof,* and those who read this prelude to hospitality either applaud or pause in surprise. Newspaper and magazine editors, publishers, and certain business firms fight a guerrilla war in the jungle of jargon and pick off—a few at a time, over and over again —some of the worst enemies of logic and usage. It is hard to imagine where we should be without this effort, and it is at least conceivable that if the pressure is kept up it will hasten the increasingly obvious and imperative reform—a resumption in our schools of the teaching of grammar and the reading of books.

In any event, fatalism about language cannot be the philosophy of those who care about language; it is the illogical philosophy of their opponents. Surely the notion that, because usage is ultimately what everybody does to words, nobody can or should do anything about them is self-contradictory. Somebody, by definition, does something; and this something is best done by those with convictions and a stake in the outcome, whether the stake of private pleasure or of professional duty or both does not matter. Resistance always begins with individuals.

Previous generations also had their cant words and pedantries, which were destroyed, not by empty time or by the indifferent, but by the choice of those who were offended or bored. Jonathan Swift, who is damned by the hands-off school for denouncing what seemed to him objectionable in 1710, actually accomplished much of what he hoped for, though he failed once. He disliked fashionable shortenings such as *mob*, from *mobile vulgus*, the fickle crowd. Since *mob* has become part of good usage, it is held proved that Swift was wrong to raise his voice. But we can well imagine that *mob* was offensive when new; it has only gradually become deodorized. The lesson is that when repeated use has worn down the novelty, the word we hear and the associations we sense are not what they were at first. That is why we would still agree with Swift about the other shortenings he reproved and vanquished: *phizz, hipps, poz, rep, incog,* and *plenipo*. One need not suppose that he got rid of them all by himself in order to see that he was right to take his chance and speak out. At any time and about any word, one should exercise the right of free speech that some would abridge. By simply using or rejecting the vocable, one casts a vote, repeatable as often as one likes, in favor of one's views. To arrive at these views and achieve consistency among them is much the harder part of the task, and it is this difficulty that brings the thoughtful to discussions of usage.

2 / ON THE NEED
OF AN ORDERLY MIND

IT IS NO DOUBT possible for a writer so to train himself, or so to be trained, that his only merit is freedom from faults. But even the most fanatical believer in the efficacy of hunting down errors will not pretend that we can distinguish at sight the negative from the positive merits of writing. It is a mistake to imply an opposition between the absence of faults and the presence of vitality, as if correct writing had to be dead writing, or as if we had to choose between power and polish. In writing as in morals, negative and positive merits are complementary; resistance to the wrong and the weak is, *ipso facto*, cultivation of the right and the strong.

For example, to eliminate the vice of wordiness is to ensure the virtue of emphasis, which depends more on conciseness than on any other factor. Wherever we can make twenty-five words do the work of fifty, we halve the area in which looseness and disorganization can flourish, and by reducing the span of attention required we increase the force of the thought. To make our words count for as much as possible is surely the simplest as well as the hardest secret of style. Its difficulty consists in the ceaseless pursuit of the thousand ways of rectifying our mistakes, eliminating our inaccuracies, and replacing our falsities—in a word, editing our prose. When we can do this habitually (even though it never comes easy) we shall find ourselves honoring the faculty that can do more toward this end than a mastery of prescriptive grammar, more than the study of etymology and semantics, more than an observance of idiom and the maxims of rhetoric. And what is this faculty? It is the blessing of an orderly mind.

No mind, to be sure, is completely and consistently orderly. But some minds are incomparably more demanding of order than others, and in consequence some writers lapse into disorder more rarely than others. Still, all writers drowse at places where they should have stayed awake; all writers are guilty of oversights without which they would have been better writers—one reason why many of the cautionary examples in this book are drawn from authors ranging from respectable to illustrious. A great deal of our language is so automatic that even the thoughtful never think about it, and this mere not-thinking is the gate through which solecisms or inferior locutions slip in. Some part, greater or smaller, of every thousand words is inevitably parroted, even by the least parrotlike.

Anyone inclined to doubt this statement can prove it to himself by a simple test. Let him skim through a book or magazine at random. Most articles and stories will require the turning of a page in the middle of a sentence. At these moments he will find that he has mentally read the next word —frequently the next several words—without turning the page at all. He will occasionally have guessed wrong but more often he will be right. Where so much of language falls into automatic and predictable patterns, there will certainly be a good measure of standardized error that the orderly mind has not even noticed. Hundreds of educated persons have written, for example, *center around* or *center about*. They know as well as Euclid that a center is a point that other things can surround, not an area that surrounds other things; their sense of order, if they used it, would tell them that circles find their centers *in* or *on* or *at* a point, and that this fact must control our metaphoric use of *center*. But this reasoning is just what does not come into play.

Order, reasoning, is sidetracked again in the construction that we may call the *one-of-those-who-is* blunder, probably the commonest in speech and print alike, in spite of being one of the most easily detected. *He is one of those who fights back:* the orderly mind sees where the singular statement about the individual ends, where the plural statement about the group or class begins, and such a mind avoids mixing the forms. But to see such matters one has to look. The many who never think of looking have therefore sprinkled millions of lines with *those who fights, prophets who goes unrecognized, children who has never known parental companionship, peaks that wears a perpetual crown of snow,* and so on without end.

This particular mistake will yield to a hint of rhetoric or to a touch of the old-fashion prescriptive grammar now in disfavor with linguists. But there are thousands of other mistakes that fall outside the grammar book, since grammar deals only with what is amenable to classification and rule. For the irregular error, the unique blunder, a superior sense of order is the sole corrective. Without its discipline, the faults can only be dealt with one at a time, laboriously, after the damage has been done. Perhaps a third to a half of the offenses against usage illustrated in the following pages would need no description or analysis if the faculty that makes for order were always alert.

Consider what pitfalls may hide even in the simple device of listing, the very basis of logical organization. Any educated person can surely make a list of items under a heading designed to govern them all. Such an arrangement will be what the track is to the train, the fence to the field, or the strait-jacket to the unruly patient: it will be inescapable. But is it? Look at the description that a widely esteemed desk encyclopedia gives of its contents on the jacket of its second edition. The inventory begins with a centered head:

HAS SEPARATE ARTICLES ON:

under which we read:

EVERY proper name in the Bible, with reference to passages where they occur.

EVERY incorporated place in the United States with a population of 1,000 or over, as well as many smaller places of historical interest.

EVERY U.S. President, every Supreme Court Justice since 1908 (plus many earlier ones), all outstanding Senators, Representatives, and Cabinet members.

So far, good—three entries, in parallel, answering to the verb and noun in their common heading. But now comes the fourth entry:

BASIC articles on major literatures, as well as innumerable biographies and shorter articles.

Where now is the link with the centered head? Forgotten, consigned to limbo, along with the orderly mind. The column runs to four more items, not one of which matches the announcement *Has separate articles on*. What we have articles on in these four is:

EXPANDED articles on music, modern literature, European geography, science, and many other subjects.

MORE economic information and social history in articles throughout the book.

ARTICLES covering thousands of species of plants and animals (and ten pages of illustrations on animals, four pages on plants).

AND countless additions and improvements that put this ... ENCYCLOPEDIA in a class by itself.

Of the eight entries under one rubric, only three have a logical connection with it. The grand culmination of senselessness is reached when we bring together the first statement and the last: *Has separate articles on and countless additions and improvements*. (As an afterthought one might also ask how, in a reference work, *separate* articles differ from just articles.) The lesson here is simply that where the orderly mind is not continuously in charge—before, during, and after the act of writing—all the signs and gestures of sound organization will not rule out blunder and chaos.

The chief trait of the orderly mind is tenacity, concentration—that undeviating attention which in various sports is enjoined in the precept "Keep your eye on the ball." What we must keep our eye on in prose is the object, idea, or wording that we start with. In any list of items, the head sets up a promise; if anything below fails to fit, the promise is broken, the thought is derailed. For all who speak or write, the road to effective language is thinking straight.

In ordinary prose the counterpart of an inventory is the simple enumeration of three or more members separated by punctuation (usually commas), with a conjunction (usually *and,* but sometimes *but* or *or*) as the signal of the closing member. This sort of series, one of the commonest of all patterns, can be represented by the formula *a, b, and c* or (when expanded) by *a, b, c, . . . , and n.* Examples: *red, white, and blue / tea, coffee, or milk / woke up, got up, bathed, dressed, breakfasted, and hurried out / Boston at Detroit, Cleveland at Chicago, New York at Minneapolis, Kansas City at Los Angeles, and Baltimore at Washington.* One might think offhand that these series provided about as little opportunity to go wrong as any standard construction in English, but to think so is to underestimate the capacity of language for laying traps and the propensity of writers for stumbling into them. The conjunction *and* is one of the most troublesome words in the vocabulary. Because it is so regularly a signal of the last member, the absent-minded writer automatically accepts it as signaling a last member that in fact never turns up. The result is a structure with the look but not the reality of an honest enumeration—a false series in which the last item is a misfit.

The new tanker has an over-all length of 736 feet, a beam of 102 feet and she is capable of carrying 16,581,000 gallons of oil. To have a genuine series of three, you must either link the *length* and *beam* phrases with *and,* or turn the last unit into a matching noun—e.g. *and a capacity of . . .* (See APPENDIX 2, pp. 480–528.)

We saw in the discussion of *one-of-those-who-is* why and how the clash of number between subject and verb should be avoided—though not all compound subjects constitute a plural. The genuine clash occurs in many other constructions, usually when the attention is distracted from the true subject by some intervening word that differs in number, or else by some inversion that causes the subject to follow instead of precede its verb. Consider such a sentence as *Mrs. W.'s list of special methods include those developed for the home as well as for the school.* Here *includes,* the singular verb that belongs to *list,* is corrupted into a plural by the intervening *methods.* The old playwright John Ford, who obviously wrote too fast, was a frequent victim of this false attraction, e.g. in Act IV of *Perkin Warbeck:*

> *I feel the fabric*
> *Of my designs are tottering.*

The attraction of a properly plural verb to an intervening singular is only a little less frequent than the reverse. *Even friends of the labor movement like Professor X. has* (have) *finally become convinced that curbs on that monopoly are necessary.* Sometimes a quasi-collective noun that might be construed as a plural provides a sort of escape hatch for the careless: *A combination of lectures and fashion shows are planned to stimulate playgoing in various cities.* The writer might protest that he conceived *combination* as a plural and was not derailed by *lectures and fashion shows;* but it may be doubted whether he would write *combination are* with nothing in between.

It is of course by means of the critical spirit that one learns the unteachable things about writing. One forces oneself to be critical about everything one reads or hears, and this must not exclude what one says or writes. Self-criticism, which begins by being an arduous discipline, ends by becoming second nature. But habit also protects familiar faults. Without a continual scrutiny of his successive drafts, even a good writer will fall into bad writing. Here is an author so intent on what he means that he fails to see what he is actually saying—all the more regrettably that he is dealing with questions of language. Of a particular level of diction he says: *It is so universal that few people in the United States escape its influence entirely, including all but a small portion* (number?) *of schoolteachers.* He is not aware that he has bundled in nearly all the schoolteachers with "the few that escape." His intention was to say the exact opposite; namely, that most people, including most schoolteachers, do not escape.

Order or the lack of it is sometimes hidden well below the surface of the words, and the analysis that would disclose error is not undertaken, because the reader's mind willingly follows the writer's concealed confusion. Thus a storyteller starts off a paragraph with these words: *Some hours later, after an excellent lunch had been swallowed untasted by a silent assembly* . . . The riddle here is: Who could testify to the excellence of the lunch?

More often, inconsistent thought gives itself away by disrupting the form, as in the opening of this book review: *The two really first-rate books of reportage under discussion today differ so widely in technique and in approach that it becomes rather remarkable to see how much alike, after all, they are in their search for truth (a word so badly abused that it may be taken to mean, for example, a television quiz show that is fixed but not illegal); their confident grasp of large, troubled areas of human experience, and their hunger—it is a hunger—for justice, explicitly in the one, by unmistakable implication in the other.* Of these ninety words, sixty furnish us only red herrings and obscurity. Mere grammar goes by the board; the ten words at the end hang in mid-air, adverbial in meaning and having no verb to hook on to. Obviously the writer, confident in his forward motion, never once looked back.

The great classics are no better off when they rely on habit or technique without self-inspection. James Fenimore Cooper, who could write superb narrative prose when he resisted his mania for calling every bullet *a leaden messenger* and every eagle *a monarch of the air,* would from time to time produce a sentence that in its perfection of chaos staggers credulity. In *The Pathfinder,* one of his Indians, startled by the smoke of an unexpected campfire, stands on tiptoe watching it: *Then, falling back on his feet, a low exclamation, in the soft tones that form so singular a contrast to its harsher cries in the Indian warrior's voice, was barely audible.*

The miscellany of common blunders here assembled shows, not that the orderly mind is a rarity, but that its lapses are frequent and easy. No one would contend that the faculty of order by itself will overcome all the difficulties of writing sound prose. It gives the security of the good tactician, but it is not the whole art of war and not even the full arsenal. What it needs as a first supplement is a command of traditional grammar and of some tested rhetorical principles. We must accordingly glance at them forthwith, beginning with what in all the Western languages but English is still officially known as grammar.

3 / ON THE NEED OF SOME GRAMMAR

As ROBERT BROWNING tells us in his "Grammarian's Funeral," the grammarian must die, but the logic and grammatical forms of the beautiful inflected language he has cherished live on. Today the cultural descendant of Jefferson or Mark Twain makes the same assumption about the permanent need of grammar to govern his own much less highly inflected language. By grammar he means primarily syntax—parts-of-speech grammar, subject-verb-and-predicate grammar, the traditional apparatus for analyzing the structure and logic of the sentence. According to that tradition any good sentence will stand parsing: it can be broken down into subjects and objects and antecedents, cases and parts of speech, modes and tenses. The comprehension of these goes with the comprehension of meaning itself: grammatical relations are the offprint of logical relations. Grammar explains how the elements of language that everybody rearranges so swiftly and easily come together to form meaning.

Any such descendant is likely to suffer shock when he comes upon the discovery that everything he was taught about grammar is now in disrepute among the scholars of language; is, indeed, officially as dead as Browning's grammarian. If someone of inquiring mind turns to the article *Grammar* in an up-to-date encyclopedia, he will learn that grammar no longer deals primarily with syntax. It has become morphology—the science of the formation of words, how they are built out of the smallest bits and pieces of meaning; e.g. the *s* that usually turns a singular common noun into a plural. Since the inquirer's troubles probably have to do with constructions rather than with the make-up of words, he turns to the entry *Syntax*. All it tells him is "See *Grammar*." Back where he started, he discovers that what he is seeking is a reprehensible doctrine called *pre-*

scriptive grammar—something now outlawed because it is unscientific: it prescribes—that is, recommends—certain uses of English as grammatical and correct, others as ungrammatical and incorrect. This is as bad as to point out correct usage in words and idioms. In true grammar it is wrong to say that anything is right.

By now our inquirer is at a loss. He wanted guidance and has been denied it in the name of science. It dawns on him that modern linguistics regards language as a set of facts and tendencies; it has nothing to impart about the successful ways of composing English or the relative merits of forms and constructions. Grammar has renounced all these concerns as so many value judgments. Yet what the seeker was after was precisely a system of value judgments, such as he can get from any mechanic or builder about the appropriate use or relative strength of materials.

There is of course much to be learned from the so-called objective or purely descriptive grammar, whose foundations were laid by an Englishman, Henry Sweet, the model of Shaw's hero in *Pygmalion* and *My Fair Lady*. Sweet's *New English Grammar* (1891) inspired the Danish scholar Otto Jespersen to perfect the method and produce *A Modern English Grammar on Historical Principles* (7 vols., 1909–1931). After these two came a host of laborious analysts and collectors of what are now called speechways. This term puts writing in its place among things artificial and unimportant, and the objectivists deride the grammar book and the schoolmarm who together tried to maintain the norms. Actually, the old grammars were in general quite objective, and it was society rather than the books that enforced correctness.

Thus do cultural ideals change and, in changing, obscure or repress permanent human needs. For the "science" established by the appeal to liberty and the tactics of ridicule during the past half century is in effect not about language at all, if language is defined as the art of skillfully conveying intended meanings. Rather, what the linguists have studied is that portion of human behavior which is articulate—a branch of social psychology. Whether the stuff of this new learning is indeed a natural product like cobalt or ambergris is something to be debated elsewhere. What concerns us here is that the other thing also known as language, language as the art of self-expression, language as a material conformable to the rules of creation, remains a subject deserving man's best care.

If, then, we assume that language is not only to be spoken and suffered but can also be used—and well used; and if we believe it possible to make words serve purposes that are more than momentary, we find the linguistic critique of grammar irrelevant and we recover the right to judge between those forms that are awkward and false and those that are delicate and expressive. To help us compare and choose, we must accept judgments of value and adopt suggested remedies—quite as if we were curing an ailment. This enterprise involves reading books about language that do not simply describe, and it means mastering that part of grammar which is the most potent aid to composition; namely, the rules of syntax.

Prose is not necessarily good because it obeys the rules of syntax, but it is fairly certain to be bad if it ignores them. Professional writers have generally felt it a duty to face and solve the difficulties of grammatical agreement, time sequence, and natural linkage, considering this effort not slavery but protection against unreadability and wrong meaning. The perceptions codified in grammar supplement the orderly mind if one has it, and serve as a substitute for it if one has it not. Examine this short, simple sentence from a widely read murder story: *And what purpose has all his objections served?* That is what happens to those who trust the ear alone: *purpose has* is a natural sequence; it sounds right. Unhappily, the question asked is not about *purpose* but about *objections*. The author has actually written: *All his objections has served what purpose?* The orderly mind being at fault, nothing is left but grammar to save it from falling victim to the reversed order characteristic of questions.

Nor does it take a question to bring about such accidents. Any singular that leads into an inverted order of words can do it. Here is an instance the more curious for occurring in a book devoted entirely to the niceties of diction: *From this use has sprung certain quaint verb-specimens;* that is, *Certain . . . specimens has sprung . . .* When instinct fails, grammar helps by naming the fault and the remedy: a singular noun ahead of the verb must not blind a writer to his delayed plural subject. This help of course presupposes assent to the principle that verbs had better agree in number with their subjects. Anyone is free to dissent, but the rebels are likely to find that the convenience won by anarchy can become terribly inconvenient. Such opportunism has all the disadvantages of changing signals without consultation or the rules of a game without foreseeing all the consequences.

It is commonly said that English is a language in which a standardized word order performs the functions assigned to endings in inflected languages such as Latin; but English is so free in its order that it is often hard to make sure where the subject is. The discovery calls for an act of grammatical discernment. *Silver and gold have I none / Gone are the days of effortless ease / Peaceful lay the valley / Desperate if not hopeless is such a diplomatic assignment* —such idiomatic inversions contribute to vigor and variety. But in dislocating the normal order they bring next to the verb some noun easily mistaken for its subject. At this point, again, a grammatical rule is a means of rescue and reassurance. As in the *one-of-those-who* construction, analysis (parsing) sets us or keeps us on the track: the subject, antecedent of the relative pronoun *who,* is the plural *those,* which requires a plural verb *are.* The demonstration will of course be Eskimo to one who does not know what a subject is, or a pronoun, or an antecedent. But to the technically equipped the explanation is quicker and simpler than the appeal to logic.

Some, to be sure, insist that errors committed so often by so many must not be called errors. One libertarian quotes a sentence of Shelley's: *I am one of those who am unable to refuse my assent* and asserts that in the United States the singular (more usually *is* than *am*) offends no one but grammarians. This is not true, to begin with—it offends every good writer; and next, the assertion misconceives the role of examples, great names, and majority rule. As Jespersen showed with his 50,000 classified examples, a precedent can be found for practically any construction or locution. At this rate anything goes and there is no use arguing either for the rules or for unlimited freedom.

But whoever has a meaning to convey finds that in order to say anything briefly and well he must choose among many possibilities. As a thinking being he cannot help responding to sound and rhythm or favoring logic and smoothness over their opposites—whereby he is once again engaged in generating rules. And to the extent that he can think straight the rules will come close to those already in the tradition. Let three thousand say *one of those who believes* while only three say *those who believe;* and as long as the three thousand do not also say *we believes, you believes, they believes,* the three thousand will be wrong from the only point of view that is relevant here, the point of view of form. Mere prevalence can sanctify many sorts of popular error—it can, for example, make words eventually mean the opposite of what they originally meant—but it cannot make a singular verb consort with a plural subject for the convenience of a writer who has not taken the trouble to find out what the subject is.

Grammatical analysis is not, of course, confined to such elementary problems as the identification of a subject to insure agreement in number. Many constructions are susceptible of both a lower and a higher interpretation, a simpler and a more complex analysis. On the cover of a popular weekly is listed an article about *What American Youth Thinks About War, Religion, Jobs, Sex, Parents, Education and Themselves.* The clash between *Thinks* and *Themselves* can be taken as that between a plural pronoun and a singular antecedent, and to see it so will disclose the ill-advised pairing of *Thinks About . . . Themselves.* But the discrepancy can also be seen as a matter of confused definitions. The phrase *American Youth* suggests the younger generation collectively, and this construction is confirmed by the immediately following singular verb *Thinks.* Yet when we come to the plural pronoun *Themselves* we find *Youth* given the quite different meaning *all the young as individuals.* Since words should not be made to carry two opposite meanings at once or to figure as both singular and plural, this second analysis—which is grammar too—makes us aware of an inconsistency more important than the merely mechanical.

Meanwhile, the example tells us something deeper about the mental activity that, if sustained, produces good writing. Among the snags that every writer encounters, many cannot be recognized without the sort of analysis that underlies grammar. Agreement presents riddles impossible to formulate except in grammatical terms. Punctuation is difficult to discuss (for example, as it relates to restrictive and non-restrictive clauses) without a good grasp of grammatical forms. Like the carpenter or plumber, the writer cannot carry on his own trade without technical terms; he cannot judge or describe his own work or confound his editors without using grammatical categories. Diction itself, the choice of words, cannot easily be discussed apart from grammatical names, for each of several synonyms may allow a construction with which the others would clash. If, for instance, we want to argue whether *commiserate* takes a direct object without a preposition, it is desirable to know what a direct object and a preposition are.

In short, if in taking up speech and writing we throw grammar overboard, we shall find that little will be left that can be generalized about. The language will have become a catalogue of forms and phrases, a confusion of idioms to be individually conquered, a jungle of irregularities; we shall be like the beginning student of Chinese, who must memorize ideograms by the thousand. For despite all its deviations and excrescences, English does have a structure, a logic at its center, a set of principles, a consistency matching that of the orderly mind. Of this structure grammar is the working diagram and teachable plan—reason enough why, to the worker in prose, grammar remains indispensable.

Powerful arguments from utility, then, confirm the value of grammar to those who take language as an art to be practiced rather than as the flora and fauna of linguistic naturalists. The opponents of grammar are quite right to say that it is an artificial analysis made after the fact, and not a statement of natural laws; they are quite wrong to think this condemns it. As much could be urged against the map that saves us from getting lost on land or against the chart that enables us to read our way about the seas. Yet we do not hear these denounced as artificial or gratuitous; the only question ever raised is whether they are reasonably accurate. All systems and diagrams are conventions, all are imperfect, and all that gain currency evidently satisfy the purpose for which they were devised.

To be sure, one hears the further complaint that what we call English grammar was framed by scholars as if English were Latin, a dead language which they knew better than English. The assumption is that an analytical description of one dead language cannot be relevant to another which is living and growing. This indictment no longer corresponds to anything in modern experience. The English grammar inherited by people now living is actually a grammar of the elements common to various modern Indo-European tongues. It applies with slight readjustments to the Romance languages and the Germanic, to the more and the less inflected; and it has long ceased to proffer definitions and distinctions that cannot be grasped without a knowledge of Latin.

The hostility to Latin among linguists and educationists is in fact perverse. Those who speak so harshly against Latin do not show much familiarity with it, whereas few of those who have even a tincture of Latin deny that it throws light on both the structural and the stylistic features of English. The English vocabulary, besides having hundreds of Latin words taken over *literatim*, consists so preponderantly of Romance elements that the reader equipped with some Latin will understand at sight a great many words of which another cannot make head or tail without a dictionary; and of course even a nodding acquaintance with this dead language opens the way to picking up a reading knowledge of French or Italian. Among the classics of English literature a large number are the work of authors who read (and sometimes wrote) Latin like their native tongue. Who more characteristically English than Milton, Dryden, Swift, Dr. Johnson?—yet how full their minds and works of Latin speech and forms of thought. It would be rash to maintain that the connection between their powers and their knowledge was accidental. Certainly one still hears of students to whom the hang of their native English suddenly became clear when they began to learn Latin grammar. For the analytic method of grammar appears all the more clearly in a language where inflections show the function of the word in the sentence, and where meaning is not so immediate as to make the form negligible. If there exists a better pedagogic device than Latin for showing how the Western languages work, it has not yet been found.

Now, if we are to keep grammar because we do not know how to replace the teaching it gives, we would be wise to keep also the best formulations of which it is capable. Afraid of everything traditional, modern theorists have devised several new terminologies (said to be easy) and various systems (supposedly simplified) to take account of the difference between a highly inflected dead language and a less inflected living one. The chief of these revisions affects the treatment of grammatical case in nouns and pronouns —a subject suitable for testing whether the simplification really simplifies.

The American grammarian's new definition restricts the idea of case to change marked by inflection. To the personal and relative pronouns that have three forms—e.g. *he, his, him; they, their, them; who, whose, whom*—the modernist grants the like number of cases, which he calls either subjective, possessive, and objective or (in the old "Latin" way) nominative, genitive, and accusative. The possessive or genitive, whether of pronouns or of nouns, we can ignore in this connection, because it acts not as a noun at all, but as an adjective. Since nouns, aside from the possessive, inflect only for the plural (*dogs, matches, counties, monkeys, oxen*), the new definition confines case to a handful of pronouns. The pronouns that have the same form whether they are used as subject or as object (e.g. *you, it*), together with all nouns, are said to be in the common case—the grammarian's way of pronouncing them caseless. His "common" means that the one form serves every possible use—subject, object of verb, indirect object, object of preposition, predicate complement, appositive, vocative, and even interjection. The grammarian is in effect asserting that case, except as it survives vestigially in a few pronouns, has disappeared from English.

Anyone is free to dispose of case in this way; but he should reflect, and we should note, that washing his hands of case makes him poorer, not freer. He remains (or rather, he keeps himself) in the dark about the way sentences hold together and words function. "Common case" describes nothing and analyzes nothing. But grammar is essentially analytic; it names things not for the fun of having a nomenclature but so as to understand the relations of working parts. One can analyze an English sentence without using the word "case"; what matters is to know that a given word is subject or object, and of what it is the one or the other. Assuming that we invoke case at all, as we do for the pronouns that show the case by inflection, we will find it advantageous to learn the broadest possible definition of case, so as to be able to name the relation of any substantive to other words, whether or not that relation is shown by a changed form of the word (*he*, subject; *him*, object). On this view, every noun has case; the case is objective if the noun serves as an object, subjective if it serves as a subject: Boy (subject) meets Girl (object); Girl (subject) meets Boy (object). Since in spite of all antigrammarians transitive and intransitive verbs still differ, as do active and passive voice, strong verbs and copulas—all matters involving case —the notion and the name *case* are indispensable for talking about sentences after seeing into their machinery. No garage mechanic would tolerate a doctrine that prevented him from naming the distributor and its role, on the pretext that to do so was arbitrarily to divide a unified electrical system.

The firecracker exploded under the horse's hoofs (intransitive verb) / *He exploded the firecracker under the horse's hoofs* (transitive verb). How can we specify and explain the formal difference here between the two firecrackers whose role as an explosive is unaffected by the form? Quite simply: we say that the first *firecracker* is in the subjective case, the second in the objective case; the first names the agent of the verb; the second suffers the action of the verb, the agent being *He*. If we say that both *firecrackers* are in the common case we brush over a radical difference of function and describe nothing. It may be remarked in passing that in Latin itself nouns may have identical forms in the nominative and in the accusative, in the singular and in the plural, yet no one dreams of lumping them in a common case or parsing them otherwise than according to their function in the sentence.

What counts, of course, is not system or terminology, but perceptiveness. For lack of it one may struggle with a vague sense of wrongness in something one has written and be unable to find or correct its cause. For example: *Your neighbors and friends will never mention, and thus may remain unsuspected and uncorrected for years, these traits that rub everyone the wrong way.* Here the word *traits* is compelled to be in two cases at once, as the object of *will never mention* and the subject of *may remain.* Nothing short of a knowledge of grammatical case will tell writer or reader precisely what the trouble is. Likewise, allowing grammar to merge ideas formerly distinct is a bar to understanding. The loss of inflection in English does enable us to treat alike an indirect and a direct object after a transitive verb that takes both. *Please grant the bearer* (= to the bearer) *time to state his mission / She threw X.* (= at X.) *a quizzical look / He read the gathering* (= for the gathering) *some of his unpublished poems.* But the indirect objects here—the objects of omitted prepositions—are called by some modern grammars objective, like the direct objects *time, look,* and *poems.* Anyone with a smattering of Latin cannot help feeling those indirect objects as datives, which illustrates again how the dead language lights up the realities of the living one. The non-Latinist who does not scorn grammar knows that the indirect object implies a preposition. Both Latinist and non-Latinist, without speaking of datives or prepositions, or even needing to reflect that the indirect object almost always precedes the direct one, use that word order instinctively, for it is usually not reversible. Why should not both speakers also share the means of knowing explicitly what they are doing?

The antigrammarians and homogenizers who have little use for case often oppose the inflecting of *who* in the objective case; they prefer *Who were you talking with just now?* to *Whom were you . . . ?* They grant that we have to say *To* (or *With*) *whom were you talking?* but demand the suppression of the *m* when the object precedes the preposition. At the same time, some of them will perversely permit *whom* in one of its fairly frequent misuses: *I got my information from someone whom I believed was in a position to know.* This *whom*, as the subject of *was* (not the object of *believed*), has to be *who*, and the defense of it by *whom*-haters raises the suggestion that what they really hate is not so much any particular locution as the general idea of grammatical punctilio. Jespersen rationalizes this false *whom* as the natural outcome of a rather involved speech-instinct; he does not recoil even from such a monstrosity as Disraeli's *individuals whom, if you do not meet, you become restless.* But you can read a thousand pages of Jespersen's own prose without encountering any such aberration.

It is, in fact, one of the striking features of the libertarian position that it preaches an unbuttoned grammar in a prose style that is fashioned with the utmost grammatical rigor. II. L. Mencken's two thousand pages on the vagaries of the American language are written in the fastidious syntax of a precisian. If we go by what these men do instead of by what they say, we conclude that they all believe in conventional grammar, practice it against their own preaching, and continue to cultivate the elegance they despise in theory.

Meanwhile the scientist who investigates words as the natural by-products of unconscious behavior and the artist who delights in words as miraculous and lovable creations are talking from opposite shores of a pretty wide gulf, and it is small wonder that they do not hear each other very well. To the scientist choice and taste are prejudice, standards are pedantry, and the distinction between fit and unfit, grammatical and ungrammatical, is reprehensible. The artist, on the contrary, could not live or work without exercising the critical faculty, which at its highest applies taste and at its lowest applies grammar. As for the great majority, in spite of being by turns careless and embarrassed, it is certainly on the side of the artist. The poorly taught, the foreign-born, the ambitious young aiming at the professions, the unassuming men of business, the mothers whose minds are not given over to total permissiveness in child-rearing—each individual for his own good reasons struggles over dimly felt obstacles to make his meaning clear. He or she may seek help in the "Words" column of the monthly magazine or in the headier manual of usage, but all hope to find somewhere the way to better means of self-expression. The professional writer, of course, is concerned not with what is allowable or defensible, but rather with what is good enough to need no defense. From the common root of their desires the artist and the user of language for practical ends share an obligation to preserve against confusion and dissipation the powers that over the centuries the mother tongue has acquired. It is a duty to maintain the continuity of speech that makes the thought of our ancestors easily understood, to conquer Babel every day against the illiterate and the heedless, and to resist the pernicious and lulling dogma that in language—contrary to what obtains in all other human affairs—whatever is right and doing nothing is for the best.

II

LEXICON

A

a, an, the. 1. Surplus *a, an.* 2. *A, an* before aspirates. 3. Misplaced *a, an.* 4. *A, an, the:* definite and indefinite. 5. *The* omitted. 6. *A* with epithet and proper name. 7. *Per* for *a, an.*

1. Surplus *a, an.* There are phrases in which idiom requires the indefinite article to be omitted, and it is a mistake to think that one is exercising extra care by including it, especially after a negative: *There is no more difficult a field of historical writing and no more capable an exponent.* The negative in such a construction supersedes the article by including it. Read *no more difficult field . . . no more capable exponent.* Similarly, write *no more expeditious way,* not *no more expeditious a way.* Omit the articles in *No braver a deed was ever performed / No wiser a teacher ever occupied this chair / no more generous a sacrifice / no more useful an invention.* Sometimes the presence of a necessary indefinite article will insidiously encourage the inclusion of an unnecessary one: *I dare say that a check in a butcher shop in the outlying provinces of France would show no worse a record.* The first *a* and the sec-

ond are needed; the third is subsumed in *no* and should be omitted.

One of the articles has no excuse for being in *a half an hour* or *a half a glass.* (A pharmaceutical leaflet recommends *a half a glass of water* eleven times in seven inches of print.) The acceptable locutions are *half an hour / a half hour / half a glass.* The more formal is *a half hour,* and though correct *a half glass* sounds stilted. To correct *a half an apple,* one had better say *half an apple* rather than *a half apple,* which would carry some obscure suggestion of a fruit half apple and half not; cf. *a half-god* or *a half-truth.* Omitting *a* is required in *I can appreciate how difficult it must have been for you . . . especially at this late a date.* (But note that the alternative *so late a date* requires *a,* because the construction is *at . . . a date* in place of *at this . . . date.*)

When *a* or *an* is not omitted at the right time, the failure will sometimes convert one person into two or more. Contrariwise, if we say *an architect, planner, and builder,* we think, or ought to think, of one person exercising three functions; but the words are from a radio program announcing a debate among three, and it should have been *an architect, a planner, and a builder.* The sentence *Y. is a fanatical fisherman and hunter* makes *fanatical* qualify both nouns equally; *a fanatical fisherman and a hunter* leaves the adjective qualifying *fisherman* only and does not specify what kind of hunter Y. is.

The phrase *what kind of hunter* rightly omits the indefinite article, and omitting it is likewise necessary in *know automatically in what kind of book a kind of fact is recorded.* After *kind, sort, species, manner, type,* and the like, the object of the following preposition is likely to be a generic term pointing to a category, not a particular one pointing to an individual. Despite examples to the contrary in the works of great writers, there is no place for *a, an* in *that sort of mistake / this breed of dog / what kind of argument / a later model of airplane / some sort of trick.* The article is an interloper pretending to specious elegance in *the broadest kind of an education / This is a very special kind of a honeymoon / could train a youngster to be any kind of a specialist from a physician to an artist / have been trying for more than a century and a half to strike some kind of a balance between dictatorship and anarchy / The only way you can get people to work . . . is to give them some kind of an incentive.*

The presence or absence of the indefinite article will commonly determine the all-important difference between the alternative and the merely additive uses of the conjunction *or.* The phrase *a democracy or a republic* denotes two kinds of political organization; *a democracy or republic* would, or should, denote one kind under synonymous names. If we say *a theological or religious contention,* we equate theology with religion, or at least make no effort to differentiate them; *a theological or a religious contention* says that theology is one thing, religion another.

The smallest mismanagement of *a* can exert a curiously disproportionate power to make our language sound as if written gropingly by a foreigner. The erudite front matter of a good desk dictionary includes the clause *whether it is a native word or borrowed one;* the unidiomatic omission of *a* before *borrowed* suggests a specialist not at home in English. For native writers' similar failures to be idiomatic or precise under the influence of journalistic compression or caption style, see 5 below.

2. *A, an* before aspirates. Some very Anglophile or very bookish Americans, and perhaps others influenced by them, are addicted to *an* before *historical, homiletic, hum-*

ble, and other words with a formerly silent *h* and before words beginning with the consonantal *y* sound (*Eurasian, euphonious, unique*); also sometimes before *w* sounds (*one, once*). The practice is traditional: *An humble and a contrite heart / Whoso breaketh an hedge.* But it is no longer current: *the establishment of an European free trade area / an one-cent rise / his official status as an United Nations employee / once an ubiquitous part of the New England scene* —all these sound affected. The normal, undoubtedly the prevalent, American feeling is that such words begin with consonants, not vowels, and that it is archaic and unnatural to precede them with *an* instead of *a.* This feeling has the right of way in speech and should have it in writing. That the older form is kept here and there by house rules but no longer corresponds to instinct is shown by the discrepancy found in some newspapers between *a 1-to-0 score* in the sports column and *an one-hundred-dollar fine* in the editorial.

3. Misplaced *a, an.* The indefinite article is idiomatically subject to an inverted order in a few constructions, especially after *so* or *too* (*so heavy a burden / too difficult an assignment*); also after *how,* as in *how deplorable an outcome!,* and after *what,* as in the title *What a Widow!* The alternative construction after *so* (*a so difficult undertaking /* [and similarly] *your so instructive article*) is generally felt to be slightly unidiomatic and vaguely French. Henry James was noticeably addicted to it, especially in his later works. It is easy, however, to get the rhythm of inversion so fixed in the mind that it will slip in where it is not idiomatic or is less comfortable than the regular order. *Even more memorable an occasion* sounds less natural than *an even more memorable occasion.* Awkwardness marks *in order,* explained R., "*to put her situation in less bizarre a light*" (in a less bizarre light). *The conviction that God had chosen him as an instrument . . . was more potent a motive than glory and personal enrichment* (a more potent motive). The least that can be said of such examples is that nothing would be lost by keeping to the normal order. The tone of latter-day English discourages avoidable inversion, and this tendency, which has been uninterrupted for many decades, may well be taken as a guide where one is in doubt, e.g. between *no less triumphant an artist than L.* and *a no less triumphant artist than L.*

During most of the eighteenth century it was idiomatic to wedge the indefinite article between the parts of a compound adjective. In *The School for Scandal,* Careless says *as stern a looking rogue as ever*

I saw. Stern-looking is now thought of as indivisible. Needless inversion sometimes leads into unnaturalness bordering on the grotesque: *the view expressed in so charmingly an unpleasant way* (in so charmingly unpleasant a way) / *I have seen too many boys who have . . . got far bigger an ego than their capabilities justified* (a far bigger ego). A sentence such as *Each year England becomes more urban a nation* looks like an attempt to combine *becomes more urban* with *a more urban nation.* Either phrasing gives the full sense; the two fused distract the reader and therefore give less than the full sense.

For the omission of *a* or *an* before the second of a pair of nouns when the first takes the alternative article, see WHAT IS "UNDERSTOOD"?

4. *A, an, the:* definite and indefinite. There is an observable tendency, likely rather to increase than to diminish, toward so confusing the definite and the indefinite article as to make each do duty for the other. They are, of course, often interchangeable: it makes no difference to meaning whether we say *The exception tests the rule* (any exception, any rule) or *An exception tests a rule;* and *the proof of the pudding* is the same as *the proof of a pudding.* But in many instances a failure to differentiate will befog meaning and at the same time make

English sound foreign. An example of *a* for *the: I do not believe very much in a success of a summit meeting of the Big Four forces* (in the success of). An example of *the* for *a: This disaster, among others, was the result of lack of foresight* (was a result of the).

The omission of either article before *lack* in the last sentence opens up a vast subject in which the confusion just noted between *a* and *the* acquires philosophical importance. The English language makes a point of distinguishing the particular from the general in a variety of idiomatic ways that puzzle foreigners accustomed to a simpler system and fewer nuances. By their streamlined speech, therefore, the many foreign nationals who as refugees or globe-trotters have adopted English during the last quarter-century have unintentionally strengthened the influence of headline style, which often omits *a* and *the,* so that the idiomatic distinctions attached to these words are beginning to become blurred for native speakers. The loss is especially noticeable in the discrimination between a particular at large and one singled out for the purpose in hand—two distinct purposes that are related as the indefinite is to the definite.

A (an) is the indefinite article; that is, the word that points to an individual without suggesting a favored position within the class to which it belongs. *The* is the definite (i.e. defining) article. It says: This is *it*, the thing in question, the important one. A ready illustration is found in the difference between the Earth as *a planet* and the Earth as *the planet*. The second is our familiar way of saying—at least until we colonize another—"the one planet that matters, ours." In moments of broader contemplation we are also able to see that *the* Earth (for there is only one of that name) is also *a* planet (there being nine of the kind).

This distinction being fundamental, it ought to be observed whenever we use *a* or *the*. To say *Then she married the relative of her theatrical manager* is to state definitely that the man had only one relative. That this implication is present appears when we try to correct the false impression. We cannot merely substitute *a* for *the*, but must say *a relative of her theatrical manager's* [relatives]; i.e. any one of a possibly numerous class. (See POSSESSIVES 2; PROSE, THE SOUND OF 5.)

The management of *a* and *the* in close articulation with related nouns sometimes causes trouble through failure to perceive the logical definiteness or indefiniteness of each. For example: *If published under a pseudonym, an autobiography* of a woman could not be told apart from a man's. It is not only unlikely that anyone, man or woman, would write more than one autobiography, but the focus of attention here is the clearly defined genre autobiography; so *an* must be *the*. What led to *an* was that the writer thought first of *a woman's autobiography*, then switched to the *of* construction without seeing that the indefiniteness was provided by *a woman* and a definite *the* was required to make clear the correct relationship of book to author. Note further that if the book were a novel—a type of work not limited to a single example—the sentence could not read *a novel of a woman could not be told apart*. It must be either *a woman's novel* (which leaves the indefiniteness of *novel* unexpressed) or *a novel by a woman*, which expresses indefiniteness twice and correctly. This is because *of* is an emphatically defining word, whose importance in this whole question we shall attend to at length in a moment. In general the sequence *a . . . of a . . .* will be found unsatisfactory because of the uncertainty it produces about the twice indefinite relation. *A bodyguard of a gangster was shot last night* is either *the bodyguard* or *a gangster's bodyguard*.

5. *The* omitted. The previous section has been concerned with singular nouns. With plurals we find that logically no indefiniteness can be expressed through *a*, which denotes *(any) one of the lot*. For a plural we must go to *some* or to the omission of *a* altogether. Except for keeping postitive and negative in their right places, *some* and *any* give no trouble. But the distinction between plural definiteness, indicated as in the singular by *the*, and plural indefiniteness, indicated by the plural noun standing alone, is one of the nuances increasingly overlooked. In *We were met at the Dublin airport by the officials of the Irish Republic* there is an implication that all the Irish officials—or at least all those that matter —were present. Had the sentence read *by officials of*, the suggestion would be that some two or three had turned up. *A revolt of the students in Paris touched off the revolution of 1830* implicates all or nearly all the students, *a revolt of students* only some. In giving instructions this difference can be important. *I want you to pack the books* puts an obligation on the helper to do the job from beginning to end. *I want you to pack books* directs him merely for the time being.

In framing titles, authors who feel the force of words recognize the effect of putting in or leaving out *The*—an effect sometimes of emphasis, sometimes of modesty, each in its way a means to accuracy.

Pleasures of Music tells the reader: "These are some of the pleasures; the work is not a comprehensive treatise"; whereas *The Economic Consequences of the Peace* professes to round them up without exception. If *The Yearling* had been entitled simply *Yearling*, the emphasis would have been shifted from the individual to a quality possessed by many individuals. The title with *The* prepares us for a character, the other for a condition illustrated by a character, as in *Shanghaied* (i.e. "It might happen to anybody").

An American writer on usage, who rightly prides himself on success in helping people to express their thoughts, recommends in his latest book that seekers after clarity and directness strike out all the *the*'s that the text can get along without. This is dangerous advice at a time when captions and slogans assail us from all sides and weaken in many of us the sense of definition. This is especially true in phrases where an *of* followed by a concrete word or a proper name defines a preceding abstraction—e.g. [the] *appointment of a new sheriff* / [the] *assassination of Diem* / [the] *accumulation of objects of art*. Newspapermen, corrupted by their own headlines, think that it makes for briskness to start paragraphs without *The*. They will write *Focus of the discussion was the issue of escalation in Vietnam,* never recognizing that their syntax amounts to *The issue of escalation was focus of the discussion.* Unmindful of both syntax and sense, they then go on to omit *the* as chance or the hope of forcefulness dictates.

The result is to reduce English to a kind of pidgin in which sentences such as the following arouse no sense of incompleteness or faulty logic: *Pronouncement of the encyclical in 1963 produced discussion . . . throughout the world / One act of desertion can cause distrust of those who remain / The Administration is not opposed to adoption of the plan described in your letter / Few are aware of the need for reorganization of courts, which as everybody knows are two and three years behind their dockets / With selection of the two final courses planned for the Community College's first degree program . . . / He wished there were more doors to close off the cubicles for purpose of privacy / Progress of native populations . . . cannot take place without a proper program of education / The leading houses paid the author or publisher for rights of a book.* And apropos of Governor Adlai Stevenson's death: *Cause of death was not immediately announced.*

In several of these examples, one can discern the workings of minds not only influenced by headline style but also confused about different constructions. In the first sentence, for example, the phrase *produced discussion* is the natural way of stating a general fact: the reference is to discussion at large, not to *a* discussion held in Paris or to *the* discussion of a particular point. But at the head of that sentence *pronouncement* is not a general term like *discussion;* it does not denote pronouncement(s) at large, but *the* unique, definite pronouncement of a set of propositions at a given time and place. No one would be likely to say *Pronouncement of encyclical in 1963 was . . .* Why then choose to omit one of two equally functional *the*'s? This arbitrariness is the most salient fact about the practice. In one editorial section of two columns in the *New York Times,* the reader finds the following: *The passage on meeting ( ) educational needs of the state would be more encouraging / Nothing is said of ( ) abolition of capital punishment / commits the nation to the suppression of this terrorism / slam the door on the legal importation of hundreds of thousands of low-wage Mexican laborers / authorize the emergency admission of large numbers of braceros / Having seen their list dwindle with ( ) desertion of the best names on it / There is no reason why the law of supply and demand / no excuse will exist for the mass import of cheap foreign labor.* On other pages of the same issue of the *Times* the same anarchy reigns: *However,* ( ) *apprehension of a 61-year-old man destroyed the public image of the thief as a young man / President De Gaulle made proposals today for* ( ) *reform of the United Nations,* the *reunification of Germany,* etc. One asks: why proposals for *reform of* and proposals for *the reunification of* in the same sentence?

A provincial newspaper unwittingly gives a clue to the cause of this variation. It says: *Since the plans were first made public, we have been opposed to construction of Bell's Walk-in restaurant at Franklin and Columbia Streets. We have been opposed to garish architecture.* The second opposition, to a kind of architecture unrestricted as to time or place (and correctly expressed without *the,* since no complement follows), colors the statement about the first opposition, which is to a particular construction—that of a restaurant at the street corner specified. A due sense of the radical difference between the two gives rise to the rule that any noun in the singular limited by a restrictive *of* phrase requires *the* in front of it, except in some common idioms of the type discussed below.

That this sense of definition is not entirely dead was shown in the violent debate that took place within one of the political parties over the insertion of a *the* in a statement being drafted for publication. One group argued that the passage *no longer tolerate the policy of exclusion* was "to direct a slap at Mr. Goldwater's campaign organization" and should be rephrased *any policy of exclusion.* The difference between definiteness and indefiniteness could not be more vividly illustrated. And almost anyone whose attention has once been drawn to this difference, produced by *the,* will begin to perceive it in much that passes under his eye. Compare *the man who should have been there to discuss insurance business* with *the man who should have been there to discuss the insurance business.*

But there is more to say; for as one reflects on the form of many phrases lacking a necessary *the,* one discovers that they are often cases of the NOUN-PLAGUE, as well as of hostility to the gerund (see -ING 1). If a writer objects to using a string of *the*'s in his prose, he can readily dispense with a few by substituting the -*ing* form of the verb for the all too common -*tion* derivative. Returning to the faulty sentences listed above, one sees how easily most of them can be so treated: *The Administration is not opposed to adopting* (instead of *adoption of*) / *the need for reorganizing the courts* (instead of *the need for reorganization of courts*). Similarly: *Nothing is said of abolishing capital punishment / commits the nation to suppressing / proposals today for reforming . . . , reunifying. . . . / we have been opposed to constructing.* In such a phrasing as *Toward defrayal of the expenses of producing the finest yearbook,* it is manifest that *defraying* is the natural word, displaced only by a love of the abstract noun. Note in the sentence that introduces these suggestions the temptation it could offer to the writer who trusts only nouns: *If a writer objects to use of a string of the's . . .* Not all sentences, of course, are amenable to this treatment, which eliminates both *the* and *-tion.* The refractory will require their logical *the's.*

What matters to precise thought in the observance of definiteness and indefiniteness is that the writer should know when he is talking generalities and when he is judging a case. Take this sentence from a modern novel: *But he had a trick of finding time to censure imprudence of unimportant functionaries.* This is nonsense because it fuses and confuses two distinct ideas about the character described. He is surely not quite the same man if he (a) finds time to censure imprudence or (b) finds time to censure his subordinates *for* their imprudence. The same sort of distinction often has to be made with *a* or *an.* Consider *They now take an interest in art that used to be shunned even by professional critics.* There is a world of difference between *take an interest in art* and *take an interest in an art* (the dance) *that used to be shunned.* The writer who thinks he can pass from *a* to *x* in this fashion is in a muddle; likewise the novelist who fends off possible suits for defamation by prefacing his work with the unqualified statement *All characters and incidents are imaginary.*

Nor is a proper care for defining worth the effort wholly as a preventive. The writer who knows how to use *the* and *a* can produce subtle effects that some, at least, of his readers will value as they should. Consider the following sentence: *But his denunciations of lust and concupiscence and his praise of chastity are not marked by the coldness and the resentment of other people's pleasures that frequently are so evident in the ascetic.* With the first *the* we are distinctly told that the coldness in question is that of the ascetic; the coldness goes with the resentment. But it was possible for the author, simply by omitting that first *the,* to attribute coldness to St. Augustine himself and add to it the resentment often found in other saints. Again, in the report of an inexplicable assault it was surmised that certain events *might have created the animosity*. To put it this way was to make an assumption, for there had been no sign of animosity. If the phrase had read *might have created animosity*, the facts and the supposition would have been differentiated, making the report truer in an important way.

It is easily seen that the problems created by *the . . . of* (and less frequently by *a . . . of*) do not arise when *of* is replaced by another preposition. In fact, a substitute can often provide a way out of the bad logic just exemplified. *He then discussed investment criteria of welfare enterprises* (for) / *The circumstances surrounding publication of facts of divorce cases* (the . . . in) / *Such a fabrication of a woman without education astonished the court and even her enemies* (by; surely *fabrication of a woman* can only denote a female FRANKENSTEIN).

There is moreover the possibility of keeping logic straight by first analyzing and then properly articulating the ideas yielded by analysis. Take *In brilliance of insights their careers as neurologists are comparable*. The first four words try to combine three separate notions: (a) the quality to be used for comparing the careers, which is brilliance; (b) the kind of brilliance, which is that of insight (singular); and (c) the brilliance of the

several insights achieved by X., Y., and Z. To make one package of these three notions is impossible. The writer must choose between *in brilliance of insight* (a homogeneous quality) and *in the brilliance of their insights* (a quality duly related to the particular deeds —insights—that distinguished the careers). In short, the defining force of *a* and *the* with *of*, like the force of *the* when omitted (whether in singular or plural phrases), will serve meaning only when logic is maintained and English idiom respected.

There remain two sorts of common locution that call for comment. The first sort, of recent growth, seems to be connected with the desire to give importance through the fixity of abstraction. For instance, the students of the history of science, or the sociology of crime, or any such compounded subject often show a wish to dignify it by removing its annunciatory *the*. They will write: *This is a contribution to history of science* / *Mr. X. is the well-known expert in sociology of crime*. The absurdity appears when from *Professor of English Language and Literature* we take out *Professor of English Language* —the former a hybrid made up of a particular and a general, the latter unidiomatic by its failure to mark particularity with *the*. In any compound with *history, theory*, and like terms, the more descriptive the complement the more it cries aloud for the anticipatory article: *a contribution to history of New England hooked-rug manufacture*. Lopping off the restrictive words back to *New England* does not remove the need: one must still say *a contribution to* the *history of New England,* and hence *to the history of science, to the history of philosophy, to the sociology of crime.*

With the names of institutions, e.g. publishing houses, a comparable question arises, and for the same reason. But since businesses are free to call themselves what they like, one can only regret that they have lately preferred *Columbia University Press* to *The Columbia University Press,* etc., with the consequences of further weakening our hold on the meaning of *the.* The ear notes a gap in *The work is published by Oxford University Press.* The names of ships, similarly, are often misrendered, as in the referral to Sherlock Holmes of *the case of Matilda Briggs,* which makes him say: "Matilda Briggs was not the name of a young woman, Watson, it was a ship which is associated with the giant rat of Sumatra." Holmes himself (or Conan Doyle) was scrupulous about writing *the Gloria Scott, the Lone Star* and italicizing the ship's name. (The usage of the British Navy about warships

omits *the* in dispatches, but historians continue to refer to Nelson's death on *the Victory.*)

The second type of locution in which *the* is in jeopardy is the introductory phrase beginning with *in.* It is idiomatic to say *in view of, in respect of, in pursuance of,* etc., because no idea remains that *the view* or *the respect* is being modified by what follows—indeed *view,* etc. have lost their literal meaning. Where the definable idea does subsist, we continue to say *with the view of* and *with a view to.* Likewise, English has long used *in the light of, in the face of,* which the abolishers of *the* are steadily reducing to *in light of* and *in face of.* Perhaps attrition here does no harm, though there is a perceptible jar when in *face of* is joined to, let us say, *destruction* and *in light of* to *ancestral wisdom.* For present in both is a feeling of personification: ancestral wisdom sheds light and destruction has a face, which makes us want *the* light of the one and *the* face of the other. In these cases the parallel with *in view of* does not help us, for *in the view of ancestral wisdom* differs in meaning from *in view of ancestral wisdom.* Examples exist of *in course of* with the meaning *during (in course of a conversation with the envoy).* They are still rare, and they may be due to an unawareness that the phrase has a standard use: *this large work is in course of publication.*

Other omissions of *the* must be judged by context. *On stage, on deck, on campus* have different meanings if *the* is inserted. An actor is *on stage* or *off stage*, but an author's play is not *put on stage.* Similarly, a gun turret is not *on deck* but *on the deck. On campus* has the same professional generality. A student may be required to be *on campus* five days a week, but a rare species of elm grows *on the campus.* There is, however, no warrant for a similar treatment of the phrase *seventh heaven.* The fortunate being is always *in the seventh heaven,* from the very nature of differentiation by numbers. The supposed example of Handel's *Messiah (The Oratorio Society is giving* Messiah) is no example at all, since Handel was hardly an accomplished user of English; and there is something contradictory in the Deliverer not being the only one. Only to His face could the word be used vocatively without *the.* If it is observed that in colloquial speech *Lord knows!* and *Lord love you!* are often heard, the explanation lies in the attraction of *God knows!,* etc., which nonetheless do not generate *Praise be Lord* or any such removal of His uniqueness.

Paradoxically, the ruthless pruners of *the* carefully save it for insertion in two phrases where idiom warrants omission in certain senses: *in future* is a synonym for *hereafter, from now on, indefinitely.* It is distinct from the merely descriptive *in the future.* Likewise *I am of opinion* means *I believe* or *I conclude,* again with a shade of difference from *I am of the opinion that holds all men to be equal.*

Lastly a word must be said about the misdeeds of translators, who too often follow the lead of the foreign original in distributing their *a*'s and *the*'s. Mistakes in this department do more than anything else to impart a flavor of stagy silliness to the Englished utterances of foreign statesmen, novelists, and travelers. To take two examples from literature, it is obvious that Chekhov's short story is entitled "In Court," not "In the Court," which would be appropriate only if the scene were a court*yard.* More recently, Sartre's autobiography *Les Mots* appeared in this country as *The Words,* which is devoid of sense. The British translation bears the correct and sense-bearing title *Words.* To sum up, *the* and *a* are excellent vocables, surprisingly difficult to use, and most helpful to lucid communication when rightly used.

6. *A* with epithet and proper name. Writers of novels and of news stories make excessive use of a locution that was tiresome the moment it was launched: *it was a reluctant William who turned homeward that night / After two rounds, the jaunty C. had no difficulty disposing of a bloody S. / . . . an output exceeded only by a later Zane Grey / A weary L.C., former governor of . . . is met by his sister on arrival / He fully expected to find a bewildered Sanford, but he was not prepared for an aggressive one.* This last example makes plain what is fundamentally wrong with this formula. It splits the person into as many different doubles of himself as there are adjectives to apply to human character. *A weary L.C.* is in fact the same man as *the weary L.C.* and should remain one and indivisible. This can be done only if he is never *a* [something] *L.C. M. expected to find S. bewildered but not aggressive* correctly states the divergent attributes of one person. But when *a passionate Tom kisses a bashful Jane* (otherwise than as a generality personified by the use of names), there is in the report something at once coy and condescending that reinforces the sense that these are not persons but puppets. To the sociologist they may be role-playing, but to the reader a sullen Joe and a blithe one and a startled one and a reassured one do not, however long the enumeration, add up to a convincing whole Joe.

7. *Per* for *a, an*. The indefinite article, when used to mean *to the* or the Latin *per*, is the idiomatic, standard, and unimprovable preposition. Only necessity should be allowed to displace it in ordinary prose. The form *eighty cents a dozen, three dollars a yard, fifty miles an hour, dollar-a-year man, three times a day* is better English than the locution *$17.50 the ounce, a cost of about $3000 the mile, ten dollars the copy.* Such a use of *the* is a Francophile affectation that is even less idiomatic than the generally gratuitous *per*, as in *wind from the southwest at thirteen miles per hour.*

It is obvious that *a, an* can find no place in such set Latin phrases as *per diem, per annum, per capita.* And by extension we grant the technicians their *rpm* (revolutions per minute), *mph* (miles per hour), and their rate of acceleration *per second per second.* Note, however, that in other, semi-technical contexts *the* is idiomatic after *to: three cubic yards to the ton, seventy pulsations to the minute, chattering sixteen to the dozen,* etc.

Where the idiomatic *a, an* would lead to an awkward repetition or another oddity, as in *an allowance of $35 a family a month*, it may sometimes be necessary to resort to *per* for one *a* or the other, or for both. But usually, as in this example, the difficulty is easily got around by *a monthly allowance of $35 a family*—a reminder that the best solution often lies in avoidance.

à, au. See FRENCH WORDS AND PHRASES.

abbreviations. 1. The modern tendency in scholarship as well as popular works is to replace the Latin abbreviations by English ones; for example, *cp.* (= compare) for *cf.*; *ff.* (= following) for *et seq.*; *above* and *below* (not strictly abbreviations but shortened directions) for *supra* and *infra*; plain *see* for *vide* or *q.v.*; *note* for *N.B.* Two of the Latin particles, *sc.* and *viz.*, which stand for *to wit* and *namely*, have almost disappeared from modern print. Yet some of these marks retain their currency. The commonest are *c.* or *ca.*, meaning *about* and modifying a date; *e.g.* and *i.e.*, which will be discussed below; the familiar *etc.*; and the indispensable *ibid.*, which saves space by telling the reader that a quotation comes from the same place as the one just preceding. *Sic* is also convenient as a sign that the original word or text is being exactly reproduced, despite a patent mistake or oddity; and *passim* discloses its meaning of *here and there* throughout the book or chapter, when one does not want to pin down a reported opinion to a particular passage.

2. *E.g.* and *i.e.* are often confused, though their meanings are rarely interchangeable. The first means *for example* (*exempli gratia*) and introduces an instance or a short enumeration of names, words, or other items. The second means *that is* (*id est*) and introduces a repetition in different words of the idea just uttered, or an amplification of the kind appropriate after an ordinary *that is* in English. Perhaps a good way to make the distinction firm after it is learned is to think of *here are* (*is*) for *e.g.* and *I mean* for *i.e.*

Less frequently *etc.* and *et al.* are thought to be equivalent. *Et cetera* (= and the rest), being neuter, can only refer to things; *et alii* (= and others) can only refer to persons. A list of persons' names should not end with *etc.* and is better with *and others* than with the legal *et al.*

See also SHORTENINGS.

-ability, suffix. See ROAD-ABILITY.

abjure, adjure. See DAN-GEROUS PAIRS.

-able, -ible. 1. Meaning. 2. *-able* with *e* preceding.

1. The root idea in this suffix is the same as in the letters *able* when they stand by themselves. *Manageable* means *able to be managed*, *potable* means *able to be drunk* (said of a liquid, not a man), *intolerable* means *not able to be tolerated*. The common features are, then, the ordinary meaning of *able* coupled with the passive meaning of a verb. This generality is not affected by the spelling *-ible*, which is found in, say, *reversible* and other adjectives clearly formed with the same intention. Yet there are in good current usage words ending in *-able* (or *-ible*) that require either a mental addition to the verb or some change of its normal object before the compound can be properly understood. *Reliable* is the prime instance. It does not mean *able to be relied*, which is meaningless, but *able to be relied on*. *Actionable* means *able to be sustained in a court action*. *Sizable* means *having some size, not insignificant*. And *knowledgeable* goes still farther afield with the meaning *able through possessing knowledge*. Such wanderings from the expected results of compounding should not be multiplied at a whim. The recent appearance in political circles of *negotiable* with the intended meaning of *willing to negotiate* is to be severely condemned by the orderly mind. *Negotiable* means *able to be negotiated* and nothing else—at least until diplomats and heads of state can be turned into cash.

2. Endings in *-able* and *-age* that tack on to ordinary words need no intervening *e* unless the preceding letter is *c* or *g*, and then only if their soft sound has to be preserved. That is the sole function of the *e*. Thus *change* gives *changeable* with the *e* in order to prevent the pronunciation *changhable* from suggesting itself on first reading. (See CATALOG.) It follows from this that *like* gives *likable*, *mile milage*, *survive survivability*, *sale salable*, *drink drinkable*, and so on. To this rule of common sense there is the exception of *lineage* (meaning *ancestry*), pronounced in three syllables lĭn′ē·ĭj. *Linage*, meaning *number of lines of print*, follows the rule and is written without the *e*. (This same *linage* and *milage* are often found with the inconsistent *e*.)

See also NONLEAKABLE; SPELLING.

aborigines. See LATIN AND GREEK PLURALS.

above, adjective. Perhaps because of its familiar use in *above-mentioned*, which we borrow from legal documents, it seems permissible to use *above* in front of the noun: *The above books should have been shipped to you earlier.* But for the demanding ear the commercial tone is still unpleasantly there, just as the legal tone is still too strong for common use in *the within letter*. Since the other indicators of place are never so used (*the without people, the below remarks* being thus far impossible), it seems best, at least in studied writing, to keep *above* in the same class and say *the books above*, like *the remarks below*.

A parallel use of *then* is sometimes ambiguous. *In his younger days he was a member of the then Air Corps.* This sentence probably means *a member of what was then called the Air Corps*, but *then* might equally refer to some superseded feature of the service. When used of persons and positions (*the then Prime Minister*) the designation of time is better given in more explicit terms: *the Prime Minister of that time | the matinee idol of the day | the former office of dogcatcher.*

abrasive. See CONNOTATIONS; VOGUE WORDS.

abridge. See MALAPROPS.

absolute words. Some words exclude comparison or partition; they denote what is superlative or complete, and they must be handled accordingly. The most familiar example is *unique*; something can be *almost unique* but not *rather unique.* Others are less commonly recognized, judging by their frequent misuse. *Discomfit*, for example, means to undo totally. It is foolish, then, to say either *partly discomfited* or *thoroughly discomfited.* Again, *essential* means *indispensable* and does not admit of *more* or *less*, or even of *so*.

Absolutes, moreover, cannot be used as it were ahead of the time when their truth would logically be seen. You cannot for this reason ask for *an excellent cup of coffee.* It is a premature superlative until you have drunk the coffee and declared it excellent. Note in this connection that *very* can be misused in much the same way. The reviewer who writes *This is not a very good book* implies that he had expected or been told that it was very good; whereas he expresses a conclusion of his own if he writes: *This book is not very good.*

Partition is excluded by a similar logic, which sometimes wears the look of paradox. Thus no man can be said to be *every bit the counterpart of Dr. Johnson:* he is the counterpart or he is not; and the *every bit* reduces to absurdity the otherwise sound notion of a counterpart. If a theory *does not hold* much *water*, the argument against it is lost: the theory has some value. Still more absurd is the attempt to hedge in *Necessity is only in part the mother of invention.* With absolutes tautology shows the prentice hand: *general consensus, universal panacea, fully completed* are blunders caused more often by carelessness than by ignorance.

There remains *perfect*, which would seem to be the absolute word par excellence. Yet the Constitution speaks in its preamble of *creating a more perfect union.* Usage has in fact authorized *more perfect* and

less perfect, it being understood, perhaps, that nothing
on earth achieves perfection
and that the degrees of approximation to it deserve to be
named. Many of the other absolutes are either abstract, like
panacea, or the mere summit
of competition, like *excellence*.

accept. This useful verb
will not admit either of two
different constructions that are
being more and more frequently thrust upon it: namely, the
infinitive and the *that* clause.
Both outrage idiom. The infinitive: *But American public
opinion will not accept to be
bullied* (will not accept bully-
ing, will not be bullied) / *we
accepted as our purpose to
give some realization of how
the scientist works* (accepted
. . . the giving of some realization, accepted it as our purpose to give). The *that* (substantive) clause: *One accepts
only because one is told so
that V. is not a native* (replace
accepts with *credits* or some
similar verb that tolerates
that).

It is implicit in these suggested corrections (1) that *accept* naturally leads to the ger-
und (verbal noun in -ING),
(2) that it can be given the
supplied object *it*, which does
lead to an infinitive, and (3)
that *accept*, unlike most verbs
denoting a mental process, is
ill at ease with a substantive
clause. The natural object of
this verb is a noun, and the

third example would be idiomatic if it read: *One accepts
. . . the fact that.* But *fact that*
is an overworked locution which
is seldom justified unless the
writer is actually referring to a
fact. As a mere stopgap in the
sentence, it is the mark of a
beginning writer.

acceptance, acceptation.
See DANGEROUS PAIRS.

accolade. Reporters who
make frequent use of *accolade*
to signify approval, praise, and
similar signs of recognition
will on other occasions report
that, after conferring a medal
or prize, a European dignitary,
acting according to custom,
kissed the recipient—soldier,
scientist, or diplomat. The fact
is that no reporter ever saw
such an act. What he saw was
an *accolade*, which consists in
touching the recipient's cheeks
alternately with one's own. The
word is from the French root
col, meaning *neck*. By extension it is often used to denote
the tap on the shoulders with
the flat blade of a sword which
is part of the ritual of knight-
ing.

according. See DANGLERS,
ACCEPTABLE.

account for. As a synonym of *explain*, this verb
phrase would be difficult to
mishandle; but it has an unfortunate currency as a synonym of *consist of*, and in this

guise it has the same disabilities as REPRESENT. *Ninety-seven per cent of the nation's exports are accounted for by* (consists of) *fish and fish products / Over half his library is accounted for by* (consists of) *musicology.* Sometimes the two ideas of *consist of* and *explain* are fused: *X. points out that most of the congestion is accounted for by tourist traffic.* In such places *account for* is legitimate.

accuse. It seems obvious that an accused person must stand accused of some crime, offense, or dereliction; if he is not, the word is misapplied. Yet it will often be found applied to situations in which someone is accused, not of any offense, but simply of being accused. *In announcing Mr. X.'s suspension, the* [newspaper] *management pointed out that "Mr. X. had neither been accused nor convicted of any charge."* Perhaps X. had not been accused or convicted *on* any charge, but as it stands the sentence states that he is not accused of any accusation. The juxtaposition of *charge* with *accused* makes the sentence describe a circle and come out meaningless.

See also CONVICT.

acknowledge, admit. We acknowledge a fault; we acknowledge being at fault. We also admit a fault or being at fault. It was formerly common to admit *to* being at fault, and this idiom is perhaps still possible, though archaic in tone. But what of *acknowledge to?* The handsome, gray-haired Jesuit readily *acknowledges to being the conqueror of a ten-and-one-half-pound bone fish that graced his outer office* (omit *to*). The extra *to* is probably an unconscious borrowing from *confess to*, an idiom that is alive, though overused for ironic effects.

Admit, when it has an impersonal subject and means permit, may take *of: Situations of this acuteness will not admit of delay or trifling. Permit* itself once commonly took *of*, but no longer needs it and is therefore better followed by its direct object.

acknowledging. See DANGLERS, ACCEPTABLE.

acquiesce. Once idiomatically followed by *to*, *acquiesce* has required *in* for at least a century and a half. Reversion to the older preposition is encountered—as in *Acquiescing to his parents' wishes, O. attended* [a particular school] —under the influence of *agree*, *assent*, *yield*, or some similar verb that combines with *to*. See PREPOSITIONS.

acronyms. See INITIALESE; OPERATION X.

additives. See LINKING 3.

addressed envelope. See SELF-ADDRESSED ENVELOPE.

adequate. To be adequate —etymologically, *level with, equal to*—is to measure up (to the requirements); and like *measure up* it is normally followed by *to* and some word denoting a quality or thing rather than by a word denoting action. *Adequate to meet the requirements* is redundant: the idea *meet* is contained in *adequate* itself; *adequate to the requirements* says all—indeed, more than all, for *to the requirements* may also be considered implicit in *adequate*. It should be added that *adequate to meet the requirements* is unidiomatic as well as redundant; for *adequate*, if followed by an action word, requires the gerund (verbal noun in -ING): *Few men would feel adequate to coping* (not *cope*) *with these responsibilities.* In this construction *adequate* is parallel with *equal*; we say *equal to facing*, not *equal to face*.

Adequate without any complementary phrase still implies one. *His income is adequate* means an income equal to all reasonable demands on it. And by context the word can be given a belittling or even pejorative suggestion not inherent in it; for example, the critic's patronizing phrase *adequate performance* denotes a performance equal to moderate or even low expectations.

We frequently meet attempts to compare adequacies, signified by such phrases as *more adequate, less adequate, insufficiently adequate, adequate enough: This explanation seemed to W. adequate enough to account for* (seemed to W. to account for) *the parcels the lady then brought to him / must make a greater use of the nation's merchant fleet so that it will carry a more adequate share* (an adequate share) *of the nation's international trade.* The second example, which tries to compare something adequate with something more adequate, should stop at comparing adequacy with something less than that. *Insufficiently adequate* merely says *insufficiently sufficient.* One may of course say *more nearly adequate, closer to adequate.* But the too familiar *adequate enough*, sometimes found in exalted contexts, is nonsense. *There are many "quiet" situations for which this style is adequate enough* occurs in a quasi-philosophical treatise on prose style. *Adequate* is no less resistant to comparison than *enough* itself.

adhere, adherence, adhesion. As an intransitive verb *adhere* seems proof against misuse. Objects are made to adhere with glue; people adhere to a cause, a party, or one another. But what about *adhere* as a transitive? It is listed as one in Webster, with the definition *to cause to adhere,* and its inclusion technically justifies the passive participle in *Then along came the "frozen wire" staples, adhered to each other in a strip.* To many or most readers this use will seem as odd as *He was firmly clung to his prejudice.* For *adhered* read *adhering.*

Of the two nouns *adherence* and *adhesion,* the first is generally for figurative, the second for literal use. One *adheres* to the principles of a party, and this constitutes one's *adherence* to it; the surgical tape *adheres* to the skin, and its firm *adhesion* holds the bandage in place. Because French has only one word for the two types of sticking, and French books tend to be translated at sight, *adhésion* has begun to make its way into English and American writings on politics as *adhesion* (to the Tories, to principle, to one's pledged word).

The surgical term to denote the postoperative sticking together of tissues that should remain separate is always *adhesion.*

adjectives, co-ordinate. See APPENDIX 2, pp. 480–528.

adjudge, adjudicate. See DANGEROUS PAIRS.

administer, minister. Medicine, first aid, or other succor is *administered* to a person in need. The person so served is *ministered to,* not *administered to.* Lately the impression has got about, unwarrantably, that *minister* has become archaic; *administer* is being written in its place by many reporters and passed by their copy desks. *After X.'s shoe had been removed and he had been administered to, he got to his feet / After being administered to, C. resumed the battle / More than 100 persons, including two doctors who administered to him, were attending the lecture.* In each of these the intransitive verb *minister* (or some intransitive equivalent) should replace the transitive *administer.* *Administration* is the act of giving or bestowing; what is received is a *ministration.*

admission, admittance. A cast-iron distinction used to be made between *admittance,* which meant the act or fact of entering, and *admission,* the right to enter, whether exercised or not. Under this rule one would apply for *admission* to a college (the privilege of entering), whereas in front of a locked door one fails to achieve *admittance* (physical access). There is a hint of support for the distinction in the obligatory use of *admission* for an entrance charge; what you buy at the box office is a permission to enter. To honor the distinction would mean to replace *admission* with *admittance* in the following: *where the current cuts the ice from* *below and open water gives admission to the air.*

But is the distinction validated by usage? What the treatment of the two words by dictionaries conveys is that both have long been used in both senses, although some regularities are found. Whereas an article in a magazine edited by precisians gives us *these seven hundred and fifty colleges received applications for admittance from some seven hundred and fifty thousand secondary-school students / judging the boy's fitness for admission to* [a college] / [X. College] *practically guarantees admittance to the A group / the once fairly placid business of college admissions,* the academic practice is to speak of *admission to college, admission blanks, officers, interviews*—never *admittance.* Again, on business premises the mysterious little door around the corner bears the sign *No Admittance,* never *No Admission.* On invitations the phrase is always *Admission Free.*

admit. See ACKNOWLEDGE, ADMIT.

admitting. See DANGLERS, ACCEPTABLE.

advance, -d, -ment. The first two of these words are treated first in their adjectival use, because they frequently cause trouble through being interchanged. Yet the difference between them is not hard to see and to retain if one asks oneself whether the desired word is to mean *in advance* (of the usual time or place) or *is advanced* (by reason of effort or accident). Thus one requests *advance notice* or *an advance payment* on salary, or one receives *an advance copy* of a new book. The passive idea in the participle in -*ed* makes it the word to use for a student who has *advanced standing* or for a pioneering mind with *advanced views.* The standing and the views have, as it were, been moved forward; they are not ahead of schedule. *Advance* connotes anticipation; *advanced* connotes progress accomplished.

Between the nouns *advance* and *advancement* the distinction is more easily manageable. *Advance* refers to any progress, literal or figurative; *advancement* is restricted to individual progress in a career, bureaucracy, or hierarchy. The schoolboy has made a great *advance* in his studies, the youth little *advance* in maturity. The soldier or cleric has won *advancement.* One seeks *advancement* very deliberately but can only hope to have made an *advance* after the labor or the cure is over. As for *making advances,* these are only attempts to secure love or friendship, generally (but not always) of an unwelcome sort. After a quarrel the more generous person *makes the first advances,* but he may be thrown back with no *advance* in mutual esteem and no *advancement* whatever.

adverbs, vexatious. 1. A clothier whose advertising takes the form of little essays quotes a former slogan of the American Institute of Men's and Boys' Wear, *Dress Right —You Can't Afford Not To,* with the comment that it "had that ungrammatical touch that nowadays seems to be considered essential." What and where is the ungrammatical touch? The answer, presumably, is that someone thinks the correct wording would be *Dress Rightly.* The truth is that many adverbs, including *right* and *wrong,* are formed without *-ly.* They do not differ in appearance from adjectives, but they are adverbs. We go *straight to the point,* not *straightly;* a transgressor of speed limits is driving *too fast,* not *too fastly.* The belief that adverbs should end in *-ly* is hard to down in the mistaken purist, and one often meets the tone of reprobation about the short forms. A newspaper will comment quizzically on the public authorities that have *given outright approval to road signs like "Drive Slow."* Would the critic not agree that *slow-growing, slow-spoken* are good English? And does he ever contend that he is *widely awake?*

Where an adverb exists both with and without *-ly* it may have, or may be given by context, an entirely different sense with the suffix. *I expect to hear from him direct* means I count on him to communicate with me without anyone's intervention; *I expect to hear from him directly* means I count on hearing with little or no delay. If we *eat right* we are giving ourselves a proper diet, but if we *eat rightly* it means, or should mean, that it is proper for us to eat instead of fasting. To *think hardly* of a person or idea is not the same as to *think hard. Hardly* has a figurative meaning; *hard* is better suited to physical or material events. Misfortunes bear *hardly* on their victims, but one part or object bears *hard* on another that receives its full thrust. As for driving, when we assert that we *drive carefully* we are describing our attitude toward the act; when we drive *slow* or *fast,* we are describing the motion of the car, not our driving in the same sense as before.

A more important difficulty that bears on both grammar and style is the choice between adverb and predicate adjective: *concluded that what comes naturally in the field of grammar would be well and good.* Shall it be *comes naturally* or *comes natural?* Obviously we can construe *comes* as an active verb, modifiable by the adverb *naturally.* Or we can construe *comes* as a connecting verb (copula), equivalent to *is;* we then modify *what* with the predicate adjective *natural.* In this instance there is perhaps not much to choose; but in most parallel instances we do well to bypass the weakening adverb and prefer the adjective, taking the verb as a mere link and the attribute as a property of the person or thing, not of the action: *the two men stood silently, engulfed in the urgency of the moment / and they all stood there silently for a few seconds.* Let the silence refer to the standers, not the standing, and obviously *they stood silent. The army was to travel as lightly as possible.* Lightness belongs to the army, not to the manner of traveling; let it *travel light.*

Cookbooks are not ordinarily prissy about grammar, but they are addicted, prissily, to *bacon fried crisply, batter beaten smoothly,* etc. Better as style and not less good as grammar would be *fried crisp* (= fried in such a way as to be crisp), *beaten smooth.* Commercial bakery bread is described as *thinly sliced;* in fact it is *sliced thin.*

Ben Jonson, who persistently had grammar on his mind, was given to writing *look superciliously while I present you,* and the like; yet *look* in this meaning is as copulative as any verb except *be,* and modern usage demands *look supercili-*

ous. A reviewer who may not be aware of Ben Jonson writes: *Mikhail Sholokov, another Russian, who is* [the] *author of "And Quietly Flows the Don."* The book itself was more happily given the English title *And Quiet Flows the Don,* ascribing the quietness to the river and taking *Flows* as a mere connective.

2. The true form of the adverb is a source of repeated, vehement debates about whether we should *feel bad* or *feel badly.* Such discussions often miss the point. *He is equally inconsistent when he feels badly about having insufficiently thanked his host for his kindness.* Strictly, this should be *feels bad.* But *feel bad* in this use is thwarted by its prevailing meaning of *feel ill* (= unwell). It might comfort everybody if we could give up *badly* as an adjective in *-ly* (cf. *likely, lovely, friendly, comely, goodly, soldierly, workmanly*) and save it for the one idiom *feel badly.* Unfortunately lexicography already records *badly* as an adjective (dialectal), and in the very meaning that we do not now want—*unwell.* ("How are you?" "I am badly, worse luck.") There is thus no way out but to say colloquially *I feel badly*—if one dislikes *I feel bad* in the sense of feeling unhappy or regretful. Then, in careful writing, one would skirt the issue with synonyms:

feel sorry, feel regret, have qualms, be uneasy.

If one writes a review in which one describes a book as *devoted entire to* such-and-such a subject, the chances are about seven in ten that the editor will "improve" the wording to read *devoted entirely to*, which is not quite what was meant. Authors should protest even though the protest comes too late (not *too lately*,) and even though the copy editor who made the change knows perfectly well that an oyster is swallowed whole, not wholly. Such a protest did not persuade the *New Yorker*, always punctilious about English, to announce its items from the press as *reprinted entire* (instead of *in their entirety*), but it is by banging away at the same points that printed English gains an inch here and there against the improvements that do not improve.

3. Idiom occasionally embalms a word having adverbial force though it may be anything but adverbial in itself. Such idiomatic words—usually nouns—had better not be tampered with. The listener to broadcasts of baseball games is distressed to hear the words *crystally clear* in a singing commercial about beer—a piece of corruption doubtless brought into being so as to companion *icily light*, which immediately precedes it. It has not yet occurred to the author of this jingle to write *razorly sharp, diamondly bright,* or *ovenly fresh.*

4. What shall we say of the writer given to modifying adjectives with an adverb that weakens or neutralizes their force? *We find this a moderately terrifying prospect.* The inherently immoderate *terrifying* is here toned down almost to extinction. The trick is characteristic of writers who have felt the power of understatement or think it a duty to depress strong emotion. Occasionally this device will produce a striking OXYMORON, but it is usually a trick, which easily becomes a bad habit. A writer should consciously guard against stylistic trademarks; for the reader will first notice, then collect examples, and soon forget the meaning of the prose in his pursuit of the game: *rather exhaustive / a little repulsive / pretty meaningless / somewhat forbidding / faintly disgusting / mildly preposterous / tolerably overpowering / slightly overwhelming / somewhat dreadful / rather appalling / just a bit lethal.*

5. Akin to the problem of CONTRARY TO is the one encountered in words of adjectival form (without *-ly*) but adverbial function—such words as *relative, preparatory, preliminary, irrespective, independent.* The problem occurs in this sentence: *This subcommittee is now conducting field*

studies preparatory to drafting much-needed legislation. The reader cannot be sure whether the author means that the undertaking of field studies or the studies themselves are preparatory to legislation. On the latter supposition, *preparatory* is an adjective that modifies *studies;* on the first, it is an adverb that modifies *is conducting.* The sentence is defective, or at least improvable, because of this doubt; a good sentence should leave no doubt.

Webster's New International Dictionary lists *preparatory* as an outright adverb, equal to *preparatorily.* Like *preliminarily, preparatorily* is cumbrous and absurd. But consider a parallel example: *The grants . . . will enable three experienced international agencies to broaden their consideration of radiation problems independent of the policies of governments.* Here the simple, natural improvement is *independently* (if it modifies *broaden);* otherwise: *problems that are independent of.* Both are equally possible because *independently* is not a preposterous word like *preliminarily.* An irreproachable sentence of Bernard Shaw's supplies a parallel: *Not until an author has become so familiar that we are quite at our ease with him . . . do we cease to imagine that he is, relatively to older writers, terribly serious.* Some good judges think that *relative* would be tolerable here, if not preferable; but other and equally discriminating writers would find it slipshod. Fewer would so regard *irrespective* in the following: *I think the Cuban people are friendly to the United States irrespective of what Dr. Castro may say / are increasingly urging Britain to join the Community, irrespective of Commonwealth ties.*

As for *doubtlessly* and *regardlessly,* they sound so odd to modern ears that one is surprised to find them recognized in dictionaries. The really bothersome pair is *preparatory* and *preliminary,* but there are ways of avoiding them. In *There were some fleecy clouds when they came down preparatory to landing,* the cure is not *preparatory* but *came down to land.* Elsewhere some alternatives are *in preparation for, as preparations for, by way of preparing for.* The recommended practice, then, is (a) to differentiate with the adverbial *-ly* for the adverbial function except where the form without *-ly* is standard and (b) to resort to some alternative construction when *-ly* will produce monstrosities. (See also OVERLY; SINGLE-HANDEDLY.)

6. Where to put the adverb in the sentence is a question that in contemporary writing receives more diverse and worse answers than all the preceding questions put together. It is a new question: until a few decades ago instinct about the rhythms of the mother tongue served instead of principles. Now explicit ones are needed to fill the place of instinct. The chief ones are these: (a) An adverb intended to be emphatic goes before the subject (*Unfortunately he could not foresee this consequence*). (b) An adverb not required for emphasis comes after the subject of a simple verb (*The Smiths generally dine with us once a week*). (c) With a compound verb—that is, one made with an auxiliary and a main verb —the adverb comes between auxiliary and main verb (*He will probably telephone before starting / I have often had that thought myself / The clock is consistently losing five minutes a day*). (d) If the verb is compounded with two or more auxiliaries the adverb comes after the first auxiliary when its force is to apply to the whole compound (*They have certainly been forewarned / He will undoubtedly have had some news by this time*). (e) If the adverb modifies the participle alone it comes immediately before the participle (*It has been confidently asserted / It will have become firmly established*). (f) An adverbial element that runs to several words is put outside a compound verb— ordinarily after it (*He has been asked over and over*

again / We have been hearing this particular argument off and on for several years past).

These principles were practiced for many generations without anyone's having to think about them. Then strange things began to happen. Some influential source promulgated the doctrine that the compound verb is an indivisible unit, and that to wedge an adverb into it is a crime akin to the splitting of an infinitive. The results are uniformly bad: *It long had been known / It officially was announced the other day / They unfailingly have been led by a brilliant passer / This session of Congress doubtless will see a lot of pot-shots fired in X.'s direction / Is "Doctor Zhivago" protected since it first was published in Milan, Italy? / The baritone finally was accepted to portray Darcy / This quiet man steadily was gaining the respect of his players / The strike that otherwise inevitably will be in effect at midnight / The people upstairs always are pounding / whether a 450-room skyscraper accurately can be termed a motel*. Most of these examples transgress either (c) or (d) above; the last one transgresses (e); *unfailingly have been led by* might come under (d) or (e), according to what it means. For rhetorical effects, especially in spoken discourse, one may put the adverb in a place where it will enforce a pause and heighten a feeling, but then the adverb must be set off by commas: *The Communists, presumably, are making headway with their propaganda.*

It is clear from this list that the position of the adverb can affect meaning. The word *also,* notably, varies in meaning according to its position. The obituary of an industrialist names the companies of which he had been president and continues: *He also had served as a director of* [six companies]. This means—or should mean—that he had served with some others on the board; the intended meaning, that he had filled other posts, calls for *had also served.* In *The next Pope also will have to decide,* we ask: Who before him had to decide what? The intention was to refer to previously named matters awaiting the Pope's decision. Other adverbs will similarly betray when misplaced. *Few of them were doubtless aware that they played on what was once Millionaires' Street* probably tried to say that no doubt few of them were aware, but managed to say instead that few were aware with unquestioning certainty.

A last principle about adverbs should encourage writers to place them before the simple verb, instead of between it and its object. That is the principle of elegance. In English the adverb should precede the verb whenever possible. Consider *Usually I understand entirely his motives.* Quite apart from the repetition of *-ly* and the awkwardness of having two modifiers of unequal power and scope struggling over the verb they flank, the putting of *entirely* between *understand* and *motives* is felt as the erecting of a wall. *I entirely understand* is the natural order. *The youngest must take part if they are to advance effectively their beliefs* (are effectively to advance; or even, are to effectively advance—see SPLIT INFINITIVE) / *I want you to imagine a state of affairs in which people would have forgotten mysteriously their past* (would have mysteriously forgotten).

affinity. This standard word for relationship by marriage has, by legitimate extension, the meaning of strong mutual attraction, as between those who fall in love at sight. An affinity is *between* two such persons; each has an affinity *with* or *to* the other. In keeping with its use in early chemistry to denote the force combining elements into compounds, *affinity* expresses a mutual relationship, not someone's attraction to a passive or insentient object—and it does not denote a propensity for doing or being something. *He has some affinity for mathematical studies* is a misuse: it could hardly be said that mathematical studies have an affinity for him. *Aptitude* is doubtless the word sought. *X. is practically devoid of affinity for pursuing such a career.* Again *aptitude* might serve, or *qualification*, or *capacity. The six-time winner of the American League batting championship has an affinity for making news when* (1) *He does something,* (2) *He does nothing.* Has a gift? A talent? An instinct? A knack? (But *knack* requires *of* not *for.*) Anyway, not *affinity.* A writer with a taste for fashionable inaccuracies might make it *flair.*

It is perhaps unnecessary to add a reminder that *affinity* is a word for the relations between persons, not for the persons themselves. *She is well known to be his affinity* and *They are affinities of long standing* produce an unfortunate effect even when used jocosely.

See also PREPOSITIONS.

-age. See -ABLE, -IBLE 2.

aggravate. See DEFENSIBLES.

ago, before. Both adverbs refer to time past, and both relate it to another time as a point of reference. Normally the point of reference is *now* when we say *ago*, and *then* when we say *before. Ago* covers the range from indefinitely far back to a fixed point already past. *I knew that long ago* is from a point of view in the present. *He had known that long before* is from a point of view in the past. *Ago* = earlier than now; *before* = earlier than then. (There is an apparent idiomatic exception in *I knew that before, The same thing has happened before,* etc., which imply a present point of view, but this *before* means nothing but *previously*; it does not call attention to the stretch between one point in time and another.) The distinction is worth a moment's notice, because popular fiction is much given to the false *ago. His thoughts turned to the time, now fifteen years ago, when* . . . The *now* of this sentence is the character's now, not the reader's; the *ago* means *before.*

The commonplace words *ago* and *before*, idiomatically used, have an obvious correspondence with the rather bookish word *hitherto* and the much more bookish word *theretofore*, respectively; and *hitherto* (= up to now) is often used by those given to this sort of vocabulary when they should use *theretofore*—exactly as *ago* is used for *before.*

When *ago* is combined with *since*—e.g. *It is two months ago since I have heard from him*— it is simply redundant; omit *ago.* Those who write this construction invite the confusion that generally overtakes the attempt to say a thing in two ways at once: (1) It was two months ago that I heard from him; (2) It has been two months since I heard from him. (See SINCE, YET 1).

agree. See PREPOSITIONS.

ague. See PRONUNCIATION 1.

-al. See REMEDIABLE, REMEDIAL.

all, adjective and predicate. 1. When elbowed out of its natural position and converted into a pronoun, *all* obtrudes itself unpleasantly and may mislead. Its natural position is before what it modifies: *All we like sheep have gone astray / All things work together for good / All the Brothers Were Valiant.* Here it is in the unnatural position: *Is this all leading toward a third round in the Palestine war or to some other violent Levantine explosion?* The inversion makes the subject of the sentence stylistically indistinguishable from the *we-all* and *you-all* of dialectal speech in the South—expressions pleasing enough in their own setting but outside the patterns of normal prose. *All we like sheep,* from Isaiah, is of course an unidiomatic combination in modern prose, but the cure is not *We all.* Where *all* modifies the subject pronoun of a compound verb, *all* properly follows the auxiliary: not *They all would be paying calls on each other at all hours of the day and night,* but *They would all . . .* In everyday unpoetic writing the sentence from Isaiah becomes *We have all, like sheep, gone astray,* or *All of us . . .*

2. A modern ellipsis with *all* should be kept for colloquial encounters only: *He has his facts wrong is all* [that's the matter with him] */ I forgot to wind my watch is all / She's gone to the hairdresser is all* [that accounts for her absence].

3. *All . . . not.* For sentences such as *All liars are not thieves,* see NEGATIVES, TROUBLE WITH.

See also NEEDLESS WORDS 2; NUMBER, TROUBLE WITH.

all but. In the meaning of *virtually* or *the next thing to* or *little short of,* the phrase *all but* is one of those crystallized idioms that brook no tampering. (See SET PHRASES.) Do not imitate the sports reporter who writes genteelly: *Sceptre was all except invisible in the haze when the Columbia swept across the finish line.* (By the way, why the article with *Columbia* if there is to be none with *Sceptre?* See (A, AN, THE 5.)

allege. In the passive voice *allege* is naturally followed by an infinitive: *He is alleged to be a Communist sympathizer.* In the active voice it is followed by a simple object or by a *that* clause: *We allege his guilty knowledge of what was going on / We allege that he had guilty knowledge.* Moreover, *allege* should always carry an implication of complaint; it is a word colored with accusation and criminality. By reason of both idiom and connotation, then, *allege* cannot be the word wanted in *all the churches which allege to have relics of St. John the Baptist.* The best word is probably *profess.* A word that might be proposed by some is *claim;* but *claim to have* would suggest a contested ownership. Other possible verbs, with the appropriate complements, are *assert, maintain, pretend,* and *declare.*

allergic. The victim of an allergy is abnormally sensitive to some substance—pollen, dust, feathers, shellfish, or what not—that has no bad effect on people in general. To whatever substance has the effect of making him ill he is said to be *allergic.* The adjective is not, then, an everyday synonym of *averse, ill-disposed, resistant, prejudiced, hostile, unreceptive.*

Once the term *allergic* (literally *other-acting*) attained currency, however, it was seized on to denote a person's attitude toward anything he happened to dislike; it is now an omnibus word that saves thought and flouts precision. We read of persons *allergic to free advice* or *allergic to bad manners* or *allergic to being dictated to* or *allergic to abstract painting.* Worse yet, we find the fundamental sense of the term contradicted by its being applied to dislikes that are normal and nearly universal: *Practically everybody is allergic to excessive and unnecessary noise.* The typical misuse: *Now and then a newcomer is so belligerently aggrieved or so allergic to work that he has to be returned to the downtown jail.* Like other VOGUE WORDS, *allergic* needs suppressing not alone for its often absurd inexactitude but also for its displacement of more apt and expressive terms.

See also SCIENTISM.

allowing. See DANGLERS, ACCEPTABLE.

all the more. The attempt to give emphasis by a seeming measurement of the terms in a comparison is common to all the European languages, and its effectiveness rests on clear signaling by correlative words which introduce the elements being compared. There is nothing archaic about the traditional and quite emphatic *all the more,* though it is now formal rather than colloquial. What has happened as a result is that the introductory particle for the second member has become uncertain. The established pair is *all the more . . . that. She loved him all the more that she had, as it were, given him back his life when everyone—his mother too—had given him up for stillborn.*

Yet anyone who follows this clear and unobjectionable form will find his text corrected without hesitation by many helpful hands. They think a word has dropped out, and they want it to read *all the more so . . . that*, which is acceptable but not required; or again, *all the more . . . in that*, which is to confuse two constructions. *He was mistaken beyond hope of self-correction in that he thought all his actions divinely inspired.* Here the *in* is essential to introduce the clause acting as a noun. If we do not choose to say *He was mistaken in his belief*, we can say *mistaken in that he thought* and go on to state the belief. But *all the more* does not need and will not accommodate *in* or any other preposition, as a simple inversion will show: *That he is qualified by training as well as experience is all the more reason for electing him = There is all the more reason . . . that he is.*

allude. An allusion is the kind of glancing mention that does not name its object but gives the reader a means of making the identification if he has the knowledge or the wit to do so. The competing word, needed nine times out of ten where *allusion* is a misfit, is *reference*. A reference *is* an identification, whether a precise one (e.g. a footnote naming the source and location of something quoted or used in the text) or an approximate one (e.g. *Seward's Folly* for Alaska or for the purchase of Alaska). The borderline between approximate reference

and mere allusion is hard to draw; we might put it that one man's reference is another man's allusion. When an editorial writer calls the conflict with Spain in 1898 *Mr. Hearst's war* he is making a reference, but one that may be taken as an obscure allusion by an uninformed reader. If, on the other hand, he represents someone as *sighing for more worlds to conquer* he is alluding (not referring) to Alexander the Great. Allusion and reference are clearly enough differentiated at their extremes, but may overlap midway.

Sometimes *allude* is carelessly used where there is neither allusion nor reference. An example: *The common phrase "the irony of fate" alludes to an apparent mockery of destiny.* This sentence is clearly a definition; for *alludes to* read *means*.

almost. One might suppose that the use of *most* for *almost* was a patent illiteracy in a class with *we ain't* or *he don't*. Fiction writers reproducing the colloquial or dialectal *most* (adverb) commonly give it an apostrophe: *'most always, 'most any schoolboy*, etc. Nevertheless this scrap of dialect does keep turning up in formal print: *An increasing number of households go in for cookouts most every pleasant Sunday.* And an eminent sports reporter for one of the great newspapers comes out with *Then came a play that* *would have unsettled most any pitcher equipped with less fortitude than the lanky . . . right-hander.* There are, then, those who can use a reminder that there is no short form for *almost.*

alone. Following a noun, as it commonly does, *alone* is often ambiguous in grammar and therefore in sense. *Cupidity alone accounts for so flagrant a violation of the decencies.* Does this mean that cupidity unassisted by other causes is enough, or does it mean that cupidity is the only possible explanation? One cannot tell. The second meaning had better be rendered by *Only cupidity accounts for*; the first by *Cupidity by itself accounts for.* In *X. alone was competent to handle the situation* read, for one meaning, *X. was the only one competent*; for the other, *X. unaided was competent.*

along with. See AS 11.

also. See ADVERBS 6; AND; TOO 1.

alternate, alternative. The principal difficulties that beset these words come under two heads: 1. The management of the noun *alternative.* 2. The tendency to confusion between the adjectival and the adverbial uses of *alternate(ly)* and *alternative(ly).*

1. To the strict-constructionist writer an *alternative* can be either (a) a problem of choice

between two possibilities or (b) one of the possibilities to be chosen; and it is often signaled (as in this sentence) by the alternative conjunctions *either* and *or.* *To be, or not to be* makes, in that form, one alternative, the choice between being and not being; and *that is the question* means *that is the alternative.* On the other view, *to be* is one alternative, *not to be* the other. But note that this acceptation creates an *and* relationship, not an *or* relationship; Hamlet would then have had to say: *To be, and not to be: those are the alternatives.* It makes, accordingly, a difference in grammar and rhetoric which definition of *alternative* a writer uses. He should not try to use both definitions at once, as in this sentence: *The deterministic conception of the universe poses clearly two alternatives for consideration of moral action—a complete pessimism or a precariously subjective optimism.* Here the second definition (implicit in *two alternatives*) masquerades (by means of the false *or*) as the first. There is a mix-up between (a) *the* (one) *alternative— pessimism or optimism*—and (b) *the two alternatives—pessimism and optimism.*

By a loose extension, *alternative* has also come to mean any one of three (or of several) possibilities. *Of these alternatives the least unpleasant is the third* (or fourth or *n*th) is frowned on by the purist, but it passes most readers without notice and is not found objectionable even by many who would not write it themselves.

2. So far there is little room for serious trouble. Confusion begins with the adjectives and adverbs, and it enters through a loophole provided by an extension of meaning in *alternate*, adjective and verb. In one of its standard meanings, affiliated with *alternation*, this word causes no blunders: *Elms and maples alternate on the south side of Main Street / Mother dines with us on alternate Sundays / The alternate angles are equal.* But in the United States *alternate* happens long ago to have acquired currency as a noun meaning *substitute, second choice.* We appoint delegates to a convention and also *alternates,* who, if need be, can serve in their stead. This use is easily transferred from persons to things. For example, a book club chooses a book for the month and, for those who do not want it, proposes an *alternate.* By this route *alternate* has arrived at a function hardly distinguishable from that of *alternative.*

Unless good writers will make the effort at self-discipline, the distinction between the two unrelated ideas will not be restored and ambiguity will continue. A spokesman for the United States Army writes to a correspondent: *Requests to use alternate* (i.e. alternative) *test dates are also received from other groups and individuals for various reasons.* Newspapers use the two words interchangeably: *Guests can drift from the formal living room to the . . . family room. Alternately* (Alternatively), *the family room can be used as extra space for food preparation / Scores of flights were ordered to alternate* (alternative) *landing fields from Pennsylvania to New England.* One can even find a perverted *alternate* and an orthodox *alternative* in the same context: *Another problem which will have to be met if Africa's wildlife is not to go the way of the dinosaur, is that of finding an alternate way of life for the tribes which do most of the poaching.* And a few lines farther: *because he has no alternative means of supporting himself and his family.*

Alternate, meaning one empowered to act in the place of another, is established and inescapable; but the overlapping with *alternative* leads to confusion (in both meaning and construing) and is therefore inexcusable: *The alternate modes of travel are by dog sled and by airplane.* Is traveling done first by one means and then by the other, or must one be chosen instead of the other?. *He asked that the experiment be continued eight months, during which the buses would have tried alternate routes.* This sentence about highway traffic suggests an experimental shifting back and forth between routes, but the context shows that the point is to try out a number of alternative routes. As for construing, note that the sentence above in which *flights were ordered to alternate . . . fields* suggests the verb *to alternate.*

Alternative in one of its standard denotations is nearly synonymous with DILEMMA.

although, though. The main doubts affecting the use of these concessive conjunctions are these: 1. What is the difference between them? 2. Is the relation of the clauses a truly concessive one? 3. If the relation is concessive, is the concession ascribed to the right clause? 4. When one of the words introduces an implied clause, is it followed by the logical participle?

1. In most uses the two words have become interchangeable. There is perhaps a slight tendency to begin clauses with *although* (as more emphatic) instead of *though,* and correspondingly to use *though* for connecting minor elements within a clause: *A rising wind kept deepening the drifts, although it had stopped snowing at daybreak / They continued to hold out, though without prospect of being reinforced / born of poor though honest parents.* But the two words could readily be interchanged in these examples, and one can easily summon up contrary

cases such as *Though he slay me, yet will I trust in him.* This scriptural *though* means *even if;* and it is true that *though* is generally preferred in purely imaginary or in contrary-to-fact conditions. Its ordinary meaning is, of course, not *even if* but *despite the fact that.* In an inverted order that shifts conjunction from its natural leading position, *though* seems to be idiomatic and obligatory: *Desperate though the situation was / Modest though his expectations were.* In this pattern *though,* nearly equivalent to *as,* is not readily replaced by *although.* Otherwise, it seems extremely doubtful whether a thousand examples at random from modern writing would substantiate any difference or validate any rule for making a distinction. There is not much to be lost by treating the two words as interchangeable and not much to be gained by attempts to differentiate them. (Note that the intensive *even* can be placed in front of *though,* but that it sounds affected in front of *although.*)

2. The real danger is the temptation to resort to one of the pair where neither belongs; that is, where there is no concessive relationship between clauses. A concessive clause is a statement of something that tends to weaken what is stated in a principal clause; it names some consideration in spite of which the principal statement is true. Where this opposition does not exist, or where it exists only between the concessive clause and something not said, a concessive conjunction is amiss. *Temperatures may rise to 280 degrees Fahrenheit although the ideal temperature is said to be between 190 and 200 degrees.* There is no opposition between stating the possible extreme and stating the desirable mean; the second clause lays down, not a concession, but a separate fact. Omit *although* and use a semicolon after *Fahrenheit.*

Consider other examples: *The remainder expressed a desire to return to Cuba. Mr. A. said that there were no objections to this, although a decision would be made later on the requests for asylum* / *The* [vaccinated] *children ranged in age from six months to seven years, although even 12-year-olds were included in some districts* / *The climate is gradually changing, although there is little agreement about the causes* / *I was lucky enough to get through the winter without a cold, though I had an attack of jaundice.* In many of these false concessions there is an opposition between the concessive clause and a thought more or less obscurely present in the author's mind. In the last example the unexpressed opposition seems to be *I was lucky enough to get through . . . without a cold, though unlucky enough to have an attack of jaundice.* The sentence as written requires the reader to fill a vacuum.

3. Sometimes a clearly concessive relationship is stood on its head—i.e. one clause is made concessive when it is the other clause that should be. *He habitually exceeded the speed limit, though he had never had an accident.* Read: *Though he habitually exceeded the speed limit, he had never had an accident.* Similarly in *Both drew large crowds, although Senator X.'s was larger,* the sense is clearer the other way around: *Though both drew large crowds, Senator X.'s was* [the] *larger.* In such sentences the writer may be supposed to have had an afterthought and to have perceived the concessive link, but not to have seen which was the broader statement and which the limitation upon it.

4. When *though* or *although* begins an elliptical clause, there may be a hidden clash between the key word of that clause—usually an *-ing* participle—and the word that would be required if the clause were fully expanded. Where we detect such a clash the sentence is at best weak and at worst off balance. *He is an extremely learned man, though wearing his erudition lightly.* Expand the elliptical clause, and what do you get? Not *he is wearing,* but *he wears*—the simple, obvious way to improve it. *I think this course the right one, though deploring* (I deplore) *the arguments commonly heard* *in its favor.* On the other hand, expansion produces no participial change in *Though overworking already, he could hardly refuse this demand on his time;* the ellipsis is perfect, and brevity is not paid for with awkwardness.

It should be noted that *though* (not *although*) can be used as a terminal adverb with a meaning akin to the adverbial *however: Our January temperatures run twenty degrees lower than yours; we have a comfortable absence of humidity, though / The flight takes just under four hours; it takes almost an hour to get to the airport, though.* This idiomatic use exempts *though* from the logically concessive relationship normally required; indeed, it serves to rein in a thought that actually goes off at a tangent. Some of the examples above that proved untenable could in fact be rectified by changing the conjunction to the terminal adverb: *He habitually exceeded the speed limit; he had never had an accident, though.*

See also WHILE.

ambiance. What is *ambiance*? To Webster's New International Dictionary it is a French word chiefly useful in English for a specialized meaning in the criticism of painting. Elsewhere it is affectation: *Luscious fabrics emphasized the ambiance of luxury and warmth that ran all through the collection.* The received English word for a surrounding medium, an atmosphere, or a fluid is *ambient* (an adjective here used absolutely as a noun). But an atmosphere can hardly run through anything or be emphasized. A pretentious word has been used to mean nothing more than *general effect, impression,* or *suggestion.* (Note the recently imported, still more fashionable, and equally affected *ambiente,* borrowed from Italian.)

ambiguity. Persons who come fresh to questions of usage after a longer or shorter life of inattention are often puzzled by the question: When does ambiguity matter? They notice that many words sound alike (homonyms) and can thereby provoke doubt or contradiction. *Toast,* a solid, is eaten in the morning and *a toast,* liquid, is drunk at night. The observer knows that such similarities of sound rarely cause confusion. Why then make a fuss about other possible ambiguities when a little thought about context will show what the speaker or writer meant? In *A woman with a snub nose appeared to conduct him to the door marked Private* it does not take long to decide that she did conduct him and not merely appeared to do so. Is it not pedantic to call for a rewriting?

The answer is no. The momentary halt, the bringing to

consciousness of the possible choice of meanings, the look at the context or at the probabilities of the case are unwarranted demands on the reader's attention. And when a writer is habitually blind to the chances of even slight misreadings, he sooner or later produces a sentence in which the doubt cannot be resolved. It may be easy to work out the intention in *She had obviously planned to ask for* [the] *identification of every single male caller,* but what is the exact purport of *All right, check that witty brain of yours; it's running away with you*? In the first sentence *single* means *alone* and not *unmarried;* but in the second does *check* mean *restrain, put in the coat room,* or *verify*? The context suggests meanings 1 and 3. The practical writer knows that *check* readily goes astray. *Seem* and *appear* are even worse: HEIRESS IN APPARENT SUICIDE may mean she probably committed the act, but it may also mean that the circumstances may have been contrived to give that impression. The further caution to bear in mind is that almost any common word can lose its straightforward character by finding itself in company that brings out some hidden weakness.

ambivalent. This pet word of amateur psychologists is already threatened with corruption and decay. A literary biographer discusses a writer's *early ambivalence between poetry and prose,* and this misuse is encountered frequently enough to prove that the term does not fill but usurps a place in our thoughts. *Ambivalence* does not mean indecision between different objects or desires; it means a state of simultaneous attraction and repulsion. An ambivalent lover is not one torn between rival affections, but one teetering between love and hatred of the same person. *I can neither live with her nor live without her* is the characteristic declaration of ambivalence. A punctilious use of the noun occurs in the following: *Such is the ambivalence of educational researchers that very often their recommendations (for discontinuing homework, for example) run counter to their experimental findings.* The noun *ambivalence* is also misused when the intention is to say AMBIGUITY. This confusion simply adapts the error above to the need of generalizing and objectifying: *X. is ambivalent* (= undecided); *there is ambivalence* (= ambiguity) *in everything he does.* The words in parentheses here are not only the ones wanted; they are stronger and clearer than the pseudo-scientific *ambivalent, ambivalence.*

among. See BETWEEN 1.

ample. Unmodified, *ample* means *roomy enough*—some-

times *enough and to spare.*
The author who writes *a niche
in Mount Washington's hall of
fame ample enough for his
sturdy frame* is committing not
only the misdemeanor of unwanted rhyme but also the sin
of redundancy. *Ample enough*
is neither better nor worse
than *adequate enough* (see
ADEQUATE).

Because it suggests absolute
size and amount in the abstract, *ample* should not be
used to define a portion or
quantity. One says *a man of
ample means,* but not *they
served ample food and drink.*
One can write *the provisions*
(abstract) *were ample,* but not
*he had ample genius for the
task;* rather, *his genius was
subtle, strong, ample.*

amplify. We amplify—that
is, enlarge on—a subject under discussion; but do we amplify *on* it? The breach of
idiom is the same as that in
expound on (see EXPOUND).
Amplify is wrong in *sought to
amplify yesterday on that part
of the X.-Y. television debate
dealing with the issue.* The debate is finished and not to be
amplified. What the speaker is
presumably doing is amplify-
ing his own views of the issue.
What he is doing to the debate
is to *supplement* it.

and. A prejudice lingers
from the days of schoolmarm-
ish rhetoric that a sentence
should not begin with *and.*
The supposed rule is without
foundation in grammar, logic,
or art. *And* can join separate
sentences and their meanings
just as well as *but* can both
join sentences and disjoin
meanings. The false rule used
to apply to *but* equally; it is
now happily forgotten. What
has in fact happened is that
the traditionally acceptable
but after a semicolon has been
replaced by the same *but* after
a period. Let us do the same
thing with *and,* taking care, of
course, not to write long
strings of sentences each headed by *And* or by *But.*

Notice at the same time that
also is not a linking word and
should not be used as if it
were. *Also* is an adverb that
qualifies by suggesting simi-
larity of form or manner.
(Hence the combination *and
also* is not, as some think, redundant.) *Also* can therefore
begin a sentence only when it
is attached to some word or
phrase in the new sentence:
*Also present were / Also
drowned in the* Titanic *disaster.* But not: *He was graduated with high honors the
following June. Also he married, to everybody's surprise.*
(The last sentence should begin *And he* or *And he also.*)

See also BUT; INTRODUC-
TORY, p. 33.

and/or. Whether a lawyer
can or cannot make out a case
for the necessity of this ungraceful expression in legal

documents only a lawyer is competent to say; but anyone else is entitled to the view that it has no right to intrude in ordinary prose. One such intrusion may stand for all: *A majority of the tourists come here with camping and/or fishing on their minds.* Suppose this to be written *with camping or fishing on their minds.* How will any sensible reader interpret it? He will presume that some camp without fishing, some fish without camping, and some do both, nothing being said or implied to prevent the three equal possibilities. Note, besides, that these possibilities would be the same if *and* alone had been used.

We see in this example one of the usual effects of borrowing phraseology from the professions: it kills the plain sense of the words formerly deemed adequate by the layman. That plain sense in the sentence under review is that *and* can sometimes suggest *or*, and that generally *or* includes *and*. The weatherman's *Snow or sleet tomorrow* is no guarantee that we shall have only the one or the other. For generations the chairman has asked *Are there corrections or additions to the minutes?* well knowing that there may be both. The phrase EITHER . . . OR was invented for situations in which it is important to exclude one of a pair. To be sure, in casual speech *you or I must go* carries the meaning *either you or I*; but *If he tries that stunt he will be hurt or killed* makes it clear that the inclusion of *and* in *or* arises naturally from the facts and is habitual for most readers.

Indeed, if the users of *and/or* were as logical as they pretend to be when they insist on the legalism, they would have to say *and or or*, since their assumption is that the two cannot coexist. That assumption is not made better by the punctuation in *well, then, there's Mackenzie and, or, his associates.* And if a writer thinks his readers have been so corrupted by the abuse of *and/or* as to misunderstand his simple *or*, he should courageously repudiate the hybrid and write—using our first example—*tourists come here to camp or fish or both.* Let him remember that, except for lawyers, English speakers and writers have managed to express this simple relationship without *and/or* for over six centuries. This truth is commemorated in the couplet:

Had he foreseen the modern use of *and/or*,
It would have sickened Walter Savage Landor.

anent. There are times and places for deliberate archaism, but the morning newspaper is not among them. It is therefore a surprise to find a well-known publicist writing *this column quoted Ambassador Z.*

as . . . *disagreeing with those who took "a gloomy view" anent this change.* The ordinary words *about* and *concerning* suffice for all the purposes of modern prose.

-ant, suffix. See RESOURCE PERSON.

antecedents. 1. An antecedent is meant to precede whatever pronoun refers to it, and in the absence of special reasons it should always do so. But it does not. The following sentence illustrates three common irregularities: *While I may not have realized it as a student, the education I received was the basis for whatever success I have achieved in life.* Here we have (a) a pronoun *(it)* ahead of its antecedent, (b) an antecedent that defies precise identification, and (c) an intelligent reflection reduced to self-contradiction by the way it is stated. You have to wait to know what the first clause is talking about; having waited, you find that you have done so in vain; and you end up with the proposition that an undergraduate did not know what produced the success he achieved thirty years later. All this is a backhanded way of saying *Though as a student I may not have realized the importance of education, my education has been the basis of whatever success I have achieved.*

Of the relation between *it* and its delayed antecedent, we may say that a pronoun is puzzling enough when it tries to put a drawstring around a whole preceding idea, and much too puzzling when it points in the dark to some idea not yet hinted at. Again, a well-regulated pronoun refers to an identifiable substantive with which it agrees in number. Yet the public prints are full of pronouns that try to extract antecedents from entirely ineligible parts of speech. Here is one that refers to something embodied in the verb *examine: There is grave doubt . . . that, however timely or hard we had tried to examine this man, we could legally have compelled him to submit to one* (submit to an examination). A railroad station in Texas used to display the warning *Don't spit on the floor,* to which some wag had added: *Spit on the wall and watch it run down.* His *it* should not, perhaps, be pedantically reproved. Writing on walls enjoys a certain license. But in common prose the pronoun whose antecedent is not an unmistakable substantive is the mark of a loose mind. A special temptation to looseness occurs when the reference is to some ostensible noun that is functionally an adjective—e.g. *shark* in the following: *In the old days no shark fishing took place, and they were caught only occasionally* (and sharks were caught). Again: *Washington is the nation's largest per capita small boat market. These are in process of production at Anacortes* (Small boats are in production). The remedy when a pronoun lacks a competent antecedent is to give up the pronoun and supply the indicated noun.

2. Other words than pronouns can suffer from the same attempt to manufacture antecedents out of thin air. *A Rumanian campaign to terrorize Jews there who have shown a desire to emigrate to Israel was reported today in* The Times *of London.* The relation between the adverb *there* and the adjective *Rumanian* is logically the same as that between *These* and *small boat* in the preceding example. For *there* we have to read *in Rumania,* though the preferable improvement is to omit *there.* A demonstrative adjective with its noun may also do pronominal duty and falsely claim an adjective as its antecedent: *has been in love with all that is English since her childhood adoration for a governness from that land* (a governess from England).

3. A noun in the possessive case, being functionally an adjective, is seldom a competent antecedent of a pronoun. *On F.'s arrival from Virginia at La Guardia Airport last night, he denied to reporters that . . .* F. would legitimately lead to *he;* F.'s cannot. Reconstruct,

then: *F., on his arrival . . . , denied.* (Of course, a possessive noun can be the antecedent of a possessive—i.e. an adjectival —pronoun: *F.'s denial was made on his arrival.*) A would-be antecedent in the possessive can be baffling: *The Angel's dearly beloved son was less than a block away from where he waited and sweated.* This *he* means the Angel (an Italian named Angelo), but the reconstruing of the sentence takes effort.

4. The maladjustment is perhaps a shade more subtle, but not less disturbing, when a noun used in general is made the antecedent of a pronoun used in particular. *President Eisenhower's address adds little to the known fact that we could hardly be closer to war without being in one.* The word *war* means the general state of war; *one* is a specific instance —*a* war. Read, then: *without being in a war,* or *at war.* Again: *Students of science who are already specializing in one* (specializing in a particular science).

5. Less common than the pronoun with a false antecedent or none, but still too common, is the pronoun repeated with a different antecedent. *N.O. lined one into deep left center where P.Q. hauled down the drive after a hard run. It was a fine play, but it was also a sacrifice fly that . . . tied the score.* The first *it* is the defensive fielding play, and then *it* recurs without notice to mean the batter's offensive stroke. The same disorder appears in the discussion of an educational problem: *But until the council completes an inquiry into the reasons for the drop, its* (the council's) *officials are inclined to believe it* (the drop) *may be due to such things as higher entrance requirements* (until the council completes an inquiry its officials . . . believe the drop may be due to . . .).

6. Negative forms are full of traps for the unwary because they entice the writer to make a pronoun refer to something previously said not to exist. The preface to an admirable biography claims *There is nothing in the book which has not already been published in some form but some of it is, I believe, very little known.* What can *some of it* be except some of the nothing in the book which has not already been published? How much simpler to begin with an affirmation—*Everything in the book has already been published, but some of it,* etc.—thus avoiding the temptation to represent something as a part of nothing.

At times a pronoun leans on an antecedent fully present but in an obscure position, where it gives no clear point of reference. *Five years' duty in India followed before World War I, during which M. was shot through the chest.* Was he shot in the course of duty in India or during the war that followed? The rhetorically natural reference to *which* is to the substantive set up as the subject, *Five years' duty in India;* but *which* also has a natural tendency to refer to the nearest preceding substantive, *World War I*—the object of a preposition in a phrase that may amount to no more than a passing mention of time. We find from the context that the wound was received during fighting in France. So we must recast: *After five years' duty in India M. took part in World War I, during which he was shot.* A principle emerges: Pronouns tend to be weak and baffling when their antecedents are the objects of a preposition, firm and clear when their antecedents are the subjects or objects of a preceding finite verb.

Sometimes an antecedent weakened by its place in a prepositional phrase is further weakened by its occurrence in an element so parenthetical that it ought to be kept in logical isolation from the main clause. *Meanwhile, at private conferences with nationalist party leaders . . . , General de Gaulle convinced them . . . that the right to future independence was solidly written into the new Constitution.* An easy matter is made hard by pretending that an essential element left on a siding is part of the train. Why not *Mean-*

while, at private conferences, General de Gaulle convinced nationalist party leaders . . . ?

7. The clash between particular and general that we noticed above will sometimes take the form of a clash of number between pronoun and antecedent. The general noun, because it denotes a class or a kind, may be felt as plural though it is grammatically singular. Thus *man* must have been felt as generic by the Bible translators of Ecclesiastes 7:29: *God hath made man upright; but they have sought out many inventions.* In modern prose the same sequence seems excessively careless: *The true swastika* (generic) *moves from right to left, and there is hardly any place in the world where it has not been found. They are* (It is) *seen on ancient Chinese carvings, on the pulpit of St. Ambrose in Milan,* etc. Nowadays a noun, generic or not, is usually felt as a singular if it is singular in form, and it ordinarily calls for a singular pronoun, though it does not always get one: *The thirty-one Oxford colleges each control their own admissions* is an ill-considered mixture of *All thirty-one . . . control their own admissions* and *Each of the thirty-one . . . controls its own admissions.* Colloquially, few patterns are more common than *Everybody ought to mind their* (his) *own business* and *Each pupil will now take*

their seats (his seat), etc. Liberal grammarians defend and even recommend the plural pronoun after these distributive words; they praise Will Rogers' aphorism *Everybody can get along on half of what they think they can.* To the scrupulous the sequence seems unbuttoned, even in speech, and it is rejected despite all innuendoes about purism and PEDANTRY. (See INTRODUCTORY, pp. 20-26.)

Pronouns are supposed to agree with their antecedents in gender and person. The problem of gender is nothing like so conspicuous in English as it is in Latin, Italian, French, and German, but it does exist. By a long-standing convention the masculine pronouns serve to denote both sexes after a genderless word. *Every person is the highest living authority on the spelling of his own name* is a standard form of statement not restricted in meaning to males. If our society were a fully evolved matriarchy the corresponding feminine pronouns would doubtless replace the masculine ones, and the standard form would be: *Every one of us must act according to her lights*, the male being tacitly included.

The implacable feminists of both sexes still object to *he* and *his* as shorthand for the whole human race and insist that women's rights include the right to equal and separate mention. The consequence is a multiplied use of the labored phrases *he or she, his or her: If anyone fails to register by 10 P.M., Saturday, he or she will be unable to cast his or her ballot on November 4.* This development may be socially good: linguistically it is unfortunate. The punctilious phrases in question have the unwieldiness of the double-duty formula *approach to and survey of, admiration of and confidence in,* etc., as well as something of the affected precision of AND/OR, UNLESS AND UNTIL, etc.

8. In the attachment of pronouns, a clash of person is a little less frequent than a clash of number, but it occurs. The Bishop of Durham, describing himself in *Perkin Warbeck,* says that he is

a man enforced
To lay his book aside, and clap on arms
Unsuitable to my age or my profession.

The shift from *his* to *my* is as dramatically natural as it is grammatically unkempt. Modern instances generally lack this excuse: *When an enlisted man got himself into that fix, they showed you* (him) *no mercy / Who could be an efficient rock-climber with that thing dragging at your* (his) *waist?* Note, in addition, that *who* as a relative pronoun is ordinarily of the third person

but should take on the person of its antecedent. *To me, who am* (not *is*) *a professional critic of art / I cannot account for this cynicism in you who believe* (not *believes*) *in him.*

When a ship or a nation that may conventionally be either *she* or *it* is called both indiscriminately, the clash is the same as if it were of person: *Communist China must first abandon her ways of conquest—direct and indirect—and by concrete acts convince the world of free nations that it* (she) *is ready to cooperate in good faith.* Stick to the gender you start with. Similarly, when the pronoun *one* stands for anyone at all, it should not serve as the antecedent of *he.* The British are inexorable on this point, both in denouncing the American habit of *one . . . he* and in doggedly going through with the implications of an initial *one,* whatever the cost in repetition: *One is entitled to do as one likes as long as one does not trample on one's obligations to one's fellows.* It is probably the laborious and artificial sound of such a sequence that drives many Americans into switching to *he* and *his* after the first *one.* The reason is good, the solution not, since it can raise a doubt whether *one* and *he* refer to the same person: *The criticisms are sweepingly extravagant, but one senses also that he must not dismiss them entirely.* Where following through with *one* and *one's* would result in too much repetition, resort to one of the other labels for the unspecified person—*we, anyone, you, people, they, every man.* Even without shuttling from one form to the other, trouble may ensue, as in: *One read one's writings to one another or in company.* There is a like defiance of arithmetic in *Each club has five games remaining but will not meet one another again* (but neither will meet the other again). *One* has an altogether different status when it is not indefinite but identified, as in *One who* or *one* (from among others): *One who holds that opinion ought to have his head examined / One who never turned his back but marched breast forward / Of the three, one became a judge—and he never came back to the old country; the second,* etc.

9. Pronouns are not the only part of speech to raise the great difficulty of precision, of exact reference to a clear subject. Any locution that refers to something either not present or not present in a suitable form will fail to point back. Try to explain the phrase *such organizations* in the sentence *Many waterless cooking sets are sold on a door-to-door basis* (see BASED ON) *chiefly because such organizations have been able to give home demonstrations that are difficult for stores to present. Sold*

door-to-door is not *such organizations.* Beyond ideas is compatibility of forms. This is violated in *Whether in the company of these rough men he visited any of the numerous brothels in the city—this was one of the lushest periods in New York history for that business—no one knows.*

10. Of all attempts at reference, whether through pronouns or through other words, the greater number are set off by either of two pronouns, the relative *which* and the demonstrative *this.* Both are liable to looseness. For example: *It should be remembered that not many Latin Americans can afford the luxury of paying for a concert, which may amount to one or two days' salary.* As far as the sense of *which* can be localized, it resides in the gerund *paying;* but *paying ... may amount* is poor joining. The true antecedent and ultimate subject is *the cost of a concert*—which is not there.

Still more common is the antecedent that consists of an entire thought: *Relative pronouns are as troublesome to the inexpert but conscientious writer as they are useful to everyone, which is saying much.* In this encircling use, *which* has attained such currency that no one is startled by the mannerism of beginning a sentence with *which*—making a relative clause masquerade as a whole sentence: *Which he did / Which was very careless of her / Which he found strangely enlightening.* This pert *which*, whether at the head of a sentence or within it, usually has no strict antecedent. The popularity of the construction goes back to Kipling, who made it a trademark in *Plain Tales from the Hills.*

Next to the offenses under *which* come those chargeable to the singular demonstrative pronouns used in disregard of antecedence. The unanchored *that* is often found but is so far outnumbered by *this* that it may be ignored. In some kinds of modern writing—e.g. editorial pages in the best dailies and weeklies—it is almost impossible to get through a column without stumbling on at least one *this* used in summary of unspecified elements that precede. *The State Department has said it will consider such action when the necessary legal procedures have been completed under the treaty. This is now being done* (when the legal procedures necessary under the treaty, and now under way, have been completed) / *Crude partisanship has on the whole been admirably restrained. The Congressional leadership can take pride in this* (in this restraint) / *Countries that suffer the maltreatment of dictatorship for many years cannot recover quickly and easily. This is a part of the heavy price that must always be paid for the evils of tyranny* (This helplessness? inability?

time lag?) / *Now, most of these experts . . . rely . . . on the same statistical data. To some persons this might suggest that their conclusions would have to be . . . of the same general tenor. Actually, of course, this is by no means the case* (this uniformity might suggest . . . Actually, of course, they are not) / *Many people in Brooklyn where apprehensive over another outbreak of cholera in the hot weather, and this may have influenced the move.* In the last specimen *this* probably refers to the moving family's apprehension, which was shared by many other people, but how is anyone to find out?

One can hardly overstate the dependence of modern writers on the unfocused *this*. The author of a standard biography uses it in the third, fifth, eighth, and ninth sentences of his preface—four times in twenty lines—and relies on it throughout five hundred pages: *He was near a crossroads in his life, and he did not know which road to take. We might guess this* (the first fact? the second? both?) *from his literary juvenilia / wrote a friend . . . his reasons for opposing the Proviso, and this was circulated for publication* (this letter?).

The remedy is suggested by the query in the reader's mind: turn the *this* (pronoun) into a *this* (adjective) by adding the appropriate word—*this letter, this awareness, this predicament,* or whatever the true antecedent amounts to when looked at in a backward glance.

anticipate. See DEFENSIBLES.

anxious, eager. In the Age of Anxiety one should welcome chances to call by their right name feelings that are free of the blight. To say *I'm very anxious to see you* plunges us back into the pit. Say rather: *I am eager.* When eagerness seems excessive, there is always *I want (very much) to see you.*

apart from. See ASIDE FROM.

appreciate, esteem. 1. It is too late now to try to hold *appreciate* to its primary and legitimate meaning: *measure the worth of, put a correct valuation on.* But if a writer makes up his mind to confine the word to these unimpeachable uses, he will find himself giving it up also as a loose synonym of *like, enjoy, approve, take pleasure in.* The business use of *appreciate* (= rise in value) is to be taken as a specialized use, which in its context will not be misunderstood.

It is of course no sin to use *appreciate* for *approve* and the rest, but such a use has the drawback of all other improprieties of language: it leaves better words idle and impoverishes the vocabulary. This result is even more noticeable when *appreciate* is used negatively. *I don't appreciate people that put words into my mouth* means that the speaker dislikes such persons. *No one appreciates being interrupted when he is absorbed in his work* means that the experience is annoying.

Used affirmatively in the loose sense, *appreciate* is often accompanied by quantitative words that war against its true meaning. We usually *appreciate very much* or *more than we can say.* Yet once we see that *appreciate* means to put a just valuation on, these modifiers appear inept, and it may become easier to use the verb in its proper absolute sense.

That sense has the advantage of being unambiguous. To be sure, when we say *We appreciate the difficulties of your position,* we can only mean that we understand these difficulties and have taken their measure. Hence a literary *appreciation* ought to be an exact critical analysis, but it often turns out to be merely a favorable review. "Appreciation" courses in art and music have earned a bad name because the term has come to suggest conventional opinion and gush. If we mean to be clear, *appreciate* should most often be replaced with either a synonym of *enjoy* or a synonym of *understand.*

2. The verb *esteem* gives rise to a parallel confusion through its two meanings: (a) regard with great respect, and (b) deem or think of as. The sentence *What we obtain too cheap, we esteem too lightly* can mean either that we honor it too little or that we undervalue it. When Spinoza, translated into English, is made to speak of *the things esteemed as the greatest good of all*, does he mean that they are venerated as such a good or merely that they are taken to be such? Clearly, just as *appreciate* should be replaced by an unambiguous verb, so *esteem* ought often to be replaced by *estimate*.

See also DEFENSIBLES.

approbation, approval. No consensus exists about the difference, if any, between these words. They are so nearly the same word that anyone can justify preferring the second for being the shorter. Nevertheless a writer might please a discriminating reader here and there if he were to use *approbation* for a favorable response on a particular occasion and *approval* for a general favoring attitude. A man's character has our approval or disapproval, a given act of his has our approbation or disapprobation. A particular expression of approval deserves to be called an approbation; thus *His fiscal policy has met with general approbation, but this particular act will hardly command widespread approval* would be better if the two words were interchanged.

Note that in the official or formal sense of concurrence and ratification, *approval* is the standard and invariable word. The meaning is neutral and carries no idea of praise. Hence it would be eccentric to replace it with *approbation* in *My memorandum received immediate approval* or *In this organization many a good idea fails to get approval*. Whatever has a chance of the notation *Approved* (or *O.K.*), with initials attached, calls for the administrative *approval*.

approximate, approximation, approximately. *Approximation* denotes the near approach of one thing to another in merit or other important characteristics. It is an affirmative word that stresses similarities or adequacies. The adjective *approximate* should therefore not be used to stress differences or inadequacies. It is forced to act as a belittling negative in *It permits a comparison, however approximate, of the relative socio-economic position of the several ethnic groups in our nation.* Here *approximate* means not close but remote, defective, short of the mark; some such expression is required in its place. We can, of course, qualify the congruence of one thing with another as *only approximate*, but we must then convert the affirmative force into a negative by the addition of the adverb.

For the reason just given, *approximately* should almost always be replaced by *about*. *He was due to arrive about half past three* (not *at approximately half past three*). As for the growing misuse in *He is approximately bankrupt*, the proper substitute is *nearly, almost*, or *just about*.

apropos. See PRONUNCIATION 2.

archetype. See PRONUNCIATION 1.

argot. Like JARGON, *argot* has a figurative meaning that is also pejorative. A man will disdainfully call someone else's speech *argot* if it seems to him full of words he cannot understand: his is the response of the man shut out, and he is right to designate this shutting out by the name of *argot*. He is probably wrong, however, in using *argot* to mean the special language of a trade or profession. That special language is a *jargon*, and its effect of shutting out the uninitiated is no more intended than the similar effect of a foreign language.

In argot, on the contrary, the effect is intended. Argot is thieves' slang, and its purpose is secretive. Despite some international borrowing, argot is generally national and even local. Hence argot is not one tongue but many tongues. An interesting variety of argot has developed in certain states among illicit distillers, and it provides a convenient illustration: *When a Third Rail with a smell warrant broke the blind string around a silver cloud, a sign trotter set off a mountain shaker*. This means, according to its interpreter, Robert Scott Milne: *When an incorruptible official with a search warrant (issued because the smell of whisky had been reported) broke the frail black thread stretched through the woods around an illegal still of galvanized iron, a lookout posted for the purpose set off a blast of dynamite as a warning*. Argot, it is clear, has a kind of poetic conciseness.

articulation. This word denotes the kind of LINKING provided by some of the small words of the language (OF, THE, AS, THAT) and by the placing of locutions close together according to conventions commonly understood. For the many forms of articulation, the reader is referred to AND/OR; AS 11; BOURGEOIS; DIFFERENT(LY) THAN; DOUBT; HAVE; HOPEFULLY; IN for BY 2; IN TERMS OF; LIKE 1; MEANINGFUL; NEEDLESS WORDS; PREPOSITIONS; RESPECTIVE; SAME; SELF-ADDRESSED ENVELOPE; SO THAT; TELESCOPINGS; THAT, WHICH; -WISE; WITH; UP TILL. And also: A, AN, THE 5; FUSED PARTICIPLE; -ING 1; GERMANISMS; REIDENTIFICA-

TION; SEQUENCE OF TENSES; TO; WHICH AND and WHICH; SCIENTISM. In those articles, and sporadically in still others, examples will be found of the ill effects of poor or wrong articulation. The present tendency of the Western European languages (including, for the nonce, American) is to neglect articulation in favor of a sort of agglutinative pidgin. Books echo educated speakers who affect this gamy simplicity: *This keeps up we go to the poorhouse* for *If this . . . we go* (or *shall have to go*). The need for this saving of effort at the expense, ultimately, of clarity and elegance has yet to be shown.

as. 1. *As* for *being.* 2. Missing *as.* 3. *As much as* or *more than.* 4. *As* in negative comparisons. 5. *As of.* 6. *As regards.* 7. *As* (= since). 8. *As such.* 9. Surplus *as.* 10. *As to.* 11. *As well as.*

1. *As* for *being.* Some of our shortest words make the most trouble and the most kinds of trouble. One of the worst troublemakers is *as*; an exhaustive account of its misdoings is next to impossible. It is absent where needed, present where not needed; it occurs as a misfit subordinating conjunction; it leads to endless mismanagement in various set phrases. And it works in insidious ways to derail locutions in which it has the sense of *being*; that is, *in the role or capacity of.* For example: *as a tax-pay-*

ing citizen, as an incorrigible skeptic.

So used, *as* will ordinarily entail no confusion within its own phrase, but it can provide temptations to leave the phrase in a grammatical void, especially when it begins a sentence. *As a man of peace, there could be no more effective way for him to protest.* Such an *as* construction requires matching with the subject of the following main clause: *As a man of peace, he could not find a more effective way to protest.* When the subject fails to match, the status of the *as* phrase is exactly that of DANGLERS, or the so-called dangling participles. (The mismatched construction is no better than *Bending his body low, the rifle was discharged.*) *As a* Times *subscriber and an ardent reader of your column, kindly tell me where to write for a sample copy of . . .* (Kindly tell a *Times* subscriber and ardent reader) / *As the son of a noted sculptor-educator . . . his talents were fostered* (Because he was the son of) / *As a dissolute and cross-grained youth . . . they foresaw that his presence would cause them endless trouble* (They foresaw that the presence of this dissolute . . . youth would cause them).

In letter writing, the descriptive *as* phrase must connect with the right person: *I am writing to you as the Mayor of the City* is proper from voter to politician; *As Mayor of the*

City, I am writing to you is the campaigner writing to his constituent. But mere propinquity does not always serve. The headline INDEPENDENCE REJECTED AS WORKABLE FORMULA FOR ISLAND should read INDEPENDENCE REJECTED FOR ISLAND AS UNWORKABLE, because the second requires no algebra of positive and negative to convey the same meaning as the first. Consider *As a completely new, independent, responsibly edited, unabridged dictionary, no other work can rival it on precisely its own ground.* Anyone who writes the first nine words has got himself irrevocably committed to *it* as the tenth—or to some other word meaning the dictionary in question. The main clause must read *it is rivaled*; that is, the clause must be about the dictionary, not about *no other work.* Moreover, it must be about what the new dictionary *is*, not what it is *as.* Why not, then, a direct statement about the subject? *This new, independent, responsibly edited unabridged dictionary is unrivaled on its own ground by any other work.*

2. Missing *as.* A person is known *as* so-and-so; this or that is described, depicted, characterized, regarded, or shown *as* such-and-such. With these verbs the *as* is necessary to sense and idiom. The need for this *as* remains, naturally, in clauses that are already introduced by the conjunction *as,*

but it is often omitted under the impression that its task has been performed by the clausal *as: Judge Hull, as he was forever after known.* No one with an ear would want to write *Judge Hull, as he was forever after known as,* yet the sense requires the second *as.* A solution is often impossible without a change of pattern; e.g. *as he was forever after called.* The same solution applies to *Marianne, as she was known to* (called by) *her intimates.* The comparison in *NRA was neither so rigid nor so ominous an undertaking as it has been depicted* is made complete and irreproachable by the simplest possible expedient—omission of *it.*

Many verbs of saying or perceiving—e.g. *view, regard, refer to, characterize*—may also require *as* for idiomatic completion and are maimed without it. *I regard the development of a comprehensive and effective labor training program one of the prime duties of my office* (add *as* after *program*) / *The other* [question] *is how important his superiors regard the case* (add *as being*) / *You see young Sean Casside, as the autobiographer refers to himself, learning the pain of hard physical labor and the pleasure of Shakespeare and Shaw* (as the autobiographer styles himself) / *Your editorial . . . can be characterized in no other way than a spiteful attack on President Z. personal-*

ly (in no other way than *as*). The error in these wordings is to treat *view, regard,* etc. as synonyms of *consider* or *deem,* which in themselves incorporate the force of *as.*

3. *As much as or more than.* This skeleton lacks an essential bone if we omit the second *as. They had as much and possibly more influence on our country than a like number of generals and statesmen.* The writer of this sentence has committed himself to *as much than*—a sequence sometimes tolerated by journeymen (but not tolerated by others) who accept linguistic kinks as evils to be submitted to. Retaining both constructions in their full forms results in an unwieldy double-purpose mechanism that seems as little at home in prose as a $\pm$ sign.

The quickest extrication is to pick the two formulas apart and handle them separately: *They had as much influence on our country as a like number . . ., and possibly more.* The device does not always work. *A Government education expert said today that some students who had taken classes over television had received equal or better marks than those attending regular classes.* What is given us here is *equal than,* which is preposterous. A solution might be *received marks as good as those of students attending regular classes, if not better,* but it is discouraging to accomplish no more with that number of words. Perhaps a better solution would be *received marks equal or superior to those of students attending regular classes.* This particular snag, like other instances of trying to say too many things at once, can be dealt with in several ways, of which the best is to sort out one's ideas before committing them to paper. (See also PROSE, THE SOUND OF 4.)

4. *As* in negative comparisons. One of the oddities of American English, as compared with the parent tongue, is the retention in the United States of the shift from *as* to *so* when the statement is negative. Apparently without effort, workaday writers and persons otherwise casual in speaking will say: *This summer is not nearly so hot as last;* whereas English speakers and writers use *as . . . as* throughout. American copy editors will pounce on this neglect of what seems to them a compulsory usage, though it would be difficult to attach a shade of meaning to the difference. Perhaps *as . . . as* suggests equality so strongly that a denial of it must be signalized by *not so.*

5. *As of.* This phrase is not a new way of specifying a date, but it has lately become so popular, as scraps of jargon will, that the public prints are peppered with all but meaningless occurrences of it. Apparently many persons think that dates need some sort of emphatic introduction. The truth is that *as of* is justified only as a device for assigning an event to one time and the report or recognition of it to another. Thus, academic documents contain references to those who took degrees in 1960 *as of* 1959. This use is official and standard for making privileges retroactive, as in an order, dated November 1, that promotes an officer *as of* the preceding July 1: he will receive four months of additional salary.

The phrase may have point, again, in a March 1966 report on the fiscal year 1965, or in an extrapolation of current trends to some date in the future. But it is useless and absurd in *The business outlook in New England as of mid-October*. Write *at* (or *in*) *mid-October*. Other typical abuses: *Earned $18,064,100 in this country alone as of July 12* (up to July 12 / *As of December 31 the amount received or pledged* (By December 31) / *Candidates must be under 45 years of age as of the deadline date for applications* (on the deadline date).

Whatever sense *as of* may carry when aptly used vanishes when the time specified is the present. *I feel strongly that our league should remain with eight teams, at least as of now* (at least for the present) / *There is little doubt that, as of the moment, the Democrats are way ahead* (at the moment) / *Lieut. Gen. X. said that, "as of now," there could be "no doubt" that the . . . weapon would be perfected by 1965* (said that there could now be no doubt) / *The Governor, at a news conference, asserted that as of now he did not know whom he himself favored* (did not know as yet). The prize for ineptitude in this class goes to the report of a medical bulletin: *The doctors now think that as of now he will be able to go tomorrow.* Omit *that as of now* to discover the plain sense.

6. *As regards.* Is this clumsy compound preposition indispensable? Would not a writer who makes frequent use of it be a better writer if he did not? Ostensibly a means of singling out a subject for special emphasis, it has the actual effect of smuggling a subject in or of stealing up on it from ambush. *As regards the satellite countries, the diplomatic problem is somewhat different. For the satellite countries* is as lucid and is more direct. A like example: *As regards his competence, I am not in a position to judge* (His competence I am not in a position to judge).

Variants of *as regards*—e.g. *as affects, as bearing on, as concerns, as relates to, as respects, as touching*—suffer from the same defects.

7. *As* (= *since*). The novice's resort to *as* with the meaning *since* or *because* is always feeble. It makes trivial what follows. Webster (1934 edition) remarks: "*As* assigns a reason even more casually than *since.*" What is worse, the untrained or heedless writer turns to this weak subordinating link to introduce a co-ordinate clause or what should be his main clause. In either case he ruins emphasis. *It was a comparatively unproductive year, as he was dogged by ill health and domestic worries.* For *as* read *for.* Readers will recognize the pattern of many feeble sentences like the following: *A good business might be built up . . . by spraying trees, as most individuals would sooner pay a fair price for this work than undertake it themselves, as it is expensive when done as individual work.* Here the important idea is merely glanced at in a subordinate clause; then a subsubordinate clause gives a glance at the glance, so that emphasis tapers down to the vanishing point. To reconstruct: *A good business might be built up by spraying trees: most persons would rather pay a fair price for this service than undertake it themselves, for it is expensive as individual work.* The colon, which points to a following explanation, takes care of what was poorly done by the first *as*; the *for* builds up strength where the second *as* tore it down.

It follows from all this that the causative *as* is useless except to tone down the reason assigned: *As it makes no difference to you, I will take the later train / We had better send the ribbon copy, as the carbon is so faint.*

8. *As such.* It is generally not difficult to distinguish between *as such* when it says something and *as such* when it says nothing. *A military expert as such has no business pronouncing on this sort of question.* The implication here is that the military expert may have something to say as a man of judgment, or as a citizen, or as a student of history, or as a Presbyterian, or as a New Englander, but that his expertise is irrelevant. Suppose, however, that we say: *Theology as such is helpless before these questions.* In what guise, we ask, would it not be helpless? It is hard to think of theology as anything but what it is. *The automobile as such revolutionized our idea of a practicable shopping distance.* No one is likely to suppose that the idea was revolutionized by the automobile as a toy or as a status symbol. What may have been cloudily in the writer's mind was *the automobile by itself.* The implication of *as such* in the following is no less shadowy: *Mr. Q.'s troubles . . . stem from personal rivalries having nothing to do with his pro-Western Government's foreign or domestic policies as such* (on their merits? per se?). A novelist who helped a politician with his campaign speeches described his employer as *a fine writer, but, as such,* *too intellectual.* His *as such* is difficult to construe if it means anything but *as a writer,* and in that meaning it is grammatically lost.

The front matter of a desk dictionary has an *as such* that is baffling in both grammar and meaning: *The dictionary has combined the facts about the frequency of the occurrence of different meanings that were tabulated by scholars with the judgments of experts in choosing the senses of each word that were to be discriminated and classified. As such, the dictionary utilizes the last forty years of scholarship in vocabulary selection and discrimination in the choice of senses of words to be defined.* The formidable first sentence seems to be saying that the meanings defined were chosen according to (a) their statistical frequency and (b) expert judgment of their importance. *As such* probably means, then, something like *in combining these two factors.* If so, why not say so?

9. Surplus *as.* Style will suffer as much from an excess of *as*'s—observe this very sentence—as sense will from a shortage of them. (See AS 2.) *If you could see the way these young men met their challenge you would have been as proud of them as Americans as I was as their commanding officer.* It is not easy to give such a sentence a touch of grammatical grace and also keep its original grace of sincerity. To write *as proud as I, their commanding officer, that they were Americans* would wipe out half the repetitions of *as,* though at a price. But *a region that, as she saw as soon as she began to read* becomes tolerable in the form of *a region, she saw the moment she began to read, that. As between an apparently pro-Communist regime in Leopoldville and a clearly anti-Communist government in Katanga, we don't have any trouble making a choice* (omit *As*) / *has concluded that Great Britain might as a member emerge as more influential* (omit the second *as*) / *The failure to recognize the needs of other groups of people as being as real as one's own seems all too common* (to recognize that other groups have needs as real as one's own) / *There can be no compromise as with the communist regimes because they are dedicated to our destruction* (omit *as*) / *we must not equate criticism as between the open and closed systems* (omit *as*).

In the following, *as* does no perceptible work: *He was designated as representative* / *She was acclaimed as queen* / *You are appointed as ballot clerk* / *I was elected as a director of the company.* (This last sentence ought to mean *I owe my election to my being a director.*) This *as* is apparently written as part of the breathing process.

In one characteristic use, *as* has the force of the concessive *though*—witness the cliché *unaccustomed as I am to public speaking* and many workaday phrases: *sick as I was, much as I hate to do it, silly as it sounds*, etc. The only difference is that *though*, slipping less readily off the tongue, is more emphatic. Perhaps to give *as* the same degree of emphasis, some writers begin with an unidiomatic *as* that, once standard, has long been obsolete: *As fond as I am of him, I think him utterly wrong-headed on this issue / As convinced as they were of his innocence, the evidence given by this witness left them shaken / As busy as the Smiths were they insisted we visit them / As steady as Florida's growth has been . . . many say this is only the beginning / constantly remind us that as tiresome, as inconvenient and as expensive as it may be, we must constantly keep up our guard / As hard as people try to defy it, young and old alike must at one time or another admit the truth / As great an all-around back as is K., R. knows that Princeton has a flock of dangerous ball carriers.*

To resurrect this opening *as* brings about not only an excess of *as*'s but also some ambiguity. The book title *As Bad as I Am* leaves one wondering whether it means *others are as bad as I am* or *bad as I am, I might be worse*. The surplus *as* has the further effect of throwing the reader off the track when a proper *as* introduces a comparison. *Some of these emancipated young executives, as indifferent as they pretend to be to status and its symbols, never pass up the chance to acquire a tonier address.* Are we to think them (fully) as indifferent as they pretend to be—a comparison? Or have we here the concessive form with a needless *as*—*indifferent though they pretend to be?* Before the vogue of surplus *as*, the reader would not have been in doubt about *As much as it is a drama of human motives, M.'s first novel is a political document.*

We should of course be careful to include the first *as* in a true comparison. *Glib as a candidate for office* can be ambiguous, at least when written. If the intended meaning is *no less glib than*, we had better make it *As glib as . . .*

10. As to. Questions, doubts, problems should never be *as to whether*; there is no reason why they cannot be simply *whether* (or, with a noun complement, simply *of*). Omit *as to* in the following: *Replying to a question as to whether there would be war / the question as to what would happen if / The question now arises as to whether this idea cannot be expanded / the problem arose as to whether some of the girls might cheat and wear another kind* [of lipstick] /

has thrust forward the question as to how much Moscow dominates. A slightly different disease and cure are shown in *There is some question as to his eligibility* (replace *as to* with *of*).

Other words than *question* and *problem* can lay the same train. *There was no mention as to whether the Nationalists had fired back* (no mention whether) / *It was anybody's guess as to which craft was leading* (omit *as to*) / *But the clubs in the other league have absolutely no interest as to who wins the National League pennant* (no interest in who wins) / *For the next twelve hours the mystery deepened as to what had happened to the ship and its crew* (what had happened . . . was a deepening mystery).

Clues are idiomatically *to*, not *as to*. Delete *as* in each of the following: *This article also gives valuable clues as to the nature of the edition planned* / *This, in turn, will give us a cule as to the size of our universe and as to* [the] *density of population at its outermost fringes.*

The word *doubt*, noun or verb, had better be followed by *whether* or *if* in clauses, by *of* in phrases, and never by *as to*. Indications, hints, evidences, proofs, intimations, statements, opinions, confessions, etc. are normally *of*. *As to* should be watched even as a replacement for *about*,

concerning, etc.; it tempts to jargon and waste. *As to that I cannot say* / *his remarks as to neutrality*: there is nothing gravely amiss in these, but it is simpler and therefore better to say *about* in the first remark and *on* in the second. To put a subject in the leading position (*as to the problem of delinquency* / *as to the method of disbursing this aid*, etc.), *as to* is passable and certainly less afflictive than *in the case of* (see CASE). But do not let *as to* drag with it *the matter of* or its like.

11. *As well as.* **a.** Various locutions, of which this is probably the most frequent and the most serviceable, are used to tuck in additional subjects before a verb in such a way that the grammatical number of the subject, and hence of the verb, remains unchanged. Other expressions of this class are *in addition to* / *together with* / *along with* / *besides* / *and not alone* / *like*. Any of these could be used with little alteration of meaning in this typical sentence: *The graduate school, as well as the college, is* (not *are*) *compelled to increase its* (not *their*) *tuition.* Here is, in fact and in logic, a plural subject, but in grammar and in usage a singular one. The phrase *as well as the college* is taken to be off the straight line from *graduate school* to *is*, as if the sentence were written: *The graduate* *school is compelled . . . and so is the college.*

As well as gives a lesser degree of subordination than other, similar expressions, as we discover when the tucked-in addition happens to be plural. *The Civil Aeronautics Administration, as well as the military services, has agreed to cooperate.* Replace *as well as* with *like* or *together with*, and the awkwardness is abolished. In effect, then, *as well as* comes closer than the others to a simple *and*, which would of course make the subject compound and the verb plural. One reason for this peculiarity of *as well as* is that it carries the implication of *and not alone*. In *The graduate school, as well as the college*, etc., the suggestion is given that we knew, or expected, that the college would raise its tuition. A new fact is added to the old by *as well as*, and hence it is important not to interchange their order.

Despite the overlapping of *as well as* and *and*, the first is not to be coupled with *both*. *The West is again being exposed to both a starry-eyed optimism, which expects miracles from these meetings, as well as to seductive voices urging the West in effect to abandon its "inflexible" and "non-negotiable" position* (omit *both* or replace *as well as* with *and* or *and also*).

b. The partial equivalence of *as well as* and *and* is fur-

ther shown in a common solecism that results from trying to make the phrase link different forms of parallel verbs. *For little if any sacrifice in comfort, I can save in miles per gallon as well as losing less per year in depreciation* (as well as lose) / *formed the New England Golf Association which conducts an annual championship as well as supervising the qualifying rounds of the U.S.G.A. championships* (as well as supervises).

To begin a sentence with *As well as* is generally to complicate what ought to be simple: *"As well as being messengers, stock boys and other unskilled workers, many are acquiring skills on the job,"* Mr. B. said. This sentence has other faults than its contorted opening, but that opening invites contortion. Some expressions are unalterably sequential, not introductory, and *as well as* is one of them.

as, connective. See SAME; SUCH 2; SUFFICIENTLY

aside from. A word capable of different meanings or shades of meaning must get its definition from its context. It follows that an inadequate context will leave the word ambiguous. *Aside from* has two radically different meanings, both idiomatic. The same is sometimes true of *apart from*, and both phrases have a ten-

ASSURE, ENSURE, INSURE • 109

dency to stray into inadequate contexts. The simpler meaning is *besides, in addition to: Aside from his accomplishments in the fine arts, he played no negligible part in public affairs / Apart from the fear of reprisals, there are some disinterested reasons for a more patient policy.* The second meaning is *with the exception of: Aside from this one brilliant achievement his career was commonplace / Apart from his fervor in collecting antique firearms, you would think him incapable of any enthusiasm.* All these contexts define. But now consider a sentence about Texas at the turn of the century. *Aside from the one-cent piece, the dollar bill was unknown in the Southwest of those days.* The meaning is *in addition to,* but the sentence is framed as if the meaning were *except for;* in other words, as if the one-cent piece were a kind of dollar bill. And consider this even more baffling sentence, about a seventeenth-century architect, from an encyclopedia of art: *His paintings, aside from the summary allusions* (references?) *of contemporary biographers, have been wholly forgotten.* Here we have an *aside from* that means neither *in addition to* nor *except for.* The form of the sentence would suggest that the references of contemporary biographers were among his paintings; the

meaning of the sentence is that without these references we should not know that his paintings ever existed.

Apart from and *aside from* can also point to mere separation, physical or mental. In these uses the phrases cause no confusion.

as, like. See LIKE 1.

aspidistra. See LATIN AND GREEK PLURALS.

assuming. See DANGLERS, ACCEPTABLE.

assure, ensure, insure. The second and the third of these verbs are equivalents, and nothing stands in the way of using whichever spelling one happens to fancy; but there is considerable confusion between these two and *assure.* The confusion occurs at the point where *assure* must be used because the reference is to persons, *ensure* or *insure* because the reference is to events. *Assure* = promise, cause (someone) to count on, and in this use it normally takes no preposition, though it sometimes takes *of,* particularly in the passive: *assured of a fair hearing. Ensure* or *insure* = make (some future occurrence) certain or reliable, and they are normally followed by *that,* as in *His present lead insures that he will not be overtaken;* or by a direct object, as in *Exorbitant* *bail insures his detention. As-sure* is obviously used for *ensure, insure* in the following: *He took steps to assure that these islands will not be a "thorn in the side of peace."* And plainly *insure* is used for *assure* in *This insured the island continent of its fifth United States title in eight years.* In the headline ROCK-AWAY ASSURED QUICK HELP TO BUILD ANTI-FLOOD SEWERS *assured* is the right word, but the omission of *of* is too free even for a headline.

In a curious attempt to fuse the two ideas, an advertiser produces nonsense—or a joke on himself: *No effort or ex-pense has been spared to as-sure you that this A.Q. brief-case will give you the utmost in utility.* This means *we have spent a great deal on advertis-ing so as to assure you . . . ,* and it tries to suggest that *we have done all we could to insure your being satisfied.*

as with. See AS 9.

at about. Since *about* can be with equal naturalness (1) an adverb meaning *approx-imately, somewhere nearly,* and (2) a preposition meaning *almost at, not far from,* the *at* of the phrase *at about* can usually be spared, with a gain in ease. True, there are oc-casions when both words are necessary: *Mail this week is running at about the same rate / at about 100 miles, the*

earth's atmosphere virtually disappears. But such occasions are rare compared with *he awoke at about 6:25 A.M. and smelled smoke,* etc., in which the *at* is superfluous. So it is in the following: *At about the same time Nationalist transport planes made a suc-cessful airdrop / the tanker will be waterborne at about 8:30 tomorrow morning / was in trouble with some of the regulatory agencies at about the time the gifts were made.* Sometimes *at* is used in a way that seems designed to bring out its uselessness: *the additional revenue required . . . will be at about $100,000,000.*

-athon, -thon. This bit of the place name Marathon has been seized on as if it were an adjective suffix that means long-lasting. The full word *marathon* has of course become official for a running race of 26 miles, 385 yards— the reference being to the feat of Pheidippides in 490 B.C.— and its extension to such uses as *dance marathon* is natural and perfectly clear. But what we get when part of the word is taken as a free building block is a series of grotesque hybrids. A *telethon* is sup-posed to mean a long series of telephone calls to induce the recipients to buy goods or to make gifts to charity. The manager of a private political poll writes about the *statistical* *results of this walkathon-talkathon;* a small-town department store runs a *sale-a-thon;* and one has even heard the endurance of a sitter on flagpoles styled a *sitathon,* which incidentally involves a curious jumble of the mobile with the static. Other scraps of Greek—see SCIENTISM—are taken as pretexts for similar formations, equally specious.

augment, supplement. We need not cavil at the statement *He augments his natural height by wearing shoes with elevated heels.* By a reasonable interpretation *his natural height* means simply the height he has reached by growing. But this interpretation breaks down in circumstances radically different: *He augmented his regular salary by occasional shrewd speculation / the hatcheries turn out 7,000,000 walleyed pike, to augment the natural reproduction / a brief main text augmented by four elaborated appendices.* Each of these increments is a supplement, not an augmentation. A salary is not raised by cultivating other sources of income; natural reproduction is unaffected when artificial reproduction is added to it; a main text stays the same length no matter what is done about the appendixes. In short, we do not augment one thing by creating a supply of another. Augmentation is the expansion of something homogeneous. A

supplement is the addition that results from putting a second thing with the first. The way out of the illogicalities quoted above is to find an inclusive term for the things added together: he augmented his *income* by adding the gains of speculation to his salary; the total *supply* is augmented by adding artificial to natural reproduction; the size of the *book* is augmented by joining appendixes to the main text.

author, verb. See NEEDLESS WORDS 1.

avail, available, availed of. When followed by an object, *avail* is inescapably a reflexive verb; that is, it requires *oneself, himself,* etc., to complete its meaning. One can not say *When hard pressed he availed of all the properties he could lay his hands on.* This misusage is but an inversion of the caption often found in business reports: *Special Reserves Availed Of,* meaning the amount actually used from that source of funds. The form is wrong whichever way it faces. The first example requires *he availed himself of;* the accountant's phrase should be *Draft on Special Reserves.*

Available has become a literary CRITICS' WORD, tiresome and precious. *But Lawrence, as he grew older, found these buoyant emotions no longer available to him / So much chiaroscuro of the mind, such a fine hesitation between the conceivable and the imaginative, could not last forever: one day he found it unavailable*. The affectation in these examples is due to the pretense that the feelings or powers described originate in some source of supply outside the man. The straightforward words are *he could no longer* do or feel or permit himself whatever is in question.

Finally, *available* has become a euphemism (see GENTEELISM) for various forms of consent. *He offered to make himself available / said he would make the room immediately available* mean only *offered to come* (or *serve*) and *said they could use the room at once*. In the negative, this euphemism is not only offensive but also ridiculous. The printed rejection slips of a certain magazine used to inform authors that their contributions were *unfortunately not available*, when the truth of the matter was obviously the opposite.

average. An average, in common speech, is the arithmetical mean of two or more quantities, determined by dividing their sum by their number. It is clear that if one literary composition is four hundred words long and another six hundred, their average length is five hundred words. It is also clear that if we try to assign an average length to one of them alone, what we have is a contradiction. *These stories, which average about 500 words apiece* (omit *apiece*) / *Each of the travel pieces . . . is short, averaging only three or four pages* (The travel pieces are short, averaging . . .). We can, to be sure, say that the average story is so many words long, or that a particular story happens to have a length which is at or near the average—just as *a valuable Book-Dividend averaging around $7 in retail value* must mean that the average book dividend offered by the club is worth that sum, but the single example cannot have an average value.

It is easy enough to guess what is meant by the foregoing examples, but what does an "Extended Forecast" mean when it states that *Rainfall during this period will total on the average over one half inch occurring as showers Sunday or Monday?* It would be hard to invent a more puzzling phrase than *total on the average* or to fashion a "scientific" sentence more resistant to analysis.

Note in addition that *average* must be treated as one of the ABSOLUTE WORDS. Two or more averages can of course be compared; but one average cannot be treated comparatively, as in *a very average upbringing*. An average upbringing must be one indistinguishable from the general run of upbringings and therefore not more or less or very average.

awed, awesome. What is awesome leaves the beholder awed. A writer will lose nothing if he reserves *awesome* for the description of awe-producing phenomena and *awed* for the persons experiencing awe. But the love of the extra syllable is a force that will not be denied, and it has its way in the reminiscences of a traveling ex-ambassador: *I gained an awesome regard for the ability of the Soviets to achieve their economic and military goals.* Since *awed* will not do here, substitute *awe-struck.*

ax to grind. Like Tom Sawyer selling to his friends as a privilege a share in the chore of whitewashing ninety feet of fence, the man with an ax to grind has ulterior and unadmitted purposes to serve. His tactics are akin to inducing another to pull one's chestnuts out of the fire. Such scraps of proverb, fable, popular anecdote, or literary allusion are often bandied about by those who either do not know or have forgotten the originals, and the result is confusion or self-contradiction. A typical error, in a serial story about a family feud: *As far as he was concerned, there were no further axes to grind between the J.'s and the K.'s.* This may have sprung from a dim recollection of *burying the hatchet.* In any event, what is meant is *no further bones* (or *crows*) *to pick* between the two families; that is, no occasion for continued hostilities. It is a counsel of perfection to tell a writer that he should not make a glancing reference to an anecdote or incident that he has not firmly in mind, yet to neglect this advice is to court risks, including the risk of ridicule. (See SET PHRASES; SOUR GRAPES.)

B

back formation. This term refers to the modern habit of making verbs from nouns by shortening: *enthuse* from *enthusiasm*, *reminisce* from *reminiscence*, *donate* from *donation*, *convalesce* from *convalescence*, etc. The four above are those in most common use, *enthuse* being the least accepted or acceptable. The reason probably is that no verb lurks in its past history, whereas Latin verbs do exist for the other three. *Burgle* from *burglary* and *sculpt* from *sculpture* started by being facetious, but they are occasionally found in print with a serious intent. The first can be replaced by *burglarize* if *break in* is not good enough; and the second should be *sculpture* (verb), since *sculp* is obsolete.

From the adjectives *groveling* and *lazy* the verbs *grovel* and *laze* have been formed, but whereas the former is now part of the language, the strong resistance to *laze* continues.

bad, badly. See ADVERBS, VEXATIOUS.

balance. There is no good reason why anyone should want to use this accountants' word as a regular substitute for the formal word *remainder* and for the informal word *rest*. Stylistically the habit is on the plane of *calculate* or *figure* for *suppose* (*His ideas were rather coolly received, I calculate / I figure he is likely to get the appointment*). In the following sentences the natural word is *rest*: *B. drew a suspension for the balance of the New York harness-racing season / The balance of the show was not particularly distinguished / replaced by Federalized National Guardsmen who remained throughout the balance of the school year / During the balance of the year the mature bulls seem to get on very well with each other / and prepared to live there the balance of our lives*. In such contexts *remainder* would be needlessly stiff, and the quasi-synonym *residue* would be both bookish and inaccurate, for it presupposes a previous taking away (*After payment of the individual bequests the residue goes to the S.P.C.C.*).

These strictures about *balance* do not, of course, apply to such standard phrases as *balance of power* and *balance of payments*, which denote not a remainder but an equilibrium.

114

barbarisms. The term *barbarism* may seem a harsh one to apply to a kind of blunder in language, but it does not imply any barbarousness of character or of manners—except as good speech is a part of good manners. What it says forcefully is what the Greeks meant when they said *barbaroi* —people who do not speak, who in fact are *babblers*. The same imitative word is related to Babel, the well-known institution which today would be called a General Confusion Center.

The opportunities for barbarisms in a highly civilized tongue such as English are endless and only a brief sampling can be given. A barbarism is an expression in the mouth of an educated speaker which is so at variance with good sense and good usage that it startles the hearer. When such a speaker says *somewheres, anywheres, everywheres, someplace, no place, go places,* he commits barbarisms. The same holds true of *irregardless, presumptious, portentious,* BENEFICIENT, and *asterik.* The hybrid *obliviate;* the confusion of *mitigate* and *militate;* the misuse of *aegis,* as in *through the aegis of the Foundation* (in a university proposal); the pronunciations *swep'* and *kep';* phrases such as *fun activities* and *leisure-time preoccupations* (found six times in a government document); the use of *various* as a pronoun of quantity (*then he showed us various*)—all these are in different degrees barbarisms. The inventor of the term *guidance counselor* had barbarism in him by birthright; that is, a total blindness to logic and to what the Germans call *Sprachgefühl,* the sense of language. Barbarisms, though unforgiveable in a professional writer, can be condoned in laymen if they will take the cure: the barbarism must first be spotted, then uprooted by conscious effort.

barbiturates. See PRONUNCIATION 1.

barely...than. See HARDLY (SCARCELY) ... THAN.

barring. See DANGLERS, ACCEPTABLE.

basal, basic. See ENDINGS 1.

based on, on the basis of, on the basis that. By the extension of a literal meaning, an edifice of thought can be erected on a *basis* of logic, a delusive theory on a *basis* of inadequate information, etc. The bases named are actually in a fundamental, i.e. foundational, relation to the structures reared. From this legitimate use the phrases *based on* and *on the basis of* have been allowed to flourish until they threaten to usurp the functions of *because, for the reason that,* *for the sake of, on the condition that, by the method of,* or of simple *by* and *for,* for all of which they are poor substitutes.

The net result is the further proliferation of JARGON; indeed, business and bureaucratic English would be nearly helpless without its *bases of.* A manual issued to copy editors by a publishing house explains: *The various forms shown are recommended on the basis of clarity, acceptability, and practicality.* Why not *recommended for their clarity,* etc.? The same source admonishes: *Given names that are spelled out in copy should not be changed to initials on the basis of their being so shown in the catalog* (because so shown). In the following sentence *on the basis of* means no more than *by:* "*A person recommended for membership is judged on the basis of whether he will be congenial with the other members,*" Mr. W. said. (Mr. W. might better have said *congenial to.*) And *basis* is quite without meaning in *Many waterless cooking sets are sold on a door-to-door basis* (sold door to door).

If *basis* must be used at all, it should at least figure in the statement as the basis *of* something; but it is frequently allowed to introduce a *that* clause, in defiance of idiom: *The Army is trying to establish an annual football rivalry with the Air Force Academy,* *but only will consider it on the basis that the games be played at mutually agreeable neutral sites* (will consider it only on condition that) / *the criticism that some members made of educational pamphlets on the basis that their effectiveness is unknown* (the criticism that some members made . . . ; namely, that their effectiveness is unknown) / *She was engaged on the basis that they live in or near Abilene* (on condition that).

The participial phrase *based on* has all the liabilities of *on the basis of* and in addition a strong tendency to defy the grammatical obligation of participles to attach themselves to something modifiable (see DANGLERS). *Based on scientific experience and our knowledge of what is occurring in southern New Jersey . . . we . . . are convinced that the New Jersey situation does not present a threat to New York City* / *Based on data and photographs recovered in this capsule, it is now considered probable that . . .* What is based? To make this good English, remove *based on* and put in *from.*

because. See AS 7; REASON . . . BECAUSE; SINCE, YET. For the use of commas with *because,* see APPENDIX 2, pp. 480–528.

become, come to be. These two expressions are as nearly synonymous as any pair in the vocabulary of English; one would be hard put to it to detect the difference between a politician who *becomes* a power in the party and one who *comes to be* such a power. Yet the exigencies of idiom can set up an impassable wall between the two locutions. *Cars are becoming more in the same category as furniture and appliances* is flagrantly un-English, whereas *are coming to be in the same category* can pass without challenge. The reason is obvious: to *be in a category* is intelligible, whereas to *become in one* raises but a confused image. In short, *come to be* can generally do duty for *become* (in the sense of *progress*), but the converse is not always true—one more reminder of the principle that, under close analysis, there are no complete synonyms.

before. See AGO; NO SOONER . . . WHEN.

begging the question. See POPULARIZED TECHNICALITIES.

beginning. See DANGLERS, ACCEPTABLE.

behoove. See BESPEAK.

being. One sign of inexperience in writing is the habit of using the participle *being* as a sort of lubricant. An encyclopedic work informs us: *The African languages follow the tribal divisions, with the related languages of Twi and Fanti being predominant.* If *being* is to be kept, the sentence should omit *with* (see WITH); if *with* is to be kept, omit *being*. A sharp disjunction would be more workmanlike than either version: *The African languages follow the tribal divisions; the related Twi and Fanti are predominant.* When *being* is used needlessly it acts as an abrasive rather than as a lubricant. *The next second they were rolling in the dust, Pedro being uppermost / The whole little army, it being mostly Calabrian mercenaries, embarked in five vessels.* Omit *it being* in the second example and *being* in the first. But note the idiomatic use of *being* with a causative meaning in *Being* (= because he was) *a patient man, he merely shrugged / The eye of the storm being now past us, the wind whipped around / Human nature being what it is, this behavior might have been anticipated.* The pattern of the last example—*politicians being what they are,* [this, that, or the other] *being what it is,* etc.—has been made wearisome by overuse and should be dropped.

See also AS 1.

belie. This useful word for *misrepresent, contradict, give the lie to* is being distorted into the opposite meaning of *betoken, exhibit,* or *evince.* Like *betray,* the word *belie* is increasingly found with this misconceived and ambiguous meaning, as in the following protest by a delegate to the United Nations: *Your editorial belies a tendentious effort to sow seeds of distrust*—the burden of the complaint being that the newspaper was making such an effort, not disclaiming or resisting it.

The distortion occurs (as in the misuse of *betray*) from the common belief that certain ideas and feelings appear to the observer only when the possessor loses control over his words or features. One can say of a man: *His speech betrays his true intentions; his face betrays his sentiments.* But from his side he could say, with *betray* meaning *misrepresent: My words betray* (= falsify) *my meaning; my face betrays* (= contradicts) *the purity of my intentions.* It is precisely because *betray* is now incurably ambiguous that it is important to keep *belie* in its original and irreplaceable meaning of *misrepresent, play false to,* and the like.

bemean. See DEMEAN.

beneficial, beneficiary. See ENDINGS 2.

beneficent. This version of *beneficent* is at present one of the popular nonwords; it is printed so often that the Shorter Oxford Dictionary lists it as erroneous. *If the action* *of time has a poor effect on the interior of buildings, it has a most beneficient one on their exteriors.* This is the kind of error that an educated person can go on making for decades, secure in the analogies of *beneficial* and of *de-, ef-, pro-,* and *suf-ficient.* It is more than an unfortunate misspelling, because it provokes a mispronunciation that shifts the accent from the second syllable to the third. See BARBARISMS.

bespeak. Some educated persons have trouble with the bookish, indeed pompous, *be*-words *befit, behoove,* and *bespeak.* For example, an important city official says: *It ill bespeaks the members of that body, however, who never permitted the bill to be discharged from committee.* He meant that the councilmen were giving a poor account of themselves, not that they were holding up the bill. His intention would have been expressed by *ill befits.* Even *ill behooves* would have come nearer than *bespeaks;* but *behooves* is customarily reserved for situations involving duty (*It behooves us to weigh this proposal very carefully*). The main uses of *bespeak* are (1) to denote advance booking (*They bespoke a pair of seats in the front row*—whence the British *bespoke trades,* which make to order only); and (2) as a synonym of *show, reveal* (*Such an act bespeaks a good heart*).

bet. See UNSAVORY PASTS.

bête noire. See FRENCH WORDS AND PHRASES.

betray. See BELIE.

between. 1. *Between, among*. 2. *Between each*. 3. *Between . . . or*. 4. *Between . . . to*. 5. Vagarious *between*.

1. *Between, among*. The hard-worked preposition *between* takes a good deal of battering from those who are too fussy about it and those who are not fussy enough. The underfussy keep denying the inherent meaning of duality in the word; e.g. in *between each* (see BETWEEN 2). The overfussy want *between* changed to *among*. We should cultivate skepticism about the standard oversimplification, which is that we should say *between* when two and only two entities are present, *among* if there are more than two. *Between* is not merely allowable, it is required when we want to express the relations of three or more taken one pair at a time. Thus it would be hypercritical to object to *between* in the following: *The main stumbling block in the present delicate exchanges between Paris, Athens, London and Ankara . . .* The exchanges almost necessarily consist of *démarches* from each capital to each of the others, not of identical and simultaneous messages from each to all. When three or more per-

sons argue or converse and each speaker addresses all the others, *among* is necessary for accuracy and clearness. The *between* is dubious if not downright false in the following: *The invasion was discussed at the house of de Tassis, the Spanish ambassador in Paris, between de Tassis, the Bishop of Glasgow, the Duke of Guise and Dr. Allen.* Whoever dislikes *among* in such a sentence —and for some reason the word makes certain writers uncomfortable—can sidestep it with *by*.

2. *Between each*. The meaning *two* (*twain*) is explicit in *between*, and any discrepancy, difference, distinction, gap, clash, disparity, or contradiction is necessarily between one thing and at least one other. To be sure, the distributive *each* ultimately means more than one thing, but the word undertakes first to consider things one at a time. For that reason *between each* is a self-contradiction pointing to an impossibility like the square circle. *She repeated it after him, a pause between each word* (pausing after every word) / *slowly uttered these words, pausing between each sentence* (between sentences) / *"No—no—no," returned Richard, speaking quickly, but making a significant pause between each negative* (after each negative) / *given five coats of primer paint, and hand-rubbed between each coat* (after each coat) / *Between each meeting there had been a gap of at least two days* (between meetings).

3. *Between . . . or.* A clash of dual with singular occurs with some frequency in the misguided combination of *between* with *or*, especially after such words as *choice* and *decision. The choice was between tackling these things through the codes or* (and) *not tackling them at all / will mean the difference between college or* (and) *no college next year / The choice too clearly lies between an honorable agreement of three or four great powers on the one hand or* (and) *a disagreement that might lead to anarchy and doom / To the average dancer, the primary difference between a rumba, a samba, or* (and) *a tango is in the spelling.*

Note that the two entities between which the choice is made must be comparable. There is no exact comparison in *the differences in standards of living between a steel worker in Pittsburgh or in Magnitogorsk,* which, even after correcting the false *or*, invites us to gaze at one worker in two places instead of a worker in one place and his counterpart in another. Logic requires *between a typical steel worker in Pittsburgh and one in Magnitogorsk.*

We may further note that *choice between* is itself often redundant, for *choice* can mean the act of choosing or the alternative confronted; that is, the force of *between* is already in *choice.*

4. *Between . . . to.* The sequel of *from* is as naturally *to* as that of *between* is *and.* When we find *between* unidiomatically followed by *to*, these idioms have no doubt been carelessly combined. *These specimens are believed to be between 70,000 to* (and) *100,000 years old / between* (from) *40 per cent to more than 50 per cent of the non-Catholics acknowledged being influenced by religion / northwesterly winds of between forty to fifty-five miles an hour* (omit *between.*) The *between . . . to* fallacy is especially noticeable in historical works, where it takes the form *between 1825–50 / flourished between 1370–1400.* A point worth noting is that *diaries which she kept daily between 1858–61* is intended to mean *from 1858 to 1861, inclusive,* and therefore does not mean *between 1858 and 1861.*

5. Vagarious *between.* Sometimes a *between* construction is allowed to lead its sentence off the rails of idiom and common sense. *Berlin's Socialist Mayor carefully distinguished between what seemed to him permissible for the Germans, but unwise for the Western powers.* So far, one thinks, the Socialist mayor has been distinguishing between one course of action open to the Germans but not good for others. We are still waiting for the *and* ushering in the second part when it dawns on us that he is through. His distinction actually was *between what was permissible for the Germans and what was unwise for the Western powers.* Such ingenious perversions of sense are not so rare as one might think: *the difference between handling a regular client's account, as opposed to one closely tied to a franchise or dealer operation* (replace *as opposed to* with *and*; the opposition is expressed in *difference*).

Occasionally, by sheer absence of mind, *between* is applied to situations logically or physically impossible. *Some time between 1889 and 1890 he began to see his problem in a new light.* Query: What time did he find between 1889 and 1890? A lady who writes tales of murder and detection made one of her characters hide a will between pages 79 and 80 of a book, a feat that would strain the dimensions of our world. This blunder went unnoticed through all the editing and proofreading, and to a correspondent who diffidently remarked that several hundred others must have twitted her already she replied that he was the fourth in the two years since publication.

biological. See OLOGY, OLOGIES.

bitter. See JOURNALESE.

blond(e). See FRENCH WORDS AND PHRASES.

both . . . and. Like *either . . . or, neither . . . nor,* and *not only . . . but also,* the formula *both . . . and* sets up a parallelism of equal and similar vocables heralding equal or similar elements. (See MATCHING PARTS.) If what follows *and* is not the logical and rhetorical equivalent of what follows *both,* the result is disappointment or shock. These are often produced by the misplacing of *both. The United States knows that it is possible both to have human freedom and economic development.* The infinitive after *both* is a commitment to another after *and*; e.g. *both to have . . . freedom and to maintain . . . development.* But what the writer probably had in mind was simply two co-ordinate objects after *have*; in other words, *to have both human freedom and economic development.* The inequality is sometimes more subtly disguised: *designed to protect both the interests of the city and of the suburban communities* (read either *both the interests of the city and those of the suburban communities* or *the interests of both the city and* [no *of*] *the suburban communities*). Usually it is mere length that induces forgetfulness of the *both* and lets the *or* usurp the place of *and: We are equally baffled both by the sudden caprice that produced this *break with his past or the steady sobriety with which he accepted its uttermost implications.*

bourgeois, bourgeoisie. The collective noun is *bourgeoisie*. The noun for one member of the class is *bourgeois*; the adjective is the same. Therefore: *he is a bourgeois, he has bourgeois manners,* and *he belongs to the bourgeoisie.* Too often one reads *he is bourgeoisie* or *he is bourgeoise* (the French feminine). To be sure, *the bourgeois* with a plural verb will also denote the group as a whole: *The bourgeois are despised by the Marxist and the beatnik alike.* But this substitute for the collective singular must not obscure the relation between the *-ois* and *-oisie* forms.

The error of *he is bourgeoisie* does not, of course, invariably come from an uncertainty about French endings. The locution has equally offensive parallels in *he is nobility* and in *he is faculty,* with the meaning *he is a member of the . . .* The minimum ellipsis that can be allowed is *he is of the nobility,* etc. Some examples of this barbarism are: *It is striking that so many characters in the late nineteenth-century Russian writers are half servant class / The reasons why their affair didn't prosper too well is that she was faculty and he very distinctly administration.* A variation on this misuse of *faculty* is now very common in colleges and universities. *One could see a little knot of men talking heatedly on the edge of the grass; two were faculty and about five were students / No plan can succeed in an institution with a good morale unless enough faculty are behind it.*

Faculty is and should remain a collective noun, like *army, senate, college,* and so on. One says *three army men* (not *three army*) *were found drunk and disorderly last night / two members of the senate* (not *two senate*) *voted "Aye" / college men are apt to wear queer clothes* (not *college are apt*). Hence, *Dean of the Faculty, not Dean of Faculty.*

See also GENTEELISM.

breakdown. See VOGUE WORDS.

bridegroom. See HELPMATE, HELPMEET.

brief, adjective. See VOGUE WORDS.

brittle. See VOGUE WORDS.

broadcast, verb. See UNSAVORY PASTS.

burgeon. See MALAPROPS.

bus. See LATIN AND GREEK PLURALS.

but. 1. *But* for *and* 2. *But* for *except*. 3. Interjectional *but*.

1. *But* for *and*. The first is adversative, the second—it need hardly be said—additive. *But* proposes to contradict something preceding or offers an exception to it; *and* ushers in an extension of what precedes or notes an application that reaffirms it. The hasty writer is tempted, especially after a negative form, to confuse extension with contradiction when a contrast occurs between the two ways of making the same assertion. *Your reviewer completely fails to understand what the author is driving at, but substitutes a preconception of his own.* The second statement extends and reaffirms the first; they call for an *and* to link them, not a *but*. Each *but* in the following should be *and* for the same reason: *Ravens and fulmars that have eaten the flesh of newly killed sharks may sometimes be so sick that they scarcely are able to fly, but tumble about erratically / Catching sharks did not begin in Greenland until the beginning of the nineteenth century, but only a few were caught for a long time.* In the second of these sentences an affirmative statement would validate the *but*: *Catching sharks began at the beginning of the nineteenth century, but for a long time only a few were caught.* The same **principle** applies to *There is too much ice on the water to permit hunting with kayaks except in a few open places, but* (and) *these diminish day by day.* There would be a genuinely adversative relationship if the form were affirmative: *Hunting with kayaks is possible in a few open places, but these diminish day by day.* We have, then, to distinguish sharply between the exception to an affirmative statement, which calls for *but,* and the repetition of a negative statement in an affirmative form, which needs *and.*

The kind of zigzag produced by beginning a string of neighboring clauses with adversatives can sometimes be rectified or mitigated by noticing that *but, yet, still,* or *however* ought to have been *and. But April still permits sledge travel, even if water is to be found at some places. But when you reach Disko Bay, you find that winter still rules there. Yet even here the seals have started coming up on the ice.* The *but* of the second sentence pretends to deny the main thought of the first sentence, but actually reinforces it; this *but* should be *and.* Make it so, and you leave the adversative *yet* of the third sentence free to turn off at an angle from both of the preceding sentences without causing any zigzag.

2. *But* for *except*. This usage constitutes one of the

most prickly topics in the whole range of English syntax. The most learned lexicographers have tried in vain to deal with it simply, and if the unlearned rely on common sense to cope with the difficulties, it is because the experts' explanations seem more difficult still.

Dictionaries agree that *but*, which is commonly a preposition or a conjunction and not so commonly some other part of speech, often defies classification. The Shorter Oxford Dictionary says: "The preposition and the conjunction are not distinctly separable." Webster's New World Dictionary says that *but* "is often indistinguishable . . . as any one of the preceding parts of speech" (preposition, conjunction, adverb). The constructions that raise such doubts are represented by the opening of "Casabianca," about the boy on the burning deck *Whence all but he had fled.* To the reader whose equipment is restricted to mere common sense such a *but* seems plainly a preposition meaning *except*, and therefore logically and grammatically to be followed by *him*, not *he*. But the dictionaries see it otherwise. The New World Dictionary illustrates the conjunction *but* with *Nobody came but I*, adding *came* in parentheses. The Oxford similarly illustrates the conjunction *but* with Cardinal Newman's *I am one among a*

thousand; all of them wrong but I, presumably meaning that after the second *I* we are to supply *am not* or *am right.*

The New International Dictionary is determined to make this *but* a conjunction to be followed by *he* and *I*, not a preposition to be followed by *him* and *me*. Stating the point in a veiled way, it defines *but* as a conjunction "connecting co-ordinate elements" and meaning "with this exception, namely;—before a noun or pronoun, adverb, prepositional phrase, in a construction involving an unexpanded clause; as, affable everywhere *but* at home." Then come illustrations, including our first example, *all but he had fled.* By this mysterious reference to "a construction involving an unexpanded clause" the New International must mean what the New World Dictionary means when it asks us to construe *Nobody came but I* as an abridgment of *Nobody came but I came.* We are to read *I can bear anything but contempt I cannot bear* and *All had fled, but he had not.* It would be interesting to know how the New International would apply this doctrine to Dryden's *None but the brave deserves the fair.* Is this to be expanded into *None deserves the fair, but the brave deserves them (her)?* How else expand the clause? And yet how can one believe that this expansion matches anything that Dryden had in mind?

These expansions are objectionable also because they transform the very meaning of *but*, apparently without its being noticed. The person who says *Nobody came but I* (or *me*) is using *but* to mean *with the exception of*; but the moment you expand and make him mean *Nobody came but I came*, you turn his *but* into the adversative conjunction meaning *on the contrary, on the other hand*. This piece of unconscious misrepresentation occurs every time we read a nominative case after *but* as the subject of a conjecturally supplied verb; and a dictionary that resorts to this explanation leaves us with the anomaly of an example cited as illustrating one definition of *but* (= except) while it is actually illustrating an utterly different definition (= on the contrary).

In contrast with the foregoing, the New International deals with the preposition *but* in the meaning of *except* by saying that it is "followed by the objective case form of the pronoun . . . ; as, all have coats but me." The illustrations are *There was no one left* but *me* (Stevenson) and *No one had the least control over him* but *her* (William Black). No expanded-clause doctrine here; merely the simplicity of a preposition and its object. What and where is the

difference between these examples and *None but the brave, I can bear anything but contempt*, and *all but he (him) had fled?* The difference is invisible to anyone but a lexicographer who wants to illustrate the historical confusion between the preposition and the conjunction, and who is ready by twists of interpretation to demonstrate that the first is the second. The expanded-clause theory would require Stevenson to have meant: *There was no one left but I (was left)*. Black must have meant: *No one had the least control over him but she (had control over him)*. Why should this theory be applied to one set of examples and not to a grammatically indistinguishable set?

The expanded-clause doctrine is at best farfetched. Anyone speaking or writing modern English who says *Nobody came but I* is not using *I* as the subject of a second understood *came*; he is joining it with rough logic but no grammar to *Nobody* as a subject of the first *came*—as if he had said *I but nobody else came*. The Shorter Oxford virtually grants as much when it says: "In colloq. use *me, us,* etc. are more common after *but* than *I, we,* etc. and equally correct." Why raise the difference between the colloquial and the literary if the two are equally correct? If *me* and *us* after *but* are correct to say, they are correct to write, except on a theory that literary English has to be unnatural English. On this showing, the quotations from Stevenson and Black, which use *but* as a preposition with an object, are to be regarded as colloquial, whereas exactly similar quotations from Dryden, Maria Edgeworth, and Lamb, which use *but* as a conjunction linking coordinates, are to be regarded as literary.

Lexicographers might be in a stronger position if they simply classified *all but he had fled*, etc. as constructions that are idiomatically right without being strictly grammatical. Note that *save*, like *but*, can be both preposition and conjunction, with the same results in usage. Logic and idiom, equally correct here, suggest that Newman might have written *all of them wrong but (save) me* and Mrs. Hemans *all but (save) him had fled*, with a small difference in stylistic effect but no change in meaning. Had they done so, they would have supplied dictionary-makers with examples of a construction easy to explain and hardly noticeable, in place of one that defies analysis and evokes explanations at variance with simple facts. Which construction sounds the better depends on the ear that hears it; that is, on what the ear is used to and has come to expect.

3. Interjectional *but*. One of the fads of the 1920's was an attempt to naturalize in English one of the characteristic uses of the French *mais*, which, besides being a conjunction meaning *but*, often expresses surprise in the manner of our interjection *why* (*Why, I never heard of such a thing!*). Sometimes this *mais* has the further effect of a passing intensive, an *oh* giving a slight stress, as in *Oh, I grant you that*. From these uses in French the adversative sense of *but* almost entirely evaporated years ago. Nevertheless, English and American speakers who frequently heard this *mais* were amused by the idea of adopting the idiom, and the mannerism has become obsessive in literature as well as in small talk: *But yes, But no, But certainly*, and, most common, *But definitely*, which presumably gives emphatic assent. (See DEFINITELY.)

buttonhole. See PEDANTRY.

by. See PREPOSITIONS.

byword. See CONNOTATIONS.

C

cake, eating and having. To eat one's cake and have it too, a proverbial statement of the human greed for irreconcilable benefits, turns up in print and talk with the order illogically reversed. Radio commercials assure us, about various "dual purpose" appliances, that *we can have our cake and eat it too. Pentagon officials,* we read, *are trying to have their cake and eat it too.* It is of course no trick at all to eat the cake that you have. The point of the saying is to have the cake after you have eaten it.

calculate. See BALANCE.

calculated risk. See JARGON.

cancel. See CORRELATE.

cannot but, cannot help. See HELP.

capsize. See CORRELATE.

caption. See PEDANTRY.

careen. American usage has substituted this word, especially in the participal form *careening,* for the original and evocative *careering* in the

sense of *run wild.* Actually, *careen* means only the bottom of a ship, and *careening* should only mean putting the ship in drydock for repairs, or heeling over in the wind, thus exposing the *careen.* The traditional use is illustrated in an early novel of Conrad's, *Romance: We turned arm in arm to look at the boat. There she was, lying careened on the deck, with patched sides, in a belt of chips, shavings, and sawdust.* By now the career of *careening* in the United States is not to be checked by the infrequent occurrence of the legitimate *careering,* which is either felt as ambiguous or taken for a misprint. (Compare the corruption of *carom* into *cannon.*)

carouse. See CORRELATE.

case. In his famous "Lecture on Jargon," Arthur Quiller-Couch makes a laughingstock of the word *case* in one of its ordinary uses—*in that case, in case of fire, in the case of Jones,* etc.—by insisting that all *case* is good for is to denote a box: *a case of books, a case of whisky.* This is culpably misleading, for Q. must have known that the first

127

set of *cases* above are like *cases* at law—not *boxes* but *events*. *Casus* (*case*), as we know from its application to the declension of Latin nouns, is what (be)falls. So *in case of fire* is correct, idiomatic, and unimprovable. What Quiller-Couch was right to make fun of is the superfluous intrusion of *case* when a simple preposition will do and there is in fact no *case*. *In the case of the Rembrandt the museum paid a million and a half* (For the Rembrandt) / *Now let us turn to the cases of the three other texts* (omit *the cases of*) / *In the case of my wife, all her baggage was lost or perhaps stolen* (As for my wife) / *In case of an emergency ring this bell* (in any emergency).

There is yet another meaning of *case*, derived from the law case, which is useful and convenient. That is *case* meaning *argument*. To sum up the case (in this last sense) against *case* in its jargon sense: One should never use *in case of* to announce what a sentence is about, or insert *the case(s) of* when a direct connection will serve. (See IN TERMS OF and AS 11.) Here are a few more examples that should encourage total abstinence from *case* until the lazy reliance upon it is broken: *In the case of production control, for example, industrial quotas were often set so high that they had no restrictive effect* (Industrial quotas for production control were often set so high) / *In the case of the agricultural program, this meant* ... (For the agricultural program this meant) / *As was a few years ago the case with Joyce Cary, the time has now come* ... (The time has come ..., as a few years ago it came for Joyce Cary) / *In those who look solely to their own security, as in the case of the two landladies* (Those who, like the two landladies, look solely to their own security) / *In the case of books the problem of distribution is rather different* (The problem of distributing books) / *Except in the case of oysters it is usual to precook the shellfish* (With the exception of oysters).

See also CHARACTER; LEVEL; NATURE; COVERING WORDS.

cast anchor. See ICECAP.

catalog, cataloged. The simplifications promised by spelling reform tempt the enthusiast to undertake them without sufficient forethought about consequences. Most persons would probably agree with the reformer that the *-ue* of *catalogue* is of little use to the language, and that these letters are destined to go the way of the terminal *-me* of *programme*. The unforeseen consequence is that the inflected forms of the verb *catalog* as they are now spelled by professional librarians and others violate common and useful conventions. The forms *cataloged* and *cataloging* denote sounds parallel with *lodged* and *lodging*, not with *logged* and *logging*. It should be a point of common sense— especially, one would think, for librarians—not to add *cataloging* and *cataloged* to such forms with uncertain pronunciation as *gill, gibbous,* and *gimbals,* or to raise a suspicion that *cataloger* and *astrologer* have something in common. If the professionals decline to restore the *-u* to the inflected forms, let them simply double the *g*.

A similar disorder is introduced by the failure to add *k* to the inflected forms of certain words ending in *c*. One comes across *tarmaced* (especially in England) and *picniced,* which are no doubt so written and printed out of a characteristically modern feeling of literalism and simplification. "Let the reader work out the formula" seems to be the writer's self-righteous thought.

See also SPELLING.

catalyst. See POPULARIZED TECHNICALITIES.

center around. Quasi-metaphorical language derived from Euclidean geometry ought not to flout Euclidean sense, yet the geometrically senseless expression *center around* (or *about*) is more frequently met than the tolerable images *center in, on,* or *at. Much of this activity centered around two auto stocks / A number of them center, in one way or another, around a girl named Mariette / Right now, this enthusiasm seems to center chiefly around homes, automobiles and bridges / And in that parallel acceptance centering about the individual / Early ideas centered around superstitious beliefs / Centered around the literature of the '20's.* The examples are from respectable sources: the *New York Times,* a distinguished novelist, the Columbia Encyclopedia, a volume of scholarly criticism. Webster's Collegiate Dictionary is not above using *center around* in definitions, and the New International Dictionary tells us that the Great White Way is *That part of Broadway . . . centering about Times Square.*

Pivot around, sometimes encountered, is a similar way of putting the core around the apple.

challenge. See METAPHOR 4.

character. What this word properly denotes is one of man's greatest assets, but as the word itself is generally used, it is a liability meaning nothing. *President Fouad Chehab is believed to be forming an emergency Cabinet,* *mostly military in character / desires to establish a dictatorial and repressive regime of a totalitarian character.* The meanings are: *a Cabinet, mostly military / a regime, dictatorial and repressive.* No sensible person would wish to deny the word its figurative extensions to inanimate things that truly have character, as workmanship may, or white oak, or handwriting. But when the word is a mere synonym for *kind, sort, cast, species,* or *description,* it is pure waste. The remedy is to use a noun in *-ness* or the buried adjective itself: Whatever is *of a slovenly character* has slovenliness and is slovenly.

See also CASE; COVERING WORDS; LEVEL; NATURE.

check, verb. See AMBIGUITY; UP TILL.

chestnut. See PRONUNCIATION 1.

chivalric, chivalrous. One might think that these two words are proof against confusion with each other, but miscellaneous reading proves the contrary. A highly praised biography contains the sentence *He found all the male characters in this production of the great tragedy extremely comical—for some reason, chivalric or otherwise* (see OTHERWISE), *he did not mention the Queen or Ophelia.* True, many dictionaries define

chivalric as *chivalrous;* but they neglect to add that the synonymy does not go all the way. For a good many decades *chivalrous* has had a pretty consistent monopoly of the specialized meanings *honorable in combat* and *deferentially courteous to women; chivalric* has almost as consistently pointed to *knightly adventure.*

See also ENDINGS 1.

choice. See BETWEEN 3.

Christmas. See PRONUNCIATION 1.

cliché. See SET PHRASES 1.

clothes. See PRONUNCIATION 1.

co-. See COHORT.

cohort. In this continually misused word, the *co-* is the misleading element. Unlike many similar words, it does not imply a reciprocal combination, as in *co-signer, co[l]laborator.* On the contrary, it is related to the word *court*—an enclosed space—and denotes a multitude. In Roman usage, a cohort was a subdivision of infantry numbering from three hundred sixty to six hundred men. The modern storyteller is therefore far from the mark when she writes: *She idly turned over the pages of a magazine, while in the tiny kitchen her cohort washed the* *dishes.* Again from a novel, this time a best-seller: *"Go ahead, boys,"* he said to his *cohorts. "I'll meet you outside."* (The cohorts here were four persons) / *At about the same time Joe Adonis, a cohort who has since been deported to Italy, moved into a house just a quarter of a mile away.* An even more aberrant use turns up in the following passage, where the word is evidently a substitute for *counterpart: The suburbanite, riding to his job in town over a new expressway, is not much concerned by the fact that his city-dwelling cohort is sweating out his trip to work on a bus that keeps getting caught in traffic jams.*

The extension of *cohort* to nonmilitary uses is natural enough, but if the word is to retain its force it should observe two requirements: (1) it should designate members, too numerous to be conveniently counted, of some sort of united group, and (2) it should imply some sort of struggle or contest. *No one of the candidates succeeded in completely marshaling his cohorts before the first ballot / To the legion of the lost ones, to the cohort of the damned*—in such uses the sense of the word is preserved.

Note further that certain words imply the relation ordinarily marked by *co-* without any prefix—e.g. *partner,* *sharer, spouse.* Do not encumber them with a needless *co-,* any more than you would be tempted to say *co-friend* or *co-twin.*

colleague. With the decay of hierarchies in recent times, the word *colleague* has come to be used outside its original sphere, which was limited to government and the professions. The Oxford English Dictionary explicitly notes that *colleague* is "not applied to partners in trade or manufacture." But since its day trades and businesses have become professions. By dictionary definition a colleague meant originally one chosen at the same time or for the same (high) office as another. By the social extension just mentioned, a plumber or electrician now refers to his *colleagues.* Formerly they were his *mates.* It is for the understanding of this last word in the classics of literature that this entry may be required. (For the pronunciation of *colleague,* see PRONUNCIATION 1.)

come to be. See BECOME.

comity. See POPULARIZED TECHNICALITIES.

comma splice. See SENTENCE, THE 4.

commiserate. See PREPOSITIONS.

commission, omission. See PRONUNCIATION 1.

commitment. See CRITICS' WORDS; METAPHOR 4.

common. See DEFENSIBLES.

communicate, communication(s). The drive toward abstraction and COVERING WORDS has brought about an excessive use of *communication* and its verb and cognates. There is a *communications industry; communications* is a university subject, elementary and advanced; there is a *problem of communication;* and people more and more refer to their *communications* instead of their *letters, remarks, messages,* or *telephone calls.* The *Washington Post,* which circulates among its writers a lively and wise critical sheet on diction and grammar called *Post-Script,* once commented on a headline: *"Communicate* is being used illegitimately and pompously, generally in connection with our own profession of journalism, so often these days that apparently some of us feel impelled to apologize for using the word at all [by putting quotation marks around it]. . . . The story under the head incidentally said *Motivated by the desire to communicate. . . .* Why not simply *Wanting to communicate . . . ?"* One might go a step further than *Post-Script* and suggest *Wanting to speak.* At any rate, the word *communication* is not needed as a substitute for the concrete carriers of ideas—letters, gestures, signals, newspapers—or for the ideas themselves. Nor need we say *he rates high in communications skill* when we mean *he is articulate.* Like hundreds of other words ending in *-tion, communication* is to be reserved for the abstract and general idea—i.e. the CONCEPT.

compare, compared. It is clear enough that one thing compares favorably, unfavorably, or otherwise *with* (not *to*) another; idiom requires it to do so. When we pass from the intransitive to the transitive verb, we compare one thing either *to* or *with* another: *to* if we are noting a striking likeness, not necessarily deep or well analyzed; *with* if we are undertaking an extended analysis of similarities and differences. We compare the United States *to* the Soviet Union in size and climate; we compare the one country *with* the other in the various factors that encourage or inhibit freedom of the press. Shakespeare is a baroque dramatist compared either *with* or *to* Racine: the comparison can be either worked out or flatly stated. There is also an absolute use with the meaning of *equal: For power over language Dickens may be compared to Shakespeare.*

Any transgression of idiom in the choice of preposition is venial beside a misuse of *compared* itself that is rampant in the public prints. The word occurs in what may be called gratuitous compar ison—the statement of absolute facts as if they were relative, or of independent facts as if they were dependent. This perversion is generally introduced by *compared with*, sometimes by *as compared with* (see AS 9). A typical example: *His new annual salary will be $20,000, compared with his present salary of $19,500.* Patently, his salary will also be $20,000 if *not* compared with his present salary, or compared with anything else. The two facts are independent, and good sense requires either that they be kept separate and the comparison left to the reader, or that the comparison be actually made, not merely promised. *His new annual salary will be $20,000; his present one is $19,500* would express the meaning accurately; so would *will be $20,000, $500 more than he is getting now.*

The frequency of the abuse, and its trifling variants, can be conveyed by a cluster of examples, all collected within a few days from some of the best metropolitan newspapers: *A crop of this size would compare with last year's small production of 10,964,000 bales* (This crop is *x* bales larger than last year's which was) /

He placed earnings at $4,542,-000, or $2.85 a share, compared with a loss of $2,542,000 the year before ("This year's earnings were . . . ," he said; "last year's loss was") / *The power rating of the device was less than one kiloton, as compared to the twenty-kiloton bomb that leveled Hiroshima* (less than one kiloton; it was a twenty-kiloton bomb that leveled Hiroshima) / *A pentomic division has five battle groups totaling 13,700 men compared with the old-fashioned non-atomic three-regiment division of 17,000 men* (13,700 men; the old-fashioned . . . division had 17,000 men) / *The cost of a black-and-white page . . . will be $25,285, without benefit of discounts, compared with $23,475 now* (discounts; the present cost is) /*Their size is limited to sixty square feet, compared with the standard 300 square feet* (sixty square feet; the standard size is 300 square feet) / *The FBI said today crime increased by 11 per cent in the first nine months of this year, compared with the corresponding period in 1957* (said that there was 11 per cent more crime . . . than in the same months of 1957) / *estimates that placed the need for college teachers at 500,000 by 1970 as compared with 196,000 in 1956* (1970; in 1956 it was 196,000). Note that several of the examples use *with* where, if *compared* were acceptable at all, the preposition might well have been *to*.

A further caution before leaving the subject: The orderly mind is not displayed or promoted by comparing things that are incommensurable. The report of a new process for concentrating hay reads: *International Harvester says that storage space is reduced by 40 per cent when compared with baled hay*. Two storage spaces lend themselves to comparison; so do two methods of concentration; but to compare storage space with baled hay is to scatter ideas at random.

See also PREPOSITIONS.

compatible. There are signs that this word is being overused and, in the excess, misused. The fault lies in a wrong inference from its contrary, *incompatible*. People will argue that an action or a decision is wrong because *incompatible* with a given fact or purpose. Careless thinkers thereupon assume that *compatible* can mean *appropriate, convenient, all right. She asked to come up and I said, "O.K." I thought it was compatible* (= would do no harm). While there is yet time, let us all remember that *compatible* does not mean simply *acceptable* but *capable of being done or thought of together with a second action or idea*. Being a poet and running an insurance company are rarely compatible, but either occupation is compatible with playing chess, being a good father, or dying in the poorhouse. The absence of conflict is the essence of compatibility, which is why the word permits itself the illogicality of a useful idiom: *a compatible marriage*.

compose, comprise. The whole is composed of its parts; the whole comprises the parts. The parts compose the whole and are comprised in it. *Comprise*, the word that produces most of the trouble, expresses the relation of the larger to the smaller, not the other way around. If we think of *comprise* as meaning *take in*, we shall escape the pitfall into which even good writers manage to stumble. *The suburbs of large cities also are avoided ... because their booming populations are comprised mainly of white-collar workers.* Not so: the booming populations are *composed* of white-collar workers, and these workers are *comprised in* the booming populations. *The denomination is comprised of three sects.* On the contrary, it is *composed* of three sects, and it *comprises* them. For *the new poems which comprise the present volume* read: the poems compose the volume (or the volume comprises the poems). *The politicians comprise* (compose) *most of that shrill group.* (The group comprises the politicians.)

Speaking mnemonically:

The whole comprises the parts;
The parts are comprised in the whole;
The whole is composed of its parts;
The parts compose the whole.

conceding. See DANGLERS, ACCEPTABLE.

concept, -ion. The vogue of *concept* as a word that will dignify any idea from a passing fancy to a full-fledged plan has blurred—probably forever—a useful distinction. But those who like to call things by their right names continue to mark a difference between *concept*, the abstract, general notion of any entity, and *conception*, the particular image, shape, or set of features with which the empty *concept* may be filled. Thus the *concept* God is the idea of a supreme ruler of the universe. All the religions propose different *conceptions*. For any namable thing there can be only one *concept*, but the *conceptions* are many. It would follow from this formerly well-understood difference that the statement PANEL WEIGHS MAN'S CONCEPT OF GOD IN AN UNFOLDING UNIVERSE should read MAN'S CONCEPTION. The panel members could not have discussed various definitions of God if their *concept* had not been virtually the same and thus defined their problem; i.e. with what new or changed *conceptions* should we now fill the unchanging *concept* God?

The negative *misconcept* (SOVIET MISCONCEPT HELD CAUSE OF RIFT) is so far only a headline word.

concerning. See DANGLERS, ACCEPTABLE.

concur, concurrence. See PREPOSITIONS.

conferee. See -EE, -ER.

conform, conformity. See PREPOSITIONS.

confrontation. See METAPHOR 4.

connect. See PREPOSITIONS.

connive. This delightful and indispensable word was undone during the Second World War, when restless spirits felt the need of a new synonym for plotting, bribing, spying, conspiring, engineering a coup, preparing a secret attack. In the end, by association with *contrive*, the old verb *connive* came to mean simply *managing, effecting, doing. By use of his native ingenuity and gift of gab he connived so well that he got all their proxies in record time.* As an adjective, *conniving* is being used to supply a totally unneeded synonym for *underhand, scheming, secretive.* Meanwhile the original idea of *connivance* cannot be expressed without circumlocution or further harm to words. This truth was shown a few years ago in an article by a well-known philosopher and publicist who, having used *connive* to characterize the main action of a political incident abroad, was forced to use nine other words to describe the action of a helpful prison guard. One of his locutions was *with the contrivance of the guard,* which sufficiently shows how much we need *connive* in its pure state. What, precisely, does it mean? It means *wink at, lower the eyelid,* presumably while something forbidden is going on. The guard turned his back while the political prisoner made his escape. This the guard certainly did not *contrive;* it was the prisoner's friends who *contrived* to overcome many difficulties—an active task. The guard's behavior was passive—*connivance.* This is neatly underlined by the required preposition: *connive at,* not *with.*

connotations. Some words and phrases of great import tend to acquire through literary or vernacular use a particular meaning or force that is at odds with the literal meaning. As a result, the purpose that such words and phrases can serve becomes limited, and these limitations can be thoroughly learned only by close listening or extensive reading; frequent repetition is needed to impress the exact scope and intention on the mind. People who use these expressions in their literal meaning, as though tradition had not done its work upon them, mislead at least some of their audience.

Thus *to have words with someone* does not mean *to exchange chitchat* but *to quarrel; to a degree* means *to a very high degree* and not *to a certain extent* (*to an extent,* by the way, is not yet an idiom in formal English); *graceless* means *lacking in divine grace,* not physical grace, hence it means *immoral,* not *ungraceful*—the *graceless nephew* of Victorian novels is usually a very graceful fellow on the dance floor; *presently* does not mean *at present* but *shortly, in a little while.* Many passages in plays and novels written before 1920 will cause bewilderment if the contemporary usage prevails. *Chance of showers tomorrow,* which the Weather Bureau discouragingly repeats, goes against a strong tendency in the word *chance* to sound hopeful: there is a *chance* of winning the lottery prize and a *risk* of losing one's money. Therefore *chance of showers* suggests the point of view of the gardener, who wants rain, not of the picnic party, who want sunshine. *Watershed* (while we are busy with liquids) properly designates the point or line in a mountain range where some streams flow in one direction and others in the opposite. The word is misused when applied to the streams themselves. The figurative use of *watershed* (= dividing line) should serve as a reminder of the right use.

Many other phrases are being similarly diverted from their useful specialization. A few more examples may perhaps induce the reader to think twice before he employs what he knows is a SET PHRASE, if he is uncertain of its ambit. To put someone *at hard labor* implies that he is a convict, not the neighbor's boy being given his first job of hard work; and speaking of *job*, the older meaning of *crooked job* (bribery and pull) should be brought to mind when one reads in a novel of forty years ago *You know there are no jobs in the Civil Service* or when one hears the song in *Trial by Jury: It was managed by a job and a good job too!* In our time, it is still useful to know that *pleasantries* are light, bantering jokes, not simply amiable conversation; that *well-spoken* means *polite*, not elegant in speech; that a *visitation* is not a mere visit but a tour of inspection for discovering errors or defects; that *bureaucrat* is a disparaging word; and that *literate* is not a term of praise for anyone who can read and write, let alone for an author or his works. Finally, though the misuse will ruffle only a few spirits, it may be pointed out that the business or social letter beginning *I am pleased to send you (give you; tell you)* is ac-

tually condescending in tone. Only sovereigns and puissant lords should say they are *pleased* to do something that the rest of us are simply *glad* or *very glad* to do.

Nuances of this kind are as uncodifiable as they are unenforceable; they rest upon an awareness of what others say and have said, and also upon a subtle feeling for what words connote, as much as for where they belong. Connotations serve good writing unobtrusively, and give the pleasure of a clear atmosphere even to those who notice none of the minute causes at work.

For the convenience of searchers and as a spur to attention, here is a short list of connotations often ignored in recent American prose:

abrasive: that which wears down by rubbing; hence not *the abrasive clatter of the garbage cans.*

astronomical: large, but for distances only; hence not *an astronomical abundance.*

attrition: breaking down by small repeated efforts; hence not (in a context of sexual violence) *taking her attritively.*

byword: always used in a bad sense; hence not *whenever a purchase of leather goods is mentioned ACME is the byword.*

concocted: means *cooked together*; hence not *clad in a uniform concocted of odds and ends.*

dedicate: applies to concrete things, such as buildings, or to life and man's energies; it is no synonym for *call by the name of*; hence not *Lawyer Dedicates Plan* *for $25 Theater Tickets to Lef-kowitz.*

emanate: for the invisible and impalpable only—an idea or a fragrance emanates; hence not *the book emanates from the well-known publishing firm of . . .*

heritage: a concrete or abstract legacy received by a person or a people rather than by an object or a place; hence not *a wall-bracket with a Moorish heritage.*

hotbed: a place where growth is activated on purpose, by fertilizers or by figurative means; hence not *Battlefield Hospital a Hotbed of Misery.*

meritorious: always of persons; hence not *any meritorious science development program must contain . . .*

opinion of, have no: always in a bad sense; it is no alternative of *have no opinion about;* hence not *I have no opinion of psychoanalysis* when the meaning is *I know too little to judge.*

plenitude: always abstract; never a synonym for *plenty;* hence not *"Plenitude from Petroleum"* as the title of an article.

usage: always of words and improperly substituted for *use;* hence not *a lecture on the usage and influence of Isaiah in the New Testament.*

verbiage: always in a bad sense and improperly used for *language* or *wordage;* hence not *in honor of three modern masters of legislative and judicial verbiage.*

-conscious. See LINKING 3.

constant(ly). It would be foolish to reprove the extension of *constant* to mean *continual.* The link between the two is the idea of steadiness. But the perception of that idea is what makes an alert writer occasionally prefer *continual.* There is a touch of paradox in *He was constantly fidgeting:* one thinks with remorse of *I am constant as the Northern Star,* which twinkles but does not fidget. Again, the exaggeration in *She was constantly having children, each more unwanted than the last* would be as effective and of greater plausibility if the writer had used *continually.*

See also CONTINUAL, CONTINUOUS.

consul. See COUNCIL, COUNSEL, CONSUL.

contact, verb. Persons old enough to have been repelled by the verb *contact* when it was still a crude neologism may as well make up their minds that there is no way to arrest or reverse the tide of its popularity. Persons young enough to have picked up the word without knowing that anyone had reservations about it may as well make up their minds that a considerable body of their elders abominate it and would despise themselves if they succumbed to the temptation to use it. In this converted noun we have the perfect example of a coinage that has thirty or forty more years of intolerance to face from a dwindling minority of conservatives while enjoying the full approval—and, more important, the increasing use—of a growing majority that will eventually be unanimous. This clash of generations—a forlorn cultural resistance or a healthy disposition to make the most of linguistic growth, according to how you look at it—is one of the standard phenomena of change.

If in doubt, contact your physician—this locution is as natural to the American of thirty as it is grotesque to the American of sixty, for whom the idea of *surfaces touching* is the essence of *contact*. The elderly can therefore see no fitness and no use for the word in its new sense, when the vocabulary already provides *consult, ask, approach, get in touch with, confer with,* and simply *see*. Their juniors can perceive no point in forgoing so plainly useful an invention.

The conservative retains one advantage: no one insists that he *must* use *contact*, and if he sticks to *consult* and other inconspicuous synonyms no one will even notice his abstention. But this argument is unlikely to persuade the addicts of *contact*, who exploit the word because it sounds brisk and comprehensive. (See COVERING WORDS.)

Two other VOGUE WORDS in the same category of nouns converted into verbs for "dynamic" reasons are *implement* and *process*. A plan or program is *implemented* when supplied with the practical apparatus—appropriations, staff, schedule, or what not—needed to carry it out. The word is perhaps a shade less harsh than *contact*, very likely because of its analogy with *tool* and *retool*, standard words for a factory's preparing to undertake new or increased production. With *implement* the layman can sound technical. As for the second word, an application, request, memorandum, or some other document is *processed* when it goes through the usual sequence of consideration, approval, and execution. The word sounds as if it should mean something more exact than *considered, appraised, weighed, handled, studied, dealt with*, etc., but does it?

It is to be noted that all three of these currently fashionable verbs—*contact, implement, process*—belong to the proliferating vocabulary of bureaucratic organization, the patter of officialdom. This is a linguistic medium that practically everyone not immersed in it systematically mocks, but meanwhile its toxic properties undermine our resistance, and in the end contemporary speech becomes, regardless of the occasion, more and more bureaucratic.

contemporary, modern (istic). The ease and grace with which a language may be handled by skillful writers depend largely on the existence of single words to denote complex relations. If instead of *a contemporary* one has to say *a person who was living at the same time as the other person we have been speaking of*, elegance suffers a setback. Accordingly, when such words have been forged, it behooves every writer to keep their usefulness intact. *Contemporary* has begun to chip and crack from careless handling as an absolute instead of a relative term. *Our contemporaries* is clear enough because the time relation is pinned down by *our*. But if after discussing events that occurred, say, a century ago a writer says *When we turn to contemporary opinion*, in the sense of *today we think*, he is helping to pervert an indispensable word. The headline CONTEMPORARIES AT THE X. GALLERY SHOW VIVID CONTRAST may be exact, but ought not to designate living artists —just as *contemporary art* is not of itself synonymous with *the art of today*.

It is always possible and often preferable to make time relations clear through the simple words *now, then, today, at that time, in the past*. If an adjective is needed, *modern* is ready to hand. But caution is necessary here too, for the application of *modern* varies with the context. Historians say the modern period began in 1500, but what Chaplin meant by *Modern Times* was the age of machinery—the present. *Modern art* may denote movements

that began in 1870, 1900, 1920, or at some nearer time. Hence the writer's obligation to define and give dates.

Modernistic, once the cant word for the art of the Cubist decades (1905–1925), is no longer used in serious criticism. It lingers on in the lower reaches of fiction and advertising, usually in the phrase *modernistic furniture*.

content(s). Teachers college usage seems to be responsible for the change of *contents* (what is contained) into *content* which, with the accent on the second syllable, also means *contentment*. A century ago T. H. Huxley could unambiguously write *I have only begun to learn content and peace of mind since I have resolved at all risks to do this* [follow wherever nature leads]. The modern reader hesitates an instant at *learn content*, which first strikes him as a familiar phrase of the P.T.A. meeting. He would be in no doubt if *contents* had retained its *s* in the schools as it has in the kitchen, where bottles and cans have measured *contents* stated on the label. Critics who like to analyze multiple meanings in works of art might also like to resurrect *form and contents*, in place of the homogeneous and uninteresting *content* that now fills the containers of art.

context. The figurative uses of this word are rapidly dissipating its important literal sense, which is: the words surrounding a term or phrase or sentence that make clearer these portions of the whole text. *Context* for *situation* is allowable only if one does not speak of a *context* for every event, difficulty, or remark. *Context* is no synonym for *connection*; the idea of a homogeneous *text* (atmosphere, tendency) must be present before *context* is appropriate.

Again, the word is not a synonym for *sentence*, *context* being wider and more indefinite than any grammatical element, and always implying aid to interpretation. See META-PHOR 4.

continual, continuous. In modern use these words have become more sharply differentiated than they once were, and no careful writer fails to draw the useful distinction between *continuous* (going on without interruption) and *continual* (recurring at frequent intervals). Normal breathing is *continuous*, a chronic cough *continual*. Telephone service is supposed to be continuous, but a talkative person's use of it is ordinarily no more than continual. Historical examples show that the distinction has not always existed, and dictionaries list *continuous* as a secondary meaning of *continual*. But a virtual unanimity of writers rejects the confusion in practice. Occasional excep-

tions stand out: *It must be remembered that this is December when* [in the Arctic] *it is dark continually* (continuously) / *having been almost continually* (continuously) *chief or deputy. Almost continually* (= almost again and again) would be felt as self-contradicting by most readers; *almost continuously* (= with but little interruption) raises no problem and no eyebrows. The opposite substitution, startling when made by a professional rhetorician, occurs in this sentence: *But there is no doubt that a continuous use of* miracle *to describe any coincidence or amazing happening is vulgar.* In the following warning, *whenever* flatly contradicts *continuously*: *If you continuously get a busy signal whenever you dial a number that is new to you and is in the same central office as yours, it may be the number of a party on your line.* Whatever happens repeatedly on like occasions is continual, not continuous.

See also CONSTANT(LY).

continuum. See POPULARIZED TECHNICALITIES.

contractions. See I'D, I'LL, I'VE; and also APPENDIX 1, pp. 477-479.

contradictory. See CONVERSE, OBVERSE, REVERSE.

contrariwise. See ON THE OTHER HAND.

contrary. 1. *Contrary* does tireless duty as an adjective (*The contrary opinion is also outspokenly held*) and as a noun (*Only the credulous can believe the contrary*). In either guise, it raises no very intricate grammatical or stylistic problems. (It may raise logical ones where it overlaps *opposite* and CONVERSE.) The commonest trouble with *contrary* as a noun occurs in the accurate and standard locution *to the contrary notwithstanding,* which has attained some currency in a mutilated form that lops off *notwithstanding.* Undoubtedly this practice defers to a feeling that a four-syllable, fifteen-letter word is something to avoid if one can. The question is: Can one? *She even believed, all previous experiences to the contrary, that her new book would restore her to favor / Runaway victory in the pennant race to the contrary, this hardly was a smashingly superior effort by a smashingly superior team / The long steady decline of the Canadian Mounties' use of horses—many movies, comic strips and stories to the contrary—received emphasis on Fifth Avenue yesterday.* Unfortunately, in all these examples the omitted *nothwithstanding* is the word that does the work. Without it the idiom is as unpowered as a balloon. For *all previous experiences to the contrary* must be negated by some word, or the meaning is lost. A writer who finds *notwithstanding* unacceptable for this negative word had better give up *to the contrary* as well. The construction can often be replaced by *in spite of* or *despite,* with a gain in brevity: *in spite of all previous experiences.*

2. Dictionaries also enter *contrary* as an adverb, with *contrarily* as its first definition, and another serious trouble with the word is adverb trouble. Attempts at the adverbial use are frequent, and most of them are so lame that they breed a total skepticism about the utility of *contrary* as an adverb. One fact is certain: *contrary* and *contrarily* are not consistently interchangeable. *Behave contrarily* is acceptable diction, *behave contrary* not. Most attempts to make the word an adverb are followed by *to,* as in *They spend the winter in the larval stage and, contrary to southern countries, pupate in spring.* The sentence is rendered absurd, of course, by the attempt to contrast incommensurables—southern countries with pupation in the spring. To express accurately and without wordiness what is meant and to keep *contrary to* is so difficult that it is not worth the effort. Better be simple, and write *pupate in spring, as they do not in southern countries.*

Contrary, then, labors under formidable handicaps as an adverb. When we say that someone *acts contrary,* the word is no adverb, but a predicate adjective describing the person. When we say that someone *argues contrary to logic,* the word is an adverb modifying *argues,* but doing it incompetently; it is quite as shambling as *due to* in such a sentence as *He caught cold, due to exposure.* (See DUE TO.) The handy adjective makes a lubberly adverb. *Contrary to his usual practice, he sent the reviewer a letter of protest* has the cloudiness of many other attempts to make a single word gather up the matter wrapped in a whole clause, but it comes as near to clean English as the adverb can manage.

See also CONVERSE.

controversial. Twentieth-century politics in the democracies has so shifted the meaning of this word that it now seldom refers to actual controversy but more often to some latent quality in a person or an object that may provoke unfavorable comment. For example, *a controversial book* today is rarely one of which the purpose is polemics; rather, it is a book, possibly neutral in itself, that a person or group may disapprove of. Similarly, *a controversial figure* is one whose presence or background or opinions have aroused criticism. Thus a scientist who declines government aid for research in biological warfare might become a controversial figure if certain persons read a political mean-

ing into his decision. By adopting this usage we soon run into queer tautologies, such as *The Vietnam war is perhaps the most controversial in American history.* And by further extension we wind up with (1) a needless synonym for *divergent: This was the play that received controversial notices;* and (2) an absurd BACK FORMATION: *a controverted production of* Huck Finn [in] *San Francisco.*

What does this kidnaping of *controversial* leave us for characterizing a public speaker, an argument, a party that challenges another (. . . *and as controversial zeal soon turns its thoughts on force*—Burke)? We surely need to distinguish between the subject of controversy and the controversialists themselves. A controversial temperament is one thing; a quiet worker who has controversy explode around his ears is another. The only suggestions are to continue to use *controversial* in its former sense and to describe in as many words as necessary the pegs on which controversy hangs. This course has other merits than the linguistic, for *controversial* in the new sense may well degenerate into a tag for discrediting everybody who is not colorless, to the detriment of both democracy and the individual.

converse, obverse, reverse; opposite, contrary,

contradictory. 1. In logic, the *converse* of a proposition results from transposing the subject and the predicate. Here care must be taken to preserve for each term the degree of generality that it had in the original form. Thus the converse of the proposition *All Canadians are North Americans* cannot be *All North Americans are Canadians*, because the original proposition does not tell us anything about *all North Americans*; what it really says is *All Canadians are some North Americans* and the correct *converse* therefore is *Some North Americans are Canadians*.

2. The *obverse* is the negative counterpart of an affirmative proposition or the affirmative counterpart of a negative proposition. If we start with *Everyone is fallible,* an affirmative, then the obverse is *No one is infallible.* Both propositions must make the same assertion, but with the affirmative and negative terms changed each for each. (See also 5 below.)

3. Still in logic, *contrary* propositions are those in the relation of affirmative and negative within the same degree of generality. *All men are honest* and *No men are honest* are contraries. So are *Some men are honest* and *Some men are not honest.* In the first pair, both cannot be true and both may be false. In the second pair, only one

can be false and both may be true. Now if we relate No. 1 of the first pair with No. 2 of the second pair and No. 2 of the first pair with No. 1 of the second pair, we get two new pairs of propositions, which form *contradictories.* In contradictory pairs, the one must be true and the other false. If *All men are honest,* then it cannot be true that *Some men are not honest;* and if *No men are honest,* then it cannot be true that *Some men are honest.*

4. These logical relationships are grouped together under the heading of *opposition;* and as everybody knows, ordinary language calls *opposite* both contraries and contradictories. Similarly it uses *reverse* for both *obverse* and *converse* propositions. There is no need to refine on ordinary usage except when formal argumentation might make it convenient to separate two kinds of opposition or of conversion, in which case it would be best to use the established terms of logic. As for the common phrase *diametrically opposite,* it has no logical significance; it is merely emphatic. By vaguely suggesting opposite points on a circle or sphere, it applies equally well to *contraries* and *contradictories* and to *obverse* and *converse* propositions.

5. In speaking of coins or medals, the *obverse* is the main surface—say, that depicting a head or figure; the *reverse* is the other side.

convict, verb. A suspect is charged *with,* indicted *for,* and convicted (or acquitted) *of* something. He may also be convicted *on* a charge. There is a tendency, especially in newspaper writing, to borrow for *convict* the preposition that belongs to *indict* and thus to pervert an idiom. *Two suspended patrolmen were convicted yesterday in Special Sessions Court for* (of) *soliciting business in behalf of a lawyer / A. had once been acquitted for* (of) *a burglary charge and B. had been convicted for* (of) *bookmaking.*
See also ACCUSE.

convince. This word overlaps much of the territory covered by *persuade;* we either convince or persuade someone of the truth of a proposition or of the advisability of an action. But the two verbs are at an absolute parting of the ways when we try to make them lead into complementary infinitives with *to*—a construction that *persuade* accepts and *convince* refuses. We can convince a person *that* a statement is correct; we can convince him *of* its correctness; we cannot convince (though we can persuade) him to believe it or to act on the belief. In all the following examples *convince* is unidiomatic: *It was thought to have convinced a considerable*

number of doubtful electors to vote for the Constitution / suggested that the President had been convinced by Secretary Dulles to follow a war-like policy / to convince the candidate by the end of the campaign to read his speeches from a teleprompter / must convince the taxpayers and their legislatures to pay more of the costs of an education in the public institutions. In each of these examples *persuade* (or *prevail on*) would serve both meaning and idiom.

correlate, noun. Since T. S. Eliot coined the evil-sounding phrase *objective correlative,* the second word has flourished in critical journals, usually in close linkage with other words in *-tive.* It is therefore worth remembering that there is a noun *correlate* (like *precipitate, carbonate,* etc.), which sounds just as scientific and profound but a little less jingly.
It may also be useful to know that *cancel, carouse, capsize,* and numerous other verbs are in good standing as nouns. With this knowledge one can help reduce the crowd of words ending in *-al, -ment, -tion, -tive,* and *-ness*—the plague of modern prose.

correlative, noun. See CORRELATE.

council, counsel, consul. The ability to spell, pronounce, and use these three words is no longer the pons asinorum of literacy. Light on the mystery is as much needed by Ph.D. candidates as by stenographers. The main point to bear in mind is that the first two words should be held separate from the third, in pronunciation and in meaning. Concentrate first on the consular *(con,* not *cown)* service of the United States. Its *consuls* are persons working in *consulates,* who deliver passports, compile statistics, and serve as business agents. The ancient Roman *consuls* were like prime ministers and worked in pairs. Bonaparte made himself First Consul in 1799, and he was the last. The connections between the roots of *council, counsel,* and *consul* no longer affect our usage and had best be forgotten by those who get entangled in the words.

Counsel, as we know from marriage *counselors,* school or camp *counselors,* and lawyers in court (= *counsel* as a plural collective noun or *counselor* as a singular title), means to give advice: *The doctor counselled him to take a long rest / If you come to me for counsel, I'll give you some, but on condition that you don't follow it.* Most often, *counsel* is advice or the giving of advice.

A *council* is a public body or committee of persons set up to make policy or advise others

about making it. It is clear that a *council* counsels and that a *consul* may also *counsel.* But the differences are no less clear. The *City Council,* a group sitting at home; the United States *Consul,* a man sitting abroad; and the commodity furnished by doctor, lawyer, and priest are distinct and, once understood, easily kept apart. The annoying fact that lawyers, singly or in groups, call themselves *counsel* is an irregularity we can forgive when we have got thus far.

covering words. The progress of abstraction due to science has had a noticeable effect on the language, a chief fault of prose nowadays being its avoidance of concrete terms and active verbs (see SCIENTISM; NOUN-PLAGUE; -IZE). One aspect of this deviation from the plainer speech of our ancestors is the evident desire of writers to use terms whose generality and vagueness will cover a variety of possible particulars. CONTACT and COMMUNICATION are good instances. *Contact* as a verb exerts its attraction because it covers *write, speak, wire, call, send a messenger,* and indeed it may wind up meaning *I'll ask your secretary to remind you. Communication* is similarly substituted for *letter, memorandum, report, summons, money order,* or whatever, These uses remind one of

French classical tragedy and pre-Wordsworthian poetic diction, in which *charms* and *flames* and *bonds* repetitiously covered the multitudinous incidents and feelings of love.

In the modern vogue one should note the direction in which the abstractness is extended. *Communication* has always meant the (abstract) idea of conveying news or information, and it is still needed for this purpose. When the same word is made to stand for the actual letter or message *(The communication I left at your house yesterday)*, the abstraction is being stretched as it were downward toward particulars that should be expressed in words unmistakably concrete. The point is still more obvious in the train conductor's request to *Please take your transportation with you*, when he means *your ticket*.

Now, it is true that precedents exist for confusing the abstract and the concrete. We say *a conversation, a definition, an imposition, an inhibition* as well as *conversation, definition*, and the rest. The expression of a generality requires abstract words: *Evil communications corrupt good manners*. But the language already has too many words ending in *-tion*, which make the writing of agreeable prose difficult, and no fresh ones should be added when their place is well filled, as by *ticket* and *letter*.

Not all covering words are old abstract nouns in *-ion*. Some are new-minted singulars from established plurals: *a facility* for *a building and its equipment; an amenity* for *a comfortable lounge*, etc. Here again it can be seen how the meaning of *facility*—a general and abstract term for *ease in doing*—is elbowed out by the wish to dignify a set of concrete objects, such as a cyclotron and all its outhouses, now *a large scientific facility*. (A proposal to a foundation assured its readers that *no special facility is required for pianists*.)

The original *facilities* was a covering word too, but it honestly disclosed its generality of intention by the plural mark of indefiniteness. Such phrases as *smokers' requisites, writing materials*, and *men's furnishings* are obviously useful, but who would want them to displace *pipe, pen*, and *necktie* as *communication* and *facility* are displacing *letter* and *building*? Very rarely indeed does the complexity of a plan or a business require covering words. *Classroom and laboratory space* is clearer and manlier than *student-station usage*. What perversity inspires the modern mind to fill workaday prose with these indefinite *essentials, basics, components, specifics*, and *co-ordinates*?

Similarly, *processing* is a word that covers *doing whatever is necessary. We will process your application, your medical history, your old raincoat, your sinful soul.* Why not simply say: *We will consider your application, study your case, repair your raincoat, purge your soul?* For the indefinable *processing* as in *The delay in delivery was due to processing,* it is better (because less pompous) to say *handling.* Again, if the speaker or writer can summon up more than one vague idea to cover all the events (he would say *eventualities*) of the day, he will find he has no need to repeat *structure* (verb), *motivation, orientation, development, expansion, potential, realism,* or *activity* (*leisuretime activity*) for the many hundreds of different events and qualities he has in mind. And, having exerted himself so far as to say what he means, he will find that his "problem of communication" has been partly solved.

See also CASE; CHARACTER; LEVEL; NATURE.

crafted. See NEEDLESS WORDS.

crave. See PREPOSITIONS.

creative. See JOURNALESE.

credulity. See MALAPROPS.

critics' words. Nothing is more difficult than writing about the arts, literature included. To do so daily, weekly, or even monthly has proved a strain that the minds best endowed for this sort of work can withstand for only a few years. One ought therefore to be charitable to those who tell us every morning what the play or concert was like or what the gallery exhibition showed forth. But critics tend to ease their labors by fashioning for themselves vocabularies which are neither technical nor plainly descriptive, and which therefore must be reproved as jargon.

The generic fault lies with epithets. The recurrent ones are metaphorical, or at least transferred from common use, and they soon cease to mean anything except approval or disapproval. The reader will recognize the excesses committed with the aid of *crisp, firm, sensitive, sophisticated, alert,* MASTERFUL, and *structured;* as well as with the phrases *imaginative control, deep-lying irony, wide context, dialectical tension,* and *repeated insight.* He may not have met *utter dispassion* or *efflorescent ambit,* but it makes no difference: none of these terms means very much. And still others, which begin by having a meaning, do not keep it long when turned to daily use: *apocalyptic, charisma, commitment, compassion, discourse, disturbing, empathy, epiphany, evocative, existen-*

tial, IDENTIFY, *ironic, insightful*, MEANINGFUL, *perceptive, persona, sensibility, simplistic, stimulating*, etc. The best critics are those who use the plainest words and who make their taste rational by describing actions rather than by reporting or imputing feelings. Whitman's advice to critics is still the best: "Nothing is better than simplicity ... nothing can make up for lack of definiteness."

See also SAKE, FOR ITS OWN; VOGUE WORDS.

crucial. See JOURNALESE.

crushing. See JOURNALESE.

cryptic. See JOURNALESE.

curtains. See SKILL (s).

D

dangerous pairs. The drawing of distinctions between related words—say by a teacher or an editor—arouses in some people an impatience expressed in a tone or gesture which seems to say, "Don't expect a person engaged in high pursuits to observe minute differences; the general idea is the same regardless of the ending or prefix I use."

Whoever is thus put in his place may think that his interlocutor is annoyed at being asked to make distinctions of meaning, but this is not so. When the words are far apart in sound, like *wet* and *damp, wildness* and *wilderness,* everybody is ready to distinguish, and anybody will be allowed to correct anybody else who, he thinks, has chosen the wrong term for the occasion. It is only when a distinction is expressed by confusable words that suddenly it appears unworthy of attention. Yet it is clear that there is economy in making the difference reside in some change of form; and it is equally clear that the refusal to observe the many distinctions-by-suffix is mere laziness of mind. The suffix, of course, is most often but not always the point of difference.

Sometimes a different root is embedded in a word whose beginning and ending duplicate another's. The richer a language is and the more symmetrical its "architecture," the more pairs and triplets will occur to betray the unseeing.

A long list could—and perhaps should—be made of the words that speakers and writers often interchange to the detriment of their meaning. A random choice would certainly include the following, of which those in small capitals are discussed elsewhere in this book. Only a few of those listed warrant the additional space for comments; all can be differentiated with the aid of a dictionary.

abjure, adjure.
acceptance, acceptation.
acter, actor.
ADHERENCE, ADHESION.
adjudge, adjudicate.
ADMINISTER, MINISTER.
AND; BUT.
ANXIOUS, EAGER.
assured, insured (see ASSURE, ENSURE, INSURE).
autarky, autarchy (see SPELLING).
bi-, semi-(weekly, etc.).
COMPOSE, COMPRISE (nothing can be said to be *comprised of* . . .).

compulsive, compulsory (the first is from within, an obsession).

CONCEPT, CONCEPTION (the first is not for daily use).

confound, confuse.

CONSTANT; CONTINUAL.

contemptible, contemptuous.

CONTINUAL, CONTINUOUS.

COUNCIL, COUNSEL, CONSUL.

deceiving, deceptive.

decry, descry.

defer, delay.

definite, definitive.

DELINEATE, delimit.

DEMEAN, BEMEAN (think: is demeanor demeaning?).

deprecate, depreciate.

discomfit, discomfort.

distinct, distinctive.

elemental, elementary (see ENDINGS 1).

enormity, enormousness.

EUPHEMISM, euphuism.

EXCESSIVELY, EXCEEDINGLY.

exhausting, exhaustive.

exposure, exposé, exposition.

feasible, possible.

FELICITOUS, FORTUITOUS.

flout, flaunt.

heartburn, heartburning (or the stomach versus the soul).

home, house (*homes* are not bought and sold, *houses* are).

IMPLICIT, EXPLICIT.

IMPLY, INFER.

import, importance.

inchoate, incoherent (the first means only *beginning*—and perhaps *not fully formed*).

infest, infect.

ingenious, ingenuous.

intense, intensive.

intent, intention.

JUDICIAL, JUDICIOUS (the first requires a bench).

labor, belabor (one labors a

point and belabors an opponent).

LIBEL, SLANDER.

lie, lay, laid.

loan, lend.

luxuriant, luxurious (see MALAPROPS).

militate, mitigate (the first *fights against*, the second *softens*).

nauseous, nauseate (what the first is like causes the second).

need, necessity.

offending, offensive.

perspicacious, perspicuous.

PRAGMATIC, practical.

precipitate, precipitous (see ENDINGS 1).

primal, primary (see ENDINGS 1).

PRIOR TO, before.

PROSELYTE, proselytize.

REMEDIABLE, REMEDIAL.

SANCTION (noun and verb).

seasonal, seasonable.

sewage, sewerage.

SPECIFIC, particular.

subject (to), subjected (to).

supposititious, suppositious.

TRANSFER, TRANSFORM.

VERBAL, oral.

visit, visitation (see CONNOTATIONS).

To show how the failure to distinguish puts the writer at the mercy of those who habitually sort out meanings, here are three examples of words not listed above and misused in conspicuous places. We read in a large newspaper ad: *Sample findings:* Life's *single issue and accumulative audience* (cumulative; an accumulative audience would be one that piled up riches). In a popular modern novel: *She looked across at his heavy brow, so suddenly bowed with grief, and on impulse suggested retirement* (retiring; the context makes it clear that a good night's rest, not a withdrawal from business, was the hostess's happy thought). In a story of crime a teacher of English tells us that a respectable person *had had an assignment with the murderer* (assignation; the obsession with school assignments may be pleaded in excuse).

See also CONNOTATIONS and PRACTICAL.

danglers. 1. It is a pity that American prescriptive grammar never put into currency a more precise name for what the textbooks call the *dangling participle*. Anything that dangles is attached at one point while elsewhere hanging free. *Dangling,* which is generally used to characterize an unattached participle, would more truly describe one that is properly hung and obedient to rule. For an orthodox participle has but one possible point of attachment, the subject of a main verb, and if it clings to that, it is performing the chief duty of participles. A participle that lacks this one fixed point is not dangling in any proper sense: it is totally unanchored, unmoored, unlinked, adrift, floating, disconnected, loose—any one of these terms would be more ex-

pressive than *dangling.* Fowler calls such a participle *unattached.* For better or for worse, however, *dangling participle* has become the label generally understood in America, and there is no getting away from it. *Danglers* is used in this book to denote, not only participles of faulty reference, but other constructions that similarly flout the obligation to maintain the bond between the subjects of related clauses.

There is no doubt that the language, which is always undergoing a loosening in some departments and a tightening in others, has been evolving since the late eighteenth century in the direction of a much tighter logic in the management of participles, especially those that begin sentences. Most of the eighteenth-century classic authors were satisfied with an introductory participle if it referred to a noun present anywhere in the sentence, in whatever construction, or even if it referred to an absent one easily supplied. The liberty claimed for participles down to the time of Lamb and Hazlitt is illustrated in the Old Farmer's Almanac version of an anecdote about Richard Brinsley Sheridan: *Sheridan was once staying at the house of an elderly maiden lady who wanted more of his company than he was willing to give. Proposing, one day, to take a stroll with him, he excused himself on account of the bad-*

ness of the weather. It was the maiden lady that did the proposing; she is present only in the preceding sentence, and only in a very subordinate construction. But the passage does not violate the canons of Sheridan's generation or the next. Today, all writers except the most heedless would feel that the second sentence must begin *When she proposed,* affixing the action to its author, or else that the subject of the second sentence must be *she,* pinning the participle to the author of the action. In the rhetorics published after, say, 1880, such sentences are cited as horrible examples, along with howlers from student themes—*Sitting on the porch last night, a comet and five shooting stars were seen*—and specimens of that order. The New International Dictionary exemplifies the dangler with *leaping to the saddle, his horse bolted* and *walking home, an accident was seen.* The modern doctrine, which codifies the modern feeling, is that a participle at the head of a sentence automatically affixes itself to the subject of the following verb—in effect a requirement that the writer either make his subject consistent with the participle or discard the participle for some other construction. A typical example of nonobservance: *Swinburne was not entirely consistent. Yet, speaking now as poet and esthetic critic, there was logic in his pro-*

nouncement. Reshaped on one system, this might read: *he had logic in his pronouncement;* on the other system, *Yet in what he said as poet . . . there was logic.*

The illustrations of danglers in textbooks run rather disproportionately to the present (active) participle in *-ing,* doubtless because beginning writers tend to overuse it. In experienced writers the fault is neither very common nor very rare. A university fund-raising campaign explains: *Feeling that proximity to X. Library was an important factor in locating a humanities center, it was determined that Q. Hall was an ideal place for such facilities.* The sentence promises to tell who had the feeling and then cheats the expectation aroused. It could have escaped the fault by beginning *Because it was felt that.* (For the use of *facilities* in this sentence, see COVERING WORDS.) In the next sentence the participle refers to the wrong person, or at least to one wrong person: *So, hastily making a few preparations for himself and his fourteen-year-old brother . . . , the two . . . left Brooklyn by train on Friday.* Note that the tense of the participle is as dubious as its reference: accuracy requires *having made.* Ease and simplicity would be better served by *As soon as he had made a few hasty preparations he and his . . . brother . . .* A new twist appears in *Lacking a new Chesterton, it is good that Dorothy Collins, who worked with G. K. C., has given us . . . a selection.* This looks like an attempt to erect the participle into a so-called nominative absolute, equivalent to *A new Chesterton being lacking.* Most participles do not lend themselves to such a use, but some do. Among the compliant are *pending* and *failing;* one could actually write *Failing a new Chesterton* (= in default of a new Chesterton).

After a sentence about the Englishman Henry Bryan Binns, a literary biography continues: *While in this country collecting material, an admirer of Whitman in California told Binns his theory of the poet's being the father of some children in New Orleans.* It was Binns, not the California admirer, who was in this country collecting material. Here it is not merely the participle *collecting* that is adrift; it is the entire opening phrase, which includes it. A sensible reading: *Binns, while in this country collecting material, was told by an admirer of Whitman.* More subtly askew is *extending* in the next sentence: *To the north of Fulton, gradually extending eastward . . . , cheap frame houses were being built for the families of the day laborers.* One could say that houses extended eastward, provided that they were there to begin with and the spectator reported their extent from a fixed point of view. What ruins this possibility is the *gradually* and the *being built,* which suggest actual motion and thus absurdity. Rewrite: *In an area north of Fulton and gradually to be extended eastward.*

Writers should not forget that the empire of a main verb, or of its subject, reaches forward in a sentence as well as back, controlling present participles to the end of the clause; that is, a participle does not have to precede the subject in order to be unanchored. *Should we win our fight in the courts, thus permitting us to use public funds* shows the point. The participle needs to go with a noun that provides a clear answer to the question Who or what permits? But there is no such noun, and the participle, essentially adjectival, is trying to modify a verb, *win.* The meaning is: *Should we win . . . and thus become entitled to use.* Slightly different underneath a superficial resemblance is *including* in *He . . . frequently wrote tenderly of children—including his perennial campaign against the cruelty of teachers in the classroom.* This *including* is the participial adjective that means *inclusive of,* and it is so nearly divorced from the verb *include* as to claim a separate entry in dictionaries, though the New International omits it. It has not the participial obligation to the subject of a main verb, but it has an obligation to the agent of inclusion, which does not appear in the sentence. It was the subject's writings that included his perennial campaign. Once more an adjective is asked to modify a verb, and the sentence will not readily accommodate *including*. A tolerable revision might be *He often wrote tenderly of children and kept up his perennial campaign . . .*

Some present participles, technically unhitched, are much less objectionable than those with a flagrantly false reference, because they actually modify a subject that is present and named, though they have to jump a gap to do it. *Being a citizeness of the world's smoothest roads it was small wonder that she was quick to recognize* could not be called a shipshape sentence; the grammatical clause that does the work is not the logical one. But at least there is no contradiction of the logical subject by the participle, which one might classify as a semi-dangler.

2. In books and periodicals —whatever may be said of student themes—the mismanaged past (passive) participle has become much more common than the mismanaged present (active) one. For example: *He regarded slavery as wrong, but until abolished by the action or consent of the states, the Constitution must not be violated even to combat slav-* *ery.* This shadowing forth of political subversion can be cleared up by the simple insertion of *slavery was* after *until*. The word *written* in the hands of the Sunday reviewer is peculiarly susceptible to isolation. *Written by one of T.'s personal friends and filled with touching anecdotes and never-before-told incidents, no account could come closer to the truth* (patently, only *this account* could bear the features ascribed to *no account*) / *Written with affection and mercy, this sensitive Mr. C. tells an old, sad, human tale* (What is written with affection and mercy by . . . Mr. C. is . . .). *Put,* when it means *phrased*, demands a vigilance that it often fails to get: *Put another way, both broadcasting and the press perform related yet different functions / Put another way, this feat has shown that the sending of rockets to the moon . . . is entirely feasible in the years immediately ahead / Put another way, the Soviet scientists would not have been willing to agree if their masters in Moscow had not said they might.* None of these says what is put another way; each *put* refers to something outside the sentence and grammatically unconnected with it. The labor-saving cure is *in other words, that is to say*, or some similar nonparticipial expression. And for every *put* that fails to tell us what is put, a BASED ON evades the question

What is based? *Based on a private survey, it* [a firm of investment consultants] *has concluded that the decline in capital expenditures by corporations is indeed over / Based on velocity data measured at Cape Canaveral, the eight vernier rockets were fired by radio command.* What is based is, in the first example, the conclusion; in the second, the firing —both absent, with the result that again an adjectival word is deprived of its mate. This unattached *based* appears all too often in writings about economics and finance, and probably springs from the desire to get away from the wordiness of *on the basis of* (or wrongly *that*), which, though grammatical, verges on jargon. The way to escape it without also throwing coherence overboard is to take the trouble of thinking out what is meant in each statement. Our first example seems to mean *A private survey leads to the conclusion;* the second, *Velocity data . . . made it possible to fire* or *were used in firing* (see EFFECTIVE). The passive participle stationed anywhere but at the beginning will, indeed, modify the nearest preceding substantive unless prevented. But like its brother, the present participle, it has to modify the intended word. It will surely miss if it is just shot into the air in the common way of *put* and *based.*

3. Various nonparticipial elements, when they occur at the beginnings of clauses, have precisely the obligation of participles to seek grammatical bonds with the subjects. Like participles, they can go adrift; like bad participles, they can miss right meanings and express wrong ones.

By far the most frequent of such intractable elements are those introduced by the grammatically identical antonyms *like, unlike.* Their mismanagement results in the comparison of incomparables: *Like another Philadelphian, Benjamin Franklin, Dr. Squibb's interests were catholic / Unlike the conditions prevailing in most verbal exchanges, some of the judges . . . have unhampered access to but one side of the issues under consideration.* By dangling like *based* or any present participle, *like* and *unlike* in the sentences above say that Dr. Squibb's interests resembled Benjamin Franklin, and that certain judges differed from certain conditions. Read: *Dr. Squibb's interests, like Franklin's, . . . / . . . , those under which some judges work allow them access to . . .* In a likeness or an unlikeness you are pledged to make your next words name the person or thing that embodies it. (See LIKE 2.)

4. *As* in its ordinary comparative meaning also gives rise to danglers, especially where it is resorted to in order to dodge a distrusted but desirable *like*. It is, in fact, one of the ironies of composition that *like*, which produces danglers when it is the wrong word, will also encourage them by its absence when it is the needed word. *As everywhere else, Massachusetts will be holding elections Tuesday* / *As with Leo Durocher, it is not for nothing he is called The Lip* (see AS 9) / *As in football, where the query went: "What's become of the Irish of Notre Dame?" boxing has had its problems.* Massachusetts holding elections as everywhere else? Someone called The Lip as with Leo Durocher? Boxing beset with problems as in football? What bizarre statements! Why not say simply: *Massachusetts, like other states* / *He, like Leo Durocher, is called The Lip* / *Boxing, like football, has had its problems.*

For similar troubles with *as* meaning *in the capacity of*, see AS 1.

5. A noun in descriptive apposition—a simpler construction than any of the foregoing —has the same propensity to go adrift from the subject with which it should agree. When you read a sentence beginning *Daughter of a millionaire, transformer of philosophies, passionate politician,* you know that the inevitable next word is *she*; alas for inevitability, the sentence goes on: *a wit of the day said of her . . .* The indicated subject is likewise tossed overboard in

A soldier's soldier, the Army would have followed any road with him / *One of the famous "few" immortalized by Churchill . . . , X.'s life . . . was full of action and drama.* The commonest position for these ungrammatical appositives is the introductory one. When they follow, the effect is likely to be even stranger—witness *The quote is his, a man of spirit.* What the writer of this sentence needed was an adroit editor. As two sentences the words would pass (supposing one can swallow *quote* as a noun): *The quote is his. A man of spirit!*

danglers, acceptable. Some present participles have so far lost their obligation to serve nouns as adjectives that they have in effect become prepositions, parts of prepositional phrases, or adverbs. *Considering,* one of the commonest, is a handy representative of the class: like many other members, it may be either an outright preposition, meaning *in view of* (*Considering the deficiencies of his education, his career has been extraordinary*), or it may remain a conventional participle modifying the subject of a following clause (*Considering his situation likely to go from bad to worse, he decided to offer his resignation*). *Considering,* then, is a sample of that middle group between the words that have practically ceased to be participles at all, such as *according*, and those, such as *going*, that remain so prevailingly participial as to seem unattached and dangling in a nonparticipial use (*And going through the city there was very little friendly response by the men in the trucks to the wildly cheering civilians*). *According*, to be sure, can still have a participial function (*According perfectly in their fundamental tastes, they achieved one of the most successful collaborations on record*), but many might think this use odd if not archaic, and certainly it has become rare; whereas almost anyone might write *the Gospel according to Mark* or might say *according to my way of thinking*. *Concerning* is another such completely transformed participle. Still another, *owing* (*to*), has the great usefulness of doing acceptably what is often asked of the grammarless DUE TO, for which it can generally be substituted.

Other words often encountered in nonparticipial uses, some admissible and some dubious, are *acknowledging, admitting, allowing, assuming, barring, beginning, conceding, depending, excluding, granting, including, leaving, looking, meaning, providing, reading* (as in *reading from left to right*), *reckoning, recognizing, regarding, speaking* (as in *broadly speaking*), *taking* (*account of, into account*), and *viewing*. This list is far from complete: there is no limit to the number of participles that writers try to enfranchise as something else. Still, it will be noticed that a majority of the converted participles denote some kind of mental or sensory activity; they are from verbs of thinking or perceiving. Some illustrative contexts follow, with all comment momentarily suspended:

Acknowledging the force of what you say, it is necessary to call attention to what you do not say / Admitting his competence, there is reason to distrust his general attitude / Allowing for reasonable delays, the job should be done by April / Assuming that the train is on time, there will be an hour for luncheon / You may count on it, barring accident / Conceding all that, there is no blinking the fact that / Granting that in thought a man may travel far from his own center, . . . experience brings him home / He looks down on everybody, including his betters / Leaving the High Arctic and going south, August is likely to show / guarantees continued support of scholarship students after freshman year, providing only that the student is in satisfactory standing / But viewing it from this distance, such fears seem at the very least exaggerated.

The difficulty of arriving at a fixed principle about this class of words suggests that they do not truly constitute a homogeneous class. What they show is a series of stages in the course of adding a prepositional or adverbial use to an original and inherent participial use. *Concerning* has become a preposition equivalent to *about* or *on the subject of;* *regarding* is perhaps similarly converted, though its effect is pompous wherever a shorter and simpler preposition would do. (Even so, it is less forbidding than *as regards;* see AS 6.) At the other end of the scale, such a word as *looking* tries to perform the nonparticipial function at so early a stage that the word will often strike an analytical observer as unmoored. *Looking seaward . . . , eleven lighthouses are visible* is of a piece with certain grotesque examples of the dangling participle in old-fashioned rhetorics. Less grotesque but hardly less loose is the *looking* in such sentences as this: *He was, looking back with the perspective of a century later, entirely justified in his contempt for the sixteenth and seventeenth terms of the Presidency.* Here the fairly observant reader wants to know who (we? anyone?) does the looking, and the careful writer will tell him. Many ill-advised laxities result from the assumption that certain participles have acquired prepositional or adverbial functions that they cannot actually perform, though they may acquire these powers in the end. Each

writer has to make his own judgments if he wants to resort to the liberalized uses of these words. He can look to dictionaries for the notation of a tendency but not for a definitive statement of how far the tendency has gone.

What is certain is that any such block of illustrations as the foregoing will draw comments as various as the status of the words illustrated. The loose constructionist will accept practically all the examples as desirable expansions of linguistic resources. The purist will deplore most of them as laxities. The less stringently critical observer will find some acceptable, others dubious, and still others revolting. The same person might reasonably defend *You may count on it, barring accident* and as reasonably condemn *Leaving the High Arctic . . . , August is likely to show.*

General principles aside for the moment, certain of the quasi-participles under review might well be avoided on the ground of accuracy or idiom or both. Two such present participles, *granting* and *providing,* are best replaced with the past (passive) participles *granted* and *provided* in the so-called absolute construction: *Granted that in thought a man may travel / provided only that the student is in satisfactory standing.* It is noticeable that in many sentences the words we are dealing with have a conditional force; they mean *if* one considers, acknowledges, assumes, begins, concedes, etc., and a gain in accuracy will often result from the replacement of a marginal or suspect participle by *if* with a finite verb. It is also noticeable that many such *-ing* forms can be advantageously replaced, as *granting* and *providing* can, with the past participle. If our imaginary arbiter has qualms about, for example, *Reading from bottom to top, the table shows*, and points out that a neater way to cover the same meaning would be *The table, read from bottom to top, shows*, only an extreme advocate of lounging English would gainsay him. A similarly desirable tightening accompanies *His competence admitted / Reasonable delays allowed for / All that conceded / his betters included*, etc.

Another anarchic word is *depending*, which invariably loses itself in a void if not attached to some substantive. In *Public response may be either enthusiastic or apathetic, depending on unpredictable factors*, it is not public response that depends, nor would enthusiasm and apathy, even if they were present in those forms. What depends is whether public response is this or that—a complex idea that *depending* is not competent to modify. The author meant *Whether public response is enthusiastic or apathetic depends*,

and he might have done worse than write it so. The faulty reference is patent whenever this dubious *depending* is replaced by its corresponding adjective: *He predicted more Friday evening sessions, dependent upon the joint decision of the council and the Recreation Commission*. What is dependent is whether the sessions will be held or not; and we see that the adjective, like *depending*, cannot work as a tolerable modifier of something left unnamed.

Speaking, as in the stock phrase *generally speaking*, can hardly be construed as anything but a participle, yet it has become completely emancipated from participial agreement: few readers would think of taking exception to *generally speaking the King's will was God's will*, in a brilliant modern biography. When, in the same book, we encounter *He was, generally speaking, Edward's younger uncle*, we are disconcerted, not by a point of grammar, but by the riddle of what is meant.

On the practical plane, it is expedient for a writer who has a penchant for converted participles to avoid uses that might confuse them with unconverted ones. That is, he should take pains to give his following main clause a subject that cannot possibly be modified by the *-ing* word construed as a conventional participle. *Assuming this docu-*

ment to be authentic, we have to revise the previous interpretations of B.'s ruling motive. This sentence ought to mean, by simple virtue of its construction, that *we* makes the assumption named; but how can we know whether the first phrase does not simply mean *on the assumption that* or *if it be assumed*? Such a sentence is ambiguous and therefore bad, or at least improvable. If it begins with *assuming*, it would do better to continue *the previous interpretations ... have to be revised*. This kind of construction stakes out an unequivocal claim to the non-participial use of *assuming* by avoiding the suggestion that there is participial agreement with the subject. Whether the sentence could not be made a radically better one by doing without *assuming* is a separate question.

dare(d). See UNSAVORY PASTS.

data. The Latin language, nothing like so dead as some people think, registers outrage when the unchanged Latin neuter plural (of *datum*) is treated as a singular—e.g. *exact data has not been available until quite recently*. Sometimes the culprits are found in unexpected places. FALLOUT DATA IS GOAL is a *New York Times* headline. A series of bulletins issued by the Department of Defense reads: *Additional information ... will be reported as the data is transmitted to the tracking stations*. On the evidence, it is too soon to say that *data* is slowly turning into an English singular like *agenda*—i.e. *data, datas*. Possibly we should think ourselves fortunate if we can escape *datae*.

Those who treat *data* as a singular doubtless think of it as a generic noun, comparable to *knowledge* or *information: How is all this data used?* The mistake is easy for anyone who has no feeling for Latin, and it is paralleled by many English usages that are not mistakes; witness the difference between *potato* (several or many potatoes converted into a homogeneous substance, as by mashing) and *potatoes* (individual tubers), or between *radio* (broadcasting in general) and *radios* (receiving sets). The rationale of *agenda* as a singular is its use to mean a collective program of action, rather than separate items to be acted on. But there is as yet no obligation to change the number of *data* under the influence of error mixed with innovation.

See also INSIGNE, INSIGNIA; LATIN AND GREEK PLURALS.

de (French). See TITLES AND PROPER NAMES 5.

decisionmaking. See VOGUE WORDS.

defensibles. Persons whose interest in words has led them to books on usage are doubtless familiar with the standard warnings about some half dozen words that are commonly misapplied. The question that the thoughtful must resolve for themselves is whether they will heed the warnings or follow the crowd. Will they say and write *mutual friend* for *friend in common*? Do they APPRECIATE a favor you have done them? And what of *aggravate, anticipate, (self-) deprecatory, meticulous, shambles,* and *trivia*?

In calling them *defensibles* in this article the intimation is that the misuses impugned have gone on long enough in the absence of good alternatives to warrant their being accepted without further cavil. Of those listed, *aggravate* is perhaps the one least entitled to mercy, for we have *annoy, irritate, put upon, rile,* and *vex* to do the work. Yet *gravel* (verb) in that same sense exerts a possibly unnoticed pull and makes *aggravating* at least defensible.

For *appreciate* in the sense of *value* (not the business sense of *increase* in value) there is no ready substitute. No one can say *I valued your saying those kind words / I value your point but must disagree with it.* No, *appreciate* now seems indispensable. Similarly, *anticipate* in the sense of *looking forward* is a great convenience. It means both

more and less than *expect,* and in expressions of politeness comes very pat: *Anticipating your acceptance I will make everything ready.* The shade here is halfway between the sense of *counting on* and that of *forestalling, jumping the gun.* In the eighteenth century *prevent* was used for this latter meaning, which now must be borne by *forestall* and *anticipate.*

To be forced to say (*self-*) *depreciatory* or *a depreciatory gesture* is to be made to say more than one intends. A *deprecatory cough* is very likely the phrase that has enlarged the meaning of *deprecatory* (= praying against) to include the acts and hints of mild or purely formal depreciation now generally called *deprecatory.* And going in the opposite way, *meticulous* has lost its overtone of fear and come to seem the right word for *exceedingly careful,* just as *shambles* has lost the idea of bloodshed and remains expressive of a general mess.

As for *mutual friend, mutual interest,* and other combinations where *mutual* means *common,* adherence to the second and preferable word would not be difficult in itself. *Common interest* is in fact heard as often as the other, and no one supposes that it means *vulgar interest. So-and-so is, I believe, our common friend* would be similarly clear. But Dickens' title has clamped down the error of one of his low-life characters upon the English-speaking world and it will probably not be shaken off.

definitely. This has been one of the persistent VOGUE WORDS of the century. It is used both in and out of print to replace with a standardized noise the meanings of *decidedly, emphatically, clearly, indisputably, certainly, absolutely, assuredly, far and away, hands down, yes indeed, beyond argument,* and numerous other expressions of assent or emphasis. For example, an often heard radio commercial assures us that a certain sherry is *definitely the connoisseur's preference.* A drama critic says a play is *definitely a vehicle unworthy* of the actress who stars in it. Most uses of the word are not grossly objectionable, merely tiresome and less than exact.

delicious. See VOGUE WORDS.

delineate. Since the prominent trial of an unscrupulous businessman some years ago, this word has come into frequent use as a needless substitute for *mark off, separate, demarcate.* In that trial, the accused, the lawyers, and some of the witnesses kept saying sentences of the type: *Now, can you delineate between the ones that have been negotiated and the ones still held by the company? To delineate* properly means to draw a line around, rather than to draw a line between. Accordingly, it is a synonym for *describe,* not for *distinguish,* and the following uses are wrong: *There should be a delineation between his views and those of other authors* (a line drawn) / *A meeting will be held in Washington to delineate offshore fishing rights* (define, mark off, establish).

See also CONNOTATIONS.

demean, bemean. An excellent and long-standing word, *bemean* means *abase, degrade, vilify,* or *impair the dignity of.* Every consideration but one is in its favor: it is self-defining and unmistakable in sense; it is unambiguous and not in request for any other meaning; it incorporates the adjective *mean,* and its prefix, *be-,* characteristically means *make, cause to be,* as in *bejeweled.* Good writers have long used it, and with frequency; rhetoricians and purists have recommended it in their admonitions against its competitor, *demean.* Meanwhile this competitor has every recommendation from usage but one drawback: it is identical in sound and spelling with the indispensable verb (cf. *demeanor*) that means *behave* or *comport oneself* and is therefore too easily mistaken for it. A characteristic sense of its prefix, *de-,* like *un-* or *dis-*, is *make otherwise, cause not to be,* as in *deform, debase, degrade,* etc. Some careful writers have used *demean* (= bemean), but some more careful ones have recoiled from it; how many or on what grounds we cannot know, since abstention and its motives are hard to prove. It is a safe guess that no writer whose vocabulary includes *bemean* would use *demean* in lieu of it.

The controlling consideration, however, is that the word with less to be said for it has virtually supplanted the one with more to be said for it. *Demean* is now so common that its occurrences far outnumber those of *bemean,* which fewer and fewer writers seem to be even aware of; and even the other *demean* (= conduct oneself) is less in evidence than the *demean* that many still frown on. *With an air that clearly implied he found the role of salesman demeaning / attempts to demean this victory by an appeal to things that are of no consequence*—such uses are familiar to multitudes of readers who find only strangeness in the strict use of the word: *Any United States citizen who demeans himself as becomes his character is entitled to the protection of his Government.* The truth that *demean* in this sense is neutral, not derogatory—just like *demeanor,* which nobody misunderstands

—is hard to get accepted. What helps to make it hard, very likely, is the reflexive: *demean oneself* seems irresistibly to imply *lower oneself,* while the unreflexive *demeanor* vaguely suggests *mien,* which strengthens the meaning *behavior.*

It is a writer's privilege to grant himself the freedom of the pejorative *demean* and to insist that usage has made it standard. But it is also his privilege to let the word alone, if only on the ground that it is often wise to avoid what some judicious persons object to. The argument from mere precedent which takes the form "If it was good enough for Thackeray, it's good enough for me," could make one's writing a mere concentration of solecisms, since every good writer has resorted to expressions without which he would have been a better writer. *Bemean* is still automatically clear for the uses that *demean* serves dubiously; there is, in fact, nothing against *bemean* except this: set from clear copy, it will come out of composing rooms as *demean* three times in ten. Not every usage that is defensible is desirable, and it may be that any writer gains more than he loses by deciding to leave the pejorative *demean* to those who care for it.

These remarks have, of course, no bearing whatever on the status of the noncommittal *demean* (from the Old French *desmener*—to manage), which means simply *behave*. But the existence of its homonym requires a writer to use the older word in a way that prevents confusion with the newer one. A great merit of *bemean* is that it requires no such precaution. The use of it in a commencement address by the governor of a New England state is of admirable nicety: *There is a compelling need in our personal lives and in the lives of all nations for a sabbatical leave so that we may ponder the nature and meaning of life, seek to learn how our conscience would have us behave, and cleanse our minds and souls of that which bemeans.*

dependent, depending (on.) See DANGLERS, ACCEPTABLE.

deprecatory, depreciatory. See DEFENSIBLES.

develop. See VOGUE WORDS.

devil to pay. A great deal of nautical lingo came ashore in the days of wooden ships and iron men, and much of it underwent alteration in the transfer. A crude example is *sheet*, which often gets into print in contexts that show the writers to be thinking of a sail rather than of a piece of cordage (or, in square sail, of chain)—or what the landsman calls a rope. Confusion is compounded by the circumstance that *sheet* was anciently poetic for *sail*. It would be entertaining to know what proportion of those who read Allan Cunningham's verse *A wet sheet and a flowing sea* think of drenched canvas rather than of a line wetted by spray. The *sheet* that means cordage and the *sheet* that means a fabric are different words, differently derived, but there is nothing in their form to tell us so.

Curious things have happened to sea talk ashore, and none more so than the fate that long ago overtook *the devil to pay*. *Devil* has been applied to all sorts of things that make or suggest mischief or behave intractably—a bird, a flower, a tree, and a machine, among others; and the dragonfly is popularly a *devil's darning needle*. Seamen applied the word to a ship's seam difficult of access and given to developing leaks—whether they meant the seam at the waterline or that at the waterways is in dispute; perhaps both. Anyway, it had to be *payed* (preferably not *paid*) from time to time; that is, waterproofed with pitch, tar, tallow, resin, or what not. (*Pay* = Latin *picare, from pix* = pitch; unconnected with *pay* = requite or reimburse.) Whence the proverbial marine expression for an impossible predicament, a hopeless fix:

The devil to pay and no pitch hot. The same *devil* appears in *between the devil and the deep* as a definition of an insoluble dilemma; in this expression *deep* probably meant, not the sea, but the part of a sounding line between fathoms. The Shorter Oxford Dictionary, though it supplies the foregoing nautical definition of *devil*, says of *the devil to pay* that it is "supposed to refer to bargains made by wizards, etc., with Satan, and the inevitable payment in the end"; and one might read miscellaneously for years without once encountering the phrase in its traditional sense. (SEE POPULARIZED TECHNICALITIES.)

dialectal, dialectical. Since the very form of these adjectives (as of their adverbs) associates the first with dialect, the second with dialectic(s), confusion ensues when *dialectical* is connected with the regional usages of a language or when, as happens less commonly, *dialectal* is connected with logical disputation. The interchange is frequent enough to get itself recorded in dictionaries, and the application of either adjective to either noun can be justified by impressive examples. In the authoritative *Words and Their Ways in English Speech* (Greenough and Kittredge) we find *the full phrase is dialectic as both noun and verb / many Scan-dinavian words did not survive the Middle English period, except dialectically / apparently a dialectic English word,* etc. (It is only fair to add that in 1901, the date of the first printing of Greenough and Kittredge, *dialectal* was much less firmly established than it is now.) Nevertheless it is common sense to ignore these permissive precedents by holding *dialectal* to the meaning for which it was made—i.e. *related to a provincial form of speech*—and by reserving *dialectical* for reference to a logic or its theory, as in *dialectical materialism*.

dialogue. See VOGUE WORDS.

dichotomy. See POPULARIZED TECHNICALITIES.

diction. Though often used for *speech, elocution, delivery,* or *enunciation, diction* should be reserved for the meaning *vocabulary, choice of words.* Ambiguity is otherwise too easy and too frequent. *He was noted for his elegant diction* —speech or choice of words? *An improved diction is often the key to social or political success.* What are we to practice—the sweet nothings of the drawing room and the public platform or the overcoming of a slovenly pronunciation? *Grammar and diction,* says this book, *are the two*

concerns of the would-be
writer.

differ. See PREPOSITIONS.

differential, noun. See
NEEDLESS WORDS.

different(ly) than. British
colloquial usage seems to make
one thing *different* to another
more often than not. Prevailing British written usage is
divided between *different to*
and *different from*. In the
United States *different to* is
almost nonexistent, and it
sounds odd to Americans when
they encounter it in British
novels. In both England and
the United States there is an
increasing tendency to follow
different and *differently* with
than. When challenged, *than*
is sometimes defended with the
argument that *other* and *otherwise*—logically equivalent to
different and *differently*—are
idiomatically followed by *than*.
Sometimes the argument is
rather that *from* after *different*
leads to wordiness.

Both arguments have merit.
But the first does not dispose
of the educated American's
strong feeling that *different
from* is idiomatic and hence
inviolable; and the second
does not dispose of the writer's
implicit obligation to find alternative ways of expressing
thoughts that work out awk-
wardly in the forms that first
occur to him. True, *the behavior of the hen now is very
different than in June* becomes
wordy if we make it *different
from what it was in June;* but
are these the only two possibilities? What would be the
matter with *has changed radically since June?* Again,
*caused the family to move to
a different place in the fall
than where they lived in the
spring* does not commit anyone
to *a different place from that
in which,* and it is foolish to
consider the choices closed:
*caused the family to change
its spring dwelling place in
the fall* would be clear, idiomatic, and a good deal shorter.

There is always some ac-
ceptable way of saying what
is meant, and it is often better
to find a way around a linguistic thicket than to bull one's
way through it. To condone
different than because it is
sometimes awkward to follow
different with the accepted
preposition is defeatism. As
for *differently than,* it can
often be replaced by *otherwise
than,* which is irreproachable;
try using it, for example, in
*apparently polar bears behave
differently here than in other
parts of the Arctic*—after
changing *in other parts of* to
elsewhere in so as to avoid
repeating *other.*

In simple sentences, then,
the remedies for *different than*
are (1) to keep *than* with
some word that fits it, such as
other; or (2) to keep *different*
and replace *than* with *from*.

For reasons different than Bonaparte's, Necker also was pressing for a settlement can equally well be *For reasons other than Bonaparte's* or *For reasons different from Bonaparte's.* Not easily repaired as it stands is the following: *They viewed this kind of subsidy in a very different light than the painless land-grant subsidies to railroads.* Translate, rather, into the root meaning: *They found this kind of subsidy much more objectionable than the painless land-grant subsidies to railroads.*

See also PREPOSITIONS.

dilemma. This word, meaning two horns, points to something more than a mere difficulty or perplexity: it signifies an inescapable choice, an enforced decision to be made between two evils of equal force, and not more than two. *It was not possible either to advance or to retreat without disaster* is the statement of a true dilemma. But consider the following sentence: *The West's dilemma was how far to go in dealing with Moscow's East German satellite.* It states a *difficulty*, a *predicament*, a *perplexity*, or as we say a hundred times a day, a *problem*. But it is not properly a dilemma. It lacks the requisite pair of horns.

dis-, prefix. See DEMEAN; also DISINTERESTED.

disagreeables. See FALSE SINGULARS.

disassemble. See NEEDLESS WORDS.

disassociate. See NEEDLESS WORDS.

disciplinary, discipline. See ENDINGS 2.

discomfit. See ABSOLUTE WORDS.

discussant. See RESOURCE PERSON.

disinclined. See DISINTERESTED.

disinterested. Wise men have declared that the battle over *disinterested* has been lost, and that writers and speakers had better resign themselves to using the word as a duplicate of *uninterested.* This conclusion shows the extent to which the word has swung back to an earlier meaning, after a period of valuable service in a post where at the moment no replacement is in sight.

That service was to indicate the nature of an act or a person devoid of self-interest. The arbitrator in a dispute, the judge in court, the official making appointments or awarding contracts should be *disinterested;* that is, he should not selfishly profit by his decisions. It is clear that *just, fair, impartial, equitable, dispassionate, impersonal, unprejudiced, unselfish, moral, ethical, high-minded,* and the like do not hit the mark. They denote general qualities, without specifying the one element that affords a presumption of fairness, justice, and the rest. Anyone who feels this important difference will probably continue to use *disinterested* for what it meant in its best period.

For practical purposes the opposite of *interest* (= concern, attentiveness) is *indifference. Uninterestedness* exists, to be sure, but it is an unwieldy word that is hardly ever used. *Disinterest,* or *disinterestedness,* as it is now employed by the careless or the desperate, not only blurs the meaning but also stops the reader who can see two possible meanings, because it is still the name of a great, sterling, and positive virtue— freedom from self-seeking motives. It is not the name of a lack, which is what the writer was looking for. *Is one of the consequences of good times a disinterest in bad news?* Here *disinterest* is the wrong word, *uninterestedness* would be a fumbling one. *Indifference* (with *to*) is the inevitable word. And so it is again in the following if we insist on a single word (those whose verbal riches can afford a phrase will prefer *lack of interest*): *They encountered only profound dis-*

interest / The division between city and suburb goes deeper than a mere apathetic disinterest in the other's problems. (Note that in the last example *each other's* is logically necessary in place of *the other's.* See EACH, EVERY 2.)

The deplorable confusion is carried further by the presence of a natural antonym for the adjective or participle *interested:* to wit, *uninterested,* which has only to be substituted for *disinterested* in such a statement as *the small ducklings . . . seem completely disinterested in which is the mother as long as they can find shelter under her wings.* Failing this substitution we may end by wondering whether the *disinterested* judge is the one who is asleep on the bench.

Interested has also, of course, the meaning of which *disinterested* is the true antonym: the meaning of *involved, having something at stake, moved by an ulterior motive,* as in *an interested party* or *interested testimony.* (Compare the common charge of *conflict of interest.*) This use, self-explanatory in context, introduces no complication or difficulty. The trouble is occasioned by trying to equate the negative prefix *un-,* generally passive, with the negative prefix *dis-,* generally active. For example, to be *un*inclined is to have a mere lack of inclination, but to be *dis*inclined argues a positive aversion, an inclination against. *Uninterested* denotes only the absence of interest, but *disinterested* (= free from the influence of personal advantage) is a highly affirmative word.

dislocate. See LOCATE.

dive, dove, dived. See UNSAVORY PASTS.

division. See *dichotomy* under POPULARIZED TECHNICALITIES.

dock, pier. It is always hard to know when one should observe in the vernacular a distinction that is habitually made in one of the trades or professions. (See KNOT and SCOOP.) One always risks being thought a pedant or being misunderstood. A rule of thumb that suggests itself is that when the layman's mistake or confusion involves, through analogy or derivatives or homonyms, more than a single term, it is best to speak like those who really know what they are talking about— the professionals. Again, when the layman is dealing with the subject semi-professionally (as in most uses of *knot*) he is bound to be exact and he will not thereby be pedantic.

The words joined in this entry refer to different parts of a ship's berth, and under the rule just proposed they should not be used interchangeably. The *dock* is the water-filled space in which the ship comes to rest. The *pier* is the structure on which the passengers stand or alight. *Drydock* sufficiently points to the difference by raising the image of the cubical space emptied of water so that repairs may go on. The confusion doubtless arose from references to the ship's *docking*. To the landsman this suggests tying up to the *pier,* and he writes: *We stood on the dock watching the great hulking monster slowly inching in* (*slowly* is superfluous with the image of *inching in*) / *"Tell you what," he said, "I'll meet you on the dock and give it to you just before you go aboard."* Note also that in a court of law the accused stands, quite logically, *in* the dock. That expression reinforces the advisability of waiting for returning friends *on the pier* and neither *on* nor *in* the dock.

Doctor. See TITLES AND PROPER NAMES 3.

double-duty construction. See PROSE, THE SOUND OF 4.

double-entendre. See FRENCH WORDS AND PHRASES.

doubt, doubtless, doubt not, no doubt. American usage expresses two shades of meaning by the choice of conjunction to follow *doubt.* The statement *I doubt that I can go* is negative and it means *I do not think I can go.* No actual uncertainty is expressed. *I doubt whether I can go* conveys uncertainty with a shade —but only a shade—of the negative. *I am in doubt whether* is neutral, the two possibilities in balance. The hitherto disallowed *I doubt if* is akin to *I doubt that* and holds out little hope to the inquirer. (For *doubt* with *as to*, see AS 10.)

I do not doubt that makes perhaps the most literal use of *doubt.* It gives the effect of conceding a point while minimizing it. *I do not doubt that you are sincere, but that is no excuse for causing offense / I do not doubt that he left oral instructions, but the matter called for more exacting measures / I do not doubt that you would recover damages, but what good would that do you?*

The *-less* in *doubtless* is not so privative as it is in other compounds; that is, *doubtless* is not so clear an expression of certainty as its form would suggest. *You will doubtless want to settle this bill immediately* states a polite hope rather than an assured faith. The formal equivalent *no doubt* ranges in meaning from *probably* to *very likely* and does not reach the point of no doubt. (For *doubting*, see DUBIOUS.)

See also ADVERBS, VEXATIOUS.

drastic. See JOURNALESE.

dual. See VOGUE WORDS.

dubious. This is an adjective the dictionaries generally fail to make clear. It springs, of course, from doubt; but in what direction does it point? When the word is used with discrimination, the doubt is elsewhere than in the person or thing described as *dubious.* This person or thing is the object of doubt by another or others, not the author or abode of doubt. An expensive series of advertisements uses the word in the heading IMPORTANT NOTICE TO ALL KING-SIZE SMOKERS AND DUBIOUS READERS OF CIGARETTE ADS. To an acute reader this carries a strong suggestion that the readers of cigarette ads are not genuine readers. What is meant is *doubting readers*— skeptical readers. What is dubious from their point of view is not themselves but the cigarette ads. *In dubious battle* (Milton) points to a struggle of uncertain outcome; *dubious loyalty* is putative loyalty that others suspect of not being genuine; a *dubious supporter* is a nominal supporter who cannot be counted on. *She took the two dollars, and said, somewhat dubiously, "Suppose he doesn't want to see you?"* She makes this remark doubtingly, not dubiously. The difference is in the point of view; it is parallel with the difference between *questionable* and *questioning*.

Dictionaries do, to be sure, record with implied approval both the objective and the subjective uses of *dubious* and thereby provide a technical defense of the misuse here illustrated. But no one writing with nicety will fall into this misuse —which could perhaps be called a dubious use.

See also TRANSITIVE, INTRANSITIVE.

due to. Over *due* as an adjective modifying substantives there is no contention; everybody agrees that an effect is *due to* a cause: a disease is due to infection, exhaustion due to overwork, insomnia due to worry, success or failure due to aptitude or inaptitude, and so on. Trouble begins at the point where *due to* is converted into a prepositional phrase used to introduce adverbial elements—a general substitute for *because of, on account of, owing to, by reason of,* etc. Can a disease be *caught due to* infection, a man be *exhausted due to* overwork? Can someone complain that *due to worry* he sleeps badly? The answer of everyone who cares about workmanship is a flat no. But to give that answer in the United States today is to commit oneself to fighting a rear-guard action. For the doctrine that any locution in wide use is right by virtue of its mere existence has validated the unanchored *due to*. Not only is the emancipated phrase frequently found in the public prints, but it also entered Webster as long ago as 1934 in one usage at least: "Prepositional *due to,* meaning 'because of' and introducing an adverbial modifier, though objected to by some, is in common and reputable use; as, he failed *due to* faulty training." About the commonness of the use there can be no dispute. But the loose and lawless *due to* is still rare in writers other than those who take advantage of every latitude.

The more demanding, when they use the phrase, ask themselves "What is due to what?" The answer is invalid if it consists of some idea not in evidence but "understood" or produced by editorial conjecture. *Due to differences in time zones, none of these games has started.* Here the wordy answer would be [*the fact that*] *none of these games has started.* Turn this around and you get: *None of these games has started is due to differences in time zones.* We can say: *Owing to (Because of, By reason of, On account of, Thanks to) differences in time zones, none ... has started.* We can say: *That none of these games has started* (substantive clause) *is due to ...* But the sentence as first quoted fails to answer the primary question that *due to* always implies.

Due to at the beginning of a

sentence or of a clause will practically always produce the same dependence on something not present at all or present only in a grammatically unusable form.

Note that if one replaces the ungrammatical *due to* with *thanks to,* it is desirable to avoid a contrast between the idea of thanks and some cause or effect that no one could be thankful for. The phrase goes with what is favorable or neutral, unless one intends irony: *No information is available from official sources due to* (thanks to) *strict censorship.* See DANGLERS, ACCEPTABLE.

durable, durational. See ENDINGS 2.

E

each, every. 1. These words are alike in their singling-out effect; both imply, in logic and in numbering, more than one, but they insist on taking the members of the plurality one at a time. They have a manifest kinship with the idea in *apiece*. (*You are to have three guesses apiece = Each of you is to have three guesses / You are to have three guesses each / Every one of you is to have three guesses.*) *Each* and *every* thus call for singular verbs and are to be correlated with singular nouns and pronouns—generally pronouns in the third person. *They shall sit every man under his vine and under his fig-tree* (not *their*; not *vines, fig-trees*) / *Each of you* (*Every one of you*) *is to show me his outline before proceeding* (not *are*; not *their*; not *your*; not *outlines*) / *Each of us* (*Every one of us*) *is required to feel that he is in some sense his brother's keeper* (not *are required*; not *we* or *they*; not *our* or *their*; not *keepers*). *Everybody* is of course subject to the same patterns: *Everybody has to mind his own business* (not *have to*; not *their*). The notion that *everybody* has become a plural through some

collective notion is denied by the fact that everybody keeps on saying *everybody has gone* (not *have gone*); *everybody has bad luck* (not *have*) *once in a while*.

To return to *each:* the prevailing pattern for *each* is not regular throughout. It no longer holds for number—and, in the first and second persons, for person—when *each* is shifted to the position immediately after the subject. We follow logic in saying *each of us* (*each of you, each of them*) *has his own difficulties*; but we give it up when we change the order and say *We each have our* (*You each have your, They each have their*) *own difficulties*. And, as if to make things still harder, the original pattern of number and person may (not must) be idiomatically restored in the first person (not in the second) when *each* is further shifted to follow the verb: either *We have each his own difficulties* or *We have each our own difficulties*, but *You have each your own difficulties*. (The third person, of course, remains unaffected: *They have each their own difficulties.*) It is therefore sensible to refrain from the order

174

that puts *each* after the verb, and the more so because a dilemma of number is involved where the object of the verb may be either singular or plural. Start with *Each of us has his own destiny.* That will give *We each have our* (*You each have your, They each have their*) *own destinies.* But it will also give, in the first person, either *We have each our own destinies* or *We have each his own destiny;* in the second person, *You have each your own destiny* (*destinies?*); in the third person, *They have each their own destiny* (*destinies?*). Is the noun to agree in number with the singular *each* or the plural *their?* It is expedient to avoid *each* after the plural verb, and at times to substitute an equivalent that raises no problems of number or person: for *All of us* (*you, them*) *have our* (*your, their*) *difficulties* read: *Nobody but has his difficulties,* etc.

The separate words are difficult enough to use without combining them into the cliché and tautology *each and every.*

2. *Each other* and *each other's* cannot be avoided. On the assumption that the phrase means two and two only, what is important to remember is that *each other* means *each the other.* Remembering that, one is safeguarded from the illogical plural *others'* and from the intrusion of an illogically plural noun. *They threatened to break each other's neck* (not

others'; not *necks*) means *Each threatened to break the neck of the other* (one other, with but one neck). There is a tendency to use *each other* for two and *one another* for more than two, but it creates no obligation. One can cite numerous instances from good authors of *each other* for more than two and of *one another* for two only. Still, it is sensible to preserve the distinction, because many readers are startled if they discover that *each other* has been used of several, and startled again, though less so, when they discover that *one another* has referred to but two. The distinction is a wholly natural one for the reason that *each other,* as we saw, carries an inherent implication of the definite article (each *the* other), *one another* of the indefinite article, which is in fact welded into a*nother,* a pronoun essentially incapable of a plural. Most readers will feel the ineptitude of *The explosions* (three) *were touched off one after the other* (another) *in separate parts of the school.* When, however ill-advisedly, *each other* is used of more than two, that use may validate the plural possessive and a plural noun: *The whole circle took each others' hands.* But they will have to take *one another's hands* and be held fast in a logical clinch, for each takes a hand of each of two others—two hands—and yet *another's* cannot be anything but grammatically singular. It would be simpler to start again and say: *They formed a circle by holding hands.*

The tangle is different in *They know perfectly well what each other is secretly thinking*, for it will not work with either a singular verb or a plural one. There is nothing for it but to pick the components apart: *Each knows . . . what the other is . . . thinking.* The nonsense is factual rather than rhetorical in *Two men walk behind each other, keeping step.* In our world, if A. walks behind B., B. cannot walk behind A. These two will have to let it go at walking *one behind the other.*

For *between each*, as in *sixty seconds between each round*, see BETWEEN 2.

ear, play it by. Musicians of whatever quality can be presumed to know what is wrong with the current use of this phrase. If they do, they should point out to their heedless neighbors that to play a piece by ear means to reproduce a composition from memory, without the score. The use of the image in everyday life implies a different situation, which is illustrated by *It's too far ahead for us to plan; we'll have to play it by ear.* The meaning here is *we shall have to improvise:* there is no score; the piece not only has not been composed, but in the present circumstances it cannot be.

The point of this trifling observation is that when a word exists that means exactly what you mean—in this case *improvise*—use it.

echelon. Borrowed from the military during the last war, *echelon* is now suffering from the overuse that invariably goes with misplaced extension. An *echelon* is a step in a scale. The French Army has ranks or groups of ranks that form *échelons,* the *échelons supérieurs* being what we know as the *top brass.* It might at first seem odd that in the United States, where hierarchies are not well thought of, *echelon* should have caught on so well. But a moment's thought shows that its purpose is precisely to avoid saying the blunt words *grade, rank, level.* This evasive use is clear in the headline LOW ECHELON WOMEN FOUND MORE NEUROTIC, which doubtless echoes the wording of the survey thus announced. The kindly intention of *echelon*, at once pretentious and genteel, does not keep the word from being an avoidance of plain fact. See GENTEELISM.

-edly, adverbs in. See REPORTEDLY.

education. Originally the sum of a man's intellectual and moral acquirements, *education* is now loosely used to mean *instruction, information, propaganda, advertising* (e.g. *a* *campaign of consumer education*), and even *course* or *curriculum* (*We offer a comprehensive yet well-balanced two-year education on the college level*).

As a result, in place of teachers' colleges and departments of pedagogy, we have schools and departments of *education*. Pedagogy is in bad repute, both as a word and as a branch of knowledge, and the ubiquitous and quite unteachable *education* reigns in its stead. There are two divisions within *education* so conceived: *methods* and *subject-matter disciplines*. Those who profess the former are *educationists*. Those who profess the latter are *disciplinary faculty* (see ENDINGS 2 and BOURGEOIS). Writers who are careful of their diction will hesitate to use *education* in its new senses and will avoid most of its derivatives.

educationese. Special terms, known legally as terms of art, naturally arise in every trade or profession for the convenient discharge of its duties. The terms may be words not used in the vernacular or common words used in a different sense. From the trade some of these words are borrowed by common speakers, often with a figurative or a mistaken meaning (see KNOT). One would imagine that the profession of teaching, presupposing in the practitioners more knowledge than is usual in the laity, as well as a greater sensibility to meaning, accuracy, and logic, would have produced an admirable technical vocabulary. One would be wrong so to imagine. The language of education is the worst of all trade jargons, perhaps because it is one of the most recently contrived. Compared with the sailor's vocabulary, which is much older and one of the best, the teacher's affords no argument for a belief in progress.

The faults of educationese are excessive abstraction and intentional vagueness, coupled with a naïve faith in the power of new terms to correct old abuses. It would be tedious to illustrate these faults in their unremitting variety. It should suffice to mention the shifting terms by which the contents of education themselves have come to be known. They used to be *branches*, on the analogy of the tree of knowledge. When the notion of change and movement replaced that of fixed, eternal knowledge, the tree seemed inappropriately static, and the *branches* became *fields*, which the scholar or pupil was said to explore or discover for himself. So far reason was still in her seat. Then came the wish to express the lack of boundaries by replacing *field* with *area*. Areas could be anything known or unknown. Several researchers could *concentrate on* (in?) *one area*, or one person could choose an *area of concentration.* But in the phrase *area studies* the areas are actual portions of the earth's surface—i.e. geographical regions. The looseness of *area* was sometimes felt, so it required the aid of a *framework.* Nowadays few academic enterprises can be discussed or curricular reforms instituted without recourse to a *framework,* and any set of remarks about it or them is made *in terms of* (see IN TERMS OF) a *frame of reference.*

All this effort is arduous; to suggest how arduous, the subjects of learning—traditionally known as *subject matters*—had to become *disciplines* (see ENDINGS 2). English, mathematics, and the rest are now *disciplines*—except that their rudiments for young children are SKILLS. In the confusion of proliferating skills and disciplines and the talk about them, it proved necessary to discern some parts that were more important than the rest—something to *focus* on. These nuggets were quickly baptized *nuclei.* In groups they formed the *core curriculum.* Meanwhile, slices of each skill or discipline had to be marked off for orderly presentation. They obviously could not be called *lessons;* they had to be *units,* absorbed in successive *learning situations* with the aid of *clinics, workshops, tools,* and *audiovisually qualified personnel.*

By the end of this ordeal *teaching* and *instruction* had well-nigh disappeared. All that was left was EDUCATION.

See also JARGON; METAPHOR.

-ee, -er. The extension of the suffix *-ee* from legal terminology (*donee, grantee, vendee,* etc.) into general English has had mixed results, some of which are beginning to verge on the absurd. The original scheme was to denote agents and the objects of their action. *Lessor* and *lessee, assigner* and *assignee, mortgageor* and *mortgagee* are readily explained by their relative positions. The *-er, -or* denotes one who acts toward another who receives the benefit or is the object of the deed. The extension of this device has been influenced by the belief that the form in *-ee* will stand for any French past participle in *é* doing duty as a noun—e.g. *employee,* which English might have chosen to render as *an employed.* We do say, in a collective sense, *the unemployed,* and less frequently we also say *the employed.* Both the *-ee* and the *-ed* forms convey a passive meaning, the agent bearing the correlative name in *-er* (employer).

This application of this reasoning has given us some standard and inescapable words, such as *debauchee, devotee, referee, employee,* and *refugee.* But the *-ee* does not play the same role in all. In some we find the normal passive meaning, which points to the direct or indirect object of the action. In others the suffix is, as the Shorter Oxford English Dictionary calls it, "arbitrary," as in *bargee* (British for a *bargeman*). In *devotee* it is possible that the notion of one devoted to a cult (i.e. given or assigned to it as by a higher power) subsists in the *-ee*.

But whether this explanation holds or not, what makes these words with "arbitrary" endings acceptable is that, being familiar, they no longer cause us to think of the meaning of *-ee*. In words newly coined the trouble can be serious—as when persons who pledge funds to a charity are called *pledgees*. They are *pledgers* if they are anything, and the charity is the *pledgee*. Again, logic and sense are at odds in *absentee*, which refers to a positive act, to an *absenter*. The same objection applies to *attendees* for *attenders* and *conferees* for *conferrers*. As for those whom an understandable wanderlust entices away from a prison or an asylum, they are surely *escapers*, though often called *escapees*: COURTROOM ESCAPEE GETS PRISON TERM / ESCAPEE FROM VIETCONG PRESENTED TWO MEDALS, and so on.

The false analogy that leads to such paradoxes must be held in check when we coin new names; one already comes across examples of *resignees* and *relaxees*. And since it is the awareness of contrivance as much as the confusion of active and passive that is annoying in these words, it is advisable to drop also those that are "correctly" formed, such as *adoptee*, *biographee*, and *persecutee*. At the cost of one more word, say *an adopted child*, *a biographical subject*, *a persecuted man*; and refrain especially from the misshapen growth that forgets part of its root, e.g. *amputee* (AID FOR WAR AMPUTEES . . . SENT TO VIETNAM), as if there were a verb to *ampute* having *amputers* as its agents.

For parallel active-passive confusions in new coinages, SEE TRANSITIVE, INTRANSITIVE; -ABLE, -IBLE.

effective. When it is not used as an epithet of praise, this word must be pinned like any other adjective to whatever noun answers the question What goes into effect or becomes operative? American business English tries with increasing frequency to pretend that it is an adverb, with the result that the question requires for its answer some noun that is not there. *Effective* remains an adjective, with nothing to modify: *The basic price of the Fairchild F-26 turbo-propeller airliner will be increased effective Nov. 30.* What is effective here, and what *effective* modifies, is the increase—not mentioned. The cure will generally be, not to supply the missing noun, but to abolish *effective*; in the foregoing sentence there is no reason not to say *on*. (The British avoidance of the difficulty by means of *with effect* is no avoidance at all.) In the following, other substitutes are suggested: *would replace it with another program, effective Oct. 30* (*replacement* is missing; *effective* might well be *to begin*) / *ordered the Norfolk schools closed effective Monday* (from Monday on) / *It will be seen at 8:30 P.M. on Thursdays, effective this week* (beginning this week).

See also AS 5.

either . . . or; neither . . . nor. 1. A complete diagram of all the kinks and turns possible with these four words would occupy a large part of any such book as this. *Either* and *neither* are adjectives (*on either hand / Neither applicant can be taken seriously*), pronouns (*Either is well qualified / Neither deserves consideration*), and adverbs (*Not that we can fully accept this proposition either*), besides being conjunctions that characteristically hunt in pairs—*either* with *or*, *neither* with *nor*. They also serve uses that grammarians are as one in approving while quarreling about their classification. Nevertheless the perplexities that bother a modern writer are comparatively few, and they occur within a fairly narrow range of the conjunctive uses. *Neither* and *either* as adverbs raise hardly any

problems. As adjectives and pronouns they require us only to know that they presuppose two subjects of discourse but treat them (as EACH and EVERY do) one at a time and therefore call for statements in the singular number. *Neither candidate has a chance* tells us that two are under consideration, but separately. *Neither of them has a chance* tells us the same, and the number of the verb is unaffected by the intervening plural. All aberrations being possible, we find an occasional sentence in which the alternative subjects are handled like a plural: *Neither the President nor Secretary of State Christian A. Herter were* (was) *informed / Neither Helen nor Paris were* (was) *in Troy when the Greeks attacked.* The last example, which occurs in a serious work, exemplifies a rather rare blunder. The feeling that *either . . . or* and *neither . . . nor* introduce separate alternatives is strong and is generally obeyed.

2. It is also rare to find in modern writing a combination in which *neither* is acceptably correlated with *or*, or *either* with *nor*. When we read: *one he could neither cow, browbeat, or intimidate*, we think at once of a misprint, or else of carelessness. (In older and statelier prose one might have found *She did not blanch; neither did she weep or cry.*) The coupling raises the question whether *either* and *nei-*

ther may be used of more than two items—a license sanctioned by dictionaries and other authorities, but still short of punctilious.

3. As for what might be called the disguised confusion of *neither . . . nor* with *either . . . or,* it is common enough and it brings up subtle considerations of emphasis and logic.

The common form of the practice substitutes *nor* for *or* in sentences where a *neither* is imagined at work though physically absent. The force of *neither* is fallaciously ascribed to some other negative word that is actually there— usually *not* or *never: Can't ever dent, rust nor tarnish* results from the impression that *can't* (cannot) is the equivalent of *can neither.* Modern English argues that it is the equivalent of *cannot either,* the sequel of which is not *nor* but *or.*

Still, the argument is not conclusive. George Bernard Shaw, who was steeped in Elizabethan and Biblical English, was much addicted to this questionable *nor* and used it often but not invariably. He wrote: [Tchaikovsky] *never attains, nor desires to attain, the elevation at which the great modern musicians . . . maintain themselves.* Analyzed, this says *nor never desires to attain;* though Shaw might reply that *never attains, nor desires* is equivalent to *not either attains or desires,* which can be converted into *neither attains nor desires.* Modern usage responds as to a double negative in *never . . . nor,* and feels that they cancel each other. Shaw similarly writes: *and think, not of his own safety, nor of home and beauty, but of England,* construing *not . . . nor* as the equivalent of *neither . . . nor,* or as if *not . . . or* limped as badly as *neither . . . or.* An American example of the same false *nor: The most important item . . . was not the title poem nor the other six poems he included.* (Among classic American writers, Ambrose Bierce is a partisan of the Shavian *nor,* but he has not generally been followed.)

Lesser writers often make their uncertainty graphic by using both *nor* and *or* in the same construction after a negative: *He does not need to become a Pangloss nor a Pascal; . . . he does not fancy himself, or any philosopher, a revolutionary or teleological planner.* The *nor* and the first *or* are parallel; the *nor* should patently be *or.*

4. This type of confusion is compounded by the existence of a functionally quite different *nor*—the separate conjunction that means *and not* and introduces a totally disjoined independent clause, generally with subject and verb inverted. Several of the foregoing examples could be recast in this independent construction by retaining the *nor* that was a miscue as written; and indeed the two constructions have so beguiling a resemblance that the authors may have thought they were writing elliptical forms of the clausal construction. *G. never acknowledged any boundaries between these, nor did she acknowledge any between public and private life:* this correct though wordy version has the radical difference that its *nor* cannot be correlated with any preceding word mistakenly assumed to perform the task of *neither*. Similarly, *there is no point nor honesty in pretending* uses a false *nor* for *or*, but might with entire correctness be written *there is no point, nor is there any honesty*.

As a connective of simple nouns *nor* is sometimes substituted for *or* where it suggests an almost calculated effort to be wrong. *The shrewd seal always keeps his blowhole open beneath a protruding piece of ice where no bear nor harpoon can strike down at him.* Obviously, here is an option of *no bear or harpoon* and *no bear and no harpoon*—the second so superior in emphasis as to be worth the extra monosyllable. For aberrant uses of *or* for *and* see BETWEEN 3; also EQUALLY 2.

5. *Neither* and *either* are subject, like other negative and alternative words, to careless misplacement, with resulting imbalance: *Americans so far have neither been permitted to learn their names and records nor their beliefs*. This becomes grammatically tenable if we put *neither* after *learn*. Note, however, that on the principle of giving a negative meaning a negative form the sentence would be better if written *Americans so far have not been permitted to learn either . . . or* . . . Written as first quoted, it implies a quite different kind of matched structure: *have neither been permitted to learn . . . nor been* [some construction balancing *permitted*—e.g. *suffered to know*] *their beliefs*. Likewise *the size of my contribution is neither a measure of my indebtedness nor of my belief in the significance of the program* becomes tolerable with *neither* after *a measure* instead of before it, but would be still further improved by writing *is not a measure of either . . . or* . . . Such examples have no bearing on the force or meaning of *neither*; they concern the order of modifiers and the general question of the misplaced negative.

6. *Neither . . . nor* does not combine two singular subjects into a plural, but emphasizes their disjunction; hence the following verb is singular when each of the subjects is. Some grammarians encourage writers to make the verb agree in number with the nearest subject; but the clash will be felt by thoughtful readers. *Nei-*

ther Judaism nor its voluntary adherents possess the characteristics of a race or a nation. This is defensible but a workmanlike writer may put his pride in not writing sentences that need defending. Nor need he, in the interest of grammar, go in for such a dotting of *i*'s as *Judaism does not possess, nor do its voluntary adherents, the characteristics* . . . He could always write: *Judaism and its voluntary adherents do not possess the characteristics* (or *lack the characteristics*) *of a race or of a nation.*

A typical mismanagement involving *neither* . . . *nor* occurs in such sentences as *Neither the experience of 1956 nor this year—the two best farm production years in Soviet history—has yet shown convincingly* . . . Here we have another form of the false comparison, the second year being matched, not with the first, but with the experience of the first. The interpolation in dashes reasserts that the experience of 1956 is a year. Perhaps the intention was *The experience of neither 1956 nor this year* . . . How much better to scrap the *experience of.*

See also AND/OR; MATCHING PARTS.

eleemosynary. See PRONUNCIATION 1.

elemental, elementary. See ENDINGS 1.

ellipsis. See WHAT IS "UNDERSTOOD"?

emanate. See CONNOTATIONS.

empathy. See POPULARIZED TECHNICALITIES.

emphasis. It is a commonplace that the emphatic places in a sentence are the beginning and the end, but this generality is subject to important exceptions. In the periodic sentence—that which begins with a subordinate clause and makes one wait for the meaning held in the main clause—the first emphasis falls somewhere in the middle of the utterance. *Although he fought a series of brilliant battles across Europe, Napoleon in 1813 could not hope to prevail over so many enemies massed against him.* Here and in all similar constructions, the expectant rush toward the subject—*Napoleon in 1813*—heightens the emphasis upon it. The end of that sentence, however, is weaker than it need be because *against him* is filler made necessary only by rhythm. If the sentence had ended *prevail over such a host of his massed enemies* the chief idea in the predicate would have gained prominence and therefore emphasis.

There is no decree that all sentences should begin and end with emphatic bangs. LINKING often depends on quiet endings or beginnings that reserve a single emphasis for the most important thought within the paragraph. A succession of emphatic sentences tires the mind. They resemble maxims or aphorisms, which do not develop an idea but rather compress it into a final utterance. If it is indeed final, there should be nothing more to say; a chain of final statements is a contradiction in terms. Hence no good paragraph can come out of recurring hammer-stroke emphases.

If a writer or speaker has thought enough about his subject to be aware of its main parts and of their interconnections, his discourse will probably find the right moments and the right expressions for the emphasis he desires. What he has to guard against is inadvertent emphases in the wrong places, for these can occur in many small ways, easily avoidable if tagged in advance and steadily remembered. Here are a few types of this common fault that will open the alert reader's eyes to other types:

(1) Muffed climax. In a progressive series there should be a logical order of increase or decrease: *We were bored, exhausted, beyond caring.* Though there is no established scale for such intensifications of feeling, a little thought shows at least which is the term that should come on the highest rung of the ladder (= scale = climax). This natural rule of oratory has been forgotten in the otherwise acceptable reversal *After years of gambling and winning, he had lost by the merest fluke, by a careless shake of the head, by inattention.* As the least emphatic, because most general, term, *inattention* should come first and *shake of the head* last.

(2) Making a point of the subordinate. The statement of an objection or a conclusion or any other affirmation must not be obscured by its surrounding details. *What is damnable about these personnel tests is that only the men who give nonconformist answers fail to get a job.* This clearly implies that the writer wishes other people would also fail, whereas he means that the tests *unfairly weed out the nonconformists*—or some such phrasing.

(3) Misleading intruders. Words like *always, both,* and *whenever* can impart a stress that throws the sentence out of shape and will sometimes puzzle the reader: he looks for a nuance that is not clear since it was never intended. For example: *The locking up was systematically done, without hurry—each door, each drawer, each window latch—whenever he came to them* (substitute *as* for *whenever*) / *I will sign an affidavit that they both attacked me, both inside and outside* (inside the house and also outside) / *At times he would go over the whole sequence in his mind invariably*

after the gap, the clue, to the mistake he had made. This needs recasting: *At . . . in his mind. What he sought persistently was the failure that would be a clue to the mistake,* etc.

(4) Emphasis by exaggeration must be sparingly used. It wears itself out just as quickly as understatement or OXYMORON. Nor should one count on the obviousness of an exaggeration to impart a light humorous touch. The sign repeated on every floor of a first-class hotel on the West Coast fails of whatever effect may have been intended: *Incredible confusion, indeed needless dismay can develop if you do not study this time-table* [of restaurant hours].

(5) The use of italics will emphasize words that ordinarily would be slurred over and hence would not convey the right meaning. But one must make sure, by hearing the words spoken actually or in the mind, which word needs the stress. In the exclamation *She doesn't need him!* any one of the four words could conceivably be italicized, according to the context and the intention. The *locus classicus* of unintended emphasis by means of italics is the following Biblical quotation as it is printed in versions that italicize words supplied by the translators: "He said 'Saddle me the ass.' And they saddled *him*."

See also PROSE, THE SOUND OF; SENTENCE, THE.

endings. 1. Alternative. 2. Misdirected.

1. Alternative. Although the difference between *basic* and *basal, supplementary* and *supplemental* is for most purposes negligible, similar differences in other pairs embody important distinctions, and their neglect can blur meaning. In our century the worst confusion of this sort has been that between *precipitous* and *precipitate.* The former refers to a sharp downward slope: *The descent for the next three hundred yards is precipitous.* *Precipitate* as an adjective means *hasty.* It follows that the action of the Chairman of the Board is *precipitate,* not *precipitous.* The decline in the company's profits is *precipitous* and cannot be *precipitate,* no matter how suddenly it occurred.

Two similar pairs must be treated with a like attention to differences. *Elementary* refers to the simple parts of a subject or a compound, and hence to the beginnings of schooling, study, explanation, as well as to the products of analysis, as in the *elementary* particles of physics. *Elemental* has the special connotation of power and a further suggestion of first in point of time: the *elemental* forces of nature, the *elemental* passions of men. (A special usage in chemistry reserves *elemental* for the free, uncombined substance—e.g. *elemental phosphorus*—while phosphorus in general remains one of the *elementary* substances.) Very nearly the same distinction separates *primal* from *primary*: the *primal* brute, *the primary* school; our *primal* parents (Adam and Eve), our *primary* needs—food, clothing, and shelter.

Generally speaking, the urge to change the endings of established adjectives should be repressed. Such changes are not necessary and may lead to trouble. The usage of a profession (e.g. *basal metabolism* in medicine) should be respected, but it is an affectation of singularity to change the *basic texts* of some years ago to the *basal readers* that publishers now bring out. See also -ION, -NESS, -MENT.

2. Misdirected. The modern desire to bestow special names that are anything but transparent on the objects of our concern often leads to absurdities that involve the meaning of suffixes. Thus a study of the law's delay found, and dealt with, a group of *durable cases* —that is, cases that lasted an inordinately long time. It may be useful to speculate that the authors, in their wish to be technical, first suggested and rejected *enduring* and *durational* and then fastened on *durable*, blind to the common meaning of that word and to the force of -ABLE. As a result, cases that should *not* endure

are denoted by a word that proclaims their power to do so. One may surmise that if *long* (or *long-lasting*) *cases* ever occurred to the legal experts, the phrase was discarded as insufficiently technical. The desire to tell all in a single somewhat abstract modifier is strong; it has inspired the awkward and needless *societal, dialogal,* and others; but it should be resisted.

A related but different type of error is to name an act or function by means of an accepted and well-formed adjective, yet one that singles out the wrong feature and sets up an ambiguity with an established meaning. The commonest instance is that of *disciplinary* and, by extension, *interdisciplinary,* as these words are used in the academic world. A generation ago *discipline* became a synonym for *subject matter;* then questions arising in research became *disciplinary problems,* on a par with naughty boys; finally links between subjects or "across disciplines" generated *interdisciplinary.* To restrict *discipline* to its original meaning is a desirable but probably utopian goal.

In a like manner, when the contractor in charge of a building under construction allows the owner to move in at his own risk before the work is completed, this is known as *beneficial occupancy,* from the fact that the beneficiary of the permission is the occupant. Coinages of this sort should be kept down; they not only mislead, but when understood seem to authorize muddled thinking.

ensure. See ASSURE, ENSURE, INSURE.

entropy. See POPULARIZED TECHNICALITIES.

equally. 1. *Equally as.* 2. *Equally . . . or.*

1. *Equally as.* For some elusive reason the coupling of these words incriminates a writer out of proportion to the gravity of the error. *Equally as* is, after all, no more than a trivially redundant mixture of constructions that should be kept separate. We can either call one man *as tall as another* or call the two *equally tall;* what we must avoid saying is that one is *equally as tall as* the other. When someone says *It is impossible to anticipate in advance*, we merely think that he must be speaking in a daze, and we may feel like asking him to try anticipating in retrospect. We are amused, for an instant, by a general's pronouncement that *We do not want bluff and bluster and tactical maneuvers that could lead to a war none of us wants*, a feeble elaboration of the thought that we don't want what we don't want. But the moment anybody writes *equally as* he provokes a surge of the censoriousness that should be reserved for worse offenses. The remedy is usually to omit the *equally* or the *as*.

Occasionally the construction turns up in disguise, as in a thoughtful letter to the *New York Times: It is unfortunate that the United States, which at one time was looked upon as the symbol of liberty and justice, should now be considered on an equal level as* (on a level with) *the British and the French.* And this suggests the cure for the infrequent type: *I was entitled to it equally as much as him* (*equally with him* or *as much as he*). See also ADEQUATE.

2. *Equally . . . or.* It should go without saying that *equally*, when it introduces a two-pronged alternative, takes the sequence *and*, not *or*, by a logic as inexorable as that which requires *and* after *both* and *or* after *either*. But to let the point go unmentioned would be to overlook the propensity to forget one's intention on setting out. *It was equally hard to imagine that he was unaware of these details or that he could be aware without doing anything about them.* Obvious patterns for the thought are (a) *equally hard to imagine* [this] *and* [that]; (b) *as hard to imagine* [this] *as* [that]; (c) *hard to imagine either* [this] *or* [that]; (d) *hard to imagine both* [this] *and* [that]. A mixture entails the usual disadvantages of

swapping horses in midstream.

See also PREPOSITIONS.

era. See PRONUNCIATION 1.

erosion. See METAPHOR 4.

essential. See ABSOLUTE WORDS; JOURNALESE.

esteem. See APPRECIATE 2.

ethic. See FALSE SINGULARS.

etymology. For some time the experts on language and stylistics have inveighed against making pupils aware of etymologies. The old practice of noting derivations is said to be pernicious because it ignores the detailed history of each particular word and sets up between ideas barriers that usage has broken down. Etymology is thus reserved as the exclusive province of the professional linguist, and professional writers are told once again that they know nothing about language, except now and then how to use it.

It is true that words lend themselves to plausible but false derivations and that to discover the actual ones requires painstaking work which writers lack the time and the knowledge to pursue. But the fact remains that writing without a sense of the interconnections or repulsions arising from the meaning of roots is likely to produce prose that is deficient in some way. It will lack the inner cohesion that comes from the linking of complementary ideas by means of those hidden meanings; or it will fall into tautology—as when someone speaks of *eradicating the root of the trouble*; or it will overlook mixed METAPHOR—as in the sentence *It was the Governor's veto of this measure that ignited a race of unsurpassed bitterness.* Obviously the last writer took *ignite* to mean *set off, start up,* as does the *ignition* mechanism of a car. That the word is inseparable from the idea of *fire* can of course be learned unconsciously from usage if one reads widely and attentively; but the knowledge is also obtainable direct, from looking into etymologies. It was one of the advantages of studying Latin that it disclosed the meaning of many roots in common words. For those who never had a brush with Latin and Greek one can recommend the etymological dictionaries by Skeat and by Weekley, and the admirably organized *Origins* by Eric Partridge. They should be the bedside books of the many persons who invent or baptize products and processes with Greco-Latin coinages of their own. See SCIENTISM.

euphemism. See GENTEELISM.

evasive. See SCIENTISM #3.

-ever. See WHATEVER, WHO-EVER, INTERROGATIVE.

every. See EACH, EVERY.

excessively, exceedingly. This is one of the numerous pairs (see DANGEROUS PAIRS) within which differentiation is convenient and not to be given up. *Excessively* tells of an unwanted surplus; *exceedingly* merely carries the stated quality to its highest point. So we should expect our protégés to be *exceedingly* grateful for the benefits we bestow upon them, but if they are *excessively* grateful they become a nuisance. The common phrases are *I am exceedingly glad / He is exceedingly tender (quick, sharp, clever, friendly) / She is exceedingly beautiful (sweet-natured, muscular, rich)*. And again: *He is excessively polite* (= obsequious), *excessively amorous* (= foolishly infatuated), *excessively rich* (= too much for his own good). Note that a quality that may be supposed regrettable takes *exceedingly*: *exceedingly shy, poor,* or *stupid*; and that words of absolute import (see ABSOLUTE WORDS) cannot take *excessively*: *excessively bald, excessively mature* go against logic.

exciting. This by now intolerable word needs no illustration from current sources: it is ubiquitous and nearly meaningless in all contexts. It has not yet displaced its exact double, *fascinating*, so that a comparison of the two is still possible and instructive. *Exciting* implies agitated motion; *fascinating* implies frozen immobility. The two are used interchangeably to say: *admirable, new, productive, excellent, pretty damn good, not half bad*, etc.

excluding. See DANGLERS, ACCEPTABLE.

execute. Ambrose Bierce, an energetic fighter of rear-guard actions in lost causes, used to protest against the journalistic use of *execute* to mean *put to death by law*. Bierce insisted that it is the sentence which is executed, not the criminal. By Bierce's time the transfer of the word to the new meaning was beyond reversal, and that meaning is now the main one. But it is not the only one. *Execute* still retains its etymological and primary meaning of *carry out, fulfill, pursue to the end, follow through*; it would be a pity to let it slough off this meaning because it has acquired the other. A writer who reports that *The sentence of five years' banishment was strictly executed* shows a nice sense of what the word originally meant and is guilty of no archaism. This is the meaning in *executive*, one who carries out decisions. *Execute* for *legally kill* is only the fourth definition in Webster's New International Dictionary; it is the sixth in the Shorter Oxford.

exodus. There are dictionary definitions that provide a loophole for the use of this word to denote the departure of only one person, but that use goes against all the natural associations of the word, which does not readily evoke anything short of a mass migration. It is an unfitting word in this sentence: *Schlegel's exodus from Jena caused little regret in the duchy of Saxe-Weimar.* Words that might take its place are *departure, withdrawal,* or the simple gerund *leaving* (without *from*). *Disappearance* will do if the leaving was secret or sudden. A one-man exodus is not much more plausible than a one-man stampede. (See POPULAR.

explicit. See IMPLICIT.

expound. To expound is to set forth in systematic order—to explain, make clear, elucidate—and the word calls for a direct object without intervention. You expound a doctrine; you do not expound *on* it. Yet *expound* seems to be gaining currency as a synonym of *expatiate,* perhaps owing to confusion with it. The misusers of *expound* would avoid error if they would notice that its associated noun is *exposition;* an exposition is idiomatically *of,* not *on. Expatiate* means to expound at length, and it conveys a touch of derision—to go on and on. *He expounded at length on the fish* / POPE EXPOUNDS ON BEES / *Harry S. Truman dedicated a portrait gallery of former Democratic Presidents today and took occasion to expound briefly on the virtues and vices of all but one—himself* / *Mr. S. was expounding on Chekiang teas and the proper method of grading them* / *T. compensates for his golf-course frustrations by expounding occasionally on his glory days as a prep-school pitcher* / *A public official in attendance will expound on the values of putting a fishing pole in the hands of a youngster and keeping him out of trouble in his idle time.* In the last specimen, omit *on;* in the others *expatiate* (without *at length* or its equivalents) will serve in place of *expound,* except that the sentence about President Truman contains a *briefly* which requires a simple *talk* or *speak.* See PREPOSITIONS.

extraordinary. See PRONUNCIATION 1.

extrapolate. See POPULARIZED TECHNICALITIES.

F

facility. See COVERING WORDS; FALSE SINGULARS.

factor. See NEEDLESS WORDS 2.

faculty. See BOURGEOIS, BOURGEOISIE.

fail in. We may fail in an attempt to do something, or we may fail to do it; but to say that we fail in doing it is self-contradictory. *They have notably failed so far in convincing Spanish or foreign business men here of their thesis* is such a contradiction; the failure is in not convincing them, and convincing them would be success. It should be put: *They have . . . failed . . . to convince . . .*

faintly. See UNDERSTATEMENT.

false singulars. The names of certain branches of study that end in *-ics* (*statistics, tactics, ethics*) have lately sprouted new and unwarranted forms without the *s* (*a statistic, a tactic, an ethic*) and not always with the same meaning as the plural. Thus *a statistic* is generally used to designate a single number or a table of figures singled out from a series. Likewise *a tactic* is used to mean *a measure* or *a step*. But *an ethic* purports to mean a system of ethical beliefs, and *an esthetic* one of esthetic beliefs. There is no need whatever for coining these singulars. A *figure* or *number* or *table* suffices for *a statistic*; a *move* or *step* for *a tactic* (*a tactical move*, if one wants to dignify it). *An ethics such as Aristotle's, Spinoza's,* etc., and *an esthetics in the tradition of Hegel and Croce* should not become *an ethic* and *an esthetic.*

Ethics, esthetics, and *mathematics* are singular nouns; *tactics* and *statistics* take a plural verb. *Mathematics is* (not *are*) *deemed a hard subject / Statistics are for the gullible.* But note that the phrase *the higher mathematics* acquires a plural meaning through the notion of various kinds grouped together as the higher branches.

Other nouns, plural in form and meaning, also tend to be forced into the singular, notably *evidences, goods* (merchandise), *facilities, instructions,* and *remains.* There is no such thing in good prose as *an evidence, a good, a facility, an instruction,* or *a remain,* no matter how strong the analogical pull of (*a*) *proof*(*s*), (*a*) *vestige*(*s*). The moralist's *virtue is a good* is not an exception to this generality but a confirmation of it, since he does not deal in marketable *goods*. Nor does one set up *an archive,* but *archives;* or approve the committee's *proceeding,* but *proceedings.* Likewise, *To the victor belongs the spoils* (not *spoil*), and it is a barbarism to speak of *a portrait in oil* instead of *oils*—though the canvas is known as *an oil.* Acts of *damage* are not *damages:* these last are compensation for the acts. Again, *talents,* once always plural because of the parable, is now current in the singular, perhaps justified by the historical existence of *talent* as a coin. *Disagreeables* is a good word not frequently seen. It means the lesser, unpleasant aspects or concomitants of an experience or of life itself. It is always plural.

As for *interests,* the idiomatic distinction that makes the plural convey a general notion and the singular a particular one determines the right usage. One says *in the interests of peace and good will* (at large) and *he was then acting in the interest of the other party to the suit.*

For false plurals, see KILT and SKILL(s).

fault, verb. See VOGUE WORDS.

felicitous, fortuitous. One might think that the resemblance of these words is remote and faint enough to preclude confusion; but no two words with an initial letter and a terminal syllable in common are confusion-proof, and observant readers become inured to encounters with *fortuitous* (occurring by chance) in lieu of *felicitous* (apt, appropriate). The hidden influence of *fortunate* is doubtless behind the illicit transfer of meaning: *Fortuitously, S. stipulated that he was to get 10 per cent of the net profits, and at last reports his share was touching $500,000.* From the book page of a distinguished daily: *This is a particularly fortuitous book for the summertime.* And again: *His remarks after the memorial dinner were thought especially fortuitous.* A fortuity may, of course, also be a felicity; but the chance occurrence is as likely to be a mischance.

fewer, less. *Fewer* is by nature a word applicable to number; *less* is a word applicable to quantity. Hence in making numerical comparisons *fewer,* not *less,* is required: *We had fewer people last night than a week ago.* This distinction has no bearing on *ten less seven* (diminished by seven); and we say, of course, *a lesser number.* But in all the following *less* should be replaced by *fewer: M. had no less than* *seven separate offers to buy it / standard equipment in no less than nine houses we visited / candidates for Directors . . . , not less than twice the number of vacancies to be filled / 30,000 men embarked for England, less than 10,000 returned to Spain / The nation's traffic death toll . . . was 377—thirteen less than the . . . pre-holiday estimate / increase its production . . . secured with about 2,000 less workers.*

The antonym of *less,* which is *more,* applies to either number or quantity. When qualifying a number it ought not to be contradicted by an associated word that applies only to quantity—e.g. *much* or *little. With little more than 1,000 Negroes in a county population of 17,000* requires *few* or a noncommittal *hardly* in place of *little.* The SET PHRASE *more or less* is an encouragement to the confusion of quantity with number: *He had chosen one of those ruthless savages, more or less of whom are to be found in every tribe / The scouts and friendly Indians, of whom more or less were always hanging about the fort.* In these, *more or less* might well be replaced by *some,* which, like *more,* serves for both quantity and number.

An occasional construction in which the ideas of quantity and number are hardly distinguishable will be equally tolerant of *less* and *fewer: The million seasonal farm workers* *normally work less than 150 days in a year.* Here *150 days* can be felt as either a specified number of days or a unitary measure of time (as *five months* or *less than half a year* would be). Sometimes an ostensibly numerical expression is unmistakably a unitary measure and, as such, excludes *fewer.* We take a *million dollars* as a sum of money, not as a number of units; *fifty feet* as a measure of distance, not as one foot added to forty-nine other feet; *thirty minutes* as a stretch of time, exactly like *half an hour.* With these expressions a singular verb is appropriate. *(A million dollars is more easily accumulated than it used to be / Fifty feet is too short a distance),* and the quantitative *less* is therefore correct in comparisons; *fewer* would sound absurd.

See also NONE.

fiction. See UN-, IN-, NON-.

field. See EDUCATIONESE; NEEDLESS WORDS 2.

figuratively. See LITERALLY.

figure. See BALANCE.

financial. See FISCAL.

first of all. Enumerating reasons, causes, arguments often requires a trumpet call to arrest attention. Usually *first, second,* and so on are felt to be adequate, but if the enumerator wants greater emphasis for his first item, he will, with a certain note of impatience, begin with *first of all*. It is just because of this emphasis that he should not follow suit with the frequent and foolish *second of all*.

fiscal. The pirating of one word after another to give a fresh look to old routines has become a mania among businessmen, from whose reports and declarations in the press civil servants, academics, and the common man pick up the habit. As late as fifty years ago, sensible people spoke of *money matters* and *money troubles*. If they were a bit Micawberish they referred more loftily to their *pecuniary situation*, and in so doing they were still within the limits of reason. But at some point since, the private citizen began to refer to his *finances*, which was at once pompous, inaccurate, and genteel. *Finance*, as *financier* still suggests, is properly the management of large sums by professional money men interested in business or government enterprise. It is doubtless impossible to recapture this useful distinction. Every school child who overspends his allowance of a dollar a week is in *financial difficulties*, and needs and *secures refinancing*.

Now, for larger entrepreneurs and corporations, *finance* itself (noun and verb) has grown too commonplace, and we hear everywhere of *fiscal* measures to be taken by the board or *funding* arrangements to be made by the treasurer. These mean respectively *raise money* and *pay* (or *appropriate*).

That first slipcover on the old reality has a colorable excuse in the accepted use of *fiscal year*. But *fiscal* in that phrase simply records the fact that business adopted the government's "year," which was *fiscal* because that is the name appropriate to governmental money matters. *Fiscus* is the Latin word for the public chest, derived from the meaning *wicker basket*. If it is argued that there is now no clear line between the private and the public moneybags, that will still not excuse a sorry decline of simple good sense.

As for *funding*, it should retain the useful meaning of setting aside capital (a fund) to insure regular payment out of the income. Hence a scientist seeking a research grant is not *looking for some means of funding his project*.

fit. See UNSAVORY PASTS.

flair. See AFFINITY.

flammable. See UN-, IN-, NON.

focus. See SCIENTISM.

folk(s). See PERSONS 2.

forbid. See PREPOSITIONS.

forbidden words. 1. By reason of obscenity. 2. As an aid to writing.

1. The words called "good old Anglo-Saxon" and also "four-letter words" are no longer excluded from high literature, though they are still rare in the periodical press and in civil conversation. In books they are spelled out in full, not with dashes following an initial or between single letters, as in the old-fashioned *d--n.* The restoring to good repute of the strongest two or three among those words has been tried in vain, yet is still being advocated. The obstacle, it is clear, does not consist in a stubborn remnant of prudishness among the public. It consists in the widespread spoken and fictional use of these words to express hate, disgust, and contempt. These are powerful emotions, which war against the return of the forbidden words in their simple and friendly aspect. The result is that there are no words but euphemisms or clinical terms for what many scenes of modern fiction profess to describe. (See GENTEELISM; SEX.)

2. Many are the books and systems advertised as contributing to the enlargement and strengthening of one's vocabulary. None is so effective as the device of denying oneself the use of fifty or a hundred words that are overworked in one's circle or profession. Among general terms, the writer obsessed by JARGON may want to outlaw first the ones listed below. They are not to be banned forever, nor are they evil in themselves. But their abuse has turned them into mere plugs for the holes in one's thought. As such, they also block the way to finding the exact word —one of several possible words. Removing these stoppers and keeping one's mind on the object in one's mind will bring about an immediate release of the vocables that the habit of thinking in omnibus words keeps imprisoned. Of the following fifty, those printed in small capitals are discussed elsewhere in this book.

NOUNS: *angle, approach, background,* BREAKDOWN (analysis), CONCEPT, CONTEXT, *dimension, essentials,* FACTOR, *insight,* MOTIVATION, NATURE, *picture* (situation), *potential, process,* (re-) *evaluation,* (my, your) THINKING.

VERBS: *accent, climax,* CONTACT, (de-) *emphasize, formulate,* HIGHLIGHT, PINPOINT, PROCESS, *research, spark, state* (say), TRIGGER, *update.*

MODIFIERS: *basic,* BITTER, CRUCIAL, CRYPTIC, *current* (ly), DRASTIC, ESSENTIAL, INITIAL, KEY, MAJOR, *over-all,* REALISTIC, *stimulating,* WORTHWHILE.

LINKS: *as of* (see AS 5),

-CONSCIOUS, -*free*, IN TERMS OF, -WISE, WITH.

foreword, introduction, preface, etc. The vocabulary to designate the elements of front matter in books has long been in disorder, and there is no prospect of putting an end to the confusion. To it *foreword* is a chief contributor. The word existed in English well before German philological scholarship became fashionable, about the turn of the century; but it is as certain as anything unprovable can be that *foreword* was reinvented late in the nineteenth century as a transliteration of *Vorwort,* in German the standard word for *preface.* So reinvented, *foreword* flourished until it has become as common as *preface* itself, a word at home in English for many centuries. We have, then, the paradox that the Latin *preface* is sound old English, whereas the upstart *foreword,* with two Anglo-Saxon roots buried in it, is foreign and relatively new.

A multiplicity of words for the same kind of composition, or a multiplicity of meanings for the same term, is a liability, not an asset, when technical details are to be distinguished. And though the components of a book are not parts that work with the rigidity of a machine, there would be some value in having the designations such that the reader or buyer of a book might know the scope and purpose of the sections designated *Preface, Introduction,* and so on. Naturally, an exact use of these terms can never be enforced. A logical hierarchy among them is suggested here only as a guide to the growth of a possible convention.

At the present time the *preface* to a book may be by the author or by somebody else; it may be one paragraph or forty pages; it may be either an integral and necessary part of the preliminaries to the subject or a mere note on the author's purpose and point of view. *Foreword* is similarly noncommittal; and *introduction* may designate a puff contributed by someone other than the author, or an editor's preface to an edition of someone else's work, or the author's indispensable survey of background matter, or a mere prefatory comment or acknowledgment. Scholarship and instruction might be better served if it were agreed that:

(1) A *preface* is a brief explanatory statement by the author; it is about the book, but not an integral part.

(2) An *introduction* is a statement by someone other than the author—either a tribute included as reinforcing the claim to attention or an expository essay by the editor of a work.

(3) An author's preliminary exposition that is an integral

part of his work—in effect a general opening chapter—may well be called *Introductory*, and it should be folioed as belonging to the main text, not in the roman numerals given to front matter.

(4) When the editor of another's work finds it desirable to include, in addition to his own introduction, a prefatory explanation about his part in it, this explanation ought to be called the *Editor's Preface*.

(5) Ornamental or quasi-poetic terminology such as *prologue*, *proem*, or *prelude* could be restricted to such special classes of works as epic drama and long narrative poems, and units so labeled should be treated as text, not as front matter. (But caution is advisable in view of jargon uses by organizers, at the White House and elsewhere: *There will be a cultural Prelude and Reception on Sunday from 5 to 6.*)

Foreword finds no place among the suggestions, the need for it being slight or non-existent except as an elegant variation of *preface*. Its one possible excuse for being is as a companion term to *afterword*. But this pairing, under the suggested scheme, could be effected less obtrusively by matching *Introductory* with *Conclusion* (or *In Conclusion*). For the occasional work in which an editor's hand supplies comments after the death of the author of the book, *Editor's Note* can be used, or—on loftier occasions—*Epilogue*.

forgiveness. See TOGETHERNESS.

format. Originally a French word spread abroad by way of the printers' international jargon, *format* properly denotes the size, shape, and general design of a book or magazine. By an extension that may be deemed excessive, the word has been taken over, first by the producers of radio and television programs, and next by anyone who finds *arrangements* or *program* too ordinary for his taste. *The format is this: cocktails at seven, dine at eight, then a short two-mile drive to the auditorium where this unrivaled entertainment awaits you / The format displeased him. He would have to sit there with nothing to do while all the lesser lights crowded him out of the limelight.*

fortuitous. See FELICITOUS.

framework. See JARGON.

Frankenstein. In 1818 a young woman prodigy named Mary Wollstonecraft Shelley published a horror story called *Frankenstein; or, The Modern Prometheus*, about a German student, Frankenstein, who fabricated a monster that ultimately became the agent of his creator's destruction. The aptness of the fable and of the foreign-sounding name popularized the plot and notion among the many who never read the novel. For decades it was therefore felt necessary to correct those who thought that Frankenstein was the monster, and in any direct reference to the story this correction is still in order. But in alluding to situations in which the creature undoes the creator—e.g. man and his machines—it seems permissible to many writers to transfer the maker's proper name to his invention. The change follows the natural process of acceptance. Thus *a mackintosh, a Ford, a silhouette*—to say nothing of *a Rembrandt, a Malaprop*, or *a sandwich*—are familiar extensions that would encourage legitimizing *a Frankenstein*, and not just by yielding spinelessly to a common misunderstanding.

French words and phrases. A recent English writer on usage offers the incidental suggestion that it would not be desirable to adopt the American habit of countering *I beg your pardon* with *You're welcome*. This example shows what pitfalls lie in the path of him who would use unfamiliar expressions borrowed from abroad. What is worse, it is not enough to know the foreign language in order to know how to use (and spell) in English the indispensable borrowed phrase, nor is it always clear what degree of agreement (by means of endings) should be shown in the foreign word playing a role in the English sentence.

Still, despite the difficulties, there are certain spellings and relationships that are cast-iron and must not be tampered with. Of the French phrases used in American prose, the one most liable to error in print is *bête noire:* the final *e* is compulsory whether the application is to a man or a woman, the feminine *noire* modifying *bête* and not the person in the given instance. Since *bête noire* means only *bugbear* or *obsession*, use one of these if the feminine spelling of *noire* bothers you. It is a good rule to use foreign phrases only when no native equivalent is to be had. *Force majeure* follows the same pattern as *bête noire:* the *e* is invariable and the phrase, unnecessary in English, means *compulsion, coercion, duress*.

But what of this sentence from a work of criticism? *The incident reminds us of the hero of Lermontov's novel and of his fatale attributes.* What coursed through the writer's mind was the phrase *femme fatale*, of which he thought the second part adaptable to his purpose. It is not. The phrase is an all-or-none affair. With the *e*, *fatale* cannot apply to a hero; without it, *fatale* loses its French connotation. The way out of the dilemma is to write simply *his fascination, his pow-*

ers of fascination, his irresistible qualities (or *features*). There is always a way to say what one means if one has to give up a conventional figure of speech, because figures only embellish what can from the outset be stated literally.

Two pairs of French locutions that give trouble may look as if they were too tangled to sort out: *à fond* and *au fond*, and *à point* and *au point*. The first pair is the easier to keep clear: *à fond* means *thoroughly*, and says it by saying *to the bottom*; the other means *after all* or *when all is said and done*, and it does this by saying (as we also do in English) *at* (the) *bottom*. In the second pair, *à point* is the absolute phrase, as is shown by the absence of the definite article. Anything properly cooked is *à point*. *Au point* occurs only with words preceding or with a situation understood. [*La*] *mise au point* is *the final adjustment, correction,* or *improvement*. The full phrase just given thereby comes to mean a meeting between contending parties in which everything is to be set straight. In English there is no conceivable sentence in which *au point* could by itself be rightly substituted for *à point*. The former is always a mistake for the latter.

Au naturel is used in French for an article of food prepared without a sauce, though menu French often reduces this to *nature*. By extension *au naturel*

is sometimes used in English for *naked,* with the emotional grade of elegance of *in the buff.*

Double-entendre is not French at all but is by now excellent English to denote a play on words whose secondary meaning is risqué or suggestive of some impropriety. The French original is *double entente* and it covers a wider range of hidden meanings—threats, allusions to the past, or anything insinuated, not necessarily off-color.

In the previous paragraph the word *risqué* illustrates the recurrent question of spelling. Should the word become *risquée* when the writer has used a word that he thinks would be feminine in French, such as *remark?* The answer is that the text is not in French and *risqué* is invariable. Who could tell what French word might lie behind the English noun? *Remark* might be translated *propos* (masculine) instead of *remarque* (feminine). The gender of the imported word is therefore best forgotten. This goes for *blond* as an adjective applicable to girl or boy. *Blonde* and *brunette* denote women and neither applies to men. The pseudo-masculine *brunet* is a figment of the pedantic mind.

Spellings and connectives in certain French phrases often used in English must be mastered by the writer who would not be thought amateurish. The spontaneous, revealing exclamation is *le cri du coeur* (not *de*); the happy afterthought that comes too late is *l'esprit de l'escalier*; violence between lovers is a *crime passionnel* (two *n*'s, no final *e*); high society is *le haut monde*—not *haute*, which belongs to *couture* and *cuisine*, both preceded by *la*. Apropos of cuisine, all designations for special dishes are in the feminine, to agree with *à la mode* understood. So it is *boeuf bourguignonne* and not *bourguignon*. *Chaise longue* is a long chair and should not be rationalized into *chaise lounge*. And *de rigueur*, meaning *obligatory*, needs two *u*'s.

A word finally about shades of meaning to be aware of when using French words. Most important, perhaps, is the connotation of the contraction *M'sieu* for *Monsieur*, which appeals so strongly to novelists who want to create local color. No educated person in France reduces the two syllables to one in addressing another; and, a fortiori, no such person uses the popular combined form *m'sieu-dame*. Writers who portray church dignitaries and high civil servants need to be aware of these distinctions, of which habit, not snobbery, is the cause.

Arrière-pensée does not mean *after-thought* but *ulterior motive* or, occasionally, *hesitancy*. The *arrière-pensée* is a thought, as it were, spatially behind the present thought, not after it in time. *Vis-à-vis*, which is nothing but the literal equivalent of *face to face*, should be used in English with a clear sense of this root meaning. There are other linking terms for use when faceless elements are joined, and the following should be recast as suggested: *Article 6 taken vis-à-vis Article 9 lead* (s) *one to conclude that the authors of these by-laws were not models of consistency* (Article 6 taken together with Article 9) / *If the officer chooses to postpone the payment of tax vis-à-vis his retirement . . .* (until, when, considering his retirement) / *Vis-à-vis what you were saying last night, I've thought it over and I accept* (Apropos of, As to, About).

friend in common. See DEFENSIBLES.

-ful, suffix. See MASTERFUL, MASTERLY; MEANINGFUL.

fulsome. See MALAPROPS.

fund (-ing). See FISCAL.

fused participle. *What's the use of me doing all the hard work if you don't even appreciate it* contains a fused participle at the point where *me* and *doing* come together. Fowler gave the form its name in 1926 and argued the strongest case against it. The ground of his objection was the absence of a grammatical bond between the two words. *Doing* is a participle acting as a noun (i.e. it is a verbal noun, or gerund) and hence requires an adjective to govern it, e.g. *my doing*. There is no denying the charge. Indeed, the faulty construction does not, even for the most casual speakers, totally displace the tenable one. People who say *What's the use of me doing* will be heard to say *My going away is my business*. In this the fused participle resembles the shifting use of *who* and *whom* where only *whom* is grammatical (see WHO(M), WHO(M)EVER). Practice, then, is in a state of anarchy.

Still, it can be argued—and this is the doctrine of this article—that there is room for both constructions, that the choice between them can express a shade of meaning, and that the fused form can be grammatically defended as a "heavy apposition"—a variation in form of that familiar link, as heavy water is of water in the realm of nature.

Before arguing the need and the nuance, let it be said that the example which heads this entry is one of the less defensible ones. Its only excuse lies in the speaker's desire to make a contrast emphatic—*what's the use of* me . . . *when* you —and perhaps it would be a good excuse if the smoother and easily uttered *my doing* were not able to bear just as strong a vocal stress. It can,

and therefore the example as it stands is adjudged careless and clumsy.

The point of view changes, however, when some preceding word that governs the *me* or *my* (let us stick to the same person for simplicity) obviously calls for a personal pronoun and excludes a possessive adjective. For example: *the spectacle of me standing in the pulpit in my uncle's robes and delivering his sermon was too much—I burst out laughing.* Here *the spectacle of me* imposes itself as the main idea— as one would experience and express it while showing a snapshot to a friend: *That's me standing in the back row.* Hence the suggestion that the allowable fused participle may be explained as a heavy (long-drawn-out) apposition. Thus a stylist as exacting as Wilde makes one of his characters say (in 1895): *I don't think there is much likelihood, Jack, of you and Miss Fairfax being united.*

The first guideline drawn from this view is, then: Whenever the idea that governs the verbal noun (participle) is one that clearly calls for a stress on the person, the fused participle may be used; whenever the stress falls equally well, or better, on the action expressed by the participle, the possessive case must be used. If we adapt one of Fowler's examples—*What I object to is women having the vote*—it is clear that the speaker's objection is not to women but to the having a vote, to *their* having it; hence to *women's having the vote*—the only satisfactory way of putting it.

This first rule takes care of a great many cases, but not of all. There remain those in which the difficulty of making a possessive, even if one wanted it, tempts to the fused participle. For instance: *The likelihood of that ever happening is slight.* No one in his right senses would say or write *of that's ever happening.* Someone may ask: Why not write *the likelihood of its ever happening* and preserve good grammar? This is always possible, but emphasis may call for the original *that.* Awkward possessives may then be considered as a subclass under our first rule, the governing idea becoming the *unlikelihood of that* [event], with the "heavy apposition" as before. Similarly one will write: *I doubt this being said in such a place at such a time.*

One may question whether the appositive interpretation will fit all situations, for example those of compounded terms: *What the Justice feared was the Constitution of the United States becoming a shield for the criminal.* Here both constructions break down. What the Justice feared was obviously not the Constitution but its becoming, so the fused participle is offensive. And yet an apostrophe after *United States* is equally absurd. The writer must recast: either *What the Justice feared was that the Constitution . . . would become*; or omit *United States* and write *the Constitution's becoming.*

This leaves one type of sentence to dispose of, the one in which the word that should take the possessive is incapable of possessiveness. Some writers, it is true, seem to lack all feeling about what may or may not own something else (see POSSESSIVES 1); but when we confront a sentence such as *The argument arose because of dialectical materialism's claiming a greater role in scientific research than it could sustain,* many will feel that personifying the doctrine of dialectical materialism is ludicrous as well as clumsy. *It* does not claim; its partisans do. The sentence must be rewritten in any of several ways to show the actual doers or proponents claiming *for* dialectical materialism (or for themselves as materialists) the role later defined. In general, ideas and abstractions from facts will not permit the unfused participle to sound like anything but an affectation and the fused one like anything but a barbarism. There is for instance no way other than recasting to repair the sentence *She wasn't risking features of her script being identified in both letters.*

The reader may want to test the thesis here propounded by examining the following:

Proposed as allowable: *The ink has matured and an insoluble iron tannate has been formed, which prevents the aniline dye associated with it escaping / But with the situation the way it is and me deciding to cut loose from them as soon as it is straightened out / I'm so used to my poltergeist now that weeks on end pass without a recollection of it ever entering my head.* And from an ad: To Stop You Skidding.

Disallowed: *I'm strongly in favor of you putting someone on to tail the young lady / What he could not see was the Eiffel Tower being held up as a work of architecture* (not to be unfused but rewritten). And from a woman scholar who also writes good novels: *Some small children can take a whole school day without it doing them much harm.* A final example is disallowed on the score of compound illiteracy: *There was no point in he and Erhard going into great detail in these matters.*

G

gambit. Allied to *gambol*, a *gambit* is a move in chess by which a step forward—*a leg up* —is achieved through the sacrifice of a pawn or other piece. An *opening gambit* is therefore something cleverer and more costly than what is implied in its cliché use as a substitute for *opening remark,* adroit or not. Note that *opening* is a good noun and will serve without *gambit: His opening was friendly, even diplomatic; he spoke of their old days together.*

genteelism. Words in this class form a subgroup under euphemisms, which are locutions designed to soften or veil the harsh contours of some reality. Euphemisms are often indispensable to pleasant social intercourse. They are likewise the stuff of diplomacy, as when it is announced that a certain step by another nation will be regarded as *an unfriendly act,* meaning a deliberate affront capable of leading to war. As against euphemisms, conventional or impromptu genteelisms are soft-spoken expressions that are either unnecessary or too regularly used. The modern world is much given to making up euphemisms that turn into genteelisms. Thus newspapers and politicians shirk speaking of the poor and the crippled. These persons become, respectively, *the underprivileged* (or *disadvantaged*) and *the handicapped.* The term *minority group,* meaning one of the nationalities or religions that may hitherto have been denied common rights, has degenerated into the genteelism *He's minority group, you know* (for the pattern of this locution, see BOURGEOIS), where the phrase usurps the place of *Negro, Jewish, Catholic, Puerto Rican, Italian, Polish, Irish,* or whatever would be the appropriate term.

Few periods in history have been so reluctant to call things by their right names as our own. Our neighbors do not go crazy, they *become disturbed;* employers no longer fire or discharge employees, they *effect a separation* or *termination.* Even important warnings come wrapped in cotton wool, not to say couched in falsehoods —witness this printed card put in the bedrooms of a first-class hotel: *For your added comfort and convenience please lock your door and adjust chain before retiring.* For

204

comfort and convenience read *safety,* and for *adjust* read *be sure to fasten.*

The trouble with all euphemisms is that they wear out. They become "indecent" from association with the object or idea that they cloak, and a new screen has to be erected. The recent history of the efforts to replace *backward countries* by something genteel shows how quickly the new coinage loses its value. First we had *undeveloped countries.* This was soon found offensive and *underdeveloped* was substituted. A taint of reproach still adhered to this, and within a short time we heard *developing countries.* The outcome of this headlong march is to introduce into articles and reports on these important subjects statements clearly implying that Europe and the United States are not in the group of *developing countries.*

Genteelisms may be of two other kinds—the old-fashioned sort that will not name common things outright, such as the absurd plural *bosoms* for *breasts;* and phrases that try to conceal accidental associations of ideas, such as *back of* for *behind.* The advertiser's genteelisms are too numerous to count. They range from the false comparative (e.g. *the better hotels*) to the soapy phrase (e.g. *gracious living*), which is supposed to poeticize and perfume the proffer of bodily comforts.

See also ECHELON; FORBIDDEN WORDS 1; SEX.

Germanisms. American English has lately developed, largely under the influence of advertisers and packagers, a construction deeply at variance with the genius of the language. We now have *easy-to-read books* for the children and *ready-to-bake food* for their mothers. This agglutination of ideas into complex phrases requiring hyphens to make them into adjectives goes against the normal articulation of thought, which is *books easy to read, food ready to bake.*

If one wonders why the habit has taken hold, after centuries in which the utmost compounding for adjectival use limited itself to a few common expressions such as *would-be, all-or-none, so-called, long-drawn-out,* one may surmise that our minds have been prepared by reading the algebra of the headlines and the pseudo-science of the ologists. From the former we get NEW STEEL PEACE HOPE and from the latter we get *non-age-discrepancy sex offenses.* In both, the insult to reason consists in the failure to articulate. The reader must unscramble the ideas for himself. In the headline it is only the *hope* that is *new,* though the adjective stands before *steel* and *peace.* The consequence is that we learn to think of **a** *steelpeace-*

hope, a single notion quite close to the *easy-to-read book.* In the *non-age-discrepancy sex offenses* one cannot even apply the same factoring formula, and that is what condemns the practice. We are not to look for *non-age sex* but for a tangle of relations nowhere expressed and no less ridiculous than the *exceptional all-butter Paradise fruit cake.*

In a certain sense all these locutions can be uttered; but when in publicity for a directory we are promised *4,000 hard-to-find biographies,* and in a dictionary we are asked to note its concern for *hard-to-say words,* we have reached a point where agglutination resembles baby talk. And indeed the advertiser's estimate of his public confirms this impression. Note the implications of *no-iron sheets / an easy-to-carry bag for many uses / a not-for-profit solicitation / an easy-to-order form*—all from recent circulars. It is little wonder that fairly well-written prose catches the trick and produces: *inflexible, difficult-to-change statutory language* and *overpasses of more or less look-alike appearance.* The counterpart of this device in the realm of social science is the discussion of such topics as *the nontaxpaid liquor traffic, the life-lethal concentration of nitric oxide,* and *the briefly-visiting prime minister.* The language has no need of such fallacious compressions. They save no time; they corrupt both style and thought; and they make the detection of fallacy less and less habitual. What, for example, does a rebel student mean when she declares: *I am quite crisis and issue oriented?*

If we wish to protect ourselves from this new assault on our wits, we must begin by avoiding every form of easy compounding—e.g. *air-conscious, air-conditioned, career-* or *action-oriented, accident-prone, teen-age-proof, budgetwise* (see -WISE), and all other lumping of words in which the relation is not either established by usage or controlled by rule. *Walking stick* deceives no one into believing it is a stick that walks, because it is formed on a regular pattern; the same is true of *hairdresser, lantern-jawed, house broken, bowling alley,* and *secretary bird*—in all these we know how the elements affect each other to denote a new fact or idea. But in *budgetwise* and *crisis-oriented* the juxtaposition merely suggests some relation, as in the still lower perversions *jeunexpo, tidescapes, guesstimates,* and their like.

These last were called by Lewis Carroll PORTMANTEAU WORDS. Except for humorous effects that can soon turn tedious, they still sound commercial or pretentious, and they should not usurp the place of older terms or of complete sentences that explain what part of experience has so far been overlooked and unnamed. It is a mistake to think that because everything is classifiable everything must be classified. And Germanisms in English are but clumsy attempts to stick labels on arbitrary groupings: *never-before-told incidents / a hair-oily shopping-district-at-three-in-the-afternoon kind / a more-honored-in-the-breach situation / a let-the-devil-take-the-hindmost attitude,* to which we may add the multitude of definitions by *non-(nonfiction, nonviolent, nonreligious, noninsured).* Some of these last may be necessary but most of them only pretend to define.

gift, verb. It seems that *gift,* like CONTACT, is now a verb. *"The gifting is just ridiculous,"* said a Highland Park doctor / *Wonderful to own or for gifting!* The second example is remarkable for the perversity with which the copy writer, for the sake of getting in the fashionable word, resists the natural symmetry of *Wonderful to own or to give.* One does not commonly find in so little room an example of parts so badly matched. Nor is the verb treated as a simple transitive. *Gift him with a shoe on Father's Day*—unlucky, one-legged, indirect object of his children's love!

Granted *to gift,* can *giftable* be far behind? It seems not: here is a manufacturer advertising for the Christmas trade a number of *Giftable Portables.* Note that the suffix of *giftable,* unlike that of *portable,* results in a double passive, since the noun *gift* itself is passive—"giv'd," a thing given. *Giftable* is therefore something that can be being given.

Speaking more generally, the turning of nouns into verbs when no need exists save that of being different and chic should be given no quarter. *To author, to research, to pressure, to position* must be left to those who find no other way to impart freshness to their prose.

glamor, glamour. No one has yet proposed leaving the *u* out of *amour,* and we do not find *dour* (like *glamour,* a Scottish word) spelled *dor.* But *glamour* has a delusive resemblance to a class of words in which the British keep the *u* of Old French where American spelling since Noah Webster has omitted it, as in the Latin *favor, honor, labor,* etc. *Glamor* is now so common in the United States that dictionaries have taken to recording it as a variant. There has been an energetic advertising campaign for *Glamor Beverages.* As a result of this misunderstanding, our Anglophobes fume at *glamour* on the assumption that its intention is Anglophile. They might as well reserve their ire, for the spelling is the normal Scottish one. Note, however, that the adjective *glamorous* does drop the disputed *u*.

A separate question is whether, or when, a judicious writer can afford to use *glamour* at all. The word needs to recover from the battering it has taken from milliners, perfumers, hairdressers, and dollar-a-word writers.

going. See DANGLERS, ACCEPTABLE.

got, gotten. See UNSAVORY PASTS.

graceless. See CONNOTATIONS.

grammatical error. There will always be a few martinets to admonish us that this expression is a contradiction in terms and itself in error, since *grammatical* means *conforming to the requirements of grammar* and hence, by defini-

tion, *free from error*. To such remarks one is permitted to listen with half an ear, for *grammatical* quite as readily means *pertaining to grammar, belonging to the province of grammar*. This sense is, in fact, recorded in most dictionaries as the primary one.

The phrase, moreover, is but one specimen of a very large class: e.g. *logical error, diplomatic blunder, musical heresy, dramatic boredom*—all these failures or mistakes being readily understood to occur in the domains designated by the adjective. Its presence is no indication of the rightness implied in *logical, diplomatic*, etc. when they stand alone. To condemn phrases that are perfectly clear and have long been accepted is PEDANTRY.

granting. See DANGLERS, ACCEPTABLE.

greenhorn. See TENDERFOOT.

H

had (would) rather (sooner). 1. One finds indications, and even statements, that in modern use *would rather* is to be preferred, but it is hard to know what they are based on. Both *would rather* and *had rather* are in common use; the first is a comparatively recent substitute for the second, which has never approached obsolescence; both have respectable standing. *I had rather be a doorkeeper in the house of my God* is no more archaic than it was in 1611. A slight element of confusion enters through the contraction *I'd,* which of course can mean either *I had* or *I would;* but we can be sure that Wordsworth, writing

> I'd rather be
> A Pagan suckled in a creed outworn,

meant *I had.* No consideration makes this vestigial subjunctive logically inferior to *I would,* and it is at least as natural idiomatically, if indeed its long and unbroken history does not make it more natural. An incidental advantage is that *had rather* sidesteps the delicate issue of *would rather* versus *should rather* in the first person and in the interrogative second person—see APPENDIX 1: SHALL (SHOULD), WILL (WOULD). *I would* (should) *rather be right than be President* | *Would* (Should) *you rather be changed for a goat than a lamb?* Etymologically, *rather* is a word denoting time, but it has gradually taken on a sense so strongly volitional that the temporal meaning is all but squeezed out of it; and it undoubtedly ought to invoke the rule against unnecessary duplication of volition in auxiliaries. Where there is as much popular reluctance to use *shall* and *should* as we find in America, a locution irreproachable in itself that avoids the issue has that added point in its favor.

2. *Rather* once meant, of course, what *sooner* can still mean; but whereas *rather* has become almost completely volitional, *sooner* is still charged with a temporal implication strong enough to determine the auxiliary, and probably few would think of saying *I should sooner cut my hand off than sign such a document.* The meaning is volitional, but *sooner* is not felt as containing the volition, as *rather* contains it; we construe such a

sentence as meaning *I would* (not *should*) *cut my hand off before I would sign*. One does encounter *had sooner* in print, but probably with not enough frequency to establish it as idiomatic; *had as lief*, now somewhat archaic, is as idiomatic as *would as soon*.

Had rather, then, is unimprovable; it is one of the normally surviving subjunctives in English, like the second *had* in *If the rope had been stronger, my tale had been longer*. Anyone who insists on *would rather* does well to treat it as volitional and to vary the auxiliary appropriately between *would* and *should*; whereas *would sooner* or *would as soon* should remain invariable in all persons.

See also I'D, I'LL, I'VE.

hamstring, hamstrung. Shall the past tense and the participle be *hamstrung* or *hamstringed?* The slave to dictionaries will not get a confident answer, for dictionaries disagree. The New International records only *hamstrung*. Other American dictionaries record both forms, preferring *hamstrung*. The Oxford dictionaries prefer *hamstringed*. Jespersen merely remarks that both forms are in use—the observable fact. There is, then, enough conflict in usage to leave anyone free to choose. It we thoughtfully choose *hamstringed* we risk sounding illiterate to the thoughtless and

the underread. If we succumb to the doubtful analogy of *string, strung* we follow the path of least resistance and probably escape notice. The analogy is doubtful for the reason that the *strung of hamstrung* is an unaccented syllable and has a meaning opposite to that of *strung*, i.e. unstrung. Also, the analogy is imperfect anyway: instruments of the violin family are *stringed*, not *strung*, and the past tense of *string* is generally *strung* when it means supplied with strings (a tennis racket) but *stringed* when it means deprived of strings (cf. *string beans*). The question for a writer, then, is whether he shall prefer inconspicuousness or a slightly defiant logic. The political writer who characterizes the Arabs as *hamstrung by . . . a congenital inability to work together* seems to have preferred inconspicuousness, but may have chosen quite without thought, unaware of an alternative. Neither choice is indefensible; neither is immune to criticism. We cannot, without loss, forgo the word altogether, because it is a necessary word in its literal meaning and a highly expressive one in figurative uses. A writer has to decide arbitrarily whether he shall be damned for conforming to an unsatisfactory analogy or for asserting his independence of it.

For a parallel dilemma affecting a different part of

speech, see TENDERFOOT. See also UNSAVORY PASTS.

-happy. See -WISE.

hard core. See METAPHOR 4.

hardly. See FEWER, LESS; NO SOONER . . . WHEN.

hardly (scarcely) . . . than. The conjunction *than* is a chronic producer of idiom trouble (see DIFFERENT(LY) THAN and PREFER . . . THAN); it is, in fact, nowhere completely foolproof except after adjectives and adverbs in the comparative degree (*safer than / more safely than*) and after *other* and *otherwise*. It is continually being asked, in defiance of both idiom and its inherent tendency, to follow the almost indistinguishable synonyms *barely, hardly,* and *scarcely: Barely had the first Europeans landed at the Cape in 1652 . . . than they clashed with the Bushman / Hardly was he dead than Nxou and Bauxhau started skinning the bull / The Frenchman had hardly uttered his anti-war remark than W. dived in to investigate / Scarcely had B. congratulated himself on bettering his own mark than he was unceremoniously picked off first base / Scarcely had the noise subsided from this play than the Bombers really sent the arena into an uproar as their uprising got under way / They had hardly got moved and settled at the new address than X. was reassigned to the Seattle office.* The idiomatic and grammatical word in each of these is *when*; an admissible, perhaps slightly less natural possibility is *before.* (See, however, NO SOONER . . . WHEN.)

Apart from idiom, this type of sentence is open to criticism because it subordinates what is logically the main clause and puts the rhetorical emphasis on the subordinate temporal clause. On principle and in practice *He had hardly got home when the telephone rang* is open to a reservation that does not apply to *As soon as he got home the telephone rang;* and *They had hardly got moved and settled at the new address when X. was reassigned to the Seattle office* will reward the trouble of rewriting it: *Almost before they had . . . , X. was reassigned . . .*

hard put. The full idiom, in the meaning of *hard pressed* —colloquially, *up against it*— is *hard put to it,* in which *to it* is so nearly the efficient phrase that the expression loses more than half its meaning without it. The original figure in *put to it* or *hard put to it* probably derives from putting a horse to the jump. Latterly, the idiom occurs almost as often in its mutilated as in its intact form. *Even Roosevelt at times was hard put to keep it* [a political system] *from flying apart.*

(Here it is just possible that the author thought it better to clip the idiom than to tolerate *it* repeated in a different sense, but he should have avoided the repetition in some other way.) *Mayor John Burns, a Democrat, says he is hard put to pin down why its employment is moving in the opposite direction from the nation's.* If *to it* is sacrificed for economy, the distortion of a standard idiom outweighs the saving of two syllables. The frequency of the abuse suggests that many writers are unaware what the standard idiom is. Others may be influenced by newspaper SHORT-ENINGS, which produce such unidiomatic phrases as *long-drawn recital, stave attack,* or PUT IN JAIL ON CHARGE HE THREATENED PRESIDENT.

See also SET PHRASES.

have, noncausative. You have yourself photographed for a passport; the principal has the class dismissed; the manager has the outfield shift to the left. These are causative expressions; the actions, each volitional, are correctly reported as proceeding from a human will. But the same verb, with a plausible counterfeit of the same force, is continually cropping up in connections whose subjects have no will and perform no action, but are acted upon. *If he detected a student in a falsehood, he exposed him in a story told in such a way "that the guilty fellow knew who was meant" without having his name mentioned* (without mention of his name) / *[He] . . . conceded he had said that Democratic candidates might have their positions "seriously jeopardized" if the Democratic city administration opposed community desires* (might find their positions jeopardized) / *The Newark team . . . had six of its fifteen games rained out last spring* (Six . . . were rained out) / *one of the best-kept secrets the city has ever had burst upon it* (secrets that ever burst upon the city) / *Occasionally the "non"* [= "no"] *stickers have had stuck upon them printed legends implying that anyone who votes against Gen. Charles de Gaulle's new Constitution is a Communist* (On some of the *"non"* stickers there have been stuck legends implying) / *It is obviously unfair both to Mr. L. and to those who paid to hear his "jazz opera" to have it presented in such shabby, self-defeating circumstances* (unfair . . . to present it in) / *Mrs. M. is used to having her young clients suffer such setbacks* (is used to such setbacks suffered by) / *The Tennessee Williams play has had its engagement extended at the Arts Theatre* (The engagement of . . . has been extended) / *The holding in the case was simply that a witness who refused to answer a Congressional question must have pointed out to* *him the pertinency of the question to the committee's investigation* (that to a witness . . . the pertinency of the question . . . must be pointed out) / [Lily Langtry] . . . *had a town in Texas named for her* (A town in Texas was named for) / *Folwells had the branches of their family tree lopped off in similar ways* (Branches of the Folwells' family tree were lopped off) / *the fury of men who had worked long and hard to bring order out of industrial chaos at having their achievements traduced* (at hearing their achievements traduced).

The solecism in these examples is not less depraved, but only less obvious, than that in *The Halpins had their water line freeze and burst* or *Poor Johnny had his father die last week.* The trouble with every such *have* is that, active in form, it is passive in meaning; it gives somewhat the effect, nearly always feeble or otherwise deplorable, of narrating action in the passive voice. The simple cure is generally a truthful active verb with a different subject: *the water line froze and burst / Johnny's father died.*

heinous. See PRONUNCIATION 1.

help for **avoid, prevent.** When we want to express the idea that we cannot avoid performing a certain act, we find that we have three succinct,

idiomatic, virtually equivalent ways of stating it: (1) *I cannot help doing it,* (2) *I cannot but do it,* (3) *I can but do it.* The contradiction between the second and the third is apparent only: one means *I cannot do otherwise,* the other *I can only.* Given this embarrassment of resources, we are often tempted to seize on a fourth way that is a grammarless mixture of the first and the second or third: *I cannot help but do it.* We read: *A novel that cannot help but hold the attention / O'Neill could not help but suspect that his writing days were over / The interests of the United States cannot help but be advanced as the cause of peace . . . is advanced / "Love Affairs" cannot help but hold the attention of anyone who . . .* It is worth noticing that three of the samples make assertions about subjects incapable of volition and devoid of control over the action named. *Help* is manifestly a verb that should not be used of an unconscious or impersonal subject.

No mistake is ever big or good enough to be beyond the power of ingenuity to make it bigger and better, and we occasionally find *cannot help but* aggrandized by the addition of *to,* as in *The result cannot help but to raise grave doubts in the hopeful British as to their chances in this mission of retrieval.* The sequel to *help* is indeed an infinitive, but idiom requires the writer to forget the *to*.

Cannot help but in the wake of quasi-negative qualifiers such as *only* or *scarcely* may be thrown into the affirmative form, and then its effect is even more disconcerting: *With the final chase scene, only retired desk sergeants and the ghosts of faithless mistresses can but help wish* (can help wishing) *that every cop in Cardiff will end up under 50 feet of water off Tiger Bay.*

What shall be said of the colloquially ubiquitous *help* in *Don't take longer than you can help?* One obvious meaning is: *Don't take longer than you can't help taking,* but he who would insist on logic here would be a contentious purist indeed. Idiom does and should prevail, though it can be pointed out that for the same price the same thing can be said compactly, accurately, and with a complete avoidance of apparent illogicality: *Don't take longer than you have to* or *longer than you must.* Howells, when he wrote *you must not lie about the fact any more than you can help,* might as easily have written *any more than you must.* Here, as in many contexts, anyone bothered by an idiom that nags at his sense of fitness can clutch at a saving principle peculiarly at home in a language so rich as English: When in doubt, sidestep.

And yet this same idiom is capable of another interpreta-

tion. To say that *more than you can help* is an illogical compression of *more than you cannot help* is true only if we limit the special meaning of *help.* If it is negative only to the extent of *avoid,* the classic interpretation holds; but if it goes as far as *prevent,* then the idiom is logical: *I can't help it* = I cannot prevent it; *I can't help myself* = I cannot prevent myself from. (Here, surely, the translation *avoid* does not go far enough.) Therefore, by logical extension, *I don't spend more than I can help* = I don't spend more than I can prevent myself from spending. This interpretation is borne out by the following dialogue from a novel whose tone is natural and representative throughout: *"Too much action but you can't help it." "I should have helped it."*

helpmate, helpmeet. Readers of Webster's New International Dictionary can give themselves the mild start of finding *helpmate* described as a corruption of Genesis 2:18, in which God decides it is not good that the man (Adam) should be alone and undertakes to make him *an help meet for him; meet* has here, of course, the meaning *suitable,* as in *My tables! Meet it is I set it down.* Patently, *helpmate* is not so much a corruption as a more or less fumbling attempt to repair one. The actual corruption is *helpmeet,* the result of misconstruing an adjective as part of the noun preceding it. The misbegotten word is still enjoying quite a career. *And be to him wife, helpmeet, tender comrade, guiding star, and all the other things he had so poignantly been longing for / What course then is open to a cautious patriot yoked to a Rightist helpmeet? / Check your helpmeet at the door and retrieve her two hours and twenty-seven minutes later along with your hat.* The consecutive definitions in Webster tend to suggest that *helpmeet* is a standard word and *helpmate* a substandard invention gratuitously devised to replace it—an entirely untenable position. Neither word has any defensible latter-day use except for archaic or jocular effects, and the sensible writer lets both alone. *Helpmeet* is outlawed, not indeed by its illiteracy—a prolific source of words now highly reputable, e.g. *bridegroom*—but by the brazenness with which it flaunts its perversion of a still living and familiar source. *Helpmate* seems to have the hollowness of most words made up in cold blood as corrections of real or assumed misnomers —e.g. RAREBIT. Apparently this hollowness was not always felt, however. Dryden wrote with seeming comfort: *Well, if ever woman was a help mate for man, my spouse is so.* It may be noted in passing that *spouse* itself, outside legal contexts, is unusable today except jocularly. This is unfortunate, for the word is often indispensable —witness Henry James's difficulties with the married pairs in *The Golden Bowl.*

highlight. See LINKING 3.

historic(al). That is *historic* which holds an important place in history. Thus Napoleon's return from Elba was a *historic* event, President Monroe's doctrine of 1823 a *historic* utterance. All things *historic* are also *historical* in the sense that they belong to authentic history, but the great mass of *historical* figures and events have nothing *historic* about them: *historic* = special; *historical* = actual. It is thus possible to use *historical* to affirm or deny the truth of a supposed event. *The great terror of the year One Thousand is not historical.* Had it in fact taken place, the occurrence would have been both *historical* and *historic.*

hopefully. The German language is blessed with an adverb, *hoffentlich,* that affirms the desirability of an occurrence that may or may not come to pass. It is generally to be translated by some such periphrasis as *it is to be hoped that*; but hack translators and persons more at home in German than in English persistently render it as *hopefully.* Now, *hopefully* and *hopeful* indeed apply to either persons or affairs. A man in difficulty is hopeful of the outcome, or a situation looks hopeful; we face the future hopefully, or events develop hopefully. What *hopefully* refuses to convey in idiomatic English is the desirability of the hoped-for event. College, we read, is *a place for the development of habits of inquiry, the acquisition of knowledge and, hopefully, the establishment of foundations of wisdom.* Such a *hopefully* is un-English and eccentric; *it is to be hoped* is the natural way to express what is meant. *The underlying mentality is the same—and, hopefully, the prescription for cure is the same* (let us hope) / *With its enlarged circulation—and hopefully also increased readership* —[a periodical] *will seek to* . . . (we hope) / *Party leaders had looked confidently to Senator L. to win* . . . *by a wide margin and thus, hopefully, to lead the way to victory for* . . . *the Presidential ticket* (they hoped) / *Unfortunately—or hopefully, as you prefer it—it is none too soon to formulate the problems as swiftly as we can foresee them.* In the last example, *hopefully* needs replacing by one of the true antonyms of *unfortunately*—e.g. *providentially.*

The special badness of *hopefully* is not alone that it strains the sense of *-ly* to the breaking point, but that it appeals to speakers and writers who do not think about what they are saying and pick up VOGUE WORDS by reflex action. This peculiar charm of *hopefully* accounts for its tiresome frequency. How readily the rotten apple will corrupt the barrel is seen in the similar use of transferred meaning in other adverbs denoting an attitude of mind. For example: *Sorrowfully (regrettably), the officials charged with wording such propositions for ballot presentation don't say it that way / the "suicide needle" which—thankfully—he didn't see fit to use* (we are thankful to say). Adverbs so used lack point of view; they fail to tell us who does the hoping, the sorrowing, or the being thankful. Writers who feel the insistent need of an English equivalent for *hoffentlich* might try to popularize *hopingly*, but must attach it to a subject capable of hoping.

See also TRANSITIVE, INTRANSITIVE.

hospitable. See PRONUNCIATION 1.

however, interrogative. See WHATEVER, WHOEVER, INTERROGATIVE.

human, noun. The word *animal* is equally satisfactory as adjective (*the animal kingdom*) and as noun (*the lower animals*). Its dual competence leads those who write English by analogy to treat the adjective *human* as a similarly satisfactory noun for a member of the human race: *The horse was a "roarer," suffering from a condition akin to asthma in a human / Also shown was a surgeon mapping the brain of a human as the preliminary to an operation / A human has more dimensions than any test so far devised can measure.* The user of the word in this way can plead historical precedent as well as logical parallel and the support of some dictionaries, but not without convicting himself of a stylistic blind spot and a defective sense of present usage. The Shorter Oxford English Dictionary characterizes the noun *human* as now chiefly jocular or affected; the very liberal American College Dictionary calls it colloquial or humorous; and the New World Dictionary merely says "a person: usually *human being*." Referring to persons as *humans* is stylistically the equivalent of calling a horse an *equine* or a woman a *female*—usages that have also had their day.

humanism, humanist, humanity, humanitarian. The authors of a political-campaign document want a candidate elected to judicial office because of his *liberalism and humanism, practiced through a long career.* It seems probable that they are thinking of his *humanity* or *humaneness*—a kindly disposition toward his fellow men—rather than of his possession of a particular cultural heritage (*humanism*). *Humanity* is something that one can indeed practice through a long career; *humanism* describes rather what one believes than what one practices. *Humanism* is accordingly applied to various philosophies that make man the measure of all things.

The confusion between *humanism* and *humanity* is frequent and easy because the plural *humanities* signifies, not humane practices, but the branches of learning that foster the attitude of *humanism.* The name for one who cultivates the humanities is *humanist,* not—as one sometimes hears and reads, even in academic places—*humanitarian.* This last term is reserved for men whose career or public doctrine serves the ends of *human kindness*—*humanity.*

I

I. See WE, EDITORIAL.

-ible. See -ABLE, -IBLE.

icecap. Submarine navigation in high-latitude waters has involved thousands of miles of sailing under the broken and shifting field of floes known to explorers and students of the Arctic as the polar pack. For some reason many journalists, including editorial writers, choose to refer to it as the *icecap*—properly the name of the accumulated glacial ice sheet that covers some northern lands to an immense depth. The polar pack appears to average not over twenty-five feet in thickness and it hardly ever exceeds forty-five: it has been found only three feet thick at the pole. The icecap of Greenland is the better part of two miles thick in places and of a weight to have sunk the land to or below sea level. Certainly no vessels are sailing under it. The commander of a submarine that had made the transarctic passage, interviewed on television, was asked if he and his crew had *ever sailed under the icecap before*. He replied quietly that they had done some experimenting with the polar pack. But this tactful and quasi-official correction in the answer has never caught up with the misnomer in the question. A California member of the House of Representatives, in a letter to the President, says it has become clear *that underground and under polar ice cap test shots* [see GERMANISMS] *can be conducted without detection*. A man of letters, addressing the Congress on the hundred-and-fiftieth anniversary of Lincoln's birth, echoes the same error. A weekly of immense circulation, printing a review that gives the polar pack its rightful name, illustrates the text and supplies a caption in which the pack is renamed *icecap*. A magazine describes an elaborate commercial amusement by saying: *Passengers . . . make a realistic underwater journey through coral gardens, then descend to greater depths to view the wrecks of old treasure galleons and pass under the polar icecap*. This usage irritates students of the Arctic as the phrase *cast anchor*, when used of a modern vessel, irritates seamen. But newspapers have remained deaf to polite protests about the distinction and unperturbed by the problem of what the Greenland icecap is

218

to be called if its established name is to be misappropriated for floating sea ice.

identical. Americans, who practically never say *different to,* an extremely common locution in British English, are addicted to *identical to,* which is probably almost as unidiomatic everywhere as *different to* seems in the United States. *The New York studio in which Mr. Kennedy appeared was designed to be identical to Mr. Nixon's / The present currency system, which is identical to the British / The bust, identical to one originally commissioned for the aircraft carrier* Forrestal / *It is almost identical to the Glaucous Gull.* In each, idiom calls for *with*; so has a thing identity with, not to, another.

See also DIFFERENT(LY) THAN; PREPOSITIONS.

identify, identification. These VOGUE WORDS, which are also CRITICS' WORDS, have by overuse acquired an indefiniteness that continually borders on ambiguity. In the jargon of business, we *identify* problems instead of *finding, naming,* or *defining* them; imminent difficulties are *up for identification.* We also expect the employees to *identify* with the corporation, the office staff, the Community Chest drive. Similarly, the critic reports that he *identified with the nonhero* of the play under review. Thus, in our JARGON, intellectual discovery of problems and the emotional state of sympathy are both *identification.* Nor is this all. The modern citizen is also required to *carry identification* in his pocket in order to cash a check or placate the guard at the barrier. In this last use, however inelegant, the idea of oneness that belongs to *identity* and *identification* (Latin: *making the same*) is preserved. The police are right when they say they are working to *identify* the corpse; they assume *he had an identity* (= he was himself) when alive. But a newborn child is not *identified* when his parents give him a first name. By the same token the businessman or civil servant should desist from *identifying* problems and simply name them. As for the critic, he could help restore the true notion in these words if he would give up *identifying* at large and resume *identifying himself with* Ivan Karamazov, Don Quixote, Mary Poppins, or whomever.

I'd, I'll, I've. American usage differs radically from English as to the possible meanings of *I'd.* No American ever says or writes *I'd no money* or *I'd a few thoughts left, not good ones,* in which *I had* is contracted and means *I owned, I possessed.* Similarly, Americans keep the full emphatic *have* in the meaning *must* and do not say *I've to shave and dress.*

For the belief that *I'll* can stand equally for *I will* and *I shall*, see APPENDIX 1: SHALL (SHOULD), WILL (WOULD), p. 477. See also HAD (WOULD) RATHER (SOONER).

if and when. The conjunctions *if* and *when*, which have obviously different meanings when separately used, produce merely a duplication and a redundancy when put together, as they continually are by jargoneers. *Let us know if and when you hear from him* says no more than *when you hear from him* or *if you hear from him*; whichever is said, the hearer is to report on receipt of a message and not to report if no message is received. Sometimes we get this formula in the shape *if or when.* With *and* it is an unconscious betrayal of duplication; with *or* it records awareness that the conjunctions have different meanings if kept apart. The AND/OR problem is skirted by the simple expedient of keeping *if* and *when* apart.

See also UNLESS AND UNTIL; WHEN AND IF.

if's and an's. Writers may please themselves and put down *if's and an's* or *if's and and's.* So far as etymology goes, *an* in the sense of *if* is actually *and. I will roar you an 'twere any nightingale,* says Bottom in *A Midsummer Night's Dream.* But since both forms are acceptable, there are two very slight reasons for preferring *if's and an's.* One is the avoidance of the duplication *and and's.* (Notice that speakers will generally slur the second *d.*) And the curtailed form suggests more clearly the redoubled "iffiness" of the person causing this impatient description.

illy. See OVERLY.

immodest. See UN-, IN-, NON-.

impact. See IMPINGE; METAPHOR 4.

impinge. Acceptably used, this verb denotes a violent hit by one object on another, which receives it passively—a one-sided onslaught rather than a collision. The output of energy being inseparable from the meaning, the word is no substitute for *approach, affect, influence, merge with, get in the way of,* etc., though it is being encouraged to become a VOGUE WORD with such diluted effect. Any modifier will turn *impinge* into an absurdity, as when a novelist describes a man's life and work as *impinging more and more closely upon the operation of the legislature.* No closeness can be added to impingement, and this novelist's meaning is only that there was a growing association without clash. The word is justifiable, though perhaps not especially apt, when used of someone claiming literary ownership who *declared . . . that he would attempt to halt the production if it impinged on his asserted rights*; but it is very likely that the word intended here was *infringed* (without *on*).

The occasional attempt to make *impinge* do duty as a transitive verb produces a merely grotesque result, as in the assurance of a general manager that his company *in no sense wants to impinge its wishes on the town*. He was apparently seeking for *impose*. As for the derivative noun *impact*, it has rapidly exhausted its force (like *thrust*) through continual repetition as a vogue word that replaces *effect, result, consequence*, and the like.

implant. See INCULCATE.

implement, verb. See CONTACT.

implicit, explicit. Both words can exert the same force and approach the same meaning. The cliché is *I trust him implicitly*—that is, without a word said, without investigation. *It is implicit* (inherent) *in his nature that he should be trustworthy and in mine that I should recognize it*. Again, the performance of a certain action may be *implicit* (unspoken but clear) in an understanding, or it may be *explicit*

through oral or written reference. The difference is of the mode, not the substance, of the agreement. In this sense *implicit* and *explicit* point to the same, not opposite, facts. Note that *implicit* offers less ground for argument than *implied* (see IMPLY, INFER). For a promise to be *implied*, it should be discoverable in some recorded form; but a gesture, a look, or sometimes a person's whole past life can make it *implicit*.

Tacit is often used in the same way as *implicit*. A *tacit* reconciliation is one that both parties acknowledge and act upon without speaking of it.

imply, infer. When the confounding of these two words is not a mere illiterate blunder, it illustrates the pitfall of using the historical meanings of words as guides to their desirable present use. *Imply* and *infer* seem to be of about equal age, and they were well established early in the sixteenth century, when they were mainly used in senses remote from any that can be considered natural today. *Imply* meant, among other things, to *ascribe* or *attribute:* You implied a motive or a quality to a person —meaning that you considered him as having it or asserted his possession of it—or you implied a given result to a specified cause. And *infer* commonly meant just what *imply* means now; that is *to* *suggest strongly, to mean without saying*. So it is used often, perhaps always, in the plays of John Ford, as when Menaphon refers to

The sweetest and most ravishing contention
That art and nature ever were at strife in

and Amethus replies:

I cannot yet conceive what you infer
By art and nature.

It is small wonder, then, that various dictionaries neglect to make the sharp differentiation that the New International makes when it says that *infer* is "loosely and erroneously" used for *imply*. Because they neglect to make it, it is possible for the loose and erroneous user to adduce official sanction of an interchange that defies the present facts of language and can only be classified as illiterate. For usage, which tends to break down distinctions in some parts of language, has built up a clear distinction here—one as clear as that between *give* and *take*, which indeed it resembles. *Imply* is a word for the transmitting end, and *infer* a word for the receiving end, of the same process of deduction. The relation between an implication and an inference is that between printer's type and paper: the first delivers an impression, and the second ac-

cepts it. This physical example of course omits the presence of a mind giving or taking the impression. To such a mind smoke *implies* (according to the proverb) fire; so that when you see or smell smoke you *infer* fire. *Imply* means *fold in;* *infer* means *draw from*. Hence the implications unfolded by evidences or clues prompt us to the inferences that we draw from them.

That *infer* now continually turns up as a substitute for *imply* does not mean that its misusers are steeped in the English classics and instinctively revert to Elizabethan or Jacobean precedents: it means simply, like other common errors, that a great many persons are heedless of clearly established distinctions. The confusion reaches to unexpectedly high places. The newspapers naturally report verbatim when a White House spokesman says: *I am not going to make public here what the broadcasts said, because they are a pretty bad thing— but the inference was that the President and the Vice President were going along with the proposition*. Again, in a bestselling thriller written by a judge, you find the same confusion: *The defense is trying to infer that the prosecution is trying to conceal something / I know you did not actually say it . . . but you have plainly inferred it | And surely you do not mean to infer that it would be an unjust verdict if X. were acquitted on the ground of temporary insanity?* Of course the implication of these sentences may be that the author was only reproducing the language of trial lawyers, for verisimilitude; or is that too hasty an inference?

impracticable. See PRACTICAL.

in-, prefix. See UN-, IN-, NON-.

in addition to. See AS 11.

in for **by, of,** etc. **1.** Noticeably on the increase is a peculiar use of *in,* usually followed by an *-ing* form of some verb, in a way that sometimes befogs the intended meaning and sometimes contradicts it. *Our political leaders are not fulfilling their responsibilities in illuminating and arousing concern in the public.* This *in* seems to concede that the leaders are illuminating (enlightening?) the public and arousing concern in it, but not sufficiently to discharge their responsibilities; whereas the writer was probably trying to say that the leaders are failing to enlighten the public and arouse concern. Using *of* (and in some other constructions *by*) would avoid the false implication; or better still, substitute the infinitives and thus avoid a cascade of participles. *We must restore America to*

its position of world leadership in achieving universal peace! This demand probably means that universal peace is not being achieved because America has lost her world leadership, but it seems to say that universal peace is being achieved under other leadership. If we substitute *in order to achieve* for *in achieving* we express the probable intention. *There will be problems in construction of some types of shelters in complying with existing building codes* (in constructing some types ... if one must comply) / *Specialists have contributed both in determining what words were to be included and in framing accurate, precise definitions* (replace each *in* with *by*).

2. Less paradoxical but no less slovenly is the journalistic use of *in* to suggest a connection without naming it: PRESIDENT IN SURPRISE VISIT HERE / STUDENTS IN PROTEST / MARRIED WORKING WOMEN IN JOB SURVEY, and so on. The meaning is perhaps sufficient for a caption, but the abuse of prepositional vagueness ends by breaking down both the sense of idiom and the particular power of the small word itself. What we need in the examples above is a *survey* of *women, a surprise visit* from *the President,* and *a protest* by *students.* A proof that articulating ideas correctly is on the wane may be found in almost any scholarly bibliography. The titles are certainly long and lumbering enough, but the prepositions used give the impression of having been scattered at random. No distinction seems to be felt between *Air Disinfection in Large Rural Central Schools,* where *in* is literal and right, and *Recent Developments in Diarrhoea of the Newborn* or *Group Attitudes in a Polio Vaccine Program,* where *in* is figurative and wrong. Clearly, the developments are *in the study of* the subject, hence they are *about* [the subject of] *diarrhoea;* the attitudes are likewise *about* the program, not *in* it. (See WITH.)

3. When describing the material of which an object is made, *of,* not *in,* is idiomatic: *I want the shelving made of teak / The small bust of Napoleon was of plaster / a robe of richest silk.* The temptation to substitute *in* arises from the shopper's natural query *Have you the same model in green? In velvet?* Here *of* is impossible because of the effect of *same . . . in another color (shape, material).* But this variation does not authorize *He treated himself to a huge tomb in marble,* for nothing is more partitive than the making of objects out of materials, and the partitive requires *of* or *out of.*

inasmuch, insofar. These trisyllables, which almost always lead to an excess of *as*'s, should be reserved for situations in which the idea of proportion or measurement is needed. *Insofar as he could see into her character he thought her a woman of honor / Inasmuch as the old storekeeper had relied on the other's political influence he was bound to suffer disappointment.* The implications in this pair of sentences are, in the first: *insofar—and not one inch further;* and in the second: *to that extent, but possibly not more than that.* It is waste to pepper the page with *inasmuch* when *since* or *because* would do as well or better; and with *insofar* when *so far* is enough.

include for are. It is apparently easy to confuse the idea of inclusion with that of identity. Witness this assertion: *Some of the 30 or more scientific and technical disciplines which this vigorous research-based organization is applying in its pioneering effort include* [a list of eighteen items]. The whole thirty, of course, *include* the eighteen; but *some of* the thirty *are* the eighteen named. The writer incurred the usual consequence of trying to say something in two ways at once; he started by restricting his subject to a part of itself, but chose a verb that can go only with the unrestricted subject.

For an even more common confusion of a like sort, see REPRESENT.

including. See DANGLERS, ACCEPTABLE.

inculcate. 1. Verbs denoting the introduction of ideas, principles, notions, or codes into a person or persons—e.g. *instill, inject, implant, inculcate*—raise a problem of point of view that some writers apparently find troublesome. Are we inculcated with a discipline, or is the discipline inculcated into us? The second is idiomatic, the first not. Nevertheless we frequently read that persons are inculcated *with* something or other: *Deductive reasoning was an absolute necessity in a military man. . . . They inculcated you with that* (That was inculcated into you). A leading military analyst writing in a leading weekly says: *Or has the novitiate to military services been inculcated—as West Point has found in a study of the candidates that apply for the Military Academy—in a system of "dollar values"?* He is stating the process wrong end to; the dollar values have been inculcated in (or *into*) the novices. The same weekly editorializes: *Any youngster who has been inculcated with the "dictionary habit" has taken a giant step toward self-education* (into whom the . . . habit has been inculcated). The dictionary habit would forestall this misuse, which is in all probability encouraged by the influence of *inoculate;* for one is *inoculated* with germs, serum, ideas. The same is true of *indoctrinate,* which calls for a following *with* or *in. Inculcate,* an emphatic word for the implanting of ideas, retains some of the force and all of the point of view of its etymological meaning, which is *to trample in, stamp in with the heel.* Webster's New International Dictionary declares that teaching is inculcated *on* or *upon* the recipient. But in current usage *in* or *into* is much more usual. *To* (*unto*) was once admissible but should now be regarded as archaic.

2. *Instill, inject,* and *implant* all share the point of view of *inculcate.* A philosophy is *instilled into* the mind, not the mind instilled with the philosophy; a new idea is *injected into* a discussion, not the discussion injected with the idea; an ambition is *implanted in* a person, not the person implanted with the idea. The misuse of all four words betrays a confusion parallel to that which often overtakes IMPLY, INFER; that is, a confusion between the transmitting end and the receiving end of a mental conveyance. See TRANSITIVE, INTRANSITIVE.

Less commonly, *interject* leads into the same fallacy: *a moral fiction which is often interjected with autobiography.* The author here is evidently fishing for *interspersed* or *interlarded,* both eligible in this impersonal passive use.

indicate. This verb has become as tiresome a word-of-all-work in print as *O.K.* has become in conversation. *Indicate* is doubly damned by the frequency of its occurrence and by the number of more expressive words that it displaces. No verb except the simpler auxiliaries (*have, be, will,* etc.) could stand the overuse of *indicate*. In a metropolitan newspaper of forty-four pages, the chances are good that *indicate* occurs in it forty-four times. In those few uses where it means *evince, betray,* or *signify* and is followed by a noun object, there is nothing wrong with it. Trembling indicates fear, smoke indicates fire, a blush indicates embarrassment. TREND TOWARD REGULARLY ORGANIZED UNITS INDICATED AS RANDALL'S ISLAND FETE ENDS does no violence to *indicate*. The trouble begins when *indicate*, leading into a *that* clause, is substituted for any one of the many words of saying, for every mode of conveying facts or thoughts from one mind to another. An acting assistant attorney general *indicates* that the antitrust division plans no action in a given case. Sixty high schools *indicate* that they would inaugurate the teaching of Russian if they could find the teachers. The chairman of the Senate Foreign Relations Committee *indicates* that he feels it would be wise in the long run to recognize Communist China. *After seven hours of conference today, ... it was indicated that ... the bout ... would be held "probably in November and not in New York."* And so on. Once in a while this colorless and noncommittal word is used expressly (and effectively) to avoid attributing a firm statement to someone who has spoken with reticence or caution. But for the most part *indicate* is a makeshift for the words that writers are too hurried or unenterprising to summon: *hint, suggest, intimate, insinuate, imply, disclose, reveal;* or *convey, announce, affirm, assert, specify, stipulate, insist, protest, proclaim;* or *propose, advocate, recommend, urge;* or *note, point out, show, signify, profess, particularize, report;* or *admit, concede, grant, confess, testify;* or *state, declare, remark, say.* Writers and speakers addicted to *indicated* should remind themselves that its root is *index,* a pointer.

One specialized use of *indicate*, adapted from the standard medical vocabulary, has become a piece of parlor slang. In a given patient's condition, such-and-such a treatment is *indicated*—i.e. rendered logical or necessary, prescribed by the circumstances; in the opposite circumstances it is *contraindicated*. Whence such remarks as *A good stiff drink is indicated,* or *A few well-chosen words of protest are indicated,* or the sports broadcaster's *Someone to pinch-hit for the pitcher is indicated?* This usage resembles the tiresome slang remark *what the doctor ordered* (for any expedient that seems appropriate), or its analogue *You're the doctor,* which means *I defer to your judgment* or *It shall be as you say* or *Far be it from me to argue the point,* or, more simply and universally, *O.K.*

indict for. See CONVICT.

indifference. See DISINTERESTED.

indoctrinate. See INCULCATE.

infer. See IMPLY, INFER.

infringe. See PREPOSITIONS.

-ing. 1. Hostility to. 2. When to omit.

1. Hostility to. It is shown under A, AN, THE 5 that the addiction to nouns and to their inadequate linking by a definite or indefinite article can easily be remedied through the use of a present participle acting as a noun. Instead of writing *The program also called for reform of the United Nations* (which is a bad fusion of *called for reform* and *reform of the United Nations*) one can write *called for reforming the United Nations.* Similarly, one can be in favor of *adopting the metric system,*

reducing taxes, discussing terms of peace, and *sterilizing congenital idiots.* These verbal nouns (gerunds) happily stand for *adoption, reduction, discussion,* and *sterilization,* which not only are ill-joined to their neighboring words but also multiply out of all reason the number of *-ion's* and *-tion's* in nearly every sentence.

The disinclination to using the participial noun in *-ing* comes from a prejudice which assumes that it is a weak form. The modern temper likes standard abstractions—in the arts, the sciences, and daily life—and as a result it feels most secure when what is offered it is a grand process labeled with a noun. *Reform, adoption, discussion, reduction* seem less human than *reforming,* etc. and therefore surer, more universal and scientific. It may be rash to quarrel with the feeling, yet it must be pointed out that as between the *-tion* and the *-ing* forms, the *-ing* is closer to the verb, hence more active, concrete, direct, real. *The discussion went on for hours* is not so strong as *We sat there discussing for hours.* (See -ment under -ION, -NESS, -MENT.)

Another form of impatience with *-ing* expresses itself in the SHORTENINGS *frypan, swimsuit, playfield,* etc., which, if they spread, will radically change the principle of compounding nouns and verbs into new terms. We shall then have *dine* *halls, sit rooms,* and *sing commercials;* that is to say, find our adjectives in amputated infinitives.

Now for some examples of the shifts writers resort to out of hostility to *-ing.* The distaste often leads to making up new words: *One is struck by the complete absence of any panderage to fashionable trends* (pandering); or to the misuse of old ones: *The noted British ornithologist who studied the Yenisei's annual dissolution* (melting); or to pseudo-technicalities: *substituting an all-civilian review panel would result in fall-off in departmental efficiency* (in a falling off of); or yet again to ambiguity: *He cannot blame anyone else. The rumor is of his own generation* (generating).

The preference for the infinitive over the participle also interferes with idiom. Ear and mind insist that we say *I look forward to going away,* not *look forward to go away.* But less common parallels to this construction are repeatedly mangled; e.g. *You're welcome to use my typewriter* (using) / *In* [his] *early years, Mr. H. did everything from set type to solicit advertising to reporting* (from setting type to soliciting—just like the final reporting) / *She was accustomed to take a little nap after her lunch* (to taking).

2. When to omit. Perhaps by way of compensation, the contrary taste—equally bad—has popularized *gracious living, my* (*your, his*) *thinking,* and the almost infallible mismatching in *The lecture adds to the required reading rather than repeating it* (rather than repeats it) / *This move is meant to increase our effectiveness rather than diluting it* (rather than dilute [diminish] it).

Where *-ing* may sound weak is in sentences that would admit of a different tense of the same verb, often with a gain in clarity. *He bought the pictures hanging on the wall* is both ambiguous and weak. A relative clause is always stronger than a pivoting participle, which in this case is not a verbal noun but a verbal adjective. Say instead *He bought the pictures that hung on the wall* and you will feel definiteness and strength return. No style is worse than that which slithers down a series of *ing's: They spent that summer lazily, the house going slowly dilapidated, they not caring. In the village nestling far down below they could see men and women trotting like ants about their business depending on the hour of the day, waxing and waning with the heat oppressing them all alike.* Except for *trotting* all these participial adjectives need a second look and a pruning knife.

But this fault or abuse is not so common as it once was when stylish novelists went in for languor and a dying fall. What is common today is the misplaced *-ing* in balanced constructions with *rather, than, but,* which call for the infinitive; for example: *She could not understand why he should stay rather than being* (be) *moved elsewhere / The officer indicated by a nod that he was willing to keep silent rather than turning* (turn) *in a report / To rescue their good name, spare her father disgrace, save his very life, she would do anything—yes, anything but marrying* (marry) *that odious Leon.* The fault is a failure of grammatical parallelism: see LINKING and MATCHING PARTS.

inherent. See PRONUNCIATION 1.

initial, adjective. See SCIENTISM 3; VOGUE WORDS.

initialese. The scientific world early discovered that its work was facilitated by the use of symbols—letters or arbitrary signs—which could be more readily associated with numbers and postulates than words could. Chemistry and mathematics were the first sciences to make the practice systematic, and it was then extended with success to other endeavors, notably to engineering and to manufacturing generally. We are all accustomed to ordering Model N-0066 and aware that the letter and the

figures not only denote the particular type of object but also connote its main features and possibly the date of its design. As chemistry enlarged its repertory of compounds and their names became longer, it resorted to abbreviation by initial letters. Instead of *trinitrotoluene,* it said *TNT;* instead of *dichloro-diphenyltrichloro-ethane,* it said *DDT.* Other sciences did the same thing with the same purpose of convenience, and so did trade. But in every one of these activities the symbols and abbreviations were distinct—that is, unique for that science or industry—and they were readily learned by those engaged in the activity, because the system was intelligible and the knowledge thus conveyed was their concern.

The extension of this clear and intellectually decent arrangement to public matters—organizations, programs, and abstract schemes and proposals—is something radically different. It lacks system, clarity, intellectual decency, and a proper respect for mankind. It is ambiguous, affected, and at times childish; and by its amplification beyond reason it has become a menace to the memory as well as to the rational mind. To take a trifling instance of this irrationality, consider the usual way in which two familiar sets of initials, A.C. and D.C., are referred to. The layman invariably says *A.C. (D.C.) current*, although the *C.* in each pair already stands for *current.*

As everyone knows, there are two types of denotation by initials—that which takes its rise from an ordinary descriptive name, such as the American Medical Association, which becomes the *A.M.A.*, and that which begins in reverse with a word or near-word whose letters then become the initials of a descriptive or common word. *AID* stands for the Agency for International Development; *CORE* = Congress of Racial Equality; the Post Office is proud of its *ABCD*, or Accelerated Business Collection and Delivery, etc.

It is always permissible for a professional group or a clique to make what abbreviations it wants, because it presumably knows what the short form means, and the occasion for using the symbols or initials supplies the context. To teachers, *NEA* stands for the National Education Association. But the public also hears of the *NEA* as the Newspaper Enterprise Association and the National Editorial Association. What then does *NEA* mean, even in the context of journalism, which at times overlaps the educational? *SRO* in the newspapers may mean *Standing Room Only* (in a theatre or a concert hall) or it may mean *Single Room Occupancy* (= a slum building). The dictionaries that have been compiled of these abbreviations cannot keep up with them or separate them for the puzzled reader. And a like uncertainty will soon arise from seeing the initials of great men, living or dead. There will come a time when F.D.R., J.F.K., G.B.S., and R.L.S. must revert to their full names if bafflement and irritation are not to be the regular concomitants of reading and listening.

Names made up of initials are called *acronyms,* and the supposed ingenuity required to invent them entices more and more persons into the pastime of devising elaborate names for very simple things. This is akin to the passion for COVERING WORDS. Thus an apparatus for breathing under water is called a *scuba,* from *self-contained underwater breathing apparatus.* If ingenuity needs exercise it should have been deployed in the traditional way, which is to find the old word that best describes (as in poetry) the new object. There is a word for *self-contained underwater,* etc., and that is *gills.* Once in a while the modern letter game produces an expressive word, as in *radar;* but what is one to think of organizations that freely call themselves JOIDES or DACOWITS, or that choose to associate federal mortgages with the names Fanny May? Nor is it a good thing for the moral man to accustom himself to the emptiness of imagination that repeats BW and CW for biological and chemical warfare.

Discussing the affectation of modern scholarship that turns books and men into initials, Mr. Gershon Legman justly says: "The index, the schema . . ., intended originally as dummy representations, as tools or perhaps tongs to help grasp a complicated living reality, entirely replace the reality. . . . Let's be specific. Why SMLJ when *Beck* requires no more than the same four letters to set down, and three less syllables to pronounce? Why SSLKFS (in six syllables) for the whole name *Cecil Sharp* (in three)? . . . Why not the dignified scientific minimum of a name or place and date, locating the human phenomenon or art expression . . . in its human and historical context, outside of which it can neither be assessed nor understood, nor in fact have any real meaning at all." In short, there is no reason why today our minds and our prose should be cluttered up with letters and vocables that, unlike the symbols of science and the abbreviations of trade, neither denote with exactitude nor connote anything whatever.

inject. See INCULCATE.

in order to. Despite pedantic objection, the use of this phrase is a kindness to readers whenever a clause expressing purpose and beginning with *to* stands at some distance from the verb that heralds it, or when a succession of *to*'s might create confusion. In the sentence *Thomas had seen no way but to borrow the foreign car which he was not sure he knew how to drive to reach the doctor's office in time*, the addition of *in order* before *to reach* and the setting off of the *which* clause with commas would improve the articulation.

Without a verb, the phrase is old-fashioned but not incorrect: *In order to the execution of the decree, a platoon of horse guards was despatched to the spot.*

in part. See PART, IN.

insigne, insignia. Because of its form, the Latin plural *insignia* is easily mistaken for a singular. The mistake often takes shape in the manufactured form *insignias*, a plural of a plural and as redundant as *scissorses* would be. Advanced liberalizers, aware that much English now established and reputable grew out of just such misapprehensions, condone and even recommend the treatment of *insignia* as a singular and invite us to forget the legitimate singular, *insigne* (pronounced *in-sig-nee*), which occurs in print so rarely that many are unaware of its existence. What these liberalizers overlook is the difference between ancient errors sanctified by the evolutionary processes natural to English and errors amounting to retroactive alterations of Latin, as if the Romans needed us to straighten out their language. A typical example of what is sometimes condoned: *Chances are you will also see this insignia bannering shop windows up and down* [the] *Main Street of your own town.*

Singular or plural, the word is not fittingly applied to emblems lacking in dignity, prestige, or illustriousness: the different branches of the armed services have their *insignia*; the caduceus is the *insigne* of the medical profession and of the Army Medical Corps. In the example quoted, the reference is to a trademark, which deserves no such honor.

See also LATIN AND GREEK PLURALS.

insofar. See INASMUCH, INSOFAR.

instill. See INCULCATE.

insure. See ASSURE, ENSURE, INSURE.

interdisciplinary. See ENDINGS 2.

interested. See DISINTERESTED.

interest(s). See FALSE SINGULARS.

in terms of. The rage for expressing everything *in terms of* something else is a disease traceable to college-catalogue English. From 1900 on a college course was hardly respectable if it did not offer to present literature in terms of its social effects, an author in terms of his influence on the development of this or that form, history in terms of underlying economic forces, geography in terms of transportation and commerce, and so on. It was not long before academic writers found themselves unable to finish a paragraph without using *in terms of*. The phrase was a ready substitute for the common prepositions *at*, *in*, *for*, *by*, and the rest, and it also supplied a loose coupling for ideas whose exact connection had not been thought out by the author.

The professorate undoubtedly had borrowed the phrase from the sciences. In formulas and equations you do express one thing in terms of another—distance as a function of rate and time, earnings as a product of volume and price, etc. But in an equation the terms are named and numbered; they are the components of the problem —physically, visibly there. As the phrase is used in general discourse no one is thinking of converting anything into anything else. The phrase is invoked to lend an air of intellectual strictness to statements that are in fact the opposite.

The on-again-off-again rhythm of the Eisenhower Administration's interest in missile development is here recounted in terms of the man who put up perhaps the hardest fight at the top civilian level for a consistent research and development program. This sentence does not mean that anything is recounted in the language of the man referred to, or even in the patterns of his thought; it means simply that his experience is used as a narrative thread or an illustration. The sense would be served by *recounted as the story of the man who* or something of the sort.

There follows a purposely long list of examples showing the extent of the blight; and parentheses suggest how they might be written to advantage. *The seating arrangements, while excellent for music, are far from ideal in terms of the drama* (for the drama) / *the industrial charters, if construed in terms of the guarantee of exclusive craft jurisdiction, could not mean very much* (construed as guarantees) / *Wilson, with his passion for decentralization, had set up operations in terms of independent local corporations* (set up operations as a system of local corporations) / *looked at the future of world affairs in terms of the key forces and events of the past decade* (as a sequel to) / *Hardships have been diminished in terms of food and clothing* (The short-

ages of food and clothing have been reduced) / *the industrialization programs are showing results in terms of factories going up and in terms of actual production* (omit *terms of* in both places) / *His major political task was to designate a new Premier, but this designation was always in terms of what was thought might be acceptable to an elusive majority of the Assembly* (was always dictated by) / *Although the Communists remained the second biggest party in terms of the popular vote* (in the popular vote cast) / *President Eisenhower today named a blue ribbon committee . . . to evaluate the U.S. military aid program in terms of how to strengthen national security* (as a means of strengthening) / *advised newspapers "to tell advertisers of your impact in terms of circulation and area coverage"* (impact by means of) / *consider the Halloween of yesterday in the terms of a great equalizer* (as a great equalizer) / *Third Avenue, in terms of entire blockfronts being rebuilt, is catching up with Manhattan's building boom* (to judge by entire blockfronts being rebuilt) / *In terms of television's much-publicized impact on the American mind, the potentiality of its negative influence is not often mentioned* (Compared to the . . . positive effect of television on the American mind, its potent negative effect is not often mentioned) / *several matters that are related to the closer cooperation of the American republics in terms, perhaps, of more significant and frequent meetings of the foreign ministers, in terms of the operation which has been initiated by President Kubitschek and called "Operation Pan America," and in terms of the decision by the United States to be willing to cooperate with a regional financial institution for the Americas* (matters related to the closer co-operation of the American republics—perhaps more significant and frequent meetings of the foreign ministers, President Kubitschek's "Operation Pan America," and the willingness of the United States to, etc.).

into, in to. 1. The two forms are not interchangeable and the second, in which the words are separated, conveys a meaning quite distinct from that of the first form. In technical language, the first is a preposition, the second an adverb followed by a preposition. Failure to distinguish them is common and damaging to sense. *While the Prime Minister leads his guests into the reception* (in to; *in* = inward to another room; leads *in* his guests *to*) / *The ominous growling sound of angry men in the streets outside reached into* (in to) *them within the building* / *For a time he had resisted this enchantment, only in the end to give into it* (give in to; *in* is an integral part of the verb phrase *give in*) / *late drivers who pulled into* (in to) *the curb, glancing apprehensively over their shoulders* / *A police car rounded a corner and skidded into the curb* (in to; this was a controlled skid, not an accident) / *where he could see the excursion boat coming into* (in to—otherwise it is a catastrophe) *the pier* / *the farmers* [in a blizzard] *just couldn't get into town.* The last is a borderline case; *get into town* is often idiomatic, but the author probably meant that the farmers were failing to reach town from the environs—*get in to.*

2. A slightly different trouble appears in *Then she placed the phone into its cradle.* For some logic-defying reason we *put* things either *in* or *into*, but *place* them *in*; she placed the phone in its cradle. This inflexible idiom runs counter to the general rule that we use *in* for simple containment without motion (*This volume is in the art collection*) or for motion within (*He was pacing back and forth in the corridor*), and *into* for motion toward (*She tiptoed into the nursery*).

invaluable. See UN-, IN-, NON-.

inversion. See A, AN, THE 3; NUMBER, TROUBLE WITH.

inverted commas. This phrase for what prevailing American usage calls *quotation marks* seems to be gaining ground in America; it is the standard expression in Great Britain. A speaker or writer will not be doing amiss by using whichever he is accustomed to, but it may also be worth pointing out that *inverted commas* is not an accurate term. The opening signs (" and ') consist of commas both inverted and reversed; the closing signs (" and ') are neither inverted nor reversed, but merely superior—i.e. above the line; and they might be described as apostrophes. There is a further snag in the circumstance that some modern fonts of type adopt a form of the opening marks that is not inverted but only reversed. (This departure makes traditionalist typographers see red.) On the whole an American accustomed to *quotation marks* has nothing to lose by sticking to his habit and nothing to gain by altering it.

See also QUOTE, UNQUOTE.

-ion, -ness, -ment. No clear distinction exists between *precision* and *preciseness*, or between similar roots that can take both *-ion* and *-ness* without making either derivative seem artificial. Perhaps a distinction would be desirable, and sometimes one suspects in reading the best writers that they consciously or unconsciously mark a difference between these two endings. When they do, or seem to, the difference appears to be that *-ion* describes the abstract act and *-ness* the concrete quality. One might say, for example: *The exercise of concision will bestow conciseness on a piece of writing.* And likewise of course for *precision* and *preciseness.* A number of words, however, do not follow the same simple pattern and form the *-ness* compound from the longer adjectives in *-ive* (or *-ate*). We say *derision* and *derisiveness, division* and *divisiveness, intrusion* and *intrusiveness, decision* and *decisiveness, persuasion* and *persuasiveness, deliberation* and *deliberateness,* etc. As a result, the distinction sought appears more clearly, because the adjective that generates the longer noun points more emphatically to *the quality of,* which leaves the *-ion* form more abstract. Surely everyone feels—or can come to feel—the difference between *consideration* and *considerateness.*

What works against establishing this distinction, or a distinction, is the need to avoid stuffing sentences with words in *-ion,* which are so numerous and, for some writers, so hard to escape. The whole question is one of style rather than of usage, and it illustrates how style must effect a compromise between contrary demands. The ear wants fewer *-ion* words, regardless of meaning; the mind wants cognate words with different endings to convey different nuances. Both are right, and we face here a dilemma akin to the one produced by the wish to make *that* the restrictive and *which* the nonrestrictive relative pronoun. (See THAT, WHICH, RELATIVE.)

In spite of what has just been said about the difficulty of absorbing more than one or two *-ion* words into a sentence agreeable to the ear, there is no warrant for seeking novelty by the substitution of *-ment* in old words that end in *-ion*. The recent campaign for the abolition of capital punishment has made some journalists grow weary of *abolition* and introduce *abolishment*. Most of them have a good enough ear to use this new creation next to *death penalty* and so avoid the sequence *abolishment . . . punishment*, though it may well be that the jingle inspired the change in the first place. In any case, the *-ment* ending has not enough life in it to displace *-ion*, except where *-ion* has been pre-empted by the same root for another meaning. We have to say *containment* because we cannot say *contention* without ambiguity. But say *detention*, and *detainment* sounds affected.

What is more, there are occasions when the established word in *-ment* has another meaning than the one intended. *Confinement*, *retirement*, *assignment*, *impressment*, and *advisement* have not the same meaning as the verbal nouns *confining*, *retiring*, *advising*, and the differently formed *impressiveness* and *assignation*. Purpose and context decide which is to be used, and the resistance to words in *-ing* (see -ING 1) should not cause the placing on *-ment* of a burden it cannot bear.

ironic. See JOURNALESE.

irony. See UNDERSTATEMENT.

irregardless. See BARBARISMS.

-ism. This Greek ending has until now been reserved largely for the designation of either a doctrine or an emotional tendency. *Anarchism* and *patriotism* illustrate these two poles of accepted usage. The useful extensions have followed this pattern, using a proper name or a general term when these implied a sufficient breadth of ideas or practices to deserve an *-ism* being created about them—e.g. *Darwinism, Marxism, totemism, Symbolism, bimetallism*. Note that in adapting proper names attention is generally paid to form and sound. Thus *Freud* has given *Freudianism* rather than *Freudism* (except in French, with terminal *e*), *Shaw* has given *Shavianism* instead of *Shawism*, etc. A difficult name like Nietzsche rarely puts on the suffix, however much the system of ideas might warrant it.

Of late, these instinctive and rational guidelines have been overlooked and *-isms* have sprouted in several directions: (1) By a superfluous expansion of established words, as when a person's *behavior* is referred to as his *behaviorism*, or when psychiatrists feel impelled to write *He is a psychopathic personality . . . with asocial and amoral trends, antisocialism, and recidivistic history.* The occupation here is serious, because *behaviorism* and *socialism* are established doctrines that have nothing to do with *anti-social* and *behavior.* In other cases, the *-ism* is unnecessary. We do not need *bigotism* because we have *bigotry.*

(2) By the application of *-ism* to tendencies that lack the intellectual or emotional quality justifying a separate name. Thus *absenteeism* is not a program of action or a cluster of ideas and feelings; it is an accidentally determined number of absences during a stated period. Again, *tokenism* is a poor word to characterize the insufficient concessions made to a protesting group; it would be an appropriate name only if a party were to advocate such a holding back of full satisfaction. One more example: from the sentence *The Provost of Columbia University writes of the communicating problems inherent in encyclopedism* it is hard to extract the intended meaning of *the difficulty of putting together an encyclopedia that will inform people of various ages and degrees of learning.* Writing encyclopedia articles is not and cannot be *encyclopedism,* though it so happens that the authors of the eighteenth-century French Encyclopedia had a doctrine that deserves the name. (Notice also in the quoted sentence the barbarous use of *communicating problems* for *problems of communication.*) See COVERING WORDS.

(3) Finally, by the practice of some historians of ideas to turn every author they treat of into the maker of an *-ism: Bucklism, Taineism, Huxleyism, Renanism, Gidism, Heideggerism.* This is foolish as well as ungainly.

issue. See PREPOSITIONS; PRONUNCIATION 1.

-itis. As an ending attached to the name of one of the organs of the body, *-itis* denotes the irritation or inflammation of that organ. *Appendicitis* is the great exemplar, surrounded by the troop of less dramatic afflictions—*tonsilitis, conjunctivitis, bursitis,* etc. To attribute to *-itis* the meaning of addiction, obsession, monomania, or simply *It's a disease with him* is a culpable affectation rooted in ignorance. *Wagneritis, projectitis, discothequitis,* and the like are needless and silly.

-ize. The Greek suffix *-ize* has proved so useful in modern science to designate a process (*electrolyze, polymerize,* to say nothing of *analyze*) that the public has acquired the habit of making up new words in *-ize* to describe its workaday doings. The words are nearly all unnecessary and ill-formed. A scholar who discloses to the world his mode of composing books says that until he is ready to write he *folderizes his ideas* (= files notes). Businessmen no longer *strike a bargain* or *conclude a deal,* they *finalize an agreement.* Pianists *concertize in Europe and South America.* In England, it is said, the Foreign Office *secretizes* when it makes a secret treaty. Over here, librarians and clipping bureaus *permanize* documents by covering them with a transparent adhesive sheet. Shipowners and janitors both *containerize* to make easier the unloading of goods and of trash respectively. Electricians *reflectorize* light, and management consultants *uniformize* procedures. Alumni secretaries write that *We don't do much at the lunches but friendlyize.* As for the child who was referred to a diagnostician as *grossly undernasalized,* it is impossible to say whether the trouble required a plastic surgeon or a speech improver. These absurdities and those bound to come in their wake call for only two comments. If the itch to *-ize* a common word is irresistible, let it be by addition to the full root. *Permanize* is amputated and can do no work (see PERMAFROST). If, again, the urge beckons, let it be after a review of existing resources. *Reflectorize* (= equip with a reflector) can be dispensed with by using *reflect: You'd like more light, madam? That's easy—we'll just reflect it for you.* The question is: Could the bill be made as large as if the light had been *reflectorized?*

J

jargon. Properly the special vocabulary or phraseology of an art or a profession—and as such acceptable—*jargon* has by a metaphor become the pejorative name given to certain faults of modern writing. It would be more exact to call their corrupting influence on prose *pseudo-jargon,* for the badness consists in the pretense of using technical words when these either have no currency or are not appropriate. Sometimes the writer makes them up as he goes; at other times he picks them up from another art or science without a sufficient awareness of their use and tone. With this obscure diction goes a heavy syntax that strings together abstractions and noun-clusters with *of*'s and *in*'s, so that the sentences lack rhythm, clarity, and force (see NOUN-PLAGUE). Here are two examples, the first and milder one being from an essay called "Plenitude from Petroleum"; the pseudo-jargon is marked by roman type: *In the* energy field *during the next twenty years the* overall position of *petroleum will not be affected other than* marginally, *although the* fuel pattern *is likely to change. The use of nuclear reactors in electric power stations and in ships may check the* growth rate *in the use of heavy fuel, and cheaper electricity may well cause the* growth curve *for domestic petroleum fuel for central heating to* flatten out; *but on the other hand there is likely to be steady growth in the utilization of petroleum in metallurgy, particularly for reducing iron ore.* (This last phrase startles by being straight English and not *iron-ore reduction.*)

The second is from a report by an industrial engineer: *After trying* a variety of methods of operations (various ways of conducting it) *this year the seminar* operated against the framework *of an outline the chairman prepared and presented at the opening meeting* (the seminar used an outline I presented at the outset). *While the various presentations did not follow, or indeed in many cases tie into, this outline* (Although some of the reports diverged from the outline), *yet it* definitely provided a greater coherence *to the seminar as a total operation and I am grateful for the distinct contributions which were made to* my thinking (yet the outline helped, and I am grateful for

239

what I learned from the discussions).

By dint of repetition, pseudo-jargon of this sort infects all our minds until it seems impossible to express oneself without recourse to its battered elements—*motivation, framework, time factor, calculated risk, positioning, structuring,* and dozens of others (see SCIENTISM; VOGUE WORDS; EDUCATIONESE; CRITICS' WORDS; and POPULARIZED TECHNICALITIES). Since the manufacture of jargon goes on at an accelerating pace, the infiltration of the product into one's mind and speech must be steadily resisted. In writing, the only cure is to deny oneself the use of an ever-enlarging list of terms; or, rather, the use of them in their jargon sense (see FORBIDDEN WORDS 2).

journalese. The best writing is done by professional writers, and among them are journalists. Hence some of the best writing done today, writing free of the faults discussed in this book and elsewhere, is done by journalists—and this despite the rush, excitement, and small opportunity for revising that go with the practice of their art. But every profession is liable to certain failings, and it is these failings that have given rise to the name *journalese* for a kind of fault in writing which, owing to the public's daily exposure to it, is particularly contagious.

In general, the tone of journalese is the tone of contrived excitement. When the facts by themselves do not make the reader's pulse beat faster, the journalist thinks it his duty to apply the spur and whip of breathless words and phrases. Since these exist only in finite numbers they get repeated, and repetition begets their weakening, their descent into journalese. That is how we have worn out the epithets *drastic, cryptic, crucial, essential, crushing, bitter, ironic,* and others that a studied writer will use only with caution. What sense of danger (or, more properly, of a turning point in a dangerous situation), for example, is left in the poor abused word *crisis?* Through frequent and automatic repetition such words find themselves in contexts where they do not belong, hence where their meaning does not come into play except as a signal to routine excitement. Thus *drastic* rightly used implies a violent action involving a sacrifice, a loss. The Massacre of the Innocents was a drastic decision of Herod's, because a king does not like to deplete his population. The shopkeeper who announces drastic reductions in all his prices suggests that he is going to lose by your gain. But there is nothing drastic in the suddenness and violence of a riot, an explosion, or a decision to move a factory to a better site.

Similarly, *cryptic* implies a teasing mystery, a provocative concealment, not just a secret. A document marked *Top Secret* is not cryptic. As for *irony* and *ironic*, the idea of an opposition of meaning between the thing said and the thing intended must be present to make the words applicable. By extension they can be applied to events, and that is why journalese has annexed them. From the *irony of fate*, which consists in the contrast between opportunity and circumstance (you have a chance to cruise around the world—you should be happy, but you are ill and condemned to bed for six months), journalese came to use *ironic* for all disappointments and defeats, regardless of their connection with some contrary appearance.

The desire for excitement tempered by sophistication leads writers to commit other faults classifiable as journalese. One is the abuse of superlatives—*the most, the first, the only*. These are rarely true, or provable if true; and even if true and provable, they generally do not add much to the interest of the subject. If the President's wife receives the gift of a piece of furniture for the White House, it is enough to satisfy any but a childish curiosity that the piece be genuine and of a suitable period; it does not have to be the oldest, most expensive, or rarest of its kind. Headline words of course overemphasize steadily. *Bar, ban, score, rap, quash,* and their kin suggest a very primitive form of social debate; just as the corresponding words for actions that are not hostile (*scan, see, urge, tie*) reduce a great variety of acts and attitudes to a very few. This overemphasis and reduction establish the atmosphere of journalese, which is that of a stock melodrama.

In such a mood, it is no wonder that every other day some event is said to *make history,* and that in the intervals nothing is reported as done without *intensity* and *speed.* Visiting dignitaries do not go or drive from one place to another of their itinerary: they are *whisked away.* Even on the pages devoted to the arts or to clothes and advice about love and cooking, the routine excitement persists. The simple little dress, we hear, can be *whipped up* in an afternoon. The deserts are *fabulous,* children's play had better be *creative,* every innovation is EXCITING or *adds a new dimension to living.*

Perhaps the worst and most characteristic of the phrases that common speech has picked up from the great mint of exaggerations is the term *mass murder* for the killing of six or seven persons by one man. Why is this half dozen suddenly a mass, and what shall we call the great exterminators of history if Landru is a mass murderer? The answer will come only when we discover why every good book or play has to be *provocative, brilliant, scathing,* or *stimulating.* Meanwhile, the misfortune is that in seeking to excite regularly and routinely, journalese does the very opposite of stimulate, and this, it might be said, is ironic.

See also SHORTENINGS.

judicial, judicious. It is possible to find a halfhearted sanction in some dictionaries for treating these two words as synonyms, but the inevitable result of so treating them is to mislead without necessity. Common sense enjoins us to make the distinction established by usage between *judicial,* characteristic of court procedure or of the legal mind, and *judicious,* characterized by judgment, discernment, or wisdom. It is patent that *judiciously* would avert confusion in such a sentence as *The problem confronting their owners is where to run them* [race horses] *judicially in order to preserve their peak competitive condition for the Triple Crown.*

K

key. Overindulgence in figurative speech tends to denature first the meaning of a word and then the figure of speech itself. (See META-PHOR.) This change in two steps has affected the word *key*. The first image is that of a device, idea, or person that unlocks. The "lock" is a difficulty or a refusal or some other form of obstruction. *The key to increasing East-West trade was the building of a railroad / The key to the establishment of peace was the prince himself / After the problem had been defined* IN TERMS OF *the increasing rate of motion, or acceleration, the key to measurement was the differential and integral calculus.* In each example here the imagined key opens a way by turning an imagined lock. By extension, the term is used as an adjective: *a key idea, a key invention.* (The old application in *keystone* is directly visual: the piece of stone that fits in the gap at the top and fills out the arch; and *keynote* is from music, in which sounds are organized in groups called keys, from their first or tonic note.)

From being used in the figure *key idea*, etc., the epithet *key* acquires the sense of *important* or *outstanding*, the chief or main element: AID TO RETARDED CALLED KEY NEED. At this point the idea of resolving a difficulty tends to disappear. Indeed, it turns into its own contradiction, and soon we read: FALTERING FUEL CELL A KEY TO FLIGHT, in which the *key* is the obstacle, not the means of removing it. Again, in *The key problem was not hard to identify, key* means *great: the great problem, the chief riddle,* and nothing else. For it is clear that a problem is not a key, though it may sometimes happen that the *solution* of one problem leads to the solution of others; in such a case the *key problem* would mean the one whose solution would be decisive as to the rest. If so, the context should make plain this connection and justify the shorthand reference to it. Such cases are rare. The interests of good writing suggest that we leave *key* in actual or conceivable locks and reinstate the simple qualifiers *chief, main, prime, important, outstanding.*

kilt. One look should be enough to show that the Scot-

243

tish garment is single, not double like trousers or pants. Descriptions that contain phrases such as *the brave and brawny lads in kilts* refer to the accoutrements of the whole troop. See also SKILL(s).

knot. What *knot* measures is not distance but rate of speed: 1 knot equals a speed of 1 sea mile an hour. Powered boats and ships are accordingly rated as capable of 6 or 10 or 25 or whatever knots.

This meaning and usage therefore prohibit two types of statement: (1) *During the night we covered the eighty-three knots between Toulon and Cap d'Ail* (substitute *miles*); and (2) *The old tub could hardly be pushed beyond 7 knots an hour* (omit *an hour*).

knowledgeable. See -ABLE, -IBLE; NONLEAKABLE.

known (as). See AS 2.

L

last, latest. The distinction between these has virtually disappeared, with odd results in usage. One may now speak to a writer of his *last book* without his taking the remark for a death warrant. He knows we mean his *latest*. Again, although no one would confuse the *last news* from a friend who died suddenly with the *latest news* from him if he is alive, yet the custom is to refer to this latest news as *the last I heard from him was ten days ago*. And certainly *last week, month, year* are the only possible expressions, even though those times are only the *latest*.

Latin and Greek plurals. As is shown in DATA, contemporary usage wobbles like a rundown top when it tries to fit into common prose the Latin and Greek it professes to despise. The chief difficulty occurs when the writer has to decide whether a Latin word in *-a* is a singular or a plural. The college *alumna* is visibly singular, since the plural *alumnae* is well known for causing a confusion in pronunciation with the masculine plural *alumni*. But beyond this point

all is *terra incognita* (singular). Because of the vogue phrase *mass media*, one hears more and more often *It's a powerful media*—an error encouraged by the fear that the correct *medium* might suggest a soothsayer. The label on one of the most highly perfected gadgets of the kind says *This cartridge is equipped with a diamond and sapphire styli*. Is this pretentious plural of *stylus* due to the two precious stones that make it up? Or is some vague notion abroad in the world that Latin (and Greek) endings are at once euphonic and optional? Certainly, one hears *a phenomena, a criteria* with increasing frequency in circles where these words are used with the right meaning in mind. But then, when a learned musicologist writes in the Encyclopaedia Britannica of *canti firmi*, obviously unaware that *cantus* belongs not to the second declension but to the fourth and forms its plural in *-us*, lesser men may permit themselves their lapses. For writers and speakers who prefer to observe the forms of the original language, the following short list may prove useful.

NEUTER SINGULARS (Latin in -*um*, Greek in -*on*)	PLURALS (original or anglicized)
addendum	*addenda*
(no singular)	*agenda*
animalculum	*animalcula*
candelabrum	*candelabra*
criterion	*criteria*
datum	*data*
(no singular)	*marginalia*
medium	*media*
memorandum	*memoranda*
miasma	*miasmas* (Eng.)
	miasmata (Gr.)
nostrum	*nostrums*
(no singular)	*paraphernalia*
pendulum	*pendulums*
phenomenon	*phenomena*
stratum	*strata*

FEMININE SINGULARS	PLURALS
alga (rare)	*algae* (pron. *jee*)
alma [*mater*]	(no plural)
alumna	*alumnae* (pron. *ee*)
bona [*fide*]	(no plural: *fides* is a singular nominative sometimes used with *bona* instead of the ablative *fide*.)
persona [*non grata*]	*persona* [*non gratae*] (rare)
propaganda	(no plural)
phantasmagoria	(no plural)
sequela	*sequelae*

MASCULINE SINGULARS	PLURALS
alumnus	*alumni* (pron. *eye*)
bonus	*bonuses*
cactus	*cactuses, cacti*
calculus	*calculi* (medical only)
coitus	(no plural)

Note that *insignia* is a neuter plural; singular: INSIGNE. *Opus, lotus,* and *octopus* are not masculines in -*us* and they give (in English) *opuses, lotuses,* and *octopuses.* (For *cantus firmus,* see above.) *Bus,* from the ablative plural *omnibus* (= for all), gives *buses.* Two regular Latin plurals, *opera* and *aspidistra,* are now singular and take *s* in the plural. *Viscera* is plural and has no English singular. *Aborigines* is plural and its infrequent singular is *aborigine*.

lavish. See MALAPROPS.

lay, lie. It is a pity that the eighteenth-century freedom of usage which permitted Byron still to write *There let him lay* did not persist and bring about a useful amalgamation of the overlapping forms. They cause more trouble than they are worth, and trip up even careful speakers. What is still more confusing is that good writers, who are not tripped up, recognize as acceptable the inconsistent form *lay of the land,* at least in its figurative sense. *The lie of the land* suggests more directly the terrain or topographical features. For the rest, what man does with his body is *lie, lay, lain;* what he does with objects is *lay, laid, laid.* A hen, of course, both *lies* and *lays.*

To this one must add the caution that the prefixes *over-* and *under-* seem to seduce into error. *Seventeen centuries of violence overlay the bloody Balkans* clearly sports a present tense. *Overlie* is the only correct form, but the ear is annoyed because the mind thinks of a pall, a layer of violence covering the country. *Underlying causes* is standard and not readily mistaken, but here again the *underlayer*—of clouds, wood, skin, etc.—will

pull one away from grammar, especially when one brushes by the meaning of untruth through the sounds of *lie* and *liar: A government of cynics and profiteers awaiting with fatalism the day of reckoning, and placidly living out their ancient lie, is the strongest stimulus to the spirit of revolution that underlays* (underlies) *all old-established monarchies.*

leak, verb. See NONLEAKABLE.

leaving. See DANGLERS, ACCEPTABLE.

legalisms. See AND/OR; AS 5; IF AND WHEN; PRIOR TO; RIGHT, IN HIS (HER) OWN; UNLESS AND UNTIL.

-less. See UN-, IN-, NON-.

less, lesser. See FEWER, LESS.

lest. See SUBJUNCTIVE.

lethal. See MALAPROPS.

level. When some sort of hierarchy of rank, authority, or power is under discussion, *level* may be the appropriate or even the inevitable word. In such contexts it is a natural extension of a general term for comparing physical elevations. Unhappily, *level* has acquired a vogue in uses unconnected with either literal or figurative elevation, and in these uses it has next to no meaning whatever; it is, in fact, one of the most dispensable VOGUE WORDS of recent decades. *Suggesting that talks be started at a technical level to work out plans for the reunification of a free Germany* (Suggesting that technical talks be started) / *political discussions that would go beyond the current talks which have been mainly on the technical level* (have been mainly technical) / *But his story has to be looked at on two levels* (from two different points of view) / *Criticism of the court's work on a professional and intellectual level has been subdued or perhaps overwhelmed* (This last sentence is insolubly ambiguous: do we reach the intended meaning by writing *Professional and intellectual criticism* or by writing *Criticism of the professional and intellectual aspects of the court's work?* / *Sales increases at the retail level have led to greater optimism in manufacturing and distribution* (Increases in retail sales) / *declarations that unemployment is an illness that breaks out at the state level and can be cured at the state level* (is a localized illness within the states and can be locally cured) / *They opposed any idea of watering down the Ph.D. degree program in order to get more teachers at that level* (more teachers that hold the degree)

/ *At the junior high school level, 58 per cent of the students are involved in foreign-language training which includes Russian* (Fifty-eight per cent of the junior-high-school students study Russian) / *a manifestation at the local level of the all-embracing love of Christ* (a local manifestation) / *The betting is good on a tripartite conference at the foreign ministers' level* (on a conference of the three foreign ministers) / *if the level of military activity was substantially raised* (if military activity were considerably intensified) / *Many laundering problems can be avoided if they are anticipated at the manufacturing level* (anticipated by the manufacturers) / *conviction that "neither party is worth a damn" on civil rights on the national level—and, in some cases, on the local level* (in the nation at large or in the towns and counties) / *wrote strong, conventional poems striving for control of emotion in language suitable to mature acceptance on both an intuitive and a cognitive level* (acceptance, both intuitive and cognitive).

See also CASE; CHARACTER; COVERING WORDS; NATURE.

levied. See MALAPROPS.

libel, slander. *Libel* may result from injurious remarks that are circulated in writing, *slander* from those that are spoken. But note that because words spoken over the radio or on television are likely to be recorded, what would normally be slander is treated as libel. In this connection it is useful to remember that, legally, *publishing* means *making public* and does not imply printing. In a college or elsewhere, a lecturer who has large audiences but who never writes books could claim that he published regularly.

licorice, liquorice. The first spelling is general if not universal in the United States; the second prevails in Great Britain. Both are distortions of the Greek *glykyrrhiza* (= sweet root). Modern French *réglisse* is a further distortion by metathesis. Americans are often startled when, on the wrappers of toffee from England, they encounter *liquorice*. It is in fact the result of folk etymology—a spelling arrived at, one might guess, under the influence of *liquor*. If spelling were made either good or bad by any consideration but the custom of the country, one would have to say that the American spelling of this particular word, being closer to the Greek root, is the better one.

lie. See LAY, LIE.

like. 1. *Like* for *as*. 2. *Like, unlike.*

1. *Like* for *as*. There is no point in discussing at length the pros and cons of *like* as a conjunction, because in workmanlike modern writing there is no such conjunction. Comparisons involving a verb are introduced by *as* or *as if*, not by *like*. *I don't dance like I once did* is not literate, any more than *He goes on like he was crazy.* For the first *like* use *as;* for the second, *as if* followed by *were,* not *was.* (See SUBJUNCTIVE.)

The status of *like* is a topic of historical linguistics, not a problem of usage. Linguists know that *like* was used as a conjunction in the formative stages of the language and that it was freely used so by writers before and for a long time after William Langland, in the fourteenth century. Isolated recurrences of it have turned up in the writing of standard authors during the last century and a half, though there is no standard author who has used it habitually. A midway stage of its literary disuse takes the form *like as,* familiar in *Like as a father pitieth his children,* etc.

Like masquerading as a conjunction is rather frequently written in Britain today and is well entrenched in spoken American, particularly in the South and West. It is heard on the floor of the United States Senate, where much diction is current that never gets into the Congressional Record. Smokers and others read and hear about the cigarette that *tastes good like a cigarette should*, and a great corporation spends several thousand dollars a page to proclaim the succinct message *Cars that can do what they look like they can do and they look like they can do more than any other cars on the road*. Such English is not a product of careless ignorance: it is the outcome of an expensive effort to be folksy or to arouse interest by shocking. Note, by the way, that in the last example *like* once again means *as if*, which was its primary meaning in 1400. The futility of the argument from history is shown by the fact that *like* is now even more repellent when it means *as if* than when it means simply *as*, and it becomes intolerable when it is used with calculated archness by those who know better: *Wartime Italy demanded opera like wartime America demands movies*.

Because of an instinctive or acquired revulsion from this misuse, some writers who are unsure of themselves fall into the opposite error of substituting *as* in comparisons between substantives where *like* is necessary. The result is ludicrous or misleading and in some cases hopelessly ambiguous: *She decided to appeal to his better nature, as her predecessor Mary, . . . / At the last minute he flung on a few rags and went to the masked ball*

as his cousin / As the night before, B. ordered martinis / This staircase, as the one in the front of the house, was uncarpeted / There was nothing left to do: he was baffled, beaten—as I. In all these would-be elegant comparisons, *like* is required—and in the last, of course, *I* must be changed to *me*.

One symptom of the blind fear of misusing *like* is to fall back on *such as* (e.g. Conrad's *such as an enormous riding light above a vessel of fabulous dimensions*). More common is *as with*, in which *with* is usually as meaningless as a word can be. *As with most things here* [in Moscow] *etiquette is politics / The Greenland birds, as with the mallards, remain in the country in winter*. Both writers have been afraid to write *like: Etiquette, like most things here* and *The Greenland birds, like the mallards*. The same hesitation appears in *And as with so many people, mere abstract ideas were not nearly as disturbing to M. as immediate actualities*. Here *as with* may be a halfhearted attempt to pin down the unattached opening phrase, but the *as with* only camouflages the impropriety without rectifying it.

The writer who thinks he can do without *like* does not know his business, and his evasions are as indefensible as the misuses of the word. When we ought to write *The Greenland birds, like the mal-*

lards, remain in the country in winter, we must not be done out of *like* by terror lest someone suspect us of meaning *remain . . . in the winter like the mallards do.* The grammatically scared end up writing nonsense: *Her breath came fast, as a small animal's;* or more pretentiously: *We must not behave as children or coax them to lie down as seemly ghosts in quiet graves* (like ghosts). The chancellor of a university declares: *I have spent my life among the private corporation, the government office, and the campus, and I understand that each of these is, as is the church and the press, a prime source of strength and thought and aspiration.* Here the awkward and unnecessary *as is* manifestly represses the spontaneous *each of these, like the church and the press, is.* A popular novelist writing as a masculine narrator does not shrink from *The words just came tumbling out: I spoke as her mother.*

It is true that some traditional examples encourage modern confusion. When we read that Jesus of Nazareth spoke *as one having authority,* we cannot be sure from the diction alone whether the Bible translators were saying that he possessed supernatural authority or simply that he talked *as if* he possessed it. Today the second meaning would require *like one having*

authority. Again, *They fell upon the supplies as men starving* should mean to us that they were actually starving men; *like men starving* should mean that they could not have behaved more voraciously if they had actually been starving. The rule of thumb is: *as* tells in what role or capacity the deed is done; *like* introduces a comparison. *He has acted as a fool* implies: he is a fool; *acted like a fool* compares him to one. (Note the logic in *acted like the fool that he is.)* See also SUCH 2.

The one area of legitimate doubt about *as* and *like* is that in which an earlier *as* or a later verb is omitted. If we read *impervious to water as ducks,* a full comparison may be intended: *as impervious as ducks;* or the intention may be *impervious to water, as ducks are known to be.* But the first meaning is best certified by a preliminary *as;* the second is best expressed by *like.*

2. *Like, unlike.* Language is called on to say that *this* is like or unlike *that* more often than for any other task. The important requirement is that we understand precisely what the *this* and the *that* are. But the mind is lazy and avoids analytical thought, and the hope dies hard that if we say an undefined something resembles or does not resemble an unnamed something else, the separate vagueness will somehow come together into clear

meaning. The twin adjectives *like* and *unlike,* though exact antonyms in sense, are exact equivalents in grammar and rhetoric. Their use at the heads of sentences in the expectation just described achieves an effect identical with that of the participle that fails to modify the subject of the following main verb—the so-called dangling participle. (See DANGLERS.) Often there is a further effect of absurdity—the assertion of resemblance or of difference between incommensurables.

Both the flouting of syntax and the comparison of incompatibles are shown in this typical example: *Like Emerson in his mystical experience on a bare common in winter time on a cloudy day, the setting of this poem would seem at first glance to be unpromising.* As soon as anyone begins a sentence with *like* he is committed to answering the question: What is like what? The only way to answer it is to make whatever constitutes the second half of the comparison the subject of the following main verb. In our example Emerson is like the setting of someone else's poem —no answer to what is like what. To introduce here the right reason that is the basis of good grammar requires a thorough overhaul. One way might be: *The setting of this poem, like that of Emerson's about his mystical experience . . . , would seem . . .* This is

no pearl of a sentence, but it does compare the setting of one poem to the setting of another, it does say what is like what, and it does pin the descriptive matter to the right subject. If we want to keep *Like Emerson* and prefer to reorganize the main clause, then there is nothing for it but to make the opening read: *Like Emerson in his poem about his mystical experience . . . , X. gave this poem a setting that,* etc.—a spate of words, but at least Emerson is like another poet.

If, however, the writer meant to compare the unpromising setting of X.'s poem with the setting in which Emerson had his wintry mystical experience (our first reconstruction), then the formula to be followed is: either the introductory *like* plus A must be made to match B (the subject of the main clause) or B must be made to match A, justifying the *like.* The principle may be tried on these jumbles: *Like any Eastern ski center, its continued success will depend on having plenty of snow* (it will depend for continued success) / *Like any clichés, its exact meaning is puzzling* (Its exact meaning, like that of many other clichés) / *Like Novalis . . . the main doctrine here is . . .* (The main doctrine here is like that of Novalis) / *Like most newspapers of the time, the size of the* Eagle *was four pages, six columns wide* (the *Eagle* had four six-column pages) / *an affectionate circle in which, unlike his own family, he was made to feel that he honored them by reading one of his poems aloud* (an affectionate circle that, unlike his own family, made him feel) / *Like those commercials of an aspirin tablet making its way into the blood stream, we see too much too clinically.* The last sentence is a puzzler. Did its author actually mean that the commercials see too much too clinically? It is technically possible. More likely he meant: *We see too much too clinically, as in those commercials.* The liability to chaos of this construction is suggested by the eminence of our sources, which include the *New York Times*, the Columbia Encyclopedia, the chairman of a university department of English, and a volume of guidance about American usage.

Unlike is of course subject to the same law of MATCHING PARTS, and its violation presents the same logical impossibilities: *Unlike yesterday, when the clubhouse door remained closed for ten minutes, it was opened today exactly four minutes after the final out* (Whereas yesterday the . . . door remained closed . . . today it was opened . . .) / *Unlike his 1954 effort, there was not the slightest impugning of Democratic patriotism when he asserted that a foreign policy of "weakness" . . . had brought on the Korean war* (Unlike his effort

of 1954, this speech contained not the slightest impugning) / *Unlike the Canaveral technique of touching off a rocket from its launching stand at ground level, the Far Side vehicles were ignited by remote control after having been borne aloft 100,000 feet in attenuated plastic balloons* (The Far Side vehicles were ignited, not by the Canaveral technique . . . , but by remote control) / *Unlike the old mechanical treadle-operated signals . . . , the controls are not visible to the motorist* (The controls, unlike those of the old . . . signals, are not visible) / *But unlike Emily Dickinson's lines . . . there is no irony in Whitman's lines* (Whitman's lines, unlike Emily Dickinson's, . . . contain no irony) / *Unlike the Soviet attitude in past crises in Europe and the Middle East, Moscow has not volunteered its services as a conciliator* (Moscow has not, as in past crises . . . , volunteered its services).

Here should be added a cautionary word about writing oneself into a mantrap by injudiciously combining *like* or *unlike* with a negative subject. *Like the drawings mentioned in the documents, none of these has survived.* This pays a deceptive tribute to logic and grammar but comes down to saying that something is like nothing. The best one can say for this sentence is that it is more courageous than *As with the drawings.* The meaning would be expressed by *All these drawings, like those mentioned in the documents, have failed to survive.* Logically and structurally similar is this sentence: *Unlike the principles formulated at Geneva, no subsequent rapprochement has stirred much real hope of a change of climate* (every subsequent rapprochement has failed to stir). Clearly, *like* and *unlike* herald affirmative subjects. See NEGATIVES, TROUBLE WITH.

limited. The euphemistic use of *limited* to mean *small, poor, insufficient,* and the like deserves to be itself limited. When a person or an organization offers the excuse that he or it cannot comply with a request because of limited funds, the answer inspires one to ask which firm or friend has unlimited ones. It is hardly descriptive to qualify in the same way supplies of different magnitudes, though all *limited.* Nor is the case improved by adding an adverbial dressing gown (SEE NEEDLESS WORDS 2): *relatively limited, strictly limited, considerably limited.* The tiresome use of *limited* is a good example of what happens when a word that is a mere hyperbole in the negative (*His patience was limitless / I have unlimited time to put at your disposal*) is turned into a dull positive.

linking. 1. If there is one principle which may be said to govern the whole art of writing, it is the principle of linking; that is, joining what should be joined and separating what should be separated. Put in these terms, of course, the principle receives general assent and does not take us very far; it remains abstract; and that is why it requires for its elaboration the many separate suggestions in this and other books about the proper ways of joining and separating the several parts of speech as well as their clusters—phrases, clauses, and sentences. The injunction to give parallel form to parallel ideas, the advice about placing adverbs and commas—all these particulars relate to the craft of correct or adroit linking, which is the prerequisite of good prose.

It is easy to choose from able writers examples of proper and skillful linking; and the reader alert to the difficulties of framing a complex sentence can pick out such passages for himself and study their instructive peculiarities. Here all that can be done is to draw attention to the subject and illustrate a few of the commonest blunders.

The first care of the writer who would be clear is to connect his modifiers and his objects in such a way that the resulting phrase slips into the mind without effort. He need not be pedantic and try to glue each adverb or epithet to its verb or noun (see ONLY and PEDANTRY), but he must avoid outlandish combinations such as *permanent artists' oil colors* (in which it is the oil colors that are permanent and not the artists) or *Ask for our cup of complimentary coffee* (when it is the cup of coffee that is complimentary). All accumulations of qualifiers without proper links between them are liable to this fault (e.g. *the nontaxpaid liquor traffic*, which attempts to squeeze ideas into a narrow space) as are all mismatings of locutions (e.g. the bank slogan *Help to people with money since 1792*, where one would expect the help had been given to people *without* money). In each the reader must unscramble and rearrange the elements for himself, and even if he succeeds in doing this correctly every time, he is halted and annoyed by having to do work that should have been done for him.

Parallelism of thought and of form is discussed at several places in this book, notably in the Introductory chapter and under PUNCTUATION (APPENDIX 2), where precepts are given for managing an enumeration that concludes with *and*. The failure to observe these pieces of advice leads to poor linking, by which the reader is jarred. For example: *Practically pays for itself* [,] *because you save subway and bus fares, money order fees, your valuable time.*

One expects a third saving in actual cash; time may be money also, but its apparent apposition with *money order fees* is bad linking.

Equally obstructive to sense is the linking of parts that need to be separated if they are to be understood correctly: Sometimes a comma will do the trick: *When I got through the table at the end of the room was ready for the meeting* (comma after *through*). But usually punctuation will not help or cannot be used: *Its significance in headaches is not clear, but by providing relief from an external application it holds intriguing possibilities.* The author of this editorial did not mean *relief from an external application*; he meant *providing relief* [pause] *from* [i.e. *by*] *an external application.* And what makes the sentence worse is that only a few lines earlier he had led us to link the same two words that should now be unlinked. He had written: *If we can get relief from pain.*

Similar trouble frequently occurs in subordinate clauses following certain verbs if *that* can be taken either as conjunction or as relative pronoun. For instance: *It was 4 P.M. and they were all turning in, but I persuaded the second taxi driver that I stopped to take me downtown.* On a first reading the mind runs: *I persuaded him that I stopped* (e.g. along his route), whereas the sense is *the second taxi that I stopped.* Unless strictly controlled, the everpresent *that* can be a capricious connective.

2. As in evolutionary theory, so in writing there are missing links. Commercial jargon has always been known for a tendency to leave out the necessary and put in the unnecessary—a curious form of fair trade. Nowadays, conciseness goes very far indeed, as in *We've gone Discount.* But the same tendency works throughout the realm of print, in an effort to be brisk or allusive. In the following sentence from a novel, the effect is pointedly literary: *It was good to be far, to be a continent, from the meaningless sprawl of Los Angeles.* Between *continent* and *from* we need a link, such as *away,* because *to be a continent* is no synonym for *far;* it is in fact much more "meaningless" than the sprawl of Los Angeles. A more confusing example calls for a structural remedy: *X. . . . shot and killed a former beauty queen who had once been his stenographer and then took his own life.* As it stands, the *then* and the *once* make a false link. One correction would be *his stenographer; then he took . . .*

The worst difficulty in linking is that which comes in the arrangement of a number of circumstantial details. There are no rules for the order in which time and place and the other bits and pieces of the full situation should come. Their length and rhythm determine their place, and so does the emphasis desired. But what is not permissible is the comical juxtaposition of parts or the dangling remnant, as in *The Police Department ordered investigations yesterday into the death of a 20-year-old grocery clerk last week, allegedly caused by a policeman at Coney Island with a billy club.* Here the placing of the billy club confers upon it a quasi-human status that makes it the policeman's companion instead of the instrument of the beating. There is no remedy but to split the sentence at *last week* and insert *at Coney Island.* Then go on: *It was alleged that the death resulted from a beating with a billy club by a policeman.* Note the incidental improvement in emphasis, each sentence ending with an important idea and the clumsy adverb *allegedly* disappearing as if by magic. Remember also that placing will have a linking effect even in the absence of links: *They took his loose change, his wristwatch, his cigarettes, his cigarette lighter (he had smoked the prisoner's during his five visits).* The parenthesis here is linked with the last noun in the list; i.e. *smoked the prisoner's cigarette lighter.* Move *cigarettes* to the last place. But placing will not work if the parts fail to dovetail, as they fail in *He smiled again—almost, now, a grin.*

Whether *grin* is hooked on to *smiled* or to *again*, the sentence falls apart.

3. A final caution against certain types of loose linking is in order here, though most examples are given notice in other entries. In the heading GUEST VALET SERVICE, the fleeting suggestion is given that a guest valet is ready to give service. The fundamental objection to the additives -WISE, -*wide*, -*conscious*, -*minded*, -*oriented*; to certain verbs, such as *highlight* and *pinpoint*; to IN TERMS OF and *with respect to* is that they generally link the neighboring ideas wrongly or feebly. What is it *to be air-minded, to launch a campaign country-wide, to be crisis-oriented, to screen candidates in terms of potential, to pinpoint the salient features, to exercise control budget-wise?* The appearance of meaning may be given, or the meaning may be supplied by someone who already knows the facts; but the simple question shows that around the central word there is nothing but a haze of possible connections. The links are not there to attach one idea to the next so as to form a chain marking the direction of the whole passage.

liquorice. See LICORICE.

literally. Writers are so often besought by rhetoricians not to say *literally* when what they mean is *figuratively* that one would expect them to desist in sheer weariness of listening to the injunction. The truth is that writers do not listen; and *literally* continues to be seen as a mere intensive that means *practically, almost, all but. He was literally speechless. He could only murmur: "Good God!"* This speechlessness would be literal only if he had been incapable of uttering the words we are told he murmured. [A golf cart] *literally floats over the roughest fairway.* To accomplish this it would have to be one of those vehicles that ride a few inches above the ground on a cushion of air. Since this particular cart moves with its wheels on the ground, the floating is figurative.

livelong. See PRONUNCIATION 1.

locate often runs the risk of ambiguity. The policeman may report of a suspect: *I located him at Broadway and 16th Street*, meaning *I found him there*. The renting agent will utter the same words and mean: *It was there I obtained a place for him to live.* And some citizens will turn this into the intransitive *I located at,* etc. *Locate* is perhaps least objectionable in the passive mood, when it becomes an adjective synonymous with *situated*, as in *The horse trough is located at the crossroads*; though in most sentences where the passive *located* occurs, *at* will suffice: *The home* (house) *recently acquired* (bought) *by Professor F. W. D. is located* . . . (is at). *Locate* is at best an unsatisfactory word, which one tolerates chiefly for the sake of its indispensable antonym, *dislocate*.

logic. Writers who do not bother to think about the interrelations of the words they use, and who take these relations ready-made in the form of clichés, often fall into the habit of referring to *a fine toothcomb*, and sometimes just *a toothcomb*. This instrument is found especially often in the literature of detection, where it is called into play for every systematic search. Now, it does not take much reasoning power to discover that (1) the very essence of a comb is to have teeth and (2) what serves to make a sifting particularly close is *the fine tooth* of the comb. In short, the battered metaphor is about a fine-tooth(ed) comb—a comb with fine teeth—not a tautological toothcomb, fine or coarse.

This brief demonstration, which could be supplemented by a multitude of others, defines the place of logic or reasoning in the use of language. Educated people who have thought about their speech are often heard to say that "logic has nothing to do with language—usage and idiom decide everything"; and they il-lustrate their dogma with telling instances of common sense defied. They are right about those instances, and every book about usage confirms and extends them; but for one piece of arbitrary arrangement in the language, recorded as idiom or anomaly, there are hundreds of thousands of expressions, ordinary and familiar or new and strange, in which the application of reason is implicit or required. Only by thinking about what we mean can we decide whether to say *the batter hit the ball* or *the ball hit the batter; she likes me better than he* or *she likes me better than him; to eat one's cake and have it too* or the reverse (see CAKE). The form of words known as an Irish bull (*If you could see the molecules in this piece of matter, they would be going so fast you could not see them*) is an embodiment of the failure—or the refusal—to make words accord as they should with the dictates of logic. The effect is ludicrous in the bull, ambiguous or irritating elsewhere.

For example, the writer who tells us that *the absence of any prepared plan thrust itself prominently in the minds of the board and left management without a loophole* is a writer whom we come to resent after a very few pages, because his neglect of logic forces us to do his work for him as we read. What is a plan, if not prepared? How can an absence thrust itself in (into) a mind and, having done so, leave no loophole? The illogicality here is due to the loose coupling of metaphors, but it will be found that the penchant for metaphorical writing in prose also comes from a weak sense of logic. (SEE METAPHOR.)

Yet the exercise of logic where it will make for tight and clear sentences is no warrant for forcing it into situations where it has been given up by the language in exchange for the convenience of mental shorthand. For example, English does not bother to analyze and to articulate the relation of many modifiers to the noun they modify: a *hairbrush* is a brush *for* the hair; a *hair shirt* is a shirt *made of* hair; a *hairline* is a line *as thin as* a hair; a *walking stick* does not walk, but a *walking delegate* or *patient* does. Persons who object to the modifying of a noun by another noun insist that one must speak of a *dramatic* (not a *drama*) *critic*, of a *musical* (not a *music*) *critic*. Usage accepts both, with a slight tendency in favor of the shorter form. And idiom is adamant, in opposite directions —for and against the noun— about two other familiar figures: a *dance critic*, because a *dancing critic* would be another kind of wonder altogether; and a *literary critic*, because a *literature* (or *letters*) *critic* would smack of intolerable affectation.

The upshot of this discussion is that when one has eliminated everything that idiom and usage clearly command, one must apply one's logical faculties to what remains. And this in turn is a warning that without a knowledge of idiom and usage gained from reading there is little chance of good writing.

long-lived. See PRONUNCIATION 1.

looking. See DANGLERS, ACCEPTABLE.

loose (un-). See UN-, IN-, NON-.

lost causes. If the Bretons and the Scots still struggle to regain their independence as sovereign states, and if we Americans continue to dream of living like Thoreau at Walden Pond, it is permissible for the student of words to keep alive his convictions about certain meanings and usages that he knows to be no longer shared by the majority, including many educated persons.

First on his list is DISINTERESTED. Next come DATA and DUE TO. After this, and not in order of importance, are such locutions as *friend in common* for *mutual friend* (not Dickens' fault—he was quoting a semi-literate one-legged man); UNPRACTICAL, *impracticable* (instead of *impractical*, and with differentiated meanings); *ep-*

och as *turning point* instead of as *era*; *fruition* meaning *enjoyment* and not *fruit-bearing* (think of *the fruition of the Blessed Virgin*); *cater for* (instead of *to*, by reason of the French root *acheter*—implying *to go shopping for*); *lend* instead of *loan*; the legitimate spelling of *rime*, not *rhyme*; *Have you a match? Yes, I have* preferable to the two mismatings of *do* with *have: Do you have a match?* and the dialogue *Have you a match? Yes, I do* (though everybody says *or what have you*); the shorter, more English and less French *chanceries abroad* (not *chancelleries*); the longer and more correct adjective *climacteric* (out of *climax*), not *climactic*; the simple *arithmetic* for the school child's homework, not *mathematics*. Again: remembering that *scotching* the plan to build a highway through your back yard does not kill it but only postpones the evil day (Macbeth says: *We have scotch'd the snake, not kill'd it*); that *tinker* calls for *at*, not *with*; and that *trivia* are crossroads, not trifles. For the popularity of this last bit of Latinity, Logan Pearsall Smith, a scholar and lexicographer, is indirectly responsible, having chosen the word as the title of a series of essays not at all trivial, but suggestive of traveled roads and chance meetings, like the verses of John Gay called *Trivia, or the Art of Walking the Streets of London* (1716).

See also RESTIVE.

lotus. See LATIN AND GREEK PLURALS.

luxury. See PRONUNCIATION 1.

-ly, suffix. See ADVERBS, VEXATIOUS; HOPEFULLY; MASTERFUL; OVERLY; PROSE, THE SOUND OF 2; REPORTEDLY; SENTENCE, THE 7; SINGLEHANDEDLY.

M

major, minor. The advertising attitude expressed in *the better hotels* is shown also in the abuse of *major* and *minor*. Every novelist's new novel is a *major event*; every breakdown in public transportation is a *minor mishap*. The standard of comparison is in each case assumed to be known to all. Since this assumption cannot be true, everyone can, without incurring responsibilities, magnify his concerns and diminish his errors until the visible world is populated entirely by *major figures* doing *major work* and suffering only *minor setbacks*. A moratorium on *m* and *m* is in order, to make room for the responsible use of positive terms such as *great* and *small*.

majority, minority. Democratic habits impel us to overuse these correlative words. They are most often (not, please observe, *in the majority of cases*) long and pretentious substitutes for *many* and *most*, *few* and *some*. By this misuse, an unwarranted connotation of *nearly all* has become attached to *majority*, and the corresponding one of *a negligible few* to *minority*; though no one needs to be told that one person more or fewer than half

the members of any group is enough to warrant the use of those technical terms.

Maximum and *minimum* are liable to a like distortion in reverse. They are made to stand for *much* and *little*, instead of *the most* and *the least*, which are their proper meanings. Anyone who wishes to speak true English today will make an effort to remember and use the neglected little words, among the first to be learned, and still as good as new.

make sense. The vogue of *make sense* wherever English is spoken conceals from its users the arrogance of the implied argument: You make a perfectly intelligible remark or suggestion; I do not agree with it or I wish to reject it; whereupon I have the effrontery to say to you that *it does not make sense*. The rejoinder obviously ignores the merits of the question. *Make sense* should be reserved for occasions when meaning is for some reason obscured. If it is argued that the comparable exclamation *Nonsense!* is well established, one must point out that its use is generally confined to people on intimate terms with one another, whereas a stranger may be told that what he has just said and what one has fully understood *does not make sense.*

In the positive, *make sense* can apply to a proposal which is nevertheless unwise or impracticable.

See also REALISTIC, UNREALISTIC.

malaprops. The matron in Sheridan's *Rivals* who requested that *no delusions to the past be made* has given her name to the class of mistakes in language that consist in uttering a word which more or less resembles the one an accurate speaker would use in the same context. Though some linguists maintain that no native speaker of a language can make a mistake—he merely incarnates the spirit of Change—most people persevere in the belief that Mrs. Malaprop's *delusions to the past* still produce delusions in the present. *Fortuitous* for FELICITOUS or *fortunate* and COHORT for *companion* are discussed in their alphabetical places. Here are a few more that are often encountered in talk and print:

A *stickler* is not a puzzle but a *precisian,* a *fuss-budget.*

Credulity is not *credibility* (*Ruby's lawyer then challenged the credulity of the witness*). *Credulity* is the tendency to believe whatever one is told; *credibility* is the being worthy of belief.

To *burgeon* means to put out

buds; figuratively to come out in a small, modest, hopeful way, not to spread out, blossom, and cover the earth.

Costive has nothing to do with *cost;* it means *constipated.*

Scarify has to do with *scratch,* not *scare;* figuratively it means to deliver a slashing attack, to flay and leave scars.

Luxuriant and *luxurious* are related but distinct. The first means of abundant growth, as applied to vegetation, hair, imaginative power; the second denotes the same copiousness of comfort and showy things. The jungle is *luxuriant* but not *luxurious;* the upholstery of a car may be *luxurious* but it should not be *luxuriant.*

I feel a repulsion against bearded men confuses the outward act of being repelled (*repulsion*) with the inward feeling of being revolted, revulsed (*revulsion*).

The too amiable man who was accused of *languishing praise on all his friends* did not in fact *languish* (= grow anemic, have a lingering illness); he *lavished* praise like a too generous (= lavish) spender.

That same man was doubtless to be described as *fulsome,* a word that turns into a malaprop when intended for *complete* or *satisfactory: We want to give these young people a fulsome education.*

Again, *noisome* will mislead if interpreted at a guess. *Noise* plays no part in its formation, which draws on the root meaning stench. That is *noisome* which is evil-smelling.

Eavesdroppers are not merely people who stand about without excuse, like the gapers at a street accident whom a journalist so designated: they are people who listen furtively at others' doors and windows, under the eaves.

Sometimes an echo between words will lead to their being confounded. Thus the professor who said *We'll have to abridge the gap* was kin to the graduate student who confessed to an *absorbent interest* in the professor's subject. Gaps are *bridged* by a construction, physical or mental; to *abridge* means to abbreviate; an *absorbing interest* takes the mind out of itself and soaks it up in the subject; *absorbent* refers exclusively to a physical quality, as of blotter, surgical cotton, natural and artificial sponges, which students may emulate but only in a figurative way.

The observer of modern speech and writing is struck by the great frequency of malaprops among educated people who write and speak extensively in the course of their professional work. It is usually not any one word or set of words that is liable to this misuse; rather, one notes the liability of any word to being replaced by some near-homonym, and not necessarily every time that it is used. Among

such words are *tinge* and *twinge, smattering* and *scattering, scan* and *span, ravished* and *ravaged, levied* and *leveled, overweening* and *overwhelming,* and the phrase *ivy-leave colleges* for *ivy-league*. There are many others that an attentive ear will catch. The causes of this tendency are not all obscure: language is freer, less bound by convention and timidity than it was a hundred years ago; again, modern literature—especially poetry—plays with words: Joyce's later prose is a mass of conscious malaprops; and then, too, language-making with an eye to surprise and simple punning has long been the advertiser's sport. All these laxities, real or apparent, confuse the ear and the mind and encourage innovation on the part of the ordinary citizen. He is no longer guided by wide reading in classic authors and he is often misled by analogy, true and false. The result is the endemic malapropism of the college-bred.

One kind of reflection, however, should protect the writer from such combinations as *the Air Force foresees a lethally vital future for its intercontinental ballistic missiles. Lethal,* from *Lethe,* the river of forgetfulness that the dead drank of in Greek mythology, means *deadly. Vital,* from *vita* (think of *vitamins,* O journalist!), connotes *life. A lethally vital future* is therefore a supermalaprop, and would be so even if *lethal* when properly used did not imply a powerful but partly disguised danger. Many plants are lethal. So is a drug when the wrong dose is given. But a revolver or an intercontinental missile is too obviously death-dealing to be called lethal except in JOURNALESE.

See also CONNIVE; DELINEATE; DANGEROUS PAIRS.

manner. The ancient phrase *all manner and conditions of men* probably explains the belief that the coupled words are synonymous. The posted request *Please leave the toilet in the manner in which you found it* will miscarry if every reader agrees with the person who wrote under it: *You mean by groping around?* The phrase *all manner of things* is an idiom from which *manner* cannot be lifted out for modern use in the old sense. *Manner* now means only *mode, conduct, deportment.*

margarine. See PRONUNCIATION 1.

massive. See VOGUE WORDS.

masterful, masterly. The distinction between the two is not disregarded with impunity, because the idea of domination, of enslavement, exercised by one human being over another, is so clear in *masterful* that it seems absurd to apply the same word to the writing of a sonnet or a court decision.

Besides, the cliché *masterly inactivity* is there to remind us that a second word exists, which in that context we could scarcely exchange. Nevertheless, some speakers are driven to preferring *masterful* at all times by its possession of an easy adverb. *Masterlily* is impossible, and there is these days a lust for single words, however uncouth, in place of phrases, however simple and brief. *In a masterly way* is wrongly felt to be feeble, so *masterfully* is used at every turn. Add to this the confusion caused by situations where both the *-ful* and *-ly* forms are applicable (e.g. a performance on the piano), and the present disorder is the result. In spite of the excuse that such anarchy affords to the heedless, *a pale, shimmering, altogether masterful water-color* remains both ludicrous and wrong.

matching parts. The heading of this entry is borrowed from Le Baron Russell Briggs (1855–1934), one-time teacher and dean at Harvard. Few men in North America can have done so much as he to teach whatever of the rudiments of good prose is teachable. The phrase "Match parts," which appeared with some frequency as an injunction in the margins of essays written for his inspection, was his private shorthand for a principle that, understood and observed, goes as far as any to make writing workmanlike; or, when disregarded, to make it shambling and seedy. This principle is the simple one that logically equal elements in a sentence had better be also rhetorically equal.

Everyone who tries to write —at least, everyone not afflicted with what is sometimes called a tin ear—has a degree of natural instinct for putting like thoughts into like constructions. Some have the instinct *in excelsis*. Macaulay had it from the cradle; it ruled his prose from first to last and is often the definitive element in its magnificence, as in his famous sentence about Frederick the Great: *In order that he might rob a neighbour whom he had promised to defend, black men fought on the coast of Coromandel and red men scalped each other by the great lakes of North America.* The translators of the English Bible attained many of their most glorious rhythms by a like parallelism of matching thoughts, corresponding to the original verse: *Canst thou bind the sweet influences of Pleiades, or loose the bands of Orion? / If I ascend up into heaven, thou art there; if I make my bed in hell, behold thou art there / Then the eyes of the blind shall be opened, and the ears of the deaf shall be unstopped / the Lord gave, and the Lord hath taken away.* Such writing seems inevitable,

but if we could contemplate the doing of it from a little in advance of the fact, we should see nothing marked out as fore-ordained, but rather a labyrinth of ways to go wrong. The truth is that most of us possess the instinct for matching parts in no more than a variable and inferior degree and must strengthen it by self-discipline and taking thought. We perversely suffer it to take charge where it is not wanted, as when we make *in whole or in part* out of the idioms *as a whole* and *in part;* and then we fail to invoke it where it would save us from disorder. (See PART, IN.)

There follow some scraps from modern works, at many of which Dean Briggs would have written his firm "Match parts." About others he would have raised the question whether they really lend themselves to parallel constructions; that is, whether the unfulfilled promise of matching had not better be given up since divergent constructions are used. *Thus he belonged to neither group, having moved away from the former and lagging behind the latter* (read *and lagged behind the latter*, the obvious way to repair an implied but broken engagement to match parts) / *Y. was thinking about the date of his competition and that he must work harder at his paper* (and the need to work harder)

/ *Something subtle and powerful in this luminous darkness suggested a vast and open landscape and that the station was situated higher up* (a noun object of a verb will almost never mate acceptably with a clause object; read: *suggested that the landscape was vast and open and the station higher up,* or else abandon parallelism, as in *suggested that the station was looking down upon a vast and open landscape*) / *She began to talk about herself as the most depraved of all mankind, and that she never could share in the heavenly grace* (this apparently says *talk about . . . that she never could share;* read, as one possibility: *to talk about herself as if she were the most depraved of all mankind and could never share*). What is fatal is to arouse an expectation of matched constructions and then to frustrate it. Even a wooden fulfillment is generally preferable to a disappointed expectation. *Disappointment with the women of Kansas City and Denver because of their delicate appearance and dressing like the women of the East* (because they were of delicate appearance and dressed like) / *believed the American people to be the "advance guard of humanity," and that they must have an art which would be truly their own* (believed.)

that the American people was, or were, . . . and that it, or they, must have).

If any two verbal formulas are hard-and-fast promises of parallel construction, *either . . . or* (*neither . . . nor*) and *not only . . . but also* are such promises. The promise of the first is broken in this typical sentence: *No evacuation has been scheduled yet either to clear the housing areas that may be needed or because of the threat of war that always hangs over this island* (either because of the possible need of some housing areas or because of the threat). And the second formula often leads into ugly mismatchings by the simple displacement of *not only.* *Readers . . . will find that they are in contact not only with a cross section of American achievement, but are invited also to enjoy a generous helping of human nature* (will find that they are not only in contact . . . but are also invited) / *The lifeboat is ready to save not only the occupants of our Ship of State, but can be dispatched to the assistance of others* (is not only ready to save . . . but can also be dispatched) / *We . . . revealed in our fellowship—not only the encouraging growth of our communion—but also that it is part of the Holy Catholic Church which includes members of every race and nation* (not only that our communion has had an encouraging growth but also that it is). The last example might perhaps be given the alternative form *not only the encouraging growth of our communion but also its unity with . . .* The somewhat eccentric punctuation does not affect the sense and is easily overlooked; not so a mismanaged *not only.*

See also EITHER . . . OR; NEGATIVES, TROUBLE WITH; BOTH . . . AND.

maximum. See MAJORITY, MINORITY.

may, might. See SEQUENCE OF TENSES 2.

me. Writers and other persons whose devotion to sound grammar could be shown by the evidence of print, and who would prove it again by other deeds in any civil war with the linguistic anarchists, are nonetheless firm in believing that the colloquial *It's me* is acceptable in speech and in writing when the tone is not elevated. The reasons for their belief are two. The correct *It is I* strikes them as forbiddingly formal for workaday use—say, for knocking on a friend's door and answering the *Who is it?* from within. And again, the tendency toward what other languages call the disjunctive form (French *c'est moi*) corresponds to a genuine need of the mind. The clergyman being sought by name who stepped forward and said *That is I* achieved a stiffness that probably concealed a last-minute avoidance of *That's me.* When you add the probability that anyone who identifies himself by voice alone is on familiar terms with the person asking the question, you conclude that *It's me* and *That's me* are indispensable to friendship and domestic life.

When the sentence is likely to carry the subject into a relative clause, *I* is the only possible predicate after *is;* e.g. *No, the responsibility's mine: it was I, no one else, who was on the spot.* In the latter-day phrase that denotes a species of claim or demand made by parties to a contract, the *me-too clause,* it is clear that *me* is not replaceable by *I.* Indeed, the ellipsis is undoubtedly *Give it to me too,* rather than *I too want it.*

meaning. See DANGLERS, ACCEPTABLE.

meaningful. There is no reason in logic or linguistics why one may not freely use the suffix *-ful* to form adjectives from nouns on the pattern of *joyful, painful, sinful, youthful,* and many other words so familiar as to give us no reminder that they are composed of stem plus suffix. There are, however, reasons apart from logic why such formations make us uncomfortable when they lack this familiarity, especially when their stems consist of more than one syllable. Many of the comparatively recent -ful words call undue attention to themselves as improvisations; they bother the ear and produce effects of deterrent ungainliness. Perhaps the most common is *meaningful*, a product of the feeling that *significant* has been overused. The fortunes of *meaningful* have doubtless owed something to the theoretical desirability of Anglo-Saxon derivatives, and in lesser degree to the interest in semantics that followed the appearance of *The Meaning of Meaning*. At any rate, *meaningful* has become fashionable—so much so that it has almost caught up with *significant* in the race of vogue and vacuity.

Note that *meaningful*, when applied to most intellectual experiences and to nearly all understandable statements, adds little more than feeble emphasis. To say *His announcement to the board was meaningful* tells us only that the statement was not gibberish. There is greater force in *Her glance was meaningful*, because glances do not necessarily carry meanings; nor do gestures, acts, coincidences, and the like. *Significant* is, or should be, similarly restricted.

Of coinages even less acceptable than *meaningful*, one, *suspenseful*, seems to belong to the desperate vocabulary of the hack reviewer: *This fast-paced, suspenseful novel / Suspenseful, prize-winning French novel centering on a homicidal maniac / It is nervous and suspenseful from the start.* The word *flavorful*, which has had a vogue in the advertising of foods and beverages, also creeps into reviews of books. *The telling is considerably like A.—warm, human, flavorful.* (The resemblance noted is not remarkable, for A. is the author of the novel described.) Other typical inventions are *insightful* (the sociologist's condescending praise), *characterful*, and *resultful*: *The balanced statement of an insightful man whose every word sounds and is authentic / I congratulate your Professor Academensis* [sic] *for his insightful piece on Academic Bureaucracy / the full-page effect is characterful and harmonious / an important and resultful medium for so many of the nation's leading advertisers.*

A disadvantage of the suffix -ful in newly minted compounds is that it tends to become ambiguous. In established and familiar words it generally means *characterized by, possessing the quality of*. *Youthful* does not mean full of youth, or *beautiful* full of beauty, or *hopeful* full of hope: the meanings are simply *having* (in unspecified quantity) *youth, beauty, hope*. But as soon as anyone manufactures a new adjective in -ful it is impossible to be sure whether the word denotes partial or total possession of the attribute named. Does he who writes *meaningful* intend to describe something as characterized by meaning or as being filled to capacity with meaning? Webster's New World Dictionary sidesteps the difficulty by not defining the word at all except as *meaning* plus a self-defining suffix. The Shorter Oxford ignores *meaningful*. When an advertiser calls a product *flavorful*, we surmise that he means *full of flavor*; but when a reviewer calls a novel *flavorful*, he may be saying only that it has a flavor of its own.

means, noun. Like *news*, *means* is at will singular or plural. *He proposed as a means to that end the buying up of all outstanding shares / The means are ready to hand.* By itself, *means* almost always refers to money. *A man of means was a rarity in that outpost of civilization.* In *They wanted to move, but did not have the means,* the writer must have in mind lack of cash, not lack of a vehicle or of suitable housing.

measure up. See ADEQUATE.

meld. This word is frequently heard at meetings of businessmen or government officials when a difficulty arises which calls for uniting two diverse plans or proposals. The obvious cause of the misuse is the urge to say *weld* while suggesting a quiet and mild operation that will escape public notice. The fact is that *meld,* from the German *melden,* means to announce. It is a technical term of pinochle. To make it anything else is a MALAPROP. An example from an admirable book reviewer: *It is a serious effort to meld reality and dream.*

meritorious. See CONNOTATIONS.

metaphor. 1. By now everybody has heard of the mixed metaphor and shuns it as an error charged with ridicule—shuns it, that is, when he is aware of it. The extreme cases alone are self-disclosing, and few writers would miss such a trope as this from a Congressman in full spate: *The Internal Revenue Service appears to be totally impaled in the quicksands of absolute inertia.* But the trouble today is not that kind of absurd yet rhetorically tempting mixed metaphor. Indeed, the scorn which mixing is met with often overshoots the mark and calls mixed metaphor what is only a succession of parallel images. The prime instance, easily remembered, is John of Gaunt's eulogy of England in Shakespeare's *Richard II,* where the *scepter'd isle* is also the *seat of Mars, a precious stone set in the silver sea,* and thirteen other discrete metaphors. It is not the mere succession of incompatible images that offends reason, but the joining of these images into, as it were, a working piece of machinery. When this is not attempted, credulity is not strained; and to the fertile mind that thinks up a series of comparisons one gives admiration—and protection from those who misunderstand the ban on mixed metaphor.

2. Far worse than any of the laughable mixings that still occur is what may be called the metaphorical style, to suggest its continuity and its difference from the decorative metaphor. That style is nowadays in common use. It is characterized by a steady reliance on images which are buried in abstract words, which therefore do not strike the speaker or the writer as figurative, but which often leave the hearer or reader perplexed as to the meaning. At the turn of the century there lived in Scotland a workingman's wife named Amanda Ros, who wrote and found a publisher for several novels written entirely in this metaphorical mode. A sentence from her fiction will show, through her exaggerated example, how she joined images without analyzing them and managed to give an impression of meaning where none is to be found. *Every morning, at the same hour, mistress and maid were at their respective posts, the former, with brightened eye, mounted on her favorite pedestal of triumphant account and gazing intently on the object of rescue; the latter, casting that grave and careworn look in the direction of the niched signboard of distress, stood firmly and faithfully until she received the watchword of action and warning.*

We know that we cannot follow Mrs. Ros because the pictorial confusion is too great; but only a willingness to lend meaning to jargon creates the illusion of sense in a letter from an executive placement bureau that describes its client as *one who seeks sharper challenge in his preferred sphere.* A succession of such loose-jointed and half-conceived images makes a page or even a paragraph so woolly that the reader's mind ceases to respond. Yet much workaday prose of the supposedly practical kind—business reports, political statements, educational announcements—consists of just such series of unexamined images. For example: *The company overextended its operations in hopes of stimulating its liquidity position, but the disastrous end-product was not hard to foresee / The road to the American dream is littered with task force reports that were lightly read, widely ignored, and then as messily dis-*

carded on the roadside as empty beer cans / I should like to focus upon the European Community the light cast by the present crisis, which in many respects throws the Community's contours into sharper relief. In particular, I believe that that light reveals its dynamic character. For the European Community is not something static, or something readymade; it is a process of continuous creation. If you like, it is a policy, an endless series of questions and answers, of continual challenges and responses. And for a prime instance of visual carelessness, in a work by the late Ian Fleming: *Bond's knees, the Achilles heel of all skiers, were beginning to ache.*

3. The tendency to write in images rather than say in direct fashion what one means has a number of causes. The most important is the desire to make one's activities or one's thoughts about them interesting in a world otherwise felt to be dull. Business and advertising men are continually framing new metaphors with this in mind. They want to sell ordinary products by throwing over them the glamour of an implied comparison, or they want to seem fashionable by coining sophisticated phrases about their own doings. To understand what is going on at board meetings and conferences, one must accordingly be familiar with the meaning

of dozens of metaphors, such as *wearing two hats, getting one's feet wet,* and *standing in the gray area* (respectively, *having two posts or capacities; learning a new job;* and— about a point or a policy— *having something to be said for and against it,* i.e. not *black or white,* itself a metaphor for *good or bad*).

The effect of these pictures when joined to others is to suddenly give a new life to older images that lie dormant in common words or in the terms of art of the profession. Thus in the bank report quoted above *liquidity* is a technical term. *Liquidity position* is already a combination that brings much too vividly to the eye the literal meaning of *liquid,* and when to this are added the idea of a stimulus and the sight of the end product—a physical object—the mind is fully wakened; reason revolts and submits that positions cannot be stimulated and that liquidity is a state, not a position.

It is important to remember that this revolt is not deliberate, this objection not the response of a hairsplitting mind. Both are spontaneous and immediate feelings; the mind's eye has been opened to these conflicting sights by the writer himself; it is he who has interrupted the flow of meaning through carelessly putting together pictures that clash. Since the writer must always rely on the reader's close attention, he cannot complain when that attention is startled by his own fault. And in smoother but still inaccurate imagery, the discomfort persists. When a journalist who is discussing the Warren Commission Report on the Assassination of President Kennedy writes *But the reality is that the commission will be judged by a far harsher yardstick,* the competent reader is vaguely aware of a series of subdued comments within himself: "He doesn't mean *the reality is* but *in reality,* or *the truth is; a* yardstick is a yardstick, neither harsh nor gentle, and hence not *harsher*—and besides one doesn't *judge* by a yardstick, one *measures.*" While this soliloquy takes place, the meaning is compromised as badly as by inattention.

A second cause of the metaphorical style is the careless use of VOGUE WORDS whose literal meaning is no longer attended to, precisely on account of the vogue. For instance, a high-school teacher writes to a newspaper that he is glad to learn *that Superintendent G. is about to make life more viable in the Paper Castle which has so long imprisoned . . . the school staff.* Lately *viable* has displaced *feasible* as the omnibus word to express an unspecified possibility; the writer just quoted did not see that the one thing that cannot be made viable (= capable of living), let alone *more* viable, is life itself.

Since the modern vocabulary borrows heavily and steadily from the professions in order to be chic and solemn at once, it perpetually transfers meanings instead of speaking direct. Metaphor begets metaphor without check, even in the writing of those whose task it is to improve writing. One of the great words in education is *approach,* a metaphor that hardly suggests a coming to grips; hence in order to give it force it is often linked with the word *functional.* The phrase sounds imposing but remains vague, even though we are assured that *Such a functional approach is of immeasurable benefit to the student and will be particularly important in future years when swollen enrollments make individual attention difficult.* In that sentence from the chairman of a college department of English, no person is named, no action shown, no result defined. In this regard there is little to choose between educational prose and commercial: [We] *announce the opening of a shop with complete facilities for the production of individually designed hand-made frames to complement and embrace all art. Personalized services to individuals, artists, and interior decorators.* Obviously the habit of metaphor suffices to transform literal words into counters of metaphorical import; for in this announcement *facilities, production, complement, embrace, personalized services,* and *individuals* have only the cloudiest meanings. Nothing is named straight out except *hand-made frames* and *the opening of a shop.* (See also EDUCATIONESE.)

4. It is of course true that "all language is metaphor" and that the growth of language, as of literature, depends on the extension of literal meanings. Yeats's Crazy Jane is so called because to be insane is to be *cracked,* and the cracking of a pottery surface is known as *crazing.* But to justify this or any other extension there must be a better motive than careless habit or silly affectation. There must be a need, expressive or evocative, or both. None such appears in the large mass of metaphors that are made today, which may be why almost all are so inexact. They lack the proper intention. For example: *Dear Developer* (first undefined image): *The World Conference of the Society for . . . Development is just weeks away* (*weeks* is a metaphor for *a few weeks*—the time would still be weeks even if the conference were five years away). *Your help is needed in making this conference a useful tool* (third metaphor) *for international, social, and economic development* (clearly, *international* has here a purely metaphorical sense, since it does not in fact parallel or exclude *social* and *economic*). Or again, to go from political science to music criticism, what confidence can be placed in the judgment expressed as *He completely deserted the dispassion he showed with the Schubert?* The loose *with* is a kind of telltale reflex showing the lack of forethought that produced the idea of desertion in speaking of *dispassion*— whatever that may be.

No doubt the search for bright, crisp, arresting headlines and broadcast words contributes to the perpetual extension of meaning which is the principle of metaphor. But as metaphor is now practiced, both the principle and its applications are turning into destroyers of right reason. Thus in the captions AIRMAN YIELDS KIDNEY and AIR OF CONFUSION GROWS IN BRAZIL, the verbs flout common sense, seeing that the man did not give up something under threat but freely offered it to save the life of his twin brother; and in the second headline, although *confusion* can grow, *air* cannot. The finance pages of the paper, like the sports pages, rely on continual transfers of meaning: GRAINS UNEVEN AS SOYBEANS RISE; intelligible, no doubt, but conducive to an ever deeper unawareness of when we are or are not thinking metaphorically. This assertion can be tested by reading the approved samples in several of the guides to clearer business English—e.g. *Creative work and printing of this caliber deserve Smith Ink.* In this same approved style advertisers *of the highest caliber* (the biggest bore?) refer to their products as *Perfections from the C. collection,* while universities that advertise their wares employ a string of images that defy visualization. So does the public. For one first-rate metaphor such as *moon-lighting* (= holding a second job at night), there are fifty foolish or tired ones—*context, thrust, impact, commitment, erosion, hard core, confrontation, package, challenge,* etc. These are what the English call *boss words,* in the belief (or vain hope) that they are restricted to the white-collar class. Actually they spread by broadcasting and print and induce the narcotic state in every kind of audience.

5. But the harm metaphor does to the power of attention is less insidious than the harm it does to thought. For there is a domain of fact, namely scientific fact, which metaphor has lately invaded, and where it has visibly weakened the hold of common sense. Both scientists and laymen, for example, now believe that digital computers think, have memories, learn, translate, make errors and correct them, and succeed each other in "generations." Likewise, scientists and laymen have been seduced by metaphor into believing that the formative elements in genetics constitute a *code,* which *transmits information,* and thus helps determine the shape and growth of living things. Finally, some theorists have come to look upon science itself as a metaphor or a series of metaphors. All this is dangerously unclear thought.

For whether the doctrine that science is a metaphor explains why scientific hypotheses succeed one another without cease is not the point. The point is that metaphor, by definition, is something different from a literal statement. In order to say, as in the old grammar books, *He was a lion in the fight,* there has to be a lion, and *lion* must be the common, literal name of that existing thing. Now, if science is "but a metaphor," what are the literal *words*—not things —that it is a metaphor of? And as for language, what is the test—hence the value—of metaphor if the words are never literal and exact? The conclusion to be drawn is plain. Any reader or writer who values his common sense and who also values metaphor must resist the pseudo-poetry that is incessantly being fed to him. He must ask, just as incessantly, What is a *developer,* a *harsh yardstick,* a *gray area,* a *liquidity position?* In other words, Where am I? Who is speaking? What is going on? See also TICK.

methodology. See OLOGY, OLOGIES.

meticulous. See DEFENSIBLES.

militant. See RESOURCE PERSON.

-minded. See LINKING 3.

minimum. See MAJORITY, MINORITY.

minister, verb. See ADMINISTER.

minor. See MAJOR, MINOR.

minority. See MAJORITY, MINORITY.

mixed metaphor. See METAPHOR.

modern (istic). See CONTEMPORARY.

momently, -arily. The difference between what lasts only for a little while (*I forgot momentarily / I was dizzy but momentarily*) and what may happen at any moment (*He is expected momently*) is worth making clear by keeping apart the uses of these two words. The merit of this is evident if, bearing in mind the *short while* meaning, we use the longer form in such a sentence as *He will die momentarily*.

moonlighting. See METAPHOR 4.

more. See FEWER, LESS.

more preferable. One thing is preferable to another. To call one thing *more preferable than* the other (see PREFER . . . THAN) is the same sort of redundancy as to say *more better* or *more farther*. There is no defense for *A cold war is more preferable than peace on dishonorable terms. More preferable* is a possible phrasing only when two or more preferences are being compared. Nothing but a certain awkwardness precludes our saying: *Cold war is more preferable to abandoning allies than nominal peace would be at that price.* The phrasing *more to be preferred* would be better, and the meaning could be still better expressed by some simpler construction; e.g. *If the choice is peace at the price of betraying one's allies or a cold war, then a cold war is more to be preferred* or *Better cold war than nominal peace at the price of abandoning allies.*

motivation. See JARGON.

M'sieu. See FRENCH WORDS AND PHRASES.

muchly. See SINGLEHANDEDLY.

mutual friend, mutual interest. See DEFENSIBLES; LOST CAUSES.

N

nature. As the immortal mother of mortals, nature deserves and generally receives a good press; but in many of its uses the word is degraded in the same way as *character*. Indeed, in these uses the two are interchangeable. Both become pretentious substitutes for *sort* or *kind*, both can usually be replaced by abstract nouns (often in *-ness*), and both carry the vice of JARGON. If anyone wants to say that so-and-so has a sunny or a saturnine nature, meaning disposition, he does no harm; but to permit that august or intimate word to mean nothing at all is to debase communication. *Both the Defense Minister and Foreign Secretary Selwyn Lloyd stressed the continuing nature* (the persistence) *of the Soviet Union's challenge to the free world / The following varied events . . . helped to picture the country's divided nature* (the country's disunity) *as Sunday's referendum on the proposed new Constitution approaches / Because of the fickle nature of the breeze, there was a twenty-minute delay beyond the appointed 11:50* A.M. *deadline* (for *fickle nature* read *fickleness* or, even better, *Because of the fickle breeze.*) A biologist seems to pun perversely when he writes *I see modern man enjoying a unity with trilobites of a nature more deeply significant than anything at present understood in the processes of biological evolution* (For *of a nature* use *of a kind*, or omit altogether).

See also CASE; CHARACTER; COVERING WORDS; LEVEL.

nauseous. See TRANSITIVE, INTRANSITIVE.

necessity. See NEEDLESS WORDS 2.

née. See TITLES AND PROPER NAMES.

needless words. 1. Variants. 2. In use.

1. It should seem as if, apart from proved duplicates or recent formations of a pedantic cast that displace the simple term, no word could be called needless. Exact synonyms are rare and there is always a feature in the apparent synonym, whether shade of meaning, connotation, length, or rhythm, by which it can make itself useful. Yet some words at some times and others at all times can be shown to be unnecessary. *Utilize* is one of the second class. The occasions when *use* will not do are so rare as to be inexistent for the workaday writer, and the bad habit of resorting to the longer word becomes incurable. If a nuance must be found to distinguish between the pair, it lies in the stronger suggestion *utilize* gives of turning an object or a material to purposes it was not meant for. Again, *utilization* carries a hint of *using up*, of *economic use*, which does not reside in the shorter word. But if *utilize* and *utilization* were to disappear tomorrow, no able writer of the language would be the poorer.

Similar variants we could do without are *author* (verb), *differential* (for *difference*), *necessity* (for *need*, but not in all contexts), *disassociate* (for *dissociate*), *disassemble* (for *strip* or *take apart*), *correlative* (noun; see CORRELATE), *crafted* (adjective for *made* or *designed*), GIFT (verb), *illy*, and OVERLY.

2. The presence of good words that were better absent from a particular phrase or sentence is a different kind of needlessness, which calls for passing notice. Surplusage is common with such words as *factor*, *field*, and NATURE (see also CHARACTER). *He considered that the time factor was essential* means only *He thought time essential*. *An object of a curious nature* is but *a curious*

object, and *a research project in the field of economics* is very likely nothing more than *a study in economics*. (See also BEING.)

Besides these staples of the jargon writer (see FORBIDDEN WORDS 2), one could make a long list of what the late Ernest Gowers aptly named "adverbial dressing gowns." These occur in official prose, academic, corporate, or governmental, and follow the pattern of cliché in coming invariably with certain verbs: *seriously consider, thoroughly satisfied, sadly lack, closely scrutinize, fully recognize, utterly mistaken, deeply resented, satisfactorily complete, carefully investigate*, and so on. The removal of the dressing gown will be found to leave, not nakedness, but strength. And this goes for the couples made up of adjective and noun, whether the exact parallel (e.g. *serious consideration*) or the separate pairing (e.g. *avowed purpose, painful necessity, personal check*; see PERSONAL).

It can also be observed that in most sentences where *all, own, whole, very*, and *real* occur, these intensives do not in fact intensify and can be left out without loss. A few examples should suffice to give warning. *He had a way of mulling over what he read, coming back and back to all the ideas he found there* (omit *all* and *there*; add *in books?*) / *They left at dawn, quietly* on tiptoe, carrying their own baggage, including sandwiches (omit own) / They expected to be bored by the famed lecturer; instead, they found him very stimulating and lively (omit very) / It was not a modest ambition—no criminal's is—to want to be known throughout the whole world (omit whole) / The big city and its bustle were to her a real novelty (omit real) / How significant is their role in the whole practice of medicine? (omit whole) / He turned abruptly away and began to pick up his own papers (omit own) / They refused to a man to admit that it was a real mistake (omit real).

negative, proving a. Someone sets down a statement that sounds like a newfound and important truth, and if it is tersely enough put, it will be unthinkingly copied by the legion of authors. Aping them in turn, the public solemnly repeats the original nonsense. Such has been the history of "You can't prove a negative." A tenth of a second's thought would have shown that if A. thinks he did not bring his umbrella home from the office, all he has to do is to walk to the hall stand or the coat closet and by inspection prove or disprove his negative proposition. Every alibi (in the legal sense) is the proof of a negative: *I was*

not at the scene of the crime; I was 500 miles away.

What is probably intended by the false maxim is the suggestion that a universal negative in matters of fact is difficult or at least laborious to prove. To try to prove that *There is no fifth gospel in existence* or *There are no snakes in Ireland* or *No one suffers as much as I do* is a tall order. Even to define what would constitute proof would be difficult, let alone carry out the search for contrary instances. But take note of two further truths. First, universal positives are equally difficult to prove: *All rabbits have long ears* seems an assured matter of fact until some are found or produced with short ears. Black swans and white crows have turned up to confound the positive generalizers. Universal propositions are the same whether positively or negatively framed. Second, universal negatives not relating to existing things are readily proved: *There is no whole number such that it is the square root of 2.* This leaves us, then, with the tenable statement, "Proving empirical generalities is usually difficult."

negatives, divergent. See UN-, IN-, NON-.

negatives, trouble with. For many reasons, negative statements have to skirt more grammatical pitfalls than do affirmative statements. An affirmation is usually a simple whole and, as such, comparatively resistant to ambiguity; whereas a denial often applies only to a part, and sometimes to an insignificant part. It requires thought and an effort at precise expression to make sure that the question What is being denied? receives an unmistakable answer. Every writer's experience goes to show that it is easy to deny the wrong thing, and many readers notice the blunder.

Of the patterns that govern misdirected denials the most common are probably these four: (1) Simple misplacing of the negative, often with resultant affirmation of what is meant to be denied, or denial of what is meant to be affirmed, or both; (2) stating an affirmative meaning in a negative form; (3) stating a negative meaning in an affirmative form; and (4) stating antithetical or alternative meanings in a form that requires us to supply a false or illogical version of words left unexpressed. Of these four the last three largely overlap; and all four may involve the fundamental problem of position: Where does the negative element belong?

(1) The misplaced negative at its simplest occurs in connection with the word *all* and its synonyms. *All of these acids are not found in complete form in protein foods.* The meaning: Some of the acids are found,

some not. As written, the sentence flirts with the meaning that none are found; rewrite: *Not all . . . are found. All of Mr. Byrnes' memories of Franklin D. Roosevelt . . . are not so happy as this* (Not all . . . are so happy) / *All of the Founding Fathers may not have acknowledged a formal faith, yet all of them profoundly respected spiritual belief* (Not all . . . may have acknowledged). The author of a questionnaire sent to some three hundred persons testifies: *All of them did not reply. But . . . we found twenty-seven people* (persons?) *in Paris who . . .* Patently, *Not all of them replied* is the shape his first sentence needs. *Our entire stock is not included in this sale* (This sale does not include our entire stock). If the warning were construed as written, there would be no sale.

The *not only . . . but also* construction, when mismanaged, constitutes a subspecies of the misplaced negative. *Not only*, usually the misplaced element, will not flatly falsify a meaning as *not* in the wrong position will, but it has an uglier effect on the shape of a sentence if placed where it upsets rhetorical balance. Like EITHER . . . OR, NEITHER . . . NOR, and BOTH . . . AND, *not only . . . but also* is an explicit promise that what follows its first member will be grammatically equal and similar to what follows its second member. When the promise is broken the result limps annoyingly: *This not only puts pressure on the parents to provide the kind of environment they have envisioned, but on the child to show the felicitous effects of his new environment.* With *not only* where it is, there is no decent escape from the wordiness of repeating *puts pressure* after *but.* What is wanted, of course, is *not only* after *puts pressure* instead of before it; that adjustment brings us to the desired balance of *not only on the parents to . . . but also on the child to . . .* Balance is similarly to be restored in *agree that to back down after taking such a stand would not only destroy the American position in Asia, but throughout the world* (would destroy the American position not only in Asia but also throughout the world) / *pick books which the youthful reader not only will enjoy, but which will also be good for him* (not only will enjoy but will also profit by; books which will not only be enjoyed by the youthful reader but will also be good for him) / *has demonstrated that he not only can survive adversity but that he is exceptionally well qualified in the art of licking it* (take out the second *that he;* otherwise it is necessary to put *not only* before the first *that*).

Note that three of the four examples omit the *also* that idiomatically follows *but* as

part of the balance with *not only.* This omission undoubtedly reflects a growing tendency, especially in newspaper writing, which is editorially encouraged to be as spare as possible in some particulars. (For example, the conjunction *that* is omitted as often as possible.) *Not only . . . but* (without *also*) should probably be regarded as now unobjectionable, but if a writer has the habit of the full, balanced construction and cannot feel that a sentence is symmetrical without it, he is certainly not open to reproach. (See THAT, CONJUNCTION 2.)

(2) Statements of affirmative meaning in negative form probably constitute the largest class of mismanaged negatives. *The fight was a quarrel between two Moslem groups. It was not believed to be connected with the recent political crisis, but with a family feud.* Essentially, this sentence is about what is believed, not about what is not believed. Read, then: *It was believed to be connected, not with . . ., but with . . .* The same pattern of complaint and cure will nearly always apply. *Soustelle does not consider himself a representative either of the political Right or Left but of the Center* (considers himself a representative of neither Right nor Left but of) / *contends the present war need not be terminated by formal treaty but by "individual cease-fire arrangements*

with various fighting groups" (This example departs from the usual pattern, and seems in need of a totally different verb after *but*—perhaps *can be terminated*) / *In this score the three saxophones are not used in a solo role but as part of the wind choir* (are used not in a solo role but) / *"It will not be concerned with day-to-day administration,"* Mr. A. added, *"but rather with the long-term goals of Indonesia's social revolution"* (will be concerned not with . . . , but with) / *It is not included in this dictionary because we think that someone might need to know these facts but simply in order to make the list . . . complete* (It is included . . . , not because we think . . . , but simply).

Sometimes, as if it were not enough to have to untie a rhetorical knot, a logical one is added. No mere shift of a negative from here to there is going to unravel such a sentence as this: *The problem, therefore, is not one just for railroad management but for the good and welfare of all of us and our progeny.* The first *for* and the second have entirely different bearings—in fact, different meanings—and what follows *but* concerns not the problem but the (unmentioned) solution of it. There is no making coherence out of the statement short of radical reconstruction, such as *Solving the problem is not merely a re-*

sponsibility of railroad management, but a necessity for the welfare of all of us and our children. The question of misplaced meaning is manifestly more important, as well as more difficult, than that of the misplaced negative; the lesser question in fact disappears before the greater is answered.

(3) In the preceding cluster of examples, negations that belong to subordinate parts are falsely applied to the whole. When a negative meaning is couched in an affirmative statement, we get the opposite maladjustment: a negation that logically governs the whole is tucked away in a subordinate part. Howells provides an example of this perversity: *I can, neither as a man of letters nor as a man of business, counsel the young author to do it.* The grammatical line *I can . . . counsel* runs counter to the actual meaning, which is *I cannot counsel.* The perversity disappears if we read: *I cannot, as either a man of letters or a man of business, counsel . . .*

For supplementary examples and discussion, see EITHER . . . OR.

(4) There are not many legitimate exceptions to the rule that a missing word to be supplied by the reader must be a word that has previously occurred, and occurred in a position and in a form that permit it to be borrowed without

a struggle. We cannot fairly ask the reader to translate a negative verb into an affirmative one. *It does not have as much merchandise as the old crackerbarrel New England store but more than the village store of ten years ago.* Logically, what must be supplied after *but* is *it has*; but the sentence as written has saddled us with *does not have.* There is nothing for it but to bring in the logically needed verb: *but it has more than.* Nor should we expect the reader to supply *always* from a context that comes no nearer to that idea than *never. We are never assured that anything is "a bed of roses" but that it is not* (but always that it is not).

In the examples that follow, logically indispensable elements not present in the originals are suggested parenthetically: *Thus the pagination would not be continuous and the table of contents* (would be) *confusing / V. never really mentions it, or* (mentions it) *only to remark that Don C. will have no priest at his deathbed / Of course, no primitive Eskimo eats by any theory, and only by the desire of the moment* (any primitive Eskimo eats not by a theory [system?] but only by) */ For a moment neither spoke, but sat mute, gazing across the current at distant Manhattan* (but both sat mute) */ The testimony showed that she was not, at the most, more than nineteen miles away from the sinking Titanic and probably no more than five to ten miles distant* (and was probably no more than) */ stated that there appeared to be no references after 1564 to the queen's own hair, only to her wigs* (that all references after 1564 appeared to be to the queen's wigs, not to her own hair) */ I am surely no philologian, and my inquiries and surmises will probably be of small value to the first successor who is* (the first successor who is one) */ Washington stopped making sense to me about one month after I got here, and it never has* (made sense) *since / The Midwest wanted none of it. He wasn't so sure he did himself* (wanted any of it himself) */ Senator M. was in no mood yet to pretend that what had happened was just a jolly romp among good friends, and obviously the others weren't either* (the others were in no such mood either).

A negative will often lead one into a snarl from which there is no extrication except to abandon the position and start afresh. Consider *as though confronted with a problem for which there was no solution; as indeed there wasn't,* in which the author has without noticing it written down *there wasn't no solution.* The cure is not to supply an affirmative verb in the last clause but to make the verb in the first negative: *confronted with a prob-*

lem for which there wasn't any solution. Conversely, the verb in the following has to be made affirmative: *There has not been a return to overt police terror, no going back on the decision against forced collectivization* (There has been no return to . . ., no going back on . . .). Still another kind of adjustment is needed to take care of *No one had yet crossed him in any serious degree . . . , not knowing what this aspect might portend.* Here the author commits himself unaware to *No one . . . not knowing.* The simplest escape is perhaps *No one had yet crossed him . . . , for no one knew . . .*

For further side lights on unexpressed elements that the reader must supply for himself, see WHAT IS "UNDERSTOOD"?

See also HARDLY . . . THAN; NO SOONER . . . WHEN; UN-, IN-, NON-.

neither . . . nor. See EITHER . . . OR; MATCHING PARTS.

news. See MEANS.

noisome. See MALAPROPS.

non-, prefix. See UN-, IN-, NON-.

none. The writers of some newspapers are instructed to treat *none* as a singular and to allow no deviation from that rule. Lexicographers, who know as well as journalists that *none = no one,* point out that it is rather more commonly treated in modern usage as a plural, as if it meant *no ones*; and the same is true of colloquial habit, as anyone's ears will tell him. Literature shows both usages without a clear preponderance: *none but the brave deserves the fair* (Dryden) and *none was worth my strife* (Landor) by no means prevail over *have found that none of these finally satisfy, or permanently wear* (Whitman). In Greenough and Kittredge (*Words and Their Ways in English Speech*) we find *None of these borrowings . . . have affected the structure of our speech.* That the second pair are American instances is merely fortuitous; the plural can as easily be illustrated from British sources, the singular from American.

Some investigators have made statistical inquiries that prove a modern preference for *none* construed as a plural, but statistics covering the incidence of a word are vain when they do not take account of meaning. The fact is that in some contexts *none* means *not a single one,* making singularity emphatic, whereas in other contexts it means *no two, no few, no several, no fraction of many.* In *None of us is entitled to cast the first stone* the singular meaning is hardly mistakable; in *None of the commentators agree on the meaning of this passage* the plural meaning is equally clear. *None*, then, is freely either singular or plural according to the sense suggested by its context. Often, the number we give it makes no difference. As style, as grammar, and as meaning there is little to choose between *None of these opinions seems to be held with much conviction* and *None of these opinions seem to be held . . .* A self-conscious writer might prefer the first as a demonstration that he is not one of those careless fellows who let themselves be side-tracked from a singular subject by the accident of an intervening plural (see NUMBER, TROUBLE WITH); but that consideration does not affect clarity.

Obviously *none* should be given a plural verb wherever a singular one would produce awkwardness. Contortion and absurdity result when the rule prescribing an invariable singular fights with the plain sense, as in *None of these authorities agrees with one another*. Here *none* is trying to be both singular and plural at the same time. Sometimes *none* will lead into a trap from which there is no escape but by abandoning the word. *None of the cities or towns in this sprawling region . . . are* (is?) *connected by road* is uneasy either way. At the cost of wordiness one might write: *None . . . is connected with any other by road*; the trim repair seems to be *Of the cities . . . no two are connected by road.*

None is often balanced against *some: Some of them may have been eccentric, but none of them was* (were?) *crazy.* The natural procedure here is that of MATCHING PARTS; the shift to the singular calls attention to itself. When *none* is used to balance *few* we sometimes get such curiosities as the following about vitamin injections for athletes: *None, or at least very few, was used before the war.* The newspaper commandment about singular *none* has pushed this writer into absurdity; *were* is obligatory. *The whole edition, none of which were for sale* is correct and natural; *none was* would be correct and unnatural.

Untouched by these comments is a *none*, inherently singular, that means *no amount, no part: None of the debris has been cleared away / None of this task has been performed / None of our skepticism is allayed by such protestations.*

nonleakable. The standard meaning of -ABLE (-IBLE) is passive—*capable of being.* But just as certainly it sometimes does not possess or imply this meaning. *Knowledgeable* does not mean capable of being known, or *personable* capable of being personed, or *irascible* capable of being irasced. (It is interesting that *knowledgeable* did once have the passive meaning, *capable of being known,* and that *personable* had the active sense of *qualified as a person, for legal purposes.*) In spite of these discrepancies, the passive idea is not easily overcome, and it asserts itself when this affix is put to words that are not accustomed to it. *Leak* is such a word, and *non-* (or *un-*) *leakable* for *unleaking* seems as perverse as it did when first used about fountain pens. (A recent example: *"Unleakable" is an epithet applied to . . . a former small businessman who got to know so many top secrets about national security that he was invited to brief Vice President Richard M. Nixon.*)

But now there enters a factor that compounds confusion. The verb *leak* itself, in our time of concern with espionage, suddenly developed a new transitive meaning and hence a capacity to be used passively. *This information is supposed to have been leaked to the press by a minor official of the department / News of this increase in the interest rate was leaked from some source before it was announced officially.* This use is virtually established: it is natural and meets a need. There is no way to stop it and no reason why anyone should want to; it is a good sample of one way in which language has always grown. Now, when *leak* in this special transitive sense has be-

come as familiar as its long-standing intransitive uses, *unleakable* will very likely acquire the passive sense *incapable of being leaked.* But its application will have to be restricted to facts and ideas, and it will remain hard to believe.

See also ROADABILITY.

nor . . . or. See EITHER . . . OR.

no sooner . . . when. *Hardly* and *scarcely,* when they introduce temporal clauses, are followed by *when* and sometimes by *before* in the succeeding clause and do not tolerate *than* (see HARDLY . . . THAN). But temporal clauses introduced by *no sooner* require *than* as a sequel and are impossible with *when. No sooner had he arrived when the familiar orders arrived from Coppet* must have its *than,* for it is the inevitable conjunction after words in the comparative degree, such as *sooner.*

Sentences of the pattern *hardly . . . when* are open to the improvement of reversed emphasis, because the grammatically subordinate clause is logically the principal one. The main statement above is that the familiar orders arrived from Coppet; the rest amounts to no more than an adverb of time. Therefore: *As soon as he got there the familiar orders arrived,* or some equivalent construction, unless the paragraph needs a connective in the inverted form *No sooner* at the head of the sentence.

not only ... but also. See BOTH ... AND; MATCHING PARTS; NEGATIVES, TROUBLE WITH; SENTENCE, THE 4.

not too. See TOO 2.

notwithstanding. See CONTRARY.

noun-plague. 1. The blue air-letters supplied at a low rate by a benevolent government recommend to the user that he *moisten flap well and apply pressure to seal.* The noun-plague is illustrated by the decline from grace in the second half of the compound sentence. *Moisten flap well* is direct and strongly based on a verb. *Apply pressure* is a weak indirection for *press down.* Influenced as it is by the mechanical impersonality of the scientific report (*pressure was then applied*), modern style tends to turn thought into a chain of static abstractions linked by prepositions and by weak verbs generally in the passive voice. "Weak" here means that these verbs do not denote any single characteristic action but, like *is* and *have,* draw their strength from the accompanying noun (*apply pressure* as against *press / give authorization* rather than *permit / send a communication* instead of *write / take appropriate action* in place of *act / lose altitude* instead of *come down*).

2. Many abstract nouns in English end in *-tion,* and the effect on the ear of stringing several of them together is narcotic. The prose of science may be left to the scientists, who are more concerned with numbers and diagrams than with words. But the prose of journalists, businessmen, scholars, lawyers, and civil servants amounts to a public act and becomes our intellectual environment. It should, if not enchant, at least inform without causing instant weariness and protracted boredom. The science reporter writes: *The prediction of the existence of antiparticles was made by P. A. M. Dirac in 1927 and its confirmation was an important reason for the construction of the Bevatron at Berkeley in 1954* (compare *Dirac predicted in 1927 that antiparticles exist. Once this statement was confirmed, the Bevatron was built*—one noun preceding each verb). Again: *The educational program of the college is a unique approach to the teaching of the liberal arts and sciences. While offering a new level of flexibility for maximum individual student growth, the curriculum welds together the natural sciences, social sciences, and the Humanities into a unified whole throughout the entire three years.* Apart from the obvious surplusage, these *approaches to teaching* and *levels of flexibility for maximum individual student growth* are unanalyzed abstractions that do not acquire meaning simply by being juxtaposed in familiar ways. The one question that must be put to any description, especially that of a college program, is: What goes on? With nothing but abstract nouns in series, the desired clarity and vividness are made unattainable.

3. The sociologist offends in the same way: *In the act of forging* [,] *an ephemeral personal reorganization occurs in response to situational interactors which may be recognized as a special symbolic process conceived to cover aspects of motivation, feeling, emotion, and the choice of adjustment alternatives. The personal differentiae we have set down here are the original broad limits within which a certain class of situations can impinge upon the person with the possibility of emergent forgery.* Even the novelists most highly praised for style and originality succumb to the noun-plague. Here are examples culled from two consecutive pages chosen at random from a "powerful" novel of the avant-garde: *He had washed the floor before his departure* (= leaving) / *I assumed that . . . harm had come to him* (= he had been hurt / *now they would suffer the proxim-*

ity they had always avoided (= be together as they had never wanted to be) / *On this occasion there was nothing faltering* (= Now) / *Her blue eyes regarded me in innocence* (= looked at me innocently) / *so compelling that I must have stared at her with evident amazement* (= stared at her, visibly amazed) / *She yawned in a pretense of indifference* (= with pretended) / *yet her restlessness was so pressing that it overflowed in another instant* (= she was so restless that she broke out again).

The words in parentheses are not proposed as improvements—that would be an impertinence—but simply to show how persistently the modern mind makes its objects out of abstract states, and how the repetition of the words denoting those states dulls narrative and description. And when the sole contrast is with dialogue written in slang that is equally repetitious, the combined effects inevitably produce an impoverishment of experience. We moderns are exceedingly fond of the word *dynamic*, but our characteristic style in many genres is unshakably static. The only way to set it in motion again is to avoid abstract nouns like the plague.

number, trouble with. The linguistic theorists (now in the majority), who despise prescriptive grammar, advocate many liberties that strike the prescriptive grammarian as license; but so far they have not carried the love of liberty to the point of decreeing that a plural subject ought to be followed by a singular verb or a singular subject by a plural verb. A good many of them do recommend that when there is a compound subject containing both plural and singular elements, the verb shall take the number of the subject element nearest it. This formula is in itself a tacit admission that in general we do expect a subject to influence the number of its verb. English has in the course of a millennium sloughed off a great many distinctions once made by inflecting words as German still inflects them; but there is no reason to suppose that it is about to slough off the distinction of number, and so long as there is grammatical number there will be a tendency toward agreement in number. If we accept the long-established conventions of prescriptive grammar—which this book does accept, on the theory that freedom from confusion is more desirable than freedom from rule—we find that the chief troubles with number in the domain that embraces subject, verb, object, and predicate complement are these four: (1) clash between subject and verb; (2) subversion of verb by predicate noun; (3) failure to identify the part of the subject with which the

verb is to agree; (4) illogical and confused shift between singular and plural.

(1) Disagreement between subject and verb is insidiously facilitated when the order is inverted; that is, in a declarative inversion that brings the verb ahead of the subject or in a question that brings about the same inversion. An example of the first: *Among the passengers was Wilhelm Grewe, German Ambassador to the United States, and his wife* (which says *Wilhelm Grewe and his wife was . . .*). An example of the second: *And what purpose has all his objections served?* (which says *All his objections has served what purpose?*). There is no way to be right about such a matter, or to know whether one is right or wrong, without some operation akin to parsing. The learned are as helpless as the ignorant if they do not examine and verify.

The converse of this accident—the attraction of a verb properly singular to a plural noun or pronoun that precedes it—can also occur: *Among those attending were George M. Humphrey, former Secretary of the Treasury, who, like Mr. McElroy, is an Ohioan.* The first verb is subverted by *those*; the second has had the benefit of a name and a phrase in apposition clearly singular. Such are the mishaps of inversion.

But do not dart to the conclusion that the normal order (subject, verb, predicate) guarantees anybody against this sort of clash. *A thirty-one-game exhibition schedule and a quick dash north has* (have) *been mapped for the . . . spring training campaign / It has the light weight and fine balance that makes* (make) *writing so much easier /* [The] *creation of two top posts . . . and* [the] *selection of officers to fill them was* (were) *announced over the week-end / estimates "conservatively" that new home construction and the demand for business and store space has* (have) *added $50,000,000 to $100,000,000 to the value of property surrounding the big housing project.*

Each of these examples advertises the plurality of its subject by means of *and*. One should note, however, as an apparent but not actual exception, that in a few instances *and* is used to join, not several subjects, but repetitions of one subject rhetorically varied, and that such repetitions are properly given a singular verb. The impassioned preacher or perfervid orator intones: *What is the end and aim and object and goal of all this striving?* His grammar is irreproachable, however windy his style. With or without *and*, a subject consisting of synonyms or reduplications in the singular number is correctly treated as singular: *This inhibition of his,*

this aversion to wearing his heart on his sleeve, this obsessive reluctance to give himself away, is (not *are*) *traceable in every one of his relationships.* It is the numerical meaning of a subject, not its numerical form, that controls the number of its verb.

Plural verb with singular subject is nothing like so common, except where the verb is carelessly made to agree with some plural noun that happens to intervene between true subject and verb. The comparatively rare examples generally involve a mismanagement of some collective noun —a word singular in form but construable as plural in sense. *The snow-fed vegetation are subjected to the most intense heat of the summer* can hardly be explained except on the theory that the author conceived *vegetation* as a collective word like *committee, majority,* or *family,* which can be treated as singular when we are thinking of the collective unit or as plural when we are thinking of the component members. Unfortunately, *vegetation* (for *plants*) cannot be forced into that class without strain; the effect is as eccentric as it would be to use *forestation* as a synonym of *trees.* In the sentence *No "public body or authority" are* (is?) *to intervene to protect the public interest,* what is at work is probably a confusion between an alternative (singular) subject (this *or* that) and a bona-fide plural (this *and* that). But here again it is possible that *body* and *authority* were conceived, in the English manner, as collectives, with awareness of the individuals composing the groups. The *are* is at worst wrong, at best awkward.

What shall be said of the increasing tendency to make a verb agree in number with the subject nearest it when it serves a combination of singular and plural subjects? A typical instance: *The criticisms from without, the feuding within, was bringing NRA down the home stretch in a condition of weariness and irresolution.* Try a reversal of the subjects, applying the same rule: *The feuding within, the criticisms from without, were bringing NRA,* etc. Either way, can anyone think the sentence admirable? Many readers cannot shake off a feeling that whichever subject comes first is abandoned in mid-air and left to shift for itself. The best writing does not leave anyone with that feeling. Suppose the subjects had been written with a connective: *The criticisms from without and the feuding within* . . . Would the author still think *was bringing* a tolerable form of the verb? Yet no real difference is made by the addition of *and*; the subject is as plural without it as with it.

The doctrine proposed in this book is that problems of this order are not to be solved, but sidestepped. Some such simple adjustment as the following is always feasible: *The criticisms from without, the feuding within—these were bringing NRA . . .* Since good writing demands an effort to please as well as to communicate—or at the least an effort not wantonly to displease—an author's dignity is not compromised by a concession to intelligent susceptibilities.

(2) The second kind of discrepancy, that which is brought on by a singular subject and a plural predicate noun, involves one of the so-called copulative verbs, generally some form of *to be*. *The only thing that made it real were the dead Legionnaires / Just about the only thing that had been left untouched were the folded pyramidal tents in the supply room / The nearest thing to "scandal" are the vitriolic elaborations of the Clemens grouch against his partner in publishing, against . . . / An encouraging note also were three cases made against persons who threw trash in or along trout streams.* The only thing *were*? The nearest thing *are*? An encouraging note *were*? Clearly, the authors have hocused themselves into seeing the predicate nouns as the true subjects. The first sentence as it stands is taken to be but another form of *The dead Legionnaires*

*were the only thing that made
it real.* Here lies the error. A
predicate adjective can come
before the verb, to be sure
(fortunate is the man that . . .),
and now and again an osten-
tatiously inverted sentence
may put a predicate noun before the verb *(Good friends
are we);* but otherwise the
noun that precedes a copulative verb is its subject, and
the noun that follows belongs
to the predicate. We cannot
reverse the two by after-
thought.

Two words that lead into
these subverted plurals with
some frequency are *all* (= the
one thing) and *what* (= that
which). The first, in this use, is
singular, and the following
sentences ignore the fact to
their detriment. *All that came
to him in that time of ultimate
clarification of his life were
voices / Well, all you need
are a cup of molasses, 2 tea-
spoons of vinegar, ¾ cup of
sugar / All we need are a few
suits of armor hanging over
the line to dry / All that remained to be done were the
small jobs of touching up and
adding refinements here and
there.* These examples are perhaps additional instances of
mistaking plural predicates
for true subjects. The word
what can be plural; it can
mean *those which* as well as
that which. But it has this insistent peculiarity: if meant
plurally, it has to be set up as
plural to begin with. Nothing

will make it plural retroac-
tively. We can say: *He well
understood what were the requirements of politeness,* but
if we say *He will understood
what politeness required,* the
what is incurably singular.
This reminder is made necessary by these typical instances
of the verb corrupted by a
plural predicate: *What to
watch for are such things as
dry, sandy layers or hardpan
/ What Jane is clutching to
her bosom are four kittens
/ What they saw were the
white sand cliffs on the eastern coast of . . . Guanahani
/ What these gentlemen need
are some new moral values.*

So much for the question of
grammar. There remains a
question of style. In this struggle against a plain grammatical requirement there is clearly
at work a feeling that it is impossible to be happy with the
combination of a singular subject and a plural predicate
complement. If a writer is
made uneasy by the disparity
in number, if he simply cannot feel right with *What these
gentlemen need is some new
moral values,* correct though
it be, he would do well to
humor his feeling. No one has
to write a construction and
like it just because it is
demonstrably correct; and the
truth is that a clash of number between subject and predicate can be awkward—e.g.
*the only thing . . . untouched
was the . . . tents.* Everybody

grows in grace by heeding his instincts about such matters, and anyone who develops fluency and force will do it partly by honoring his sense of how to make the rough and tangled places smooth and plain. Whoever is disturbed by the assertion of identity between one thing and several things, as in our examples, should learn the many ways of circumventing the difficulty. A few random hints: *Nothing but the dead Legionnaires made it real / Almost nothing was left untouched but the . . . tents/ There is no nearer approach to "scandal" than the vitriolic elaborations.*

(3) The effective subject of a verb is often more extensive than its strict grammatical subject, which governs its number; and the extensions of a singular subject often include plural nouns, usually objects of prepositions. In that event the man who writes by ear is under temptation to give his verb the number of the intervening noun. *On islands like the Aleutians and Iceland, the number of species increase* (increases) */ with a feeling of friendliness and accommodation that were* (was) *quite genuine and sincere* (the statement is about the feeling: friendliness and accommodation, by the way, are necessarily sincere). The false attraction of a properly plural verb to an intervening singular is a comparative rarity, but it does occur: *Even friends of the labor union movement like Prof*[essor] *Edward H. Chamberlin has* (have) *finally become convinced that curbs on that monopoly are now necessary.* The author perhaps thought he had written: *Even such a friend . . . as Professor . . . Chamberlin has finally become convinced.*

Additions to a singular subject are often made by the use of subordinating expressions of prepositional effect —*with, together with, as well as, besides,* etc.—and these additions are sometimes mistakenly allowed to affect the number of the verb. *P., with four other men, were* (was) *put on Omala to set up and operate a little observation post. P.* [and] *four other men* is a plural subject; *P., with four other men,* remains grammatically singular. (See AS 11.) A corrective addition to a subject that changes its number *ought* to influence the verb, but one sometimes finds such additions treated as grammatically null. A waitress in a restaurant at a missile base is said to be able to *tell by who is not there what missile* —*or missiles*—*is going up.* The author perhaps fancies that he has taken *or missiles* out of the operating grammar of the sentence by enclosing it in dashes, but the punctuation makes no structural difference, and we are left with a verb that first one subject but quarrels with the other. In this particular sentence *is going up* happens to mean *is to go up* or *is about to go up*, and therefore the issue can be neatly evaded by writing *what missile —or missiles—will be going up*. But if evasion is not resorted to, what is the correct solution? The graphic device occasionally encountered—*If any document or documents from this period ever turn(s) up*—merely advertises the problem at the expense of style. Such a trick would require at times the still clumsier *has* (*have*) and *is* (*are*). To meet the difficulty head on, only two courses are open: (a) *tell . . . what missile is— or missiles are—going up* or (b) *tell what missile is going up—or what missiles.* The first has the pedantry inseparable from the double-prepositional construction (*aversion to and distrust of*, etc.); the second, which leaves it to the reader to infer *are going up*, is only a little less grating. Neither is attractive; and indeed the construction that drives a plural and a singular in one harness always poses a choice of evils.

(4) The axiom that if one person has one head, heart, or torso two persons have two seems to be a stumbling block to a good many writers, and their failure to make terms with it results in a confused shifting back and forth between singular and plural.

When the water is hot they [garfish] *require* [a] *frequent recharge of their oxygen bladder.* The author failed to make up his mind whether he was saying *The garfish requires . . . recharge of its oxygen bladder* or *They require . . . recharge of their oxygen bladders.* A school superintendent discussing salaries says: *Until teachers can get to the point where they can make a substantial salary adjustment above a teacher's salary, they've got to be either a high school principal or assistant superintendent* (He should have begun *Until a teacher* or else ended *either high school principals or assistant superintendents*) / *Such thinking is alien to the Soviet philosophy that there would be no survival on either the Russian or American sides if nuclear war broke out* (on either . . . side).

The last example shows that the conjunction *or* is a continual temptation to inconsistency of number. *There are none of the taut discords of the Fourth or Sixth Symphonies* (Here the confusion is between *the Fourth and Sixth symphonies* and *the Fourth or the Sixth Symphony*) / *It is urged that this subject be begun in the third or fourth grades* (grade).

An interesting variant of the one-head-to-one-person axiom turns up in a piece of popular fiction: *Charley suggested that one of the* [pack] *animals' load be stowed in a wagon.* Much thought—the author's or his editor's—went into the choice of a version that can hardly strike anyone as natural and will probably strike many as ungrammatical. The problem is really two problems: *animals'* versus *animal's*, and *load* versus *loads.* Both problems can be skirted without drawing attention to them: *one animal's load* would be both accurate and easy, and *the load of one animal* would be at least accurate.

What is the number of an organization with a plural noun as the nucleus of its name? Shall we say *The Daughters of the American Revolution is* or *are?* Forms of reference that are extremely common, whether consistent or not, are (a) *The Daughters of the American Revolution are* and (b) *The D.A.R. is.* Theoretically, such a name can be felt as either the plural that it is in form or the singular that it is as the name of an organization. The title of a literary work with a dominant plural in it is treated in modern usage as a singular; no one would now say that *"Conversations in Ebury Street" are an autobiographical work,* though eighteenth-century usage shows a high incidence of *"The Two .Gentlemen of Verona" have been performed,* etc. Perhaps the most we can require is that an author be consistent with himself and stick to the singular or plural with which he begins. It is odd to read: the *Veterans of Foreign Wars has given a cancer research center, and the Masons have contributed the Masonic Memorial Hospital.*

Similarly, phrases that embody a single idea with plural contents accord better with a singular verb; e.g. *I don't think two bathrooms is too much for such a large family.* One may of course say *two bathrooms are* if this is followed by *too many;* but the true sense is: this proposal, this request, this plan—of two bathrooms. In *six thousand dollars is too little insurance to take out,* the singular is inescapable. But beware of nouns denoting single objects in plural form e.g. *scissors, bellows, tongs, pliers, spectacles,* etc., which invariably take a plural verb.

For a discussion of the commonest error in the realm of number, see ONE OF THE, ONE OF THOSE; INTRODUCTORY, p. 30.

nympho, psycho, etc. See SHORTENINGS.

O

oblivious. Some judicious minds might prefer to see this word among DEFENSIBLES; that is, in the sense of *blind, unaware*. The reason for dealing with it as an undesirable is twofold: when misused it brings with it a dubious preposition—*oblivious to;* and it lives side by side with *oblivion,* undivorced in meaning: *oblivion* and *oblivious* both denote forgetting. *Sinking into oblivion* is fading from the memory of men. The adjective is manifestly needed. *Much as he had loved this only daughter, the passage of time, the press of events, the weariness of advancing age made him oblivious.* To take this last word in order to say that X. did not see what was in front of his eyes is a waste: *Struck, suddenly, with her beauty, he was oblivious to all else.* A sense of time passing goes with the finer use: one becomes *oblivious of* one's early follies. When diverted to a cruder use, the word has to take *to* because, instead of the passage of time, it describes a state or an instant: *As soon as they reached the heavenly spot they were oblivious to all their troubles / He had seen her flush of anger but, resolved to keep his own temper, he made himself oblivious to it.* For the sake of idiom and preciseness let us not be oblivious of the usefulness still to be had from *oblivious.*

See also PREPOSITIONS.

obverse. See CONVERSE, OBVERSE, REVERSE.

obviate. The root meaning —*against the way*—restricts the use of *obviate* to those contexts where the removal of a difficulty is being referred to. Mere removal does not justify the use of *obviate,* and the following sentence overlooks the distinction: *The author must see proofs promptly and react quickly, before the pressure of the publishing schedule obviates an opportunity for making changes.* Substitute *removes* (or *precludes*) *the opportunity,* etc.

octopus. See LATIN AND GREEK PLURALS.

of. See A, AN, THE 5; IN FOR BY, OF; POSSESSIVES.

often. See PRONUNCIATION 1.

O.K. This world-conquering Americanism has also the incarnations *okay* and (once upon a time) *okeh*. It is noun, adjective, adverb, and verb. *We are hoping for your prompt O.K. / This arrangement seems okay to me / He is doing okay so far / Kindly O.K. and initial the reset pages.* The accounts of its origin, to which this book will not contribute, are many and for the most part hard to believe. In the form *O.K.* it is a standard and unexceptionable mark of approval or acceptance on documents and particularly on printer's proofs, on which *O.K. as set* and *O.K. with corrections* are familiar formulas. In conversation the uses range from the humdrum to the fantastic. *O.K.* is an understood answer to almost anything from *You won't forget my errand, will you?* to *Thank you very much*, after which it stands for *Don't mention it* or *You're welcome.*

Those who refuse all the uses of *O.K.* except the initialing of documents are probably few. The habitual users do include, however, an appreciable remnant who have never lent their lips to the reduplicative *okie doke* and who hear it with pain. Further to beslang such a word as *O.K.* would seem impossible, but even that goal is attained in *oke*, pronounced *oak*.

ology, ologies. The logos of a thing or activity, from which we derive our fast-multiplying *ologies*, is its reason or theory—the discourse about it. The very length and roll of the word thus formed tempts the heedless to use it whenever the thing or activity itself, and not its theory, is what they have in mind. The flagrant example is *technology*, which should mean the theory of our mechanized world, instead of the machinery itself. This confusion has led some modern writers to use *technics*, *techniques*, and *techne* (Greek for *art* or *craft*) to mark the forgotten difference and properly designate the machine civilization. These writers' books on the subject would then constitute the *technology* of the *techne*.

That particular long word is doubtless not to be salvaged from misuse, but there is no reason why others should be let go as well. It is inexcusable, for instance, to lengthen the wordage by writing *methodolgy* when one means *method* (*I approve of his aim but the way he went about it—his methodology—is all wrong.*) It is as if a man were to refer to his *gastronomic juices* when he meant *gastric*. Again, the events and tendencies we observe about us, whether we do so as amateurs or as scholars, are not *sociological*; they are merely *social*.

The mind or temperament of a human being or of a fictional character is, or should be, just those things—his mind or temperament or both, not his *psychology*. As for his bodily needs or urges, they are not *biological* but *organic*. And so for all the *ologies*, present or to come. In making new ones, note that they require the full root unless it ends in a vowel (*psyche, techne*). One must therefore say (if unavoidable) *symbolology* and not *symbology*.

It is a question, incidentally, whether an *ology* has to be minted every time someone thinks it profitable to look into a new subject. The study of how close people may safely be packed in hospitals, schools, office buildings, and the like has recently been baptized *proxemiology* (and also *proxemetics*.) It is only one of dozens of vainglorious terms the public could do without.

Finally, there is warrant in good writers of the last century for the revival in ours of *ology* and *ologies* as independent nouns designating, with some irony, the wondrous new sciences. Thomas Hughes in 1849, and after him Froude and others, used the word without the self-consciousness of quotation marks, which suggests that it had some currency in speech.

omission. See PRONUNCIATION 1.

on, upon, up on. Everybody uses *bookishness* as a derogatory term, but many of those who bandy the word about betray the same fault by a habitual use of *upon* for *on*, a substitution that in modern prose does as much to produce a bookish effect as any single word can do. Apart from a few set phrases in which *upon* comes automatically to lips or pen—e.g. *Depend upon it!* and *Upon my word!*—this form of the preposition should be reserved for (1) idioms (*put upon*); (2) the avoidance of ambiguity, as when *on* would link a nearer word and *upon* correctly links the farther one (*the effect of the short brisk word on* [upon] *style*); and (3) very occasional effects of emphasis, rhythm, or archaic tone. Why should we not in this enlightened and rapid century *bank on, count on, rely on, comment on, depend on, enlarge on, trespass on, verge on, seize on, land on, hit on, recline on, meditate on, sermonize on, work on*, etc.? This recommendation has, of course, no bearing on *up* as an adverb followed by the preposition *on*. We go *up on* the roof, get *up on* a horse, climb *up on* a scaffolding, etc. This construction requires two separate words, and *up* is given an intonation very different from that of the first syllable of *upon*.

one (= I). This somewhat overworked pronoun does very well in its standard use as a designation of the unspecified person who stands for all persons, or for all persons in an understood category; as in *One can thrive in the Arctic on food that violates every low-latitude definition of a balanced diet.* (For the sequence *one . . . he*, see ANTECEDENTS 8.) It does not do so well as surrogate for the first person singular as some writers tend to believe. Much depends on the intention, frequency, and tone of its employment. *One was left somewhat at a loss by this unexpected retort* / *One could not comfortably appeal to one's parents for further indulgence.* Jespersen collected sentences from Jane Austen in which the identification of *one* with *I* is so absolute as to evoke the first-person auxiliary: *one should* (= I should) *not like to have Sir Thomas find all the varnish scratched off.* This is now felt as prissy; the implication is that to say *I* is too self-assertive, and at the same time that to give an impersonal coloring to a subjective remark heightens its force. This inherent contradiction in the use of *one* for *I* has been exploited by some novelists for comic characterization. English writers are more likely to adopt this usage than Americans, and to do so without the motives of modesty or egotism. Thus the anonymous author of a light essay about the ill-advised purchase of a boater (straw hat) calls himself *one* for some eight hundred words for no reason but that *I* is forbidden by house rules (see WE, EDITORIAL). *Upon arriving home one again tried on the boater. . . . "It looks wonderful," she said. But one knew. . . . One recalled, painfully . . . So the new boater went back into its box . . . And one was hatless.* An incidental drawback to so prolonged a use is that *one* is bound to crop up in different uses: *One entered a shop on Fifth Avenue, asked to see some boaters, tried on one or two and, with a furtive glance into a mirror, agreed to purchase one.*

one another. See EACH, EVERY 2.

one of the, one of those. These words introduce the most widespread of all defiances of rudimentary grammar: the coupling of a plural subject with a singular verb. Eric Partridge characterizes the fault as a product of bad thinking, and that is indeed what it suggests. But it is so nearly universal that it can perpetuate itself without any thinking at all. A batch of examples will illustrate: *Captain B. is one of those people who has the good fortune to have "a happy face"* / *The American Gas Association is one of the few trade groups that keeps* *tabs on the activity of their members' stocks* (note the odd clash of *keeps,* singular, with *their,* plural) / *one of the customs that both shapes and expresses the life of* [a village] / *one of the few writers in the country who has made a living being funny* / *B.'s is one of the many stores that supplies this service* / *one of many farmers interviewed who was disturbed by the price situation* / *one of the most important constitutional problems that has confronted the world organization* / *one of the best things that has happened to British historiography in a long time* / *one of those phrases that after four or five hundred years of constant use has lost all sense of its original meaning* / *The author of these lines is not one of those who feels that Germany would be incapable of dealing directly with the Soviet Union without losing her own independence or jeopardizing the interests of the Atlantic community.*

The contributors to this miscellany are all educated men; some are literary artists; not one of them would ordinarily put a singular verb with a plural subject. Yet, seduced by a certain set pattern of words, they will automatically commit themselves to *people who has good fortune, trade groups that keeps tabs, customs that shapes and expresses life, writers who has*

made a living being funny, and so on. Moreover, most of the specimens can be presumed to have passed under the eyes of experienced copy editors.

The error is easy to fall into; even a writer who is on his guard against it will find it in his own draft or proofs. Why does the desire to state that some one person or thing (singular) belongs in a stipulated collection or class (plural) deviate into the statement that the class = the one? This is the cause: the definition of the class is given solely in order to define the individual, but by a mental short circuit the *one* in whom or in which we are interested is allowed to jump over the class and to link itself with the defining words.

Some apologists give it as an excuse that the many who commit the mistake are still thinking of *one* when they come to the plural—*those people,* or another class name. True—that is just what is the matter with the construction. And as long as the language keeps its few remnants of inflection, the word-respecting writer will habitually aim at plural verbs for plural subjects. The best of writers, when he falls into absent-mindedness, yields no better precedent than the worst.

only. The last word on *only* was uttered by Fowler forty years ago. He made it clear once and for all that an over-nice effort to put *only* in front of the word it modifies goes against good sense, sentence rhythm, the customary placing of adverbs, and the whole English and American literary tradition. When a special exactness or emphasis is desired, *only* may and should be moved close to its partner. *The tribesmen fought from within their stockades only when the moon was down.* Otherwise its place is before the verb; it is torturing the sentence and the listener to make a point of saying *He died only yesterday.* To establish the opposite, the advocates of the officious *only* must lead the way by saying *Only God knows.*

on the other hand. Can *the other hand* come into play in a sentence if *the one hand* has not preceded it? The need of a phrase on which to pivot, an adversative to what has gone before, a springboard to give new impetus and new direction, is often felt in English and is not to be had as readily as in other languages. *Contrariwise* is lumbering and too much in opposite; *per contra* is foreign and will strike some readers as an affectation. More and more writers resort to *on the other hand,* which by itself conveys something a little different from its meaning when paired, this something being what they

want. And yet the construction, inescapably elaborate, dangles horribly when halved. "*What* other hand?" is the inevitable question. All things considered, it is best to effect the quarter-turn by purely rhetorical means: *So much for* [the preceding subject] / *Enough has been said about* . . . / *I now turn to* . . . , etc.

opera. See LATIN AND GREEK PLURALS.

Operation X, etc. The Second World War produced a great flowering of code names for military, naval, and amphibious plans and undertakings—e.g. *Operation Sea Lion* —and they have stamped their imprint on the peacetime language in ways not to be escaped by any reader of news. The official and quasi-official utterances of departments and bureaus read more and more like a sort of algebra—a medium not of words but of symbols that people no longer bother to translate into words. Much of the algebraic effect is accomplished by acronyms— terms compounded of initials or of initial syllables, such as *NATO, SEATO, UNESCO,* etc. (see INITIALESE). Adults are moved to such ingenuities by the same pleasure that children find in devising secret languages, and much the same motive perpetuates the habit of naming projects "operations." Enterprises that have no need of military or diplomatic secrecy adopt code names or attempt to poeticize their work, more or less aptly. Thus the worthy project *Head Start* is really a *First Start* for children deprived of early nurture; a *head start* is what their luckier competitors have had. It is unfortunate that a special and arresting name should turn out a misnomer. What is worse, when undertakings are not given such special names, the lack is taken as a sign of unimportance: *Possibly because of the haste no customary code name was adopted for the series. At a press briefing at the Las Vegas City Hall today A.E.C. officials said reporters were welcome to christen the operation. After discussion of possibilities including "curfew" and "under-the-wire" the name "Deadline" was decided on.* The account of a book given in a news story reads: *This personal story begins in 1947 with Operation Windmill to establish ground control points. It continues through Operations Deep Freeze I and II to the planning of Operation Deep Freeze III in 1957, when the scientists were already at work.* Again: *Project Farside . . . which aimed at orbiting a rocket around the moon by firing it from a balloon 100,000 feet in the air / The once-secret world of Project Matterhorn, seeking to harness the power of the hydrogen bomb for peacetime energy / Project*

Man High, which is studying the stratosphere and space flight. After all this, one can but applaud the journalist's remark about two politicians who abominate each other but go through friendly motions for show: *Operation Patchup is in full blast.*

operative. See VOGUE WORDS.

opposite. See CONVERSE.

opus. See LATIN AND GREEK PLURALS.

or. See AND/OR; BETWEEN 3; EITHER . . . OR; MATCHING PARTS.

oriented. See LINKING 3.

osmosis. See POPULARIZED TECHNICALITIES.

otherwise. This word is a useful, even an indispensable adverb in the meanings of *differently, in other circumstances, for the rest,* and *if not,* provided that the context makes clear which of these meanings it carries. *How could he do otherwise? / We must act promptly: otherwise the situation will become untenable / She took top money . . . at the latter place, was an also-ran otherwise / It must be baked in a slow oven: otherwise it will curdle.* Such uses raise no problems. Ambiguity takes charge, with unintended effects, in *At Cambridge, in his rambling old Edwardian brick home, Mr. G. reviews books, reads Dickens and Trollope and lives an otherwise normal life with his wife and three sons.* The reader must decide for himself whether reviewing books and reading Dickens are components of a normal life or deviations from it.

Much more frequent than this blunder affecting meaning is the misuse of *otherwise* as an adjective. The approbation of dictionaries and the frequent use both lend sanction to such forms as *reckless recollections, true or otherwise / Mrs. J.'s own interest in man's social and family ties, legal and otherwise / A.'s retirement, imminent or otherwise / prevailing political morality, Republican or otherwise / for some reason, chivalric or otherwise.* To pronounce this *otherwise* inadmissible would be to fly in the face of a strongly established usage. But usage, which can allow it on sufferance, cannot prevent it from being rejected by more exact writers. In *true recollections, legal ties,* and *imminent retirement,* we have ordinary adjectives each describing a noun; but what is the status of *otherwise recollections, otherwise ties,* an *otherwise retirement?* The New World Dictionary gives as an interpretation: *his answer could not be otherwise,* but no one on the dictionary staff would dream

of writing *an otherwise answer.* Nor does the example quite settle the issue, because *otherwise* may be deemed to modify *could* rather than *answer.*

In its straight use as an adjective paired with another (*true, legal,* and the rest), *otherwise* continues to strike attentive ears as awkward and fumbling—and gratuitously so, for the alternatives are natural and neat. Why not say *reckless recollections, true or false / social and family ties, legal and other* or *legal and extralegal / A.'s retirement, imminent or not,* and so on? Note, in passing, that the standard idiomatic phrase for *some reason or other* paves the way for *some reason, chivalrous or other.* No one is likely to say or write *for some reason or otherwise.*

A plausible conjecture is that the currency of *eligible or otherwise, guilty or otherwise,* etc. came about through the catchiness of the once sparkling witticism *wise or otherwise* (or *wise and otherwise*), which the Shorter Oxford Dictionary traces back to 1680. This jewel has long outlived its luster, but some still expect it to shine and others echo it unknowingly in the phrasing here analyzed.

ought (not) (to). From the Midwest, ordinarily so punctilious in uttering every syllable, comes the growing practice of omitting *to* after *ought* in the negative, at least in speech. One hears *I wonder whether I oughtn't take an umbrella / If that's the way she acts, she oughtn't put on so many airs.* In the East, headlines are written on the pattern PONTIFF SAYS WIDOWS OUGHT NOT REMARRY, and even better sources reflect the tendency. *It seems to me,* says a well-known federal judge, *that we need not, and ought not, resort to our mere unchecked surmises.* This omission of *to* must be watched for and the particle restored; for habit and euphony will long support *I ought to go,* and it would be foolish to have linkage with *to* in the affirmative and without it in the negative.

over-. See LAY, LIE; OVERLY.

overlie. See LAY, LIE.

overly. It is hard to think of the reason why this adverb does not show itself up as superfluous and prove its right to be thrown into the discard. *Over-* as a combining form in all adverbial, adjectival, and prepositional uses has made a clean sweep of the role once assigned to *overly,* and the simple way to say *overly generous* has long been *overgenerous.* Webster's New International Dictionary lists twelve or thirteen hundred of these combined forms with *over-,* besides nearly six full pages of them in the main vocabulary; and all of us can and do freely improvise additional combinations without risk of affectation or obscurity.

The recent revival of *overly* can only be ascribed to a mistaken view of what is correct in adverbs; it is in fact just as useless as *illy. An overly pessimistic* (= overpessimistic) *view of American policy / There was no reason to be overly alarmed* (overalarmed) */ Admiral F. said today that he was not overly optimistic* (overoptimistic) *but not discouraged over the supplying of the blockaded Nationalist islands / The pedant is overly exact* (overexact). When the sentence requires the idea as a complement or predicate, the words *too much, excessively* will do the work: *He fusses not overly but too much.*

The gratuitous *-ly* here objected to brings on unpleasant repetitions of this sound, to which English is prone anyway. *Naturally not feeling overly hospitable to terrorists* no longer afflicts the ear if we substitute *overhospitable.* With the substitution of *overfond* a better rhythm is conferred on *Neither was overly fond of Benjamin, and both had solemnly promised . . .* If anyone argues that there is a shade of difference between *overly timid* and *overtimid,* he must be left to his own subtlety, for it is incommunicable. Some insist that they see a different shade when *gray* is spelled *grey*, though no two judges agree what the difference is.

Akin to *illy* and *overly* is the superfluous *doubtlessly*, *doubtless* being both the adjective and the adverb. If not a principle, it is at least good tactics to refrain from an adverb in *-ly* whenever there is an equivalent without the suffix.

See also ADVERBS, VEXATIOUS; SINGLEHANDEDLY.

overt, covert. See PRONUNCIATION 1.

owing to. See DANGLERS, ACCEPTABLE; DUE TO.

own. See NEEDLESS WORDS 2.

own, on one's. Headlines have introduced a new ellipsis that calls for reproof, because it can work against reflexives and articulation generally (see AVAIL). The incriminated form runs: SCHOOL WHERE PUPILS ARE ON OWN IS ORDERED SHUT DOWN BY STATE / BUCKLEY ALLIES MAY RUN ON OWN. Seeing the effect of the caption writer's omitted *the* on common prose today (see A, AN, THE 5), one may reasonably fear the effect of omitting the possessive in the idiom *on my* (*your, his, her, its, our their*) *own.*

oxymoron, or the pointedly foolish. The Greek and Latin writers liked the juxtaposition of contradictory terms for effect, and students who translate from the classics quickly learn not to be startled by expressions that have to be rendered "small to a great degree," "enormously little," "arrogantly modest," or what not. The classifying rhetoricians came to list this device among figures of speech as *oxymoron*, which means pointed foolishness or dull acuity—itself an oxymoron. Webster illustrates with *cruel kindness* and *laborious idleness*; the Oxford Universal Dictionary cites: *Voltaire . . . we might call, by an oxymoron, an "Epicurean pessimist."* Such expressions as *politely insulting*, *sour pleasantry*, and *eloquent silence* are not strange to English, and no volume of quotations would be likely to overlook Tennyson's *faultily faultless, . . . splendidly null.* James Thurber has told us that he once described a building as *pretty ugly* and *a little big* for its site, in order to confound an editor who fiercely hunted down all discrepancies, real or apparent. *Pretty ugly* is, of course, an oxymoron only by a sort of pun, the adverb being an accepted synonym of *moderately*. Nevertheless, the joining of the two words revives the literal meaning of *pretty* and makes the pairing undesirable.

The same may be said of *even odd* in this sentence from a *New York Times* editorial: *Sometimes it requires devious and even odd ways to accomplish good purposes.* In this common class of accidental oxymorons the pointedly foolish becomes pointless. A spokesman of the British Foreign Office is reported to have said *The situation in Iraq is clearly very confused.* A novelist writes *they had found increasingly little to talk about.* A broadcaster promising to make a long story short says that he will practice *economy of verbiage;* in other words, a shortage of excess. All these inadvertencies are to be deplored. The good oxymoron, to define it by a self-illustrative phrase, must be a planned inadvertency.

There is a type of purely mental oxymoron in certain ambiguous statements of the kind favored by advertisers—

e.g. *We stand behind every gun we sell*—or in `the old catch phrase of the borrower *If you will help me I will be forever indebted to you.* An official in the Treasury Department once tried to make his colleagues more aware of their diction by circulating a memorandum on economic ups and downs that paraphrased the usual jargon in a series of oxymorons: *It should be noted that a slowing up of the slowdown is not as good as an upturn in the downcurve, but it is a good deal better than either a speedup of the slowdown or a deepening of the downcurve; and it does suggest that the climate is about right for an adjustment to the readjustment.*

See also ADVERBS, VEXATIOUS 4.

P

package. See METAPHOR 4.

parallelism. See MATCHING PARTS.

parameter. See POPULARIZED TECHNICALITIES.

parliament. See PRONUNCIATION 1.

part, in; whole, as a. Two idioms so firmly established that they cannot be violated without drawing undue attention to themselves are *in part* and *as a whole*. Neither by itself provides much temptation to mishandling, but when combined, as is often done, one or the other may undergo a distortion. The instinct to make regular and exactly parallel a two-part construction takes hold and leads to *in whole or in part* and the like. Legal documents and their imitations are especially likely to show this tendency: *Provided further that the compensation in whole or in part is not contingent ... upon action by such agency* / *No Councilman or other officer, employe or person whose compensation or salary is payable in whole or in part from the city treasury.* But lawyers have no monopoly: *Whether the re-sponsibility for the present situation is a reflection—in whole or part—of that basic decision by the Administration* / *After all, about one-quarter of the school districts of the South are already integrated in whole or in part.* The matching instinct could be placated by writing *wholly or partly.* Otherwise there is no ready escape from *in part or as a whole.* Fixity of idiom is worth the extra syllable.

See also MATCHING PARTS; SET PHRASES.

particular. See SPECIFIC(S).

passed (past) master. See SPELLING.

passed (past) muster. See SPELLING.

passive voice. See NOUN-PLAGUE 1; VOICE.

pedantry. A pedant is a man who says *As sure as eggs are eggs* and who, when his wife refers to *Grand Central Station*, corrects her by pointing out that it is not a station but a terminal. The reason why such remarks are pedantic is that they miss the point either of the expression or of the occasion. There might be an occasion when distinguishing between a station and a terminal—say, in wartime, for air strategy—would not be pedantic at all; but to make the distinction at a fireside when the point of the conversation lies elsewhere is pedantry. Similarly, if one is going to use the rural emphasis of *sure as eggs is eggs* one has no business dressing it up in formal grammar: it loses its force and the corrector gives himself away as weak in judgment.

The question of who is being pedantic and when becomes more complicated the moment one leaves colloquial speech and approaches the written word—or even the diction of formal occasions. At that point pedantry becomes variable, relatively to mood, temperament, and circumstance. The definition implied above, that to take visible pains over trifles is pedantic, will not hold if one person calls a particular point a trifle and the other calls it important. And it is a commonplace that in many situations one person can do or say with impunity what another cannot. As far as speaking goes, the freedom conferred by character, reputation, or the lack of them extends in both directions. A. will shock if he swears, drops his *g*'s, and says *that there*, and B. will shock if he suddenly abandons these familiar modes of expression. This is part of what the linguists contend for when they say that everybody's speech is entirely right—it suits him and sits well on him. What they forget is that this general fitness is a matter of habit and chance merely, and that it takes no account of any goal or ideal. At that rate any man's posture or manner of dress would be perfect. As soon as someone wants to stand or speak or dress better, he must deliberately change some of his habits; and if he wants the change to become indeed habitual, he must take pains over trifles. At first his concentrated attention to details will doubtless strike him and others as pedantic; it will look just as silly as the athlete's exercises; but presumably a new power and, what is even better, a new flexibility will develop. He will express himself more fully and easily over a wider range of fact and feeling. That this is desired by many unassuming people is shown by the way in which they repeat themselves in identical words three or four times, with a final pathetic *See what I mean?* They feel within themselves notions and facts they cannot bring out; they have glimpses of a truer emphasis they cannot achieve, for lack of the exact words and the freedom to arrange them in more than one way.

Now, everything in these matters being relative, everybody except the great poet or prose writer finds himself tongue-tied at some point. The impediment comes from ignoring or not knowing the expressive resources of the language. One might suppose that a dictionary would open up these resources, but although vocabulary is an important part of the expressive means, it is not, as the popular advertisements would suggest, the sole means. Grammar, syntax, LINKING, and above all the awareness of what one is doing or can do with the means at one's command—these are the disciplines to which the writer or speaker must subject himself if he wishes to really say his say. And in this effort he cannot help being at times a pedant. Only practice and the company of people to whom good speech comes as if by nature, people miraculously unspoiled by school or society, will give power over language and the ease without which power lacks fitness and grace.

Meanwhile it may induce caution to consider a few examples of misplaced care that will almost always strike the hearer or reader as finical— here the casual speaker will say *finicky*—and that he may be so much annoyed by as to call pedantic. The list may as well begin with the pedantry that consists in the observance of imaginary rules. Among these are the injunctions against the SPLIT INFINITIVE and against ending a sentence with a PREPOSITION; the effort to put ONLY as close to its object as possible (*Tender noodles made from only the golden yolk of fresh eggs*—where's the flour?); the avoidance of *just* (*I just don't like it*) in the belief that it is a misuse of *just* as in *justice*, whereas it is from *juxta*, and means just what it says; the effort to place epithets next to the word they apply to (avoiding *a good cup of coffee* in favor of *a cup of good coffee*); or the studied rejection of CASE and SINCE (causal) without reason.

Next, paying excessive attention, at least in speech, to an earlier form of a current phrase (e.g. *it is* of *no use*); or substituting the more formal (e.g. *it is for you to* in the place of *it is up to you to*); or going back to origins when what they suggest is likely to sound archaic or even mistaken (e.g. *buttonhold* for *buttonhole*, verb; *Frankenstein's monster* for FRANKENSTEIN; *legend* for *caption*; or again, referring to dead presidents or authors as *Mr. Jefferson, Mr. Longfellow*; and many others). The collector of words and their niceties may treasure his out-of-the-way bits of knowledge and may even parade them, as Charles Lamb did, in a mood of conscious self-parody—a mood not to be indulged in too often or too long, for it can easily become tedious to the spectator. But if the possessor is really vain about his baubles and shows them off to get applause for superior knowledge, what he shows at the same time is the ridiculous face of the pedant. The call for nicety is always to be met by the question of relevance—what's the point? To hang on to the earlier meanings of DISINTERESTED, *presently*, and COHORT can be justified on other grounds than the pleasure of showing off and being better than one's neighbor. But to write *As he walked, his powerful arms swung like pendula* is to make the intelligent reader hoot.

people. See PERSONS.

per. *For two dollars per hour, wind from the southwest at eighteen miles per hour,* etc., see A, AN, THE 7. In general, it devolves on the user to make up his mind where *per* is a necessary evil, where it is an unnecessary one, and where it is not an evil at all. It is not an evil in the set Latin phrases *per diem, per annum, per capita,* which, if used, must be kept intact. If we convert them into *per day, per year, per person,* or *per head,* the Latin preposition has become an unnecessary evil and should be replaced with the indefinite article—*eight hours a day, four times a year, two inspections a head. Per* should

perhaps be accepted as a necessary evil in a few such contexts as *overtime averaging forty minutes a day per worker,* where it cannot easily be replaced with *a.* Of course, the use of *per* in business jargon —*as per your letter of the 3d* or *as per your memorandum of last week*—is uneducated and always unnecessary.

per contra. See ON THE OTHER HAND.

permafrost. This mongrel word suggests a manufacturer's invention for keeping oneself or one's larder cool. But *permafrost* is in fact the scientific word for that layer of the earth's crust which in arctic or subarctic regions is permanently frozen. The plausibility of thinking that the word belongs to trade or advertising (cf. the trade name *Permalloy,* in which *perm* is *permeable* clipped) is an indication of the mutual influence of science and commerce in matters of language; the word itself is a good example of the passion for Latinizing in persons who do not know Latin and who declare it dead and useless.

The trouble with *permafrost* and others of its kind is that the sense-bearing root is incomplete, even though it is only three letters long: *man* (from *maneo, manere*) contains the idea of *stay,* just as it is *mea* that contains the idea of *flow.* The *per* being only an intensive in *permanent* and meaning *through* in *permeate*, *perm* or *perma* conveys nothing. Obviously, *permanfrost* was impossible in English, but there are always native words to work with. Just as physics recognizes the *steady-state theory*, so it was possible in geophysics to speak of *steady frost*—equal in length with *permafrost*, English throughout, and intelligible at sight.

personage, personality. One of the curiosities of current usage is the widespread attempt, in print and out, to replace *personage* with *personality*. Any prominent figure in the news, and more especially in the columns of gossip writers, is a Broadway or Washington or Hollywood *personality*. He would once have been a *personage*. The advantages of having a personality (see PERSONS) are manifest, but when we mean to speak precisely, we may say that it is better to have than to be one. *Personality* is or ought to be the name of a quality, not of a man. *One of the most sought-after personalities in Hollywood* and *various home beauty treatments evolved by Hollywood personalities* are samples that disclose a geographical clue to the milieu in which the misplaced word began to thrive. It is now to be found in every kind of prose: *They write candidly of world problems and of their experiences with the personalities controlling other governments as well as our own* / *A first-rate description of one of the most dramatic periods of our history, written with a rare understanding of the personalities who made it so exciting.* Anyone who finds himself writing *personalities who* would refurbish his style by stopping to think of *persons* and dropping the *-alities*.

The occasional need for a word to denote someone less than a personage who is locally or transiently conspicuous (*Come meet this prolific personality on our second floor at 11:30 Saturday*) can be met by *a notable, a notability, a celebrity, a somebody*, or even *a Somebody*.

personal. The loss of the sense of individuality, which is said to be the curse of modern man, has endowed with magic the words *personal* and *personalized* (see -IZE). *Personal* is now attached to many words that need no such qualifier and that make of *personal* a mockery. Thus, commenting on the resignation of a close associate, a President tells the press: *I am fond of him as a person.* Aside from making one wonder to whom *person* refers, the declaration raises a puzzle as to the nature of fondness. Authors receive requests for their *personal autograph.* The bereaved are told *I'd like to offer you my personal sympa-*

thy, or *Her death was surely a personal loss to all of us.* Novelists report of an ordinary woman *She came in supported by her personal physician and her lawyer*—what's the matter with the lawyer that he isn't personal? Banks entice you to print your name on your *personal checks;* a dealer urges the purchase of etchings as a *personal gift;* and a newspaper interview with a philanthropist is set cozily at breakfast in his *personal dining room.* In that same paper we read that PERSONAL GUIDANCE IS KEY TO HEAD START PROJECT. What is guidance—whether given to students, tourists, the poor, or the puzzled—if it is not personal?

The height of absurdity is reached in the frequent references to our *personal lives*—as if we had some other kind—and one begins to suspect that *personal* is being substituted for *private,* to avoid the suggestion of secrecy or withdrawal from the group. "*When you say that,*" he retorted, "*you invade my personal feelings*" (read: *intimate*) / *When such an employee is discharged or laid off, he shall be given, either personally or by registered mail . . . a written notice* (given, either by hand or by registered mail) / *I tell you I knew Crosby personally, I mean apart from golf* (I knew Crosby apart from playing golf with him) / *It was his personal opinion that the Secre-*

tary of State should succeed next after the Vice-President (make it *private opinion* if it differed from his publicly stated views, or omit *personal*).

Personal appearance has been an ambiguous phrase since the movies introduced a doubt as to what one was about to see in a theatre—a celluloid phantasm or a flesh-and-blood creature. To *appear in person* is by now a legitimate way to denote the second possibility, though a probable etymology of *person* (= through the mask) would accommodate the first equally well. In its other meaning, *personal appearance* has the sense of dress and bodily grooming, not good looks or their opposite. Finally, it is worth observing that certain SET PHRASES such as *personal friend, personal stationery* are justified only in a context that offers clear contrasts—e.g. *political* (as against *personal*) friend; *office* (as against *personal*) stationery. Otherwise, *friend* and *stationery* suffice, and the addition of the qualifier makes one doubt the writer's familiarity with note paper or his awareness of what friendship is.

persons. **1.** This is a much-needed everyday word that is too absent-mindedly replaced by *people. Reports . . . from last week's emergency examinations for teacher candidates showed that 500 exist-*

ing vacancies probably will be filled, but not always with the right people / Three people in the company's down-state areas recently were awarded Vail Medals / being one of those people who, as the English say, can cope. When we say *persons* we are thinking, or ought to be, of *ones*—individuals with identities; whereas when we say *people* we should mean a large group, an indefinite and anonymous mass. A retiring President of the United States becomes one of the people again, though probably without ceasing to be one of the persons whose counsels are influential in his party. History, which had been a chronicle of persons up to the time of John Richard Green's *Short History of the English People* or thereabouts, has tended since to be the history of societies—peoples. John McNulty, according to a commemoration by James Thurber, *was concerned mainly with men, not Man, with persons, not People.*

The word *person* comes from, though not straight from, the Latin word for the mask worn by actors. Doubtless few of its users are aware that a good deal of human behavior is acting and that the countenance presented to the world by a man is often a mask and not his proper face. But on or off the stage, everybody is a person to himself and to a limited number of others. Only a few

are persons to a nation or to mankind—the few with personalities that lend themselves to public projection. (See PERSONAGE, PERSONALITY.)

2. This scarcity of persons is perhaps due to the relative infrequency with which persons resist standardization and manage to be themselves, to be oneself being the only known way to be anybody in particular. If, as many believe, the English cherish individuals and individuality more than Americans do, we find in this a clue to the difference in the British treatment of the collective noun as a plural—*the committee are of opinion, the government have committed themselves,* and so on, with the stress on the component persons. Americans tend to say *the clergy is almost unanimously opposed, the jury has been locked up for deliberation,* etc., with the stress on the collective entity.

It may be noted by the way that the form *the jury is divided, the committee is agreed* is self-contradictory, since the subject of discourse is the clash or the meeting of individual opinions. *The committee are agreed* is better logic and better English, as reporters concede when they say *The jury are rumored to be nine for conviction and three for acquittal.* Even that fictive person, the chartered corporation, is made up of persons—a hydra whose heads do not necessarily think alike. Sometimes, in quoting a British source, the American newspaperman juxtaposes the British usage and his own in one sentence: *A Foreign Office spokesman said the Government was aware of the United States position . . . and "fully share the concern of the Government of the United States at any attempt to impose territorial changes by force."* The clash of number so produced is even more noticeable than the clash of tenses.

The difference between *people* and *persons* is roughly parallel to that between the literary word *folk* and the colloquial word *folks*. The folk generates its folklore and folk songs and folk epics and, nameless and faceless, is expressed in them en masse; but a reporter out to record "what folks are thinking about" goes down the block interviewing Tom, Dick, and Harriet in order to quote them individually —that, is as *persons* representing *people*.

persuade. See CONVINCE.

picnicking. See CATALOG, CATALOGED.

pinpoint. See LINKING 3.

pivot around. See CENTER AROUND.

place in, put in(to). See INTO, IN TO 2.

pleasantries. See CONNOTATIONS.

pleased. See CONNOTATIONS.

pled. See UNSAVORY PASTS.

plenitude. See CONNOTATIONS.

popular. Some words carry so inescapable a meaning of multitude as to sound foolish in a context from which this meaning is absent. *Popular*, in the meaning *acceptable to or welcomed by a group or groups of people*, is such a word. Except for deliberately comic effect, it is reduced to nonsense when applied to one person or to a few persons: *That kind of procedure will never be popular with me / It was a favorite of John Wesley, with whom Eliza Haywood's rowdyism would hardly have been popular / This mania for privacy did not make him popular with his inordinately sociable family.* The intention in this misapplied word finds no ready substitute. There is no recourse but to think out what it is supposed to mean in its context —*acceptable to, welcome to, tolerated by, congenial to.* (See EXODUS.)

popularized technicalities. The title of this entry explains itself. In our time what is technical and professional is in high repute; what comes from the amateur is regarded as amateurish. Consequently many phrases have been borrowed from the sciences, the techniques, and the professions to adorn and lend expressiveness to ordinary prose. The choice and application of these words and phrases have naturally not been controlled by the experts; the transfer has been indeed amateurish, and examination shows that a good many of the new terms simply duplicate or replace simple words long in use. A full list of the borrowings is beyond the scope of this book, but the enumeration of a few, with comments, may encourage speakers and writers to prefer simplicity.

allergy: a pathological sensitivity to certain foods or materials that do not harm the healthy. One would have to experience great discomfort in the presence of a person most other people liked to warrant describing one's feelings as ALLERGIC.

AMBIVALENT: see the word.

begging the question: not to be used when one has a feeling that the other's argument is unfair. It means only: using as an argument some disguised form of the proposition to be proved; e.g. if the issue is the immorality of cannibalism, the argument "How can such savages be moral when they kill people in order to eat them?" begs the question. (See also MAKE SENSE; REALISTIC, UN-REALISTIC.)

catalyst, catalytic agent: part of the true meaning is that the

agent, while it aids in furthering the union of substances, remains unchanged in the process. So the term will scarcely do for an active participant.

category: a long and inaccurate word for *class* or *group.*

comity: from international law, where it means the courtesy traditionally expected of nations in their dealings with one another; not the *company* of nations.

continuum: a whole without parts—rarely applicable to workaday experience.

dichotomy: a pedantic way of saying *division into two* or simply *division.*

DILEMMA: "two horns"; therefore it cannot denote the perplexity of choosing among three or four careers, mates, or anything else. The sense of a forced option, is, moreover, very strong in the word.

empathy: not a synonym for *sympathy,* for which it is being substituted. The word means *feeling in* not *with.*

entropy: does not mean disaster or the end of the world; the term relates only to the nonconvertibility of a part of energy into mechanical work: once the steam has vaporized, it turns no wheels. But it is true that increased entropy means less order in the universe—hence the loose use here decried.

extrapolate: carry a pattern or quantity established by data beyond the point where the data stop. In common speech, a piece of pedantry for *project* (verb), *surmise, guess.*

fixation: will not do in *As soon as I met him I knew I had a fixation for him.* It should be *fixation on,* and it refers to an exclusive concentration of immature love feelings, as of a child for a parent, with a resulting lack of emotional development.

FORMAT: see the word.

gunsel: not one who totes a gun but a young homosexual, armed or not.

idiosyncrasy: not a peculiarity but the sum total of a person's peculiarities.

-ITIS: see that heading.

MELD: see the word.

neurotic, psychotic: difficult to use accurately outside a given system of psychiatry. As synonyms for *unhappy, troubled, crazy, deranged,* or *I can't stand her* they are improper.

of the essence (time is, etc.): does not mean merely important or even essential; it means that the fulfillment of a promise or contract on the specified day is as important as any other provision. Hence not a substitute for *we must get busy.*

osmosis: the slow penetration of a membrane by a liquid when the concentration of some dissolved substance is not equal on both sides. Therefore it is far-fetched to say in a novel that one of the characters must be pretending because, by association with actors, *osmosis must have set in.*

parameter: in mathematics, a quantity that varies with the conditions under which it occurs. Hence in ordinary life a pedantic substitute for *the task before us, the limits of our problem.*

percentage: = hundredths; that is, a measure expressed in hundredths of some quantity; hence not to be used merely for *advantage, profit,* etc. Note that *percentage points* is not the same as percentage. Consult a textbook on statistics.

polar opposites, polarity, polarized: why not say *opposites, enemies, division, two factions, marital discord;* i.e. what the *polarization* boils down to.

pragmatism: see .PRAGMATIC(AL).

reaction: is by definition automatic, unconscious, uncontrolled. Hence what one thinks about a book or a play is better described as a *response,* unless one reacts to it altogether as the finger to the hot stove. See REACTION.

status quo: this implies a return to a previous state, the complete phrase requiring the two additional words *ante bellum* (= before the war.) At the utmost stretch *status quo* can mean society or the government as it is, but not in future. A *happier status quo* is gibberish for a *happier state.*

subconscious: to write *Again, my subconscious didn't get through to me* is to confuse memory or presence of mind with the riddles of conscious and *unconscious* mind.

synchronized: refers only to bringing timepieces or other devices—and by extension the actions of men—into exact coordination. *Time* must be involved. The interior decorator does not synchronize the colors in a boudoir.

values: borrowed from painting, where it means the choice of tones relatively to one another. As a synonym for *moral principles, political and social beliefs, ethics, code, rules of conduct,* it is by now worn out and virtually without meaning.

vital statistics: these have to do with births and deaths in a given jurisdiction, not with the measurements of breasts and buttocks.

See also SCIENTISM.

portmanteau words. See GERMANISMS; TELESCOPINGS.

positioning. See JARGON.

possessives. 1. False. 2. Obligatory. 3. Neglected. 4. Paired.

1. One magazine started it as a device among others designed to save space, to startle, and to sound knowing; now every newspaper thinks it normal and right to speak of *Florida's governor, Berkeley's Clark Kerr, the town's high school, Cornell's division of Industrial Relations,* and *the nation's capital.* The truth is that these possessives in the *'s* form are newfangled and false. The error in writing them is to assume that *Florida's governor* means the same thing as *the governor of Florida.* At that rate *the Book of Revelations* would be the same as *Revelations' Book.* The *of* in these phrases is not a true possessive but a defining and partitive *of,* as in *loss of breath, piece of wood, ruler of men.* It being inconceivable to translate this last into *men's ruler* (*Caesar was a . . .*), we must stick to the ancestral rule which, with a few exceptions, reserves possessives in *'s* for ownership by a person.

Usage is so clear on this point that it differentiates between the descriptive term used, say, as the title of a painting: *The Death of Nelson* and the subjectively "owned" event—*Nelson's death* (occurred on October 21, 1805). And the irrationality of the the modern misconception is shown in the more and more frequent adoption of the possessive form where possession is contrary to fact; for example: *The figure is obtained by multiplying the number of school-age children from low-income families by half of the per-pupil public-school expenditures in the district's state.* Unless we are to think that the state belongs to the district, we must consider this altogether ill-kempt sentence as ending in BARBARISM. The remedy in this case is not the usual one of replacing *'s* by *of* and inverting the nouns. One cannot say: *expenditures in the state of the district.* One has to give up stinginess and spend a few words: *expenditures in the state in which the district lies.* Similarly: Washington is *the national capital;* Mr. Clark Kerr is *the executive at Berkeley; the governor of Florida* is now Mr. X; *the town high school* is full to overflowing; and *the Cornell division of Industrial Relations* (or, even better: *the division of Industrial Relations at Cornell University*).

The apt employment of the defining *of* may make a serious

difference in the implications of a statement, and hence in the responsibility for making it. To write that a citizen as yet untried has been indicted *for murdering his grandmother* is a libelous statement; it is not libelous to write that he has been indicted *for the murder of his grandmother*. The latter phrase refers to an event not in dispute and leaves the author of the crime unnamed, whereas the former statement implies that the accused and the criminal are one. Similarly, to say, as one historian has done, that *Voltaire was the Enlightenment's pope* conveys the false impression that the Enlightenment was a corporate person led by a pope; whereas the idea behind the phrase is a metaphor or analogy—Voltaire was to the Enlightenment as the pope is to the Church. That remoteness calls for the construction with *of*.

2. Now take the headline NEGROES ACCUSE CLIENT OF ZUBER. On first reading, the thought does not occur that *Zuber* is a proper name. The mind gropes for a meaning parallel to *A. Accuses B. of Arson*, and the absurdity of this leads at last to the right conclusion that Mr. Zuber's client is being accused. The reason for the misdirection is that here the obligatory possessive has been disregarded. To keep the sentence in the general form designed for it, it

should read: *accuse a client of Zuber's; that is, one of his clients*. The 's stands for this plurality of clients, and the neglect of this possessive mars the all too common mode of referring to *a book of Conrad, a letter of Lincoln, a canvas of Picasso*. Yet we do not say *an admirer of her, a friend of me*. All these require changing to the possessive 's (with, of course, *hers* for *her* and *mine* for *me* in the last pair), or else the replacement of the preposition. One can always say *a book by Conrad, a letter from Lincoln*, and by being exact in either of these ways one is able to differentiate between *a portrait of Sargent* (= his likeness) and *a portrait of Sargent's* (= a painting by him).

3. As so often happens nowadays, the passion for a false form has gone with an apparently studied avoidance of the right one: the desirable 's is given up in favor of the *of* where the former would tighten the structure and clear the meaning. The typical pattern is *The dislike of a peaceable man for violent action had been communicated*, etc. To the attentive reader the opening phrase remains ambiguous until the mind takes in the complement. *A peaceable man's dislike* would preclude from the start the possibility that the sentence might turn out to read *The dislike of a peaceable man is*

always vaguely embarrassing.

4. Paired possessive adjectives that refer to different persons or things and come before a noun will not give trouble to the ear or the mind if one is put before and the other after the noun. *Your and my children seem to like each other* sounds odd and tempts to the error *yours and my* because of the unnatural separation between the first possessive and its noun. Hence the suggestion of a shift: *your children and mine.* If for any reason this straddle does not suit and the writer goes back to the paired form, at least the tryout saves him from error by making clear the need for *your* in any case, after which *mine* shifts to *my* without effort.

practical, practicable; unpractical, impracticable. The confusion of prefixes, endings, and meanings that attends the current use of these four words is probably not to be dispelled. In speech there is usually not time to choose among the nuances offered to the discriminating, and the written word quite properly tends to echo the spoken—though not invariably or completely. For those who try to make their writing more exact than their conversation, here are the distinctions generally observed by careful writers: (1) The negatives are UN*practic*AL and IM*practic*ABLE, without interchange of prefixes or suffixes. (2) The meanings of those negatives follow exactly the distinction between their positives; namely: *practical* is the general term, applicable to men and things; *practicable* the term for a particular thing or project, never for a person. For example: *a very practical fellow / over the years all their proposals have proved practical / the bridging of the river in its swollen state was not practicable / the artistic temperament is often unpractical / to raise a loan from a bankrupt is impracticable.*

Practical gives *practicality* and its negatives; *practicable* gives *practicability* and *impracticability*, but this last pair is not often found when *(un)feasibility* and *(im)possibility* are to be had. See DANGEROUS PAIRS and PRAGMATIC(AL).

pragmatic(al), pragmatism. The use commonly made of *pragmatic* is to suggest (1) hardheaded practicality and no nonsense or (2) crude action, scornful of theory and of finer feelings. Another common and inexact word for the first meaning is *realistic*; a synonym of the second is *anti-philosophical* and, possibly, *unethical*. The older *pragmatical* meant *officious* or *opinionated*. The trouble with the modern use is that it is both ambiguous and false to an important idea. Pragmatism is a philosophical theory of truth, whose relation to practicality in the business or political sense is no closer than that of a dozen other philosophies. It is therefore misleading to use the term loosely and according to one's mood of approbation or the reverse. Thus an editorial greeting a Supreme Court appointment marks out in the incumbent his *activism, enthusiasm and pragmatism—these are qualities*, etc. Again, from one column by a political analyst: *The aim is to produce a more pragmatic and flexible posture toward China / this highly desirable pragmatism / It is desirable to be pragmatic.* Since in their vulgar applications *pragmatic* and *pragmatism* fail to denote any intellectual position, but rather confer praise and blame alternately and on erroneous grounds, it would be desirable to give the words a rest until that position is better known. See also REALISTIC.

precipitate, precipitous. See CORRELATE; ENDINGS 1.

prefer . . . than. The comparative *rather* is logically and idiomatically followed by *than*. Because of the closeness of meaning between *had rather* and *prefer*, the second is often incorrectly followed by the construction that fits the first; *If they prefer to sit still until catastrophe arrives, than get up and exert themselves / Several members of this class prefer spelling a word by guess* *than bothering to look it up.* Ideally one thing is preferred *to* another—playing solitaire to watching television, a winter vacation to a summer one, etc. But where the object of *prefer* is an infinitive—e.g. *I prefer to wait and see*—the completing alternative cannot be introduced by another *to* and a matching infinitive without a confusing excess of *to's*. When this difficulty looms, one has to make shift with a different construction, using, say, *instead of: I prefer to wait and see instead of jumping to conclusions.* More loosely one could resort to *rather than jump to conclusions.* Note that *instead of* requires the *-ing* form of the verb, *rather than* takes the plain infinitive.

It is also possible to prefer one thing *over* or *above* another, or to prefer one thing *and not* the other. Remember, though, that a preference can be stated in a single, lucid statement only when it employs *to* and a noun object, or an infinitive, or an *-ing*. All substitutes require two statements instead of one: they hark back and begin over—*I prefer this thing, and do not prefer that*, etc. Single statement: *He prefers travel books to traveling* (orderly and compact) / *He prefers to read travel books and be a stay-at-home* (double idea, equally clear but not compact). The writer who chooses *had rather* will find it much easier to manipulate: *If they had rather sit still . . . than . . . exert themselves / had rather spell a word by guess than bother to look it up.* In short, *prefer* is a shackled, restricted word; it often generates labored or wordy constructions. Its natural alternative *had rather . . . than* is free from its drawbacks.

preferable. See MORE PREFERABLE.

prepositions. One of the greatest difficulties in learning the European languages is the mastering of the idiomatic use of prepositions with verbs, adjectives, and nouns. Usually there is only the faintest glimmer of logic or system in these compulsory matings, and English is particularly willful in its disregard of the obvious clues provided by prefixes; so much so that usage has here and there created double possibilities, equally valid, as in *averse to* and *averse from.* But this concession is not always to be relied on, for *agree to* and *agree with* are not really interchangeable, any more than *compare to* and *compare with.* A mastery of all the differences and subtleties is rare, yet nothing gives away the foreign speaker or the insensitive writer like the misused preposition, or again the tenable preposition which turns out to be wrong for the meaning intended. A full repertory of these compounds and their meanings would run to many pages, especially if it were to comprise the idioms that employ two prepositions. Here follow some of the combinations that seem to be most often stumbled over:

acquiesce: always *in* (see ACQUIESCE).

affinity: with (sometimes *to*) (see AFFINITY).

agree: to = give assent; *with* = concur in opinion.

aim (verb): always *at* with a verb in *-ing.*

analogy: with; analogous to.

angry: with or *at,* the second suggesting confrontation.

answer: never *to* with a person; *answer to* (a specification, a description) means *correspond to it, coincide with it.*

approximate: no preposition, but the noun *approximation* takes *to.*

apropos: always *of.*

ask: of.

averse, aversion: to and *from.*

behalf: on behalf of = as somebody's representative; *in behalf of* = in his interest.

belong: to with indirect object —e.g. a secret society; *with* = to be classified among.

blink: with *at* = flutter the eyelids; with no preposition = overlook on purpose.

capable: of.

capacity: to with a verb; *of* with a measure.

cater: to is American usage, despite the derivation, remembered in England, from *acheter,* meaning *to buy.* With that etymology in mind it is difficult to say *to* and easier to say *for.*

commiserate: no preposition.

compare: to means *liken; with* means *place in comparison* (see COMPARE).

concur, concurrence: in an opinion, *with* other persons.

conform: to a rule; but *in conformity with* the rule.

connect: to (a wire or a pipe); *with* (a person, group, or idea).

continue: no preposition.

correspond: to means *match; with* means *exchange messages.*

crave: no preposition (but a craving *for* sweets).

dabbling: in (but dabbing *at*).

differ: from means *be unlike; with* means *disagree with.*

different: from is preferred; *to* is British; *than* is suspect. See DIFFERENT(LY) THAN.

difficult: to; but *difficulty of* or *in.*

divergent: from.

encroach: on.

equally: with, never *as* (see EQUALLY 1).

forbid: to after indirect object *you, her,* etc.

grate: on, not *with.*

infringe: no preposition (though a few writers who watch their language have adopted the unnecessary *on* or *upon*).

inside: (as preposition) no preposition for literal meaning; *inside of* with expressions of time is colloquial for *within.*

issue (as passive verb): no preposition; never *with* (*The GI's were issued boots*).

knack: of, not *for.*

lavish: on, not *to* (*He lavished a great deal of attention to detail* is wrongly influenced by *attention to*).

market: in the market = as a buyer; *on the market* = offered for sale.

meet: no preposition before persons; *with* before abstractions: meet with rebuffs, difficulties, delays.

mistake (verb): *for,* not *as.*

name (verb): no preposition; never *named as editor-in-chief*

necessity: of or *for* (*need* with verb, *to*).

oblivious: always *of* (see OBLIVIOUS).

ought: always *to* (see OUGHT).

outside: (as preposition) no preposition when physical meaning is intended; *outside of* is colloquial for *except, other than.*

partake: of.

participate: in.

practice (noun): *of;* (verb): *to.*

prevent: always *from* after a person named as object.

privilege (noun): *of* (but one is privileged *to*).

prohibit: always from after an indirect object.

promote: with title, no preposition (*promoted Captain*); with office, *to* (*promoted to a captaincy*).

recommend: no preposition when followed by the substance of the recommendation—*He recommended that I decamp at once;* use *to* with indirect object—*I recommend him to the President* (see RECOMMEND).

reference: to = a pointing toward; *on* = books or articles about.

report (noun): *of* and *on* are used interchangeably, though there is a shade of difference in that a long study tends to be a *report on,* whereas three breathless words can be the *report of* a disaster.

separate: from, never *out.*

subject(*-ed*): *to* (with the adjective means *liable to;* with the verb = underwent—e.g. punishment).

sympathy: with means *sharing another's feelings; for* means *having pity or compassion for another.*

tamper: always *with.*

temerity: to, not *of.*

tend: no preposition; *attend* takes *to.* (The mixture *tends to the furnace* is wrong).

tinker: with is American usage; *at* is British.

view: with a view *to; with* the view *of.*

visit: no preposition. (*Visit with* is colloquial for *chat with*).

wait: for has literal meaning; *on* means to serve; *upon* means to pay a formal call.

write: always *to* when direct object is absent. Also: *I will write you a note at* Chicago, not *to.*

WITH and *by* are often interchangeable after a verb in the passive. The implication of a human agent is stronger in *by:* a man is *surrounded by his enemies; he is surrounded with books.* As a result, the verb recovers something of its energy when *by* follows it. In the sentence above, the enemies are actively surrounding their victim, whereas the books are just lying about on shelves.

Note further that the more common the verb (*take, get, hold, put,* etc.) the more easily it joins itself to a variety of prepositions; but each time the meaning differs, and sometimes a coupling acceptable on the surface proves wrong on analysis; e.g. *De Gaulle has made it clear that he means to take France from NATO.* One takes *candy from a child* or

comfort *from a friend's sympathy,* but in the newspaper sentence *take from* should be *take out of,* since NATO is an alliance and does not own its members.

In joining two verbs that act on the same object it is important that the required preposition accompany each (*to make use of, and account for, every penny*). Such a construction is heavy and inelegant, and suggestions are made in PROSE, THE SOUND OF for getting around it. But it is a superstition to believe that when one of the verbs takes no preposition it is rendered false by the following verb that does. *To employ and account for every penny* is correct and easy, the *for* after *account* having no effect whatever on *employ.* Obviously, in such pairings, the verb without preposition had best come first.

See also RECOMMEND; REDOLENT WITH; SUFFICIENTLY; THAT, CONJUNCTION 1.

prestigious. Carlyle called *prestige* "a bad newspaper word," but it being now the name of what matters most to twentieth-century people and peoples, we must accept it. What we need not accept is *prestigious,* which still carries the connotation of *magic, sleight-of-hand,* and which, even if cut loose from this influence, will not readily turn into what seems to be wanted. *X. University is now a prestigi-*

ous institution means *has acquired prestige.* The word *prestige,* like *reputation,* is an absolute rather than a quantitative term, and just as we do not say *He is full of reputation,* so we ought to find it awkward to say *He is full of prestige.* This makes *prestigeful* and *prestigious* clumsy and moreover unnecessary when we have *reputable, renowned, famous, illustrious, excellent, meritorious, notable, respectable, praiseworthy, admirable,* and *glorious* to be going on with.

See also ABSOLUTE WORDS.

prevail on. See CONVINCE.

primal, primary. See ENDINGS 1.

printing shop, print shop. American dictionaries lend countenance to the breakdown of a useful distinction by listing *print shop* as both a place where prints and engravings are sold and a place where printing is done—a printing shop. The directory board on the ground floor of a university-press building lists *print shop,* but anyone who takes the elevator to the floor indicated will walk into a clatter of linotype machines, not into the sedate hush of an art gallery. This usage is not new in American speech or American literature and the distinction is probably beyond recall.

prior to. This phrase is used interchangeably with *before* at the cost of losing a useful shade of meaning. From its origin in the law, *prior to* carries with it the idea of necessary precedence: *The application to the company must be executed and filed prior to the expiry of the policy.* By extension, the philosophic statement *Concepts are logically prior to the existence of particulars* implies an idea of necessity which would not be felt in a rewording such as *Concepts come before,* etc. It is because of this additional idea, and also a certain starchiness in *prior to,* that the growing neglect of *before* is to be deplored: *She twisted her ankle prior to getting home* sounds to the trained mind as if some important point of time were being established in court. And *The boy ate all his bread and butter prior to tackling the vegetables* suggests not a simple description but the carrying out of a doctor's orders.

prise, prize. Most dictionaries prefer the spelling with *s* for both of the common meanings: (1) to pry, to free by prying, and (2) to value greatly. But many American publishers evidently prefer to differentiate the two words. By and large, spelling is not of prime importance, but the sort of reader who notices spellings may well be brought up short by *Our combined weight on the* *crowbar would not prize the boulder loose,* or by *It was like prizing pearls from oysters to get her to talk about herself.* The verb *prize* is outside the class that British usage spells *-ise* (*criticise, recognise*) instead of the *-ize* of American and Oxford usage. Hence there is nothing in the way of our distinguishing *prise* from *prize* by their spelling if we want to. It is sensible to want to, for the failure to distinguish will strike some readers as odd, whereas observing the distinction will pass unnoticed.

proceeding(s). See FALSE SINGULARS.

process, verb. See CONTACT.

Prof. Because it is pronounceable (unlike *Mr.* and *Dr.*), and reminiscent of *Doc* besides, *Prof* is not an abbreviation that those entitled to it favor or accept as fit for formal address. On an envelope or at the head of a letter it is simple courtesy to spell out *Professor,* just as one would *Senator.*

See also SHORTENINGS; TITLES AND PROPER NAMES.

profitability. See ROADABILITY.

prohibit. See PREPOSITIONS.

project. See OPERATION X.

pronunciation. 1. English. 2. Foreign.

1. The art of speaking words correctly and agreeably is the subject of many volumes, and it cannot be condensed into an article. Precept, moreover, is useless without practice, and no guide can be of help that does not aim at preparing for a well-defined end—speaking on the stage or on the platform, in the pulpit or in the living room.

Each of these is a different art; and when one adds, first, that different regions and occasions permit different degrees of exactitude; and, second, that many words have two or more acceptable pronunciations, it is easy to see that the advice that can be given here under this head is small indeed.

For convenience one may distinguish and illustrate several kinds of common mispronunciations: (a) newfangled, (b) illogical, (c) inattentive, (d) overnice, (e) eccentric. The reader may then keep his ears open for what he considers further examples in each class.

(a) The newfangled grow up, no one knows how, in the teeth of the prevailing habit. Perhaps an old word is suddenly caught up by people who have never heard it spoken. Thus *era* pronounced *ayra* is, in educated circles, a phenomenon of the last ten years; so is *inhairent* for *inherent.* Akin to these is the pronunciation *vahrious* for *vayrious, hilahrious* for *hilayrious, Sahrah* for

Sayrah, and so on. It used to be that West of the Mississippi a boy named *Harry* expected to be called *Hairy;* now the reverse is happening in the East to long-established *air* sounds.

(b) Illogical pronunciations are of the order of *zoo-ology* for *zo-ology.* The word would need three *o*'s at the beginning to permit the *zoo* effect. Similarly, *height* ends with a *t,* not a *th. Luxury* has no hard *g* before the *x,* but *margarine* has a *g* as hard as in the name *Margarita; margerine* would be right only if so spelled. There are moreover two pairs of words that some speakers insist on distorting for the sake of audible parallelism: *overt* and *covert* are properly *oh-vert* and *cuv-ert.* Likewise the comprehensive sins of *omission* and *commission* are to be spoken of together just as they would be separately—*oh-mission* and *comm-ission.* (See also COUNCIL, COUNSEL, CONSUL.) Remember, too, that the double *l* in COLLEAGUE prevents it from sounding like *co-league. Colander,* however, is *cull.*

(c) Inattentive mispronunciations result usually from misreading or misspelling. One of the advantages of knowing how to spell is that the eye can guide the tongue and prevent, for example, *salutory* for *salutary* or *esculator* for *escalator.* Again, one ending is often taken for another and the rest of the word is adjusted to fit. Thus *heinous, grievous,* and *mischievous* all end in *-ous* without a preceding *i.* They should not be spoken as *heenious* but *haynous;* not as *greevious* but *greevous;* not as *mischeevious* but *mischivous.* Notice should be taken of the second *r* in *deteriorate:* it is not *deteria-ate;* and the sleeping drugs are *barbiturates* not *barbituates,* despite the convenient jingle with *habituates.* Finally, the word *pronunciation* itself gives no warrant for saying *pronounc-.* (See also UNWIELD[L]Y.)

(d) Chief among the overnice pronunciations is the sounding of the *t* in *often.* It should be seen and not heard. Similarly, the *th* in *clothes,* which is properly *clo'es;* the first *g in suggest(ion),* which is *sud-jest(ion);* the first *t* in *chestnut* and the *t* in *Christmas* as well. As for the replacement of the common *sh* sound by a clear *s* in *issue, tissue, sugar,* and *sumac,* it can only be called *preshous. Forehead* almost rhymes with *horrid; extraordinary* sounds no *a-o* in the middle, only a simple *o;* but *eleemosynary* requires the two *e*'s separately sounded, even in rapid-fire dialogue. And to make things hard after condemning overniceness, the opposite advice must be given about paired words that tend to overlap: say *pine needles,* not *pieneedles,* and *health center,* not *helcenter.*

(e) Eccentric pronunciations are by definition isolated,

but it is likely that every person retains from early days one or two homemade deviations from usage. Thus, cultivated speakers have been heard to say *laxadaisical* for *lack-* and *laythal* for *lethal*; *cut-and-dry* for *cut-and-dried*. The only advice here is "Look and listen."

In closing, it may be useful to suggest the value of certain traditional pronunciations now widely flouted. English accent is recessive; that is, it goes as far toward the beginning of the word as tongue and breath can manage. As a result, *hospitable, exquisite, despicable, secretive,* and *conversant* are best accented like *ádmirable, théatre,* and *cónfident.* For the first three words in this list, this has the advantage of preventing accents on *spit, quiz,* and *spic.* And speaking of accents, the word *research,* both noun and verb, is generally accented on the second syllable by those who are most familiar with the thing it denotes. Traditional again are: *parl(i)ament,* without sounding the *i* before *a; sism* for *schism; ark* in *archetype; zellous,* not *zeelous,* for *zealous; aigyou,* not *aig,* for *ague;* and *long-lived* as *long-lyved,* whereas *livelong* is *livlong.*

2. Little advice can be given about the pronunciation of foreign words and phrases, because the capacities of speakers for approximating unfamiliar sounds vary widely. Anyone who feels self-conscious about shaping such sounds should naturally reduce his employment of foreign phrases to a minimum. But within that minimum which ordinary usage requires, it is best to Anglicize the pronunciation up to the point where it does not render the words unrecognizable. It would, for example, be foolish to try to say *apropos* or *Schadenfreude* with their respective *r*'s; but equally foolish to say *ayproposs* and *shaydenfroody.* On the other side, the salesgirl's illusion of speaking French when she says *lahnjeray* for lingerie only shows what misplaced effort brings about. Many words lend themselves easily to Americanization. Thus *foyer* is now part of the real-estate man's vocabulary, and to give it a French pronunciation would be both silly and misleading, since in French the word does not mean an abbreviated vestibule but the *home* as an abstract entity.

The same applies to proper names. It is difficult at best to make one's lips and tongue and uvula shift gears in the middle of a sentence, and one moreover runs the risk of not being understood at all if one slips in a foreign name with the value of its vowels and consonants unexpectedly different from the rest of the discourse. Say *Flaubert* or *Tetrazzini* in conversation as the French and the Italians would say those names, and the first will sound like a murmur and the second like an affectation. All that duty requires is to avoid *Flaoburt* with the *t* sounded and *Teetrazinny* without the *ts* sound of the double *z*. To sum up: Give the nearest equivalent, with English sounds and without straining. Our ancestors had a better notion than our pedantic pretense at accuracy when they decided on *Paris* and *Lyons* and *Venice* and *Berlin* in place of *Paree* and *Leeong* and *Venetsia* and *Bayrleen*.

So much for Western Europe and its nomenclature. When we approach Russia and the East, all common sense departs; for the transliteration of those languages is evidently difficult and it has been correspondingly arbitrary. Those who know Russian or Polish or Chinese do not need English letters to tell them how to spell and pronounce names drawn from those languages. So there was no reason why we should be asked to read *Khrushchev* and say *Krushchoff*; to read *Chiang Kai-shek* and say *Chung*; to read *Mickiewicz* and say *Mitskievitch*. Letters were invented in order to indicate sounds as far as possible according to system, and one would have thought that transliteration would mean the rendering of one system as effectively as may be in the letters of another. But it is not so, and just as translation is often considered finer if foreign idioms are given word for word in English, so transliteration is a hodgepodge of direct visual counterparts and true sounded equivalents. The height of pedantry is reached in the improved transliteration which one occasionally finds adopted in library catalogues, and which requires that one forget traditional spellings in order to hunt down the composer *Chaikovsky* and the novelist *Dostoevsky*—the *t* in the one and the *y* in the other being eliminated because they were so useful to pronunciation.

See also RATIONALE; RECREATE, RE-CREATE; SPELLING; X.

proper names. See TITLES AND PROPER NAMES.

prose, the sound of. 1. No doubt, most of the prose that finds its way into print is read aloud by very few persons; some of it is perhaps never so read by anyone. Nonetheless, prose that cannot be read aloud with pleasure is probably bad prose. Euphony is not the highest virtue of prose, but one of its rudimentary requirements. The reason is the simple one that persons not tone-deaf, when they read silently, hear with the inner ear and are quite as much disturbed by clashing sounds as if they were reading aloud or listening. This effect is independent of the tempo at which their silent reading is done. So defiant of time are some departments of the mind that we can read at express train speed and hear the result as if reading at a crawl. Anyone who can read musical notation and inwardly hear the analogous but opposite effect: he cannot, at sight, read at a performing tempo, but he can hear at a performing tempo while reading at a crawl. The writer who fills his pages with ugly dissonances and tells himself that they are not worth the trouble of rectifying, because not one reader in fifty will ever test him by voice, is deluding himself. His bad readers may not mind, but his better readers will follow him with pain and inward protest if they are sufficiently interested in his contents, and otherwise not at all.

2. Of the interferences with euphony the two most common are, on the one hand, careless assonance and fortuitous rhyme, and on the other, rhythmic jolts comparable to tripping over an obstacle or trying to go another step down after reaching the bottom of the stairs. Of course, calculated echo has a place in prose and can achieve telling effects. Most of the force of *Man proposes, but God disposes,* or of the aphorism about the correlation between inspiration and perspiration as ingredients of genius, belongs to the intentional repetition of sounds. Echo also helps emphasis in *Retaliation is, after all, one kind of compensation / as dramatically natural as grammati-* *cally lawless / a society that seems to us at once despicable and improvable.* Deliberate rhyme confers a touch of style on *The greater exaltations are also the greater consolations,* which would be comparatively humdrum if the last word were *solaces* or *comforts.* But uncalculated echoes generally tend to nothing but otalgia; and the writer too careless, too lazy, or too busy to keep his lines clear of unplanned repetitions of *-tion, -ation, -ing, -ly, -ex, -pose, -press,* and so on is neglecting his duty.

Such repetitions are easier to find than to escape, even in respectable writing: *An instinct quite distinct from thought / the things that he was formerly determined to reform / I would never have made any such to-do over something that my own dignity admonished me to do / would seem completely inert if it did not encounter the counterstrokes of actions that gainsay it / Giving us all the facts as they did was a great factor in preventing panic / undertaking the staggering task of writing one myself / The commission has taken the position that / I think he would deserve very considerable consideration from the labor movement / No immediate official reaction to the action made known this afternoon / Both compositions reflect a concern with the expressive resources of limited forces / asserted a concerted campaign of vilifi-*

cation had been conducted against him / to roar like a wounded lion at the slightest slight.

The words *say, way, day (to-day), may,* and *play* (with its compounds) must be watched with particular care, tending as they do to introduce rhymes within adjacent phrases or sentences. Adverbs in *-ly* jingle unpleasantly when close together; and making a trademark of such repetitions of sound, as a well-known novelist has done, does not make them more tolerable: *S. drew himself up drunkenly formally in the camp chair and stared at the other woodenly / went into the kitchen of C.'s restaurant irritably, with P. following cursing chokingly and impotently angrily / They sat looking at each other absolutely inarticulately furiously.*

The sound of prose is likewise affected by accidentally irregular rhythms. Here again the placing of adverbs is a subject for caution and a test of skill. A parenthesis in an unnatural position or with insufficient grammatical moorings can be even more disruptive, as in *chapters describing the past and present of that great gouge cut by the now-invisible (from the rim) Colorado River.* This is to compound an adjective in English as German freely does: *now-invisible-from-the-rim* is of the same order as Freytag's *the on-the-other-side-of-the-river-lying mountains.* A

like affront to the ear is felt in the following: *Yet things have drifted so far without—until very recently—the needed sense of moral leadership at the highest levels . . . that . . .*

Interpolated elements of any length within the components of a compound verb will produce similarly bad effects: *Ireland had—as Thomas Davis had long ago feared, and Æ repeatedly warned—been made safe for commerce.* The interpolation in dashes might well have begun the sentence. One of the anomalies of English is that, whereas a single adverb should go after the auxiliary of a compound verb unless there are overwhelming reasons for putting it elsewhere, an adverbial clause cannot go there without extreme awkwardness. *It is . . . difficult to understand how Fish, with his intimate knowledge of the widespread corruption that existed under Grant, could have, as he did in 1880, supported Grant's attempt to obtain a third term.* Besides stopping the stream of thought by a parenthetic clause, the syntax sets up an absurd suggestion of the impossible form *did supported.* Note that the ungainliness of this sentence is a by-product of excessive wordage. No more is said than *How could Fish, familiar with the widespread corruption under Grant, support him in 1880 for a third term?*

A hiatus in rhythm will invariably occur when for variety the writer of fiction resorts to the modish trick of interpolating elaborate modifying elements between his subject and a verb of saying: *"Nothing," W., who could not forget the day S. took him out on the green, said.* The gasp for breath is even worse when virtually inseparable words are kept apart by long explanatory clauses, as in *the Immigration Quarantine Station on the other side where they had the six Germans who had given up off an injured merchant vessel interned.* The passage can be made readable by the simple adjustment *where they were keeping interned the six Germans.*

Higher in the scale of literacy, but equally defiant of the reading voice, are such sentences as the following, from a novelist generally praised for style: *What but the spite of annoyance informed A. W.'s wish (like M.'s) to visit some trouble on the troublesome, entertaining if only tentatively the, in E. A.'s word, vindictive, peevish thought that, R. being apprehended, bailor's option to surrender R. to proper authority might be exercised, R. might be enabled to enjoy a day or two in jail?* And again: *Modestly, he could be seen asking himself, waiting anxiously to hear, what standards of conduct that G. (abashment said so) privately thought the highest possible would proceed* *to find on these artful, extralegal, and as G. himself saw them, if not definitely dishonest, perhaps dishonorable goings-on.* Unnatural parentheses in unnatural positions, subordinations out of place, and coy approaches to fairly simple meanings make pretense at the intricate architecture of a Ciceronian period and confront the reader with the task of parsing that used to bedevil the student decoding his second-year Latin.

3. Not so common as unintended rhyme and assonance or pretentious impairments of rhythm, but equally deplorable, is unintended meter. The public thinks of good prose rhythm as easy to achieve and of verse meter as difficult, but there are times when one who cannot imagine himself a versifier finds his prose falling into meter in spite of every precaution. At such times there is nothing for it but to break up the unwelcome regularity by devices invoked in cold calculation. The pattern that dominates such unwanted regularity is generally iambic, and a great deal of prose yields an occasional unnoticed line of iambic pentameter, or even a full line and several iambic feet over. Four consecutive feet will be picked up by a reasonably good ear, and a full line of blank verse is very noticeable. *For days on end the mound of Hissarlik / He has the look of nightfall on his face / and laid before an unbelieving* *world / the thought of all the pain he had to bear / Conflicting feelings crowded in his breast.* What is in verse a grave or even exalted pattern becomes in prose a kind of trivializing gallop. Dickens in his Christmas stories abandoned himself to the singsong of blank verse. Jerome K. Jerome made the same mistake in a few paragraphs of *Three Men in a Boat,* with the result that the effortless pervasive charm of his pages instantly explodes into bathos.

The intrusion of blank verse into modern prose seems to be mostly the product of oversight. *But more and more they felt that it was time to stop* (six iambic feet) / *Though small, it was a brilliant work —the horses modeled lightly* (seven feet) / *the other places which had not yet felt the excavator's spade* (eight) / *such freedom as is not enjoyed by any other people in the world* (nine). When this jog trot takes charge it is hard to throw off. One must then give up for the time being and return when the mind's ear has regained its independence.

4. Of the sundry constructions and mismanagements that offend the taste for prose, most raise questions of syntax or logic that are dealt with elsewhere. But there are two that are objectionable not in their form but in their sound. The first is what may be called the double-duty construction—

the familiar pairing of two meanings with two prepositions, which is awkward only because of the pairing: *A first-hand knowledge of, and deep fellowship with, those who are our brethren in Christ.* This arrangement denies itself the easy flow of straight constructions; it is all bumps. Separate the two ideas and all is well: *A first-hand knowledge of . . . our brethren in Christ and a deep fellowship with them.* Some writers seem to think they achieve profundity, or at least analytic power, when they go in for the double-duty formula, and they treat us to it every few paragraphs: *It is appropriate for us to feel a sense of pride in and to offer congratulations to the many hard-working men and women who / that the only hope for the future of Nationalist China lay in close cooperation with and assistance from the United States,* etc., etc.

Akin to this is the *as much as, if not more than* estimate of things difficult to measure. Usually this tiresome cliché is aggravated by the omission of the second *as: The competition for these abilities from government and industry is increasing as fast* [as] *or faster than the colleges' need for them.* One would think that *as fast . . . than* might give the writer pause, but even after grammatical repairs the sentence still sounds harsh. Sometimes a writer tries to sidestep the trouble he foresees, only to plunge into worse awkwardness: *The responsibility . . . rests as much if not more heavily on state and local governments.* (See also AS 3.)

5. The second construction that frequently afflicts the modern reader's inner ear is that in which an article, definite or indefinite, follows a possessive (or, sometimes, reduplicates an article) in the citing of a title: *Shakespeare's "The Tempest" / Poe's "The Raven" / his "The Ordeal of Richard Feverel" / Stevenson's "A Child's Garden of Verses" / the symbolic "The Secret Rose."* Such locutions do not occur to anybody except when mentioning a book. No one dreams of saying *his the hat* or *her a lipstick* or *Parkinson's the law.* It is an implicit property of the possessive that it swallows and contains whatever article would be in order if the possessive were not there. *Parkinson's law* is the inevitable way of saying *the law of Parkinson,* and *his hat* the way of saying *the hat of him.* But when a title is involved, the natural resistance to such incredible locutions runs head on into an imaginary rule that titles must be repeated precisely as they are. This new and fanciful commandment (actually simple pedantry) overcomes the resistance and we read: *His "The Wreck of the Mary Deare," which was published two years ago / The allusion is to Williams' introduction to his "The Figure of Beatrice" / In his "The Lost World of the Kalahari" Colonel van der Post has written . . .*

The prevalence of this usage—which is so prevalent that some copy editors are empowered to insert articles sensibly omitted by authors—shows how widely reading matter has come to be thought of as sense without sound, as something for the eye to glance at, with the ear in total abeyance. If people nowadays did not think of printed prose as akin to a graph or an algebraic formula, they would never go out of their way, as they continually do, to produce such repellent absurdities as *Homer's "The Iliad," Dante's "The Divine Comedy,"* and *Chaucer's "The Canterbury Tales."* It has never been true that in prose a title has to be cited as it is found on a title page. It must indeed be so cited in bibliographies and in bibliographic footnotes, which obey the canons of the library card; but in prose—not just print but *prose*—all that is required is that the work be clearly identified and that the mention be introduced smoothly enough to be readable. Since the definite or indefinite article of a title is ignored in determining the alphabetic order, its inclusion is no help to identification and does nothing whatever for the consultant of reference books. In any normal

PROSE, THE SOUND OF 5 • 333

sentence *Mark Twain's "Tom Sawyer"* is quite as competent a reference as *Mark Twain's "The Adventures of Tom Sawyer,"* besides being stylistically decent. In the nineteenth and the early twentieth century, rhetorics taught by express rule that the articles in the titles of books must be omitted when a possessive precedes. The prescribed forms were: *Shakespeare's "Tempest"* / *Goldsmith's "Vicar of Wakefield"* / *his "Rime of the Ancient Mariner"* / *her "Mill on the Floss."* These forms, which can be read without gagging, are still the only ones suitable for prose.

A secondary point is that a good half or more of the possessives that introduce titles are needless and should be omitted simply because they perform no function. As often as not, context settles the authorship without the trouble of including a possessive. *In his "The Lost World of the Kalahari" Colonel van der Post has written* is exactly as clear without the *his*. Why should an encyclopedia article about an author keep pointing out that his works are his, as an article on Yeats, for example, persistently does? (*Yeats's "The Countess Cathleen," His prose "A Vision,"* etc.) These possessives add nothing but cacophony. And works that are household words do not need identifying by author anyway. *Hamlet* is as unmistakable as

Shakespeare's "Hamlet" (else, why not *Shakespeare's "The Tragedie of Hamlet, Prince of Denmark"*?). It is a pure waste of space to mention the author of *Paradise Lost* unless the work meant is *not* Milton's. To be sure, obscure works or works the titles of which might be subtly altered in meaning by the omission of *A* or *The* may occasionally require being named in full, even when a possessive precedes. In such cases, interpose a noun: *Philip Macdonald's novel "The Rasp"* / *J. M. Keynes's study "The Economic Consequences of the Peace."* Far from being fussy or redundant, these insertions make the sentences exact and euphonious both.

Newspapers and magazines that have the definite article in their titles firmly insist on retaining it, capital T and all, whenever they mention themselves, regardless of what they may do about the names of other publications. Some persons respond to this insistence by writing such forms as *the editors of "The New York Times,"* as the *Times* itself would do, instead of the more usual form *the editors of the "New York Times."* But what happens when the name of the publication is approached by way of a possessive, as in *Arthur Krock's "New York Times" column of August 17* or *Your "New York Times" editorial on X. will doubtless be widely reprinted?* And what happens when the title is approached by way of the indefinite article, as in *A "New York Times" reporter has ascertained* or *A "New York Times" correspondent in London sees indications that?* The *Times* itself would convert these expressions to *Arthur Krock's column in "The New York Times," The editorial in "The New York Times," A reporter of "The New York Times,"* etc. But it has no power to enforce this expedient on others. Now, the same commandment that insists on *Hawthorne's "The Marble Faun," Howells's "A Hazard of New Fortunes,"* etc., if it were to be consistently obeyed, would equally insist on *Arthur Krock's "The New York Times" column* and *Your "The New York Times" editorial* and *A "The New York Times" reporter has ascertained*. But the commandment is not consistently followed, for the good reason that it would sound at once pedantic and unspeakable. Yet the same persons who let it govern their mentions of books, poems, paintings, and concertos reject it as absurd in their references to periodicals. It is as absurd in the one connection as in the other. The only way to push unnaturalness farther would be to follow a possessive with a possessive; and that combination can be found in Mencken's Supplement I: *Thus, when Percival Pollard published his "Their Day in Court"* ... (See A, AN, THE 4.)

See also SENTENCE, THE.

proselyte is the noun meaning *a convert*; the verb is *proselytize*.

proven. See UNSAVORY PASTS.

provided, providing. The obvious distinction is that *provided* serves as a conjunction introducing terms and conditions, *providing* as the participial modifier it patently is. This gives us: (1) *Members shall be eligible for a reduction of the annual dues to the nonresident rate provided that* (= only if) *they establish residence at a distance of at least fifty miles from the city; and provided also that they shall have resided at such a distance for not less than six months before making application for the reduction;* and (2) *The most important clause of the new bill is that providing* (= which provides) *for the inclusion of self-employed persons among those eligible for social security benefits.*

See also DANGLERS, ACCEPTABLE.

psychology. See OLOGY, OLOGIES.

publishing. See LIBEL, SLANDER.

purge. The metaphor that supplies the name of a favorite device of modern governments leads to paradox when applied as it usually is in newspaper writing. The physical body is purged of its poison or peccant humors. The body politic is purged of its (supposedly) harmful citizens. Consequently, Senator Q. and General Z. are not themselves purged; it is the assembly or the bureau they belonged to which is now the healthier for their removal. Accordingly, we should say—

though there is little chance of our doing so—*General Z., who was removed by the October purge / Senator Q., the Maurefluvian purgee of the Bangup coup.*

purport. See THAT, CONJUNCTION 1.

put in(to), place in. See INTO, IN TO 2.

put to it. See HARD PUT.

Q

qualification. This word is a trap: its two meanings prolong an ambiguity worse than most because they are subtly opposed. *Qualification* means (1) reservation, restriction, exception, and (2) ability, competence, preparation. *I believe in his integrity without qualification / a political novice without qualification for office.* The careless writer will disconcert or misinform, as when a reviewer declares a novelist to be one of the greatest living writers of English *without any qualifications whatsoever.* What is presumably being said is not that the novelist lacks all qualifications but that the reviewer lacks all reservations about his merits.

quotation. See QUOTE, UN-QUOTE 3.

quotation marks. See IN-VERTED COMMAS.

quote, unquote. 1. As a noun, *quote* is heard more often than it is seen, but it is seen too often. *The quote is Carlyle's / There is more in this quote than meets the eye / I am not responsible for the sentiment: it is a quote.* The innovation delights those who

do not mind crudity if they can have succinctness. Whoever makes this choice must expect after a time to see *The cite is Browning's / The refer is not clear / The allude leaves me baffled.*
2. The broadcaster's practice of using the words *quote* and *unquote* in lieu of visual quotation marks is often copied by lecturers and persons reading aloud informally. *Unquote* is from the jargon of newspaper cables, and some who realize that it is not a word in the ordinary sense take pains to substitute *end quote*, which is perhaps better in one way but worse in another. We have all had to get used to hearing such a sentence as *The White House spokesman said there would be a further announcement "in a matter of hours"* read: [He] *said there would be a further announcement quote in a matter of hours unquote.* But this is an affliction no one should be required to get used to. For one thing, the quotation marks around such phrases ought not to be there for anyone to read. It is implicit in *spokesman said* that another's words are being reproduced in indirect discourse, and it often makes no differ-

336

ence whether they are being exactly reproduced or not. For another, men so accomplished as those who broadcast should be able to make their pauses and intonation convey quotation marks wherever these are needed around such mere scraps and shards of utterance. When a quotation is read *in extenso,* there is no need to say *quote* after one has said *General B. made the following explanation.* When the end is reached, a perceptible pause and a change of pitch will do the business of *unquote* without that clumsy and affected intruder into speech. At the worst, one need but say flatly: *That is all from General B.* A broadcaster too pressed for seconds to wedge in *end of quotation* can catch up with the clock by skipping an adverb somewhere (perhaps REPORTEDLY). Some persons, in speaking informally, signal opening and closing quotation marks by the device of raising and crooking two fingers of each hand. This is an attempt to be scholarly at the cost of elegance, but it might suit television and save its precious time.

3. Apropos of *quotation,* it is worth recalling to the exact-minded that speakers make statements, not quotations—unless they repeat other speakers' statements. Thus the *New York Times* feature "Quotation of the Day" should properly read: "Statement of the Day." The words become a quotation only when the newspaper reader repeats them to his fellow commuter. If it is argued that the *Times* is quoting the notable words, then every article in the paper is a mosaic of quotations from known and unknown authors, which is absurd. A newspaper reports statements that its readers may turn into quotations, spoken or written.

R

rack, wrack. These homonyms involve some trifling problems of spelling that are nearly insoluble. *Rack* is several words, differently derived (some of the derivations are conjectural) ; and *wrack* is at least two different words. The old alliterative phrase can be either *rack and ruin* or *wrack and ruin.* Cloud *rack* is also cloud *wrack.* There are other overlappings. Small wonder that some writers prefix a *w* to every *rack,* for insurance. Copy editors, at a loss to know what they should do with the *w,* do nothing. Yet one simplification is possible. It is this: any sort of framework, including the historic instrument of torture, is a *rack,* not a *wrack;* and *wrack* contains the core meaning of *wreckage* or *destruction.* If, then, we will consent to stick to a differentiation that is clear in modern usage, forgoing the etymological hair-splitting that can make out some sort of case for almost any variant use, we can at least say that the *w* is gratuitous—is, in fact, a misspelling—in words that refer literally or figuratively to some kind of framework, or to the kind of mental stress described as *on the rack. Clothes rack, hatrack, hayrack,* etc. are clearly right. Clearly wrong are the following: *An American traveling abroad really does not appreciate how wracking things must be in the United States until he hits Bucharest | Algeria, wracked by nationalist rebellion for nearly four years / the fogbound, storm-wracked Gulf of St. Lawrence / the cancer-wracked body of her sister Mary / wracked by illnesses, Vincent Van Gogh came to painting in 1880 / the film made from X.'s wracking novel of love without hope | The* [pinball] *machine was wracked with more tremors and seizures / The remaining tedious, pain-wracked three years and three months of X.'s life / Taking photos of complex diagrams and formulas in physics is less nerve-wracking and more accurate than copying them with pencil on paper.*

The expression *rack up* (= score, achieve, accumulate, be credited with) probably derives from the abacus framework used in scoring pool. The sports writer was using up a space he did not need when he wrote *D. wracked up another strikeout, his fifth for his brief stay on the mound. (Rack up* has in Great Britain the altogether different meaning of fill-ing an animal's rack with fodder—and hence of providing oneself with food.) What is certain is that writers and copy editors, if they could associate the plain *r* with pain or, figuratively, with twisting and straining, would cut off nine in ten of the misspellings of *rack* and *wrack*.

-rama. See SCIENTISM 2.

range without an indication of the attribute being spoken of is quasi-meaningless. *In his seven months' tour of the world, Mr. Stevenson spoke to a wide range of the populations he encountered* (to a great variety of men?). The appropriate use of *range* is illustrated by *The range of their intelligence is narrower than for the control group of those differing only in social and economic background.* In short, something can exhibit a *range* only when it is a namable feature or characteristic— age, health, stature, color, income, or what not.

rarebit. This word, if word it can be called, is one of the triumphs of literalness over fancy. On virtually every American menu one reads the pedantic *Welsh rarebit* for the simple and harmless joke *Welsh rabbit*. Latter-day cookbooks follow suit and obliterate the original name for melted cheese (cooked with beer) on toast. Webster's New International Dictionary lists *rarebit*

as a product of false etymology working on *Welsh rabbit*. The original form follows a familiar pattern found in nearly every Western tongue—the disguising of a plain dish under a lofty name: *Cape Cod turkey* for codfish, *prairie oyster* for a raw egg eaten with pepper and vinegar, etc. *Welsh rabbit* is said to have been coined by a Scotsman, and to have drawn from the Welsh the retort-in-kind, *Scotch woodcock*, as the name of an eggs-and-anchovy preparation served on toast. (See HELPMATE.)

rather. See HAD (WOULD) RATHER (SOONER); PREFER ... THAN.

rationale. How shall we pronounce this indispensable word for (1) the intellectual structure or underlying principles (of an action or outlook) or (2) an orderly statement of such principles? American dictionaries, including the New International, have given in to the popular delusion that the word is French, and hence recommend a French or quasi-French pronunciation in three syllables with the accent on the last. The delusion is of long standing. James Fenimore Cooper made his Lieutenant Muir in *The Pathfinder* say: "That is just the *rationale,* as the French say, of the matter." But Muir is a pretentious ignoramus as well as a scoundrel, and it is possible that Cooper, who knew his French, was simply showing up Muir's fraudulent learning by one more example. At any rate, *rationale* is unknown to the French; it is the neuter form of the Latin adjective *rationalis,* and to give it a French pronunciation is to ignore the principles of three languages at once. The reasonable pronunciation may now be beyond saving. It is that based on the usual Anglicizing that lawyers apply to Latin terms and it is the one listed third in the New International: *ray-shun-ay-lee,* with the accent on the third syllable.

ravaged. See MALAPROPS.

ravished. See MALAPROPS.

re-, prefix. See RECAP; RE-CREATE, RE-CREATE.

reaction. There are fashions in words and also prejudices against them. Some of the best-based prejudices are those that run against the fashions. Of these prejudices none needs less apology than that which snubs *reaction* in its fashionable meaning of *response, opinion, impression. What was your reaction to so-and-so?* has become a cliché for *What did you think of it?* A publisher sends a novel about prizefighting to a retired prizefighter celebrated for his urbanity: "My reaction," he replies with prompt courtesy and candor, "was not propitious,"

thereby justifying an impression that his vocabulary is not quite up to his former command of ring tactics.

Reaction in this sense is a figure of speech derived from science—first from Newtonian physics, then from chemistry, and finally from physical psychology. In physical science a reaction is an effect produced in matter or motion by another motion or piece of matter. Now, the chief characteristic of a good figure of speech is that it makes a meaning more simple, by making it more graphic than it would be if literally stated. The trouble with the figure from science is that it makes the meaning more difficult and complicated. Man being a thinking creature, the question *What do you think of America?* is more appropriate than *What is your reaction to America?*—an invitation to act like the knee joint when tapped or like a chemical compound when disintegrated by the addition of a reagent.

The absurdity in the use of *reaction* is brought out when, under the heading No OFFICIAL REACTION, the article states: *Officials in Western capitals were reluctant to react officially to Khrushchev's remarks since they were made at a political rally and particularly since they had not seen the texts.* (Note in passing the loose mooring of the second *they.*) A reluctance to react is patently an anomaly, reaction being what follows inevitably by the operation of natural law. The heading quoted means nothing more than No OFFICIAL COMMENT, and a reluctance to comment is intelligible. A secondary fault in the borrowed term is that the proper link after it is *from*, not *to*.

The case against *reaction* does not apply to this same word when it means the advocacy of a return to some earlier political or social state. *Reactionaries* and *the forces of reaction* we have always with us, and their names are established in the language.

See also POPULARIZED TECHNICALITIES.

readership. See TRANSITIVE, INTRANSITIVE.

reading (as in *reading from left to right*). See DANGLERS, ACCEPTABLE.

real. See NEEDLESS WORDS 2.

realistic, unrealistic. Except as the historical name of a school of novelists, *realist* and *realistic* have been virtually emptied of meaning. Like MAKE SENSE, the terms are now used to put one's opponent in the wrong. When one says to another *Be realistic!* or when one claims for one's project that it is *realistic*, whereas the other man's is not, one is accusing him of living in a dream world, or at least of

being out of touch with reality. It is a question-begging vocable that conceals the point of one's objection and the merit, if any, of one's counterproposal.

In related uses *realistic* may also mean *approximate, not exaggerated, conservative*, as in *This is a realistic figure for what we expect to spend*. By further extension it takes the place of *practical* or *expedient: With the realistic Russian temper they simply killed their prisoners of war when it was difficult to feed them*. An earlier sense is still found, which derives from the rise of realism in the novel, and in that sense it becomes unavoidably ambiguous. Fictional scenes are *realistic* when they are copied from life, and since much of life is unpleasant or ugly, *realistic* becomes a synonym for *sordid*. George Gissing was already complaining of the uselessness of the word in 1895. "Not long ago I read in a London newspaper, concerning some report of a miserable state of things among a certain class of workfolk, that 'this realistic description is absolutely truthful.' . . . When a word has been so grievously mauled, it should be allowed to drop from the ranks." The suggestion is still excellent.

See also MALAPROPS; POPULARIZED TECHNICALITIES.

reason . . . because. 1. Anyone answering the question For *what reason?* would naturally say *For the reason that . . .* , not *For the reason because . . .* But when *reason* is the subject of a declaration, with or without a verb wedged between *reason* and what follows, there is a strong temptation to substitute *because* for *that*. The substitution, besides being a breach of idiom, is an obvious redundancy: *because* = for the reason that. Therefore *The reason is because* means *The reason is for the reason that.* Typical instances: *The reason for nominating him is because* (that) *he commands the pacifist vote* / *The reason for this return is not because of feeding problems* (omit *because of*) / *A psychiatrist suggested that the reason Hamlet could not kill his uncle was because he himself had wanted to kill his father* (omit *the reason* and *was*) / *One of the reasons the Republican party is in trouble today is because . . . we have allowed people to criticize our policies and we have not stood up and answered effectively* (for *because* read *that*). Substituting *that* for *because* will generally restore grammar; but, as some of the examples show, it may result in a wordiness that requires attention. *He was nominated because* and *He was nominated for the reason that* are correct equivalents, but the second is labored.

2. We sometimes get the same redundancy with *why*:

Why she was willing to marry him was because he could take her right away from those unpleasant scenes (omit *Why* and *was*). A worse variant occurs when an initial *because* is treated as a noun: *Just because someone twitches the strings doesn't necessarily mean that we should dance,* which yields the paired words *because . . . doesn't mean.* Change *Just because* to *that* or invert and start: *We needn't dance just because,* etc. In the next sentence *because* is expected to serve as the subject of *inclines: Because* (That) *he went no farther, but instead directed his 1501 expedition to the Labrador coast and thence south, inclines us to group him with Columbus under the head of westward search.* If *because* is kept, we must write *we are inclined.*

recap. A new verb with attendant noun is in process of manufacture by the well-known clipping action which long ago resulted in *mob* from *mobile vulgus. Recap* is already standard in the sense of renewing an automobile tire, turning it into a *recap* or *retread* by means of a new cap or new tread. (This last coinage, incidentally, makes it desirable to hyphenate *re-tread* when we wish to say tread again, as we hyphenate *re-create* [= create anew] to distinguish it from RECREATE [= divert or amuse].) The newer term *re-*

cap, already common colloquially, is the clipped form of *recapitulate* or *recapitulation* and it means *summarize* or *summary*. *That was a rather complicated play; I will recap it for you / Here is a recap of the eight-o'clock weather report*. These words, now indispensable to the broadcaster, probably do not shock or baffle anyone. They are a handy way of avoiding a polysyllable that is felt to be out of place in the colloquial style, and as neologisms go they are simple and inoffensive. The lexicographer of the future will have to establish whether the inflected forms shall be spelled with a doubled consonant, like *replanned*, or without it, like *rabbeted*; that is, in keeping with the accented syllable.

reckoning. See DANGLERS, ACCEPTABLE.

recognizing. See DANGLERS, ACCEPTABLE.

recommend never takes a direct object followed by an infinitive, but always an indirect object followed by a *that* clause. *He recommended to his students that they should read all of Gibbon*, not *He recommended his students to read Gibbon*. The only way a teacher *recommends his students* is as objects of his solicitude during their search for employment. He then recommends them *to* an employer *for* a job; he may at times recommend the job *to* the student; or (as was said before) recommend *to* the student that he take a particular job. Bear in mind also the logical relation of the parties. The guest does not say *I was recommended to this hotel*, but *This hotel was recommended to me*. (See PREPOSITIONS; TRANSITIVE, INTRANSITIVE.)

recreate, re-create, etc. American practice does not hyphenate the prefix *re-* (again, anew) in the huge class of words represented by *reread, relight, reprint, retype*; but the hyphen is indispensable in a small group of such words that without it run the risk of proposing a different meaning. Only the hyphen can distinguish *re-create* (create anew) from *recreate* (amuse, divert); or *re-form* (change the shape of) from *reform* (correct, improve); or *re-treat* (reprocess) from *retreat* (withdraw, fall back); or *re-pose* (put again) from *repose* (rest). Of this group the commonest member by far is *re-create*, a ubiquitous word in book reviewing and a frequent one in historiography. Hyphening it is especially important because the companion word is pronounced differently and, in American practice, differently syllabified. Nevertheless a prolonged observation of the leading American periodicals gives the impression that *recreate* appears without its hyphen as often as with it. In any week one can collect from reviews, book advertisements, publishers' catalogues, and miscellaneous sources at least fifty such specimens as these: *The gaudy aristocracy of Tsarist Russia is vividly recreated in this novel | The author recreates the great Alaskan gold rush | Mr. Pasternak has recreated in Russian "Hamlet," "Romeo and Juliet" | makes his bow . . . by recreating fictionally the lost autobiography of Lucius Cornelius Sulla | How a computer can help recreate the process of thermonuclear fusion in the sun | a coherent recreation of events where the documents are inconsistent or nonexistent.* At times the omission of the hyphen makes for an annoying ambiguity: *For such a recreation few readers can fail to be properly grateful.*

redolent with. This is an unidiomatic mismating of words: *redolent* insists on *of*; *redolent with* is almost as uncouth as *smells with* would be. Those who write *the whole house is redolent with the clean tang of spruce and balsam* may be under the influence of *reek*, which takes either *with* or *of*, but is even so more frequently followed by *of* than by *with*.

reform, re-form. See RECREATE, RE-CREATE; also RE-CAP.

regard (as). See AS 2.

regarding. See DANGLERS, ACCEPTABLE.

rehabilitate. If one is bent on knocking down all barriers, especially those one does not see, one can use *rehabilitate* for things and services as well as human beings. One then goes to the corner shop to have one's hat *rehabilitated,* and during a newspaper strike one reads in the improvised journal that it is *designed to rehabilitate for the people of this city . . . the zones of communication so dangerously curtailed by the current* [strike]. (Note in passing that it is not even *communication* that is rehabilitated here, but *the zones,* after they had been *curtailed.*) In that same city the inhabitants are informed by large signs that this or that roadway or power line is being *rehabilitated.*

In better prose *rehabilitation* applies solely to persons or to their names, characters, or reputations, and this only in the abstract sense of restoring privileges, dignity, self-respect, the moral capacity to earn one's living or hold up one's head. *Rehabilitation* requires a previous degradation, punishment, or exile, just or unjust. *The fundamental aim of modern criminology is rehabilitation*—but it is not the aim of surgery. *The men who perished in the Stalinist purges of the 30's were rehabilitated twenty*

REMEDIABLE, REMEDIAL • 345

years later in one of the most surprising turns of Soviet policy. If words, as we often hear, are living things, can we rehabilitate *rehabilitate?*

re-identification. Except in documents likely to be brought before a court, the re-identification of persons or subjects by repeating the name or noun in parentheses is always awkward and to be shunned. Pronouns were invented for the purpose sought in that clumsy way and they must be handled so as to perform their role— even though it is true that, for lack of gender in nouns, English pronouns are extremely intractable. In *He told his brother that he would buy him an interest in his firm if he would give up his share of his house,* nothing good is achieved by putting in *John('s)* and *George('s)* in alternation. What is needed is a new sentence— e.g. *George told his brother John that by giving up the share in the house they owned in common John would receive as payment an interest in George's firm.*

The deplorable by-product of the habit of saying *he* (*John*) and *his* (*George's*) is that names are inserted when pronouns have done the work. In the following example the name and the subject have been changed to maintain anonymity but the principle remains: *Armand Jones told the members of the Senate committee investigating crooked ping-pong that he (Jones) had never played the game or been near a table. He* is equal to representing *Jones* and does not need his presence.

See also ANTECEDENTS; THAT, WHICH, RELATIVE.

remainder. See BALANCE.

remediable, remedial. One might naturally think of these words as exceptionally resistant to the tendency of cognates to mingle; but they now and again succumb. *Remedial* (curative, tending to remedy) is active; *remediable* (curable, capable of being remedied) is passive. The writer was confused who wrote: *X. believed that evil was mere sickness of the soul, therefore temporary and remedial.* The context offers proof against any suspicion that evil is being condoned as a therapeutic agent. The meaning is plainly *remediable.* The confusion is possibly occasioned by the instances, rare in English, of words in *-able* or *-ible,* a passive suffix, that overlap in sense words in *-al,* an active suffix; e.g. *practicable, practical.* The author just quoted fails to differentiate between these much more common words also: *the practicality* [i.e. practicability] *of settling national disputes without war.*

See -ABLE, -IBLE; DANGEROUS PAIRS; PRACTICAL.

repeat. This is one of the really dangerous words. An act that is repeated has to occur at least twice, and one might think *repeat* entirely foolproof thanks to this minimum requirement, but it is not. We read *Every repetition* [of a choral performance] *has been received with tumultuous enthusiasm* in a context showing unmistakably that the first performance is included with the repetitions. The meaning is clearly *Every performance has been received* . . . When we come to the requirement that something repeated twice must have occurred three times, and so on, we find writers so commonly careless that it is impossible to be sure how many times the occurrence took place. *"No—no—no!" she protested passionately; and at the third repetition* . . . Here again it is fairly clear that the first *No* is called a repetition. But what to make of the following direction, in which clarity is all important? *Indicated dosage may be repeated every 3 hours but not more than three times in one day, unless prescribed by your physician.* If the indicated dosage may be repeated three times in one day, it may be taken four times. But we are so conditioned to the loose use of *repeat* that most of us would probably construe the direction as a warning against more than three doses in all; that is, two repetitions. In short, *repeat* has become risky to the point where accurate communication calls either for a total avoidance of the verb or for a precautionary translation: [The medicine] *may be taken . . . not more than three (or four) times in one day*, or *may be repeated three times (four dosages in all).* The equation to bear in mind is $R = t - 1$; i.e. number of repetitions = total occurrences minus one. To repeat: if something happens twenty times it is repeated nineteen times. Only thus can something repeated once occur twice.

repercussive. See VOGUE WORDS.

reportedly. Newspapermen and broadcasters live on a steady diet of this adverb, which is now recognized as a technical term thanks to its acceptance by dictionaries. Yet it is so lacking in the characteristics of a respectable adverb that one would like to see its use confined to cable messages, where it saves money and can await translation into English. *Forty-one passengers and five crew members reportedly died in the crash.* How does anyone reportedly die? And what a way of saying *are reported to have died!* *Such convictions are extremely rare, and reportedly there had been only four previous ones since the law was passed* (only four previous ones had been reported) / *However, the own-*

ers of one franchise reportedly favor the appointment of a temporary commissioner to preside over the draft (are said to favor) / The reportedly severe epidemic broke out about two weeks ago in the southwestern part of the state (the epidemic, said to be severe, broke out).

In general, adverbs made by adding -ly to past participles are deplorable—acknowledgedly, despisedly, allegedly, discouragedly, etc. Reportedly is among the worst, and it is perhaps the commonest. The test of legitimacy for an adverb made from an adjective is that it fit the formula in [x] manner. Thus wisely = in a wise manner; forbiddingly = in a forbidding manner. Now try reportedly: in a reported manner. It does not fit. We must supply some roundabout notion such as according to report or as report has it. It strains charity to treat such a word as belonging to the language. (See HOPEFULLY.)

represent. Representation is essentially an arrangement whereby few stand for many, a part for a whole, or a token for a fulfillment. Things do not represent themselves except in the mood of irony: Congressman X. represents no one but himself. At all other times things or persons merely are themselves. But because are and is seem weak, the urge is great to replace them by the noble-sounding represent. The verb is thereby overworked and misapplied to mean compose, constitute, or simply are. The Catholics represent a trifle under a quarter of the voting population / Almost 3,000,000 people in and around Paris, representing three out of five persons, have never seen a live performance of any kind (omit representing or substitute amounting to) / His support of the N.R.A. and his 1946 proposal for a High Court of Commerce represented attempts to devise institutions to control the modern market (were attempts) / Contestants who try to make a living from contests represent about one in each 200 entrants. However, contest hobbyists—those who enter contests frequently and work hard at it—represent one in four of the contestants (for represent read constitute). In this collection the absurdity of 3,000,000 in and around Paris representing three is evident. At this rate 20,000 constituents represent one Congressman.

repulsion. See MALAPROPS.

residue. See BALANCE.

resource person. The pastime of holding conferences as a simulacrum of work has led to the creation of several new and needless terms. A resource person, be it said for the benefit of the fortunate stay-at-homes, is an able man or woman whom the chairman of a group can rely on for a few sensible words at the right time. The phrase, besides being an offense to all the other members of the group, is formed on the vicious principle of linking ideas without a clear joint between them. Everyone knows what a *resourceful person* is and how he differs from a *person possessing great resources*. The new phrase wants to turn the resourceful person into one of the chairman's resources without indicating the twist. This conversion is in fact not possible. Knowing, moreover, the origins of the phrase, one is entitled to suspect that its creator and proud users vaguely think of *recourse person* as they utter their nonsense.

A second character in the cast of conference members is the *discussant*. He is needed, it seems, to insure that some discussion, instead of benumbed silence, greet the speakers' papers. The obvious *discusser* was probably rejected because of *cusser* (= curser), but *commentator* was available, though not elegant. New creations in *-ant* have a bastard look and sound, because of the leaning of that ending toward passive or intransitive meanings. A *consultant* is one who may be consulted (passive); a *disputant* (rare in the singular) is one who does not so much dispute as belong to a disputing group (intransitive). Sometimes, of course, *-ant* merely marks a distinction. Thus an *informant* is one who informs but who is not an *informer*, i.e. a paid spy or a stool pigeon for the police. (Compare *militant*, which should remain an adjective.) *Discussant* is on all counts an unfortunate birth.

For the third name bred by innovation out of conference, *conferee*, see -EE, -ER.

respective(ly). These words are pointless whenever they are not given the task of clarifying a member-to-member correspondence between one series and another. Jane, Susan, and Ann can be married to Tom, Dick, and Harry respectively; W., X., and Y. can be elected respectively moderator, town clerk, and auditor. The word has an unfortunate currency in sentences where no such correspondence exists, only one series being enumerated. *Three of them are married and live in California, Connecticut, and Washington, respectively.* The excess baggage of *respectively* may betoken here an earnest apprehension that without it someone will infer that all three live in all three states. No one will; and what the word more probably betrays is a widely felt fondness for polysyllables that make one's meaning sound more technical than it is. An encyclopedia article about Hieronymus Bosch tells us: *Two versions of "The Adoration of the Magi" are in Princeton University and the Metropoli-*

tan Museum of Art respectively. The *respectively* is futile unless we are told which version is where, for no one is likely to suppose that both versions are in both institutions or two in each. A novelist is guarding against equally groundless misunderstanding when he writes: *B.M. and the Vice President came onto the floor together and went to their respective chairs / The four of them stopped to talk . . . then broke up and went to their respective desks.* If they had swapped chairs and desks or run amok and invaded other places than their own, the circumstances would be mentionable, but an author can afford to take for granted what every reader will take for granted.

The ultimate affectation of *respective* occurs when it not only fails to match one series with another but also fails to mention any series at all: *Each will spend six months or more meeting American counterparts and observing conditions in his respective field.* In a context so firmly singular, *in his own field* is the utmost that the traffic will bear.

rest. See BALANCE.

restive. Contemporary writing shows that the majority of those who use this word suppose it to be a synonym of *restless, nervous,* or *fidgety. Growing restive, he took to pacing back and forth* will do

for a sample. The word (from *restare,* to resist or hang back) has no kinship with *restless,* and what it means is *balky, refractory, rebellious.* To be sure, the two ideas have a connection and may overlap: a fidgety horse may be on the point of kicking over the traces, and restlessness in a man may be the first stage of recalcitrance. But children's spring-fret (restlessness) does not necessarily mean their refusal to go to school (restiveness). Associating *restive* with *restless* is a natural enough error, because *restive* (unlike French *rétif* = stubborn, as in the name of Restif de la Bretonne) has nothing in its form or pronunciation to suggest that its first two letters are really a prefix. The image properly evoked by *restive* is a horse that either will not move or backs obstinately. An expressive synonym of *restive* is *mulish.*

retread, re-tread. See RECREATE, RE-CREATE; RECAP.

retreat, re-treat. See RECREATE, RE-CREATE.

Reverend. See TITLES AND PROPER NAMES 3.

reverse. See CONVERSE, OBVERSE, REVERSE.

revulsion. See MALAPROPS.

right, in his (her) own. A peeress in her own right is

one who was born to a title instead of acquiring it by marriage. Loose thinking by modern journalists has extended the phrase until it is nothing but a lofty and lengthy substitute for *also: We welcome Mr. P.'s "Anthology of Victorian Verse." A poet in his own right, Mr. P.* (Himself a poet) */Senator F.'s wife greeted the guests; a public figure in her own right* (also a public figure) */ Lady H. was chairman of the committee that invited the orchestra from Prague to open the festival. A violinist in her own right* (Lady H. has musical interests; she plays the violin) */ The cup was awarded by George F., an athlete in his own right* (himself an athlete) */ Suzanne Valadon . . . the mother of the painter Maurice Utrillo and a painter in her own right* (also a painter).

In short, when the jargon phrase is used, some semblance of meaning, direct or derived, should attach to the word *right*. A man is a poet or an athlete as the result of his efforts to develop his talent, not as the result of any right. The permissible extension of the original phrase is therefore narrow. One may speak of a woman as *an American in her own right*, not by marriage; *an heir in his own right*, through birth, not bequest. One may even say in the vein of sarcasm *an idiot in his own right*—i.e. congenital or hopeless, not an idiot by physical injury, overwork, or senility.

See also JARGON; SAKE, FOR ITS OWN.

roadability. This term became common in description and advertising very early in the history of the automobile. By analogy it ought to mean (see NONLEAKABLE) *capable of being roaded*, if that can be called a meaning. What it has always actually meant is *road ability*—ability to hold the road. That is, its *-ability* seems to be not the substantive form of the passive suffix *-able*, as in *readability, visibility*, etc., but the independent noun *ability*. Other nouns in *-ability* convert handily into *readableness, inscrutableness*, etc. without change of meaning, but *roadability* does not translate into *roadableness*. It is a freak word and a kind of pun, likely to hold its place because needed, but not likely to gladden anybody's ear until it has long lived down the history of its formation.

Note, however, that no one can circulate such coinages without inviting consequences that he may not foresee. Along comes the same independent noun *ability* simulating a standard suffix in *performability*, meaning not *capacity to be performed*, but simply *able performance:* DISCOVER LARK PERFORMABILITY YOURSELF. The same play on words occurs in *profitability*, which means *like-*

lihood of yielding profits, and again in *wearability*, which ought to mean *capable of being worn* but actually means *durableness, ability to wear: Plastic tile . . . combines* [the] *appearance and resilience of ordinary cork tile with* [the] *wearability of plastic.* These inventions, unlike *roadability*, answer to no need that is not better taken care of by words long available. A play might be said to have performability,

or a garment wearability, if one could think of no more graceful way to convey these meanings; but the words cannot mean *ability to perform* and *ability to wear*. Of one point we can be sure: once the pattern is set, such trick formations are certain to proliferate, and we are as far from seeing the end of them as from being sure of their meaning.

See also -ABLE, -IBLE; SCIENTISM 4.

S

sake, for its own. This phrase harbors an ambiguity that has led some critics astray in their efforts to popularize the distinction between the practical and the fine arts, or more especially between communicative and so-called pure art. When a "purist" critic says that he listens to music, not in order to follow a story or titillate his emotions but *for its own sake,* he successfully suggests that he is pursuing a nobler course than his neighbors and doing proper honor to the high art of music. But a moment's reflection shows that *its* in *for its own sake* cannot refer to music, which, not being a person, has no sake. The phrase, that is, is not parallel with the one in *I am going to stay with my husband's old aunt, not for pleasure, but for her sake.*

But if the art of music (or any other) is without needs or wishes to be fulfilled, then what is the tenable meaning of cultivating it *for its own sake?* The meaning seems to be *capturing the true essence rather than a by-product.* One listens, inevitably, for one's own sake, for one's own good, but in accordance with the exacting demands of the medium, rather than the easy indulgence of reverie, sentimentality, and the like. So understood, *for its own sake* becomes intelligible, but it still leaves open the question what the essence of art, or of each art, really is. Debate is not over on that point, and *for its own sake* should not by its high tone hoodwink the common reader into thinking that a confident assumption is a proof.

The common phrases *for goodness' sake, for clarity's sake* are not affected by the caution just offered. They mean *in the interests of goodness, of clarity;* and these are on a par with the interests of any person, as cannot be said of music above.

same. A needless anxiety haunts some minds about the proper sequel to use after *same* to introduce a relative clause. The fact is that both *as* and *that* are acceptable. *I want the same brand that I bought the last time / After that experience he was never the same as he was before.* If one or the other particle is to be preferred for a given sentence, the choice is made by deciding whether the idea of comparison (*as*) predominates over the mere wish to define (*that*). Except in O.C.E. (Old Commercial English) or for facile humor, *same* is never a pronoun. The following is not acceptable in serious discourse: *We have your order for three ornamental cast-iron frogs and are shipping same immediately.* But Bret Harte made humor out of inelegance in:

Ah Sin was his name
And I shall not deny
In regard to the same
What the name might imply.

See also SUCH.

sanction. The verb and the noun *sanction* have played tag with each other until they have acquired almost opposite meanings, an oddity that often puzzles newcomers to the literature of international politics. *To sanction* a move or course of action is to authorize or permit it. To apply *sanctions* (economic or other) is to take coercive measures against a person or nation. Thus *to sanction* is to say "Go ahead"; to carry out *sanctions* is to say "You mustn't."

The history of this mix-up is not worth retracing. What deserves attention is a new derived meaning that increases the confusion. It comes from sociology and occurs in discussions of the law, whose punishments it correctly interprets as *sanctions*. But then, by using the verb in its participial form, and speaking of the *sanctioning system,* it fuses the two opposed meanings in one doubly ambiguous modifier. It is ambiguous in meaning and in grammatical function: *We expressly disclaim the view that sanctioning problems are "strictly legal questions"* / *Any competent observer of what happens in a courtroom or in any other sanctioning situation* / *The field of sanction law as we understand it is the entire process of sanctioning.* And as headings: SANCTIONING MEASURES AND THE SHARING OF WEALTH / THE IMPACT OF SANCTIONING UPON POWER. In reading these and other examples that might be adduced, the mind has to judge by trial and error whether permission or punishment is intended, for in ordinary speech *sanctioning measures* does not mean *punitive measures.* Let us hope that it never will. As for *sanction law,* it seems a redundancy beyond the license generously granted to sociology.

sanguinary, sanguine. A biographer of Walt Whitman's remarks: *By New Year's 1857 even the sanguinary Whitman could hardly have avoided realizing the seriousness of his failures.* The writer never dreamed that he was calling Whitman either bloodstained or bloodthirsty; his intention was to say that Whitman had a hopeful, confident—what is popularly called an optimistic

—disposition. That is, he was *sanguine*.

See also ALTERNATE, ALTERNATIVE; FELICITOUS, FORTUITOUS; DANGEROUS PAIRS; MALAPROPS.

save. See BUT 2.

scarcely . . . than. See HARDLY (SCARCELY) . . . THAN.

scarify. See MALAPROPS.

schism. See PRONUNCIATION 1.

scholar, -ship. A child who attends an elementary or a secondary school is a *pupil*, not (as formerly) a *scholar*. In college or at the university he becomes a *student*, and he attends the lectures of *scholars* (= learned men), distinguished for their research. When published, research is known as *scholarship*, and so is the quality of the work: *His scholarship is minute, exacting, tireless; one cannot see what monograph could surpass this one in point of research and intelligence.*

It should not cause confusion that *a scholarship* also means a sum of money given to a student, usually an undergraduate, to pursue his studies. A *fellowship* in the United States is the name of a *scholarship* awarded to a graduate student; in England, it is an appointment as member of a college. Again, in the United States there is no difference between a *graduate student* and a *postgraduate student*. The former term is by far the more common. A *post-doctoral fellow*, as his name indicates, has finished his studies as far as the highest degree, the doctorate, and is studying with one of the masters of his guild.

scientism. 1. The deserved admiration in which science and technology are held today has had the effect of making the lay world want to share in their reputation by borrowing their trappings. The result is all around us in many forms, from the design of household objects to the new hybridized vocabularies of trade and the professions. To be trusted, everything must wear the technical, the scientific, look. The frame of mind and the feeling that produce and reproduce these imitations, crude or subtle, are properly *scientism*.

Whether crude or subtle, scientism has a harmful effect on language, simply because it is not the product of genuine need or thought; it is by definition affected, and affectation in an advanced culture is the chief agent of linguistic corruption. Some of the corrupt results and their particular demerits will be found discussed under other headings, notably POPULARIZED TECHNICALITIES; COVERING WORDS; -IZE; NOUN-PLAGUE; TELESCOPINGS; and INITIALESE. Here the general tendency will be described and examples given that belong to still other categories than those in the entries just cited.

In its most direct manifestation scientism simply borrows a word from technology or science and reduces it to vulgar uses. *Focus* is one of thousands of such words, words unknown before the camera, the internal-combustion engine, the electric light, or the statistical chart. In daily prose these words emerge, if one may say so, slightly out of focus: *Would you like to sharpen the focus of your investment objectives?* The proffer of help in this sentence is clear enough, but its goal is by no means precise—which may be appropriate, though not if the technical term *sharp focus* is there to tell us the opposite: it is not possible to focus on an unspecified group of things.

The writer might object that it is unfair to hold him to the strict meanings appropriate only in science or engineering. If he did, he would be supplying the ground for objecting in turn to his use of scientific terms. Why could he not write in the first place *Are you sure you know why you invest and what choices are the best for your purpose?* But no: the air is filled with the germs of scientism—with *objectives* and *processes*, with *potential* and *focus*—until few persons are left who can think at all with such unscientific terms as *goal*,

purpose, know, and *choose.* Even the poet can be found using words such as *correlation* and *entropy*, with an imperfect grasp—necessarily—of what they mean, and hence with a diminished force in his verse.

If, then, one wishes to avoid scientism in one's speech or prose, the first group of words to reject is that which draws on the vocabulary of science and engineering. It includes, among many others: *allergy, continuum, entropy, empathy, potential, focus, nucleus, process, sibling, experiment, laboratory, co-ordinates, motivation, impact, component, critical, median, end-product, -itis, order of magnitude.* It is understood, of course, that some of these terms are out of place in ordinary prose only when they are used to suggest the solemnity of science. One may still speak of a *critical article* in referring to a book review; but to say, with a vague notion of *critical mass, That's a combination of people that can go critical* (i.e. explosive) is to fall into the error deprecated.

Similarly, one may refer to the Argonne National Laboratory, for that is its name; but to print *All our work in creative writing is given in laboratories* is raw scientism. Even *language laboratory* is a misnomer: since it is a place in which to practice the speaking of foreign languages it should be called—if a metaphor is required—a *language gymnasium.* And as truly sensible people know, trying this or that food, this or that domestic arrangement is not in the least an *experiment.*

The advertisers and the public authorities need the same reminder. Iceboxes may have two compartments; they are not for that reason *dual-zone refrigerators.* Nor is the middle strip on a highway a *median divider.* So much pomposity should fool no one. Yet the effect is there, that of a new kind of theology. For the use of improper words leads to the belief in the existence of imaginary entities, each given would-be technical names. It is bad enough when a woman's suit comes to be called a *set of coordinates* and she feels *insufficiently accessorized* without a handbag to match. But one is alarmed about the collective mind when "grave concern" is expressed about the ambiguities of doctrine in the advertising industry: *Mr. C. said he knew exactly how to define sales promotion, though his definition may stir dispute in some quarters. Sales promotion, under his definition, encompasses "basic merchandising tools, such as premium incentive promotions, point-of-purchase display material, direct mail and package design." Some ad men consider sales promotion to be a part of merchandising, not the other way around, and consider point-of-purchase displays to be part of advertising.*

2. The parallel of this playing at science by forming and naming entities can be found throughout the world of art. *Cemations* have been so christened by their maker in this way: *To the root* cem *(from the Latin* caementum) *was joined a familiar ending* -ation, *which the dictionary points out means a concrete result or thing. Mr. G.'s cemations are concretely realized; they are no imitations or images of other things.* It would have been a pity if handling cement had yielded no concretely realized result or thing.

In education, the like tendency has long been evident. It is years since a student went to college to learn something: he (and she) have gone to *further their educational objectives*—just like the investment counselor about *his* purposes—and it is these objectives the students are asked to INDICATE on the application blanks. On their side, the faculties tell us that their reports REPRESENT *the distillation of a series of discussions* and that they are *contemplating the stimulation of international interest* in their *uniquely articulated experimental programs.*

Throughout this fake engineering of simple things the urge to coin new words is unabating. *Cemations* is typical, by reason of the belief born of science that every new object or entity or compound needs a new name. What differentiates science from scientism is that science defines what it names, after making reasonably sure that it exists and that it is new. In trade, of course, the proliferation of names records not so much novelty or uniqueness as varieties of makers and sellers. And this is the pattern that the artist of *cremations* has followed. Scientists in their occasional mood of advertising do the same: a planetarium cannot simply invite us to look at the stars; it must promise *Nocturnal Sky Spectaculars.* Or again: *The name "Quadri-Science" signifies the four great areas to which the corporation devotes its resources: earth sciences, oceanography, atmospherics, space research.* For *devotes its resources,* which suggests a charitable foundation, read: *will provide consultants and perform research.*

Quadri-science reminds one of Winston Churchill's wartime neologism *triphibious* (attack), for which he was justly reproached, since the *phi* in the word is a broken-off piece of *amphi,* meaning *both.* How much better to use *three-way* or even *three-pronged* to make the same point. But Churchill's temporary lapse illustrates yet another aspect of scientism. Science has traditionally forged its new terms from Greek and Latin roots; it was able to do so systematically and intelligently because its practitioners until recently knew the rudiments of these languages. Now the businessman picks up the roots or their parts without knowing what they mean and tacks them on to others or to English words indiscriminately. Thus we have the meaningless -*tron* (half of *electron,* the whole of which means *amber*) attached to *magni-, puri-, cavi-* (from cavity), *post-, laundro-, reserva-,* and so on. The same has happened to -*rama* with no greater attention to sense (see -ATHON, -THON). It is a pity that early in the game of christening discoveries or new products no effort was made, except here and there, to find combinations of native words, as did the English physician who found the *knee jerk* (American: *patellar reflex*) and the English mechanic who made the *loudhailer* (American: *megaphone*). One shudders to think of the words we should have to use if it had been left to our age to name *table, chair, luggage, house, father,* and *mother.*

3. Nor is this all. The scientific aim is ultimately that of the classifier and enumerator. Scientism responds to this sober outlook and imitates it as best it can; for example, through the number or name affixed to a denoting word, as

in botany and chemistry: *Operation Simplex, World War II, age 20, phase three, zone 5.*

Again, scientism spreads the habit of thinking in clusters of undetachable words no longer analyzed by the mind, but set down next to other clusters: *What the need is, for a longitudinal study of the sexual development and sex education of a woman.* Or *Both craft reportedly took violent evasive action / The pilot . . . was forced to take sharp evasive action to avoid collision.* The sense of a perpetual echo is reinforced when, as in the last two sentences, *evasive* is misused for *avoiding,* and when *to take sharp evasive action* clearly classifies rather than describes the event. Once again, what is proper and admirable in science, which aims at generality, is wrong in common prose, which is vivid only when particular.

The influence here being retraced goes deep: it is responsible for the quasi-universal habit of saying *initial* for *first* —*the initial phase* instead of *the first step; additionally* for *besides* or *also*—*you have additionally our assurance that; position* for *put*—*After Deposit Plate and deposit slip have been properly positioned in the imprinter face up, move handle to extreme left.* This last process is supposed to go on daily in a bank, where *name plate, slip, printer,* and *far left* would be too primitive,

not technical enough. And while needless verbs are made out of nouns, needless adjectives are produced for every noun that acquires a vaguely technical sense. Thus we have *societal, dialogal, interdisciplinary* (see ENDINGS 2), *interpersonal, group-dynamical* (why not *group-dynamicable?*), and dozens of others. We already misuse those in *-ological* (see OLOGY), and the conviction grows that the best way to express our thought is to write *Backers of the rose as a national floral symbol* instead of *Backers of the rose as the national flower.* Another says apropos of a truck strike that only five per cent *of the company trucks were mobile as of last night* (see AS 5). Or, to take another form of the same classificatory impulse, it now seems grander to say: *For the convenience of passengers* (whom else?) *this bus is restroom equipped.* The universe of buses is manifestly divided into *rest-room equipped* and *non-rest-room equipped* and ours belongs to the superior species.

4. In still other groups of words, the pretense at scientific impersonality destroys the intention or direction of the word. Thus in sociology and psychiatry *responsibility* is sometimes used in its normal sense, sometimes in the sense of *ability to respond;* in computer circles *capability* is being taken for *capacity*—i.e. of

so many words or characters. All words in *-ability* and *-ibility* are in danger (see -ABLE, -IBLE and ROADABILITY). In law and criminology SANCTION is being similarly twisted, the effect in every instance being to set up ambiguities that might conceivably be guarded against by the writer if, aware of the distortion he imposed upon the word, he regulated his practice accordingly. But it is all too clear that writers enamored of *technicity* notice only what they think they mean.

The spirit of scientism will not die out from horror at seeing its effect on language and thought. But alive or dead, scientism can be repudiated without peril to oneself, and this at the moderate cost of always trying to say what one knows, wants, or remembers, instead of always trying to utter abstractions and generalities. When a renowned choreographer and teacher of the dance was honored by many of her pupils on her birthday, one of them said: *She gave us a foundation to move in any direction we liked.* Leaving out the bad grammar, one detects in this remark both a descriptive idea and a wish to offer a sincere compliment. Those two things might have been phrased: *She taught us how to dance and let us make our own styles.* It is in those two words of the original, *foundation* and *direction*, that we can

see the subtle symptoms of our trouble and it is there that we can begin to attack it.

scoop, beat. As recently as thirty years ago, journalists distinguished between these two words. A *beat* was the getting and printing of a story ahead of one's competitors by the use of flair and honorable resourcefulness. A *scoop* was the same result achieved by dishonorable means, such as breaking a pledge of secrecy or a date of release. This distinction has disappeared, the journalists retaining *beat* and the general public using *scoop* with no awareness of its once disparaging sense. In ordinary prose, *scoop* is entitled to its place, being both well-entrenched and expressive; *beat* would only startle and confuse.

scotch, verb. See LOST CAUSES.

self-addressed envelope. There are those who reprove this standardized phrase on the ground that envelopes do not address themselves. Their position seems dubious. Any locution, especially when long established, is entitled to a reasonable interpretation of its intent. A self-addressed envelope is not one that addressed itself: it is an envelope addressed to oneself. (Compare *self-mailer*, the prepared sheet for convenient reply.) But the *self-* is a surplus syllable and might as well be spared for that reason alone. Why not simply *addressed envelope?* The phrase has the further virtue of removing one of the gratuitous sniper's targets.

But this latitude about *self-* must not be abused. As soon as a true self is brought into action, ambiguity or absurdity or both may result. A *self-learning center* may, for all one can tell, be a place where the Greek injunction *Learn Thyself* is carried out. The notion of *learning by oneself* is not evident in *self-learning* as that of *helping oneself* is evident in *self-help.*

senior citizens. Retirement and pension systems have suddenly confronted younger people with the discovery that the old are a large and increasingly numerous class—a sort of Fifth Estate with vested interests, votes not to be overlooked by the astute politician, debilities worth the attention of those who purvey patent medicines, and perhaps even feelings that should not be hurt. Thanks to the modern mania of political euphemism, a group of such numerical strength comes to be known by flattering names, or such as are thought flattering. Accordingly, we no longer have old men and women, the elderly, the aged, the superannuated, the retired, or the old fogies, but *senior citizens.* The phrase is generally preceded by *our.*

Such a label for the old could only be a young person's invention. It shares the blight that overtakes every GENTEEL-ISM. There may be someone here and there who would rather be a senior citizen than an old man. But the phrase that delights the social psychologist and enriches the jargoneer's hoard is hard to imagine being used in the street. The old man accosted by a stranger will not hear himself addressed as "Mr. Senior Citizen." From some he will hear "Sir"; from most others "Mister"; from the rest "Pop."

sentence, the. 1. Attempts to define the sentence, from the school formula *complete thought expressed in words* to the intricate elaborations of the semanticist, boil down to the assertion that a sentence has to be *about* something. Hence in framing a sentence the first move is to set up a subject, and to do it overtly, unmistakably, and promptly. This may sound too obvious to need stating; but a little investigation of actual sentences in print will show that their framers are often coy about revealing their intentions and excessively inventive of ways to hide or mask the subjects of their discourse. One would naturally expect a writer to make his first care the lighting up of his subject so as to insure that the wayfaring reader will not easily miss it; but in practice many a writer hides his light under a bushel.

Reasonable persons must, of course, make reasonable allowance for the sentence aiming at special effects, where the reader is deliberately kept guessing for the sake of a delayed surprise; and also for the sentence in which the requirements of variety or rhythm distort the natural order of parts; for the sentence composed under the license granted to poets; for the sentence in which the full meaning emerges only at the close, as the tumblers of a complicated lock fall into line with the last twist of a dial. But after every allowance is made, it is still a principle of lucid writing that sentences are the better for naming their subjects at the outset.

Restated in negative form, this principle comes close to summing up the secret of good writing: No one should ever be called on to read a sentence twice because of the way it is constructed. We may like to read a sentence twice or twenty times because its contents are profound, subtle, suggestive, and challenging. A man may have singing in his head for decades such a sentence as Joseph Conrad's definition of the novel, without ever needing to see it again. (". . . what is a novel if not a conviction of our fellow men's existence strong enough to take upon itself a form of imagined life

clearer than reality?") But the writer who keeps making us retrace because of the way his sentences are put together is foisting on his reader his own proper work. To do so is laziness; and whatever it may be deemed elsewhere, laziness in a writer is the gravest sin.

An important book review begins: *Nearly a century after his death, having evoked a personal literature numerically unsurpassed and of unparalleled intensity* ... After seventeen words you still do not know who or what is being talked about. The least the author could do, you think, is to end this guessing contest by naming his subject; but his perversity goes on: *the image of Abraham Lincoln* ... And there, at last, is your subject, not even dignified with a subjective case, but smuggled in as the object of a preposition. Since it was Lincoln that died nearly a century ago, and not Lincoln's image, the grammatical subject is a misnomer that leaves the long opening completely adrift. The first half of the sentence unmistakably implies one subject, Lincoln; the second half switches to a quite different subject, Lincoln's image, under the lax impression that it is the same. Then it concludes: *except to the prejudiced or the uninformed, remains, in many of its conspicuous features, indistinct.* To write so is first to baffle, then to irritate, and finally to madden. The one clear point is that the sentence ought to begin *Abraham Lincoln.* The initial flapping modifiers could have been taken in tow, with some such result as this: *Abraham Lincoln, despite his having evoked a personal literature numerically unsurpassed* (an awkward phrase; see PERSONAL) *and of unparalleled intensity, remains, nearly a century after his death, except to the prejudiced or the uninformed, an indistinct image in many of his conspicuous features.* It is not a good sentence—the original does not provide the makings of one—but it has at least the negative merit of not mystifying anyone about its who and what.

2. The chief agent of perversity in this example is the use of the pronoun before its antecedent. That device—or vice, rather—probably outnumbers all the other ways of fuddling readers about the subjects of sentences. Let us inspect a few typical examples. Here is the beginning of a news dispatch: *An aerial camera was fastened in its nose, four or five big tin cans equipped with white parachutes and firecrackers were loaded into its cabin, and the red-and-white twin-engined aircraft raced down the uneven, short runway, took off and roared low toward the north.* A good editor, even in a drowse, will make this sentence begin: *The red-and-white twin-engined aircraft, with an aerial camera . . . and four or five big tin cans . . . , raced . . .* Other illustrations, with parenthetical suggestions, follow: *For roughly thirteen years, or ever since the publication in this country of his first work, a book of short stories called "Fireman .Flower," William Sansom has undergone the peculiarly grating experience . . .* (William Sansom's first work . . . was published in this country thirteen years ago, and ever since, its author has undergone) / *As a result, for the first time in her six-year-old career as queen of the American passenger fleet, the 53,239-ton liner* United States *failed yesterday to make a scheduled Atlantic sailing* (Consequently the . . . United States, for the first time . . . , failed yesterday) / *With their restatements this week of the Far East policy of the United States, the President and Secretary of State Dulles have outlined a position* (The President and Secretary of State Dulles, in their restatements this week) / *By calling off their battle against television and taking giant steps to diversify into videoland, the movie companies have finally found a way* (The movie companies, by) / *The suspension of passenger car production at its assembly plant here was announced by Ford* (Ford announced today the suspension) / *during the early summer when, after*

SENTENCE, THE 3 • 363

reaching its low point of last April, business activity . . . turned abruptly around and headed upward (when business activity, reaching . . . , turned) / *The Ultra-royalists, though kept out of his government by Louis XVIII, were in all other respects masters of the field* (The Ultra-royalists, though Louis XVIII kept them out of his government).

Here is a sentence that is as opaque as if artfully planned to be so: *The preparations for the queen's marriage were going forward, and the emperor was turning over in his mind the desirability, since he could not have her put to death, of removing the heiress to the throne from her country before his son's arrival.* The emperor is Charles V of Spain; his son is Philip, later Philip II; the Queen is Mary I of England; and *her* and *the heiress to the throne* are identical, both meaning the queen-to-be, Elizabeth. Interchanging the two expressions would spare the reader some needless floundering. A pronoun is by nature a word anchored to something already identified, not to something that awaits identification. Its function is to avoid repetition, not to contrive suspense or pose a conundrum. (See ANTECEDENTS.)

3. A reader is entitled to know not only what is being talked about, but also what is being said about it. That is, a sentence does not become one

except by virtue of possessing (or clearly implying) (a) a subject and (b) a predication, or statement about the subject. Lacking either, it is only a part masquerading as a whole —a phrase or clause cut loose, a sentence either orphaned or struggling to be born. Such fragments are frequent in the essays of student writers, as every teacher of composition knows; but they are not confined to the untrained. Many writers entertain the belief that a nonsentence is preferable to a long sentence; the headless or tailless effort is thought to give zest to popular fiction, journalism, and even reference books. For example, here is a subject without predicate: *Among them International Business Machines and United States Steel.* What precedes is *During yesterday's trading some well known stocks set record highs.* Here is predication without a subject: *But also is an influential man with the ladies.* What precedes is *He dresses like a dude and sometimes subdues his opponents with a walking stick.* The following examples show ostensible sentences similarly crippled by lack of essential elements:

Kodak has since given birth to such trademarks as Kodachrome, Kodacolor, Kodaslide and Kodascope. All because Mr. Eastman was enamored with (of) *"K."* (—all because Mr. Eastman) / *He . . . quite frankly says his authorship of* [book title] *did him no harm. In fact, did much good* (no harm; in fact, did) / *We can only pray that responsible leadership will reassert itself in the South. And that the Southern States . . . will find their own solution within the meaning of the court's decision* (will reassert itself . . . and that the Southern States). A bank that has established two main offices in one city proclaims: *Meanwhile we plan to smile as patiently as we can at jokes about people with two heads. Sustained by the knowledge that this is a case where two "heads" are better than one* (Meanwhile, sustained by the knowledge . . . , we plan).

It is possible to object by asking: "Why make an issue of the formal completeness of a sentence that manages to get its contents understood?" One answer is that the maimed sentence is often an acceptable part of a longer construction that requires a subtler punctuation. But the chief reason is that the writing of prose is a public act subject to rules that range from good manners to artistic standards. At a lecture or in the library we take notes in strings of detached phrases, and with luck we can later interpret the bits and pieces correctly. But we should not print the result as prose, nor is the prevailing form of newspaper headlines a criterion of what prose should be. Ana-

logies are not proofs, but it is suggestive to remark that a good bricklayer throws out defective bricks on sight. The sentence is the smallest unit of composition that has an independently complete structure, and a confusion of a part with the whole is usually a sign of the fumbling mind, which soon shows its disorganization in other particulars as well.

There are, of course, admissible and even admirable sentences devoid of main verbs. With them the foregoing observations have nothing to do. The good verbless sentence, unlike the grammatical shards just exhibited, is not a part of anything else; it stands alone; and it affirms whatever is omitted with even higher force than if the absent were present. Ernest Legouvé, when asked how a play is made, replied: "By beginning at the end." The answer is more telling than "A play is made by beginning at the end." Eckermann wanted Goethe to tell him how the moral element came into the world. Goethe answered: "Through God himself, like everything else which is good." No one would take away from the writer of fiction his right to describe or narrate in clipped sentences: *A quick look astern at the carrier / And then that final word, the word they have been leading up to, the word they have all studiously avoided pronouncing until now. "Fire!" / Over the deserted plaza, a blaze of sunshine.* Probably the most that we are entitled to demand is that the sentence without main verb be saved for special effects. As a mannerism or habit it only induces gasping, and by claiming a false importance for the commonplace it ends by making mere attendant circumstance so emphatic that no means is left to raise the pitch for great crises.

4. Rhetorical unity in prose is equally destroyed by the opposite of fragmentation— namely, the presence of two or more wholes pretending to be one. Examples from sources of some dignity and prestige follow: *Posthumous examination of her teeth gave away her youth, she was less than a year old / Often the sketchy quality of joined lines in space makes for a static illusion, a line drawing cannot work in all four directions at once / There were times when P. felt a special quality in himself, a strange unpleasant quality that seemed to force everyone he touched into making drastic decisions about their own lives, no wonder people did not like to be around him / pull out the jar rubber with a pair of pliers, then there is no danger of injuring either the lid or the jar.* Because the sign of this piling up is the presence of a comma between independent clauses unconnected by a conjunction, this error is called the comma fault or comma splice. These labels serve as a pedagogical device for the young, but as a description of what is wrong they contain elements of fallacy: (a) the trouble is more than one of punctuation, the comma being only a symptom of the failure to grasp the relation between clauses; (b) the implied corrective of the comma splice takes in altogether too much territory. It suggests that independent clauses not joined by a conjunction need more than a comma to separate them. This rule encourages the semicolon as a panacea. Many teachers would recommend it in each of the foregoing examples, and it is indeed possible in each; but what is really needed is a sharpened awareness of the true relation between clauses, which may be marked by a semicolon, a colon, a dash, a new sentence, a sentence in parentheses, or an expressive conjunction to be supplied.

Moreover, independent clauses separated by a comma are often desirable and not to be improved upon, especially when the second clause is to be understood as looping back to catch up and carry forward the sense of the first. Caesar's well-known dispatch *Veni, vidi, vici,* commonly rendered *I came, I saw, I conquered,* is to be understood as something more than an a, b, c series of equal members. It makes use of what in a ballad would be called incremental repetition;

we feel it as a condensed and witty version of *I not only came but also saw, and I not only saw but also conquered.* There is an extreme of pedantry that would insist on *I came; I saw; I conquered,* but these semicolons would neutralize the cumulative force that each clause gains from its predecessor. They would do the same in many modern examples: *Conventions may be cruel, they may be unsuitable, they may even be grossly superstitious or obscene / Life is the higher call, life we must follow / This is not due merely to the daring splendour of the speculations and the vivid picture of Athenian life, it is due also to something analogous in the personalities of that particular ancient Greek and this particular modern Irishman.* In each of these, the comma bids us turn back and gather up what precedes, very much like a *not only . . . but also* construction. Such an effect would be vitiated by the semicolon or other divisive substitute. The distinction between desirable and deplorable commas of this class is often subtle and paperthin. *He composed this symphony in 1885, it was never performed until after his death* is illiterate. *This was not only his first concerto, it was his best* is neither illiterate nor colloquial: it is swift and emphatic. The difference is definable, yet difficult to define for those writers who most need the def-inition. Whoever finds it hard to perceive the difference between the comma fault and the legitimate splicing by commas will do well to avoid the second form and seek safety through semicolons, conjunctions, or separate sentences.

5. Another trespass against the unity of the sentence, probably more common than either fragmentation or agglutination, occurs when the sentence is made a catchall for statements either lacking in logical connection or so expressed as to disguise the connection. Consider an example of total irrelevance: *Unlike the Nazi swastika, the true swastika moves from right to left, and there is hardly any place in the world where it has not been found.* Whether the swastika moves from right to left or from left to right has no connection with its universality; one can only ask: What are these facts doing in the same sentence? Similarly incoherent is *Nelson A. Rockefeller is to be inaugurated as* (see AS 9) *Governor of New York on Thursday and will immediately face several difficult problems.* Obituary notices are peculiarly liable to this smuggling in of irrelevancy, as a way of saving space: *Mr. G., who was born in St. Paul, Minn., entered the steamship business after six years with the United States Shipping Board in Washington / Mr. M., who attended Columbia College, is survived by a* *son, D., of Concord, Mass., and by his brother, G., the playwright.*

This gorged-snake type of sentence has become virtually standard in news about forthcoming publications: *To be called "The Valadon Drama," it will be brought out in the spring by . . . / To be published Oct. 20 by X., the book is the result of seven years of research and interviewing of old timers | Illustrated by A., the volume contains . . . sketches wherein Miss S. gibes at the idiosyncrasies* (oddities?) *of life.* With less excuse, some writers act as if any attendant circumstances could be slipped into a sentence by mere grammatical subordination. The general form (and ridiculous effect) might be termed "fraudulent unity," of which the following are only slightly exaggerated examples: *An avid reader of detective stories, he married his secretary in 1938 / A firm believer in metempsychosis, he has made a hobby of collecting water colors.*

The sentence that has an actual unity of substance nullified by its form will sound not so much ridiculous as naïve: *One could stand in front of Willard's Hotel and sooner or later nearly every soldier in the Union Army would pass by* (One standing . . . would sooner or later see . . . pass by). Forgetfulness often makes a writer begin with one subject and finish with a predicate that

belongs to another, generally the object of some intervening preposition: *A visit in summer to such a bird colony with its variegated vegetation is a marvel of beauty* (Visited in summer, such a bird colony) / *The brilliance of her entourage at her home in exile, the Château of Coppet, was called by Stendhal "the Grand Assizes of European opinion"* (Her brilliant entourage . . . was called). Sometimes the predication is about a subject not present at all and perhaps even contradicted by the actual subject: *Few, if any of us, know what we're looking for and so are likely to browse on the Lord knows what* (and therefore many of us browse).

It is, in fact, all too easy to cobble a sentence together on two incompatible lasts. *The reason is a simple supply-demand relationship: fewer investors are interested in Southern school "names" than there once were.* The second clause is a baffling mixture of *There were formerly more investors interested* and *Fewer investors are now interested;* either will serve, but both are wrecked when combined. *Inevitably in a book written so casually, much of it dictated only as a means of self-amusement, its parts are not equally good.* The phrase *in a book* leads off at a tangent from the conclusion; a possible repair: *It is inevitable that in a book written so casually . . . some parts should be better than others.* Even a novelist whose style is reputed a model of precision and grace can slip into the confusion of this sentence: *Every time he had ever seen her, there had never been the repetitions that threw most human relationships into lines of boredom.* Here the clash is between *Every time he had seen her* and *never.* The meaning is *Whenever he had seen her there had been none of the repetitions.*

6. Some of the foregoing examples skirt the pit of ambiguity without quite falling into it. When a sentence does fall in, the cause usually is either a neglect of the principle that negative meanings should not be stated in an affirmative form (see NEGATIVES, TROUBLE WITH) or else the omission of words essential to the intended meaning. A simple instance of the first difficulty is the sentence *The Warsaw negotiations can come to nothing,* which means equally (a) that the negotiations cannot possibly come to anything and (b) that they may conceivably fail to come to anything. It is deducible from the context that the intended meaning is *The Warsaw negotiations cannot come to anything,* but the reader is entitled to hold any tenable view of what the author has said and to be spared work in reaching that view. The same ambiguity keeps recurring for the same reason when *all . . . are not* is substituted for *not*

all . . . are, as in *All men are not so amenable.*

A further cause of ambiguity, the omission of needed words, appears in such sentences as *The truth is that commercialism is not per se the enemy of intellect, but something much deeper.* Is commercialism something much deeper than the enemy of intellect, or is the enemy of intellect something much deeper than commercialism? The sentence cannot tell you without an addition. The first meaning would be covered by *but is something much deeper;* the second by *not per se the enemy of intellect; its enemy is something much deeper.*

7. The question of the order of parts must always be present to the writer's mind. Yet many authors seem not to have heard that it is expedient to put modifiers somewhere within hail of what they modify. *Mrs. Dwight D. Eisenhower will visit the school where she attended kindergarten during the Oct. 17 appearance of President Eisenhower at the national corn-picking contest near here.* Begin: *During the Oct. 17 appearance.* A protest to city authorities reads: *The Department of Welfare persists in placing persons in these buildings that are not fit for human habitation at outrageously high rentals*—suggesting that the buildings would be fit for habitation if the rentals were reasonable. *It has not the slight-*

est intention of backing down from the course it believes to be right because of popular opposition / *The camp was divided on the matter of eating into the savers and the nonsavers* / *One wonders if archeologists of the future who excavate artifacts of our civilization will recognize the strange weapon found by almost every campsite for what it is—a can opener* (change *by* to *near* and omit *for what it is*) / *Bolex points to a week-long demonstration of five of their new movie cameras, including the new 20/20 Compumatic, which has an electric eye behind the taking lens, to be held at Willoughby's through Friday* / *Judas saith unto him, not Iscariot, Lord.* (See also LINKING.)

Such laxities disclose the carelessness of competent writers; there are also writers, incompetent rather than careless, who seem incapable of framing a lucid sentence except by chance. Some of them have a way of devising tangles in which their meaning stands little chance of being seen, and they then try to extricate themselves by complications that would daunt a talented and resourceful writer. Other makers of sentences go in for a vagueness so pervasive that it continues to infect the whole even after one has mended the defective parts. Consider this representative: *Just as on the national level some powerful farm organizations bitterly—and usually successfully—resist any Federal regulation that affects them (except increased subsidies, of course), so too on the state level is the farm worker left unprotected.* The minor faults here include the JARGON word LEVEL, the piling up of *-ly* adverbs, and the violent inversion in the last clause. But these do not touch the main trouble, which is that although the whole is meant to be about the hard lot of migratory farm workers, most of the sentence ignores them in order to explain the position of their hostile employers. Such a sentence cannot be made to cohere by any means short of getting it born again. Extricated, the thought runs something like this: *There are Federal regulations to protect farm workers, but farm organizations bitterly resist or evade, often with success, all national provisions except those for increased subsidies; and the states give farm workers hardly any legal protection.* Enough of the original is left to produce constraint and discomfort, but at least the revised sentence is on instead of off its subject.

8. Consider finally, in one representative specimen each, three different types of malformation that combine problems of structure with problems of style to such a degree that it is hard to disentangle them. The first type is what may be called the gasper—the sentence that begins with so exces-

sive a subordination, carried through so many modifiers, that when a predicate finally turns up, one has forgotten the point and one has no strength to go on. *As the quarrel over whether the country's "missile deterrent" strength is sufficient now and for the foreseeable future in relation to the Soviet Union continues to embroil members of Congress and high military strategists in angry contradictions, the findings made here in the field by the technicians become increasingly critical.* The crevasse between *quarrel* and *continues* is a ditch so broad that it takes two jumps to get across it. The sentence needs breaking up: *Is the country's missile deterrent strength sufficient now and for the foreseeable future in relation to the Soviet Union? This question continues to embroil members of Congress and high military strategists in angry contradictions. Therefore the findings made here in the field by the technicians become increasingly important.* You get three sentences for one; but the three are together a little shorter than the one, and they do not leave you breathless.

The second example is of sentences that seem to consist almost entirely of packaging—wrappings and insulations of verbiage that have to be undone phrase by phrase if you are to come at the relatively small and simple core of meaning within. *The influence exerted by Christianity upon the arts extends to painting and sculpture in so far as their relationship to Christian religious experiences corresponds to that part of this experience which consists of images; and it extends to architecture, both with regard to edifices dedicated to worship and to the settlement of religious communities.* Whoever struggles with this farrago must rely heavily on guesswork, for a mind that uses such indirections is not readily penetrated. Admitting the possibility of being way off the mark, let us ask: Does the copious accumulation of excelsior and cotton batting cover a purport such as this? *Christianity affects painting and sculpture, because much Christian religious experience is expressible in images; and it affects architecture in the form of cathedrals, churches, and chapels, and of monasteries, convents, and abbeys.*

Our third and last sentence is one of those that, after the promise of a closing member that will raise the pitch to exaltation, break that promise and fall into anticlimax and bathos. *For most of the year the man whom many regard as the most distinguished writer of his generation lives, not in his Moscow apartment, not in the active, kaleidoscopic world of Soviet intellectual life, or within the frenzied orbit of international commerce in liter-*

ary styles and trends, but in a quiet two-story wooden house. After *styles and trends* there is nowhere for this sentence to go but up to the summit of the steady ascent already pursued to that point. Any sentence of the *not this, not that, but the other* mold is irrevocably committed to a climax: *This is the word of the Lord unto Zerubbabel, saying, Not by might, nor by power, but by my Spirit, saith the Lord of hosts.* For the last member of the sentence about Pasternak you expect at the very least *but in the impregnable tower of his own integrity* or something of the sort. All you get instead is a two-story wooden house, which is surely the most confining terminus in critical writing.

See also PROSE, THE SOUND OF.

separate. See PREPOSITIONS.

sequence of tenses. 1. In English as in other modern European languages, much latitude is now given the writer to express his thought by coupling tenses according to logic rather than convention. Except in a few situations to be discussed, the true relations between one time and another can be expressed by the tense —present, past, or future— which is marked out for the purpose by its name. Thus the statement of an immediate reality or a universal truth can take the present tense even though the statement reporting that truth in indirect discourse starts with a past tense. *He argued that the song could not have been composed in that year, because the manuscript is extant and can be examined for internal evidence of the date.* Here the time of the argument (last night's lecture = past) is not allowed to affect, as it once would have done, the time predicated for the existence of the manuscript (= is, now and for an indefinite time).

But the acceptance of this present-of-actuality in sequences where traditionally the past tense had to be sustained must not be extended to cover situations in which the actual times demand two identical pasts or a past before a past. An instructive confusion resulted from the neglect of the second of these requirements when, in a report of De Gaulle's news conference, the General was quoted as saying that *the United States overcame its great depression and then, after the Second World War, ruined the currencies of Western Europe by unleashing inflation upon them, it was only natural,* etc. The correction soon came over the wires, requesting that the comma after *Second World War* be deleted so as to permit the reading *after the Second World War ruined the currencies,* etc. What went unnoticed is that a proper sequence of tenses would have made the comma disclose its own intrusion: *and then, after the Second World War had ruined the currencies.* For no simple past can precede another past if an *after* is interposed. The *after* dictates a sequence embodying an earlier and a later past. The earlier is in the pluperfect, the later is in the simple past. If one begins this sequence backwards, by putting the *after* ahead of the simple past, or the other way around, the relation must be kept clear by the distribution of the two tenses. The normal order is *I was . . . after I had been;* not *I was . . . after I was.*

But there are occasions when the times do not differ in the main clause and in the subordinate, and the past must occur in both. *These two, small as they were, felt they were rejected because their mother was.* This pattern is common in narrative. It will not admit of *because their mother is* or any seesawing of tenses in the first pair of verbs, *were* and *felt;* and if it read *because their mother had been* the implication would be given that the mother had been cast out, divorced, displaced, at some point earlier than the children's awareness of their rejection. A young woman who refused a judge's offer of probation was reported, no doubt correctly, as having said: *It would be the height of dishonesty if I accept.* Her present

choice was too vivid for good grammar. The *it would be* is a past in the conditional mood and it requires *if I accepted,* a past subjunctive. Her other (grammatical) option was to say: *It will be the height . . . if I accept.* But the meaning would then be that she had not made up her mind to refuse. Again: *My sealed bid is $24.03, but maybe by the time you open the bids I have earned a little more* logically requires *will have earned,* for *by the time* clearly means *in the future* and *I have* just as clearly *the past.*

2. The past is not invariably used in narrative, even when it relates past events. The historical present may break in for vividness, but again see-sawing disturbs the easy flow. Moreover, the present may express a permanent truth or state of fact in the midst of a recital all in the past, and then it is made more assimilable by an occasional perfect tense. For example, one may write *I am ready to go after I eat my breakfast* or *I am ready to go after I have eaten my breakfast;* and in strict past-tense storytelling, *I was ready to go after I had eaten my breakfast.* If one needs to push the time relations farther back, one must have recourse to a participial phrase which adapts itself to the tense of the main verb: *I had been ready to go, having eaten my breakfast.*

When a writer commits himself to one form of the past in a sentence he must adhere to it; this has not been done in *Surely the faucets must have leaked once in a while, or the refrigerator went out of order, or the drains stopped up, so that the handyman would be called to the apartment.* The *must have leaked* suggests the false parallel *must have (went)* and requires *would have been called to the apartment.* This is probably no more than a slip. It occurs, for some reason, much more frequently and deliberately with *may: It was occupied now by a Mr. and Mrs. Schneider, who'd been particularly annoyed because the detectives seemed to think they may have found some papers that Brown left behind that might be a clue.* Why the author of a well-jointed sentence wrote *may* after *had been* and followed it with *might be* is something of a puzzle. Usually it is in speech and cruder prose that we find *He went expecting they may hire him.* The relation of past to past, past to present, and past to present-meaning-future may well have become too subtle for accurate analysis while one is speaking. Once the old cast-iron sequence of tenses was broken up to permit the vivid present, a wider breakdown was inevitable. But writers of good fiction ought to persist in observing what will faithfully render their intuitions of the human mind. For

instance, despite any compelling rule, the following dialogue would keep the characters more exactly in their roles —the man anticipating the woman's feelings in a protective way—if the next-to-last verb were a pluperfect: *She nodded. "It certainly did," she said, and launched into the narrative. The telling of it, as he expected* (had expected), *steadied her.*

In relating past or present to future it is important to remember that in English the present can be used with a future meaning, and it therefore does not authorize any tampering with the normal parallelism in statements that merely resemble those in which the present has the import of a future. To say *If you go, I go* is the same as to say *If you will go, I will go,* and the two forms may be mixed without alteration of the future sense in both parts of the sentence *If you go* (present = future), *I will go* (literal future). Now, a common error is to ascribe that present feeling to a past time and to write *I went thinking that you will follow* (= my thought was then "he [she] will follow"). Usage does not permit this transfer and the only educated phrasing is *I went thinking that you would follow* (= my thought was then "he [she] will follow").

3. With an anterior (pluperfect) past, the error to guard against is putting both verbs on the same plane of pastness, so to speak, for this kills the idea of future action which is all-important. If you write *I had gone, thinking that you would follow*, it is clear that the past thought looked to the other person's following-in-the-future. But write instead *I had gone, thinking that you would have followed* and you put the speaker in the place of one who knows what did happen—for example: *I had gone and you would have followed if I had not sent you that puzzling message.* In the desirable phrasing the participle *thinking* is what determines the time and the tense: "I was *thinking* (then) that you *would follow* (later)."

This set of relations, once grasped, is easier to remember and express than it is to analyze on paper; and professional writers of news and fiction work it out for themselves in practice. But conversation and letter-writing so often lead to confusions and bad verbal habits that the analysis is worth the trouble. A friend tells another of a pleasant excursion, picnic, or fishing trip which that other was not there to join. The absent guest probably says simply *I wish I had gone*, and all is well. But if he is in any way prodded by his friend and made to regret his absence, he may say: *I'm sure I'd want to have gone;* or *You know I'd have wanted to go;* or *of course I'd have wanted to have gone.*

All these *would have*'s are the consequence of an unspoken *if . . . circumstances had been different.* Only one of the three expressions correctly conveys the time relationships: *I (woul)'d have wanted to go;* that is, *had I been here, I would have wanted*—what? *To go;* not: *to have gone*, which has the effect of putting the excursion earlier than the wanting to go on it. As to the first of the three, it errs by replacing the pastness of the plans with an untoward future: *Had I been here I'd want* is a break in the sequence *Being here I want . . . ; Were I here, I'd want . . . ; Had I been here, I'd have wanted . . .*

Is there then a use for the too-often heard *to have gone?* There is: it should be reserved for that rather rare occasion in which one looks fore and aft. Any ordinary expression of regret about a lost opportunity should end *to go, to see, to meet, to dine.* But any forecast of future feeling, or any thought in the past about a still earlier past, will require the following expression: *You don't want to go to this party (now), but (some day) I'm sure you will want to have gone* (= in the future your feeling will be: "I wish I had gone"; I will want *to have gone*). This may be more simply said *you will wish you had gone*, yet there is a shade of impersonality and finality about this less usual phrasing. The usual form is the simple future with the perfect participle. Another, still more complex occasion calls for the doubling of the perfect tenses: *If events had not turned out as they did, you would have wanted to have seen him first and spoken your piece.* This means, in context, that except for luck, *it would have been natural, at that time past, that you should deplore not having got to see him first* —but all came out well just the same. The point is not the luck, but the feeling at a time past about a time before that. This sequence never applies to the common occasion, *I'd have liked to go.*

4. Note in conclusion a vulgar error with the form of the perfect *would have.* The *would* is commonly contracted to *I'd.* This is also the contraction for *I had.* Hence colloquial speech uses *If I'd hit him, I'd have killed him,* in which the first *I'd = I had* and the second *= I would.* But the two tenses are not interchangeable merely because they share a contraction. It is therefore an illiteracy to say *If I would have hit him I would have killed him.* No *would have*'s can succeed each other in that fashion; the only *If I would have* that is possible is one that is followed by a direct object—*him, the house, this desk;* which is to say, it is an emphatic and self-contained locution and not the auxiliary *have* with a verb to come. All other meanings require *If I*

had (*hit him, married him,* etc.) *I would have . . .*

See also SINCE, YET.

set phrases. 1. Uses. 2. Inviolability.

1. Uses. Despite the indiscriminate condemnation of clichés that has become fashionable in the last twenty-five years, a great many set phrases are indispensable both for easy conversation and for effective writing. Such phrases offer as their main advantages brevity, clarity, and unobtrusiveness. To try, for example, to explain in fresh and deliberate words the ideas conveyed by *wear and tear* is simply to affect originality where it is not wanted and to draw attention in the sentence to a part of it that should properly stay neutral and vague.

2. Inviolability. Accordingly, the attempt to liven up old clichés by inserting modifiers into the set phrase is a mistake; the distended phrase is neither original, nor unobtrusive, nor brief, and sometimes it has ceased to be immediately clear, as in *They have been reticent to a tactical fault.* What purpose, except showing off, is served by inflating the familiar phrase into *steady wear and accidental tear?* These are precisely the ideas embodied in *wear and tear* by itself. For these various reasons, leave *at its best* alone; it is not improved or made more telling by the advertiser's

at its tastiest best or by the ironist's *We saw him at his unexpected best.* Again, if a narrator thinks in ready-made images, he will not conceal his lack of invention by redundant filler, as in *like a dog wagging an obviously gratified tail.* The egotism of this stretching and pulling is perhaps best seen in a recent example of would-be lively prose: *He would have none of their suggestions and innovations. The status, he announced, was to be strictly quo.*

The writer who feels no need for trumpery ornaments, and who rightly values the modesty of the set phrase, will accordingly strip off, in his own writing, the modern additions he is daily exposed to, from a Supreme Court judge's *at his (very good) best* to the journalist's *does not mince (many) words.* He will write: *second by second,* not *second by leaping second; a quid pro quo,* not *a dubious quid for a nonexistent quo; turn about is fair play,* not *a slow turn about is hardly fair play;* and so on. The possibilities of distention and distortion in this genre are infinite, and infinite also the boredom engendered.

See also CAKE; HARD PUT; FRENCH WORDS AND PHRASES; SPIRIT OF ADVENTURE.

sex, noun and verb. Writers of fiction and of "frank" marriage manuals are hard put to it to find simple unscientific terms to denote the physical act of love and its attendant organs. (See FORBIDDEN WORDS 1.) The search for words that are not either euphemistic or clinical has evidently led to the misuse of sex in two senses.

With sex as a noun the verbal phrase *have sex* has been devised to mean *have sexual intercourse. Whenever he came to town they would have sex, though it no longer mattered much to either of them / In college, for instance, the big question is not "to be or not to be," but "to have or not to have" and the omitted word is "sex."* Strictly speaking, every creature that is male or female *has sex* in the sense of possessing distinctive sexual characteristics. In the same sense one would define a hermaphrodite as having not one but *two sexes* at once or *both sexes combined. Sex,* moreover, has a distributive sense that denotes all of one or the other sexes—*the fair sex, the weaker sex,* or simply *the sex* (old-fashioned).

It should seem, therefore, as if novelists could find some other phrase for their purpose than the one under discussion, which distorts the word *sex* into naming not even an activity but only an act, when what it properly denotes is an organic difference, or else the group characterized by it. (The usage found in the autobiography of Frank Harris and by which sex means the sexual organs is a gallicism to be repressed). *Sex* is properly *that which divides* half a population, human or animal, from the other. Hence there is something trivial in a locution that uses the word in parallel with *have food, have fun* and like them suggests an acquisition independent of the self.

A cognate transformation has begun to affect the verb *to sex,* hitherto used only by farmers and biologists to mean *determine the sex of an animal;* it is now also pressed into service for *having sexual intercourse.* This usage is common among the advocates of promiscuity on principle, and its form does reinforce the idea of an inconsequential act. But at the same time it destroys the idea rooted in the word and restated above. The result of thus changing both noun and verb may be to change the applicability of *unsexed.* Instead of denoting a person rendered neuter or whose sexuality has been altered by mutilation physical or emotional, it may come to describe an evening or an encounter in which *no sex* (ual act) *took place.* It will then be difficult to interpret the words *She was the glory of her sex.*

See also GENTEELISM.

shall. See APPENDIX 1: SHALL (SHOULD), WILL (WOULD), pp. 455-479.

shambles. See DEFENSIBLES.

sheet. See DEVIL TO PAY.

-ship, suffix. See TRANSITIVE, INTRANSITIVE.

shortenings. ABBREVIATIONS are recognized ways of symbolizing very common words in fewer letters than they are entitled to: *Mr., Hon., Advt., M.P.* are abbreviations. Shortenings differ from these in being possibly current but not yet part of conventional usage. This being so, they always carry a tone of vulgarity or impertinence, and if they are applied to persons they are resented by those whom they mean to designate. Among the vulgar ones are *glads* for *gladioli, mums* for *chrysanthemums, nympho* for *nymphomaniac, psycho* for *psychological* (or more exactly *psychiatric) case* or *patient,* etc. The curtailed titles *Doc* and *Prof* can only be uttered as a sort of joke between intimate friends; and the supposedly collegiate words *grad, undergrad,* and *frat* (ernity) are chiefly in favor with makers of movies and other strangers to campus life.

A different reason explains the sometimes uncouth curtailing of words and idioms in newspaper headlines. Phrases like *slay suspect* (= slayer) and *Sooner Quota Set* are an offense against plain language. So are some half words. *'Copter* for *helicopter* is rapidly becoming *copter* without the apostrophe and descending into the text below. It is to be hoped that this will not happen to other words that exceed the column width. *'Bama Politics* (for *Alabama*) is but a step away from baby talk.

See also PROF.

should. See APPENDIX 1: SHALL (SHOULD), WILL (WOULD), pp. 455-479.

shuttle back and forth. Most of the persons who have not seen a shuttle in operation will at least know shuttle trains. They, like the weaver's shuttle, go back and forth. This knowledge does not deter many of us from writing four words for one. The sin is venial and its commission may be caused by the lack of a set preposition after *shuttle*, which is felt as weak or inconclusive. But whether one gives up or retains *back and forth* in speech, a reminder of its redundancy may help lighten a written sentence here and there.

significant. See MEANING-FUL.

since, yet. 1. There is a groundless notion current both in the lower schools and in the world of affairs that *since* has an exclusive reference to time and therefore cannot be used as a casual conjunction. On that view it was a grievous error to write: *Since you are prejudiced, I cannot argue with you / Since you're dying for a vacation, why don't you borrow the money?* No warrant exists for avoiding this usage, which goes back, beyond Chaucer, to Anglo-Saxon: *siththan, sithence, sins, since* meant literally *after that* and soon generated the figurative meaning of *given that* = because.

Again, in the temporal meaning there is no ground for prohibiting *since* in the place where *ago* is usual. *How long ago was it? Oh, many years since.* Walter Scott, whose command of idiomatic English equalled his grasp of Scots dialect, gave his first novel, *Waverley* (1814), the subtitle *'Tis Sixty Years Since.* Observe the necessary change of tense: Scott would have had to write *'Twas Sixty Years Ago.*

2. Instead of these imaginary niceties, it would be better to adhere to the logical usage which calls for the perfect tense in the main clause to denote what has happened *since* the event named: *I haven't seen him since he left town, and I didn't see him . . .* The logic referred to consists in the perception that the period of time referred to is continuous, being bounded at one end by *since* and stretching to the moment when the speaker makes the statement. He thus sees the whole as a single connected action, which calls for a tense with the aux-

iliary *have.* A simple past tense carries no such intimation: *During all those years I didn't see him, but now we meet regularly.* Try to substitute *During all those years I haven't seen him, but now we meet regularly,* and the force of the perfect (completed) tense will appear from the absurdity of its employment to denote a mere past. Contrast again: *I looked everywhere for my watch but I didn't find it* and *I've been looking everywhere . . . and I haven't found it. Since I was a boy things changed* is impossible: *have changed* imposes itself on the deafest ear. One says to the waitress *I've finished,* not *I finished.* And what is true of these short commonplaces is true of longer, less automatic utterances.

3. The last examples remind us that temporal *since* has, on this point of tense, an exact counterpart in temporal *yet.* It, too, calls for the perfect tense with the negative: a short set phrase supplies the model *I haven't given up yet.* To say *It's been recommended as a good play but I didn't go yet* shows the influence of foreign tongues regrettably distorting English. Like *since, yet* unrolls a strip of time up to the very spot where the speaker is standing, and everything along its course is regarded as forming one with the present and the future that is implied: *I haven't gone yet (but I will go).* The true past, once again, is indefinite and its events are isolated. Compare *He didn't serve his country in either war or between the wars* with *He is still healthy and active but he hasn't served his country yet / Since he lost his mind he hasn't been as entertaining as before.*

Of course, this temporal *since* (and *yet*), which require a perfect tense in the main clause, are not to be confused with the causal *since* discussed under 1. *Since* meaning *because* is treated like *because* and takes present and past tenses without the limitations of temporal *since. Since the Pope was also a secular ruler like any king, he was continually embroiled in Italian politics / Since he gambled and lost he must pay.*

See also AGO, BEFORE.

singlehandedly, etc. Dictionaries that concede the word *underhand* a status as both adjective and adverb, thereby making it possible for writers to dodge the *-ly* of *underhandedly,* record *singlehanded* as an adjective only and for the adverb require *singlehandedly.* It is conceivable that here lexicography misses the mark. It could be shown, if the point were worth the labor, that a great many able writers today use *singlehanded* as an adverb, and that it is quite as reputable as *underhand.*

What reduces the importance of the point is that the wall between *singlehanded* as adjective and as adverb is often paper-thin. Suppose that the author who, deferring to his dictionary, writes *Virchow almost singlehandedly succeeded in arranging that all the other demands were met* had written *singlehanded* instead, and suppose that the form without *-ly* were admitted to have adverbial standing. It would then be impossible to be certain whether the author meant an adjective modifying *Virchow* or an adverb modifying *succeeded*. The like observation applies to a sports story in which a quarterback *almost singlehandedly turned a scoreless stalemate into a rout*: only the *-ly* discloses that the writer meant to qualify *turned* and not the quarterback. The intention to modify the verb is clear in each of the following: *It was Wagner who was almost singlehandedly forcing a reluctant administration into a national labor policy / an institution large enough to start a trend singlehandedly.* The first might as easily, and with slight improvement, have been written *Wagner who, almost singlehanded, was forcing*; in the second, the coupling of singlehandedness with *an institution* seems infelicitous at best, if not contradictory—*singlehanded* being misplaced when not used of a person working alone. In any event, it seems improbable that the writer, if he had chosen, say, *unassisted,* would have written *start a trend unassistedly.* To some ears, at least, every one of the citations would be improved by *singlehanded* in lieu of *singlehandedly,* without any reference at all to whether it should be construed as adjective or as adverb.

If we were to speak with semantic rigor, *singlehandedness*—the fact of operating without help—would invariably be treated as an attribute of the actor, not of the act; that is, the attribution would always have adjectival, not adverbial, force. But that kind of rigor would amount to a denial of the whole identity of English, a language that has its being in transferred attributes; the habit of transfer is, in fact, primarily what makes it a poetic language. We say *He faced these adversities bravely,* aware without thought that the bravery is a property of the man, not of the facing; *a brave act is* poetic shorthand for the act of a person who shows bravery by performing it; and by the same token we can comfortably speak of *a singlehanded endeavor,* although the only singlehandedness at play is that of the one who endeavors. Calling an endeavor singlehanded analyzes into a logical absurdity; but this constant transcendence of logic is the wonderful privilege of our inheritance and what turns the plainest prose of our Monsieur Jourdains into poetry after all.

The practical bearing of these considerations is on a point, not of grammar, but of style. It is a commonplace of theory, reinforced by a pervasive instinct, that -*ly*, our standard adverbial suffix (from Anglo-Saxon *lice*), produces forbidding lapses and soft spots in rhythm unless artfully managed, especially when the -*ly* sound is recurrent. There is a trace of this instinct in the general feeling against making -*ly* adverbs of words that, as adjectives, already end in -*ly*. Such forms as *lonelily, lovelily,* and *lowlily,* are nonexistent for practical purposes, even though they exist theoretically and even though Bliss Carman managed to get out of one of them the haunting line *Lonelily on Arrochar. Likely,* a dependable adjective (*a likely story / a likely prospect,* etc.) and a comfortable enough adverb in such phrases as *very likely,* is incurably awkward in normal adverbial positions: *He will likely think better of this decision / There is likely no traversable route between these peaks.* Probably no one ever tries to resort to *likelily,* which would add a third *lic(e)* to a formation with two already buried in it.

Conversely, we add -*ly* for ridiculous or jocular effects to forms that are already adverbs: *muchly, thusly.* Consciously or not, -*ly* is sensed as enfeebling to prose; it contributes to the sinuosities of style, but enervates its muscle. Two neighboring -*ly*'s seem one too many (*Accordingly, it is widely assumed here*); three are two too much (*Obviously Moscow cannot be happy about this. Equally obviously it is more important . . .*). Again, some technically allowable adverbs are so hideous that no one with half an ear would write them (*acknowledgedly the worst position in the company sector*). With the rough justice of oversimplification it is often decreed that the fewer adverbs writing can get along with, the better it is. What can safely be said is that an adverb without -*ly* should as a rule be preferred to one with -*ly* if the two are equivalent in meaning.

skill(s). Until the educationists laid their hands upon it, *skill* was a generic term that fused the meanings of intelligence and dexterity. A diplomat showed *skill* in his negotiations; *diplomatic skill* was required for their success. The adjectives *skilled* and *skillful* retain the attractive idea that has been battered out of the false plural *skills.* These *skills* are nothing more than *talents, abilities, techniques, methods, ways, rudiments* (= basic skills), which is enough to show that there was no need to destroy the qualitative element in *skill* in order to throw another synonym on the pile.

A curious plural, which is idiomatic but also contrary to logic, is *curtains,* meaning *a sudden end, death.* The image obviously refers to the lowering of the curtain at the end of a play, but that curtain is always singular. When theatrical people say *curtains* they mean the draperies at the back and sides of the stage which sometimes do duty for scenery.

slander. See LIBEL.

smattering. See MALAPROPS.

societal. See ENDINGS 2.

somewhat. See UNDERSTATEMENT.

sooner. See HAD (WOULD) RATHER (SOONER); NO SOONER ... WHEN.

so that. This conjunctive phrase is above reproach when it leads into a descriptive clause or a clause denoting result or purpose: *So teach us to number our days that we may apply our hearts unto wisdom / Arrange the pieces so that they slightly overlap.* In both examples the phrase means *in such a way that.* (The first could be written *Teach us . . . so that,* the second *So arrange the pieces that.*) But the phrase is potentially ambiguous and actually unidiomatic

when it means *to the amount that* and introduces a measurement of quantity or degree, as after *enough* or *sufficiently. The ice is still thin enough so that his powerful head can make a hole from beneath* (thin enough for his head to make; thin enough to let his head make) / *to propel large masses of human artifacts far enough away from our planet so that the gravitational pull of the earth becomes relatively minor* (far enough . . . for the . . . pull to become minor; far enough to render the pull minor) / *But it has changed enough and improved some of the worst features enough so that it is not nearly so intolerable as was Stalin's Russia* (enough to make it not nearly so intolerable).

For *sufficiently . . . that* see THAT, CONJUNCTION 1; see also ADEQUATE.

sour grapes. To make the best use of this and other phrases drawn from the literary tradition, it is necessary to remember the point of the fable, legend, or story. The language does not need *sour grapes* as a synonym for jealousy or envy. The distinctive idea in *sour grapes* is that of envy leading the envious one to belittle publicly the thing he inwardly desires. The fox wanted the grapes; being unable to reach them, he declared them sour and hence not worth having. The defeated candidate, suitor, athlete is not chargeable with the sour-grapes attitude if he is simply a bad loser: he must also declare that the office, the girl, the prize were not worth having. (See also AX TO GRIND.)

speaking. See DANGLERS, ACCEPTABLE.

specific(s). Though generally overlooked, occasions exist when it would be useful to reserve *specific* for its strict use as the adjective of *species* or *kind,* and to contrast it in those contexts with the word for the single item, which is *particular(s).* For example, in the very common phrase *specific cases,* it would frequently help the listener or reader to know whether the cases represented whole species—i.e. were *specific* in the sense of *typical* —or (as is all too likely) were mere *particular* cases, occurring at random and brought together by chance. *Name a specific instance* ought to be a request to name an instance which is capable of standing for a good many others. But usually the demand means no more than *name an instance.* Of course, *instance* should suffice, since it implies a generality, but it is just because instances are often not *good* instances that the force of *specific* should have been kept. So now we are forced to say *a specific instance you consider typical* or *a specific and repre-sentative instance,* which is saying one thing three times over.

The trouble comes from the standard uses of *specify* and *specifications.* The first was doubtless felt to be better than *particularize,* and once this preference was established *specifications* destroyed *particulars* for trade and technical purposes. Of late, the remaining uses of *particulars* in common speech are being displaced by *specifics,* which has all the air of jargon. "*Get down to specifics,*" he begged / *We referred above to the two-way interplay between concepts and specifics* / *A nice fellow, he thought, but weak on specifics.* This last is doubly unfortunate in that it reawakens memories of the medical term *a specific,* which means a drug that disposes of a particular disease. *Quinine is a specific for malaria; digitalis for heart disease.* Medicine long sought for *specifics* that would among them cure all ailments. Now, with antibiotics, the tendency is rather to treat many troubles with a few substances. Maybe they should be called *generals.*

spelling. It is hardly more than three hundred years since spelling began to be made uniform by convention, and already people are restless under the conveniences of it. On the pretext that English spelling is difficult and at times highly irregular, they want to change it radically, whether by using the present alphabet in some more representative way, or by devising a new alphabet of thirty, forty, or more letters.

Now, spelling reform is possible; it has taken place within the memory of living man, even though the many proponents of reform have rarely agreed about their recommendations. But a revolution in spelling can be faced with equanimity only by someone for whom the accumulation of knowledge has no vivid reality. For in a single school-generation everything in our libraries, public and private, would, under a new system, become as unreadable to the vast majority as Cretan Linear B. And to suppose that "everything worthwhile" would shortly be transliterated and republished in the new alphabet or scheme is to know nothing about publishing or economics.

The gain, moreover, would soon prove illusory. The object of the revolution in spelling would be to make spelling easy by making it conform exactly to pronunciation. This sounds sensible until one asks: Whose pronunciation? The slightest variation from the norm (however defined) would lead to one of two results—different spellings of the same word or a single spelling which for many people would be arbitrary since it would no longer conform to their pronunciation.

A Southerner driving a car stops for the night at a *mote-coat,* a New Englander at a *motacaught,* a Midwesterner at a *moterrcort*—and this is to give but the barest differences of three extremes within which dozens of different vowels, dentals, and *r*'s can be detected by the trained ear. The more an expanded alphabet distinguishes among the many possible vowel and consonantal sounds, the farther apart spellings will spread and the harder reading and writing will become. Or else, the present disparity between a set spelling and a variable pronunciation will return, much aggravated.

Those who can see difficulties before they are on top of them are nonetheless willing to consider and adopt modest changes in our present spellings—e.g. the reduction of unneeded double consonants, and the like. But to carry out such changes is delicate work and of limited scope. Above all, the general outline of the word as spelled must remain what it was in Shakespeare and Bacon and Locke and Addison and Swift, or we are throwing out known good things for a dubious exchange. It is only conventional spelling, "false" to the eye, that keeps such a word as *year* common to English and to American, despite the marked difference between the sounds *yeer* and *yurr.* And there is plain nuisance to be apprehended from misspelling, whether systematic and reformist or casual and coy. Even the schoolgirl *alrite* and *alnite* are harmful as affecting *all* and *right* (what is a Bill of Rites? and *alnite* (= akin to the alder tree or *alnus?*). The spellings we have are far from perfect but their irregularity has been much exaggerated, and the attainment of perfection is not so easy as the impatient destroyers think. No system of spelling, it can be safely affirmed, is going to be so simple and obvious as to teach itself, be learned in childhood without pain, and leave no uncertainties to middle age and beyond.

While tenable reforms are being devised, some few spelling difficulties and distinctions may be profitably listed here. For the example of *blond* and *blonde*, see FRENCH WORDS AND PHRASES. Note that *aneurysm*, the billowing out of a blood vessel, is no sort of *-ism*, but requires *y*. Observe that the *strait and narrow path* and *strait is the gate* and *strait-jacket* are all *strait* = narrow, without *gh*, and hence the first phrase says *narrow* twice. Remember the *s*'s in *consensus* (= sense) and *supersede* (= *sede*ntary) and the *u* in GLAMOUR—not an English spelling—which is dropped in *glamorous*. For *likable*, *salable*, etc., see -ABLE, -IBLE 2. And apropos of *e*, the way to avoid misspelling *sacrilegious* is to recall *sacrilege*

instead of *religious*, with which the word has no connection. If it is necessary to write *desiccated*, think of the dried flowers in the hortus siccus— one *s* and two *c*'s. The great difference, often overlooked, between a boat and an airplane is that one *bales* out a boat and *bails* out of an airplane. For *rack* and *wrack*, see RACK, WRACK. *Accommodate* has two of each of the consonants typists are in doubt about, and so has *embarrassed*; but *harass* has only one *r*.

Words in *-able* and *-ible* have to be learned one by one. Because of *responsibility*, most people spell *responsible* correctly with *i*; but they fall into *irresistАble* and *permissАble* because the nouns are rare. Similarly, the *correspondent* group with *e* and the *ascendant*, *confidant* group with *a* (there is also *confident* with *e*) must be memorized—or at least those words in each group that give one particular trouble. The doubling of final consonants or the failure to double them is often harmless. Everybody acknowledges the right of *traveller* to be *traveler* and vice versa. But *combatting* and *benefitted* each have by common consent one *t* too many.

Those who care about etymology will spell *autarky* when they mean economic or other self-sufficiency. The usual *autarchy* misleads by suggesting *self-rule* in a sense other than the modern one. Again, the phrase *passed master* should be so spelled when it refers to one who has become a master by passing the test—of the guild or of public opinion; for one writes that he has *passed*—not *past*—the examination. Hence *past master* is ambiguous unless one clearly means the former master of a Masonic lodge or incumbent of some other mastership that the person referred to no longer holds. The same relationship obtains between *passed muster* and [a] *past muster*. A different distinction is made with *e* in *therefor, therefore*. The first means *for the purpose just mentioned: He lacks the ambition and the ability therefor*. The second is the far commoner transitional word meaning *in consequence, accordingly: Man is mortal, therefore anxious*.

For the young who are learning to spell, the great art is to close eyes and mind to the incessant misspellings forced upon everybody by the advertiser. How natural that the school child, who reads predigested books of narrow vocabulary, should succumb to misspellings (mostly wrong vowels), when the newspaper and the magazine, the billboard and the television screen show him *expaditer. Eesyfit, Hydramatic, Fiberglas, Holsum, Finast, Tak-Ome, Shado-Shades, Enna Jettick, Fotochrome, Porus Krome*, and thousands of other pseudo-phonetic renderings of ordinary words, all carefully wrong in order to qualify as trademarks.

See also LICORICE, LIQUORICE; PRISE, PRIZE; PRONUNCIATION 2; RACK, WRACK.

spirit of adventure, the. Many blunders encountered in print are the result of a single sally into the unknown, not to be repeated and perhaps never noticed by any critical user of the language. Charity should no doubt be shown to solitary lapses, but the restraining thought occurs that there is no telling when the venturesome flight will not inspire others. And when it does, everybody is brought face to face with the misused *abrasive*, VOLATILE, COHORT, DISINTERESTED, *mutual friend,* and the rest.

The originators of possible disasters are to be found in all walks of life, just like geniuses. One of them is inspired to say *the make-ready* for *the preparation;* another speaks of his *upcoming play*—i.e. from the depths instead of from wherever it would come if it were merely *forthcoming.* From a college dean comes the sentence *Mr. F.'s inauguration was a happy and impressive event with abundant* good augury *for the future of the college.* The head of a foundation, addressing a committee of consultants, says he will *leave them to* coagulate *their thoughts*. A law reporter told newspaper readers that *lawyers, jurists, and heads of law schools* dominated *the list*. Diversity *was given by the presence of Lady J. who is*, etc. A State Department official confides: *I can say* in a distilled form *that the cultural treaty with Russia amounts to a detente*. A novelist tackling his obligatory sex scene describes his hero as *taking her* almost attritively. The music critic, not to be outdone, advises *Don't miss this* exuberant concert. And the amiable executive who wants to promote TOGETHERNESS suggests that names be exchanged around the table *so that everybody can* earmark *everybody else*. All these locutions illustrate that spirit of adventure (or novelty hunting) which lacks judgment, incurs ridicule, and may cause permanent harm to the language.

split infinitive. Like parallel fifths in harmony, the split infinitive is the one fault that everybody has heard about and makes a great virtue of avoiding and reproving in others. Again like the musical bugbear, the split infinitive has its place in good composition. It should be used when it is expressive and well led up to. Long before Fowler's defense of splitting, Shaw had delivered the controlling opinion: "Every good literary craftsman splits his infinitives when the sense demands it. I call for the immediate dismissal of the pedant on your staff [who chases split infinitives]. It is of no consequence whether he decides to go quickly or to quickly go."

One fact has not been noted, or if noted, not made enough of: the temptation to split an infinitive is extremely rare in spoken English, because the voice supplies the stress needed by the unsplit form or conceals by a pause the awkwardness of the adverb placed before or after. It is in written work that splitting is called for, and desk sets should include small hatchets of silver or gold for the purpose.

spoil. See FALSE SINGULARS.

spouse. See HELPMATE, HELPMEET.

statistic. See FALSE SINGULARS.

strait. See SPELLING.

strive, strived, striven. See UNSAVORY PASTS.

structuring. See JARGON.

subjunctive. Except in a very few tenacious forms, the subjunctive mood has almost disappeared from English speech and is retreating, though more slowly, from written prose. The purposes it once served, of expressing doubt, contingency, or matters contrary to fact, are now taken care of by explicit phrases added to a verb in the indicative. The Authorized Version of the Bible is full of subjunctives—*if it die, lest he forget,* etc. This last conjunction, *lest,* has virtually dropped out of use together with the subjunctive, and when one hears it one has the impression that it is being assimilated to *unless* in some vague way and with a corresponding uncertainty about the proper form of the verb.

It comes as a surprise, therefore, when a broadcast editorial contains a sentence that goes: *Much is being made of the possible effect on police morale if, as some suggest, civilians be given responsibility to weigh complaints of misconduct lodged against New York City's men-in-blue.* (This is being quoted from the written text.) The *if . . . civilians be given* is archaic. The normal mood is the indicative *are,* the doubt being sufficiently expressed by *if* and the preceding *possible* and *as some suggest.* The same indicative mood suffices for supposition, contingencies, and the like: *If I am a fool to go into this thing, you'd better tell me straight out.* No one today would think of saying *If I be.* But this concession to simplicity does not as yet carry over to statements—or rather hypotheses—contrary to fact.

The dividing line between educated and uneducated speech is as clear about this usage as it is about *ain't.* One does hear *If he was to move to California,* but educated speakers say *If he were.* A writer would still entitle his play *If I Were King.*

A further use of the subjunctive that educated writers and speakers find compulsory is the one traditionally called for in subordinate clauses after verbs of saying, thinking, hoping, wishing, or their equivalents. Perhaps no one is tempted to say *I wish that he lives here,* but one runs into carelessly written novels in which one finds *His grandmother gave him the house on condition that he lives here,* which is the same fault hardly concealed. Again—and this example will explain the retention of the subjunctive—one reads in a volume of musicians' letters in translation: *But how? He has no tenor for Aeneas. Mme. Viardot suggests that she plays both Cassandra and Dido.* If she suggests that she *plays* both, she must be doing so right now in some fashion kept secret from the world and first revealed by her suggestion. The forms *she suggests that she play both* and *on condition that he live here* not only present the distinction, but correspond to the expanded forms *suggests that she should play both / on condition that he should live here.* Again,

It was vital to their case that not one but both drugs were present is correct if it is a statement of fact; it must read *be present* if, as the context shows, the supposition is false or in doubt. As long as the construction with *should* remains as common as it is, the subordinate verb will have to reject the marks of the indicative.

As for the rest of the tenacious forms mentioned above, they are so usual that they cause no one any trouble. *The Devil take him; God forbid; Lord love a duck; I'll go south come Easter; come what may;* and *be that as it may* have the force of idioms, and no one not a grammarian need even know where the subjunctive lurks or why. (See also HAD RATHER.)

such. 1. Pronoun. 2. *Such as, such that.*

1. Pronoun. Except for comic effects that always run the risk of falling flat, *such* is not a personal pronoun; that is, *such* by itself will not replace *it* or *them.* Put back one or the other of these genuine pronouns in the following sentences: *He declared that he had never in his long life had to depend for his safety on bodyguards and had no intention of having recourse to such / The point at issue is whether a six-four chord is adequate to play[-ing] this role, despite the* use of such in many passages that could be cited.

2. *Such as, such that. Such as* is close in meaning to *like* and may often be interchanged with it. The shade of difference between them is that *such as* leads the mind to imagine an indefinite group of objects: *man's great inventions, such as the wheel, the steam engine, . . .* The other comparing word *like* suggests a closer resemblance among the things compared: *direct satisfactions of sense, like food and drink.* It is owing to this extremely slight distinction that purists object to phrases of the type *a writer like Shakespeare, a leader like Lincoln.* No writer, say these critics, *is* like Shakespeare; and in this they are wrong; writers are alike in many things and the context usually makes clear what the comparison proposes to our attention. *Such as Shakespeare* may sound less impertinent but if Shakespeare were totally incomparable *such as* would be open to the same objection as *like.*

Such must be followed by *as* instead of *which* or *that* if *such* is adjectival and immediately precedes the noun. *As* then introduces the defining clause. The following are wrong: *The price reached such a level which would endanger our position;* and (from an American playwright) *the set, which contains only such pieces of furniture (a sofa, a chair, etc.) that are required by the action.* The correct use of *such that* is rigidly controlled by idiom. *Such* is a predicate adjective followed by a defining clause, as in *The terms of the contract were such* (or *Such were the terms*) *that no self-respecting firm could accept them.* In this construction *such* is never glued to its noun, and *that*, relative, introduces the clause.

See also THAT, CONJUNCTION 1.

sufficiently. For reasons difficult to disentangle, this adverb, like ADEQUATE, has a way of subverting idiom. Its natural sequels are a *to* infinitive and *for* with a noun: *sufficiently persuasive to make him reconsider* / *sufficiently distinct for reception by amateurs.* It is a mistake to follow *sufficiently* with SO THAT, as in *The hoofs of the young are sufficiently strong and hard so that they can walk everywhere* (sufficiently strong and hard to let them, sufficiently strong and hard for them to). A worse aberration, and one more harmful to idiom, is the interposition of an unassimilable *as: its assumption that an individual firm could sufficiently control economic conditions as to deserve reward or punishment for its employment record.* All is well if we abolish the *as.* In answer to what desire does it get in? Undoubtedly the desire is to supply a link between *sufficiently* and its sequel after three long words; and this wish in turn is born of confusion with the other idiom *so far control . . . as to.*

suffixes. See -ABLE, -IBLE; -EE, -ER; ENDINGS; -ING; -ION, -NESS, -MENT; -ISM; -ITIS; -IZE; TRANSITIVE, INTRANSITIVE; -LY.

suggestion. See PRONUNCIATION 1.

superlatives, abuse of. See JOURNALESE.

supplement, verb. See AUGMENT.

supplemental, supplementary. See ENDINGS 1.

suspect. This verb is occasionally applied to subjects that cannot be deemed objects of suspicion. *Arms are suspected of having been smuggled to the island by parcel post.* This statement is disqualified to begin with by the fact that arms can be neither guilty nor innocent, and further by the passive voice: a subject cannot be suspected of something done to it. We really must not say that X. is suspected of having been murdered. Find his last visitor and suspect *him.* The acceptable form for the kind of statement here impugned is the active voice with the acting agent as subject. If the agent cannot be named, the impersonal will serve: *It is suspected that arms have been smuggled / that X. was murdered.* (See TRANSITIVE, INTRANSITIVE for *suspect,* adjective.)

suspicious. See TRANSITIVE, INTRANSITIVE.

swimsuit. See -ING 1.

sympathy. See PREPOSITIONS.

T

tacit. See IMPLICIT, EXPLIC-IT.

tactic. See FALSE SINGULARS.

taking (account of, into account). See DANGLERS, ACCEPTABLE.

tarmac(k)ed. See CATALOG.

technics. See OLOGY, OLO-GIES.

technology. See SCIENTISM.

telescopings. Lewis Carroll called them *portmanteau words,* because they packed several meanings into one container, like one's belongings in a suitcase or portmanteau. The author's purpose in the "Jabberwocky" and other parts of *Alice in Wonderland* was comic. When James Joyce went back to the device in *Ulysses,* the purpose was the serious one of expressing related or divergent ideas simultaneously. Between the two writers the inventors of trademarks had made the practice familiar by their coinages. *Band-Aid* and *Frigidaire* are among the most sedate of these compounds, whose aim is partly to amuse the mind, as in Lewis Carroll,

and partly to suggest a fusion of powers, as in James Joyce.

In the last forty years a tendency that was limited in purpose as has just been shown has become a common pastime. Whenever a proposal is made to join two places by a bridge or a road, writers to the newspaper are sure to suggest bizarre composite names as the obvious and desirable ones to designate the structure. Whenever a new appliance is brought out, its virtues must be recorded in a similar hybridizing of names to show "dual" or "all-purpose" uses: *travelodge, transistor, selectric,* etc. (The *Wooletin* is published by the American Wool Council.) Nor are the enterprises of government or education, however sober, free from the desire to embrace and record multiple intentions by agglutinating words and parts of words into awkward yet fashionable designations. This desire is quasi-scientific in its search for COVERING WORDS.

The vogue will have to run its course, though it can be pointed out right now that the cleverness of these manufactured names is beginning to seem tawdry, even for articles of trade. And it may also be suggested that if compounds must be made, they will have a better chance of surviving if they (1) sufficiently articulate the paired meanings, (2) denote a distinct contraption, and (3) can be pronounced without distorting the constituent sounds. By this test *vistadome* is tolerable and *scenicruiser* (for a long-distance bus) is not.

tenderfoot. This fine American coinage, a counterpart of the fine English coinage *greenhorn*, comes under the attraction of *foot, feet*, very much as the verb HAMSTRING comes under that of *string, strung*. O. Henry tried to obliterate the plural form *tenderfeet* by a jeer in "The Call of the Tame": "No damage was done beyond the employment of the wonderful plural 'tenderfeet' in each of the scribe's stories." His point was well taken: the tenderfoot is one who is tender of foot, and two, ten, or twenty of him are likewise tender of foot. But the plural *tenderfoots* is recorded as an alternative by Webster's New International Dictionary for the first time in 1961. *Tenderfeet* being illogical, use *tenderfoot* (collective plural).

tense. See SEQUENCE OF TENSES.

than. See HARDLY (SCARCELY) . . . THAN.

than whom, than which. See WHO(M), WHO(M)EVER 4.

thanks to. See DUE TO.

that, conjunction. 1. Mistreatments of *that*. 2. *That* omitted.

1. Mistreatments of *that*. As the connective that introduces nearly all indirect discourse and follows the many verbs of saying and thinking, *that* is probably the most frequent subordinating conjunction in the language; indeed, it may be the most frequent of all conjunctions except for the coordinating *and*. No word that occurs with such persistence is secure against mistreatment. The commonest faults are four: (a) absent-minded duplication; (b) use after verbs of saying to introduce constructions idiomatically hostile to *that*; (c) use after substitutes for verbs of saying or thinking idiomatically requiring other sequels than *that*; and (d) unidiomatic substitution for *as, to, for*, etc. to complete comparisons begun with *such, sufficiently*, etc. . . .

(a) In a longish sentence containing indirect discourse approached through parenthetical matter, it is natural to follow the verb of saying with an immediate *that*; and on resuming the main line of the sentence after the parenthetical matter, it is easy to slip in a second *that* without noticing that its function is already performed. *Fourth, it must be evident to all that as more than three hundred Bish-*

ops at Lambeth debated the deepest problems of the day—racial and group tension, nuclear warfare, the problems of the family—that these debates were often charged with the deepest emotion. The second *that* is the first one repeated. Which, then, should be omitted? Ordinarily the first: a verb of saying or thinking (*it must be evident to all*) is well able to carry its force over an interpolation without the suspension of a *that,* and the conjunction is of maximum help as a signal of the conclusion—what is said or thought.

In the quoted sentence, the principle just given would apply if its author had not written himself into a snarl with an ambiguous *as.* His *as* may mean *since;* it may mean *when.* On the first supposition, we get the following bearable pattern: *It must be evident to all since more than three hundred Bishops debated . . . , that these debates were often charged . . .* Better still would be a reconstruction that would eliminate both the suspense and all temptation to repeat the conjunction: *Since more than three hundred Bishops debated . . . , it must be evident to all . . .* It is a reasonable guess from internal evidence that writers of sentences like our original example sometimes deliberately repeat *that* on the theory that they are thereby smoothing the reader's path. Considerateness

would be better shown were the reader given a sentence requiring no such scaffolding. In any event, it is clear that the common duplications result from oversight.

(b) An imperative or a direct question would never be introduced by *that* if it were isolated and stripped of qualifiers. No one would write *He told them that why should such things be permitted,* or *He demanded that let the question be publicly debated.* Yet when just such constructions are approached through an interpolated modifying clause, we often find them heralded by a *that* which has nowhere to go. *The electorate seems to be saying that if the Republican politicians cannot govern themselves, why should they be allowed to govern the state?* (seems to be asking why, if the Republican politicians cannot govern themselves, they should be allowed to govern the state) / *I shall tell you that since you have believed in the possibility of so many tragic and romantic villains having existed, why can you not believe in the reality of P.?* (I shall ask you why, since you have believed . . ., you cannot believe) / *This brings us around to that second pregnant comment inspired by the remark of Skeffington that politics is the most popular American spectator sport. It is that if such may be reckoned as any-*

thing close to the truth, why haven't we had more movies about American politics? (namely, that if the remark is true the dearth of movies . . . is unaccountable) / *She rounded on the Council . . . and told them that if they wanted to convert Catholics to Protestantism, let them do it by the example of their lives* (they should do it by) / *There is a growing feeling among bird people that if a long, cold winter will end this bitter controversy involving both birds and people—let it come* (it should be welcome).

(c) It may be difficult to explain why *hopeful* can be followed by *that*, whereas *optimistic* requires *about* or *as to*; the reason is perhaps that *optimism* began as a doctrine, not a feeling. But there is no doubt about the requirement. *Optimistic* and *pessimistic* are samples of adjectives incompetent to govern *that*, yet they are continually being asked to do so. *They nevertheless are optimistic that eventually they will be able to* (hopeful that; optimistic about being; confident of being) / *Many are optimistic that an acceptable substitute can be provided* (Many trust that; are optimistic about the provision of) / *Mr. D was absolutely firm . . . that no measures looking toward demilitarization . . . could be taken while the Communists continued firing* (firm about

the impossibility of measures; absolutely insistent that).

(d) The word *sufficient*(*ly*) is likewise an impossible prelude to *that*; it takes, not *as*, but *to* or *for*. *The Russians may feel that their political positions in the satellites will soon be sufficiently consolidated that they can* (for them to) *maintain control using only the light side arms allowable for internal policing.*

There are also verbs in this category of incompetence. *Purport* is one. John Quincy Adams is quoted as having referred in 1818 to an *article in the "National Intelligencer," purporting that* (to the purport that) *General Jackson had taken Pensacola by storm.* Another such verb is *look; appear* takes *that,* but *look* has to take *as if,* on pain of outraging idiom: *After he finished reading his statement, Mr. H. said that it looked to him "from present indications" that* (as if) *District Attorney F. would be elected.* Here the false *that* may be induced by *indications,* which has no jurisdiction over what follows. (Of course, *it looked like . . . F. would be elected* is rampant in colloquial speech and sometimes wedges its way into print, but this construction, standard in the fourteenth century, has long been a stranger to good usage. See LIKE 1.) *Purport* and *look,* like *optimistic* and *sufficient,* exemplify locutions that fail to qualify as equivalents of saying and thinking. But they seem almost satisfactory in that role, compared to certain slang expressions such as *have one's fingers crossed*, in the sense of hoping for luck: *Network executives understandably have their fingers crossed that time and TV's narcotic influence will persuade set owners to forget insinuations that broadcasters deal in packaged phoniness* (crossed in the hope that). (See also PREPOSITIONS.)

Dryden, when he wrote about

> the herd of such
> Who think too little, and
> who talk too much

was undoubtedly using an idiom of his period, but it has long been obsolete, and there is no latter-day alternative to the sequence *such as*. Dryden's repeated *who* is, of course, a pronoun; and the modern error with the same construction consists precisely in the resort to *that* as a pronoun where a conjunction is required. The following samples must be recast with a *such as* instead of *that*, if they are to remain on cozy terms with modern usage: *Mr. M. wrote that such flight operations that* (as) *still might be desirable in the area could be consolidated with . . . / serving plate luncheons with such food only that may* (as can) *be cut readily with a fork while the plate is held in mid-air / Come spring, it will be necessary to rake up such leaves that* (as) *have not blown away / You indicate only such conditions that* (as) *would make it clear that this is a man of action.*

The construction requiring *as* in place of *that* must be distinguished from the irreproachable sequence *such that* to denote result, as in *His campaign was such that it won him more respect than votes*, a radically different pattern from *His campaign was such as to win him. . . .*

See also SO THAT.

2. *That* omitted. The tendency to omit *that* as a conjunction coupling a noun clause to its verb is justified by the desire to reduce the number of *th* sounds in an English sentence or to avoid a succession of *that*'s. Two considerations govern the omission: (a) the sentence must be short and simple, or it will lose clear articulation; (b) the verbs with which the omission is easiest are those of saying, denying, thinking, feeling, hoping, fearing, etc.; but not all those of cognate meaning will do without *that*. Verbs of answering, retorting, rejoining, complaining, and others known only by one's idiomatic sense will rarely tolerate the omission. Here are acceptable sentences: *He thought she had already gone and he was in a fury / The consul hoped the case would not come before him again / We felt we could not renew the loan / Unless she hopes* *he is dead, I see no reason to condemn her.* With the wrong verb or at the slightest hint of complication on any plane, even that of rhythm, the need for *that* makes itself felt. *That* is injudiciously omitted in the following: *I think I may say I do not know a better man in a pinch* (here the *that* would come best after *say*) / *They could all certainly remember he was the best of the bunch* / *Yet why should any one refuse to acknowledge he had passed through the town at an earlier time?* / *If you sifted through all those words, they came down to this: he complained he was underpaid* / *Aristotle thinks (contrary to what others think he thinks) the ideal springs out of the natural in regular progression.* In this last sentence, putting the parenthesis at the beginning and winding up with *Aristotle thinks the ideal,* etc. would make the omission acceptable.

It is obvious, too, that when the omission of *that* gives a false lead, it must be restored. This misleading will occur every time that the noun clause is the direct object of the verb and begins with a noun that fits the meaning of the verb—e.g. *We know the purpose of his trip is to make money* must be rewritten *know that the purpose,* etc.

that, which, relative. **1.** An old schoolboy riddle asks what travelers across the Sahara would use to sustain life if their provisions ran out. The answer: They would live on the sandwiches (sand which is) there. The joke relies on an English rather than an American pronunciation of *which* and—what is to the present purpose—on a choice of pronoun that many now think undesirable. The relative pronoun that should follow *sand,* they say, is not *which* but *that.* There are sentences in which either *that* or *which* can be used without calling undue attention to itself; there are perhaps sentences in which the two are equally good; there are many sentences that call for the demonstrative superposed on the relative (*A great city is that which has the greatest men and women*). But there are also numberless sentences in which *that* ought to be felt as mandatory and *which* ought not to be uttered without a sense of its uncouthness. A succinct model to follow is Kipling's title *The Light That Failed.* A cogent illustration is "The House That Jack Built" *in extenso.* Try substituting *which* for *that* in

the cow with the crumpled horn,
That tossed the dog
That worried the cat
That killed the rat
That ate the malt
That lay in the house that Jack built,

and you will have a final demonstration of the difference between the natural and the unnatural idiom, and incidentally of the stylistic havoc that can be wrought by very simple means.

What is under discussion here is whether *which* or *that* shall serve as the subject of a restrictive relative clause—what the English generally call a defining clause. (For the difference between restrictive and nonrestrictive clauses, see APPENDIX 2, pp. 492-495.) There is no problem about the pronoun in dependent clauses of the second, the nonrestrictive type. In them everyone uses *who* of persons and *which* of things (*the citizens of Denver, who live a mile above sea level / the Greenland* ICECAP, *which covers the whole interior of the country*). In these also, every reasonably careful and educated person sets off the relative clauses with a comma or a pair of commas. But about the first type, the restrictive clause, there is no such unanimity. Many writers begin such clauses habitually with *which*, not *that*; and many use *which* and *that* interchangeably without any attempt to be consistent. Now, if this scheme or absence of scheme is adopted—if, for example, we write *the schools which educate our children*—there is nothing but the absence of commas to tell you whether the clause means that some schools educate and some

do not (restrictive) or that all the schools educate (nonrestrictive). A fundamental, often crucial difference of meaning is thus left to turn on the mere absence or presence of the least of the punctuation marks, the comma, which is so easily lost on its way to the printed page. In short, a great responsibility is delegated to a small sign; to one, moreover, that is relied on to perform this most important task by not being there.

It is only in recent times that restrictive clauses have had even this inconspicuous way of proclaiming themselves. It was formerly standard practice to set them off exactly as we now do nonrestrictive clauses. In Dryden we read without surprise: *All, that can bring my country good, is welcome.* This pattern was common in prose until about 1850 and traceable after that through a lingering obsolescence. For several decades we find the juxtaposition of a newfangled usage with an old usage that was dying hard, in both America and England.

For no more than a lifetime, then, omitted punctuation has been a nominal clue to restrictiveness. Until this device became standard there was only plausible inference to distinguish between restrictive and nonrestrictive clauses if they began with *which*. The habits of writers are bound to be affected by familiarity with the works of four centuries in which all relative clauses were punctuated alike. Moreover, the punctuation that is still necessary for nonrestrictive clauses is often heedlessly omitted, with the result that the nonrestrictive clauses thus made to look restrictive impair the reliability of omitted commas as the token of restrictiveness. In fine, the frailty of this expedient is manifest.

What such considerations point to is the desirability of distinguishing the restrictive clause from the nonrestrictive by some additional device, more nearly proof against accident. The one that is available and has long been entrenched in idiomatic usage is the pronoun *that*. It might well be systematically used as the characteristic signal of the restrictive clause.

The case for this usage, which saves *which* as the corresponding signal of the nonrestrictive clause, was proposed in the Fowlers' manual *The King's English* in 1906 and cogently argued and illustrated by H. W. Fowler in *Modern English Usage* in 1926. Those arguments have been very influential on both sides of the Atlantic. Fowler's discussion is not likely to be improved on unless our language should undergo modifications not now foreseeable. The years since 1926 have brought forth no serious challenge to his main point, which is this: "If

writers would agree to regard *that* as the defining [restrictive] relative pronoun, and *which* as the non-defining, there would be much gain both in lucidity and in ease."

2. It cannot of course be maintained, and Fowler did not try to maintain, that there is any such general agreement among writers. The two points that can be maintained—that cannot, in fact, be gainsaid—are (a) that disagreement in practice is paid for with losses in lucidity and ease and (b) that there is enough solid historical underpinning for *that* in the restrictive use to show a widely diffused instinct and to justify Fowler's recommendation. In support of the first point it is enough for the moment to refer again to "The House That Jack Built." In support of the second it would be possible to cite tens of thousands of examples, from Marlowe (*Who ever loved that loved not at first sight?*) to Mencken (*Nothing can come out of an artist that is not in the man*) and Hemingway (*the little new that each man gets from life*).

No one should pretend or believe that a cluster of examples would tell the whole story. It would be easy to assemble the same sort of collection in support of *which*. Some of the classic authors between Marlowe and Hemingway used *which* restrictively as often as *that*, some of them oftener.

There are authors—Macaulay is one—in whom the restrictive *that* is a rarity. Many writers go through a phase of imagining that there is something lax and colloquial about *that*, and they adopt *which* for both kinds of clauses. No one could plausibly insist that *which* as a restrictive relative pronoun is indefensible or incorrect. A statistical survey of the present generation of writers, if it were feasible or worthwhile, would show nothing but confusion. For many still think it an unwarranted limitation of freedom—and sometimes a source of momentary confusion—to differentiate the uses of *which* and *that*. They doubt the greater lucidity and deny the greater ease. These dissenters can point to many instances where being forced to use *that* leads to an intolerable repetition of sounds, to awkwardness and loss of emphasis in the correlated *that . . . and that, that . . . but that,* and even to absurd collocations with the demonstrative and conjunctive *that*'s (We *believe that that machine that we built that year does just that*). As to euphony, it may well be that English is too full of swish-woosh sounds, but—the opposition argues—its aural elegance is not improved by a reinforced dose of lisping over *th-the-that*'s.

One can adduce, then, an impressive array of advocates for each system—and no clear majority. But the confusion need not obscure the fact that the followers of the Fowler doctrine often contribute to greater certainty in one large department of writing. And even when we make the fullest use of *that, which* remains indispensable. Restrictive clauses in which the relative pronoun follows a preposition must make that pronoun *which*—as if it were the objective case of *that*: we can say *the abilities that he owed his promotion to,* but we have to say the abilities *to which* he owed his promotion. Though we are free from the superstition that sentences or clauses must not end with prepositions, we must be aware that there often are sound objections to ending them so; and when the restrictive pronoun immediately follows a governing preposition there is nothing for it but *which*. This inherent limitation of *that*, which can be the object of a preposition only by preceding it, accounts for many recurrences of *which* and puts a further premium on the use of *that* wherever it is idiomatically possible.

3. What are we to do about parallel restrictive clauses led into by a common antecedent? We rather often encounter sentences on the model of these: *The training that we got in the Army, and which we could have got nowhere else, stood us in good stead in civilian life / The critics that have*

studied this score, and who have heard it performed repeatedly, have a quite different opinion of the work. The conservative grammarian shudders at the mixing of *that* and *which* in parallel, when restrictive and nonrestrictive ideas are brought into one construction. There are so many simple ways of putting such sentences to rights that no one has any real excuse for letting them go as quoted. In the first, note that the second clause can be taken as either restrictive or nonrestrictive without the slightest difference in meaning. Therefore: *Our Army training, which we could have got nowhere else,* or *The training that we could have got nowhere but in the Army.* And the second specimen is made bearable even more simply: *The critics that have studied this score and heard it performed,* or *The critics that, after studying this score, have heard it performed.* These expedients dispose of a grammatical question that should never have been allowed to arise, while they tighten the prose by reducing wordiness.

There remains in this connection one problem that may as well be met head on: whether, in parallel restrictive clauses, *that* is to be repeated as the subject. *The training that we got in the Army and that we could have got nowhere else / The critics that have studied this score and that*

have heard it performed. Is this pattern endurable? These sentences would never be called graceful. Moreover, their construction will sometimes result in a second *that* hard to tell at first glance from the demonstrative pronoun. Nevertheless the writer who insists on putting himself into this box can be assured that his repetition of *that* is in every way better than the switch from *that* to *which* or *who*. The partisan of the all-purpose *which* never hesitates to repeat *which* in such sequences: let the partisan of *that* similarly stand to his guns and go through with the pronoun first invoked, in pursuance of the principle that equal elements should be kept rhetorically similar. *No man that has had this experience, and that can talk about it with sincerity and candor, will ever want for listeners* is not a model sentence; but it is more workmanlike than *No man that has had this experience, and who can talk about it . . .*

The repetition of *that* in parallel clauses finds authoritative sanction on the very first page of *Words and Their Ways in English Speech,* where Kittredge and Greenough write about *strange terms that force themselves upon our attention because everybody employs them, and that rapidly die out only to be replaced by equally grotesque novelties.* Both authors may be called, if not arbiters, at least rigorous analysts of style. Their agreement on *that . . . that* is the more impressive because both show a noticeable preference for *which* in restrictive relative clauses: *words which . . . must have been . . . added to our personal vocabulary / a series of phenomena which no thinking man can contemplate without a kind of awe / a peculiar cadence which pleases the ear / an influence, indeed, which it has not altogether lost.* Nor do we have to go back to 1901 to find *that* repeated in parallel restrictive clauses. The two following sentences are from recent newspapers: *The current scandals have spotlighted conditions that have existed for a long time, that are acute and that demand correction / Otherwise it was the same missile that has performed so successfully in test firings and that is now being installed at launching sites in this country.* Still, in contemporary usage the question of *that . . . that* is so involved with the differentiation of *that* and *which* that both remain open. The conflicting arguments lie deep in the structure of the language and may never find a satisfactory resolution.

that, who, relative. As is shown under THAT, WHICH, RELATIVE, there is a fairly strong historical tendency to use *that* as the characteristic pronoun of the restrictive or defining clause, and many writers conform to it by consistently beginning such clauses with *that,* thus distinguishing them from nonrestrictive relative clauses beginning with *which.* But a great many of these same writers do not feel comfortable with *that* as the signal of the restrictive clause about persons, for which they retain the *who* of the nonrestrictives. Kipling, for example, seems not to mind whatever appearance of inconsistency there may be in shifting from *The Light That Failed* to *The Man Who Would Be King* and *The Man Who Was.* As a matter of fact, the dislike of *that* applied to persons is not to be written off as a mere caprice. It is a usage that unquestionably leads into more frequent and more extreme awkwardness than we can charge to the same *that* applied to things. Any writer or editor has to wriggle through a variety of such snarls as *fully persuaded that children that undergo the handicap of teachers that have only a perfunctory grasp of these fundamentals are to be pitied;* and it will not take many of them to persuade him that the substitution of *who* has its advantages.

Historically there is not much ground for objecting to *that* as a personal relative pronoun. *He that hath clean hands / the world, and they that dwell therein / He that is most knowing hath a capacity to become happy / They that on glorious ancestors enlarge / vile man that mourns / thou that listenest to sighs of orphans / I am he that walks / children that belonged to a man I didn't even know / An optimist is a guy that has never had much experience.* Such a scattering, which happens to reach from the King James translation of the Old Testament to Whitman, Mark Twain, and Don Marquis, could be extended to prove that the relative *that* refers to persons quite as naturally as to things, and quite as naturally as *who* refers to persons. Perhaps only habit will help one choose between *He that hesitates is lost* and *He who hesitates.* It often happens that *that* is obligatory and *who* impossible; for example, in Marlowe's line *Who ever loved that loved not at first sight?* it would be distracting to pile a relative *who* on the opening interrogative *Who.* We are, then, free to use *that* instead of *who* for a sign of the restrictive clause about persons, exactly as many elect to use it instead of *which* in a restrictive clause about things —and for similar reasons. Consider, for example, the ease with which we can remove the blight from *a couple who like* (s?) *music* by making it *a couple that likes music.*

Yet it is fair to say that the advantages of using *that* for *who* in personal restrictive clauses are not so clear and consistent as those of using *that* for *which* in impersonal ones. For the writer who altogether rejects *that* in restrictives and sticks to *which* for all impersonal uses, there is of course no problem: he will also stick to *who* as a matter of course. But even the writer who makes a general policy of the restrictive *that* for *which* will encounter more snags and drawbacks in the use of *that* for *who*—more causes of awkwardness, more occasions for making exceptions. The recommended practice, then, is: (1) Use *that* as an auxiliary sign of the impersonal restrictive clause except on those occasions when difficulty or ungainliness results; and (2) shift freely between *that* and *who* in personal restrictive clauses, according to which produces the greater ease and naturalness in the sentence. To these precepts a third might be added: (3) Do not force yourself to use *that* in personal restrictive clauses if you think it an artificial way of referring to persons. A writer, after all, does not owe it to anyone to swallow his aversions. Style is, among other things, a product of what we avoid as well as of what we do; and there are writers to whom the use of *that* for *who* seems strained, or archaic, and not to be validated in prose by examples from the Bible or the poets; to their ears *that* now carries a thing-like connotation. In the titles of books—short ones especially—they feel that the excess of *th* sounds calls for relief by the euphonic insertion of the maligned *w:* just as we must have *The Week That Was,* because *which* would make it a tongue-twister, so we must have *The Man Who Was* and *The Man Who Did,* because *that* would bring on teething trouble. To all such analysts of prose and of their own sensations, one can only pay respect while reminding oneself of Henry James's dictum that there is nothing in the world that anyone is obliged to like.

the. See A, AN, THE 4 and 5.

then. See ABOVE.

thinking, noun. See VOGUE WORDS.

this. See ANTECEDENTS 10.

though. See ALTHOUGH.

thrust. See IMPINGE; METAPHOR 4.

thusly. See SINGLEHANDEDLY.

tick. Clock mechanisms, insects of the deathwatch class, and sundry lizards are welcome to ticking on indefinitely with everybody's blessing, but it is time to call a halt to the ticking of human beings. The application of this onomatopoetic word to the analysis of motive or character (*what makes him tick*) was originally a good enough metaphor to atone for its reduction of men to machines. But with every repetition the original stroke of wit becomes less and one's annoyance greater. When we are told of *two paragraphs that pretty well answer the question: What makes a missionary tick?*—in plain English, Why is a missionary a missionary?—it is time that good taste should step in: discard the phrase, invent a fresh metaphor, or resort to unfigurative language.

See also METAPHOR.

tie-in. See VOGUE WORDS.

time factor. See JARGON.

-tion. See NOUN-PLAGUE 2.

titles and proper names. 1. *Mr.,* etc. 2. *Née.* 3. Professional titles. 4. Authors' initials and first names. 5. When to use French *de.*

1. In spite of democracy, or perhaps because of it, many persons are wanting in directness and simplicity when they announce their names, and the misuses resulting from their embarrassment have been faithfully reproduced in fiction and journalism. *I went to the house expecting to meet a woman named Mrs. Herbert. She proved to be a man named Dr. Harvey.* Nobody's *name* is *Mrs.* or *Dr.* anything. These are titles, and everyone has a

full name long before titles are acquired. Accordingly, in introducing oneself one should say *My name is Tom Jones* or *I am Dr. Jones / My name is Violet Sherman* or *I am Mrs. Sherman.* In a recent Supreme Court case a point in evidence was the unwarranted familiarity with which a Southern judge had treated a Negro defendant. She had every right to be called *Miss* like anybody else, though what she should have insisted on was the proper use of her *title,* not her name.

2. A similar point occurs in the use of the term *née,* meaning *born* and applicable only to females. In logic and usage the word goes only with a last name: *Lady Asquith, née Tennant,* not *née Margot Tennant;* for it is clear that she was born without a first name, though already tagged with a last.

3. Habits vary about the use of the optional titles assigned to the professions, but certain usages are so well established that neglecting them is a solecism. The chief of these is the requirement of the article *the* and a first name (or a *Mr.* or *Dr.*) with *Reverend*—*the Reverend Daniel Blake* or *the Reverend Mr.* (or *Dr.*) *Blake,* but not *the Reverend Blake.* A moment's reflection shows why good form makes this demand. The meaning of *reverend* is still active in the title, thanks to the preceding *the,* and the respect it implies calls for the full designation of the man.

It is not *Blake* or *some Blake or other* who is reverend, but *Daniel Blake* or *Mr. Blake.*

For reasons hard to define, the use of *Professor* as a mode of address without a name attached is no longer in good repute in this country, although the parallel use of *Doctor* to a physician is acceptable. This difference may have to do with the degradation to which *Professor* was subjected in the last century, when sellers of patent medicine and instructors in the art of self-defense made free use of the title. In many American colleges and universities today, the preferred form is to overlook all titles and follow the common uses of *Mr.* for everybody. Whatever the practice may be, it is never permissible to make play with the modifiers of *Professor* by writing or calling out *Assistant Professor Stone* or *Adjunct Professor Prendergast.* (See also FRENCH WORDS AND PHRASES and PROF.)

4. The same subtle but strong feelings lead one to condemn without appeal the practice of certain magazines that make a repetitive title out of a man's calling—*Author Hemingway, Sculptor Moore,* and so on. It is offensive, even though the appellation is incontrovertible. One just cause of the resentment is that, as author, the person is entitled to the public form of his name; as a man, he is entitled to the prefix *Mr.,* with or without initials or first name. The public form of a notable man's name is the form he chooses for labeling and publicizing his works. Accordingly, nothing is more annoying than to have *H. G. Wells* made unrecognizable by being turned into *Herbert George Wells; Arnold Bennett* expanded into *Enoch Arnold Bennett;* and *Lenin* supplied with a *Nikolai,* which is somebody's imagining of what the pseudonymous *N.* stands for.

It is true that in an index initials do not always suffice to distinguish namesakes. But the determined pedantry that flouts a public man's manifest choice should be left as the pastime of librarians and lexicographers. The editors of the third edition of Webster's New International Dictionary are particularly headstrong in this regard, as are also the makers of reference books who take advantage of the fact that the French bestow three or four Christian names on their offspring. Instead of using, or at least indicating, the familiar, established first name (e.g. *Eugène Delacroix*), these compilers insist on printing *Ferdinand Victor Eugène,* omitting the hyphens that belong to French usage, and leaving the unlearned reader in doubt which and how many of the given names form part of the historic name.

5. There remains, apropos of French names, the trouble-some question of when to use and when to omit *de.* Of course, the name in full presents no difficulty: *de* is indispensable —*Alexis de Tocqueville, Alfred de Vigny.* Likewise if a title is used—*Comte de Gobineau.* But what of the last name when taken by itself? The answer may seem complicated at first; in reality it is easily mastered.

To begin with, *de* is invariably used when it is attached: *Robert Delattre* gives by itself *Delattre;* it never appears in any other form. All other names, with *de* separate, fall into three classes: names of one syllable, names of more than one syllable, names of more than one syllable that begin with a vowel. All the names of one syllable must always have *de* before them—*De Thou, De Retz, De Mun.* All the longer names, unless they begin with a vowel, *must* drop the *de: Tocqueville says . . . ; Vigny's poems are austere; Gobineau was no racist*—and hence: *Maupassant* (not *de*) *wrote innumerable short stories.* But names longer than one syllable that begin with a vowel break the rule for long names and require *D':D'Argenson, D'Artagnan.*

The simple aid to memory about this rule-of-three is to think of an example of each: *De Gaulle, Tocqueville,* and *D'Artagnan.* A further comfort: all the foregoing applies exclusively to *de. Du* and *des* are invariably used with the last name, short or long, voweled or not: *Des Brosses, Du Guesclin.*

to, missing. Like *as,* the word *to* when present in one construction may be saddled with responsibility to another construction that cannot survive without it, and it is generally unequal to this double load. (See AS 2.) *It was Rousseau, however, whom Madame de Staël singled out to acknowledge her intellectual debt.* Here the *to* that is present as the sign of the infinitive will accept no other function; but the acknowledgment is *to* Rousseau, and it takes a separate preposition to say so. Read, then: *singled out to acknowledge her . . . debt to.* More often than not, the overdelicate who object to terminal prepositions will amend a sentence of this type by inserting the additional *to* before *whom*; and the device would work here had the sentence been *It was Rousseau . . . (to) whom Madame de Staël chose to acknowledge . . .* But with *whom* set up as the object of *singled out* no such adjustment is possible—a telling reminder to schoolmarms that the dogma about terminal prepositions is rendered null by the raw fact that it is inevitable.

See also PREPOSITIONS.

together with. See AS 11.

togetherness. The rise of this word may have started with Kahlil Gibran as far back as 1923. In *The Prophet,* which is a publisher's dream of the inspirational gift book—a work for which limp leather would have had to be invented had it not existed—Gibran wrote of marriage: *Let there be spaces in your togetherness.* It is a civilized sentiment, but there was the dreadful word, and it has come under the eyes of millions in that one aphorism. It attained the full flood of its prosperity when, after some thirty years, a periodical for women appointed itself *The Magazine of Togetherness.* But nothing fails like success, and popularity may have killed the word, at least in the minds of sensible men. They began to celebrate it with gibes. A columnist writing about the desirability of summer vacations for parents says: *Over the years I have watched—at first with amusement, then with contempt, finally with dread—the spread of the concept of togetherness into almost every part of our national life.* One should imitate this writer in his contempt, but not in his CONCEPT. A correspondent of the *New York Times,* enraged by the use of *forgiveness* as a term for a year's remission of income tax, writes: *Having already had a certain amount of "togetherness" imposed on us from the outside, the feelings of group guilt aroused by* *the use of "forgiveness" by the state authorities seem hardly consonant with our ideals of democracy.* For his objection to both the *-ness* words, one readily forgives him the deviant participle and false *had* (see HAVE, NONCAUSATIVE).

too. 1. Introductory. 2. Meaning *very*.

1. Introductory. A mannerism that has become rather modish among writers of short stories for the popular magazines—it is but rarely found anywhere else—is the sentence begun with *Too* (= also): *Too, while he was walking the safe, sure line of the street, it would be wise to think of other matters than the cold, the snow and the empty dark.* Though hardly distinguishable from *too* in meaning, *and, furthermore,* and other additive words can open a sentence with naturalness and grace; *too* is inherently sequelant, backward-facing, and stoutly resistant to taking precedence. (See AS 11.)

2. Meaning *very*. The slovenly distortion of usages which is now in favor with many academic minds has affected the simple word *too* in such a way that in one of its frequent and necessary functions it is incurably ambiguous. The corruption began by attacking the excellent idiom *none too: As he entered the examination room, Robert was aware that he was none too well prepared.*
By analysis this gives: *he was not too well prepared by even the smallest margin,* and this thought is an ironic rendering of *he was not prepared enough.* By ignorance and distortion, the idiom became *I am not too well prepared / I don't know too much about it / I think he's not feeling too well.* In this version there is neither logic nor irony, but self-contradiction and ample room for the ambiguity that now plagues us. The reader who encounters sentences such as *As a collection of first poems it cannot be praised too much / This material is not too good for the purpose* is unable to tell whether the poems are bad or good, whether the material is of just the right quality or quite unsuitable. And there is no way out of the impasse, for these expressions, which may mean yes or no despite the immediately surrounding words, are the direct and normal ways of saying very necessary things.

to the for **per.** See A, AN, THE 7.

transfer, transform. These two words look confusion-proof in spite of their sharing a first syllable plus two consonants, but in fact they are not so. An advertisement that internal evidence suggests was designed by one of the high-toned agencies and printed in a magazine quarterly, sumptuously assures us that an expensive little clock *transfers a mantel into a showcase*. (See DANGEROUS PAIRS and MALAPROPS).

transitive, intransitive. The words that form the heading of this entry apply in the first instance to verbs, and much might be said of the differentiation and its effects. But as the sort of error aimed at in this brief article results from a broader failure than that of confusing verbs, the caption must be taken as denoting a general blindness to what may be termed *the point of view*. This ignorance or indifference affects not only the use of verbs but the choice of nouns and adjectives. When, for example, we have two adjectives, *nauseous* and *nauseated,* it should be clear that the first applies to the substance that causes the state named in the second. To call oneself *nauseous* except in self-depreciation is to ignore the point of view of the word.

On the side of a truck in the service of a leather-and-findings firm one reads *We carry all needs for the shoe.* Now, it is obviously not *needs* that are carried by the firm, but the wherewithal to supply those needs. The word wanted is possibly *requisites.* A peculiarity of words is that to the careless they will seem equivalent when they are not. *Needed* and *required* are close; hence

needs and *requisites* should be just as close. But *needs* concerns trade only as unfilled wants, whereas *requisites* means the objects required. In short, *needs* is, in the special sense here adopted, *intransitive.* (The terms *objective* and *subjective* could have been used, had their loose employment in common speech not dragged in irrelevant ideas.) Names matter little; the point is that most words possess an inherent direction, ascertainable from usage and to be preserved for the sake of rapid and exact communication.

These differences are established sometimes by usage, sometimes by conventional endings. For example, the latter-day coinage *readership* is unfortunate in that it shifts the intransitive quality marked by *-ship* (the quality of being a reader or the state of being engaged in reading) to a transitive use—a collection of readers. This is not an impossible shift (the Fellowship of the Rose may be a society), but it is undesirable as contributing to the general diffuseness of aim that is weakening many words. It is just as easy to say *The readers of this magazine are adults* as *The readership . . . is adult;* and the more concrete word prevents the frequent *Our readership are . . .*

But to return to the aspect that a word may present to the exclusion of other aspects:

When a member of the United States Foreign Service is capable of sending a letter to the press stating that *The Secretary of State is attributed as writing*, etc., it is not too soon to utter a word of caution. A. *attributes* a statement *to* B.—it is a transitive act; B. cannot be *attributed as* doing anything whatever. Similarly, *rankle* is intransitive and cannot be used as in *if her remarks have rankled anybody* . . . The remarks have simply *rankled* (= festered) in the person they offended.

Often, as in *nauseous-nauseated*, the correlative ideas have bred paired words. To use them interchangeably is to destroy good work done. Thus, *suspicious* should designate the persons harboring a suspicion and *suspect* the person who is the object of it. From this it follows that one cannot be *seen carrying a suitcase in a suspicious manner.* Consider also: *The agency was authorized programs in all fields* (Programs proposed by the agency were authorized) / *It is called the Foundation for Aging Research* (whiskey but not research is improved by aging; say: *Foundation for the Study of Aging*). In VIET ATTACK UNLEASHED it is not possible to know who attacked whom: the article showed the meaning to be ATTACK AGAINST THE VIETCONG. *An excellent compensatable compass* (compensating) / *All is*

not roses for the permissive child (permissively reared child). (See also DUBIOUS.)

Sometimes the blunder is more subtle; it lies in the meaning rather than the usage of the word. Consider *His whole being registered annoyance.* Does *registered* mean (as it should) *recorded*—a purely inward act? Or did it not in the writer's mind stand for *expressed?* The jargon of the movie studios is no doubt responsible for the confusion. Many other words are heedlessly deformed in this all-important respect of the direction they point to. *A corporation is the one place left where a man can accrue a considerable amount of power* (power can *accrue to* a man; the man cannot *accrue*; he must *acquire*) / *I am constantly reminded to serve you with all the knowledge and ability I possess* (this advertiser can *remind himself*, can be *mindful*, or simply *remember*, but unless nagged by someone he is not *constantly reminded*). Again, *these were some of the foreign lands hied to during his travels* (he hied himself to is required if such a verb is to be used at all) / *Our speaker will envisage you the future of this great institution* (the speaker can only *envisage* for himself; *will describe to you*). Other examples that show the extent of the damage being done: *but his prospects to succeed the next time are said to be good* (his prospects *are* his chances of succeeding) / *The lack of plumbing will not deter its being leased* (a circumstance *deters* a person from doing something; the verb wanted is *prevent*) / *The new office will enable a closer liaison between X. Co. and its public* (a device *enables* someone to perform his task; substitute *make possible*).

Writers on scientific subjects are apt to think they are achieving compression when they adapt a common word to a new use in disregard of what was called above its direction. Scientific practice leads to saying a *signed graph* for one bearing plus and minus signs and *lawful behavior* for a process of which the law is known. These extensions are neither necessary nor condonable. It is just as easy and much less harmful to logic to say a *sign graph* and a *process that is understood.* (If *sign graph* sounds like *sine graph,* then there is no help but from the expenditure of two more syllables: *plus-and-minus graph.*)

Another kind of grammatical anarchism has inspired the use of *cladding* to denote the *clothing* of a metal with another substance—quite as if *clad* were not a past participle, which makes *cladding* = *clotheding.*

With adverbs the trouble is less one of misdirection than of no direction at all. *Thankfully, the Governor vetoed the bill* (presumably this means *we are thankful that . . .* ; see HOPEFULLY) / *Incredibly, the results will have to be gone over* (in context this may mean either *Hard as it is to believe* or *Being hard to believe*) / *Reportedly, both were not available for comments* (*It is reported,* or *According to report*).

At other times the error consists in taking the antonym of a word well understood as pointing in the exactly opposite way and thus as suitable for the desired meaning. In a statement from the Quebec police addressed to women wearing shorts, we read: *Involuntarily you have committed an infraction of By-law 784 concerning decency.* Now, wearing shorts or not wearing them is a voluntary act; the infraction of the law by doing the first is an *unwitting* act; the police draftsman did not sufficiently consider in what direction the opposite of *voluntary* (willful) pointed, and he used its opposite to mean *without intending to.*

See also ACCOUNT FOR; AVAIL; -EE, -ER; PURGE; REPORTEDLY; UN-, IN-, NON-.

transpire is the old, rather pompous word for what we now call *leak out.* Accordingly, it is not a synonym for *happen, occur, take place.* The familiar *What transpired at the* *meeting is not yet known* says the exact opposite of what the writer meant. If anything had *transpired* we should already know it. Hence the wrong-rightness of the *New York Times* comment: *Since little transpires that does not leak out, the Vatican itself is somewhat embarrassed.* Use *happen* and *leak* and leave *transpire* to die quietly.

trespassers will be prosecuted. It may be pardonable pedantry to point out that criminal trespass, which might justify prosecution, has been abolished nearly everywhere. Trespass now gives warrant only for a civil suit. Ergo, all the stout trees bearing the familiar printed notice are unconstitutional and should be relabeled: *Trespassers Will Be Sued.*

trigger, verb. From the moment of its adoption to signify the device for activating an atomic bomb, this word was foredoomed to become an omnibus VOGUE WORD for *set off, touch off, produce, induce, precipitate, be preceded by, occasion, initiate, incite to, lead to, bring about,* and simply *cause.* It has in fact become one of the most overworked words of the century. *Some 1,000 undergraduates ... staged a noisy demonstration that apparently was triggered by fire sirens / What made that handclasp especially dra-matic was the chain of events it triggered off / The sight of her standing there . . . triggered a quick, unreasoning anger / lest a false move, as in a Grade B Western, trigger bloodshed / If this glandular overactivity is continually triggered by stress, it may upset almost every system of the body / Unintentional or irrational triggering* [of a nuclear attack] *is conceivable in a time of tension.* Is *trigger* so apt that it must displace the whole vocabulary of causation and precedence? (See FORBIDDEN WORDS 2.)

triumvirate. The need for Latin is demonstrated in many curious ways. COHORT is perverted by writers whose understanding stops at its first syllable. *Triumvirate* is similarly misapplied, though not so popularly, by those whose grasp is limited to the prefix *tri-*. "The third 'great triumvirate' in American Lutheranism," Dr. F. said, "is the 3,000,000-member Lutheran-Church-Missouri-Synod." For the extension of *triumvirate* from its basic meaning of government by three men to administration by three parties or powers there is some dictionary sanction; but if the word is to escape absurdity the parties or powers must be represented by individuals—there must be something akin to personification. To call the Missouri Synod a triumvirate because it has three million members, or to call American Lutheranism a triumvirate because it is composed of three sects, is to strain language beyond its strength. Moreover, if each of these three sects is a triumvirate, as the form of statement implies, then there must be nine triumvirs altogether —three threes.

The ultimate perversion occurs when *triumvirate* is divested of all connection with human beings. A financial note about the offerings of an investment house reads: *Now, National Investors will be the growth fund of the triumvirate,* meaning three diversified stocks. *Triumvirate* is pedantic as a substitute for *triad, trinity,* and *trio.* Sanity calls for its return to the root idea of three *men,* and to the connotation of men entrusted with authority. Jerome K. Jerome would have been foolish to call his book *Triumvirate in a Boat.*

trivia. See DEFENSIBLES; LOST CAUSES.

try and. Not suitable, perhaps, for the highest reaches of eloquence, *try and* is nevertheless an idiom in good standing that need not be avoided or changed to *try to.* There is in fact a shade of difference between them. *Try to* is unmistakably purposive. Nobody thinks of saying *I will try and climb Mount Everest:* I will *try to* is compulsory. But the very casualness of form in *try and* makes it worth preserving for occasions when no definite time or effort of will is stipulated. *He knows we want one; he'll try and pick one up for us.*

type. The use of this word in apposition with the name of a person or a thing is not yet acceptable syntax. Even in speech *a champagne-type drink, an accommodating-type girl* are felt to be either slovenly or jocular—slovenly because the locution comes raw from dealers' catalogues (*a snake-skin-type plastic*), jocular because there is some faint humor in talking like a catalogue.

U

un-, in-, non-; -less; divergent negatives. Bottles containing certain liquids (notably gasoline) for domestic use, like the tanks and trucks that store or carry these materials in bulk, are apt nowadays to display the word *flammable* in a prominent place. This relatively new word came into being when it was found that more and more people took the word *inflammable* to mean *not capable of burning.* They were reasoning by analogy from the many words in *in-* in which the prefix means *not* and forgetting the smaller number in which it either means *in* or serves as an intensive (or locative) particle—*inhere, infect, inspire, incarcerate, incandescent, insure,* as well as *intensive* itself and, of course, *inflammable* in its original meaning.

The change to *flammable* is justified if it helps to avert accidents due to misjudging the properties of materials that flash, burn, or explode. It should be noted, however, that the shortening of the word has not touched *inflammatory* or *inflamed.* Speeches that incite to violence are still called by the former, as living tissues that are red and swollen are

called by the latter. Perhaps, too, the figurative use of *inflammable* (= easily aroused) will remain unaffected by the practical change. Novelists and biographers will continue to speak of an *inflammable* temperament, rather than a *flammable* one.

The use of negative prefixes in general will likewise continue to perplex writers and speakers who do not make a point of attending to the usages that prevail in this realm of mixed anarchy and strict rule. There is in truth no guide through it but from wide reading or recourse to a dictionary, coupled with conscious effort to follow in practice what has been learned or observed. Still, a few hints can be given about what to look for.

(1) One group of words can take either *in-* or *un-* with no change in meaning and no oddity of sound suggestive of unfamiliarity with usage: *inopportune* and *unopportune, inalterable* and *unalterable, inconsolable* and *unconsolable,* etc.

(2) Two other groups divide between them the invariable *in-* and invariable *un-* words: *incoherent, inescapable, indelible, indistin-*

guishable, intolerant, etc. / *unmentionable, uncontrollable, undiscovered, unusual, unacceptable, unenforceable,* etc.

(3) Some words take *un-* in some of their forms (usually those based on the verb) and *in-* in others (usually the adjective forms): *undecided* but *indecisive, undivided* but *indivisible, undefended* but *indefensible, unsupported* but *insupportable, unvarying* but *invariable, unstable* but *instability, undifferentiated* but *indifferent, uncertainty* but *incertitude.*

(4) Words that are being negated for the occasion and that are not likely to be of frequent utility take *un-*: *Despite their promise, they left the equipment unrepaired / He seemed pleasant enough by nature, but he was obviously undomesticated / At that point the stream became unnavigable.*

(5) Some words that take both *un-* and *in-* undergo a slight shift in meaning—or at least in connotation—when the form changes. One would be likely to say that a remark or assertion was *inadmissible* and that a person was *unadmissible*; that a course of action was *inadvisable* but that a man in anger was *unadvisable.* The difference usually shows *un-* to be literal and *in-* figurative.

The difficulty of threading one's way through this irregular maze tempts the cautious to avoid it altogether and take refuge in *non-.* This easy path has recently been made still more attractive by the increasing desire to classify everything into two groups like a digital computer; e.g. *fiction* and *nonfiction, alcoholic* and *nonalcoholic, age-determined unemployment* and *non-age-determined unemployment.* This tendency is to be deplored, both because of the ugly, unarticulated compounds it produces, and because the twofold division with *non-* is likely to suggest a strictness that it does not always possess. For example, *fiction* is now used to denote novels and short stories; that is, *prose* fiction alone. But poetry, which is also properly fiction (i.e. invention), thereby comes to be classed with nonfiction. Moreover, the *non-* forms are often unnecessary, either because established *in-* (or *un-*) forms exist, or because the contrast would be better made between a positive and a negative word. There is no need to say *weapons can be classed as defensive and nondefensive* when the pair *defensive* and *offensive* is in common use.

Usage has set for certain words that bear negative appendages a positive role. *Invaluable* is the chief of those; it means *highly valuable,* as does *priceless.* If one wants to say *without value,* one must say *valueless* or *worthless*; and for the literal sense of *lacking a price* one must say *unpriced,* because *without price* has also come to connote high value.

These results of idiom and rhetoric combined should put a writer or speaker on his guard against believing that negatives are always what they appear to be and can therefore be coined or turned into their opposites by the simple addition or dropping of a familiar prefix or suffix. The fact is that numerous words diverge in meaning from their ostensible opposites. Thus *modest* means unassuming, having a small notion of one's talents; but *immodest* means lacking in decency or sense of shame. *Shame*(*d*), in turn, is not the direct opposite of *shameless*, which again refers to some flouting of morality or convention. (See under CONNOTATIONS: *graceless, ungraceful*.) The obvious example of *canny* (= shrewd) and *uncanny* (= ghostly, mysterious) should serve as a reminder of divergence in negatives.

Two other words that cause confusion or paradox deserve mention—*unloose* and *unbend*. The meaning of *loose* as a verb puzzles no one, yet the practice of writers and speakers shows a strong desire to intensify that meaning by saying *unloose*. It is as if *he loosed the dog* might create confusion with *lost*, or at any rate seemed incomplete without an additional syllable. By a similar means *loose off* is merely rein-

forced in the sense of *discharge, let fly*; but the idea of *untying* doubtless suggests the illogical *unloose*. If this common mistake can be resisted, the urge to commit it can perhaps be satisfied by saying *made loose, set loose*, and, in situations where the subject himself is in bonds, *get loose*.

Unbend (past *unbent*) is similarly in contradiction with itself, but beyond recall. The figurative idea is that of a stiffness of manner relaxing under the influence of civility, kindness, alcohol, or some other emollient. One should therefore write: *After a cocktail or two he bent*. But we say and will continue to say *he unbent*. The confusion is made worse by the equally fixed use of *unbending*. A man of *unbending* courage or honesty is obviously one whose virtues will remain stiff and strong against pressure, fear, or temptation—inflexible virtues. So we are left with the linguistic curiosity of *unbend*, which means *soften, relax, become amenable;* and *unbending*, which means *stiff, braced*, and *unamenable*.

See also NEGATIVES, TROUBLE WITH.

unbend. See UN-, IN-, NON-.

under. See LAY, LIE.

underhandedly. See SINGLEHANDEDLY.

understatement. Like exaggeration, understatement must be sparingly used or it loses its force and grows tiresome. And however used, understatement is not attained by the mere pulling down of strong words with the aid of contrary adverbs—*faintly, slightly, rather, somewhat*. These marks of the so-called casual style are getting increasingly hard to bear. This is true whether or not the juxtaposition is logical or antilogical. For example, it is possible to be—hence it is logical to say—*faintly nauseated*. But this mode of expressing weary distaste is no better than the impossible and illogical *somewhat appalling*. In other words, irony and sophistication are not to be bought so cheaply, even if they were proved to be finer ornaments than sincerity and good sense. Examples of what to avoid: *As I looked down the long room, despite my prejudice against baronial halls, I was rather overwhelmed / The addition of that blue feather, though she did not know it, was somewhat disastrous / He smiled again in that set way of his and lisped his "Doubtless," and I wondered if everybody felt his hypocrisy and was faintly nauseated like me.*

undue, unduly. The danger in this pair lies in its tendency to produce a statement which, by saying a thing twice, says nothing. You may, for example, instruct a messenger *to avoid delay*. But if you tell him *to avoid undue delay*, you are telling him nothing he did not know before as a general proposition; namely, that all undue actions are to be avoided. Comparable illogicalities occur with other words in *un-* whose meanings imply rule or necessity. Thus the police force that excused itself by saying that *they did not coerce the accused unduly* was making a poor case, unless it thought coercion permissible in small amounts. Again, there is no reassurance in the treasurer's report that boasts of *a reduction in unnecessary expense.*

uninclined. See DISINTERESTED.

uninterested(ness). See DISINTERESTED.

unique. See ABSOLUTE WORDS.

unleakable. See NONLEAKABLE.

unless. The meaning of *unless* always holds within it the idea of a real choice. *Unless I go to Rome, I shall not see the Pope* implies: *I may or may not go; if I do not, then I shall not* . . . This presupposition of doubt disqualifies *unless* from expressing what a sentient being is compelled to do or undergo under some stated conditions. Hence *un-*

less is misplaced and even ludicrous in *You cannot step into a small boat unless the owner feels it.* Here the *unless* tries to denote necessity and fails. In some dialects the speaker of the maxim about small boats would say *without the owner feels it.* But standard English regards *without* as a preposition, not a conjunction, and calls for *without the owner's feeling it.* See WITHOUT for UNLESS.

unless and until. Like IF AND WHEN, this formula is a way of combining conjunctions that have different meanings if kept apart but achieve only duplication when combined. *Unless and until this quota is reached, the allotments will stand as at present* gives the same result with either conjunction as with both; nor is the result changed if for *and* we substitute *or,* as is sometimes done. One wonders why those who fancy this bit of JARGON do not go the whole way and write *unless and/or until* (SEE AND/OR).

unlike. See DANGLERS 3; LIKE 2.

unloose, verb. See UN-, IN-, NON-.

unpractical. See PRACTICAL; LOST CAUSES.

unquote. See QUOTE, UNQUOTE.

unrealistic. See REALISTIC.

unsavory pasts. Despite the hardening of usage in the conjugation of verbs, certain forms of the past (preterit) and past participle remain uncertain. Among these are, first, the alternatives to the dominant form: *proven* instead of *proved, gotten* instead of *got, pled* instead of *pleaded.* In American usage *pleaded* is educated, *pled* is not; *proven* tends to slip in with the negative, probably because of the familiar verdict of the Scotch courts: *not proven. Proved* is surely the prevailing form in the positive. *Gotten,* however, is more widespread in the United States than *got,* but it causes disquiet even in those who use it, by reason of its echoing *begotten* and of the difficulty of sticking to it when one wants an intensive for *I have.* When that need occurs *I've got* is the only usable form, because *gotten* implies a progressive movement: *I've gotten steadily worse since the doctor came;* but *I've got two tickets and the price of a dinner*—to say nothing of *I've got to go.* The advocates of system and simplicity use *got* throughout. Note that the British meaning in *Nobody had got to know he was there* requires *had come to know* in the United States. With *got,* the American meaning of that sentence is *Nobody had to know, got* being a mere intensive. And by its progressive sense the American *gotten* would give the exact British meaning—*had come to know*.

In the next class are the variables resulting from accidental similarities or compulsory differences. For example, *a drunken man* uses the compulsory form of the past participle; this makes *drunk* seem to be exclusively a noun; and the upshot is a temptation to say *I have drank*, which is sometimes heard on the lips of those who are neither drunk nor drunken. *Showed* and *shown* present the same instability, whether on account of *shown-shone* is hard to say. The fact remains that *I have showed* slips from the mouths of educated people and does so again and again, even when they correct themselves after each lapse. Still more confused are *sawed* and *sawn*. Thanks to gangster stories a *sawed-off shotgun* seems the only possible form, but *he had sawed off the projection* sounds rustic for *sawn*. To put *weave* in the past calls for a decision as to the degree of its literalness. *He weaved in and out of the heavy traffic* sounds acceptable, but not *San Francisco weaved its early life around Telegraph Hill*. A reason is at work here though it defies analysis.

The third class is due to an inexplicable embarrassment arising from what the speaker thinks is the making of a weak verb in -*ed* out of a strong verb ending in a dental. *Fit* and *bet* are the chief representatives. The educated woman who tells her husband that she bought a *fitted* nightgown will also say that she *tried on a suit and it fit*. Her husband is almost certain to say that *he bet on a horse* the previous week and has not the money to buy *the suit that fit*. It remains the truth that *betted* and *fitted* are the only recognized forms, at least for publishable writings.

In the class of *dream, learn, pass*, etc., both -*ed* and -*t* serve to make past tenses of equal acceptability, though distinctions other than of sound may be (and are) attached by some writers to each of the variants. (See *passed master* under SPELLING.)

Dare has the past *dared*, which should be used without hesitation, despite a tendency to use *dare*, at least in speech, as both present and preterit.

Dive and *strive* also give uncertain pasts; namely, *dove, dived* for the preterit, but only *dived* for the past participle; *strove* for the preterit and *striven, strived* for the past participle.

A special case arose when broadcasting came into being. The logicians argued for the past *broadcasted*, because compounds give weak verbs in -*ed*, and they instanced *forecasted*. But *cast* was so strong—at least in the United States—that neither -*ed* has survived on any plane of speech or writing: It is *broadcast* and *forecast* throughout present, past, and past participle.

unthinkable. This is one word that cannot sensibly be taken as meaning what it says. The very fact of calling an idea unthinkable is an implicit assertion that someone has thought it. *"It is unthinkable on the part of labor,"* said G., *"that we should go back, after having taken such a forward step in economic planning."* Clearly, G. could not have made this remark unless he had envisaged the dread possibility and rejected it. Raymond Moley's *Industrial laissez-faire is unthinkable* names a perfectly thinkable historical reality. If the word is not to be banned altogether in mere fussy literalism, it has to be taken as meaning *preposterous, impracticable, unacceptable,* or *totally repellent*— meanings for which it is a reasonable enough shorthand. Not even a square circle is unthinkable; it is merely unattainable as an actuality. Whatever can be named can be thought.

until. See UP TILL.

unwield(l)y. One still hears and sees much too frequently this mistaking of an adjective ending in *-dy* for a nonexistent adverb ending in *-ly*. The corrective sequence of ideas is *wield, wieldy, unwieldy,*

though the term in the middle is not in use.

upon. See ON, UPON, UP ON.

up till; up until; up to. The wish to give more and more emphasis by gathering prepositions and other linking terms in little clusters between or around main words is very strong in American English. First we *check,* then we *check up,* finally we *check up on* somebody's identity or good faith. The practice may be wasteful but it is harmless, except when the words so joined contain a hidden overlap or duplication, as in the phrases before us. *Till* means *as far as* a certain point in time or space; that is, *up to* that point. In consequence, *up till* actually says *up up to,* and so does *up until,* which has the further disadvantage of resembling a stutter. The traditional forms are best in their simple elegance: who would want to pledge love *up until death do us part?*

usage, use. The word *use* in the singular can be interchangeable with *usage;* a word fitly spoken is in either good use or good usage. But *usage* has no use outside the subject of language. To substitute *usage* for *use* when the meaning is usefulness or employment or wear is a solecism that illustrates the spell exerted on many of us by an extra syllable. A literary gossip column remarks of an officer whose military career was helped by his authorship of a book: *Literature sometimes has surprising usages* (uses). An article about the changing habits of buyers says that motorcars are now *chosen more for usage* (use, usefulness) *than for their prestige,* and an article about the expanding utility of the station wagon grants that its predominant function is still *family usage* (use). We read in an editorial: *It is an unfortunate*

fact that relatively few . . . American schools take a positive stand by offering strong courses in "dictionary usage" (the use of the dictionary). Everyone commands the idiom *make use of,* and probably no one is under temptation to convert it to *make usage of.* To do so would be no more unnatural than *usage* in the foregoing examples. See CONNOTATIONS.

utilize. See NEEDLESS WORDS 1.

V

values. See POPULARIZED TECHNICALITIES.

verbal means *relating to words* without specifying whether the words are spoken or written. Consequently, the common phrase *verbal agreement* to mean one that is not written down is a misnomer. The proper term is *oral agreement—oral* meaning *by* [word of] *mouth.* To capture and preserve the distinction, think of *oral exam* and *verbal aptitude test.*

verbiage. 1. The idea of excess or waste is inseparable from this word; it applies only to words that ought not to be there, like weeds in a garden; it is an offensive label, whether true or untrue, and no synonym for *speech, words,* or *wording.* When a baseball broadcaster turns man of letters between innings and, promising to make a long story short, says that he will practice *economy of verbiage,* what he is practicing is a contradiction in terms. *Economy of verbiage* signifies a shortage of excess, or not too much too-muchness. Accordingly, *You make the policy decision, and I'll provide the verbiage* becomes ambiguous by reason of verbiage; for rightly understood, the statement implies that the policy is going to be wrapped up in a cloud of words designed to obscure the point. If, contrariwise, *verbiage* was intended for *wording,* the speaker was either ignorant or self-depreciating. For denoting the number of words in a piece of writing, use the term *wordage.* (See also CONNOTATIONS.)

2. As to what constitutes verbiage, opinions may differ in particular instances. What is fullness, abundance, a rich fancy to one critic is excess and redundancy to another. But in ordinary prose, verbiage is almost always present. The excuse is the classic one that the writer of the memorandum, the article, the topical book did not have time to make it shorter. Conciseness takes not only skill but patience, and these are not within the reach of the journeyman. Still, he and almost everybody else can profit by a reminder that verbiage is an evil to fight against. The young or inexperienced writer particularly needs encouragement to be succinct. His first promptings to write have perhaps come from a love of words, and this love often takes the form of a belief that the more words *and syllables* he can use, the better. Only with experience and discipline does the natural man learn to express his love of words by making fewer of them count for more.

Getting rid of superfluous words has an advantage commonly overlooked: the automatic suppression of weaknesses that flourish in diffuse writing but are starved out by economy. There is nothing like terseness for protecting the writer against himself—except silence. Anyone who will struggle to reduce his hundred words to fifty without losing meaning will see looseness, inconsistency, and aberration vanish.

To test this by example, take a passage from a book about life within the Arctic Circle—a book crammed with information about human and animal behavior, weather, travel, scenery, and other phenomena of the high latitudes; a book that has everything one could ask for except good, tight writing. Here is a representative paragraph about one of the ways of catching seals:

Another way of luring the seal —although not so profitable as the first—is to fool him while he is under the water. Two men walk behind each other, keeping step with one another, so that the seal down below hears them. To the seal it sounds as if only one man were walking. When they reach the blowhole, the location of which must be known first, the first man continues on, while the other takes a stand by the hole without moving at all. The seal thinks that the man has passed by without noticing the blowhole, and after a while he confidently comes to the hole, only to find out too late that he has been fooled.

Notice the defects. First is the illogicality of *Two men walk behind each other*—A. walks behind B., B. behind A. Next the clumsiness of calling the pair *each other* and *one another* in the same sentence. Notice also the chance echoes of *another* repeated, of *first* repeated, of *seal* occurring four times. Why write *continues on,* and mention *luring the seal,* since that is the subject of the whole section from which this passage comes? Why point out that the seal is under the water? *Blowhole* is enough, and it is obvious that the two men could not approach it if its location were not known. Further waste occurs in having the seal listen twice to their footsteps (*hears them; it sounds as if*). And a good reader will not care what the author thinks a seal thinks about what the hunter thinks. The writer talks as if to feeble minds. By the right kind of effort he could have said his say in a paragraph as short as this:

Another, less profitable way is this: Two men approach a blowhole, keeping step, so that the seal hears them as one. The leader walks on past the blowhole; the harpooner stops by it, motionless. Soon the deluded seal confidently comes to the hole and is caught.

An element of suspense has doubtless been lost in reducing 119 words to 46, but such an exercise in compression shows how much bad writing and bad thinking disappear in the boiling down: there is no longer room for them.

Verbiage and loose thought are at once the cause and the result of JARGON. In attempting to dignify the commonplace while permitting composition to be absent-minded, jargon lengthens the expression of every idea. As A. P. Herbert pointed out: "Today, instead of 'fun,' we learn to speak of 'entertainment-value'; instead of Tories we have 'the forces of reaction'; instead of games, 'recreational facilities.' Instead of swords and guns there are 'casualty-producing weapons.' We no longer work together; we 'co-operate according to a co-ordinated plan. . . .' We do not hunger or starve; we 'exhibit evidences of malnutrition,' or 'our diet is characterized by protein deficiency.' "

The very words themselves suffer from the general inflation. The verb *orient* (for *set right*) has become *orientate*; *delimit, delimitate; difference, differential* and *differentiation; interpret, interpretate;* and so on through the vast realm of our earnest vocabulary for public use. Verbiage is the rule, readable prose the exception. Since readers complain of the length and dullness of what their curiosity or their work puts before their eyes, they have an obligation, when they write in their turn, to reduce as much as they can the world output of verbiage.

verbs. See SUBJUNCTIVE; TRANSITIVE; INTRANSITIVE; UNSAVORY PASTS; VOICE; WHAT IS "UNDERSTOOD"?

very. Speakers and writers seem to feel less and less sensitive to the idiomatic as well as logical difference between true adjectives (such as *sorry*) and adjectives formed from verbs (such as *disappointed*). The result is that *very disappointed* sounds in their ears as acceptable as *very sorry*. The fact remains that finer ears are offended by past participles modified by *very* without the intervention of the quantitative *much*, which respects the verbal sense of an action undergone. Such writers require *very much disappointed, very much pleased, very much engrossed, very well satisfied,* etc. Only a few adjectives from verbs—*tired, drunk,* and possibly *depressed*—have shed enough of their verbal quality to stand an immediately preceding *very*. For the rest, a careful writer would no more put down *I'm very delighted* than he would *I'm very lost, he was very feared by his family, her new book is being very read by the intelligentsia,* etc. See also NEEDLESS WORDS 2.

vested interest. By association with attacks on trusts and other powerful groups, the phrase has acquired the connotation of *sinister, powerful,* or *corrupt. Vested interests* may well be so in any given case, but the words do not imply this and their neutral sense is useful. Everybody has a vested interest in some institution or organization to the extent that he has given his time, labor, or money to make it flourish. The philanthropist has a vested interest in the hospital he helps to support, the housewife has a vested interest in the family she is bringing up, the fisherman has a vested interest in the pond he keeps restocking, and so on.

via. Airmail envelopes printed in France and Germany read —along with *Par Avion* and *Mit Luftpost—By Airmail.* Those printed in the United States read *Via Air Mail.* The difference is an indication that Europeans still respect the literal, geographical meaning of the Latinism *via* and do not extend it as we do on the analogy *by way of = by means of.* Americans tend to take it as meaning both. Easterners can certainly go to the West Coast via Chicago or via St. Louis; can they, properly speaking, go there via train? Many think they can, and we are continually reading of the man that made a fortune via market speculation, the juvenile delinquent that got into trouble via bad company, the manufacturer that promotes his product via radio, and so on: *Presidential candidates can appear throughout the country in far less time than ever before, both in person and via television / the belief that the public has a "right to know"—via courtroom photographs and TV.* It is always a pity when a word or phrase becomes an omnibus expression, for it displaces more exact names or connectives. If *via* is not to be reserved for itineraries and timetables, why not give it a rest altogether and resume the use of *by, through,* and *by way of?*

viable. See METAPHOR 3; VOGUE WORDS.

view (as). See AS 2.

viewing. See DANGLERS, ACCEPTABLE.

vis-à-vis. See FRENCH WORDS AND PHRASES.

vogue words. Public men no less than poets strike off phrases that fit a mood or an occasion, and their words become for a time the means by which men of smaller invention can appear witty or wise.

Finally the charm wears off, but long before then the point has been blunted through excessive and mechanical repetition. That is, the repetition is more and more frequently *in*appropriate; this drives out meaning and leaves only irritation in the hearers. Thus *agonizing reappraisal* turned into a nuisance from the moment when every reappraisal had to be called agonizing regardless of the facts. Likewise *calculated risk* when only *risk* is meant, and so on with dozens of others.

It would be tedious to list all the phrases of this sort that gain currency at a certain time and place. The caution here offered is to remember the principle just stated, that a catch phrase must fit, or it will impart both staleness and stupidity to the conversation or the article. Again, those phrases are soon boring that follow an odd yet too imitable formula for their construction; for example, the now intolerable definition by *is* with a plural or an abstraction: *X Country Day School is people* / *America is neighborliness* / *Z. Magazine is places people keep to themselves* / *A diamond solitaire is once in a lifetime.* The flaunted untruth of these equations is matched only by the childish cleverness of the *is* form. A comparable vogue is that based on *sound of,* after *The Sound of Music.* We now have the *sound of genius,* the *sound of*

success, etc. Reserve *sound* for what can be heard—music, prose, protest, porpoises under water, etc.

Another type of vogue-mongering consists in replacing expressive yet neutral words by synonyms which at first make the hearer wonder whether something else is meant. *Analysis* was for decades the accepted word for business and government statistics and reports until displaced by *breakdown,* which has the disadvantage of occasional ambiguity. *He had a breakdown before the meeting and I took a good look at it* / *This was a report on the population of the U.S. broken down by age and sex.* Similarly, the word *now* has gone into eclipse. Everybody feels an irresistible urge to say *current, currently, presently. He is presently Vice President in charge of sales* / *currently ambassador to Thailand* / *We want it to go out to our people in current form, not later.*

The same pretentious tone, but mixed with archness, occurs in the cant use of *operative*—e.g. *the operative word* / *the distinction is especially operative in Coleridge's religious teachings*—and again in *any resemblance . . . is purely coincidental.* Shall we ever again hear *is a coincidence, is accidental?*

Among single words whose vogue is suspect, the attentive will note *viable* (for any form of success), *delicious* (for things other than food), *repercussive* (for things that do not clang), *brittle* and *abrasive* (to describe character), *fault* (as a verb), *massive* (as an omnibus sign of magnitude or importance), *decisionmaking* (in one word and where *deciding* has prior claim), *tie-in* (for any connection whatever), *thinking* (as a noun: *your thinking, my thinking*), *develop* (for gather or compile facts, figures, etc.), VOLATILE, *dual* (for *double*, or simply *two*), *brief* (for *short*), *initial* (for *first*), and *dialogue* (for *conversation, negotiation, interview*).

Finally, the conscious user of words has an obligation to keep alive in their established meanings the words that politics may suddenly restrict to one emotionally charged sense. In Europe after the last war it was impossible for a time to refer to a *collaborator* in an enterprise: the word was a term of abuse. Now in the United States *discrimination* is in danger of meaning only (unjust) discrimination (in matters of race and nationality). And not only *segregate* and *integrate* as well, but also words and phrases such as *sensitive, security, rights, civil rights,* and *pleading the Fifth Amendment,* which topical use has narrowed down or misapplied out of all recognition. *Civil rights* now often means *political rights,* and the appeal to the amendment against self-incrimination now implies a charge of Communist affiliation. Words are too valuable to be clipped in this way; their integrity must continually be restored by proper use in clear contexts.

See also CONTACT; EDUCATIONESE; IMPINGE; JARGON; METAPHOR; POPULARIZED TECHNICALITIES; SCIENTISM.

voice. 1. *Voice,* active or passive, is the name of the linguistic apparatus that doubles the resources of expression by giving us a choice whether to say that so-and-so performed such-and-such an action or that the action was performed by him. *The Niagara Falls Suspension Bridge was designed and built by the elder Roebling* says in the passive voice what is said in the active voice by *The elder Roebling designed and built the . . . Bridge.* There is not the slightest difference between the two in contents, but the difference in effect is considerable. The first sentence presupposes a context about the bridge, or perhaps about suspension bridges; it would be a bad sentence in a context about the Roeblings. The second fastens attention on the designer and builder, and it would be bad in a passage about bridges. Voice, in short, is an expedient for throwing the weight of a sentence where it is wanted. Voice is technically and grammatically a property of verbs alone, but actually it controls the whole pattern of a sentence by determining its subject—what it shall be written *about*. *"Scheherazade" was used by Diaghilev as ballet music* (passive) and *Diaghilev used "Scheherazade" as ballet music* (active) have the very material difference that one is about Rimsky-Korsakov and music, the other about Diaghilev and ballet; the subject of the first is the object of the second. To talk about voice, then, is to raise a topic of which the mere form of a verb is a minor and incidental aspect.

2. Most rhetorics and most teachers dwell on the natural primacy of the active voice as the vehicle of ordinary exposition and narration, and they together with native common sense have done their work well enough to make an addiction to the passive comparatively rare in print. Except in bureaucratic, military, and scientific English, where the passive is sometimes required by the rule (*After six months of patient efforts, all hope of completing this arrangement was abandoned by the Bureau*), the systematic neglect or avoidance of the active is uncommon enough to be noticeable. Even unpracticed writers seem content to cultivate variety by other devices than the capricious alternation of voice. The derailments that result from the mismanagement of voice occur for the most part, not through the injudicious substitution of the passive for the active, but through the opposite fallacy of treating the passive as if it were active. Against this danger, if we are to judge by the printed evidence, there is not enough warning and instruction.

It is not generally recognized that the structure of English imposes an agreement in voice that is quite as rigid as any other kind of grammatical agreement—that of pronouns with antecedents in number, of verbs with their subjects in number, or of participles with the subjects of main verbs. To refer to a foregoing passive voice by a construction implicitly assuming it to be active produces the same kind of clash that we get from any other faulty reference, and hence the same kind of damage to logic and coherence.

This sort of trouble with voice frequently occurs with the verb *do* in some form or other. A typical illustration: *This rug may be sent to a laundry. If you do so, ask to have it tumble-dried.* Here *do so*, an active voice, clearly implies the active voice in the preceding sentence: *You may send this rug. . . . Do so* can refer to an act that you perform, but not to an act that is performed by you. Begun as quoted, the example would have to go on: *If you send it*—a recapitulation that frankly shifts to the active voice without harking back like *do so* to an active verb that is not present. To secure agreement, restate the first sentence in the active voice or the second in the passive: *If sent, it should be tumble-dried.* The problem can also be sidestepped with *If you send this rug to a laundry, ask . . . ;* but so simple a cure is not commonly to be had.

A collection of examples will show how frequent the difficulty is, and a parenthetical suggestion with each will show how one can restore agreement. *The Organization of American States must be asked by one of the parties to intervene or mediate, and neither has done so* (neither has asked it) / *We have always felt that those who perform this friendly service should be personally recompensed in some way—and this method of doing so* (method of recompensing them) *has been our practice / These berries . . . may* (can?) *even be gathered under the snow in winter, which the inhabitants of southwest Greenland actually do* (as they actually are by) / *It is doubtful that it could be said as well or as meaningfully as Rand has done* (as Rand has said it) / *If a plan had to be altered, delayed, or abandoned to fit a political necessity, he was quick to do so* (quick to alter, delay, or abandon it) / *The degree of recovery from the trough is shown, wherever it is possible to do so* (possible to show it), *as a percent of . . . / Agreeing that severe pressure must now be put upon the queen and admitting that no one but Burleigh could do it* (could apply it) / *And staff meetings will be held regularly three times a week unless wars or politics prevent his doing so* (prevent his holding them; or, perhaps better: And he will hold staff meetings . . . unless wars or politics prevent) / *Economies must be sought mostly in other directions than ultimate reduction in the civil service forces. The responsibility for doing so* (for seeking them) *rests / . . . other receptacles that were used as we do wastepaper baskets* (as we use).

This disregard of agreement in voice is not confined to the lower or the higher journalism. The preface of an excellent dictionary announces that *the reader is given the necessary additional connotative information, even if it means devoting a good deal of space to doing so* (to it).

3. An alternation of active and passive necessarily confuses the point of view, and it often leads to a construction in which one part is dangling (see DANGLERS). For instance, one wants to know who are the agents and how they are related in such a sentence as this: *By calling the volunteer office at Bellevue, duties can be more specifically described.*

The meaning is that an applicant for part-time hospital work can find out by telephone what the work consists of.

Cookery books, in which one of the main subjects is mixing, seem encouraged thereby to mix voices: *By using both white and dark breads in this manner particolored sandwiches may* (can?) *be achieved.* The errant participle could be avoided by beginning *By the use of;* but if the participle is kept, the simple sequel is *you can achieve* ... Voice is also at stake in the ambiguous imperatives that are both addressed and not addressed to the cook herself: *Turn into a preheated earthenware dish.*

The double passive—usually a passive finite verb followed by a passive complementary infinitive—is often the unseen agent of awkward changes in the point of view. In *New trustees would not be permitted to be appointed if they were older than sixty-three* the permission is denied to the wrong subject: the recipients of it instead of the authors. Read, then: *The appointment of new trustees older than sixty-three would not be permitted.* Straightening out is not always so easy: *By these expedients the inevitable consequences were attempted to be averted* is —or should be—obvious nonsense, pretending as it does that *consequences* can be the subject of *were attempted to be averted.* But to substitute *These expedients were attempts to avert the inevitable consequences* is a poor makeshift. What is really needed is a fundamental reconstruction with a new subject naming the person or persons who did the attempting. The first step in straightening out the confusions of thought that arise from mishandling voice is always to ask: "Who is doing what?"

volatile. Etymologically, *volatile* means *able to fly.* We might call birds and airline pilots volatile, but we don't, because from the beginning of its use the word has been figurative or abstract. Liquids are volatile when they evaporate rapidly. It is not stretching the acceptation too far to say of a person that he or she is volatile if the intention is to suggest flightiness, for the image is the same in both words. But of recent years *volatile* has acquired a vogue in the sense of willful, unpredictable, short-tempered, and— by false inference—explosive, none of which is in accord with the quality of light airiness in the adjective.

W

wait. See PREPOSITIONS.

we, editorial. *We* is good —or good enough—when it is genuinely editorial; that is, when it stands for the consensus of an editorial board or the collective force of an organ or organization. It is inevitable when used by the authors of a collaborative work. And of course there is nothing against the noneditorial *we* signifying the members of any understood collectivity, from a committee of two to the entire human race. Sometimes *we* in a book means you, the reader, and I, the author, conceived as prosecuting a joint enterprise.

But we also find *we* used, though less often than formerly, where it clearly means a single person who should step forth as *I*. A great deal of the literary criticism written between 1800 and 1920, though signed by an individual and claiming none but individual authority, used the editorial *we*. The reasons were complex and partly contradictory: *we* combined self-effacing modesty with the pretentious assumption of spokesmanship for a larger body of opinion. We find the same inconsistent motive in the first-person use of ONE. This editorial *we* is still rather common in works of scholarship. Graduate students brought up in a language of Western Europe are schooled to think it unprofessional, a misdemeanor, to say *je* or *ich* in such a work; Americans acquire the same point of view, and it is sometimes difficult to persuade them that the modest tone calls for *I*. They insist on *A prolonged but unavailing search has forced us to the conclusion that,* when the *us* is a solitary youth on a Fulbright grant.

Occasionally, by a freakish accident, the editorial *we* of a work produced by collaboration involves absurdity. A book in which the anecdotes are supplied by one writer and the scientific matter by another records: *We have had a coat of unborn musk-ox calf that lasted for three or more years.* One is to understand, not that the coat was shared, but that the authors felt bound by the *we* of TOGETHERNESS. In such a work statements inherently singular should be presented impersonally: *A coat . . . has been known to last three or more years.*

431

Akin to the *we* convention is that of the signed newspaper dispatch in which the author keeps referring to himself in the third person—*this writer, this* (or *your*) *correspondent, the interviewer, the* [present] *writer* [of these paragraphs], etc.—because the first person singular is forbidden him by his editors. A reader of political and literary weeklies will even come across the euphemism *This desk,* as in *This desk has always maintained that it is impossible to mix a real whodunit with a full-blown love interest. This writer* risks ambiguity whenever a writer other than the *I* has just been mentioned, and yet the phrase is bound to be brought in at that very point if a contrast between two men's views is to be made. The difficulty leads to *the present writer*—a metaphor, since the writer is indubitably absent. Resolve to take the great leap and say *I.* Everybody should by now recognize that a mask is more conspicuous than a face.

whatever, whoever, etc., interrogative.

1. The adverb and suffix (-)*ever,* apart from meanings that relate to time, has a merely intensive force, as in the relative pronouns *whatever* and *whoever* (*Give the package to whoever is on duty* / *Do whatever you think best*), the adjective *whatever* (*Use whatever method you prefer*), and the adverbs *wherever* and *whenever* (in the last of which only the first syllable denotes time). It is doubtless the attraction of these words that has produced by false analogy the interrogatives *whatever* and *whoever* (*Whatever possessed him to act that way?* / *Whoever could have imagined it?*), to which we sometimes find added *whenever* and *wherever* (*Whenever will he outgrow his foolishness?* / *Wherever could we look for anyone to replace him?*), and even *however* and *whyever.* In all these the -*ever* is nontemporal; the effect is approximately that of *What in the world?, Who on earth?,* etc. The fallacy behind these forms consists in failing to treat them as two words, but the single word can show an impressive body of printed usage and a somewhat confused recognition by dictionaries. The New International of 1934 does not list the interrogative *whoever,* but records *whatever* as colloquial, "expressing surprise or perplexity; as, *whatever* do you want?" It omits the interrogative *whenever,* but includes *when ever,* "used in questions expressive of surprise or puzzlement." Then it enters *wherever,* "used in questions expressing astonishment or puzzlement;—also written *where ever.*" Webster's New World Dictionary lists *whatever* and *whoever* with no cautionary label, illustrating with "*whatever* can he mean by that?" and "*whoever* told you that?" Then it classifies both *whenever* and *wherever* as colloquial. It ignores the two-word version of each of the four words. The Shorter Oxford, comparatively free from the "scientific" American fear of calling an error erroneous, states firmly that *whatever, whoever,* or *whenever* in the interrogative use is properly written as two words; but for some reason it omits this stipulation with *wherever,* and it classifies all four forms as colloquial. Fowler, as always definite, insists that an emphasizing *ever* must not come next to *who,* and for *Who ever could have imagined it?* he requires *Who could ever have imagined it?*

2. These variations are enough to show that we are free to make our own discriminations. The first one called for is that *whatever, whoever, whenever, wherever, however,* and *whyever* are rhetorically equivalent and should be treated alike. Any attempt to put them in different categories has to resort to historical logic-chopping without present utility. Secondly, each of these interrogatives had better be written as two words. The solid forms originated in, and perpetuate, a careless confusion between the interrogative words and their replicas. There is obviously a sharp difference between the

-*ever* of *Whoever could have imagined it?* and that of *Whoever applies will be given the standard test.* In the second the -*ever* truly does emphasize *who,* but in the first it is a question whether it does not emphasize the verb (*could have imagined*). To be sure, dividing our six interrogatives into two words each ignores a great bulk of printed usage, rather more of it British than American; but there is no harm in ignoring it, because no one objects to the two-word forms, and no one would ever notice them except those who are annoyed by the confusion embodied in the solid forms. Those who say that we may write *Whenever will he arrive?* do not insist that we must write it at all, and they see nothing amiss in *When ever will he arrive?* Division is the only way to make the logical differentiation between the non-interrogative *ever* and the *ever* that intensifies interrogatives.

3. Next we must consider the dictum, rather emphatically laid down by Fowler and others, that these interrogatives are merely colloquial and should, in print, be confined to the reproduction of popular speech. Current printed usage strongly suggests that the dictum has lost its validity. Indeed, Fowler quoted enough examples in 1926 to show that even then these forms had won sufficient literary footing to necessitate his reasoned answer

to the question: One word or two?—an almost frivolous question if asked about forms that are colloquial only. No one, of course, would maintain that the interrogatives *what ever, when ever,* etc. are at home in a grave style, but they are good enough for common use, quite apart from reproducing others' speech. *What ever possessed the city fathers to make them imagine that such a regulation could be enforced?* is perfectly fit for the correspondence column of any newspaper or periodical.

4. Finally, what of the presumed rule that *ever* must not immediately follow the interrogative *who?* If, in the sentence *Who ever could have imagined it?*, you shift *ever* to the normal position after *could,* you create an almost irresistible implication of time. *Who ever could?* means *Who in the world could?* or *Who by any hook or crook could?* whereas *Who could ever?* is naturally construed as *Who could at any time?* The difference, negligible in the particular sentence, might produce ambiguity elsewhere. If we insist on the division of interrogative *whatever, wherever,* etc.—and it is slipshod not to insist on it—then we must put up with the adverb in its exceptional and unidiomatic position, the only position in which it can carry the meaning assigned to it.

what is "understood"? If for the sake of saying our say we overlook the cynic's remark that language was given man for the concealment of his thoughts, we come to see that writing is the art of saying part of what we mean and of setting up clear implications of what else we mean without saying it. For example, every well-placed pronoun sets up such an implication; it is the task of the pronoun to do just that. No one is grateful enough for the blessing of pronouns until he has counted the cost of not having them. Consider this simple sentence: *A member of the House of Representatives, if he did not have the privilege of extending his remarks, would be cut off from a principal means of communicating with his constituents.* But for pronouns it would have to read: *A member of the House of Representatives, if a member of the House of Representatives did not have the privilege of extending the remarks of a member of the House of Representatives,* etc.

Other economies that approach, and possibly exceed, those of pronouns are effected by innumerable words and phrases of reference: *thus, such, so, hence, thence, accordingly, respectively, likewise, same, former, latter, vice versa,* all the demonstratives, all transitional words and phrases, and hundreds of other locutions that point backward or forward (or both ways) to related matter. Furthermore, all of our commonest nouns can serve in context the purpose of pronouns. Every time we say that a problem is insoluble or a truth self-evident, a theory unsound or a proposal unacceptable, we are using *problem, truth, theory,* or *proposal* to stand for some idea already expressed. We avoid its repetition by using the noun, exactly as if we had said *it.* What with all the pronouns, all the pronominally used nouns, and all the reference words, the management of language becomes an intricate and subtle adjustment of names and pointers in sequence; it resembles not so much the erection of a structure out of separate building blocks as the weaving of a fabric on a loom, or the mixing of colors from a palette.

Granted the stupendous miracle that language exists—by so much the greatest fact in human history that it has no close rival—few facts of language tend more to inspire awe than this freedom of substitution, whereby a few words take the place of many and what is left unsaid is nevertheless present through its delegates. And yet even the magic of this power is eclipsed by that of another, equally ubiquitous; namely, the force of words that are present without any delegation at all —words that appear only in

the form of a communicative vacuum. We can convey now a greater and now a smaller part of our meaning, but always some useful part, by ellipsis. *I will come in and sup with him, and he with me / The earth belongs to the living, not to the dead / Priests are no more necessary to religion than politicians to patriotism / It is easier for a man to be loyal to his club than to his planet / Render therefore to all their dues; tribute to whom tribute is due; custom to whom custom; fear to whom fear; honour to whom honour.* The twenty-four words of the last example become thirty-five if you fill in those that are invisibly at work; and even that ratio understates the truth, for all the ellipses occur in eighteen words, which do the work of twenty-nine with an incalculable gain in trenchancy. The saving and the gain are nearly as great in *It is easier for a man to be loyal to his club than* [it is for him to be loyal] *to his planet.* Such examples, so common we would hardly notice them in context, give force to Carlyle's observation that literary men ought to be paid by the quantity they do not write. To the trained writer it is second nature to go through his copy for the removal of every syllable he can do without. Those that skip this stage may know the A and the B of composition, but they have yet to arrive at its C.

This privilege of making words work for us *in absentia* entails, like all privileges, responsibilities and risks. The chief responsibility is to see to it that the words omitted in the writing will infallibly be those supplied in the reading. And the chief risk is that our way of handling the gaps will put forward the wrong words—words that will miss our meaning or belie it, or commit us to declarations so inexact and unkempt that we are thrown on the mercy of the reader for a reasonable interpretation.

The mismanagement of ellipses is easy and therefore common, though it is usually awkward rather than ambiguous or false. Many elliptical sentences that fail to say what they mean are technically rather than actually open to misconstruction. One of the most tolerable of false ellipses is that by which we "understand" an *a* or an *an* in front of a word when all we can borrow from the spot in front of a previous word is the wrong article. We ought to say *an awkward and a stupid man*, but we often say *an awkward and stupid man*. And sometimes the presence or absence of the right form in front of the second word gives to the passage the tone of deliberateness or of impetuosity. Note the solemnity of *an humble*

and a contrite heart. Akin to the frequent incorrectness with *a* or *an* is that of borrowing a verb in the wrong number in order to avoid a lumbering repetition: *His trousers were wet, his coat also.* Clearly what the first sentence supplies is *were*, which does not go with singular *coat*, but the statement will pass in headlong narrative, especially if attributed to a speaker. The more exacting way would be to write: *His trousers were wet and so was his coat.* But the very care bestowed on the sentence takes away from its vividness, so that recourse to "understanding" is justified by stylistic merit at the expense of grammar.

In more violent ellipses, the reader can piece out the sense if he is willing to do for himself part of the task that should have been done for him. *No true insect-eaters . . . could exist in the Arctic, and certainly could not rear a brood* will not deceive anyone about the intended meaning, in spite of its saying that no true insect-eaters could not rear a brood. We rearrange to suit the intention: *No true insect-eaters could exist in the Arctic or could rear a brood there.* But the author himself has failed to supply the answer to the question he must not evade: What is "understood"?

The foregoing example, it will be noticed, is faulty through mismanaging negative expressions—a contributory cause also in the specimens that follow. For further discussions of the reasons why these errors occur, see NEGATIVES, TROUBLE WITH.

The question "What is understood?" gets wrong answers —sometimes foolish ones—in the following: *The time will probably never come—we hope it won't—when the live teacher will disappear entirely* (we hope it never will; the author has tacitly put forth the impossible *we hope it never won't*) | *Last night's program was prepared on electronic tape. So will tonight's and tomorrow evening's* (as tonight's and tomorrow evening's will be) / *The question had no answer, nor will it have until the American's Cup Committee decides it has seen enough* (nor will it have one; the author does not see that he has said *nor will it have no answer*) | *Such judgment need not be intuitive, but rather the result of long living, practicing good taste in the social body* (but may rather be the result of) / *Thus, your message can be distributed overnight throughout each major marketing area—or to any one or combination of areas* (or to any area or combination of areas) / *The party . . . , claiming a membership of more than a million, has a lot to brag about, but tactically prefers not to* (prefers not to brag; *tactically* may be trying to say

for tactical reasons or may be simply a foiled attempt at *tactfully*) | *"Voice crying in the wilderness" is often used to indicate that the foretelling will go unheeded because it is uttered where none can hear or, if hearing, cannot or will not understand* (where none can hear, or to hearers that cannot or will not understand).

It will be noticed that some of the attempted ellipses, misconceived in the first place, have to be sacrificed to clarity and order. To permit an ellipsis, the opening words must be given a form which the words to be understood will readily match. This amounts to saying that an ellipsis must be prepared; it cannot be hit upon in mid-sentence.

Awkwardness is frequently produced by the demand that the reader supply some form of a verb that clashes with the form already present. *Although military vessels have and do navigate the bumpy waters of Pillsbury Sound* / *Although the West was confident that it could ride out this crisis as it had the previous two* / *Sports can continue on the present basis by dropping the freshman eligibility rule, as it was during the war* (as was done). Note that the last example contains also a clash of VOICE. In the first example, notice that the implied form is *have navigate;* and in the second, that the suggestion of *had ride* is only less overt because the clashing constructions are not cheek by jowl.

We may suppose it was the second sort of mismatching that Thomas Jefferson had in mind when he approved small grammatical negligencies that impart terseness. Many grammarians approve of them even more emphatically. Yet it remains true that false implications about an absent verb always distress acute ears and, when flagrant, suggest a tone-deaf writer. The advice offered here is that it is worth the extra trouble and the extra syllables to write *have navigated* and *do navigate* and *had ridden out*—unless one can think of other expedients. These in fact exist. Why not say *military vessels continue to navigate?*

The absence of a logically necessary verb form usually draws attention to itself; it is doubly conspicuous when the order is inverted to achieve emphasis. *He was chosen to provide leadership, and provide leadership he has.* Emphasis is indeed achieved; but most of it falls on the author's misfortune in accepting the faulty compound *has provide.* One can see that he has shied away from the ungainliness of *provided it he has.* It would moreover destroy the emphasis striven for, which depends on an exact echo. The reasonable solution is *provide leadership he did,* or *does,* or (if past action continued into the pres-

ent is material) *did and does.*

At times we find miscalculated ellipses that leave the reader stranded until he has rescued himself by conjectural emendation. *Their efforts are not limited to aiding victims of polio but helping all who suffer from physical disabilities.* We do not get out of this impasse without supplying something after *but* that will balance and neutralize *not limited to.* The presumable meaning is *but extend to* or *include helping all who.* (Note in passing that the question whether *but* should not be *and* deserves attention; see BUT 1.) Here is an even more baffling sentence: *The July increase in production of the steel industry was secured with about 2,000 less (fewer) workers than in the preceding month.* It states among other anomalies that the July increase also took place in June; for what the construction invites us to supply is *2,000 fewer workers than it was secured with in the preceding month.* What the writer wanted us to supply was doubtless *2,000 fewer workers than there were in the preceding month,* and what in the end he hoped to impart was that *in July the steel industry obtained more production from fewer workers than in June.*

Akin to the demand that the reader supply some verb form not contained in the sentence is the demand that he infer a repetition of some form that is present but with a different grammatical bearing. *In their completed race and the one that was not, Columbia has proved b e y o n d reasonable doubt . . .* The word to be supplied after *not* is indeed *completed;* why, then, does the sentence limp so badly? Because the word to be repeated as a past participle after *not* was set up as an adjective modifying *race.* Grammatical parallelism is as necessary as verbal identity. The two ways to achieve it are (1) *In their completed race and the uncompleted one* and (2) *In the race that was completed and the one that was not.* The converse of this attempt to impose incompatible duties on one word also turns up: *He seriously advised the city papers to have the streets cleaned, and kept so, regardless of the expense.* Here *so,* adjectivally used, is supposed to act as surrogate for the participle *cleaned,* but neither will do what is asked. The obvious repair: *have the streets cleaned and kept clean.*

The reference is similarly twisted in the statement *genteel reviewers who never have and never will read the original texts.* The *read* to be supplied is the past participle (pronounced *red*), whereas the word in evidence is the infinite of a future tense (pronounced *reed*). The gymnastics called for here are beyond most of us, as they are also

in this tribute to a sympathetic man: *Your problems were his, to talk over with and advise you.* (For an important group of allowable ellipses, see WHICH and AND WHICH.)

when. See NO SOONER . . . WHEN.

when and if. An exact parallel to *and/or, when and if* is a piece of legal JARGON that tends to make people forget the mutual implication of its parts. Suppose that you resolve to *leave the city when the tax rate is raised again,* you resolve at the same moment to exile yourself *if* the rate is raised. And conversely, when you promise a friend to *give help if he needs it,* you promise to do so *when* he needs it. The attraction of *when and if* lies perhaps in the intimation that the promised or threatened act will occur at the instant when the stated condition is fulfilled. But emphasis on that point can be secured without sounding like an overwritten lease. (See IF AND WHEN.)

whereas. See WHILE.

wherever. See WHATEVER, WHOEVER 1.

whether. See AS 10; DOUBT.

which, relative. See THAT, WHICH, RELATIVE; THAT, WHO, RELATIVE.

which and **and which.**
Next to the prejudice against
splitting infinitives and ending
sentences with prepositions, no
pretended rule is more popular with the eager and ill-in-
formed than the prohibition of
an *and which* or a *but which*
not preceded by an earlier
which. Yet as Fowler showed
nearly half a century ago, the
rule in its absolute form is no
rule at all. One cannot avoid
the suspicion that all three of
these "rules" are held in honor
solely because they are easy to
remember and apply.

Taking the question not as
a problem by itself but as an
instance of a more general
proposition, one asks: What
is wrong when *and which* is
indeed bad? The answer is:
The joining of what should not
be joined. Let us look at the
first of two sentences by classic authors. Horace Walpole
writes to a friend about Queen
Caroline: *She never could
make my father read* [Bishop
Butler's] *book, and which she
certainly did not understand
herself.* The *and which* is illogical and objectionable here because it sticks a conjunctive
and between *book* and its pronoun. Those two need no joining whatever. Grammar unites
them in the ordinary way—*the
book which the Queen never
understood.* No one would
dream of saying *This is the
book and which the Queen never understood.* The superfluous *and* was imported by Wal-

pole from a construction never
actualized. We may suppose
that he started out with the
vague intention of framing a
compound sentence, really two
sentences: (1) *The Queen never could make my father read
the book* and (2) *The Queen
herself never understood the
book.* In midstream he changed
his mind, seeing that the second *book* could be replaced by
which (since it was the same
book) and the two sentences
fused into one. His mistake
was to keep the co-ordinating
and after he had espoused the
subordinating *which.*

We arrive, therefore, at the
proposition that *and which* can
only co-ordinate. The *and* permits nothing else. What it co-
ordinates, in turn, must be
members of equal or equivalent
status. Note the word *equivalent* as we now turn to Fielding, who in 1758 writes to the
Duke of Newcastle an *and who*
that will serve our purpose:
*Nor would I, unless in obedi-
ence to your Grace, have anything to say to a set of the most
obstinate fools I ever saw, and
who seem to me rather to act
from a spleen against the Lord
Mayor, than from any motive
of Protecting innocence.* This
sentence allows the *and* to effect a co-ordination between
two of its members that are
of equal or equivalent status—
*fools (whom) I ever saw and
(fools) who seem to me to act.*
In other words the preceding
who, though absent, does its

work thanks to a familiar ellipsis and puts the first clause on the same level as the second, thus justifying the *and*.

Now test this conclusion by omitting the *and*: *the most obstinate fools I ever saw, who seem to me to act from a spleen.* The sentence is no longer in balance. We stumble at the *who seem to me* because we have unconsciously registered the presence of a first defining clause (*I ever saw*), so that when a second comes introduced by *who* we instinctively require an *and*. Just as no one can think or say *the person I love who loves me*, so no one should thoughtlessly repeat the rule that *and who* and *and which* require a preceding *who* or *which*.

But the ellipsis of a *who* or *whom* is not the only form in which a clause of equivalent status can occur to justify a later *and*. In the sentence *Men determined to succeed and who will stick at nothing*, we readily supply *Men* (who are) *determined . . . and who . . .* But we can also reduce the defining element to a single adjective: *Determined men, and who will stick at nothing* offers a shade of meaning easily distinguishable from *Determined men who will stick at nothing.* We have obviously reached a point where, grammar being satisfied, style and thought must make the decision. Burke, one of the greatest stylists in the language, made

frequent use of this hidden parallelism (as do the French), perhaps because it makes the sentence lighter than when the double *who* or *which* comes down audibly one foot after the other. Burke writes: *When the only estate lawfully possessed and which the contracting parties had in contemplation at the time . . . happens to fail / Instead of reconciling himself heartily . . . to the States of Brabant as they are constituted, and who in the state of things stand on the same foundation with the monarchy itself . . .*

To sum up, the test of the licit *and which* (*who*) is the logical validity of the *and*. It is not enough to remove the *and* and see whether the sentence survives, for as was shown above, style or nuance may dictate one of two tenable forms (*Determined men who* [or *and who*] *stick at nothing*). The common rule against unprepared *and which* is therefore null and void. The rule against co-ordinating what refuses to join on an equal footing holds good. We conclude with a few examples of wrong co-ordination. Remove all the *and*'s and *but*'s: *We face a serious problem, and which we will not soon see resolved / "Jane Eyre" reminds one of "Rebecca," and which is written in a livelier style / Men raised in a democracy develop high hopes for themselves, but most of which are not realized*

/ He is a four-flusher, an idler, a sneak, and whom I could never marry. Note that in each of these sentences the co-ordination could be maintained, though at the cost of a certain awkwardness, by contriving to repeat the idea after the *and,* so that the *whom* or *which* could take hold direct of what it defines: *and one which we will not see* / *and it is the second which* / *but it is these hopes which* / *and a man whom.* In short, the *and*-linked *which* needs a close and visible subject to cling to.

while. This conjunction has overflowed its primary meaning, *during the time that,* into realms that belong to *although, whereas, and,* and the semicolon without connective. *Fifty-nine of the eighty-four female victims were pedestrians, while the 316 male victims included only fifty-six pedestrians. . . . Only sixteen of the female victims were drivers, while nine were passengers.* The first *while* plainly means *whereas* (= *but by contrast*); the second means nothing (sixteen were drivers; nine were passengers). *He said his son has a Q. savings account, while* (= *and*) *his wife and mother-in-law have been Q. depositors for years* / *recalled . . . that while* (although) *born left-handed, he had learned to bat right-handed* / *In the past six years alone college enrollment has jumped 45 per cent, while* (and) *in the next decade this heavy figure is expected to double* / *Cash prizes . . . will be presented the first day of the show, while* (and) *two popular prizes . . . will be given on the last day.* What is worth noting about these specimens is that the facts linked with *while* belong to times expressly stated to be different. To write that something happened today *while* something else happened ten years ago is to work hard at achieving contradiction.

Ideally, the conjunction *while* should be restricted to the linking of simultaneous occurrences in a situation where simultaneity has point. (*Then it is the brave man chooses, while the coward stands aside.*) No writer, surely, can do himself harm by declining to use it otherwise. Yet as things stand, it is impossible to make much headway against such a use as *While there have been over 100 people* (persons?) *soliciting in this area, it has not been possible to call on everyone.* This *while* is a concessive that means *although,* and its claim to grudging acceptance is that it entails no temporal clash between facts. To tolerate *while* as a link between events patently not simultaneous is to misapply tolerance: *In the daytime he's star of his own . . . show, while at night he becomes general announcer . . . on the A. O. show.* The mind accustomed to ignoring what *while* means will soon not respond to its true meaning in *One idles while the other works.*

See also ALTHOUGH, THOUGH.

who, relative. See THAT, WHICH, RELATIVE; THAT, WHO, RELATIVE.

whole. See NEEDLESS WORDS 2.

whole, as a. See PART, IN.

who(m), who(m)ever. 1. The objective form of the pronoun *who* is having a hard time asserting its hereditary rights. On one side it suffers the mistreatment of those who will put in the *m* where it does not belong, out of fear of being thought uneducated; on the other, it is belabored by emancipated grammarians who find it bookish and affected in most uses and favor almost any construction that avoids it. Between those who are afraid of sounding ignorant and those who are afraid of sounding superior, *whom* falls into comparative disuse and causes increasing discomfort in its users.

The first kind of fear takes shape in such locutions as *I know perfectly well whom you are,* in which the speaker takes *whom* as the object of *know* (it is the subject of *are*—the construction that Franklin P. Adams of "The Conning Tower" was wont to deride in the tag line *"Whom are you?"* said

Cyril). The lapse is far from unknown in writing put forth under the best auspices: [He] *asked them, saying, Whom say the people that I am?* (Luke 9:18) / *He resists a reconciliation with his sweet wife, whom he insists is a social butterfly* / *Ahead of them on the Nonesuch Road they descried Lord Grey de Hilton, whom Essex declared was his enemy.* The victims of this trap would save themselves if they would think of the interpolated two-word clause as parenthetic and within commas: *who, he insists, is a social butterfly,* etc. (This is not a recommendation that such commas be retained.) One of the paradoxes of the time is that some liberal grammarians who are implacable toward *whom* in its orthodox uses will tie themselves into knots in the effort to condone *whom* in this particular construction. Apparently they have a feeling that it ought to command the blessing of the learned because it tramples on prescriptive grammar. But the New International Dictionary, no shrine of purism, takes pains to enter a special note under *whom:* "Often used ungrammatically for *who* in a dependent, esp. relative, clause when erroneously regarded as object of a verb; as, those *whom* we thought would come."

It is important, however, to remember that in a construction superficially similar, that in which the pronoun is the subject of a complementary infinitive, the objective *whom* is required: *The woman whom I took to be his wife was in fact his daughter / The character whom he professes to admire most is Mr. Micawber*. Note that the first of these sentences is equivalent in meaning but not in form to *The woman who I thought was his wife . . .*, where the verb *I thought* is an interpolation which could be set off by commas and even removed altogether. Try the same surgery on *the woman whom (I took to be) his wife* and you will see that what remains yields no sense. This is not because *took* turns *who* into a direct object *whom*, for in the parallel sentence about Mr. Micawber the verb *professes* is not capable of taking a direct object. In both sentences the required *whom* is the subject of the infinitive construction. This requirement can sometimes lead to what seems an inconsistency: *our concern was to find out who we were and whom* (not *who*) *we wished to be*. In such a case, change the *whom* to *what* and spare the reader a puzzle.

2. The other kind of fear, that of the savant fending off the imputation of letting too much grammar show, prompts a historian to write: *M. departed eight days later in humiliation as the man who, more than anyone else, the President had repudiated*. The radical grammarian grants this usage his full approval, undeterred by the fact that *who* makes you anticipate a clause of which it is the subject and leaves you jolted when you find that this clause is never coming. Here again the New International Dictionary (under *who*) hangs up a red lantern: "Use of *who* for *whom* as object either of a verb or of a preposition which follows intervening words, though ungrammatical, is common colloquially and is still found in good writers, esp. in interrogations and indirect questions; as, *who* are you thinking of?; I do not know *who* you can ask"—locutions that similarly gratify the libertarian. The implication of *still* would seem to be that a looser past usage is giving way to a more strictly grammatical present usage—a prospect bound to make the anti-*whom* faction indignant or incredulous. We read in a popular novel: *The matter of who asks who to do what* and recognize a very common pattern; and in everyday speech *Who's kidding who?* is virtually expected.

3. Yet even now, those who consider it admissible or preferable to say *Who do you think you're talking to?* will concede the necessity of saying *To whom do you think you're talking?* That is, they draw a clear distinction between the pronoun immediately following preposition or verb and the pronoun preceding or

separated from it. But it is no great step from the one construction to the other, and if the *m* of *whom* is to succumb in the first, it is not likely to hold out forever in the second by reason of the difference in position. The echoing sound may protect it for a while, but the time may come when it will take a historian of the language to explain what is being ungrammatical in Bierce's jingle about the decline of love-making among men and owls:

Sitting singly in the gloaming and
    no longer two and two;
As unwilling to be wedded as un-
    practiced how to woo;
    With regard to being mated
    Asking still with aggravated
Ungrammatical acerbity: "To
    who? To who?"

Meanwhile there is no good reason to distinguish two forms of the objective case of *who*. We should continue to use *whom* as the object of verb or preposition without any hairsplitting about its place in the sentence. This precept has the merit of simplicity and the reason for it is definable.

4. A further paradox in the doctrine of the liberal grammarians is that like everybody else they find *whom* obligatory in the construction *than whom there is no man wiser, than whom none ever wrote a purer style*, etc. The logic of grammar calls for *who*; nothing about *than* requires the objective case; and it would be a

solecism to say *no man is wiser than him*. Yet the *whom* construction is universally taken as natural and right. It has long lived in the domain in which idiom exults over grammar. Those who like syntactical conundrums can puzzle their wits by substituting the uninflected *which* for *whom* (*than which there is no wiser counsel*) and asking themselves whether *which* is objective. Is, in fact, *whom* itself objective after such a *than?* Since the answer has no possible effect on how we shall handle either *whom* or *which*, and since latter-day grammar prefers to deny the existence of case outside inflected forms, wisdom suggests letting well enough alone. The modern writer will not be depriving himself of anything important if he lets the bookish *than whom, than which* construction alone too. He can relinquish it with the less regret because only extreme care can keep it invariably clear and correct. Derailment of sense occurs easily, as in *a truly ecstatic telegram from Bob Benchley, than whom there was nobody whose praise a cartoonist or humorist would rather have had*, which has only to be transposed into the normal order to reveal its confusion: *there was nobody whose praise a cartoonist would rather have had than whom.* Grammar and meaning can be reconciled thus: *than whose praise there was nobody's that a cartoonist would rather have had.* But such a correction is verbal juggling and close to comic. The direct statement is always best: *whose praise a cartoonist or humorist would rather have had than anybody else's.*

5. *Who(m)ever,* meaning *any person who(m),* is regulated by the same principles that govern *whom.* It is, of course, subject to the same confusions: *answered that not only did Henry mean to maintain* [the peace] *but that he would wage war with all his might on whomever should be the first to violate it.* Here the object of *wage war on* is not *who(m)ever,* but the whole following clause, of which the subject is necessarily *whoever.*

See also WHATEVER, WHOEVER.

-wide. See LINKING 3; -WISE.

will. See APPENDIX 1: SHALL (SHOULD), WILL (WOULD).

-wise, suffix. There is at first sight no reason why this syllable, interchangeable with *-ways* in many combinations (*lengthwise* or *-ways, endwise* or *-ways,* etc.), may not be appended to any given noun—call the noun X—to make an adverb meaning *after the fashion of X, in the manner of X* (*crabwise, clockwise,* etc.), or simply *in connection with* or *in relation to X* (*coastwise, moneywise,* etc.) ; *-wise* is also

sometimes appended to other parts of speech than the noun, as in *leastwise, likewise,* OTHERWISE, *nowise, anywise.*

But the privilege of performing this simple operation on any single noun becomes an instrument of havoc when taken as a license to perform it on the whole vocabulary. The habit of doing so has grown on writers and speakers in some quarters, and perhaps more frequently in the world of investment and finance than elsewhere. Various experts seem to feel that they are not living up to their rights over English unless they pepper their analyses with *profitwise, marketwise, marginwise, percentagewise, depreciationwise,* and so on. What was handy as a device has thus been made hideous as a mannerism, and it deserves to be outlawed from decent use. Until the rage abates, a sensible writer will resort to such coinages in *-wise* only to make fun of them, as S. J. Perelman does when he speaks of *what was going on, prosewise, from 1930 to 1958.* An early instance, from Ruskin, already sounds the satirical note: *Just because it is deep* (my respect for Dickens' genius), *I have not the least mind to express it dinnerwise* (November 1, 1867).

What is reprehensible about the vogue is its re-enforcement of inarticulate English; that is, the use of words in juxtaposition without a clear joint, explicit or conventional, to articulate the ideas so combined. Sometimes the deficiency seems sought after, to produce an effect of briskness. The head of a great corporation tells a colloquium of employees: *How we do netwise is in your hands.* One suspects that he first wrote or dictated *Whether we make a profit or not is up to you* and then translated it into the current jargon. An article about submarine photography in a scientific magazine says: *But fathomwise, intensity of light is less than half the story* (the meaning being simply *underwater intensity of light*). And the sober mind rebels at the looseness, intellectual and moral, of *Touristwise, this area is virgin!*

As for writers who think they can at once exploit the trick and despise it (*Virtuosity . . . tends to be damaging saleswise—to use the dreadful coinage*) they should know that their awareness earns no credit with their readers. The addicts will be hurt by the insult to their favorite locution; the perceptive will mark them down for lacking the judgment to write *tends to hurt sales.* (Compare *-wide* and *-happy*, as in *population-wide* and *gin-happy*, where the suffix lends itself to repeated compounding, only to produce joint disease and loss of vocabulary.)

wist. See WOT.

with. The preposition *with* is clear and tight enough when it introduces the instrument or agent of an effect: we sweep with a broom, survey the ground with binoculars, reach the high shelves with a stepladder. The word is also managed without difficulty when it serves description by naming simple accompaniment: we speak with (or without) eloquence, calculate with precision, contemplate the future with hope. A third meaning that gives no trouble is *at the time of: With the arrival of these reinforcements the whole battle picture changed / With the development of wireless the sea lost some of its old terrors / His prophecy was upset in 1914 with the publication of the Tenth Edition.* In this construction the idea of causation is often more or less in evidence, but it rarely misleads. And causation can easily be brought uppermost: *The arrival of these reinforcements changed the whole battle picture.* These uses are as clear as that of *with* signifying association: *He was no longer living with his parents;* or reciprocity: *Don't you want to talk it over with me?;* or opposition: *fight with, argue with*—this last being the original force of the word, which is found in *withstand, withhold,* and curiously, in the draft animal's *withers,* the part that strains against a load. But lucidity is lost when *with* is employed, thoughtlessly, to bring attendant circumstances into a sentence without analyzing or making clear their relation to the central fact. That relation may be anything from fully causal to casual or irrelevant. A typical instance: *With the ever diminishing number of caribou it is difficult to avoid having to fast or even to starve once in a while.* Here is evidently a cause-and-effect relation, but nothing in the fabric of the sentence says so. Its fumbling looseness becomes graphic if we reverse the order: *difficult to avoid having to fast . . . with the ever diminishing number of caribou.* Some glimmer of the intended meaning appears if we rewrite: *Because of the steady decrease . . . it is difficult* or *The steady decrease . . . makes it difficult.* The wordiness is a separate problem. No more is being said than *The gradual disappearance of the caribou means fasting and occasional starvation*; though one cannot be sure whether *once in a while* applies to both *fast* and *starve* or only to *starve.* (A diminishing number, by the way, cannot be a cause; the cause is the diminution of their number.)

When the linkage of *with* is loose, no generally applicable repair is possible; one must puzzle out in each case what is meant. *At other times (as with the Normans), the victors adopt the language of those whom they have subdued* (the victors, like the Normans, adopt). Emphasis and meaning obscure each other in the following: *It seems probable that these two roots were once identical, and so with many others.* Is the statement about the others a repetition of the fact, or only of the probability? If the first, read: *and so were many others*; if the second, *and so apparently were many others* / *The most detailed reminiscence of Whitman's personality and habits during his editorship of the "Eagle" comes again, as with the "Aurora" period, from a young printer who worked on the paper.* Note, to begin with, the falsity of *again:* a young printer supplies the testimony once, not again, for each of the two periods. Read: *comes, as in the "Aurora" period, from a young printer.* / *As with any other criminal, she can see no one* (Like any other criminal). See AS 9.

Not quite so simple is the rectification of the errant *with* here: *But their employers, the Florida orange growers, have made handsome profits because the freeze put oranges in short supply and the frostbitten fruit could be marketed as "fair" frozen orange juice at a high price per can. So too with other fruit and vegetable crops.* Obviously, other fruit and vegetable crops were not marketed as frozen orange juice. To say what is meant calls for some such adjustment as *Other fruit and vegetable crops were likewise profitably salvaged* or *were similarly turned into profit*. The *with* contradictory needs still another rearrangement of the sentence. In *The theatre was completely filled with many people standing hopefully outside*, the simplest solution is divorce: *The theatre was completely filled; many stood outside still hoping to get in*. The writer addicted to the facile but evasive *with* is shirking the rigors of thought about what he means and how to say it, but he cannot be let off. The burden of communication is on him, not on the reader.

See also PREPOSITIONS.

with, missing. Like *as* and *to* (see AS 2 and TO, MISSING), *with* is sometimes asked to perform a double duty of which it is incapable, in a construction that requires another *with*. A typical instance, the more surprising because found in a very learned work on accidence and syntax, is this sentence: *So, too, with other inflections—tense, with all the complicated and unnnecessary terminology that grammatical reports and grammarians have overburdened it . . .* Here *with* already occurs twice, and the dislike of further repetition probably stalled off the indispensable third occurrence. But the *with* after *tense* means

simply *together with* and is helpless to complement *overburdened* as it seems expected to do. We have to read either *with all . . . that grammatical reports . . . have overburdened it with* or else *with all the terminology with which . . . grammarians have overburdened it*. All this withery can of course be avoided, but at the cost of some reconstruction: *The same is true of other inflections—for example, tense, which is overburdened with all the complicated and unnecessary terminology of grammarians and grammatical reports*.

without. Unlike WITH, this preposition generally does not tempt to omission or false linking. Because it is negative, it is not so handy a catchall. Yet, when abused, it is likely to produce even more disconcerting results than *with*. Especially in the introductory position and followed by what is variously called a gerund, a verbal noun, or a verbal, it has to be watched lest its cargo of sense fly off into the void. *Without wishing to be obstinate, it is difficult to see much pertinence in such an analysis* cannot be cured until the wishing is ascribed to whoever does it—I, one, we, anyone (see DANGLERS).

Worse confusion greets us in a university statement about the need of free funds: *Without in any way detracting from the desire of some to support specific activities, unrestricted gifts continue to permit a college to make prompt and maximum use of its ready funds to take advantage of changing needs in higher education.* No one, of course, supposes that unrestricted gifts can detract from anyone's desire to make restricted ones; one therefore concludes that it is the spokesman himself who does not wish to detract, and that he has been drawn into this fog by a wish for self-effacement. *Detract from* here means *disparage* or *belittle.* Thus we arrive at some such interpretation as this: *It is no disparagement of the desire to support specific activities to point out that unrestricted gifts . . .*

One of the consequences of muffled beginnings is the insidiousness with which they lead into greater and greater embarrassment—in this instance to a purposeless *continue to,* the odd co-ordination of adjectives (*prompt, maximum*), the use of *advantage* for a difficulty to be coped with (the advantage is the availability of ready funds, not the changing needs), and the duplication in *ready funds* after *unrestricted gifts.* The troublemaking *without* is best corrected by omission and a new start.

without for **unless.** The use of *without* as a conjunction is a rare survival that may crop up in the colloquial inheritance of Americans who have grown up in a nonliterary background. The English are likely to brand it a crude Americanism; it is actually reputable English now obsolete and deemed illiterate in both countries, but felt as quaint and amusing by some educated speakers. It is sometimes heard in broadcasting: *The Braves will never in the world repeat without they plug that gap at second base / You couldn't expect him to sign up without he is offered better terms than that.* Mencken cites among syntactical peculiarities: *I'll call you up, without I can't* (= unless prevented). (See also UNLESS.)

with respect to. See LINKING 3.

worthwhile. It is not worthwhile to use *worthwhile* unless you split it up first to see whether the *while* portion fits the context. Time, in other words, must be involved in the thing labeled *worthwhile.* This is why we say *worthwhile activities,* such as sports, hobbies, reading, etc. But a sandwich cannot be worthwhile, or a pair of shoes, or a short story, except on the farfetched pretext that since the consumption of these goods takes time, the goods themselves are *worthwhile.* It is better and simpler to say *worth eating, worth buying, worth reading* and leave *worthwhile* a little distinctiveness among terms of praise.

wot. This long-obsolete synonym of *know* must be about the most useless member of the class called by Fowler Wardour-Street English (from a London street once celebrated for shops offering dubious antiques)—the class represented by ANENT, *nay, ere, prithee,* etc. A present tense, *wot* is used idiomatically (for rhyme's sake) in *A Garden is a lovesome thing, God wot!* But all feeling for the reality of the verb is so long extinct that when revived for jocular effect the word is likely to be misconceived and misapplied. The author of a sophisticated short story writes: *As the bards used to say, little he wot of things to come.* What the bards used to say, for past tense and participle, was *wist* ("But had I wist, before I kissed"), and they followed it with a *that* clause, not with *of.* Writers fall into this mistake by the attraction of *got* and *forgot.* Even in Elizabethan days *wot* had become so unfamiliar that Shakespeare himself could write *wots,* a nonexistent inflection.

would. See APPENDIX 1: SHALL (SHOULD), WILL (WOULD).

would rather, would sooner. See HAD (WOULD) RATHER (SOONER).

wrack. See RACK.

X

X. The transformation of the normal sound of *x* into *egs*, as in *exaggerate*, *exult*, etc., occurs only when *x* falls after *e* and before a vowel. The altered sound should not be heard after any other vowel. The common words *luxurious*, *uxorious*, *oxygen* should not begin with *lug*, *ug*, or *og*, but rather with *luks*, *uks*, and *oks*. See PRONUNCIATION 1.

Y

yet. See SINCE, YET 3.

Z

zealous. See PRONUNCIATION 1.

zoology. See PRONUNCIATION 1.

III

APPENDIXES

1 / SHALL (SHOULD), WILL (WOULD)

CONFUSION AND CONFLICT IN USAGE

THE AUXILIARIES *shall* and *should*, *will* and *would* lead the user of English into as confused a jungle as he is ever called on to clear a way through. Outside the elementary-school grammars, which have often laid down confident laws that no one has ever consistently obeyed, most of the advice on the future and the conditional in English (to say nothing of the other uses of these auxiliaries) has been given in a tone of despair. In those who stress American-English differences and treat the American side as a separate language, this despair takes the form of a total surrender of the distinction between *shall* and *will*. For example, H. L. Mencken in *The American Language* (4th ed.; 1949) says that "except in the most painstaking and artificial varieties of American" the distinction "may almost be said to have ceased to exist."

In the defenders of the common heritage, despair takes the more muted form of deploring the frequency of unorthodox usage and of treating the observance of the rules as the mark of a superior caste. The Fowler brothers, whose twenty-one pages on *shall* and *will* in *The King's English* (1906) may be taken as a definitive statement of the rules, begin by reading most of us out of the party: "It is unfortunate that the idiomatic use, while it comes by nature to southern Englishmen . . . , is so complicated that those who are not to the manner born can hardly acquire it." Otto Jespersen, whose historical survey of the four auxiliaries requires a hundred and seventeen pages of *A Modern English Grammar on Historical Principles* (1909–1931), betrays no despair himself, because he is writing as a scientific chronicler of usage. But he provokes despair, because what he records is seven hundred years of inconsistency and groping in darkness. In fine, no rules and no digest of usage can reduce this department of the language to order and harmony or altogether get rid of the exceptional, the optional, and the doubtful.

This despair which descends on the subject from on high is reinforced in the Fowlers' account by their failure to attain the clarity that graces their treatment of most other topics. They begin with a self-defeating attempt to show that sundry uses of *shall* and *should* arose from the pre-emption of *will* and *would* for other uses. Their discussion is conducted largely in sibylline pronouncements such as this: "Indefinite clauses, relative or other, bearing the same relation to a conditional or future principal sentence that a conditional protasis bears to its apodosis follow the same rules"—a prescription lucid only to someone already aware of its purport.

Moreover, they repeatedly try to explain away various obstinate discrepancies by insisting that apparent exceptions are not real ones. The Fowlers on *shall* and *will* must often have discouraged the seeker after guidance, though they surely meant to give help. The authors themselves feared that their exposition was "in danger of being useless"; and it is noticeable that when H. W. Fowler came to grapple with *shall* and *will* twenty years later in his *Modern English Usage,* he greatly simplified his treatment and did not cite the earlier one, even though he had originally warned against "the short and simple directions often given."

Now, it is simply not true that "the idiomatic use . . . is so complicated that those who are not to the manner born can hardly acquire it." It is not true—that is, if we take the statement as applying to the hard core of useful distinctions. Many thousands of persons who were not born or reared in the south of England have so thoroughly acquired this idiomatic use by schooling or self-education that it has become second nature.

If, on the other hand, we take the Fowlers' pronouncements on the finer distinctions and the rarer subtleties, we quickly discover that these do not come by nature to the southern English themselves. No two of them completely agree on all such points; hardly any agrees with himself at different times or even in parallel expressions written at the same time. The Fowlers quote with equal copiousness from those to the manner born examples that they consider wrong and others that they consider right; they also give examples in which either of the two auxiliaries can be justified. No one who is well read in English literature or who reviews attentively the great mass of examples collected by Jespersen can continue to believe that there is a canonical usage which by a large consensus writers regularly apply throughout the domain bounded by *shall* and *will* and *should* and *would*.

What we have and have always had is (1) a relatively small nucleus of orthodox principles indispensable to those who care about accurate expression, and (2) a wide surrounding territory in which every man goes his own way and is prone to consider every other man lost. The inevitable first task, then, for anyone approaching the subject with a hope of being useful is to put together the clearest possible statement of the orthodox practices that materially affect clarity.

By way of preliminary encouragement it should be noted that a great many uses of the four auxiliaries raise no problem whatever and provide no opportunity of going wrong. *Should* when conditional is the same for all three persons: *If I should die, think only this of me / If you should fail the first time, don't give up / If A. should refuse, ask B.* In the meaning of *ought to, should* is similarly invariable: *I (you, he) should think twice before taking such a step.* The conditional *would* when it denotes volition (consent, choice) is likewise uniform: *If we (you, they) would stop guessing and really investigate, we (you, they) might undergo a change of mind.* The past-tense *would* that expresses habitual or often repeated action is unvaried: *On weekends I would go for a sail / When there were chores to be done, you would generally manage to disappear, and so would Harry.*

The same uniformity holds for the *would* that expresses determination, obstinacy, or incurable propensity: *I had plenty of excellent advice, but I would go my own way / Your allowance was ample, but you would fritter it away on nonessentials / In spite of all protest he would go without proper food, sleep, and exercise.* This *would,* given special stress in speaking, has a corresponding present-tense *will: Boys will be boys / You will get excited about these trifles / I ought to be more systematic, but I will keep putting things off.*

The *will,* usually not future, that denotes capacity or ability is equally unproblematic: *The hall will seat three hundred / You two will meet all the requirements / I will probably do if you can't get anyone better. Would* is used in all three persons for behavior regarded as inevitable or according to inherent disposition: *That is what you (he) would say / Of course, I would say just the wrong thing.*

A quasi-volitional *will* that means something between *choose* and *can* is entirely regular: *Try as I will, I make no headway / Say what you will, I stick to my opinion / Protest however he will, he knows he is in the wrong.* This *will* has a correspondingly regular past tense, *would.* The everyday *will* of consent, agreement, or concession does not shift with changes of person: *If you will telephone for reservations and Henry will pick up the tickets, I will meet you at the train gate.* And of course the independent (nonauxiliary) verb *will,* which has the regular inflections of other verbs, invites no confusion: *And If He Wills We Must Die / And, if thou wilt, remember / What the gods will, man must accept.*

EXPRESSING PLAIN FUTURE
OR SET PURPOSE

There is, then, a fairly broad area in which it is difficult or impossible to go wrong. The real difficulties are thus reduced to a number that can be coped with by anyone minded to take the pains without which expression can be accurate only by chance.

These difficulties can be grouped under four heads:

(1) The distinction between emphasis on plain-future fact and emphasis on a mental posture of intention, determination, or choice—i.e. volition;

(2) the avoidance of duplication through the auxiliary when volition is already inherent in the context;

(3) the echo principle, whereby an indirect statement or question copies the person (first, second, or third) of the auxiliary that would be used in the corresponding direct statement or question;

(4) the application of this same principle in a direct question by anticipating the auxiliary expected in the answer.

Let us first describe and illustrate these four categories in their purity, forgetting for the moment the variations, borderline cases, and real or seeming exceptions. Afterward, we shall supplement these fundamentals with notes on situations that they do not exactly cover.

(1) *Plain futurity versus volition.* Several grammarians have shown—Jespersen perhaps more cogently than the rest—that the English verb system lacks a normal future tense, so that the futurity expressed in Latin and the Romance languages by a regular tense has to be denoted in English by other expedients: such phrases as *to be going to, about to, on the point of,* etc., and even more commonly by the simple present tense (*I am to testify tomorrow / I testify tomorrow / We sail next Saturday / Henceforth you are my enemy / They convene in Chicago just after Christmas*). This is the reason why the headline in a country weekly SELECTMAN B. DIES THURSDAY reads like a prediction. Adding THURSDAY turned the normal present into a future. Another way of conveying futurity is by the progressive present (*I am seeing him Wednesday if not before / He is taking over X.'s job next week*). Futurity, then, does not have to be expressed by *shall* and *will*; they are but one way of expressing it, and a way marked by subtleties and ambiguities. Hence to ignore these is to throw on the reader or hearer a burden of interpretation that properly belongs to the writer or speaker.

Consider two radically different sentences: (a) *I shall be in my office from three to five* (the speaker's regular procedure, requiring no special decision or thought) and (b) *Then I will stay in my office until 5:30* (the speaker's concession to someone else's convenience; a declaration of willingness). The distinction between this *shall* and this *will* is the one that Mencken describes as having almost ceased to exist in America. It is true enough that multitudes of Americans—and, for that matter, most Irishmen and Scots and an increasing number of Englishmen—do not habitually make the distinction. But it is equally true that virtually all educated persons hear the distinction when it is made by others, and hear it with the intended meanings just noted.

In that fact we have a demonstration that the difference is real, living, far from obsolete. A linguistic pattern is dead, not when there is a large amount of deviation from it —as there has always been in the use of these auxiliaries— but when it has ceased to make a clear and uniform impression upon those who attend to words. And whatever may be the confusion in some minds between *I will* and *I shall*, there is certainly none in any minds about the force and purport of *you shall* and *he shall*. Hence the general understanding of *shall* and *will* correctly used still offers a solid barrier to obsolescence. Without these auxiliaries a vacuum is felt and remains unfilled. Mencken himself showed his sense of this vacuum by habitually using all four auxiliaries—with one odd exception presently to be noted—in the orthodox, traditional way as punctiliously as if his name had been Fowler.

We have, then, *shall* in the first person to express futurity, *will* to express volition. The rest of the pattern is: for futurity, *will* in the second and third persons; for volition, *shall* in the second and third.

Future	*Volitional*
I (we) shall	I (we) will
You will (thou wilt)	You shall (thou shalt)
He (they) will	He (they) shall

This conjugation, surveyed by itself, looks like a contrivance of school grammarians cunningly devised to torment the young and to make English complicated for the foreigner. Actually, it is the product of a slow and intelligible evolution. It was in answer to the practical necessities of communication that Old English *willan* and *sculan* (*sceal*) grew into what they are. Given a firm hold on the foregoing paradigm, the remaining tenses and moods present no stumbling block, because they involve either no change of auxiliary or only a change of *shall* to *should* and of *will* to *would*.

The paradigm is, of course, the key to the way the auxiliaries are used in direct and indirect questions and in indirect statements. If one does not accept it and master it, one cannot grasp and retain the complications that follow. Anyone who does not bother to acquire it, anyone who dismisses the distinction as pedantic or un-American, may as well indulge his prejudice and stop at this point. The standard idiomatic usages, future and volitional, are divested of avoidable complications in the following examples:

I shall see him next week (factual statement of expectation).

I shall be seeing him next week (slightly more casual equivalent).

I will see him if he wants to see me (consent).

I will see him, whoever disapproves (determination, defiance).

You will receive our proposal in tomorrow's mail (factual prediction).

You (he) shall have cause to regret your (his) action (threat).

You shall be the first to know our decision (promise).

He will think I meant to deceive him (factual conjecture).

He shall never have cause to doubt my word (resolve).

She shall have music wherever she goes (promise).

We will receive their proposals with an open mind (concession).

We will study your idea carefully (promise).

The driver shall not receive or discharge passengers except at bus stops (prohibitory order).

No doubt many of you will be in the Army soon (factual prediction).

All of you applicants shall receive identical treatment (promise).

They shall not pass (resolve of the spokesman and others).

They will not give up so easily (factual prediction).

Violations shall be punished by fine or imprisonment or both (warning).

I should have written to him if I had had his address (hypothetical fact).

I would have signed the petition if I had been asked to (hypothetical choice).

You would have doubted his story if you had heard him tell it (hypothetical fact).

You should have been told if I had known myself (hypothetical promise).

You shall be told as soon as I know myself (promise).

They should have been invited if I had known they were in town (hypothetical promise after the fact).

On the 20th, I shall have been here a year (factual).

You (he) will have had some news by that time (statement of probability).

By that time you (he) shall have been informed of our decision (promise).

We shall see what we shall see (passive waiting).

We will see about that! (threat of decisive action).

We would accommodate you (him) if we could (conditional concession).

OVERLAPPING, DUPLICATION, AND BORROWED FORMS

A little study of the inventory just given will show why the analyst cannot construe *shall* and *will* as agents of a pure and simple future tense. What is called the plain future often has a tincture of will in it; and the will is generally of the present, even though the act belongs to the future. An utterance as simple as *I shall see him next week* states a present intention about a future act, and an intention is inherently volitional, for the wish to see him obviously existed before the utterance. Thus elements of past, present, and future are superposed in the six monosyllables, together with some undertone of volition.

Moreover, a statement that is empty of volition so far as the speaker is concerned may carry a strong implication of volition in its subject: e.g. *They will not give up so easily.* Again, *We shall see what we shall see*—originally a sort of epigram but now little more than a cliché—is future in form but largely present in sense; it means that for the moment there is no need to do anything.

When we come to the volitional future we find still greater discrepancies. The volition expressed is practically always of the present, even when the action contemplated is future or past. *I will see him, whoever disapproves* asserts a present will about a future occurrence; and *You should have been told if I had known myself* states a present reassurance about a past event. In the second and third persons the volition is not that of the subject, but only of the speaker; the promise in *You (he) shall be the first to know* says nothing about the will of the one spoken to or of. *The driver shall not receive or discharge passengers except at bus stops,* an ostensible future, applies to any time, but most emphatically to the present. In short, *shall* and *will* so persistently mingle elements of tense, intention, and simple fact that only by convention can they be pinned to the two ideas of pure or plain futurity and pure or plain volition.

It is possible to support by selected examples the sharp differentiation that *The King's English* makes between the "plain-future system" and the "coloured-future system"; but what we find in the living language is a series of almost imperceptible gradations between statements that are mostly future with a little volition and others that are mostly volition with a little futurity. Where the element of volition is suppressed, secondary, or absent, we should in the interests of clarity use the plain future forms; and where that element is unmistakable or uppermost, the volitional forms.

It follows that there is a mid-region in which either form can be used and defended. Jespersen gathers numerous specimens of *shall* and *will* used in the same context for the same purpose. For example, Johnson writes in *Rasselas:* [The] *time will surely come, when death will be no longer our torment, and no man shall be wretched but by his own fault.* All three auxiliaries might have been the *shall* that expresses inescapable destiny, the impersonal promise of fate (as in *One shall be taken, and the other left / one of you shall betray me*); the reason for Johnson's first *will* may have been the thick sound of *shall surely*. But all three might equally well have been the *will* of simple third-person prediction. Right either way, Johnson was probably letting euphony decide. Many much less literary uses of the auxiliaries involve the same option with a noticeable difference in sense. *I shall (will) never forget what he did for me* means, with *shall*, that the speaker cannot help remembering, whether he chooses to remember or not; with *will*, that he is determined not to forget. His grateful memory in each case is potent.

(2) *Avoidance of duplication.* The governing principle here is the simple one that volition should not be expressed twice over—an application of the maxim against redundancy. The general rule can be formulated thus: Use the simple future auxiliaries, not the volitional ones, where volition is embodied in the main verb or in the whole context. *The King's English* called the breaking of this rule "the mistake that is out of all proportion the commonest"—an assertion doubtless true of England in 1906 and possibly still true, though probably not true of America today. The practicality of the rule is compromised by two factors: (a) the growing tendency to overwork *will* and *would* while letting *shall* and *should* rust; and (b) the immense number of overt or hidden volitional expressions in English—*think better of, think twice about, hesitate to, consider, reconsider, question, shrink from, resist, demur to*, and countless more, including sometimes verbs so simple as *feel, think*, and *say*.

The violations of the rule against saying *will* in those ways and saying it outright immediately afterward are almost necessarily restricted to the first person, because there is no temptation to put the volitional *shall* for the simple future *will* in the second and third persons. The commonest error is *I would like*—which the Fowlers diagnose as *I should like to like*. The speaker ought to choose one or the other, saying *I* WOULD *ask* (volitional) or *I* SHOULD LIKE TO *ask* (nonvolitional auxiliary with volitional verb). To join the two is redundancy arising from confusion.

A small sampling of the typical misusages:

We would like to enter a complaint (should like; the volition is in *like to*).

I will be glad to see him (shall; *be glad to* is volitional).

I would hesitate to take such a risk (should; *hesitate to* implies decision).

We would be pleased to consider the manuscript you describe (should; *be pleased to* is volitional).

I would think the effort likely to succeed (should; *think* = judge).

I would say he will be elected if nominated (should; *say* = suppose).

We will take it for granted that his silence is consent (shall; *take for granted* states a choice).

I would say so! (should; *say so!* is emphatic agreement).

I would hope so (should; *hope* is volitional).

We would prefer to have it in writing (should; *prefer* is optative).

We will require some time to investigate the possibilities (shall; *require* defines a volitional attitude).

I will have made up my mind by that time (shall; *made up my mind* carries the volition).

To these improvements there are, as we shall see, some exceptions that open up choices. But let the rule stand in its simplicity for the moment. The time to ignore it comes rarely.

(3) *Echoic auxiliaries in indirect discourse.* The principle here is that the auxiliary in an indirect question or statement copies the person (first, second, or third) that would be idiomatic in the direct version. To restate the idea, the shift of person resulting from the indirect discourse leaves the auxiliary unchanged: it is determined, not by the grammar of the indirect version, but by that of the direct. Direct: *I shall be too busy to spare the time.* Indirect: *He says he shall* (not *will*) *be too busy to spare the time,* or *He said he should* (not *would*) *be too busy.* In such shifts of person, *shall* may become *should,* and *will* may become *would,* but (with exceptions to be noted) there is no conversion from *sh* to *w* or vice versa. The principle is easy enough to grasp if one is already in firm possession of the standard plain future and volitional forms, and of course very difficult if one is not. In framing an indirect statement or question,

we must catch in the mind's ear the idiomatic form of the direct version. Fussy as this demand may sound, its neglect breeds confusion between the volitional and nonvolitional meanings. The following indirect statements and questions exemplify principle and practice:

He says he will accept our terms. (His words: "I will accept your terms.")

He said he should be glad to contribute. ("I shall be glad . . .")

He says he will contribute. ("I will contribute.")

He asked me if I would serve on the committee. (His question: "Will you . . . ?")

They imagine that if they give me an inch, I will demand an ell. (Their thought: ". . . he will demand . . .")

I told him I should be glad to co-operate. ("I shall be glad . . .")

He seemed to be certain he should be invited. ("I shall be invited.")

He seemed to be certain they would invite him. ("They will invite me.")

You are implying that you shall refuse the appointment. ("I shall refuse . . .")

He is afraid I will ask him embarrassing questions. ("You will ask me . . .")

He is afraid he shall be asked embarrassing questions. ("I shall be asked . . . ")

He wanted to know if I should go by the usual route. "Shall you go . . .?" For a discussion of the auxiliaries in this example and the next, see below, pp. 474-477.

They have made it clear that they shall be expecting us. ("We shall be expecting you.")

We want to know whether you shall be free to entertain an offer. ("Shall you be free . . .?" Note that if *will* replaces *shall*, it carries a suggestion to the one addressed that he free himself by some deliberate act—e.g. resignation or refusal of other commitments; with *shall*, the question is only whether he expects to be free in the ordinary course.)

Some of these auxiliaries will sound highly artificial to those who are not used to hearing them. But everything about language is artificial until we make it our own. What is amazing is the rapidity with which, under a conscious incentive, new locutions are acquired. A new word in the vocabulary is a risky adventure the first time we utter it, but by the third time self-consciousness has evaporated, and presently, if we do not watch, we are making an overworked mannerism of the vocable that it once seemed daring to speak out. A person accustomed to the Irish-Scotch-American pattern of extending *will* and *would* to every use, but observant and not hostile to the idea of self-cultivation, becomes convinced by reflection that a command of *shall* and *should* means a gain in lucidity and force.

In the mood for taking his fate into his hands, and feeling horribly conspicuous, the thoughtful adventurer remarks: "They haven't decided where they shall spend their honeymoon." The ceiling does not fall on the speaker; he does not find himself being stared at. His terror of seeming pretentious quickly dissolves, and soon enough his new mode of speech has become a habit. He ceases to be struck by the usage of those who make the standard distinctions; possibly he takes to pitying those who speak as he was lately speaking himself, for there are no mistakes so audible as the ones we have just outgrown. In the end he speaks the orthodox auxiliaries without calculation, because he thinks them. With a little practice he has made one minor improvement in diction his own. The process is simply that by which, under schooling and other influences, the great majority of us slough off provincial, dialectal, or merely illiterate English, and gradually acquire a vocabulary more precise and flexible, more consistent and unassailable than that we grew up with.

(4) *Anticipation of auxiliaries in questions.* As in indirect discourse the person of the auxiliary is determined by reference to what the direct version would be, so in direct questions its person is determined by anticipating the auxiliary that will be idiomatic in the answer. Here again the principle is simple for anyone who commands the basic conjugation given in (1) above. And, as before, the result of slighting the principle is a misleading substitution of a volitional meaning for a nonvolitional one or vice versa. In

direct questions the shift of person is commonly from second to first. For example:

Shall you be taking your vacation in July? (The anticipated answer: "I shall" or "I shall not." The actual answer may be "No, in August," which is elliptical for "No, I shall be taking it in August." The answer may, of course, go off at a volitional tangent; e.g. "I will wait until September [volitional offer] if the office is shorthanded." Such a volitional answer, being impossible to anticipate, will not affect the form of the question, which is determined by the speaker's normal expectation.)

How shall you know which train to meet? (A possible answer: "I shan't"; another: "By his telegram" [= I shall know by the telegram he will send].)

When shall we three meet again? ("[We shall meet] when the battle's lost and won.")

When will you pay me? ("[I will pay you] when I grow rich.")

"Dear me," cried Mrs. Spaniel, "what will the neighbors think?" ("They won't," said Gissing. . . . "Thinking is very rare.")

Would you believe him on oath? (In expectation of "I would not.")

Should you care to look over his prospectus? (Expects "I should like to" or "I should prefer not to"; nonvolitional auxiliary because the verb expresses volition.)

Will (would) you look over his prospectus? (Request; expects *will*).

Will X. be back by the end of the month? (Expects *will* or *will not*; there is no shift of grammatical person in an answer in the third person, but the question still anticipates the auxiliary of the answer.)

Shall you be back by the end of the month? (Expects "I shall" or "I shall not.")

Shall I have B. take over the filing in C.'s absence? (Expects *shall* theoretically. Actually, such a question is a request for instructions, which are idiomatically given with *will* by exception to the standard volitional pattern. In practice the hortatory second and third person—*you shall, he (they) shall*—are confined in the affirmative to bookish uses. They occur in questions because they *might* be used in the answers, not because they will be. The question follows the rule, though the questioner knows that the answer will not.)

THE REALM OF DOUBT AND CHOICE

So much for the reign of comparative law and order. Beyond the four enumerated categories, rule-defying idiom takes over. Yet one cannot dismiss the subject of *shall, will, should,* and *would* without commenting on some of the troublesome discrepancies, variations, exceptions, and dilemmas that obtain. The survey will be made in parallel with the four earlier categories.

In the first category, begin with a minor but insoluble puzzle: what auxiliary shall be used in a plain statement about a plural subject that comprises two or three grammatical persons? For example: *You and Henry and I shall (will) probably be on the committee.* Answers that have satisfied grammarians are these: *will,* on the score of simple politeness and self-effacement; *will,* on the principle of majority rule, there being two subjects that call for *will* to only one that calls for *shall; shall,* because *You and Henry and I* are felt as an equivalent of *we; shall,* on the ground of a modern tendency to make a verb harmonize with the subject that stands nearest it. All the reasons sound good, but none of them makes either version of the sentence good. Anyone who wants to avoid reproach and argument at the same time had better be a resourceful grammarian and rephrase his thought: *You and Henry will . . . , and so shall I* or *The committee will probably include you and Henry and me.* To such a writer what matters is to get a shipshape sentence, not to assign plausible reasons for an untidy one.

A similar form of the puzzle: *All of us will (shall) probably be on the committee. All* is technically third person, calling for *will,* but *All of us* is morally first person plural, suggesting *shall.* We can use whichever we prefer; *will* is the more usual, and it seems to draw some logical enough support from *Neither* (or *None*) *of us will offer any objection,* where *shall* is nearly or quite inconceivable. Even odder things, however, can be found in the classics. In

Jane Austen, who was addicted to ONE in the first person singular, Jespersen unearthed such curiosities as *One* [=I] *should be a brute not to feel for the distress they are in*— a pattern that to most modern ears will seem unacceptable. It is not always easy to determine whether formal grammar or underlying sense shall prevail, but it is clear that less discomfort is entailed if we treat *one, all, neither,* and *none* as third-person pronouns taking *will* or *would.*

A more serious uncertainty can follow from the first person plural by reason of an inherent ambiguity in its pronoun, *we.* Grammarians have been prone to treat *we* as a pure plural of *I,* meaning *I and I and I,* etc. This interpretation works out well enough where there is palpable identity of interest, as when *we* signifies all of us, or mankind (*We shall see even stranger things come to pass within a decade*), or all of those implied by context (*We shall have our twenty-fifth reunion next year*). But *we* often means *you and I,* or *we three,* or *I and sundry others,* between or among whom there may be no solidarity whatever beyond the fact that they can be mentioned collectively. Such a *we* combines elements of the first person with elements of the second, or of both second and third—a fact illustrated by the chairman of a large committee or by the moderator of a town meeting when he says: *What is your* (not *our*) *pleasure?* and goes on with: *Those opposed will raise their* (third person) *hands.* It follows that *we shall* is the natural nonvolitional form when there is no possible conflict of opinion in the speaker's mind (*We shall have rain before night*). When unanimity cannot be assumed, deference to the point of view of others comes into play: *We will* (shall?) *put this item on the agenda, I take it / We ought to decide how we will* (shall?) *apportion the proceeds.* In such situations the presence of those included in the *we* exerts a pressure in favor of what looks like the volitional auxiliary; but such a *will* is probably to be understood, not as a volitional first-person but as a sort of transferred second-person *will,* meaning in effect *Perhaps you others will agree with me that* . . .

Jespersen reminds us that the grammarian Henry Sweet argued for a rule to make the various equivalents of *we*— *you and I, we two, we all*—take *will* instead of *shall,* lest the speaker seem to be assuming a nonexistent right to pronounce for others. Sweet's hearers at the Philological Society disagreed; Jespersen himself, assembling examples from writers high and low, showed that there was support for Sweet and dissent from him in nearly equal amounts. The facts of usage, then, leave us exactly where we were; that is, in an area where each may do as he likes. A sensible prescription would seem to be: Use nonvolitional *we shall* where the context precludes any conflict of opinion or interest; use either auxiliary at discretion where conflict is conceivable but hardly expected; prefer *we will* and *will we* when there is no clue to the position of one's associates and one is inviting them to agree or disagree.

By a well-established idiom, orders to subordinates, a teacher's instructions to a pupil or a class, and the like are given in the plain second-person future form *will*, in flat disregard of the quasi-imperative *you shall* theoretically called for: *You will at once report to this office by telephone / You will review the first three sections and go on to the end of the chapter / You will bear in mind that at least ten days must be allowed for proofreading.* In such directions *you shall* is virtually impossible—though it is idiomatic in a promise (*You shall have whatever clerical help you need*) and in a threat (*You shall hear from our attorney*). This conventional *will* is sometimes explained as a polite softening of an order, to avoid a *you shall* that would sound overbearing; but *you will*, however it may have originated, has become by usage at least as hortatory as any other mode of command. It is in fact a calm assumption that the speaker's wishes are above question or demur, as if he were the spokesman of universal destiny. This *will* is in purport a totally different auxiliary from the *will* of simple futurity: the *you will* of an order means *you are required to*. By most persons *You will wear your uniform at all times* is probably heard as more lordly than *You are to . . .* and far more lordly than the simple imperative, *Wear your uniform . . .* In fact, the *you will* of an order has so absolutist an undertone that it is rather sharpened than blunted by seemingly mollifying additions: *You will kindly refrain from interrupting me / You will be so good as to make a fresh copy, omitting the mistakes / You will please spare me the unnecessary details.*

Still another defiance of rule under our first category is a firmly assertive simple future in the first person that attains an actually higher concentration of resolve than the normal volitional form: *I will not* (standard volition) *be interrupted / I shall* (volition reinforced) *disconnect my telephone and not answer my doorbell.* Here the *will* (orthodox volitional form) expresses determination; the *shall* (nominally simple future) intensifies the determination by an overtone of grimness. Such a *shall* utilizes the well-known force of understatement; it invests simple fact with a more urgent intention than would be shown by the conventional assertion of will. Similar locutions: *We shall take legal measures / I shall tell him to publish and be damned / If he calls, I shall not be at home / Either they will agree to my terms, or I shall offer the idea elsewhere / If I cannot get better service, I shall take my patronage elsewhere / I shall not contribute to any such cause.* Every such *shall* says: "This is the way it is going to be"—a palpably stronger affirmation than "This is the way I want it to be."

There is also a subtly volitional *shall-should* that states the actual or intended result of purposive action: *He is frankly trying to compose music that shall be popular without being cheap / They were working out a reorganization that should eliminate waste / The mirror was so placed that it should show who was approaching the entrance / If anyone wanted to execute a piece of writing that should be . . . the densest possible concentration of . . . solecisms / She had learned how to insult people in a way that should leave them paralyzed between resentment and amusement.* In each of these, *will* or *would* is possible and unassailable, but lacking in the reassuring, quasi-promissory effect of *shall* and *should*, which express the volition of the planner as if it were transferable to the thing planned. The volitional auxiliaries, so used, are an equivalent of *will (would) succeed in, will (would) manage to.* For example, *I can state it in a way that shall convince them* = in a way that will succeed in convincing them. The auxiliary expresses purpose, though not the purpose of its subject, which is commonly impersonal.

So much for irregularities affecting the simple declarative uses of the plain future and the volitional auxiliaries. There are also some idiomatic exceptions under our second category, the one governed by the rule against duplicating in the auxiliary a volition already expressed.

Rigidly applied, this rule would call for *I shall not hear of it*—clearly a volitional verb meaning *consent to, tolerate, regard as admissible*—but idiom imposes *I will not (won't) hear of it*. There are a great many other expressions—too many to list—with which, in the first person, we not only may but must use *will*, redoubling the volition and ignoring the rule. Most of these expressions denote doubt or hesitancy. We say *I shall consider him an opponent henceforth*, but *I will consider his protest / I shall advise them to drop the matter*, but *I will take it under advisement / We shall not consent to that sort of compromise*, but *We will consent if there is no other solution / I shall accept the invitation*, but *I will accept your conditions*. In such examples of reduplicated volition the *will* used is the indeclinable auxiliary of consent or concession, and *shall* is either not possible at all or else prim and pedantic.

It is to be noted, too, that the shift from a verbal to an adverbial way of expressing volition has a strong tendency to cause a shift to the duplicating volitional auxiliary. When we say *I shall be glad to do as you suggest*, the *shall* is conformable to the rule; but *I will gladly do as you suggest*, which defies it, is preferable because the weakened force of *gladly* needs bolstering. The rule is properly followed in *We shall be reluctant to accept such an arrangement*, and properly transgressed in *We will accept such an arrangement with reluctance*. We cannot, however, formulate a rule for using *shall* with volitional verbs and *will* with volitional adverbs, for we have to say both *I shall dread to face such a contingency* and *I shall face such a contingency with dread*. There is nothing for it but to admit that here is a domain, governed by tact, to which rule does not reach. The final arbiter is the ear. Some ears are of course better than others, and perhaps no ear is perfect. It is small wonder that foreigners whose general command of English is a lesson to most of us are often uncertain in their grasp of details such as these, which frequently elude even the best native speakers and writers.

It is not uncommon to find statements with volitional verbs that can take either the simple future auxiliary or the volitional auxiliary, sometimes with a shade of difference in the meaning. *I shall (will) not decide without further thought* is, with *shall*, a statement of fact: the speaker is going to think the matter over and then decide. With *will* it is a refusal to be rushed into a decision: the speaker insists on time to decide. For the second meaning, reduplicated volition is proper and necessary. There is a similar option in *We should (would) have accepted such a compromise if it had been proposed a year ago. Accept* is of course volitional with either auxiliary, but *should* gives the factual meaning that the compromise would have been acceptable a year ago though it is not now, whereas *would* says that a year ago we could have brought ourselves to accept it, though reluctantly. *I (we) shall approve* and *I (we) will approve, I (we) shall resist* and *I (we) will resist,* and other locutions of the kind are equally idiomatic; hence the precept against the double expression of volition cannot be considered by any means absolute.

PUZZLES IN INDIRECT DISCOURSE

How absolute, how resistant to exceptions is the rule of our third group—that in indirect discourse the auxiliary reproduces the person properly used in the direct version? All one can say is that it presents puzzles and dilemmas, some of which give pause even to speakers described in *The King's English* as to the manner born. *What are these formidable difficulties that you say I will (shall) encounter?* Which auxiliary? What you say is *You will encounter formidable difficulties:* therefore *will,* under the rule of agreement between direct and indirect. But *I shall* clings to its rights as the expression of the simple first-person (nonvolitional) future, as we can see if we contemplate the same thought in this form: *I shall encounter formidable difficulties, you say: what are they?* Clearly, *shall* would be unexceptionable if the original sentence lacked *you say,* though it would still be the echo of a second-person warning. It is hard to pronounce either auxiliary right or wrong.

The Fowlers grappling with the analogous sentence *You say I will (shall) never succeed*, declare that "nearly every one" finds *will* "intolerable, however reasonable and consistent." They mean that they themselves find *will* intolerable. This amounts to excepting from the rule of correspondence the entire first person in plain-future meanings converted into direct discourse. The conversion from second-person direct to first-person indirect produces a head-on collision between the instinct to make direct and indirect correspond and the basic force of *shall* as the signal of the plain first-person future. *The King's English* recommends giving precedence to the second pattern; but a large number of the best writers have followed the rule with no apparent feeling that the resultant *will* is "intolerable, however reasonable and consistent." Usage is too hopelessly divided to prove anything except that *shall* is defensible on one ground and *will* on another—hence either can be used.

It is worth noting, too, that the grammatical person of the direct version is sometimes hard to determine. *You evidently doubt whether I shall (will) pass the examination* may be an echo of your imaginary question asked of someone else in the third person—*Will he pass the examination?*—or an echo of a question asked in the second person—*Shall you pass . . . ?* Or the speaker may believe that his interlocutor has expressed doubt both to him and to others. If we disregard the Fowlerian preference for *shall* regardless and stick to the rule of correspondence between direct and indirect, the first supposition gives *will*, the second *shall*, and the third both. It is difficult to see how either auxiliary can be called indefensible or above criticism.

Sometimes an ambiguous meaning will attach to the auxiliary of indirect discourse, with resultant dilemmas. *You assumed that I would (should) take your word for it*. If the direct version is *You will take my word for it*, the meaning can be (a) *You will take my word for it as a matter of course*, reproduced by *would* in the indirect; or (b) *You will consent or decide, after thinking it over, to take my word for it*; or (c) the sentence can even be an authoritative command: *You are to take my word for it without question.* If we say that, for the first meaning, it would be better to switch to *should*, against the rule, in order to avoid the false implication of a struggle to decide, we plunge into fresh difficulties; for *should* in the indirect will imply *You should* (= ought to) *take my word for it* in the direct. Here we have an illustration of the truth pointed out by many grammarians—that in *shall*, *will*, *should*, and *would* the English language has too few auxiliaries for the great variety of tasks assigned to them.

All such difficulties lead to the important suggestion that, *shall-will* problems being often insoluble, we should try to make our meaning clear by other means. For example, the four possible senses of the sentence last examined can be disentangled by (a) *You assumed that I was going to take your word for it*, (b) *You assumed that I must come around to taking your word for it*, (c) *You assumed that I should* (would?) *submit to taking your word for it*, and (d) *You assumed that I ought to take your word for it.* The increasing tendency to resort to such alternatives, with a consequent disuse of the auxiliaries, is on the whole a salutary preventive of ambiguity.

But note in the foregoing examples a standard exception to the law making the auxiliaries correspond in direct and indirect discourse. When, in the common shift from second-person direct to first-person indirect, retaining the second-person auxiliary would introduce a false idea of volition, the auxiliary is properly shifted from a *w* to an *sh* form. *You are afraid I shall* (not *will*) *set the place afire* is necessary to express *You will* [by carelessness or clumsiness, without meaning to] *set the place afire*, not because of the Fowlers' distaste for echoic *will* in the first person, but because *will* would convey a deliberate intent to commit arson. Avoiding the false implication is more important than any awkwardness in the use of the "wrong" auxiliary. Similarly, *You will not get along peaceably with him* [because of the way you are constituted] must be reported in the form *You think I shall not . . .*, because to keep *will* would mean a deliberate intention to pick a quarrel. *My doctor thinks I shall be out of circulation for some time* denotes the prospect of a slow recovery; *will* would suggest malingering. In short, the rule of correspondence between direct and indirect has to be interpreted with discretion and rather frequently broken.

When we come to the fourth category, the direct question, we think at once of an idiomatic usage that runs counter to the rule of anticipating in a question the person of the auxiliary expected in the answer. Consider such first-person-plural questions as *Shall we dance?* / *Shall we sit down on this bench and talk it over?* / *Shall you and I* (construed as *we*) *go down to the pier and let our feet hang over?* It would be nonsensical to say that these expect *We shall* or *We shall not*. It would be equally outlandish to frame the questions with *Will we . . . ?* Any such question is actually a proposal that includes a request for assent—a moral and social equivalent of *Will you . . . ?* The auxiliary is chosen by idiom without the slightest expectation of either *shall* or *will* in the answer, which may be *Let's*, or *A good idea*, or *I don't mind*, or some form of refusal. The question is interrogative in form only; its effect is that of a conciliatory or coaxing imperative, not much different from *Let us, please . . .* The *we* of such questions is *you* in disguise; we can make it equivalent to *will* and a second-person volitional expression: *We will dance if you wish* / *If you agree, we will sit down and talk it over* / *We will go down to the pier if you like.*

There is also an element of the disguised *you* in the *I* or *we* that asks for instructions or orders. These are idiomatically given with *will*, but they are invited with *shall*: *Shall I send him the usual form letter?* / *Shall we call another rehearsal for this evening?* / *Shall I call a doctor?* These mean *Is it your wish that I* (*we*) *do so-and-so?* A second-person volition is wrapped up in a first-person plain future, and there is a total lack of correspondence between the person of the interrogative auxiliary and that of the expected answer.

CONTRACTIONS AND THEIR INFLUENCE

A final word must be said about the colloquial contractions *we'll*, *you'll*, *I'd*, *he'd*; they are, of course, unaffected by intention or context. Some grammarians—among them the

American authority George Philip Krapp—have maintained that *I'll* can stand indifferently for either *I shall* or *I will*, and *I'd* for either *I would* or *I should*. Jespersen, speaking with unaccustomed emphasis, assures us that the sound of initial *sh* is never lost, whereas that of *w* frequently disappears; so that the contractions necessarily stand for the *w* and not the *sh* forms. The instinct of many, if not most, readers undoubtedly harmonizes with the historical fact: only a minority would after reflection insist on interpreting *we'll* and *they'd* as meaning anything but *we will* and *they would*. Indeed, such forms as *I sh'll* are not unknown in print.

Nevertheless, some writers have clearly supposed that the contractions are also acceptable equivalents of the *sh* forms and have shown this supposition by writing *I'll*, *I'd*, etc. where they would have written *I shall*, *I should*, etc. if they had been using the full forms. It is clear from internal evidence that H. L. Mencken was one such writer. His habit is invariably orthodox when he is not using the contractions: *I shall be grateful, as in the past, for corrections and additions sent to me / I have arranged that all my* [materials] *on speech shall go . . . to a place where they will be open to other students.* But he also writes: *It is highly improbable that I'll ever attempt a Supplement III / Meanwhile, I'll be glad as always to hear from such students / If I tried to get all the new material into it I'd have a volume of forbidding bulk.* If his contracted forms denoted a lapse into the alleged American contempt for the distinction between *shall* and *will*, he would hardly be so consistently conventional in the spelled-out auxiliaries.

A contraction taken by itself does not tell us whether the writer has the wrong auxiliary in mind or is under the erroneous impression that the contractions cover both *sh* and *w. With a lighter bat . . .* [Babe Ruth] *might have connected more often with balls he missed entirely and thus more than made up for the homers he lost. We'll never know.* This *We'll* may be either the *we will* of the careless or a misinterpretation of what the contraction can stand for. But when a pen that unfailingly writes *we should* commits itself to *for a while we thought we'd have to spend the rest of the winter on the west side of Mendon Mountain* we can safely infer an attempt to extend the contraction beyond its tenable meaning of *we would*.

(Note in passing that the contraction *'d* can stand for *had* as well as *would*; whence its interesting contribution to the dilemma of HAD RATHER versus *would rather*, etc. See also SEQUENCE OF TENSES.)

It is obviously no easy task to survey the essentials of the usage governing *shall* and *will* without either oversimplifying to encourage the inquirer or else disheartening him by exhibiting the full list of complications. It is no service to anyone to represent the difficulties as trifling or nonexistent; or to pretend that there is a clear, cogent, and uniform set of practices; or to deny that certain problems are insoluble and the constructions that breed them are best avoided. Even so, no one should be left with the feeling that, defeated in advance, he may as well give up and leave all discrimination to born hairsplitters. With a little effort anyone can gain a command of the main principles and learn to bypass dilemmas. Neither overconfidence nor defeatism need—or should—rule the mind of those willing to cope with *shall* and *will*.

2 / PUNCTUATION

PUNCTUATION, whether we call it a science that contains touches of art or an art reared on underpinnings of science, is a graphic device for showing how sentences are constructed. Wherever it fails to show their construction it is useless; wherever it misleads us about their construction it is culpable. This truth is more far-reaching than it sounds, because punctuation is equally positive in effect whether present or absent. That is to say, marks that do not appear can and will convey as much about the structure of a sentence as the marks that do appear. To the writer who properly values clearness, knowing which marks to leave out is not less imperative than knowing which ones to put in. Since it is a cardinal principle of good writing that no one should ever have to read a sentence twice because of the way it is put together, it follows that the system of showing eye and mind how it is put together is a first requisite. To punctuate a sentence right is a part of building it right, for the wrong punctuation will tell the reader, even if the words do not, that the sentence was built wrong.

This reciprocity between punctuation and structure means in practice that the better the sentence, the easier it is to punctuate. The workmanlike sentence almost punctuates itself. Commas and colons are not emergency devices for first aid to the ailing sentence; they are aids and witnesses to the soundness of the sound sentence. The writer who has to torment his mind about the punctuation of a passage does well to inquire whether he is not struggling with something that he should not have written, or should have written differently. Punctuation will signalize coherence that is there; wrongly applied, it will introduce incoherence that would otherwise not be there; but it will not supply or serve as substitute for coherence that is lacking. Sentences that are mispunctuated usually need reshaping; when properly reshaped, the problem of punctuation disappears.

Yet we must not oversimplify: punctuation is not a precise

system that all competent writers and editors can be counted on to apply uniformly. The truth is—and the sooner it is understood, the better—that there are two different though overlapping codes, both solidly established, both defensible historically and logically. One, the loose or open system, corresponds to the natural pauses of the voice in speaking or in reading aloud; it may be called the oratorical or even the rhetorical principle. Not so very long ago, schoolbooks used to teach that when we read aloud we should pause to count one at a comma, two at a semicolon, three at a colon or dash, and four at a terminal mark (period, question mark, or exclamation point). Rhetorical punctuation is designed to facilitate this manner of reading. The second code of punctuation is the tight, closed, and structural; it depends, not on the pauses of the reading voice, but on the grammatical—which is to say logical—relations of parts.

The two systems coincide at many points, since the natural inflections of the reading voice often correspond with the structural relations and are determined by them. But they do not *have* to correspond. The customary punctuation of Hamlet's soliloquy is *To be, or not to be*; but there is nothing to prevent an actor's discarding the comma and pausing after *or* to walk halfway across the stage. Good readers have always distributed their pauses, as they do their intonations, to bring out nuances that commas and dashes do not indicate. No one is compelled either to read according to somebody else's punctuation or to punctuate a passage to suit the inner ear. In being logical the modern system sometimes flouts both ear and eye, as a simple example makes clear: *Of the undergraduates still up at Cambridge Ainsworth, Lytton Strachey, and I used to go* [to the Easter reading party]. It is obvious in this sentence that the pause between *Cambridge* and *Ainsworth* is longer than that between *Ainsworth* and *Lytton Strachey*, yet the "logical" comma marks the shorter pause, throwing together the meaningless pair *Cambridge Ainsworth*.

The two systems of punctuation, then, part company at many places, but perhaps not at so many as those at which they coincide.

There is a further cause of discrepancy. Nearly everybody

whose punctuation inclines to one system is bound at times to use the other. Good writers who are not partial to oratorical punctuation will resort to it now and then for particular effects. In fiction, the words of the dying are commonly broken up with dashes to suggest extreme feebleness or gaspings for breath. A single dash often denotes a pause followed by an unexpected, more or less tangential afterthought; such a dash is quasi-oratorical. All of us tend to put a question mark after the sentence that is affirmative in form but interrogative in sound (*You see my point? / You will meet me at the train gate? / My application is ligely to be acted on fairly soon?*). A speaker's effect, that of tight-lipped implacableness, will be suggested by such eccentric devices as *I, will, see, him, damned, first!* And the speaker-punctuator, however strong his convictions, yields like anyone else to logic and grammar in such matters as omitting the comma from restrictive relative clauses and including it in nonrestrictive ones.* In fine, nearly everybody leans toward one system but shows the influence of the other.

The historical trend for the past three or four hundred years has been away from the rhetorical style of punctuation. To the modern eye the prose of the seventeenth, eighteenth, and nineteenth centuries was needlessly peppered with marks. We tend to be sparing to the point of insufficiency. This greater simplicity is partly a result of our having gradually simplified the sentence itself and made a fetish of brevity. But many simple sentences that we speak without effort or ambiguity can no longer be punctuated—or indeed written—under the modern system; for example: *What will happen if they do not need not be considered now.* Put a comma after the first *not* and the logical copy editor will take it out. Omit it and all is confusion—though the sentence is short and straightforward.

The drive toward a lean punctuation is such that even if we still wrote the complex, periodic sentences of Johnson or of Macaulay, we should punctuate them much less heavily. Just as in the preceding example logic prevents us from sep-

---

* *The lovely piece that you see here I bought for a song* (restrictive). *This piece, which you may think gaudy, comes from a country auction* (nonrestrictive). See THAT, WHICH, RELATIVE.

arating subject from verb, so after a long, involved subject we feel no obligation to put a comma showing where the predicate begins. Again, we tend not to set off introductory adverbial phrases and clauses, even when long: *Apart from an old uncle* (,) *he has no one left.* Modern reading habits enable the mind to construe without the once idiomatic marks. The reader will have noticed that this book is punctuated mainly from the strict-constructionist, non-elocutionary point of view, which has long been gaining authority and seems likely to retain it.

Nevertheless this point of view denotes only a preference. It does not impose a law. The two systems exist side by side, each with practitioners who know what they are doing and why, and the argument between them is one that nobody wins. Consider this sentence: *Q.'s attempt to do justice to the old, and to his generation lost, liberator is thrilling.* This is punctuation by the voice, which treats *and to his generation lost* as an interpolated phrase to be islanded within commas. The structural punctuator sees the sentence quite differently. To him *old* and *lost* are logically equal adjectives connected by *and* and qualifying *liberator*; he sees no need for a comma between an adjective and its noun; and what he construes as really parenthetical is *to his generation.* He will, then, punctuate: *do justice to the old and, to his generation, lost liberator.* A similar example: *It is assumed that he too wants the backing of a majority, and having gained it will enjoy power.* The sentence is punctuated the way it might be spoken. But its logical line is *wants the backing of a majority and* (. . .) *will enjoy power.* The strict-constructionist punctuation, then, is *wants the backing of a majority and, having gained it, will enjoy power.* This has the incidental recommendation that it is normal practice to avoid, if possible, separating the two parts of a compound predicate—*wants . . . and will enjoy*—and if need be to set off a participial phrase. Yet these considerations will not move anyone committed to the doctrine of punctuation by ear.

In practice an author who prefers one system will be undone if his work is entrusted to a copy editor committed to the other system. For that reason we cannot be sure how an author punctuates unless we have studied his manuscripts, or unless we know from his high reputation that his copy is followed without change. The punctuation that we find in the public prints and in most recent books is likely to be not the author's but his editors'. Copy desks and house rules dictate it. An author, for all his readers can tell, may be irked by the way he is punctuated, pleased with it, or completely indifferent or unaware. A surprising number of those who write for print disclaim any grasp of punctuation or taste for its subtleties. They leave the commas to be put in by copyists or secretaries, sometimes implying that their own minds are intent on higher things. But so much of punctuation is inseparable from meaning, it is so integral with the truth or falsity of what we write, that anyone can write himself down a fool through wrong punctuation as readily as through wrong words. It is a frivolous abdication of responsibility for a writer not to know more than a copyist does about what he is trying to say, or not to respect the means of making it clear.

However time and evolution may have changed the shape of the sentence and the fashions in separating its components, there are at least two basic principles that remain constant from age to age. The first is relativism, which bids us gauge the comparative weight of this part and that, measure their degrees of subordination, and punctuate them accordingly. On this principle we put a mark of greater separation at a major node because there is already one of lesser separation at a minor node—a semicolon here because there is a comma there, a full stop and sentence break in this place because a semicolon or colon was required in that, and so on. The second unchanging principle sets off certain kinds of subordinate elements fore and aft with paired marks—commas, dashes, parentheses. Both these incarnations of logic solicit the writer's attention again and again. Between them they cover a large part of the difficulties that occur, and they will accordingly be noticed more than once in the exhibits that follow.

The modern simplification of the sentence has so far reduced the intricacies of punctuation that mastering the art is almost synonymous with mastering the lowest mark—the comma. The use of every other mark can be described in brief generalizations and a few rules apiece, but the comma has become a many-armed monster which takes a deal of taming. Not only is it needed much more often than all the other marks put together (the period, which is frequent too, raises only a few trifling problems), but the idiomatic uses of the comma have become steadily more exact and more exacting. Today, every comma that cannot be rationally explained looks ridiculous, and every comma irrationally omitted or irrationally placed will be interpreted as a lapse. More important, the gratuitous comma will interpose an obstacle between reader and writer. We begin therefore with the uses of the comma that observation shows to be most liable to error and confusion.

THE COMMA

Enumerative Series: *a, b, c, d, . . . , and n.*

The number of members most often enumerated in prose is three—the pattern *a, b, and c: Hurrah for the red, white, and blue! / a confusion of stone tombs, caves, and newish residential suburbs / He had gone clandestinely to Athens, acquired a residence in the Piraeus, and become one of the privileged underprivileged / He looked about nervously, dismounted, and crept forward on his stomach.* This pattern is so recurrent as almost to suggest that a trinitarian principle is rooted in the language. But series that go beyond three members are fairly common too: *They wore Prince Alberts, striped trousers, high silk hats, and bright green sashes / Acquire skill in your profession, be diligent in the exercise of it, enlarge the circle of your friends and acquaintance, avoid pleasure and expense, and never be generous but with a view of gaining more than you could save by frugality / eager inquiry on the faces of Sonia, Chattie, Meredith, Bod, Fritz, and Virginia Hadley.* The formula *a, b, c, d, . . . , and n* will serve to represent such enumerations extended to any number.

It will be noticed that such series can consist of any *kind* of element, so long as the members are truly in parallel. They may be nouns, adjectives, phrases, or clauses, and of any length. Series of adverbs are not unknown: *up, down, and sideways.* Even a series of prepositions is thinkable: *motion to, from, or within the circle.* Whatever the number of units, the characteristics of the series tend to be the same two: (1) rhetorical equivalence among the members and (2) a conjunctive word, usually *and*, which signals the arrival of the last member. Sometimes *and* is replaced by *or*—*Is a man in such a fix to advance, stand still, or retreat?*—and sometimes by *but.* The omission of the conjunctive word occurs when the members reduplicate a meaning, as in *He was tired out, exhausted, finished.*

How to punctuate these enumerations is argued with more heat than is called forth by any other rhetorical problem except the split infinitive. Leaving aside a few poets and a handful of crotcheteers who want to abolish all punctuation, everybody favors the use of commas between all members up to the last two; but there the shooting begins. A large body of opinion that includes nearly all newspapers insists on *a, b and c*—that is, they omit the last comma. A smaller body, numbering many of the most respectable book publishers, sticks to *a, b, and c:* they demand a comma before the cadence signaled by *and, or,* or *but.* Schools that teach composition are divided; so is the counsel of rhetorics, manuals, and teachers of freshman English; so is the practice of authors, whose printed works tell us nothing of their preference. Readers will have noticed that this book retains the closing comma—the *a, b, and c* formula.

A widely parroted dictum is supposed to settle the issue: if you have the conjunction, you don't need the comma. That is bad reasoning or no reasoning at all. A conjunction is a connective device, as its name announces; whereas a mark of punctuation is nothing if not separative. To insist that the first perform the duty of the second is rather like prescribing sand in the bearings. Whatever is to be said for punctuating *a, b and c* (i.e. without a comma before *and*), it is not that the *and* replaces the missing mark. The comma, when present, separates *b* from *c*; the *and* joins *c* and *b* and (just as much) *a*—a material point commonly overlooked. It is implicit in the standard form of a series that when you write *red, white, and blue* you mean *red and white and blue*—three equal terms. The form itself is a convention for making the conjunction work between *a* and *b* though it is present only between *b* and *c*; one conjunction at the end serves for all the intervals.

What, then, are the arguments for omitting the last comma? Only one is cogent—the saving of space. In the narrow width of a newspaper column this saving counts for more than elsewhere, which is why the omission is so nearly universal in journalism. But here or anywhere one must question whether the advantage outweighs the confusion caused by the omission.

This confusion can be illustrated by a series in which all or some of the members, being compound, call for *and* within themselves: *The semifinal round was completed by the matches between A. and B., C. and D., E. and F. (,) and G. and H.* Omit, by the newspaper rule, the closing comma after *F.*, and your series ends in a hash, despite our knowing from the outset that the series falls into pairs. Usually we are not given this hint, and we flounder, especially if we encounter a series within a series: *The magazines were filled with such accounts of virtue betrayed, fatal infatuations of the innocent for the wicked, romantic Indians, patriotic love for old sights, relics, traditions (,) and sentimental folk tales.* Such a series, baffling at best, defies extrication if you leave out the last comma. Is it a series of four that omits an *and* before *patriotic* and lumps *sentimental folk tales* with *sights, relics, traditions?* Or is it a series of five, having *traditions and sentimental folk tales* for its last member, co-ordinate with *virtue betrayed*, etc., and omitting a helpful *and* before *traditions?* One guess is as good as another.

The lesson here is that a series with the last comma omitted will often leave you unable to answer the rudimentary question: how many members was it meant to consist of? If you happen to be used to the *a, b, and c* pattern, the commonest list will momentarily ditch you if punctuated *a, b, c, . . . and n.* This is especially likely if there is a chance that the meanings of the last two will be taken as forming but one. Consider *In the following year he will be able to specialize in gynecology, immunology, orthopedics or diseases of the bone. Or* in this sentence could be introducing an explanation of the previous term; actually, it is a fourth term, left floating by the absence of a comma. One tends not to recognize an *and* or *or* as terminal unless a comma precedes it. Omission always tends to confusion and sometimes guarantees it; inclusion can never possibly confuse.

The following sentence supplies a particularly strong example for the case against omitting the comma before the last member of a series: *The Socialist party's many aims include an early end of the dictatorship of Generalissimo Francisco Franco,* [the] *acceptance of a period of constitutional monarchy until the Spanish people can freely vote their own constitutional future and sweeping fiscal, agricultural and educational reforms.* The third member, *sweeping . . . reforms,* is inevitably first read as part of the second; that is, as an additional object of *vote.* You do not discover until the period that you have misread: the reforms were meant as a third object of *include.* Supply the comma after *future,* and there is no such derailment. (In this system there would of course be another after *agricultural.*) The same trouble in smaller compass turns up in this sentence: *The three Presidential "imperatives" for the year were defense reorganization, extension of reciprocal trade and foreign aid.* You first read *reciprocal trade* and *foreign aid* as co-ordinate objects governed by *extension of,* and you are still waiting for the third member with voice suspended. A comma after *trade* would identify the third member for what it is.

A series of four, meant to list some of the summer attractions of a city, shows how natural is the *and* within a member just before the last and how easy it is for the *a, b and c* punctuator to mistake such an *and* for the last. Numbers and indention make graphic what was clueless in the series as originally printed:

(1) *concerts,*

(2) *dance recitals by a visiting Filipino troupe,*

(3) *presentations by the Comédie Française and the Gilbert and Sullivan company from the Stratford Ontario Festival,*

and

(4) *offerings by the Bunraku Theatre of Japan.*

The punctuation is *a, b, c, and d,* by the established code of a weekly magazine that printed the passage; but anyone habituated to *a, b, c and d* is bound to take the *and* after *Française* as the signal of a fourth and closing member, only to be disconcerted when the true fourth member leaps out at him. Inserting a second *by* before *the Gilbert and Sullivan company* might protect the reader, but it is certain that this sort of confusion will frequently recur as long as both conventions exist side by side and all readers have to adjust to each in turn.

Some journals that enforce the *a, b and c* pattern also recommend using the final comma, in conscious exception to the rule, where ambiguity threatens. But that system requires perpetual awareness for handling one very simple problem. It is hard enough to enforce a single rule with reasonable consistency, and newspapers that mean to punctuate *a, b and c* wherever possible will inadvertently stumble into the alternative practice. It would mean perfect clarity—and without wear and tear—if we could have but one code, simple enumeration being one of the few devices of writing governable by unvarying habit. But of course this is a utopian hope. Periodicals edited under strong convictions that have dictated a given practice for decades are not going to change it for the sake of a uniformity they view with skepticism. In this state of things each individual must weigh the alternatives and choose for himself. The recommendation here is that he use the comma between *all* members of a series, including the last two, on the common-sense ground that to do so will preclude ambiguities and annoyances at a negligible cost.

Superposed Versus Parallel Adjectives

The comma can cause trouble equally by its absence, by its presence, and by wrong placement. Perhaps the most serious trouble caused by omission is that inflicted on relative clauses made to look falsely restrictive (SEE THAT, WHICH, RELATIVE). But the most frequent and irritating trouble occurs in connection with adjectives falaciously interpreted as equal and parallel qualifiers of the same noun. Reporters and men at copy desks are trained to put commas between all adjectives that belong to the same noun, letting the chips fall where they may. The rule is not the helpful simplification it seems. It is, rather, a gross oversimplification which, unless clearly understood and properly limited, can produce bad results.

The comma is rightly used in such a construction as *this wise, farsighted policy* (a policy that is, for one attribute, wise, for another farsighted) ; or *a firm, forthright, unequivocal answer* (an answer having the three properties of firmness, forthrightness, and unequivocalness) ; or *a lazy, restful weekend*. These adjectives are co-ordinate, equal, and parallel qualifiers of the noun; they could be used with it separately and independently. The commas are the conventional signs of their status. We must likewise keep the comma in a *pretty, tall girl*, lest *pretty* be taken with *tall* as an adverb meaning *rather* to form the compound *pretty tall*.

But suppose we want to write *He was wearing his battered old canvas fishing hat*. Are the adjectives here parallel to one another? Far from it. A thoughtful, constructive, entertaining speech is a speech that is (1) thoughtful, (2) constructive, and (3) entertaining; but a battered old canvas hat is not a hat that is (1) battered, (2) old, (3) canvas, and (4) fishing. The adjectives lie in different planes and bear unequal relations to one another and to their noun. One might truthfully say that each modifier belongs to everything that comes after it; that each is welded to what follows; that together they make a lengthening chain in which every link drags the following links. In reality the object—and hence the noun—is not *hat*, but *canvas-fishing-hat*. This single thought or object is described by the common adjective *old*, to which is added the participial modifier *battered*. There is no license that permits a comma between a single adjective and its noun. Hence none should go between *old* and *canvas*. Next, analysis tells us that each descriptive word in the chain is attached to the following in such a way as to be integral with it; hence no comma between *battered* and *old*. There is in fact no place in this sentence for a legitimate comma.

Nevertheless, anyone who writes *his battered old canvas*

fishing hat will be prepared, if he had much experience, to see his phrase printed as *his battered, old, canvas fishing hat.* He is lucky if there is not a third comma after *canvas.* He can rely on finding at least the two surplus commas put in, even by a paper that is so hard pressed for millimeters that it cannot afford the *s* of a possessive and will print *the Rev. Mr. Jones' parish.*

These lean-to adjective phrases grow like a snowball or an avalanche. When we say *a red brick Georgian house* we are talking, not about a house that is red, brick, and Georgian, but a Georgian house (unitary expression) of red brick (unitary qualifier). It is punctuated exactly like a *summer day;* that is, not at all. The rule should accordingly read: Commas are to be put between parallel adjectives that are independent of each other and separately modify a noun. They are not to be used with adjectives superposed on the noun and on one another.

To be sure, expressions occur in which adjectives can be construed either way—e.g. *a condensed* (,) *popular edition* or *a handsome* (,) *compact unit.* But these are rare. Ninety-nine times in a hundred the difference between parallel and superposed adjectives is unmistakable. Book editors seem to know this better than newspapermen. In the following group of phrases from newspapers, there is only one comma after an adjective that would appear in a well-edited book— the first one, after *charming: A charming, energetic, little gray-haired lady* (why no comma after little?) / *a well-dressed, elderly woman* / *a willowy, brunette singer* / *a disease of the skin characterized by red, scaly patches* / *an energetic, retired businessman* / *the pretty, little mountain village* / *a dimly lit, stone house on the outskirts of Taipei* / *in keeping with a stern, age-old tradition* / *enjoying the mild, autumn sunlight* / *daughter of the late, distinguished composer, G. H.* (the comma after *composer* is an interloper too) / *the impressive, Stanford White building with a beautiful Spanish tower built in 1890* (note that such logic as puts the comma after *impressive* should put one after *beautiful;* also, that one after *tower* would help convey that the building, not merely the tower, was put up in 1890).

Restrictives and Nonrestrictives

The principle of restriction is obviously inherent in language. Even terms that we call universal—e.g. *man, mankind, mortal man, human beings*—set one kind of living creature apart from other kinds, real and imaginary (gods and demigods, quadrupeds, insects, reptiles). If we say *civilized man* or *modern man* it is a further restriction—the limitation of a class, *man*, to a specified part of itself. Restriction might be defined as the chief function of the adjective. If we say *people* we mean all, but if we say *European people* or *nineteenth-century people* we mean only some; the adjective restricts. And we should remember that many of the words we call nouns embody this function of the adjective. The hunter is a hunting man, the nomad a wandering man, the townsman a town-dwelling man, the inventor an inventing man. In short, in one way or another practically all language is restrictive. Its very purpose is to single out, to identify, to define, or to limit.

It is accordingly remarkable that written English was slow to evolve a convention for making clear whether, when we employ the commonest form of sentence, we are referring to all, or only to some, of whatever class is the subject of discourse. That commonest form is the one based on the relative clause, which can be either restrictive or nonrestrictive; and throughout almost the whole history of English the two have been punctuated alike. It is only recently that we have standardized the way to tell them apart. The device when finally evolved was so simple that it quickly attained universal acceptance, and today, after only a few decades, it is difficult to imagine that we have not always used it. All it involved was the omission of enclosing commas for a restrictive element and the retention of them for a nonrestrictive one, coupled with a noticeable (though not mandatory) tendency to make *which* the idiomatic relative pronoun of the merely descriptive clause and *that* the sign of the restrictive one.

The difference can be shown by a very simple two-part paradigm:

(1) *Wild geese, which migrate semiannually, fly high.*
(2) *Wild geese that are molting are commonly unable to fly.*

The first of these sentences is nonrestrictive. It speaks of *all* geese and throws in a *which* clause merely to describe another habit of wild geese generically—again, all of them. This added fact between the commas is relevant but not essential; the main clause would still have meaning without it. Sentence number 2 is restrictive. The *that* clause cuts down the class of *wild geese* to a part of itself—the part that is unable to fly, for the reason given. Without the restrictive clause the sentence *Wild geese . . . are commonly unable to fly* would be false. The *that* clause is indispensable and would be so even if the *that* were changed to *which*, as it could be without violating any rule. The *that* clause is the equivalent of *if they are molting* or *when they are molting*, or of a simple restricting adjective—*molting wild geese*.

The sign of the restrictive clause, then, is the omission of the commas that would set it off if it were nonrestrictive. The absence of commas means: "this part of the sentence you cannot do without." In the first example, the commas around the *which* clause tell us about it: "take it or leave it." The upshot is that omitting such commas is obligatory in a sentence containing a restrictive clause. And with this characteristic mark of restriction we often find a second pointer in the relative pronoun *that*, whose tendency in recent years has been to supplant *which* as the introducer of the restrictive idea.

How quickly we have got used to these devices is shown by our puzzlement when we meet words that suggest a nonrestrictive meaning but that are printed without the comma of nonrestriction, and vice versa. *He has had great success working with the tribal medicine men who enjoy letting him serve as their consultant.* This may mean either that all the medicine men accept him as a consultant or that some do not. The context hints at the first meaning, but the absence of punctuation declares the second. *The Japanese beetle has spread rather widely through many of the states east of the Mississippi, where conditions of temperature and rainfall are suitable for it.* Are conditions suitable for it throughout these states, or only in some? The second meaning calls for a removal of the comma. (Note that *where* and *wherever* are logical equivalents of the relative pronoun.) *I am especially grateful to Mr. R. T. for his . . . many editorial suggestions which have materially improved the book.* Did he also make suggestions that have not improved the book? The lack of a comma implies the answer yes.

Such examples remind us that the mere omission of a comma—a mark easily left out by oversight or obscured by accident—is a flimsy expedient on which to stake the difference in meaning between restriction, which defines by narrowing, and nonrestriction, which merely offers a comment. This truth is one of the arguments for adopting *that* as an additional sign of the restrictive clause—a point more fully discussed in THAT, WHICH, RELATIVE.

Simple appositions can be either restrictive or nonrestrictive, the difference depending on (1) the order of elements and (2) the absence or presence of a pair of commas. *My cousin, Henry Little,* set off by commas, should mean that I have but the one cousin named, whereas *my cousin Henry Little* should signify that I have other cousins from whom Henry is the one singled out. The pattern is obvious in *my aunt Jane, my brother Paul,* etc. However, *Henry Little, my cousin,* implies neither restriction nor nonrestriction. The most frequent trouble with appositives results from the false comma that is put in under the delusion that every appositive must be set off. The commas in the following should be removed: *a design conceived by nationally famous jewelry designer, F. G. /* [the] *reviewer and critic, D. L., discusses / California sports car enthusiast, Jim T., sums up / meteors showering all night out of the constellation, Leo / school superintendent, J. L., complained.*

Whether we put a comma or not after the month in dates of the form *March 1863* or *December 1941* is a matter of arbitrary choice. Both forms can show respectable usage. Writers and publishers apply their own codes, and logic has little to say. The restrictive form *August 1962* (equivalent to *the 1962^d August* A.D.) is gaining ground, no doubt as a by-product of the general modern aversion to dispensable punctuation.

It is an interesting minor point that when the antecedent of a relative *which* or *who* happens to be singular, the meaning may not be materially affected by the presence or the absence of the comma. Such relative clauses can be construed as either restrictive or nonrestrictive without serious alteration of sense. *The novel . . . follows the adventures of a Greek, who becomes involved in the struggle between the supporters of the prophet Elijah and the arrogant Queen Jezebel.* The *who* clause was probably meant to be defining —i.e. restrictive—but the comma is not actually misleading, because the singular is in itself a restriction. *The February commercial treaty, under which the Soviet Union has agreed to purchase 5,000,000 tons of sugar during the next five years and give Cuba a credit of $100,000,000 is held up as the most advantageous ever signed by Cuba.* This example should either dispense with the first comma or supply a second after *$100,000,000.* In *the oldest firm with membership on the New York Cotton Exchange, in which the business is conducted by the descendants of the founders* the comma should be removed, but its presence is not the cause of the confusing effect that calls for rephrasing—e.g. *the oldest member firm on the . . . Exchange still conducted by descendants of the founders.*

A difficulty is encountered when a comma is omitted in a nonrestrictive clause containing a phrase that also requires commas; for example, *an interview with the President who, for understandable reasons, would promise nothing.* The comma needed after *President* is omitted because of a feeling that two commas are all the traffic will bear. But there is still only one President; he is thereby "restricted"; hence the *who* clause is not restrictive and should not seem to be. Removing the two commas would cause less havoc than leaving out the one needed after *President.* The same observation applies in the following: [They] *renegotiated the contract which, as a result of such developments, had obviously become untenable.* Even where the parenthetic commas cannot be spared, they have no bearing on the need of the more important one: *uncovered the infield (,) which, thanks to a superior ground crew, was in tiptop condition.*

Obsolete Commas

Of the punctuation, once standard, that has virtually disappeared from modern printed English, the mark that survives with a curious tenacity here and there is the comma that formerly separated subject and predicate when the subject of a sentence ran to some length. It was natural, almost obligatory, for James Boswell to write: *For though there is no doubt that he who performs the part of a peasant well, is better than he who performs the part of a king ill* . . . His comma, if found in writing since 1900, would be felt by most of us as wrong or perhaps inadvertent. So would the one in *The sea violently agitated and rolling its mountainous waves against an opposing body, is at all times a sublime and awful sight.* If this comma belonged to 1918 instead of to 1818 we should surmise that it was meant to companion an accidentally omitted comma after *sea.* For recent commas of this kind we instinctively supply a similar explanation. *Mr. H., who is far ahead of all other American players in tournament victories for the year, and Mr. S., are younger players.* The writer is seduced by the comma after *Mr. H.,* but that is occasioned only by the interpolated relative clause. In the following, the commas in parentheses are superfluous: *Since 1947* . . . *rebuilding along Park Avenue* (,) *has totaled thirteen blockfronts / Both Mr. S. and Mr. F. (absent from the Broadway scene since 1948)* (,) *have been associated with musical hits* (here the comma is possibly a result of the author's confusion between his pair of parentheses and the pair of commas that he might have used instead) / *While the English eighteenth century gave the patterns of the satire which Yeats, Shaw, and sometimes their Irish contemporaries* (,) *wrote* . . . The writer of the last specimen may have thought of the third member of his series as an interpolation to be set off as a whole, but his last comma is as functionless as it would be in *the satire that Yeats, Shaw, and Wilde* (,) *wrote.* Modern sentences that are really helped by a comma between subject and predicate are extremely rare, and when a comma in that position is desirable it is made so by some consideration unconnected with the beginning of the predicate. For example: *All these people, except the professor and the two old women, believe that life would be wonderful if, if, if* . . . The second comma is dictated by the first; together they set off an interpolated phrase. Both could be omitted with no effect beyond a faint change of emphasis, but if either is included the other must be. The second is unrelated to the division of subject from predicate.

In contemporary prose the comma after a subject is likely to be a half-conscious apology for carrying the subject to such length and complexity that the reader can but finish it with a gasp of relief. It is the author's tacit admission that he ought to have provided a more easily graspable subject. An example: *The impetus toward improved conditions generated by the National Advisory Committee on Farm Labor and its public hearing in Washington* (,) *continues* (note that the way the subject is mismanaged makes the rhythm of the sentence fall dead—a defect reparable only by some such reorganization as *The . . . Committee . . . and its public hearing . . . generated an impetus . . . , and this continues*).

All such examples are reminders that few of the troubles connected with mispunctuation are problems of punctuation only. Most such troubles are, in one way or another, structural.

Co-ordinate Clauses

The comma that should, but often does not, appear between the clauses of a compound sentence can be a gravely misleading error, for it affects our sense of the relations between the parts of clauses connected by *and*—especially those with different subjects. Nine times out of ten the omission lures into false senses and compels rereading. Here is an instance of its characteristic effect: *The road went on over a bridge and the river Kezhma swirled beneath it*. The missing comma after *bridge* traps you into thinking that the road went over a bridge and a river. For lack of a separating mark you take the subject of the second clause as a second object of *over* in the first. The trouble-saving rule is this: Punctuate between grammatically independent clauses that are joined by a conjunction; do it invariably when they have different subjects. The reason for the rule is that nothing but punctuation gives warning that the words ushering in the new clause are not the continuation of something in the old one. *She had never acquired any taste for the social activity of the university and reading and music . . .* We think we are still safe on deck with the author, but the sentence goes on *had their limits,* and we suddenly perceive that we are overboard for lack of a comma after *university.*

The punctuation just recommended may seem to go against the modern preference for abolishing unnecessary commas. But "unnecessary commas" is not a self-defining term; the necessity of a given comma has to be determined by taking thought. The comma that averts a misreading is by definition necessary. To omit such commas as those missing from our examples is to revert to the times before punctuation was invented. Only very short compound sentences in which the first words after *and* prohibit a junction with what precedes may safely be written without the comma—e.g. *Bernard Shaw is a Puritan* (,) *and his work is Puritan work.*

Note, however, that the comma required between linked independent sentences has no business between *dependent* co-ordinate *clauses: When a novelist has begun his careeer with a rousing success and the critics have been no less responsive than the public, his next work is bound to be produced under abnormal strain.* Here a comma after *success* would remove the second clause from the government of *When* and would form an obstacle to clarity.

Preventive Commas

All punctuation is preventive in the sense that it is put in or left out to forestall misreading and misunderstanding. But in addition to what may be called structural punctuation covered by general rules, there exists a use of the various marks—particularly the comma—for functions that have to be thought out each time in their particular place. And sometimes exceptional uses to forestall ambiguity demand what may be called the stitch-in-time comma.

This kind of preventive punctuation is often needed with a word or phrase that can be read as either of two or more parts of speech. For example, the word *before*, being equally natural as adverb and as conjunction, will often mislead if left unpunctuated where it is the adverb. *The year before Cromwell and Cranmer had laid Elizabeth Barton by the heels* is the beginning of a sentence. Is the sense *before Cromwell and Cranmer had* or just *the year before?* There is no way of knowing until the end, when you may discover that you have guessed wrong and must go back to take up the other option. A comma after *before* would have made it instantly clear. In general, expressions of time and place (*ever since / five days after / within / outside / above*, etc.) can produce the same difficulty.

This particular problem of clarity is relatively new in English. Many persons now living were instructed when young to set off with commas *all* introductory phrases and clauses. Contemporary usage lays down no requirement of punctuating introductory adverbial units, even if they are fairly elaborate; but we should need no rule to make us put a comma where the lack of it will entail misunderstanding.

Another old practice put a comma in place of a word or phrase elided and supposed to be supplied by inference. We can still find sentences so punctuated: *In ingenuity he excelled most men of his generation; in energy, all.* The comma after *energy* is supposed to stand for the inferentially repeated words *he excelled.* In the mid-twentieth century many writers—though not all—punctuate thus: *In ingenuity he excelled most men of his generation, in energy all.*

Still another rule required a comma to mark any conspicuous variation from the natural order of subject, verb, predicate. *His propensity to act first and think up rationalizations afterward* (,) *we credulously took for a sign of pre-eminent executive ability.* To the modern reader such commas tend to seem superfluous. But they continue to be used, and sometimes the intrusion interferes with one of the small but sharp distinctions that modern punctuation makes clear when exactly handled. Consider, for example, the difference between

(1) a substantive clause used as the direct object of a verb that happens to come after it, and (2) a clause of the same words in the same position, but used quasi-conditionally— i.e. as an adverb:

(1) *Whatever charges are incurred* (,) *I will pay on notification.*

(2) *Whatever charges are incurred, I will pay them on notification.*

If the needless comma is used in the first, the really functional comma in the second loses its value as the indicator of a radical difference—that between a clause that means *the charges that will be incurred* and one that means *if there happen to be some charges.* Moreover, the unwanted comma raises a possible doubt whether *pay* is a transitive verb or an intransitive. Without the comma the first sentence is unmistakable in meaning; with the comma it can either promise quick payment of a sum as yet unknown (*I will pay whatever charges there are*) or, like the second sentence, merely promise to meet the charges if there are any (*If billed I will pay up*). Here, then, is another case in which modern punctuation marks a difference and tightens expression. But of course this gain is lost unless the outmoded practice is consistently dropped.

Some of the crystallized phrases of daily routine are resorted to so often that we lose all sense of their contents and hear them as mere formulated sound. For example, *No, thanks* can become so automatic that the user overlooks its union of two quite separate notions: (1) polite refusal and (2) gratefulness for an offer. Now consider the heading of a chatty advertisement: NO THANKS. Omitting the comma, probably in an attempt to imitate the inflection often heard, converts a phrase meant to be polite into a rasping rejection. ("I hope you got the information in time?" "Yes, I did—no thanks to you.")

Conversely, a gratuitous comma can thoroughly subvert meaning: *An extension telephone in color is just about the most sensible, low-cost gift with which you could surprise a young bride.* The ill-advised comma tells you that the gift is the most inexpensive as well as the most sensible. What the advertiser intends to say is merely that the gift is the most sensible for a modest price—a restrictive rather than an additive meaning. Sensible is meant to qualify, not *gift*, but *low-cost gift*.

Meaningless Commas

The obsolete rule that we must set off adverbial phrases leads to quite meaningless commas. A description ends with the words *and, behind us, crept the night*. No intelligently worded rule ever condoned such commas; who would ever put punctuation into *and the night crept behind us?* Yet a well-edited newspaper can print *And, by no means, does your responsibility stop there.* The test is to see how the sentence reads without the words between the commas. If this test gives the incomplete meaning *and . . . crept the night / and . . . does your responsibility stop there*, it is certain that the punctuation caused injury.

Not so foolish, but equally misdirected, are the commas that split into worthless halves the so-called absolute (or nominative absolute) construction (*this resolution having been passed / these preliminaries completed / the program being already printed*, etc.). Here is a case: *The next day, being a Sunday, the highways were busy* (delete the first comma). Again: *Next day, being a schoolday, nothing much happened* (delete the first comma). These false commas result from a confusion of the absolute with the participial construction. This last is generally set off from its main clause: *The grand old man, having done his best and failed, offered his resignation.* The absolute construction is on the contrary a tight grammatical unit that must be set off as a whole.

Many a functionless comma that only impedes reading is dropped into places where it seems to obey an imaginary rule about punctuation before quotations. *Answers to such questions as, "What was daddy like when he was a boy?"* The comma after *as* contributes nothing to the sense. *He, too, believed that (,) "A poet participates in the eternal, the infinite, and the one" / admitted that (,) "It is impossible to sympathize heartily with the greatest thoughts . . . and not . . ."* Quotations ordinarily require punctuation (comma, colon, or dash) when introduced by a verb of saying, but not when the quotation follows a conjunction that would take no punctuation if the quotation were indirect: *He, too, believed that a poet participates in the eternal.* Punctuate according to the structure of the sentence, and let the quotation marks fall where they must.

Commas with *Because*

Ambiguity will follow the insertion of a wrong comma or the omission of a necessary one in a *because* clause (or its equivalent) having negative force. (Equivalents are *for the reason that, for the sake of,* etc.; and the same principle sometimes comes into play with directly negative or quasi-negative connectives—*that . . . not, lest,* etc.) No such problem ordinarily arises from affirmative statements. *L. and R. married (,) because they wanted comfort and security.* With the comma this statement emphasizes the fact of their marriage; without the comma it emphasizes the reason for it; but either way it is perfectly unambiguous as to the fact. Now survey the negative version of the same statement in two forms, identical save for punctuation: (1) *L. and R. did not marry, because they wanted comfort and security;* (2) *L. and R. did not marry because they wanted comfort and security.* The first should mean, and as punctuated does mean, that they considered marriage an interference with comfort and security, and for that reason refrained from marrying. The second as clearly means that they did marry, but for reasons other than their desire for comfort and security.

We confront, then, the remarkable fact that after a negative clause a comma before *because* throws the reference of *because* far enough back to include the negative, whereas omitting the comma throws the reference far enough forward to exclude the negative and to take in only the affirmative verb. In other words, after a negative the *because* clause without comma assigns or contradicts a reason why; with a comma, it assigns a reason why not. An example of the comma rightly omitted: *X. did not put in all those laborious nights and days because he coveted the rewards of fame.* (He did put them in, but not for the reason mentioned; *because* contradicts a false reason why.) An example of the comma wrongly omitted: *C. did not last long as editor because his indiscretions created so much rancor and opposition that the politicians who had secured his appointment saw fit to get rid of him.* (By omitting the comma, the reason why he did not last long is represented as a reason why he should have lasted; the logical intention is, of course, to make the *because* clause state a reason why not.) The needed comma is omitted with disconcerting frequency in books and articles that in most other particulars show careful editing. The effect of its omission is invariably a logical absurdity. A typical instance: *The sea is never completely covered with ice because of the comparatively warm water.* Obviously, if the sea were ever completely covered with ice it would not be so because the water is warm. A comma after *ice* is necessary to make *because* lead into a reason why not—and one might add that *the comparative warmth of the water* would make the point still clearer.

Most errors with *because* and the comma are occasioned by omission, not by inclusion: *A new hinge that can't possibly rust, corrode or discolor because it's formed from rigid polyethylene / There can be no compromise with the Communist regimes because they are dedicated to our destruction / is expected to show only a slight increase in output this year because of a drought.* The nonsense or radical differences of meaning resulting from wrong pointing suggest that one should not entrust one's intentions to such a fugitive mote as the comma. Sense surely matters enough to be taken care of in some more determinate, less equivocal way. In fact, a reason stated or contradicted after a negative is best dealt with, not as a problem of punctuation, but as an instance of the poorly handled negative (see NEGATIVES, TROUBLE WITH).

In general and in principle, it is better to assert a positive meaning than to deny its opposite. *L and R. did not marry because they wanted comfort and security* is a correct way of saying that they married, though not for comfort and security. But a better way, and one that would spare much mental algebra, is to say outright: *L. and R. married, not because they wanted comfort and security, but . . .* or *married, but not because . . .* Thousands of sentences by generally admirable writers start with negative statements that are not really negative. For example: *I do not dwell upon the point* (on which the writer has just dwelt) *for any such purpose but merely to show . . .* It would be a better sentence, and its writer to that extent a better writer, if it ran: *I dwell upon the point, not . . . , but . . .*

The translator is peculiarly liable to these perilous flirtations with ambiguity when he renders literally a negative statement that may not have been open to misconstruction in the original. *Molière did not invest his entire moral capital in comedy for the sole reason that he had had but ill success in the tragic mode.* The meaning of this pseudo-English is that Molière did invest his moral capital in comedy, but not exclusively for the reason cited. A comma after *comedy* would make the sentence say—falsely—that he did not invest his moral capital in comedy. Except for special effects that presuppose a high order of professional skill, every consideration urges that we set down what is true, rather than explain that in some specified connection the statement we lead off with is not true. Modern expository writing is too prone to characterizing things, ideas, and persons by what they are not.

Paired Commas

So many commas hunt in pairs, each partner useless without the other, that one might have thought this relationship would lead to a typographical sign, such as the reversal of the first member, as in quotation marks. These, indeed, are referred to in England (and sometimes in this country) as INVERTED COMMAS. We have other correlative marks that open and close around interpolated and subordinate matter—namely parentheses and brackets—but we lack the full indication in paired dashes; like commas, they do not show which way they point. Yet where commas are paired the first belongs logically to what follows, and not, as appearance might suggest, to what precedes. If we had the device

here imagined, it might serve to prevent the chronic carelessness that includes one comma of a logical pair and omits the
other. Lacking the device, we can approximate it by thinking of two parenthetic commas as the complementary halves
of a single contrivance—halves that work together in opposite directions, like the jaws of pliers. But even more important, we should remember that many seemingly single commas stand for a pair. Clauses or phrases at the beginning
or the end of sentences do not look parenthetical, but often
they might just as well have been put in the middle, in
which case they would be found enclosed—that is, punctuated at both ends. When at the head of a sentence, such an
element is set off by what should be thought of as the second
comma of a pair; when at the tail, by the first of such a
pair. Observe the three possible positions illustrating a
parenthesis of this kind: *However public opinion may later
change, it is practically unanimous now / Public opinion is
practically unanimous now, however it may later change /
Public opinion, however it may later change, is practically
unanimous now.* Except for slight changes of emphasis, the
meaning remains constant. And—this is the point—the single
commas of the first and second sentences have the same
parenthetical function as the paired commas of the third. All
of them mark a kind of separation very different from that
made by the nonparenthetic commas of an enumerative
series, or those between adjectives qualifying the same noun,
or those between independent clauses. To perceive this difference and act on it habitually and unerringly are indispensable to a working command of sentence structure.

When both commas of a logical pair have room to appear
and one or the other is omitted, stumbling and annoyance
result: *Although these personal sacrifices are, by most individuals accepted as a condition of public service* ... In this
plain case of the both-or-neither principle, the comma after
are is senseless and irritating without its necessary companion after *individuals.* We could, at a pinch, do without
either. We could also do very well with an order of parts
that would naturally dispense with both: *Although by most
individuals these personal sacrifices are accepted*—an illustration of the truth that faulty punctuation often goes with

sentences that cry out for reconstruction. What we cannot have without the sensation of a missing step at the foot of the stairs is No. 1 without No. 2: *The campaign will start when, and not until one candidate or the other faces the vast unreality that overshadows everything else at this moment* (comma after *until,* or else none after *when*). The second comma is especially easy to overlook when the interpolation is long and enumerative: *most standard pieces of equipment, such as bulldozers, power shovels, draglines, clam buckets, front-end loaders, and trenchers can be used.* The syntactical line is *most standard pieces of equipment . . . can be used;* hence the whole *such as* construction is parenthetic, and a comma after *trenchers* is obligatory.

The annoyance is the same when the first comma of a pair is overlooked: *It is otherwise however, with a zoogeographical or faunal boundary.* Such connectives as *however, moreover,* and *nevertheless* are more and more often left unpunctuated. Omitting the first comma with such words is doubtless encouraged by their position at the head of sentences, but when they come later they require both commas if given either. The same principle applies to phrases and clauses. *An official of the C.A.B. in response to questions, said* (comma after *C.A.B.* or none after *questions*) / *The present contract which expires October 31, is being made the subject of daily negotiating sessions* (comma after *contract*) / *The truth if it must be told, is that I don't believe a word he says* (comma after *truth*) / *an admission that although some international progress is being made in space, very little has so far been made in disarmament* (comma after *that;* the syntactical line is *that . . . very little has so far been made*).

Of course, combinations occur in which one comma or the other is required for some reason other than the completion of a logical pair, and this situation can be confusing. A geographical entry in a desk dictionary reads: *defeated by Lysander, 405 B.C. leading to the termination of the Peloponnesian War.* The comma after *Lysander* is optional; one after B.C. is necessary if one is put after *Lysander;* but one after B.C. is necessary in any case, to set off the closing participial phrase—which, by the way, is grammatically adrift.

The punctuation of participial elements, as the example just given shows, is not reducible to a precept or two. Where the participle restricts or identifies, commas would ordinarily be intrusive and wrong: *pathways leading to the light / daily sessions beginning at 10 A.M. / the number of flights operated by the three airlines / the traditional welcome accorded by the port to new vessels*. Where the participle offers supplementary facts that could be omitted without changing the sense, commas are desirable and often necessary: *Airline companies, including those of Winnipeg's International Airport, are indignant that . . . / They acknowledged that their boat, stationed at the entrance to a channel leading to the . . . fuel tank area, had been ineffective in . . .* The punctuation or nonpunctuation here parallels that of nonrestrictive and restrictive clauses.

Comma Splice or Comma Blunder

Many teachers and some rhetorics still affix the label "comma splice" or "comma blunder" to a disjointed pseudosentence of the form *This engine is hard to start, the timer needs adjusting*. But the transgression in such specimens is not so much against good punctuation as against the idea of what a sentence is, and for that reason the discussion of this is reserved for a different context (see SENTENCE, THE 4).

Janus Elements

Janus, the Roman god who protected gates and doors, was the prototype of Mr. Facing-both-ways; he was portrayed with two faces turned in opposite directions, whence the use of his name for an expression left adrift between what precedes and what follows. Often the difficulty results from leaving the phrase or word afloat between two commas, one of which should be either suppressed or changed to something else.

Although many of these [letters] *are routine and dull, taken as a whole, they are interesting as the record and sig-*

nature of an artist. What is to be taken as a whole, their dullness or their interest? If the second meaning is intended, the second comma should disappear, despite the rule about setting off participial phrases. The rule cannot be allowed to interfere with clarity.

Janus elements of greater length are subject to the same principle: *While Imagism and Spectrism were both programs of revolt in the field of expression, Mr. M. maintained in his introduction, they were diametrically opposed.* If the clause enclosed belongs with the final clause, it should read: *Mr. M. maintained in his introduction that . . . ;* if with the opening clause, *While* (Although) *Mr. M. maintained . . . ;* if with both, *Mr. M. maintained . . . that both Imagism and Spectrism were programs of revolt . . . , but that they were diametrically opposed.*

THE SEMICOLON

Relativism in Punctuation

Relativism in punctuation is a shorthand term for the principle that we often need a fuller stop in one place because we have had a less full stop in another. For example, practice requires a semicolon at a point of greater separation because points of lesser separation are already marked by commas. Here is the opening of a passage about a young intellectual: *From the moment he gets off the train, he seems to be under a spell of alienation. He makes friends; he is competent at his job; he studies the city around him, but he can never shake off a sense of hopeless passivity and bafflement.* The punctuation of the second sentence is elaborately wrong. The chief break occurs at *but,* where it gets the least punctuation mark; the lesser breaks, denoted by semicolons, are comparatively less important. The *but* clause takes exception to all three of the preceding clauses, not merely to the last. The appropriate punctuation, then, is *He makes friends, he is competent at his job, he studies the city around him* (an *a, b, c* series without *and*) ; (semicolon) *but he can never shake off . . .* Pedants may think these clausal commas objectionable, and may want to keep the semicolons, starting a new sentence at *but*. This applies relativism, but sacrifices unity by separating the two halves of a single thought.

The same principle governs such a typical sentence as the following: *This was a highly successful voyage and even if it did not reveal the sought-for passage, it did something to compensate.* The major point of division is after *voyage,* and a semicolon is needed there if the comma is to be kept for the minor division after *passage.* (But note that the rule requiring a comma to set off a conditional clause is obsolescent; if, then, we omit the comma after *passage* a comma after *voyage* will suffice. We get the same relationship in sentences of the following shape: *This candidate has carried his campaign direct to the voters and everywhere, they have responded with mounting enthusiasm for the man, his message and his mission.* The comma after *everywhere* is needless and intrusive, but one after *voters* is obligatory.)

A semicolon is also likely to be called for wherever an introductory explanation with *that, that is,* etc. is left afloat, Januslike, between commas: *Dignity is the important thing, says Mrs. M., that, and a real desire for an education* (semicolon at the major break after *Mrs. M.*) / *This was only another term for "Prudence," which could be interpreted in an Epicurean sense, that is, enjoy life, but act in such a way as to prolong the enjoyment* (semicolon or dash before *that is*).

Some sentences are veritable object lessons for those who regard the semicolon as obsolete and who aver that modern prose is better without it. Consider *He agreed with Victor Hugo that Germany would become a republic in time, and that she had power to invade other countries* . . . At this point the reader is sure that the second *that* clause is parallel with the first and states a second point of agreement with Victor Hugo. But not at all; the sentence continues: *was of very little interest, since she would herself be invaded in her turn.* It is, of course, important to give logically parallel statements a parallel form; but because of that very principle it is imperative to give nonparallel statements unmistakably contrasted forms. The way to do so here might be *He agreed with Victor Hugo that Germany would become a republic in time; her power to invade other countries was of very little interest, since* . . . Any misreading is forestalled at once by the simple substitution of a semicolon that marks the major break for a comma that does not. To be sure, the sentence is still faulty, for it gives no notion of whether Victor Hugo's agreeing extends to the second clause or stops with the first. But that disability is structural; the author is withholding pertinent information.

Series with Semicolons

When an enumerative series of the *a, b, c. . . . , and n* form includes elaborated members having conjunctions or commas within themselves, it is often desirable, and sometimes necessary for clarity, to close each member before the last with a semicolon instead of a comma. *By this means they became every day more licentious, and the Campus Martius was a perpetual scene of tumult and sedition* (first member) ; *armed slaves were introduced among these rascally citizens, so that the whole government fell into anarchy* (second member) ; *and* (third member) *the greatest happiness which the Romans could look for was the despotic power of the Caesars.* Fail to use the two semicolons, rely on commas, and you add gratuitous perplexities for the reader. *He suggested* [the] *continuation of the International Geophysical Year or some similar form of international cooperation;* [the] *international exchange of tracking data and of navigation and signal codes; agreements on* [the] *use of radio frequencies and on international projects like relay or postal satellites or missiles; and agreements for advance notice* [about?] *and* [the] *coordination of launching schedules.* For these four members commas would theoretically suffice, but with such a recurrence of *or* and *and* the semicolons make the sentence digestible.

So far, good. But we do not get clear of the topic without once more crossing the trail of the *a, b* and *c* punctuator. The practice of omitting the comma between the last two members of a simple series is cited in favor of either omitting the closing semicolon of the more complex series or else of reducing it to a comma. And at copy desks there is trouble deciding whether to go for reduction or for abolition. Comparable examples of each occur frequently in our best newspapers. Reduction to comma: *The House backers of the rose as a national floral symbol include Representative Hugh Scott, Republican of Pennsylvania; Lindy Beckworth, Democrat of Texas, and James C. Davis, Democrat of Georgia / Among those mentioned for the job have been Henry Cabot Lodge, United States Ambassador to the United Nations; Fred A. Seaton, Secretary of the Interior; General Gruenther, and Clifford Folger, United States Ambassador to Belgium.* Abolition: *Other factors included Senator X.'s acceptance of favors from J.V. . . . ; the emonomic recession, which has hit Maine harder than many other states; the long-term drift of textile mills from New England to the South and* [the] *continued deterioration of traditional party loyalties / For years he toyed with the idea of . . . "three Vice Presidents"—one to help with the ceremonial duties of the Presidency; one to help coordinate foreign affairs and one to supervise the administration of domestic affairs.*

Now, all the reservations about omitting the final comma from a simple series apply equally to tampering with the final semicolon of a more complex series—particularly the reservation that you have to read twice to make sure where the final member begins and how many members there are. Indeed, the argument against leaving out the last semicolon or reducing it to a comma applies with even more force to these more complex series, since the reason for using semicolons in series at all is to distinguish a whole member from such parts of a member as require separation by commas. The likelihood of confusion under the usual newspaper rules is vividly illustrated by sentences such as the following one, where two separate *a, b* and *c* series occur as parts of the basic *a; b; c,* and *d* series: *Areas returning to Standard Time this week-end include all of New England, New York State, New Jersey, Delaware, Washington, D.C.; parts of Pennsylvania, including Philadelphia and Pittsburgh; parts of Illinois, including Chicago, and parts of Ohio, Kentucky and West Virginia.* The five-member series before the first semicolon might well be given a terminal *and* before *Washington* (though by the newspaper code that would delete the comma after *Delaware*); and certainly the whole would be improved by the logical semicolon after *Chicago,* where the stop is rhetorically equal to the stops after *D.C.* and *Pittsburgh.* In fine, not to use the same punctuation to separate *all* the equal members of any regular series is to ask for trouble while flouting the principle of relativism.

Gratuitous Semicolons

Whatever is done by way of punctuating before the closing member, it is hard or impossible to see any advantage in semicolons between members so simple as not to require commas or conjunctions internally. The semicolons are gratuitous frills better replaced by commas in the following: *A number of important laws . . . were enacted, including* [the] *creation of a committee on outer space; * [the] *development of Niagara power;* [the] *sharing of atomic secrets with our allies; assistance to the European Power Community, and* [the] *approval of the "Eisenhower Doctrine" for the Middle East.* (In newspaper practice this improvement would, of course, destroy the comma after *Community,* with the usual unhappy effect of making the last member look like an appendage to its predecessor.) Commas would likewise suffice in the following notice of a panel discussion: *Participating are architect D. F.; Builder* (why capital *B?*) *G.H.; and New York City Planning Commissioner J.L.* Note, however, that the semicolons would be useful and good if the notice were given the form *D.F., architect; G.H., builder; and J.L., . . . Planning Commissioner.*

A false relativism prompted by commas that have no excuse for existing will of course generate superfluous semicolons: *The gloaming lay around us, wrapping the world in rainbow shadows; and, behind us, crept the night.* As shown above in the discussion of commas, there is no need to set off *behind us* with commas, and hence the semicolon is removable.

Standard Semicolons

The absolute (as against the relative) use of the semicolon in modern prose is (1) to separate grammatically independent clauses connected in meaning but without a connective, and (2) to separate independent clauses joined by one of the co-ordinating conjunctions that have a quasi-adverbial force or by one of the adverbs commonly used connectively—e.g. *however, moreover, therefore, furthermore, nevertheless, whereupon, on the other hand, indeed,* and sometimes *because, hence, whence,* and *whereas.* Examples of the conjunctionless use: *They had started with provisions for three years; they had been in the field sixteen months / But it could be endured for one night; tomorrow they would be on their way / But truth is complex; we see it, not whole, but in bits and pieces; half-truth makes its contribution.* Examples with a conjunction or another connective: *She could sustain a conversation on court, theater, and social gossip more entertainingly than most; hence those who met her only at large gatherings thought her disappointingly superficial and frivolous / replied that she was pleased to see part of her debts paid; whereupon Madame Y. retreated from the room in a huff.*

THE COLON

The colon is used to introduce formally. It furnishes this service for lists, tables, and quotations, or for the second member of a two-sentence statement when the first raises an expectation or makes a promise to be fulfilled by the second. In introducing lists and tables the colon is often followed by a break in the line and the start of a new paragraph. This form is so common and so plain that it requires no illustration. In introducing a quotation, the colon is followed by quotation marks or by a line break and indention right and left. Usually, but not always, a capital letter begins the first quoted word. If it is desired to quote without quotation marks, as when the reported matter is not actual but imaginary, it is better not to use the colon and to rely on the unpunctuated natural order after some verb of saying. The two contrasted forms follow: (Formal) *He rose and said: "Ladies and Gentlemen, I am not going to make a speech."* / (Informal) *Then he wondered How the dickens did I ever get into such a fix?*

The use of the colon for uniting expectation and response is fairly standard; it presents no difficulty and little variation. *Recognize the amount of work that has gone into the product: you may be severe on serious faults, but you must forget trifling errors / The remedy for this is simple: insert a cushion word or phrase / Shaw was anything but indolent: he threw himself into the task of reorganizing the society / Let's be frank: I'm after your scalp and you're after mine.*

When the words before the colon in either of its uses end in a group within parentheses, the colon follows the closing parenthesis.

THE DASH

Despite Keats's and some young ladies' use of the dash as a universal mark for either joining or separating the parts of a paragraph or a sentence, the dash has but few legitimate uses. Most of them derive from its primary function of interruption. It is a mark of great power and should accordingly not be overused. As an interrupter the dash indicates first a break in the thought, from hesitation, suspense, sudden conviction of ignorance, fear, or what not. *We can go on and on increasing our armaments until—well, I don't know until what or when.*

As the introducer of an afterthought or explanation the dash separates but also completes: *He dispenses an enormous amount of energy in that concern of his—to stop the gaps, supervise the help, plan the next moves / We prefer to write as we speak—or so we believe.*

But the most frequent use of the dash is in pairs, to interrupt and set off a thought, long or short, which does not form an integral part of the sentence. In this capacity it serves somewhat the same purpose as the parentheses, though writers who like distinctions tend to think of the latter as slipping in a thought under the breath, perhaps for explanation, whereas the paired dashes throw in a fresh, not easily assimilable thought. *They came to agree—how inconceivable they hadn't felt it sooner!—that they were unsuited to each other / What the contemporaries believed happened is in fact truer—more genuinely "the past"—than anything discovered by later research / Sometimes circumstantial evidence convinces at sight, as when—to use Thoreau's example —you find a trout in the milk.*

The danger in the use of paired dashes—apart from an excess which will give the reader the feeling of being continually jerked out of his stream of thought—lies in the placement of two or more pairs so close together that the reader does not know which opens and which closes the interruption. For example: *The cultivation of the arts—or of one or more of them—will indeed conduce a people—at least the most favored—to take a gentler view of human society and its obligations.* The repeated break in that sentence makes it a difficult one to grasp visually and therefore intellectually. Unless one stays on the rails through an intuition of the meaning intended, one may take *will indeed conduce a people* as an interpolation. Still worse is the mixing of a pair with a single dash, as in *They are planning— and have actually reserved the space for—a huge exhibit of machinery—the pride of the new country.* Substitute parentheses for the conflicting pair or a comma for the single dash.

In the older punctuation a dash was sometimes combined with other marks, especially the comma, the period, the colon, and the semicolon. This practice is now obsolete, except possibly at the head of a formal letter, where some persons like to write *Dear Sir:—.* In running prose the rule about the use of dashes with other marks is: Give it up.

PARENTHESES AND BRACKETS

The curved marks known as "parens" among printers are called after the object of their embrace: a parenthesis is a thought that intrudes and is enclosed within another, not indeed irrelevantly, but without the link between the two being made explicit. The marks prepare the reader for this intrusion and tell him when it is over.

It may be that the intrusion is very slight, as when in the course of prose we wish to place numbers: *I shall make three points: (1) . . . , (2) . . . , (3). . . .* Or again: *The price is fifty (50) dollars.* But usually the interloper has more substance. It may be an explanatory word or phrase: *The common rat (rattus rattus or house rattus) can give a lethal bite.* It may be a complete sentence: *We must not forget that Spencer and many others wrote on evolution before Darwin (it was Spencer, not Darwin, who coined the phrase "Survival of the Fittest") and consequently we must not keep on thinking and saying that the theory of evolution broke upon the world in 1859.*

Whether to use parentheses or paired dashes is often a matter of taste. As is said under THE DASH, some writers think parentheses less abrupt in marking an interruption. Their very shape suggests rather the insinuation of related matter than the stoppage of discourse for imposing an extraneous thought. Again, parentheses may be used instead of dashes when a succession of interruptions is called for, though in this use there should be not mere variation but some principle of choice—let the short explanatory phrase shelter between parentheses or commas and the longer outburst sport dashes fore and aft.

With other marks, parentheses follow simple logic: The period or question mark or exclamation point is put inside the closing parenthesis when it belongs to the parenthetical matter. It goes outside, like the comma, colon, or semicolon, when it belongs to the whole sentence.

Brackets are the square form of the mark of parenthesis and their use is restricted by convention to one infrequent but important purpose; namely, to indicate the word or words that a writer has added to a quoted text. Thus an author who, while quoting from another, wants to inform the reader about some matter left indefinite in the original— say a pronoun—will write: *He* [General Smuts] *then took over the task of reconciling the parties.* Another frequent insertion in this form is that of [*sic*] to indicate that the preceding word or words are being reproduced truly, though obviously misspelled or ill-chosen.

Other uses of brackets and parentheses are determined by the needs of the professions and their journals and reports. Thus lawyers have a convention about enclosing in parentheses a capital letter that is wanted for the quotation but does not exist in the original. Such uses must be learned for each particular purpose or publication. They do not affect general prose even when they go against its common practice. In any prose the use of brackets, round, square, or pointed, to enclose an ironic mark of exclamation or interrogation is rightly considered sophomoric and intolerable. (An exception is the bibliographer's [?] to point out spelling errors on title pages.)

THE MARKS OF INTERROGATION AND EXCLAMATION

In Spanish usage the reader of print is warned that a question or exclamation is coming by the presence of the familiar mark upside down at the beginning of the passage characterized by these moods. He can inflect his voice or adjust his mind accordingly. In English and American usage we are limited to the final mark right side up, but this does not abolish the need to put it where it logically belongs. Some publishers and printers who believe that looks matter more than sense may insist that these two marks of feeling must always go inside the quotation marks. But this makes nonsense of any quotation within a quotation. Compare *"Then she said to me: 'Where are you going?'"* with *Did I really want to know, I reflected, what she had been up to when she had, to use her own words, been "gadding about"?* These examples point to the simplest, most defensible rule: Determine what the question or exclamation is and put after it the denotative mark. In the second sentence, clearly, the question mark belongs to the whole sentence and should appear outside the quotation mark.

What is not so simple is to decide when a sentence that begins with an interrogative word is in fact exclamatory. *How wrong I had been!* is clear enough, and so is the pure question *How had I been wrong?* But what about excited speech in the negative interrogative form? *What haven't I done to make you happy!* requires a question mark, not an exclamation point. Similarly, in correspondence the polite request *Would you be good enough to send me,* etc. remains a question and needs its mark. Only when the question is rhetorical, not actual, does the exclamation mark appear and make this plain: *How have the mighty fallen! / What numbers of people saw the coronation! / Why did he go and kill himself!*

THE HYPHEN

Spelling and Compounding

The hyphen is used more often to show the reader that the end of the printed line is not the end of the word than for any other purpose. But before we discuss the complicated business of how words should be split, two other uses of the hyphen deserve attention.

The first and by far the greatest help to reading is the compulsory hyphening that makes a single adjective out of two words before a noun: *eighteenth-century painting / fleet-footed Achilles / tumbled-down shack / Morse-code noises / single-stick expert.* Nothing gives away the incompetent amateur more quickly than the typescript that neglects this mark of punctuation or that employs it where it is not wanted. It is not wanted between an adverb and its adjective before a noun: *a serenely unconscious man / a verbally inept proposal / a remarkably pretty girl.* But when the adverb *well* is linked with a past participle, again only before the noun, the hyphen is required: *a well-liked actor / a well-intentioned fool / a well-translated poem.*

The reason for hyphening emerges from these examples: it is to warn the reader that he must fuse two ideas before he can perceive how they apply to the subject. With the ordinary adverb this signal is conveyed by the form itself: *serenely* cannot modify a noun directly; rather, it falls forward on the adjective *unconscious* and the necessary fusion is accomplished. *Well* needs the hyphen to link it with a participle because neither is obviously adverb or adjective: we can say *a well man,* and we tend to think of *liked, beaten, intentioned, protected* primarily as verb forms. The full-fledged adjective (*full* here plays exactly the same role as *well*) arises only from the combination marked by hyphening. After frequent use the mark may disappear, but only by means of amalgamation into one word: *thoroughbred, scapegrace, bluenosed, fatheaded, bittersweet,* and so on.

This agglutination brings us to the hyphening of nouns that are made up of other words and that seem unable either to stand side by side independently or to fuse into a single new noun. Hundreds of these occur daily in ordinary print, but from the anarchy that gives them a hyphen or withholds it no exact rule can be derived. Dictionaries and editorial codes agree on some but not on others. Some that are hyphened in one place are printed as one word or as separate words elsewhere. The progress, so to speak, of each two-part word is toward the single word, and there are some who spell *talkingshop* (= parliament) as they spell *sidewalk.* Most nouns beginning with *non* readily become one word— *nonconformist, nonalcoholic, nonadhesive.* Yet other combinations—say *nonoperative*—were felt at first to be misleading without a hyphen after *non,* since the unaccustomed eye read *no-no* at the first glance. Misreading will still occur if a distinction by means of the hyphen is not made between RECREATE and RE-CREATE, *repose* and *re-pose,* and similar pairs.

Some writers would like to follow John Dos Passos and write *picturegallery,* on the strength of frequency and inseparability in thought. But this is going too far and too quickly for most readers, and the writer or editor who wants with the majority, neither lagging nor leading, simply has ... learn a long list of words and note their hyphening or their fusion. For the rest he has only two guides: (1) a new combination whose meaning differs from that of its parts taken literally together—e.g. *dancing-girl*—requires a hyphen to show this deviation from the literal; (2) combinations that add their meanings literally—e.g. *movie house*—must not be hyphened. Between those boundary cases stand all the rest, some of which will doubtless ascend after a time into the blessed state of being made one continuous substance.

With double-barreled proper names (and also with expressions, themselves hyphened, that are preceded by *ex-* or *mid-*), the use of the hyphen remains uncertain and hence unsatisfactory. *The Harold Wilson-Lyndon Johnson dialogue* presents to the eye and the mind an illogical arrangement. No doubt the shortening to *Wilson-Johnson* is felt to be insufficiently clear because the last names are not distinctive. Some printer's manuals and publisher's style books call for the en dash (–), slightly longer than the hyphen, to link up proper nouns, and this device is at least indicative of a greater force of fusion. The careful writer, however, should avoid using typographical signs as substitutes for words and recast: *the dialogue between Harold Wilson and Lyndon Johnson.*

Avoidance is likewise recommended in the corresponding predicament with *ex-* and *mid-*. Some writers have accustomed themselves to *midfifteenth-century painters*, but whoever dislikes *midf* as a first syllable to a word must write *painters of the mid-fifteenth century*, which has the further advantage of not making a quality out of an adventitious date (compare *the 1954 proposal, the eight-o'clock fire alarm*, with *the mid-day bulletin* and *the six-o'clock news*, which are properly defined by the regularity of their occurrence in time). The way to avoid *ex-* trouble, as in *the ex-American League player*, is to use *former* instead of *ex-* whenever the descriptive term consists of more than one word. The common loathing of Latin as a dead language should help root out all *ex-*'s anyway.

Splitting Words

From speaking of the way separate words are joined, we turn to the opposite use of the hyphen, that of dividing them. The division of words into their syllables is called *syllabation, syllabication, syllabification*, and even, absurdly, *syllabism* (see -ISM). To perform this operation is to *syllabize, syllabicate, syllabify*, or *syllable*. The terms generally used by American printers and preferred by some American lexicographers are *syllabicate* and *syllabication*. It should seem as if an aspect of language so well panoplied in synonyms ought to be as nearly systematized and settled as anything about living language can be, but the syllabication of English is a chronic annoyance to linguists, who seem to suffer equally under the British system, based on etymology, and the American system, based on pronunciation. Their dissatisfaction is succinctly expressed in the New World Dictionary: "To decide where one syllable ends and another begins . . . is a matter of such difficulty that linguistic science is still unable to provide a simple formula for syllable division in English. Neither the system of division used in this dictionary nor any other yet devised really squares with the observable facts of the English language. The separation of syllables in this and similar books is merely a graphic convenience, intended to help printers to be consistent. Its virtues are esthetic, not linguistic. . . . [We] continue to use, and, unfortunately, to have represented to us as factual, a system which is neither logical in itself nor based in any degree on the ascertained characteristics of our language."

While the scholar is nettled by the lack of correspondence between the graphic device of syllabication and the physiology of speech, the common reader is confused by alternate exposure to the American system (reduced to ten remarkably condensed "Rules for the Syllabic Division of Words in Writing or Print" in Webster) and the British system found in the books we import. American readers have to recognize the variation in codes—the one that marks a difference between the noun *prog-ress* and the verb *pro-gress*, the noun *proj-ect* and the verb *pro-ject*, etc., and the one that does not; the code that divides *photog-raphy* phonetically and the one that sticks to etymology and *photo-graphy*. Sometimes we find a mixture of the two systems in the same book; for example, a reprint of Francis Hackett's *Henry the Eighth* shuttles between Websterian divisions of the sort that strike the English as the most perverse possible (*noth-ing, acknowl-edge*) and such un-American breaks as *lament-able, frivol-ous*, and *pro-cess*—a clash made particularly graphic in the parallel words *signif-icant* (American division) and *magni-ficent* (British division).

Under this bombardment of contradictory usages and compositors' aberrations (*tena-city, negotia-ting, bru-sque-ness*, etc.) the American writer or proofreader cannot even approach consistency without intense thought and attention. He must either acquire an absolute mastery of Webster's ten rules—no light tax on the mind—or else look up every division about which he has the slightest doubt, precisely as he would look up doubted spellings. Ideally, a manuscript typed for print should contain no line-end hyphens except such as are part of the text; that is, a line of copy may end with the hyphen of *first-born* or *first-class* or *first-rate*, which the printer is to set regardless of its place in the printed line, but not with the hyphen of *first-hand*, which denotes only a syllabic division and will not appear in print unless it happens to end a printed line. But in practice it is impossible to induce a typist to carry out this counsel of perfection, which would require her never to begin near the end of a line a word that she has not room to finish on that line. She is trained to make lines of standard length and not trained to forestall syllabic errors.

Granted, then, a manuscript sprinkled with line-end hyphens indicating syllabic division, an author who cares about consistency would be well advised to mark either the hyphens that the printer is to keep (=) or else those that he is to eliminate (+). In practice most authors leave the whole question to their typists, few of whom look up syllabications, and to copy editors, whose work varies under varying pressures. Compositors, with few exceptions, have ceased to feel much responsibility for syllabication; and printers' and publishers' proofreading is no longer very thorough, except in a few houses specialized in technical books; so that an author who wants his syllabifying to conform to the American working code will generally have to take responsibility for it himself. Since many authors are not good proofreaders, it is remarkable that flagrant misdivision is not more frequent than it is.

A difficulty formerly of concern to compositors, and one which ought to concern them still, is that not every word division deemed correct by the code is desirable, and that some undesirable ones must be condoned for spacing or other visual reasons. In general, a division is bad that ends a line on the false suggestion of some other word, generally a monosyllable. The broken-off portion causes a mental mispronunciation and thus requires the reader to retrace his steps. For example, whereas *face-saving* is a good division, *face-tious* is a deplorable one, though correct; make this, if possible, *fa-cetious*. Similarly, *tar-ry* is a good enough division of *tarry* meaning *covered with tar*, but an undesirable one of *tarry* meaning *dawdle* or *linger*. There is an astonishing number of these misleaders in English; some of the commoner ones, at random, are *char-acter, char-ity, reappear, read-just, coin-cidence, opera-tion, bar-riers, fun-erary, pale-olithic, cog-itate, mate-rial, tar-iff, scar-city, pane-gyric, car-amel, par-agraph, par-amount, par-allel, rein-force, rearrange,* and *bin-ocular.* All but one of these can be divided elsewhere than at the point of false lead, and so they ought to be wherever the spacing permits. In proofreading his own text, an author sensitive to such awkward divisions might add or delete an occasional word or syllable to provide a reading without a break or with a better break. The editor of a text not his own has, of course, no such option. In the narrow measure of a newspaper column there is often no available cure; in books and magazines this kind of mischance can be greatly reduced if authors or editors will attend. If it were possible to interest compositors as well, such accidents could be reduced almost to the vanishing point.

This last supposition suggests another. If the hyphen is designed to warn the reader that a word or part of a word is to be attached to the word or part that follows, and thus prevent misreading, then there is an obvious use of the hyphen that has never been taken advantage of. To suggest this possible use here is to make an exception to the defined contents of this book, which are matters of usage. What is being proposed for the hyphen is not practiced anywhere in the English-speaking world; at this point we leave usage to enter utopia.

As printers now print, there occur phrases composed of separate words which form a single meaning (and should therefore be read together) but which the end of the line will occasionally divide. If those words, usually a pair, do not normally need a hyphen, no hyphen will be printed between the first at the end of the line and its mate at the beginning of the next. Now, if the first of the pair happens to make a complete meaning with what precedes, then the reader gets a jolt when he finds a further word dangling at the head of the line following. For example:

With but a few changes to modify the speech
form, it would make an excellent essay.
What she vainly tried to do was to destroy her father
fixation.
Our aim then is to measure the socially necessary labor
time.

There occurs a natural example of such breaks eight lines up from the bottom of page 520 above, where *eight-o'clock fire* gives a complete meaning and *alarm* lies bereft at the beginning of the next line.

The definition of the hyphen in the manuals—a mark to carry the reader across the break in the line—defines also its fitness for the situations just illustrated. If even a few writers, editors, and printers were disposed to try the device, our reading would be made as consecutive for ideas as it is now made at the end of the line for syllables, or as it is now made anywhere for compounds. It cannot be objected that the hyphening at line-endings of certain phrases that elsewhere stand unhyphened would encourage a misuse of the mark, for the presence of a hyphen at a split word does not now breed the desire to see it split and hyphened everywhere. It is only a foolish consistency that would refuse the aid of a sign whose sole purpose is merely to keep the eye—and with it the meaning—moving forward to embrace a natural cluster, whether of syllables or of words.

DOTS OF OMISSION AND SUSPENSION

The effort to quote other men's words with fidelity entails the use of a mark to show where one or more words have been omitted in quoting. That mark consists of the familiar three dots, sometimes known as ellipses.

They are followed either by the word that resumes the quotation or, sometimes, by the mark appropriate to the spot—e.g. a period if the omission runs to the end of the original sentence; a comma, semicolon, or colon if one of these marks concludes the omitted passage. Occasionally, these marks may be omitted for the sake of visual clarity if the meaning is not affected. A mark occurring in the original after the last word quoted before the omission is usually kept in that place. For the omission of a paragraph or more, it is usual to run a full line of dots across the page.

A second use of the three dots is to suggest the trailing off of a thought or an unwillingness to complete it. *His mind was not grappling with the question; all he could think of was "After all he had done . . ."* Writing that makes excessive use of this device, which is supposed to represent the normal workings of the mind, runs the risk of producing not lifelikeness but irritation.

THE APOSTROPHE

The commonest use of the apostrophe is to mark the possessive case—*Uncle Tom's Cabin*. This use derives from the more general one of indicating by the apostrophe the omission of a letter. In an earlier phase of English the possessive and the nominative plural had an *e* which was later omitted. The marking of the omission produced the forms *James's, fox's, folio's*, etc., and by extension the apostrophe came to be used for the possessive case in words where no *e* had ever existed (*man's, children's,* etc.).

In the two centuries before the First World War, convention had settled some of the difficulties arising from this improvised system. Phrases full of sibilants, such as *for goodness' sake, for Jesus' sake, Socrates' Apology, Xerxes' fleet,* and others resembling them, were spelled and pronounced without the additional *s.* This held also for words lacking a written *s,* such as *conscience', reverence', Berlioz',* and *Beaux'.*

The possessive adjectives and pronouns ending in *s* take no apostrophe: *its, yours, ours, hers, theirs* are so spelled. But the indefinite pronouns add the apostrophe and the *s: a room of one's own, somebody else's opportunity, nobody's business.* In measurements of time the habit is growing of doing without the apostrophe in plurals: *six months leave without pay* is fairly common. This apparent simplification actually complicates matters; for no one as yet writes *an hours delay, a weeks extension,* and it is a complication to have one rule for the singular and another for the plural. This book recommends the retention of the apostrophe in *six months' leave* until writers are ready to jettison it in *a day's grace, a minute's inattention,* etc.

The apostrophe has been discarded by fiat in the names of certain institutions, chiefly educational and financial—*Teachers College, Investors Trust, Merchants Bank, Authors Guild,* etc. There is something arbitrary and illogical about this departure from common habit, and though one can read in it the intention of having a "real" name—a clear-cut formula rather than a description—one does not see so readily where the line should be drawn. *Mens room* and *womens colleges* show up on signs or in print from time to time, often at the hands of those who are careful to put an apostrophe, wrongly, in the possessive *its.*

The further wide use of the apostrophe is to make plurals for special occasions—*cross your t's and dot your i's / the 1920's / the Montgomery's*—though in recent years the stylebooks of certain editors and publishers have tended to enforce *the 1920s, the three Rs,* and even *the Montgomerys.* This last instance is unfortunate as leading to possible confusion about the correct spelling of the name in the singular; the other two are sometimes hard to read, the numbers especially.

Among the lesser uses of the apostrophe are the marking of slurred pronunciation (*perishin' blighter*); the spelling of *o'clock, Tam o' Shanter*, etc., and of standard contractions (*can't, won't, I'll*); the indication of missing letters (*sicklied o'er / pronounced "med'cine"*); and the forming of past participles out of letters or intractable names (*K.O.'d in the third round / in his youth he had been Beethoven'd and Bach'd to within an inch of his life*).

THE SLASH

The diagonal mark (/) is used to separate lines of verse when they are not printed in the conventional way on successive lines. It also occurs in abbreviations, such as *a/c* for *account*, or to mean *a* or *per* in designating rates; e.g. *25 miles/hour, an acceleration of 16 ft/sec/sec.*

In works of reference (such as this book) the slash is occasionally used to simplify the reading by marking off examples more sharply than periods can do when the sentences or phrases are not consecutive in meaning.

THE PERIOD

The period comes appropriately at the end. Anybody who knows a sentence when he sees one knows where to put the period, provided the sentence is not a question or an exclamation. (It is worth remembering, however, that the interrogative and exclamatory sentences have their period merged with the special marks denoting their kind.) The period goes inside the closing quotation mark. Indeed, the only question ever raised about the placing of a period is whether it should follow all abbreviations or only those that stop before the last letter of the full word. According to one system, abbreviations such as *Wm* or *Thos* would appear without a period because *m* and *s* are the last letters of *William* and

Thomas, but *Jno*. and *Geo*. would require a period because *o* is not the end of *John* (or *Jonathan*) and *George*. Likewise, *Mr* without a period and *Esq*. with one, *Sgt* without and *Gen*. with. Nevertheless the principle here recommended is: Periods throughout, for simplicity's sake. And this goes for abbreviations that consist of initials only (see INITIALESE). It is tiresome to have to remember that the CIO has chosen to close ranks between its letters, whereas some other organization (e.g. the A.M.A.) prefers to keep a distance by means of periods. The strain on the memory and the waste of effort imposed by such trifles on all who write and print and edit are a standing reproach to our collective judgment. We mistake the observance of these childish variations for accuracy, while we are content to miss the truths of substance and the virtues of style.